MW01028547

Foundational Texts of Mormonism

Foundational Texts of Mormonism

Examining Major Early Sources

Edited by

MARK ASHURST-MCGEE
ROBIN SCOTT JENSEN
SHARALYN D. HOWCROFT

OXFORD
UNIVERSITY PRESS

OXFORD
UNIVERSITY PRESS

Oxford University Press is a department of the University of Oxford. It furthers the University's objective of excellence in research, scholarship, and education by publishing worldwide. Oxford is a registered trade mark of Oxford University Press in the UK and certain other countries.

Published in the United States of America by Oxford University Press
198 Madison Avenue, New York, NY 10016, United States of America.

Library of Congress Cataloging-in-Publication Data
Names: Ashurst-McGee, Mark, editor. | Jensen, Robin Scott, editor. |
Howcroft, Sharalyn D., editor.
Title: Foundational texts of Mormonism : examining major early sources/
edited by Mark Ashurst-McGee, Robin Scott Jensen, and Sharalyn D. Howcroft.
Description: New York, NY : Oxford University Press, [2018] |
Includes bibliographical references and index.
Identifiers: LCCN 2017029609 | ISBN 9780190274375 (cloth) |
ISBN 9780190274382 (updf) | ISBN 9780190274399 (epub) |
ISBN 9780190274405 (online content)
Subjects: LCSH: Mormon Church—Sacred books. |
Church of Jesus Christ of Latter-day Saints—Sacred books.
Classification: LCC BX8621 .F68 2017 | DDC 289.3/2—dc23
LC record available at https://lccn.loc.gov/2017029609

3 5 7 9 8 6 4 2

Printed by Sheridan Books, Inc., United States of America

For
Dean C. Jessee
scholar, mentor, friend

Contents

Foreword

IN THE SUMMER of 1971, Mormon historian Dean C. Jessee's article "The Writing of Joseph Smith's History" appeared in *BYU Studies*—the Mormon studies quarterly published by the flagship educational institution of the Church of Jesus Christ of Latter-day Saints. Jessee's article attracted little attention in the professional historical community, but in the world of Mormon scholars and others interested in the foundations of the church, it signaled a revolutionary moment in Mormon history. Before the publication of the article, both scholars and laypeople generally assumed that all the writings bearing Smith's name were, in fact, written by Smith. But through careful textual analysis and handwriting comparisons, Jessee established that the original manuscripts behind the published writings attributed to Smith were in the handwriting of more than a dozen different scribes and clerks. Jessee built on this careful documentary research, tracking down the journals, letters, and other documents on which the manuscript history had been constructed, and began editing *The Papers of Joseph Smith*. Several historians joined with Jessee in the early years of the 21st century when the project was professionalized and reconceptualized as the Joseph Smith Papers.

Such is Dean C. Jessee's accomplishment that he ranks in the company of such stellar scholars as Julian Boyd, Lyman Butterfield, and Perry Miller, the founding editors of the *Papers of Thomas Jefferson*, the *Adams Papers*, and the *Works of Jonathan Edwards*. Boyd was elected president of the American Historical Association, and Miller was arguably the greatest American intellectual historian who ever wrote. Though bearing fewer academic accolades, Jessee belongs in this accomplished class of editors.

His great editorial achievement in Smith scholarship may also be compared with the contributions of the late Thomas A. Shafer to the *Works of Jonathan Edwards* during my own tenure as general editor. In both cases, these textual scholars were not widely known for their books and articles but contributed a scientific precision and accuracy to documentary editing without precedent in their respective areas of study. In both cases, earlier scholars and editors had tended to be filiopietistic and would make unfounded assumptions that passed as facts. Schafer explored the vast trove of original Edwards manuscripts and demonstrated how earlier editions were sloppy in execution and actually deleted portions of his writings that they deemed embarrassing! Thanks to the meticulous and comprehensive editing of Shafer and Jessee, it is now possible to access these major religious thinkers on their own terms.

Jessee's careful methodology has been taken up by a new generation of scholars. The team of historians editing volumes for *The Joseph Smith Papers* is producing exceptionally meticulous work and is publishing Smith's papers at a remarkable pace that promises to match the scope of the Edwards edition in a fraction of the time. Already scholars are revising their arguments in light of the careful transcription and annotation that is going into the edition.

This book exemplifies Jessee's influence. In one way or another, the chapters in this collection build on his rigorous methodological foundations. Each author focuses on a particular document, probing deeply into the background, intention, production, transmission, and reception of the text, offering novel insights into America's most successful new religion in its formative years. Together these chapters provide an estimable collection of documentary interpretations that will inform readers and inspire further studies by other researchers. What began with the work of Dean C. Jessee has evolved into one of the premier scholarly editions in the world today. The chapters collected in this volume bear further witness to the importance of his labor.

Harry S. Stout
Jonathan Edwards Professor
of American Religious History
Yale University

Contributors

Mark Ashurst-McGee is a senior historian in the Church History Department of the Church of Jesus Christ of Latter-day Saints and the senior research and review editor for the Joseph Smith Papers Project. He is the co-editor of several volumes in *The Joseph Smith Papers*. His writings have appeared in several scholarly journals, including *Journal of Mormon History* and *Brigham Young University Studies Quarterly*.

Ronald O. Barney is past senior archivist and historian in the Church History Department of the Church of Jesus Christ of Latter-day Saints. He was an associate editor of *The Joseph Smith Papers* and has served as the executive director of the Mormon History Association and as editor of *Mormon Historical Studies*. His three books are *One Side by Himself: The Life and Times of Lewis Barney, 1808–1894*; *The Mormon Vanguard Brigade of 1847: Norton Jacob's Record*; and *Mack Watkins: A Biography*.

Richard Lyman Bushman is Gouverneur Morris Professor of History Emeritus at Columbia University, and more recently Howard W. Hunter Chair of Mormon Studies at Claremont Graduate University. His several books include *From Puritan to Yankee: Character and the Social Order in Connecticut, 1690–1765*; *The Refinement of America: Persons, Houses, Cities*; and *Joseph Smith: Rough Stone Rolling*.

Jeffrey G. Cannon is a doctoral student in world Christianity at the University of Edinburgh, where his research explores how churches have used different media, particularly photographs, to influence attitudes toward Africa. Previously, he was an archivist for the Church History Department of the Church of Jesus Christ of Latter-day Saints. His writings have appeared in several scholarly journals, including *Brigham Young University Studies Quarterly*.

David W. Grua is a historian and documentary editor for the Joseph Smith Papers. He is the author of *Surviving Wounded Knee: The Lakotas and the Politics of Memory*. His writings have appeared in several scholarly journals, including *Journal of Mormon History* and *Brigham Young University Studies Quarterly*.

Grant Hardy is professor of history and religious studies at the University of North Carolina at Asheville. He is the author of several books, including *Worlds of Bronze and Bamboo: Sima Qian's Conquest of History*; *The Establishment of the Han Empire and Imperial China*; and *Understanding the Book of Mormon: A Reader's Guide*. He is the editor of *The Book of Mormon: A Reader's Edition* and co-editor of the first volume of the *Oxford History of Historical Writing*.

Andrew H. Hedges is associate professor of Church history and doctrine at Brigham Young University. He is the co-editor of the second and third volumes of the Journals series of *The Joseph Smith Papers*. His writings have appeared in several scholarly journals, including *Journal of Mormon History* and *Journal of the Illinois State Historical Society*.

Sharalyn D. Howcroft is an archivist for *The Joseph Smith Papers* specializing in handwriting identification and custodial history. She has an MLIS with an archival studies concentration from the University of Wisconsin-Milwaukee and is a member of the Academy of Certified Archivists.

Robin Scott Jensen is an associate managing historian and the project archivist for the Joseph Smith Papers. He is the co-editor of the first three volumes in the Revelations and Translations series of *The Joseph Smith Papers*. His writings have appeared in several scholarly journals, including *Journal of Mormon History* and *Brigham Young University Studies Quarterly*.

Jennifer Reeder is the nineteenth-century women's history specialist at the Church History Department of the Church of Jesus Christ of Latter-day Saints. She has edited documentary collections of Mormon women's writings, and her writings have appeared in several scholarly journals, including *Journal of Mormon History*.

Alex D. Smith is a historian with the Joseph Smith Papers. He is the co-editor of two volumes of the Journals series and three volumes of the Documents series of *The Joseph Smith Papers*. His writings have appeared in several scholarly journals, including *Journal of Mormon History*.

William V. Smith is emeritus professor of mathematics at Brigham Young University. His writings have appeared in several scholarly journals, including *Dialogue: A Journal of Mormon Thought*.

Harry S. Stout is the Jonathan Edwards Professor of American Religious History at Yale University. He is the author and editor of several books, including *Upon the Altar of the Nation: A Moral History of the Civil War; The New England Soul; The Divine Dramatist: George Whitefield and the Rise of Modern Evangelicalism*. He is general editor of both *The Works of Jonathan Edwards* and the Religion in America series for Oxford University Press.

Laurel Thatcher Ulrich is 300th Anniversary University Professor at Harvard University. She is the author of several books, including *A Midwife's Tale: The Life of Martha Ballard Based on Her Diaries, 1735–1812; The Age of Homespun: Objects and Stories in the Creation of an American Myth*; and *A House Full of Females: Plural Marriage and Women's Rights in Early Mormonism, 1835–1870*.

Grant Underwood is professor of history at Brigham Young University. He is the author of *The Millenarian World of Early Mormonism* and a co-editor of three volumes in the Documents series of *The Joseph Smith Papers*.

Thomas A. Wayment is professor of ancient scripture at Brigham Young University. He is the author, with Lincoln Blumell, of *Christian Oxyrhynchus: Texts, Documents, and Sources*.

Foundational Texts of Mormonism

1

Introduction

Mark Ashurst-McGee, Robin Scott Jensen, and Sharalyn D. Howcroft

It is possible today to study that incredibly rare event: the rise of a new world religion.

RODNEY STARK

RODNEY STARK, a professor of sociology and comparative religion, has often looked to Mormonism as an ideal case study of new religious movements, not only because of the rapid growth of Mormonism but also because of the wealth of information available in the documentary record its founding prophet initiated.[1] Among the thousands of documents Joseph Smith wrote, dictated, or commissioned, there are several highly significant sources that scholars have turned to again and again in their study of the beginnings of Mormonism, with little appreciation of how and why these sources were produced in the first place. But due consideration of the general context for these documents and their particular circumstances of production often make a significant difference in how they ought to be used in historical analysis.

This book insists on the importance of taking a closer look at the essential texts that historians use to reconstruct the founding era of the Church of Jesus Christ of Latter-day Saints (LDS Church). In expressing our special

1. See, for example, Stark, "A Theory of Revelations," *Journal for the Scientific Study of Religion*, 38, no. 2 (June 1999): 289. The epigraph is taken from Rodney Stark, "The Rise of a New World Faith," *Review of Religious Research* 26, no. 1 (September 1984): 18–27; reprinted with slight modifications in *Latter-day Saint Social Life: Social Research on the LDS Church and its Members*, ed. James T. Duke (Provo, Utah: Religious Studies Center, 1998), 10.

interest in these sources, we use the word *foundational* in two senses. First, we refer to Mormonism's founding period—specifically, between 1820, when Joseph Smith experienced his first vision, and 1844, when he died. Second, we mean those major sources that historians repeatedly use in their research when they study Joseph Smith and early Mormonism and upon which they primarily build their historical narratives and arguments. The purpose of this book is to provide a deeper level of understanding of these sources so historians and other scholars can use them more critically in their work.

Scholars working in American religious history often recognize Mormons as a record-keeping people. This is usually a shorthand way of suggesting that the Latter-day Saints have a source-rich history or of acknowledging the global reach of their church's genealogical resources. During the second half of the twentieth century, the practitioners of the "New Mormon History" made great use of these primary sources, bringing to bear their academic training and situating their Mormon sources in wider American, Atlantic, and even international contexts. As fruitful as this was, much was lacking in the way of source criticism. Because the archives of the LDS Church had previously restricted access to so many records, historians had often simply focused on obtaining access to documents and then mining their contents. Even with considerable interest among these historians in documentation and document provenance—spurred in part by the 1980s criminal investigation of several newly "discovered" sensational documents that turned out to be the work of forger and murderer Mark Hofmann[2]—there was seldom a deep scrutiny of documents *as* documents. Interrogating documents as *products* of history rather than just as sources of historical information results in potentially significant insights not found in the words of the document itself. Rarely have scholars approached Mormon documents using the disciplined rigor of archivists, descriptive bibliographers, and documentary editors, asking routine methodological questions of textual intention, production, transmission, and reception.

One notable exception in this historiography of content-driven writing is the work of Dean C. Jessee. More than anyone, Jessee showed that

2. Linda Sillitoe and Allen Roberts, *Salamander: The Story of the Mormon Forgery Murders*, 2nd ed., with a new afterword (Salt Lake City: Signature Books, 1989); Richard E. Turley, Jr., *Victims: The LDS Church and the Mark Hofmann Case* (Urbana and Chicago: University of Illinois Press, 1992).

sources are not always what they appear to be at first glance. Perhaps the best example of his work is his analysis of the most frequently cited source in Mormon historical writing: the church's official history. The first six volumes of this history carried the subtitle *Period I: History of Joseph Smith, the Prophet, by Himself.*[3] This title easily gives the wrong impression. For decades, historians used this source as if Smith himself had personally written the entire multi-volume work, quoting passages from the history as if from the prophet's pen. In 1971, after years of careful research, Jessee published his article "The Writing of Joseph Smith's History," showing that none of the extant manuscripts behind the printed history were in Smith's handwriting. Nor were they in the handwriting of a single scribe taking down Smith's oral dictation. Instead, the history was written by more than a dozen different scribes and clerks, combining their efforts to review the journals, letters, and other extant documents left behind by Smith and his close associates and to copy, revise, or otherwise utilize those documents to create a seamless narrative written in an autobiographical voice. While Smith had initiated the production of this history and oversaw the ongoing effort, his initial involvement apparently gave way to that of his office staff. When he died they had finished little more than half of his years as church president. The historians and clerks continued on after his death, completing the last several years of his life a dozen years later.[4]

The chronological backbone for the history was Smith's corpus of journals. However, even the journals themselves cannot be seen as ordinary productions since they were, for the most part, kept by Smith's scribes. There was often a lag of days or even weeks in the journal keeping—between the events of his life and the time of recording them—occasionally colored by subsequent developments. Willard Richards, who was keeping Smith's journals during his final years, was also working on Smith's history, and seems to have begun keeping Smith's contemporaneous journal entries with an eye toward their eventual use as the source text for creating the history. Mormon history has never been the same since Dean C. Jessee pulled back the curtain and revealed Smith's history for what it is. The

3. *History of the Church of Jesus Christ of Latter-day Saints. Period I: History of Joseph Smith, the Prophet, by Himself,* ed. B. H. Roberts (Salt Lake City: Deseret News Press, 1902–1912). Roberts only completed one more volume in the series, which covered the period between Smith's death and the reorganization of the general church presidency with Brigham Young as the church's new leader.

4. Dean C. Jessee, "The Writing of Joseph Smith's History," *BYU Studies* 11 (Summer 1971): 439–73.

document is still a valuable resource, because it was produced by people who knew Joseph Smith well and were eyewitnesses to many of the events recounted in the text. Nevertheless, it must be used cautiously and critically with an understanding of its own origin, authorship, and production history.[5]

While the complex production of Joseph Smith's history may make it the archetypical example of the need to understand how and when and by whom a document was created, there are several other foundational sources, used frequently by those researching and writing in early Mormon history, that are not what they appear to be on their face. Jessee also did pioneering work on the original manuscripts of the Book of Mormon, on Joseph Smith's sermons, and on other significant sources, and became the founding editor of the Joseph Smith Papers Project.[6] And his work has endured. Because of his careful study and rigorous analysis, his publications have easily withstood the winds of historiographical fashion, as Jessee's articles from the 1970s and 1980s are still standards upon which serious scholars of early Mormonism depend. In recent years, a few others have, like Jessee, ventured deeply into documentary analysis. Royal Skousen has devoted his professional career to his Book of Mormon critical text project.[7] Lavina Fielding Anderson produced an excellent edition of the family biography created by Lucy Mack Smith, the founder's mother, with extensive introductory analysis.[8] The volumes of *The Joseph Smith Papers* have provided essential information for most of Smith's documents. However, the editorial apparatus of *The Joseph Smith Papers* allows only for terse annotation tied closely to the document itself. More thorough documentary analysis is in order for some of the major sources of the founding era of Mormonism. This book contributes several such

5. See also the recent work on the history by Dan Vogel, *History of Joseph Smith and The Church of Jesus Christ of Latter-day Saints: A Source and Text-critical Edition,* ed. Dan Vogel (Salt Lake City: Smith-Pettit Foundation 2015), especially vol. 1, pp. ix–xxviii.

6. See Dean C. Jessee, "The Original Book of Mormon Manuscript," *BYU Studies* 10 (Spring 1970): 259–78; Dean C. Jessee, "Priceless Words and Fallible Memories: Joseph Smith as Seen in the Effort to Preserve His Discourses," *BYU Studies* 31 (Spring 1991): 19–40; and the volumes of *The Joseph Smith Papers* (Salt Lake City: Church Historian's Press, 2008–).

7. See, for example, *The Original Manuscript of the Book of Mormon: Typographical Facsimile of the Extant Text,* ed. Royal Skousen (Provo, Utah: Foundation for Ancient Research and Mormon Studies, Brigham Young University, 2001).

8. Lucy Mack Smith, *Lucy's Book: A Critical Edition of Lucy Mack Smith's Family Memoir,* ed. Lavina Fielding Anderson (Salt Lake City: Signature Books, 2001).

studies investigating and analyzing some of the most important primary sources used for researching early Mormonism and its founder.

Joseph Smith, portrayed in Figure 1.1, was born in Vermont in 1805. During his adolescence, his family moved to New York, where he developed a deep interest in religion. He studied the Bible and attended several revival meetings. Smith began experiencing visions, and claimed to have talked with God, the Father, and the resurrected and glorified Jesus Christ. Smith also claimed that an angel led him to the location of an ancient book of scripture written on a set of golden plates and that he was blessed with a spiritual gift of "translation" by which he orally dictated the text of the Book of Mormon—an English rendition of the ancient American record—to scribes. The book was published in 1830 and shortly thereafter Joseph Smith founded a church. Smith dictated several "thus saith the Lord" revelations to his early followers, commanding them to travel, preach, and proselytize, or giving instructions on how to administrate the new religion, or directing the "gathering" of converts into a community

FIGURE 1.1. Joseph Smith. Portrait by David Rogers, 1842.
Courtesy of Community of Christ Library-Archives, Independence, MO.

of social harmony and holiness. The revelations were taken down, copied into record books, and eventually published. Smith was always more comfortable with the spoken word than with writing. Scribes also began helping him with his correspondence and journals, and newly appointed church clerks kept minutes of meetings. Personal and institutional record keeping grew in fits and starts, partly disrupted by the movements of the body of church members from New York to Ohio to Missouri to Illinois. However, by the early 1840s, Smith had established an office staff that helped him with fairly consistent record keeping. His textual output—of letters, legal papers, land records, and all sorts of documents—was fairly heavy during his final years in Nauvoo, Illinois, before he was murdered in 1844.

Among these thousands of sources, in all their variety, some of the most important are Smith's revelations, correspondence, journals, and sermon texts. This book offers case studies representing each of these major types of sources used by historians of the early Mormon experience. Rather than focusing on a given incident, episode, or development in early Mormonism, each author focuses on a particular document, or set of documents, as his or her primary subject. In a way, each chapter considers the *production* of a document as an historical event, with its own background, purpose, circumstances, and consequences. As stated above, careful study of a document often reveals things about history beyond the content of the record itself. The chapters in this book consider documents not just as sources of information, but artifacts that reflect the culture in which they were created.

Each chapter in this book is an original and significant contribution, shedding new light on an important source or set of sources. This is the case even for sources that have previously received considerable treatment. For example, the Book of Mormon has been the subject of rigorous textual analysis, but in this volume Richard Lyman Bushman provides a new and insightful reading of its complicated narrative structure. Bushman's "The Gold Plates as Foundational Text" turns our attention to the Book of Mormon's account of its own creation. In contrast to the controversies over the recovery and translation of the plates, the translated text is detailed and precise in explaining its construction. Even the complicated insertion of the "small plates" into a narrative based on the "large plates" is explained and rationalized. The small plates were not just a back-up text to fill in the space left when the earliest batch of translation work was lost, but a cultural and political force within the story. The first book in the

Book of Mormon was clearly a political document created to justify the leadership of the ancient American prophet Nephi, its purported author. Furthermore, its spiritual and prophetic emphasis made it a model for the abridgment of the large plates made by Mormon, one of the last prophets to write in the book. Following Nephi's lead, Mormon added prophecies, missions, and conversions to the record's political focus. The Book of Mormon, Bushman argues, seems to have been precociously written in the spirit of higher criticism. It comes through as a divinely inspired and yet very human text pieced together by mortal men drawing on disparate source materials.

Beginning with Bushman's study, the chapters in this collection proceed in roughly chronological order. Whereas Bushman explores the idea of the gold plates as a document within the Book of Mormon narrative, Grant Hardy provides an overview of the original Book of Mormon manuscripts. In "Textual Criticism and the Book of Mormon," Hardy, a historian of world religions and their various works of sacred writ, provides his assessment of the Book of Mormon Critical Text Project conducted by Royal Skousen, a linguist. Hardy plumbs the value of Skousen's work in terms of what it might reveal about the original dictation process and the subsequent transmission of text, as well as Joseph Smith's attitudes toward the scripture he produced.

Shortly after the publication of the Book of Mormon, Joseph Smith initiated a revision of the Bible, which he also considered, and called, a "translation." In "Intertextuality and the Purpose of Joseph Smith's New Translation of the Bible," New Testament scholar Thomas A. Wayment examines the impetus of the Bible revision by looking closely at the first document produced as part of the project and how that effort led Smith to re-envision the Bible. The Bible project initially sought to expand upon a revelation Smith had dictated that related an encounter between Moses and God. In pursuing greater clarity on that early revelation, Smith turned to Genesis for more information. He began revising Genesis, and then continued through the entire Bible. Wayment shows that Smith revised the synoptic gospels to be more in harmony with each other, Christianized the Old Testament to make it more compatible with the New Testament, and affixed his revelation about Moses to his revised Bible in order to reconcile the Bible with his own revelations. Wayment makes a compelling case regarding the pervasiveness of the harmonization impetus in Smith's Bible revision. Going forward, Mormon scholars who look for doctrinal meaning in any revised passage of the Bible must consider the possibility that modifying the passage was primarily motivated by the effort to bring it into closer agreement with some other part of the Bible or with Smith's own revelations.

The production of the Book of Mormon and the Bible revision occasioned many of the earliest "thus saith the Lord" revelations issued by Smith. In "The Dictation, Compilation, and Canonization of Joseph Smith's Revelations," Grant Underwood tracks the evolution of Smith's revelations from their original dictation and inscription through their preservation and revision to their eventual publication and canonization. While the revelation texts are widely available in the Doctrine and Covenants, one of the "standard works" of the LDS scriptural canon, Underwood complicates the role of Smith and his associates in copying, revising, and publishing the texts. Underwood draws on newly available documents and research to show the complexity of the development of the revelatory texts during Smith's lifetime—especially in the early manuscript copies. While many scholars look to the revelations as texts received by early Latter-day Saints as sacred texts spoken from God, Underwood discloses and explains the human intervention that occurred in the presentation of the revelations.

Religious persecution drove Joseph Smith from Ohio to Missouri, but things did not work out better there. In October 1838, Missouri Governor Lilburn W. Boggs declared all Mormons to be enemies of the state who would be driven out or "exterminated." Missouri officials charged Smith and other church leaders with several crimes and imprisoned them. During the winter of 1838 to 1839, the Latter-day Saint people faced an existential crisis. David W. Grua's chapter, "Joseph Smith's Missouri Prison Letters and the Mormon Textual Community," places Smith's epistles to the church during this time within the historical genre of the prison letter. Grua contends that Smith used his epistles to render the catastrophe in Missouri comprehensible by connecting suffering with a foundational tenet of the Mormon religion—revelation. Grua also provides a reception history, showing that the letters succeeded in holding the exiled Latter-day Saints together as a community.

After escaping from state custody, Smith reorganized his people in Nauvoo, Illinois, where several prominent women of the church organized a benevolence society. Typical of contemporary women's organizations, the Relief Society was comprised of officers and members who kept careful records of their benevolent efforts and theological discussions. In "The Textual Culture of the Nauvoo Female Relief Society Leadership and Minute Book," Jennifer Reeder shows how the society's minute book cannot be taken at face value as a ledger of names and donations. Of particular interest is that most of the leaders of the Relief Society were polygamously married to Joseph Smith, and yet this was never openly discussed in meetings and was therefore never recorded in the minutes. This chapter examines the polygamist relationships, tracks the work of the secretaries, and shows that scholars must read between the lines to fully understand what was and was not recorded.

In Nauvoo, church members began to take notes on Smith's sermons in earnest. In "Joseph Smith's Sermons and the Early Mormon Documentary Record," William V. Smith treats Smith's preaching record in chronological fashion, showing that the documentary record of Smith's sermons expanded with the growing importance attached to his preaching, and offers an explanation for how this importance developed. He also shows that the character of Smith's preaching record and its subsequent evolution as a published source of authority in the church is a complex issue that bars the historian from a simplistic use of the resulting corpus of sermons.

The reports of Smith's sermons increased in Nauvoo in part thanks to Willard Richards and William Clayton, record keepers working for Joseph Smith and also helping him keep his journals. "Joseph Smith's Nauvoo Journals," by Alex D. Smith and Andrew H. Hedges, provides a thorough analysis of the journals kept during the last two and half years of Joseph Smith's life. Smith and Hedges explain how the journals were kept and reveal their more corporate, less personal, nature. They also examine the Nauvoo journals in the context of closely related documents that were being created at the same time, including the "History of Joseph Smith," financial records in the "Book of the Law of the Lord," an account of Smith's activities made by William Clayton, and the journal of Willard Richards. The article also overviews the results of this production, evaluating the contribution the journals make to our understanding of the final years of Smith's life and the Nauvoo era of Mormon history.

Next to the journals of Joseph Smith, William Clayton, and Willard Richards, the journals of Wilford Woodruff provide one of the most informative sources for early Mormon history. Laurel Thatcher Ulrich, who has elucidated the early American diary of Martha Ballard in *A Midwife's Tale*,[9] asserts that Woodruff also produced one of the great American diaries.

---

9. Laurel Thatcher Ulrich, *A Midwife's Tale: The Life of Martha Ballard, Based on Her Diary, 1785–1812* (New York: Vintage Books, 1990).

In "The Early Diaries of Wilford Woodruff, 1835–1839," she looks beyond the surface content of the record and shows that the meticulous care with which Woodruff kept his diaries reflects the way in which he lived his life and his religion. When read closely, his journals indirectly document his understanding of earthly and heavenly family bonds, ambitious hopes for his newfound faith, zeal for proselytizing converts, and the challenges of missionary work away from his family. Ulrich, in other words, reminds readers of the ways in which diaries and journals represent not just the thoughts and words of their authors but their lived experiences.

One of the most important sources for understanding Joseph Smith's early life was written shortly after he died. His mother, Lucy Mack Smith, narrated the family's history in 1845. Previous scholarly treatment of Lucy's narrative has utilized other historical sources to understand the origins of the book and the work of Martha and Howard Coray in transcribing Lucy's words, editing them, and compiling the history. In "A Textual and Archival Reexamination of Lucy Mack Smith's History," Sharalyn D. Howcroft applies the archival concepts of fonds to the history by reconstructing the original order of the rough manuscript, shedding new light on the document's composition methodology, and inventorying its extant and non-extant manuscripts. She also points out the lack of textual indicators for dictated transcription, suggesting the rough manuscript is not the dictated urtext described in historical sources; rather, the rough manuscript and extant fair copy both appear to be the amalgamation of two separate manuscripts. Drawing on her knowledge of archival history and the history of archival practice in the LDS Church Historian's Office, Howcroft also sheds light on the complicated provenance of the history and associated papers that were later amalgamated into one archival collection.

Written texts are not the only primary sources documenting early Mormon history. Jeffrey G. Cannon, in "The Image as Text and Context in Early Mormon History," considers photographic images from the nineteenth century as texts for historical research. Photography came to America only a few years before Joseph Smith was murdered and the Latter-day Saints left the country for the Great Salt Lake Valley of northern Mexico. Thus very few images from the Smith era were taken (or are extant). However, many images of early Mormon people and places were created years or even decades later in attempts to document or illustrate the movement's origins. Scholars writing on the history of the founding era often use the same photographs over and over again to illustrate their work, without any consciousness of the circumstances under which they were created. Cannon shows that many of these images were created in the context of rivalry and insecurity over competing succession claims following Joseph Smith's untimely death.

Despite the gravity and heft of Joseph Smith's documentary corpus, there are significant variations in the coverage and texture of his papers and even large gaps in time. The concluding essay by Ronald O. Barney, who spent his career as an archivist for the Church of Jesus Christ of Latter-day Saints, provides a mature assessment of which records were created, where the gaps are, and what this uneven documentary record can tell us about early Mormon concepts of record keeping and even Joseph Smith's personality. Barney's essay, "Joseph Smith and the Conspicuous Scarcity of Early Mormon Documentation," shows that Smith was often remarkably reluctant to share the experiences he held sacred, that he seldom utilized the early church newspapers at his disposal to publish his writing, and that he neglected to prepare or preserve his sermon texts. There has been little done in early Mormon history exploring the nature and causes for what was *not* recorded. Barney's analysis is a fitting conclusion and complement to the other chapters in the book about the primary records that *were* created.

As the editors, we wish to acknowledge the various contributors to the volume for their dedication to this project, as well as many others who have helped to make it possible. We would like to thank Dean C. Jessee, the founder of the Joseph Smith Papers Project, for mentoring us. We also thank Jeffery O. Johnson, Ronald K. Esplin, Ronald O. Barney, Christy Best, and other mentors from our years on the project. We thank the Church History Department of the Church of Jesus Christ of Latter-day Saints for providing a grant to help fund some of our production needs and Jana Riess for most of the developmental editing. Several editors who work for the Joseph Smith Papers Project generously donated time to help with further editing: R. Eric Smith, Nathan Waite, Nicole Fernley, Suzy Bills, Rachel Osborne, Keaton Reed, Shannon Kelley, Stephanie Steed, and Leslie Sherman. Angela Ashurst-McGee also helped edit some of the chapters and Reilly Ben Hatch helped with some of the source checking. Alex D. Smith provided expert assistance with the book's photographs and Matthew C. Howcroft helped with diagrams. We thank Cynthia Read, Theo Calderara, Gina Chung, Cameron Donahue, Drew Anderla, Sivaranjani Chandramouliswaran, Raji Nirmal, Sangeetha Vishwanthan, and Carol Neiman with Oxford University Press for working through the volume with us. We also thank Kate Mertes for creating this volume's index. Finally, we thank our spouses for their patience and support all along the way.

With all of this assistance, we have attempted to craft a book that will help historians working in the founding era of Mormonism gain a more solid grounding in the period's documentary record by supplying important information on major primary sources that will enable them to use those sources more critically in their own work. This book does not cover all of the major texts of early Mormonism. And the very nature of the extant documentary record skews to the (male) leaders of the church and the better educated among the early Latter-day Saints, many of whom were poor and illiterate. More work needs to be done, for example, on Smith's letter books, financial papers, and the minute books of the organizations over which he presided. In addition, several documents created by ordinary early Mormon men and women, while not foundational in the sense that scores of historians have used these records, also deserve close investigation. The editors hope that this book will encourage other scholars to engage at a deeper level with these and other sources and develop a more critical understanding of Mormonism's founding era.

2

The Gold Plates as Foundational Text

Richard Lyman Bushman

JOSEPH SMITH SAID that the Book of Mormon was the "keystone of our religion," an assertion his followers accepted at the time and have never given up since.[1] From the beginning it was the premier foundational text of Mormonism. The first and the largest of Smith's publications and the message that missionaries took with them when they first went into the field, the Book of Mormon set Mormonism apart from the scores of other religions springing to life in the nineteenth century and gave the church the nickname it has been unable to shake ever since. Moreover, the book's importance has not faded over time. If anything, the Book of Mormon has grown more influential through the church's history. The criticism of skeptics has not diminished its centrality for Latter-day Saints, and the erosion of faith in the Bible has not spilled over to the Book of Mormon. Mormons are more devoted to the Book of Mormon today than when it was first published in 1830.[2]

Behind the Book of Mormon, and even more captivating than the book itself, stood its purported source: the gold plates recovered from the Hill Cumorah with the help of an angel. For Smith's followers, the plates were the ur-text, the mysterious original of the English translation, and so for them the true foundational text, allegedly written in a derivative of Egyptian and never read by moderns save for Joseph Smith himself. So

1. Scott G. Kenney, ed., *Wilford Woodruff's Journals*, vol. 2, 1841–1845 (Midvale, Utah: Signature Books, 1983), 139, 28 November 1841.

2. Noel Reynolds, "The Coming Forth of the Book of Mormon in the Twentieth Century," *BYU Studies Quarterly* 38, no. 2 (1999): 39–40.

compelling was the image, the gold plates threatened to swamp the Book of Mormon as a text. Even for believers, the backstory of the text's production defined the book more than its actual contents. The plates were a gift from heaven, brought by an angel, making the very existence of the Book of Mormon a marvel. At the same time, the plates came out of the earth. They were an artifact recovered from a stone box on a hillside near the Smith farm, where, according to Smith's story, they had lain for fourteen centuries. Like a pot dug up by an archeologist, they put the nineteenth century in touch with biblical Jerusalem and ancient America. All this was in the plates' story before the pages of the book were even opened.

For outside observers the plates were, of course, wholly imaginary and likely a hoax, yet they defined the Book of Mormon for them as well. The first known newspaper notice regarding Joseph Smith was an article in the *Wayne Sentinel* in June 1829 reporting the imminent appearance of the "gold bible."[3] The text itself—the lengthy, detailed history of an ancient civilization—was less newsworthy than the plates on which it was purportedly inscribed. It excited reporters to think that the Book of Mormon was supposedly written on a six-inch stack of thin metal plates inscribed with ancient hieroglyphs and presumably of immense value. The reporters were aware of the writing on the plates: The *Wayne Sentinel* spoke of a supposed "ancient record, of a religious and divine nature and origin, written in ancient characters."[4] But the image of a gold bible stood out, the greed of the gold joining with the holiness of the bible to create an irresistible image.

The story of the plates has made interpretation of the Book of Mormon so contentious that readers coming from differing perspectives can scarcely agree on anything about Mormonism's foundational text. The plates cast doubt on everything. They move the Book of Mormon into the realm of the fantastic. Without the plates story, the Book of Mormon would have seemed like a simple literary fiction dreamed up by a talented folk writer. The book would have been classed with Solomon Spaulding's *Manuscript Found*, a novel of Roman voyagers who visited pre-Columbian America, with its own fictional backstory of translation from a manuscript

3. *Wayne Sentinel* (Palmyra, NY), 26 June 1829, [5]. There is some evidence of earlier publications. See Matthew Roper, "Early Publications on the Book of Mormon," *Journal of the Book of Mormon and Other Restoration Scripture* 18, no. 2 (2009): 40.

4. *Wayne Sentinel*, 26 June 1929, in Dan Vogel, ed., *Early Mormon Documents*, 5 vols. (Salt Lake City: Signature Books, 1996–2003), 2:219.

found in an Ohio cave in 1812.[5] The Book of Mormon would have been amusing but not dangerous. Add the angel and the gold plates, and the Book of Mormon becomes an insidious fraud. The *Wayne Sentinel* reporter called the whole matter "a gross imposition, and a grosser superstition."[6] By sticking to his story of an exotic artifact delivered by an angel and withheld from public view, Joseph Smith took a great risk. He rested his own veracity, the historicity of the Book of Mormon, the reality of his prophetic mission, and the legitimacy of his church on the existence of the plates.

The plates perplex even believers. Latter-day Saints themselves cannot agree on how the writings engraved on the gold surfaces relate to Joseph Smith's oral dictation to his secretaries. Assuming their existence, as Latter-day Saints do, how exactly did the translator use the plates? Artists' depictions of the translation process sometimes show him looking at the plates with a finger on the character he was translating, as if puzzling out the meaning of each mark.[7] Presumably then, the Book of Mormon text would be an exact translation of the words on the leaves. That may have been Smith's method in the early phases of the translation—when he was looking at the plates through the lenses of the "spectacles" he found with them—but later descriptions have him looking at one of his seer stones in a hat with the plates wrapped in a cloth on the table.[8] The plates themselves were not even visible to him. During parts of the translation, the plates were not even present—Smith claimed they were hidden away to keep them safe.[9] Was the dictation, then, really coming from the plates like a computer sending information to a wireless printer or like a cell phone using Google Translate? Or was the seer stone delivering something else?

---

5. Solomon Spaulding, *Manuscript Found: The Complete Original Spaulding Manuscript,* ed., Kent P. Jackson (Provo, Utah: Religious Studies Center, Brigham Young University, 1996).

6. *Wayne Sentinel,* 26 June 1929, in Vogel, *Early Mormon Documents,* 2:219.

7. See, for example, Harold Kilbourn, *Joseph Smith Translating,* circa 1970; Del Parson, *Joseph Smith Translating the Book of Mormon,* 1996; Robert Barrett, *Joseph Smith Translates the Golden Plates,* 1988.

8. James E. Lancaster, "The Translation of the Book of Mormon," in *The Word of God: Essays on Mormon Scripture,* ed. Dan Vogel (Salt Lake City: Signature Books, 1990), 99.

9. See, for example, Martin Harris, Interview by John A. Clark, 1828, in *The Episcopal Recorder* (Philadelphia), 5 September 1840, 94, qtd. in Vogel, *Early Mormon Documents,* 2:266; Joseph Smith Sr. Interview by Fayette Lapham, ca. 1830, in "The Mormons," *Historical Magazine* 7 (May 1870): 308, qtd. in Vogel, *Early Mormon Documents,* 1:464; Oliver Cowdery, *Defense in a Rehearsal of My Grounds for Separating Myself from the Latter Day Saints* (Norton, Ohio, 1839); also *Saints' Herald,* 20 May 1907, 229–30.

What was it Smith saw, or believed he saw, or at least told others that he saw? Accounts of believing Latter-day Saints do not agree.

The entire process of translation has been the subject of debate among Mormon scholars. Even those who believe the text came by the inspiration of God, as Joseph Smith said, differ on the relationship between inscribed plates and translated text. Was it word-for-word, an exact conveyance of meaning from "reformed Egyptian" to English; or did Smith get impressions of meaning that he couched in his own language?[10] Some have suggested that he injected commentary of his own to expand the translation, thus introducing nineteenth-century content.[11] Other Mormon scholars offer evidence from the translation manuscripts that the translation was tightly controlled, implying that the resulting English text closely conformed to the words Smith saw in the seer stone.[12] The space between the wrapped plates sitting on the table and Joseph nearby looking into a stone in a hat symbolizes the interpretive gap where various explanations of translation have been inserted even by those who accept the premise of the plates' existence.[13]

What then can be said about the relationship of the current edition of the Book of Mormon to its original text on the gold plates? The subject is so fraught there is no agreement at any level. Can the subject be addressed with any hope of common understanding? One resort is to the text itself. The prevailing ambiguity about the Book of Mormon's foundational text dissipates inside the book. In contrast to the uncertainties about the very existence of the plates and the nature of translation, the Book of Mormon is surprisingly exact about the production of the text inscribed on the plates. Once a reader moves inside the text and suspends judgment

---

10. See Brant A. Gardner, *The Gift and Power: Translating the Book of Mormon* (Salt Lake City: Greg Kofford Books, 2011). See also John W. Welch and Tim Rathbone, "Book of Mormon Translation by Joseph Smith," *Encyclopedia of Mormonism*, ed. Daniel H. Ludlow, 5 vols. (New York: Macmillan, 1992), 1:210–13; James E. Lancaster, "The Translation of the Book of Mormon," in *The Word of God: Essays on Mormon Scripture*, ed. Dan Vogel (Salt Lake City: Signature Books, 1990), 97–112; Dallin D. Oaks, "Book of Mormon, Language of the Translated Text of," in *Book of Mormon Reference Companion*, ed. Dennis L. Largey (Salt Lake City: Deseret Book, 2003), 116–19.

11. Blake T. Ostler, "The Book of Mormon as a Modern Expansion of an Ancient Source," *Dialogue: A Journal of Mormon Thought* 20 (1987): 66–123.

12. Royal Skousen, "How Joseph Smith Translated the Book of Mormon: Evidence from the Original Manuscript," *Journal of Book of Mormon Studies* 7, no. 1 (1998): 24.

13. The state of the debate is summarized in Brant A. Gardner, *The Gift and Power: Translating the Book of Mormon* (Salt Lake City: Greg Kofford Books, 2011), chaps. 14–16.

about the background story, the text generously explains itself. Few books are more self-conscious about their own making. Even when regarded as historical fiction, the book illuminates itself.

Nephite Records and Record Keepers

The pains taken by Book of Mormon authors to explain how the book came into existence begins with the title page. Rather than epitomize the contents, the lengthy title explains where it came from: "The Book of Mormon: An Account Written by the Hand of Mormon upon Plates Taken from the Plates of Nephi." It was an unusual title. Titles do not ordinarily say that a book was written on parchment or printed on paper, but Mormon's son Moroni made a point of saying that his book was written "upon plates" and "taken" from plates. The phrase "Taken from the Plates of Nephi" identifies Mormon's major source for his narrative, like a writer informing the reader that she located most of her material in the National Archives in Washington, D.C—and doing so in the subtitle.

It is less clear why Moroni wrote "Written by the Hand of Mormon upon Plates." As with any text, fictional or historical, the author of course needed to establish the provenance and authority of the work. Nephi, the character in whose narrative voice the book begins, did the same in the book's opening sentence: "I Nephi . . . make a record of my proceedings in my day."[14] But why, within the parameters of the book, did Moroni add "upon Plates"? The words may suggest that an account written on plates possessed greater authority than ones recorded on a more fragile medium, the durability of the material attesting to the importance of the text. One Book of Mormon prophet had said, "whatsoever things we write upon anything save it be upon plates must perish and vanish away."[15] That was why, as another prophet in the book explained, "we labor diligently to engraven these words upon plates, hoping that our beloved brethren

14. 1 Nephi 1:1. All references are to the chapters and verses in the edition of the Book of Mormon currently published by the Church of Jesus Christ of Latter-day Saints. This is the most available text of the Book of Mormon for both scholars and church members. (*The Book of Mormon: Another Testament of Jesus Christ* [Salt Lake City: The Church of Jesus Christ of Latter-day Saints, 2013].)

15. Jacob 4:2.

and our children will receive them with thankful hearts."[16] Texts of lasting importance called for durable materials.[17]

According to the Book of Mormon itself, the plates of Nephi came into existence about 590 BCE, ten years after Nephi's father Lehi and the entire family fled Jerusalem in hopes of finding a new promised land.[18] Lehi's son Nephi manufactured plates to record the family's history. From that time on, the plates of Nephi threaded their way through a thousand years of Nephite history as each generation added its bit. These, however, were not the plates Joseph Smith received. They were their source. After nine and a half centuries, one of the last prophets, Mormon, manufactured another set of plates on which he summarized the history written on the plates of Nephi.[19] Mormon passed his own plates to his son Moroni, the final prophet, who buried them in the early fifth century CE for their long sleep in the ground.[20] Joseph Smith recovered them from a stone box in a hill in 1827,[21] as portrayed by an early Mormon in Figure 2.1.

The Book of Mormon tells the complicated story of each history-writer taking up the plates to add his portion and usually includes a note about how each conceived his responsibilities. In a way, the Book of Mormon is a book about writing a book. Of all the historians to touch the Nephite plates, Mormon knew them best and was as self-conscious as any about his mission.[22] He was given responsibility for the Nephite plates when he was a child, an unprecedented occurrence in the chronicle. The previous curator, Ammaron, did not select him to guard the plates because he was a prophet, a king, or the son of the previous caretaker, the usual qualifications. Mormon was chosen because he was a prodigy. Ammaron told him about the plates when he was just ten years old, explaining his selection only by saying "I perceive that thou art a sober child, and art quick to

16. Jacob 4:2–3.

17. When Nephi secured a set of brass plates from an elder in Jerusalem to take with his family to their new land of promise, his father Lehi prophesied that these plates "should never perish; neither should they be dimmed any more by time" (1 Nephi 5:17–19).

18. 1 Nephi 19:1.

19. 3 Nephi 5:10–11.

20. Moroni 10:1–2.

21. Joseph Smith History 1:52, 59.

22. Mormon 2:2; 6:5; 8:2–3. Mormon lived approximately 311–385 CE.

FIGURE 2.1. C. C. A. Christensen (1831–1912), *The Hill Cumorah*, c.1878, tempera on muslin, 80 ½ × 116 inches.

Brigham Young University Museum of Art, gift of the grandchildren of C. C. A. Christensen, 1970.

observe."[23] Mormon himself said modestly that by age ten he "began to be learned somewhat after the manner of the learning of my people."[24] Five years later, when he was fifteen, his people chose him to lead the Nephite armies.[25] "Notwithstanding I being young, was large in stature," was Mormon's modest explanation for his unlikely selection.[26] One of the gaps in Book of Mormon history is an account of where he came from. He speaks of traveling at age eleven with his father to the land southward, suggesting his father was a diplomat, merchant, or military leader—a person

23. Mormon 1:2.

24. Mormon 1:2.

25. Ammaron recommended that Mormon recover the plates at age twenty-four (Mormon 1:2). According to his account in the three hundred and forty and fifth year, when Mormon was thirty-four, his armies fled to the land of Jashon where Ammaron buried the plates. Mormon says "and behold I had gone according to the word of Ammaron and taken the plates of Nephi, and did make a record." (Mormon 2:17) Either he went at this time, when thirty-four, to recover the plates, or, as the past perfect tense suggests, he had gone earlier, possibly at age twenty-four.

26. Mormon 2:1.

with elite status.[27] Something must have brought Mormon to the public's attention. Even so, selection to head the armies at fifteen suggests prodigious capacities. The year he was chosen general, he had also been "visited of the Lord," adding visionary precocity to his other virtues.[28] Ammaron recognized Mormon's abilities and, against all precedent, selected him to receive the records.

Despite the burdens of leading a wartime army, Mormon became intimately familiar with the collection of plates that had been handed down by Nephite prophets and kings for nearly a millennium.[29] To add his bit to the collection of records, Mormon first wrote of his own time, the "continual scene of wickedness and abominations" that had passed before his eyes since he was young.[30] Then sometime over the next thirty years, he made a major decision. Instead of adding only his portion of history, he would write a complete history of his people from their first arrival in the sixth century BCE until their last decimating wars in the fourth century CE. The previous dozen or so authors wrote only of their own times; Mormon manufactured more plates and summarized all of Nephite history in one volume.[31] He was the maker and author of the plates Joseph Smith took from the ground in 1827. His son Moroni added his own history and prepared the title page naming his father's history the "Book of Mormon."[32]

His experience as a general may have convinced Mormon that now was the time to write his people's history. By the end of his life, he knew that his civilization was doomed. His people, roughly characterized as "Nephites," continually warred with their distant kin, the "Lamanites," in gory and degrading battles. Mormon had little confidence that his armies would prevail; their moral decay had gone too far for heaven to help them. They were ferocious and bloodthirsty, so much so that he turned his back on his armies for a long period and refused to lead.[33] After a time he relented, but with no more hope than before. "O the depravity of my people!" he

27. Mormon 1:6.

28. Mormon 1:15.

29. Mormon 2:16–17.

30. Mormon 2:18.

31. 3 Nephi 5:10–11.

32. Title Page of the Book of Mormon.

33. Mormon 3:11.

cried. "They are without order and without mercy."[34] He lamented, "I cannot recommend them unto God lest he should smite me."[35] He inscribed the long history of the Nephites in an atmosphere of constant gloom, with no expectation that any of his contemporaries would see the book. It was written to be buried and preserved for a future time, like a message in a bottle written in hopes that someday someone would find it. He could only desire that future generations might benefit from the grim history of his fallen people.[36]

Ironically the title page written by his son said the book was "written to the Lamanites," Mormon's enemies in the grueling wars that eventually effaced the Nephite nation. Mormon saw the Nephites going down under Lamanite swords; and yet he wrote the book for them. It was "written and sealed up, and hid up unto the Lord," in order that sometime this "remnant of the House of Israel" might know the "great things the Lord hath done for their fathers; and that they may know the covenants of the Lord, that they are not cast off forever."[37] When Joseph Smith as the modern translator read those words on the plates, he may not have appreciated the bitter irony of the story. The native peoples for whom Mormon wrote were kinsmen but also enemies, both chosen and fallen, the object of yearning and the object of enmity. Mormon had slain them by the thousands, and eventually they slew him and all of his armies. Yet he devoted his life to writing a redeeming text for them. The plates were a memorial to that ambivalence.

Mormon's Discovery of the Small Plates of Nephi

Mormon repeatedly stated that he wrote only a "hundredth part" of Nephite history.[38] He hinted at piles of records to be sifted through. He drew primarily from the extensive plates of Nephi, the core history kept by the nation's leaders, but there were more plates in the cache Ammaron had buried.[39] At the end of his life, as Mormon was about to pass along his

---

34. Moroni 9:18.

35. Moroni 9:21.

36. Words of Mormon 1:8.

37. Title Page of the Book of Mormon.

38. 3 Nephi 5:8; 26:6; Words of Mormon 1:5; Helaman 3:14.

39. Mormon 1:1, 4.

history, he wrote a revealing note called "The Words of Mormon," about the process of history making. In his opening sentence, he offered the last testament of a dying man speaking for a doomed civilization:

> And now I, Mormon, being about to deliver up the record which I have been making into the hands of my son Moroni, behold I have witnessed almost all the destruction of my people, the Nephites. . . . and it supposeth me that he will witness the entire destruction of my people.[40]

Trying to make clear what his history was made of, Mormon explained that most of it was an abridgment from the plates of Nephi, but after he had completed the first portion down to one of the kings named Benjamin,[41] he found another intriguing set of plates. "I searched among the records which had been delivered into my hands, and I found these plates which contained this small account of the prophets, from Jacob down to the reign of this King Benjamin, and also many of the words of Nephi."[42] In other words, the newly discovered "small account" covered the same period Mormon had just abridged from the plates of Nephi but dealt more with prophets than with kings.

Mormon liked the "small account" so much that he decided to add it to his own abridgment. "I shall take these plates which contain these prophesying and revelations, and put them with the remainder of my record, for these are choice unto me," he explained.[43] Somehow the two were spliced together, perhaps bound into the same set of rings, like adding pages to a looseleaf notebook.[44] The plates Joseph Smith received would include two accounts of this period—Mormon's original abridgment taken from the plates of Nephi and this shorter account by Nephi, Nephi's brother Jacob, and Jacob's descendants down to King Benjamin.

---

40. Words of Mormon 1:20.

41. King Benjamin reigned circa 130–124 BCE (Mosiah 6:4).

42. Words of Mormon, 1:3.

43. Words of Mormon 1:7.

44. The men who claimed to have seen the plates later described them as being connected with rings (David Whitmer Interview, *Chicago Tribune*, 24 January 1888, in *David Whitmer Interviews*, ed. Lyndon W. Cook [Provo, Utah: Brigham Young University Press], 221; Martin Harris Interview, *Tiffany's Monthly*, May 1859, 165.)

At this point, modern events thrust themselves into the story in a way that complicates the reading of the Book of Mormon. Through the winter and spring of 1828, Joseph Smith had dictated Mormon's abridgment of the plates of Nephi down to the reign of King Benjamin—the so-called "large plates account." He was helped by a Palmyra friend, Martin Harris, who believed Smith was translating real plates. Harris lent Smith money, went to New York City for an expert opinion about the translation, and wrote down the text as Smith dictated. But Harris's wife Lucy was deeply suspicious and feared Smith was setting a trap for her husband. When the trap was sprung, Smith would run off with Harris's money, and he would be left with nothing.[45] To allay his wife's doubts, Harris pled with Smith to lend him the translation manuscript for a few weeks. Smith reluctantly agreed and was aghast when the worst case scenario unfolded. Harris lost the manuscript, representing several months of labor. Smith was horrified and at a loss about what to do. For months he stopped translating altogether.[46] He believed the manuscript had been stolen, and in his distress dictated a revelation in the voice of God saying that if he retranslated the text, the thieving conspirators would doctor the original—which, when it was found to vary from the new text, would be used to prove Smith a fraud. Skeptics, of course, were sure there were no plates to translate at all; the "translation" was purely Smith's fabrication, so of course he could not dictate a second version that would exactly match the first.[47]

These circumstances have produced two conflicting readings of the small plates of Nephi. Under the assumption that Smith made up the "translation" himself, it seems obvious that his loss of the manuscript forced him to retrofit the Book of Mormon text. In this skeptical reading, Smith had the prophet Nephi inscribe a second set of plates, parallel to the first, and conveniently pile them in with the first plates of Nephi where Mormon could stumble across them. Nephi admitted in the text that he knew not why he was asked to double up on his history, only proposing

---

45. Lucy Mack Smith, *Biographical Sketches of Joseph Smith the Prophet, and His Progenitors for Many Generations* (Liverpool: S.W. Richards, 1853), 116–17.

46. John W. Welch and Erick B. Carlson, eds. *Opening the Heavens: Accounts of Divine Manifestations, 1820–1844* (Provo, Utah: Brigham Young University Press, 2005), 88.

47. D&C 10:14–33. All references herein are to the edition of the Doctrine and Covenants currently published by the Church of Jesus Christ of Latter-day Saints. (*The Doctrine and Covenants of the Church of Jesus Christ of Latter-day Saints* [Salt Lake City: Church of Jesus Christ of Latter-day Saints, 2013].)

that the Lord had his purposes.[48] For skeptics, of course, the real purpose was Joseph Smith's, not God's; it was to get himself out of a jam.[49] On the other hand, believing readers could credit God's foresight for the presence of this convenient "small account."[50] In this view, God directed Nephi to write a second history so Mormon could one day discover it and fill the gap that would be created by the missing manuscript—an instance of divine providence preparing for a distant contingency.[51]

Either way, the small plates raise a question about the Book of Mormon text itself: How do the small plates fit into the Book of Mormon story? If Smith was retrofitting the text to get out of a tight spot, how did he do it? On the other hand, if Nephi actually did the writing, what did he make of the second set of plates? Even in a skeptical reading, we must ask how the small account was made to fit into the storyline. As it turns out, the small account became more than a convenient replacement for the lost history. Inside the Book of Mormon, the plates have a significant part in the plot, virtually becoming an actor in the history.

The Creation of the Small Plates

Nephi began the large plates of Nephi—the ones Mormon would later abridge—soon after his father's party had reached the land of promise.[52] After nearly an eight-year journey to the sea from Jerusalem and an extended voyage across the water, Lehi's family found themselves in a rich new land (exactly where is never made clear). Nephi reported that among the resources they found "all manner of ore, both of gold, and of silver, and of copper."[53] Nephi made "plates of ore," as he wrote, "that I might engraven upon them the record of my father, and also our journeying in

48. 1 Nephi 19:3.

49. See, for example, Fawn M. Brodie, *No Man Knows My History* (New York: Borzoi Books, 1972), 54–57; Jerald Tanner and Sandra Tanner, *Covering Up the Black Hole in the Book of Mormon* (Salt Lake City: Utah Lighthouse Ministry, 1990), 9–12; Grant H. Palmer, *An Insider's View of Mormon Origins* (Salt Lake City: Signature Books, 2002), 6–7.

50. See, for example, 1 Nephi 9:2–6.

51. See Words of Mormon 1:7.

52. This occurred circa 589 BCE (1 Nephi 19:4).

53. 1 Nephi 18:25.

the wilderness, and the prophecies of my father; and also many of mine own prophecies have I engraven upon them."[54]

These plates were to become the plates of Nephi that Mormon drew from for his abridgment. At the time, Nephi thought these original plates were all he would write on. "Wherefore, the record of my father, and the genealogy of his fathers, and the more part of all our proceedings in the wilderness are engraven upon these first plates."[55] He then told his people that when he was gone, "these plates should be handed down from one generation to another, or from one prophet to another, until further commandments of the Lord."[56]

Then about twenty years later, some three decades after Lehi had left Jerusalem, Nephi was commanded to make another set of plates: "The Lord God said unto me: Make other plates; and thou shalt engraven many things upon them which are good in my sight, for the profit of my people."[57] To distinguish the two sets of plates, Nephi explained that on the small plates he engraved only "that which is pleasing unto God." And, as he further reasoned, "if my people are pleased with the things of God they will be pleased with mine engravings which are upon these plates."[58] For "the more particular part of the history," the story of kings and wars, they would have to go to the other plates he had been working on since their arrival. So the two sets of plates were characterized roughly as historical and spiritual. The original plates contained the particulars of the history; the second set of plates said more about "the ministry and the prophecies."[59]

Within Nephi's narrative, however, the small plates served a far more serious purpose. They were not merely a collection of sermons, visions, and prophecies; they were a potent political document in Nephi's longstanding feud with his brothers. Nephi began the small account just after a violent split within the family. Until the death of their father, the six brothers fought and argued but remained one family. Lehi held them together despite his misgivings about his two oldest sons, Laman and Lemuel. He

54. 1 Nephi 19:1.

55. 1 Nephi 19:2.

56. 1 Nephi 19:4.

57. 2 Nephi 5:30.

58. 2 Nephi 5:32.

59. 1 Nephi 19:3.

diverted their complaints that Nephi spoke too sharply by saying the Spirit of the Lord had moved him, placating the two contentious sons while rebuking them.[60]At the end of his life, Lehi delivered a long admonition and blessing to the two of them, and then blessed his other sons.[61] "And it came to pass," Nephi recounted, "after my father, Lehi, had spoken unto all his household . . . he waxed old. And it came to pass that that he died, and was buried."[62]

Almost immediately, the long-brewing animosity between Nephi and two of his older brothers Laman and Lemuel burst into the open. Nephi could not restrain himself from rebuking them, and they did not take it lying down.[63] Finding it unbearable in this patriarchal society for their younger brother to rule over them, they determined to slay him.[64] Nephi was compelled to flee, taking with him three of his brothers—Sam, Jacob, and Joseph—and his sisters. After a long journey through the wilderness they found a new land on which to sow seed, raise animals, and work ore. Acknowledging Nephi's leading role in their deliverance, the people made him their king.[65] The division that was to characterize Book of Mormon society until the end had been opened. Where there had been a single family, two nations in embryo came into being.

At this critical juncture in the history of Lehi's family, Nephi was instructed to "make other plates."[66] They were begun at the exact moment when the tension in the family reached its breaking point. Laman and Lemuel had sought Nephi's life before, but this time Lehi was no longer there to reconcile his sons' differences, and Nephi was unable to keep the peace. His own animosity boiled over onto the plates. God, he wrote,

> had caused the cursing to come upon them, yea, even a sore cursing, because of their iniquity. For behold they had hardened their hearts against him, that they had become like unto a flint; wherefore, as they were white, and exceedingly fair and delightsome, that

60. 2 Nephi 1:26.

61. 2 Nephi 2:1; 3:22–25; 4:3–11.

62. 2 Nephi 4:12.

63. 2 Nephi 4:13–14.

64. 2 Nephi 5:3–4.

65. 2 Nephi 5:6–19.

66. 2 Nephi 5:30.

> they might not be enticing unto my people, the Lord God did cause a skin of blackness to come upon them. And thus saith the Lord God: I will cause that they shall be loathsome unto thy people, save they shall repent of their iniquities . . .. And because of their cursing which was upon them they did become an idle people, full of mischief and subtlety, and did seek in the wilderness for beasts of prey.[67]

Underlying his anger was the great issue that divided him and his brothers from the beginning. Nephi believed that God had told him he "should be their ruler and their teacher," and the brothers would not yield to this fate.[68] They thought he was a usurper, not the chosen instrument of the Lord. The resulting break could be seen as the failure of Lehi's project. The small plates were written to explain the divide and to vindicate Nephi's claims.

The new account did contain the pleasing "things of God," as Nephi said, but it was also driven by his explanation for the recent break with his brothers.[69] The moral of story after story was that Nephi acted with the blessing of God and of his father Lehi, while Laman and Lemuel resisted both. The point was always the same: "Wherefore, the word of the Lord was fulfilled which he spake unto me, saying that: Inasmuch as they will not hearken unto thy words, they shall be cut off from the presence of the Lord. And behold, they were cut off from his presence."[70]

In Nephi's account, the brothers fully deserved the curse of black skin;[71] they were loathsome with good cause. Their degraded lives, "full of mischief and subtlety," were all that could be expected of a people who had rejected Nephi's divine commission from the beginning. The first book of Nephi and what is now the first five chapters of the second book of Nephi were an extended apology for the split with Laman and Lemuel.[72]

67. 2 Nephi 5:21–22, 24.

68. 2 Nephi 5:19.

69. 2 Nephi 5:32.

70. 2 Nephi 5:20.

71. 2 Nephi 5:21–22, 24.

72. The vexed issue of race in the Book of Mormon is discussed in Armand L. Mauss, *All Abraham's Children: Changing Mormon Conceptions of Race and Lineage* (Urbana and Chicago: University of Illinois Press, 2003), 17–40. See also W. Paul Reeve, *Religion of a Different Color: Race and the Mormon Struggle for Whiteness* (New York: Oxford University

Perhaps Nephi feared that he had failed his father.[73] He certainly was driven to despair by the split in the family. Immediately after describing the divide and the Lamanites' base condition, he lamented his own failings as if he were at fault: "O wretched man that I am! Yea, my heart sorroweth because of my flesh; my soul grieveth because of mine inquities."[74] He had failed to maintain the unity his father had spent his life preserving. Depressed and perhaps conscience-stricken, Nephi had to explain to his posterity why he had failed. Nephi's first book was the justifying text.

The Transmission and Influence of the Small Plates

Political aims drove the writing when Nephi was the chief historian, but as the small account passed to his younger brother Jacob and down through Jacob's lineage, its underlying purpose shifted. It became a different kind of record. As the Lamanites became a more distant threat rather than an ever-present reality, the immediate need to justify Nephi's rule faded, and the small account assumed a new character. Up to the point of division, Nephi had told story after story to prove he was the righteous one who was favored with visions and wisdom to guide the people, while Laman and Lemuel dragged their feet and resisted. After the division, instead of an indictment of Laman and Lemuel, the account took the form of religious instruction to the Nephite people. Its aim was to keep the Nephites on the straight path and help them understand their place in the history of God's people. No longer was it necessary to discredit the wicked brothers. Jacob, Nephi's brother, even acknowledged that the Lamanites had become more righteous than the Nephites, an admission Nephi would have found hard to make.[75]

The struggles over the right to rule played no part in the subsequent accounts made by Jacob's descendants.[76] The righteousness and

---

Press, 2015), 52–74. For a literary analysis, see Jared Hickman, "*The Book of Mormon* as Amerindian Apocalypse," *American Literature* 86, no. 3 (2014): 429–61.

73. For an elaboration of this possibility, see Grant Hardy, *Understanding the Book of Mormon: A Reader's Guide* (New York: Oxford University Press, 2010), 50–56.

74. 2 Nephi 4:17.

75. Jacob 3:5–9.

76. Jacob 1:9; 7:27; Enos 1:1; Jarom 1:1, 15; Omni 1:1, 2, 8, 10, 12, 25.

wickedness of the Nephite people and the teachings of the prophets became the leitmotifs. The kings were keeping their own records of politics and war. Because "the record of this people" was "being kept on the other plates," Jacob explained, he was content to record only his spiritual teachings.[77] A later descendant justified his brief entry by referring to the full history: "And I, Jarom, do not write more, for the plates are small. But behold, my brethren, ye can go to the other plates of Nephi; for behold, upon them the records of our wars are engraven, according to the writings of the kings, or those which they caused to be written."[78]

Apparently it was this non-kingly, prophetic quality of the small account that attracted Mormon. He liked the small plates' spiritual emphasis, in the sections Jacob and his son Enos wrote, rather than the sibling conflicts of Nephi's time. Indeed, within the Book of Mormon storyline, the small plates can be seen as changing Mormon's own way of writing history. Until this point he had abridged the account of the kings, presumably following their political narrative. Mormon may have originally written his record in the Israelite genre of the royal chronicle, like the books of Kings and Chronicles in the Old Testament. After discovering the small plates, his account frequently diverged from a strictly royal history. In the book of Mosiah, he wrote of King Benjamin and his son King Mosiah at some length, but in the course of telling their histories Mormon went off into ancillary accounts of an expedition to another land where the prophet Abinadi had arisen and after him Alma, prophets rather than kings. King Mosiah disappeared for pages and pages while the warnings of the prophets and the rise of Alma's people as a church took center stage. The lengthy Book of Alma began with Alma as the chief judge, but after his resignation from that office, Mormon followed him as a prophetic voice, omitting entirely an account of the chief judge who succeeded him. Alma recounts the missionary journeys of the king's sons rather than the reign of their father. In Mormon's history, the fortunes of the kings and chief judges yield to the missions and teachings of the prophets just as they had in Jacob's history.

Mormon seems to have taken a leaf from the small plates of Nephi on what mattered in history. He says in the Words of Mormon that once he had the small plates in hand, he decided to "finish my record upon them."[79] This could not mean he wrote on the actual plates that Nephi forged since,

---

77. Jacob 7:26; compare Omni 1:11.

78. Jarom 1:14.

79. Words of Mormon 1:5.

as the previous chronicler had specifically noted, "these plates are full."[80] Mormon's words suggest that he was basing his approach upon the model of the small account, using new plates he manufactured himself, but writing in the spirit of Nephi's second record. In selecting the "hundredth part" that he condensed into his account, his criteria became spiritual and prophetic rather than political and dynastic.[81]

Whatever motivated Joseph Smith's "translation" of the small plates, their use went far beyond the simple need for a backup account. Initially the small plates were the instrument of Nephi's anger, regret, and political need, reflecting the anguish of separation. Then with the divide, the character of the narrative shifted to serve the revised purposes of Nephi's successors. Mormon showed no sign of valuing Nephi's political maneuvers; he read the small plates as preachments of Christ. If we speculate a little about the world within the Book of Mormon, the small plates may in turn have altered Mormon's own writing to emphasize spiritual over political themes.

The Book of Ether

In the Book of Mormon's complicated architecture, Nephi's large and small plates provided two major sources for Mormon as he prepared his summation of Nephite history on a third set of plates. As these various sources imply, the book proposes its own documentary hypothesis to account for the final text. The implicit presence of differing sources behind a text, a radical idea of advanced German biblical scholarship in Joseph Smith's time, is made explicit in the Book of Mormon with its blending of various narratives into a summary text. To these three sets of plates can be added two more: the plates of Ether; and Moroni's abridgment of those plates, called the book of Ether, a history of an independent civilization that preceded the arrival of Lehi's people in the promised land.

The book of Ether, which Mormon's son Moroni summarized, was inscribed on twenty-four gold plates that came with an elaborate backstory. In the second century BCE, a party of explorers from a Nephite colony had stumbled on them while searching for a route back to the main body of Nephites. King Limhi's explorers failed to locate the return route but came

80. Omni 1:30.

81. Words of Mormon 1:5.

upon the remnants of an ancient civilization, including rusted armor and gold plates inscribed with writing.[82] Although immensely curious, Limhi had no way of interpreting the writings on the plates. Not until he made his way back to Zarahemla were they translated. Limhi turned the plates over to Mosiah, king of the Nephites, who possessed a miraculous instrument for translation. Through Mosiah, the story was at last read to Limhi and his intensely curious people.[83]

The plates came into Moroni's hands in the late fourth century CE when, at the very end of the Nephites' sad history, the dying Mormon turned his record over to his son Moroni to make the final entries. Mormon's armies had been vanquished, and Moroni was a fugitive from the marauding Lamanites. Inexplicably, Moroni did not immediately finish up the story and die. He lived on for another thirty-six lonely years. During that time he made his own entries on the plates of Nephi and then turned to the twenty-four gold plates that contained the history of the lost civilization Limhi's explorers had happened upon. Moroni set out to write their history the way his father had told the story of the Nephites.

The resulting book of Ether, named after the ancient people's final historian, is the history of a people called Jaredites who migrated from Eurasia following the confusion of tongues at Babel. Ether was a Mormon for his people, writing their history on twenty-four gold plates and leaving them for Limhi's scouts to find.[84] Ether mainly chronicles dynastic struggles over the long course of Jaredite history, but in the opening chapters he recounts the experience of a prophet known in the Book of Mormon as "the brother of Jared." A man of immense faith, the brother of Jared witnessed the finger of the Lord and then saw through the veil to view God's entire spiritual body and a vision of all of God's dealings with his human children.[85] The brother of Jared was commanded to write all this,[86] and presumably Ether inscribed it on the twenty-four gold plates.

Since he wrote in a language that might not be known to future peoples, the brother of Jared received aids for future translators: "And behold," the Lord told him, "these two stones will I give unto thee, and ye

82. Mosiah 8:9.

83. Mosiah 28:12–13.

84. Ether 15:33.

85. Ether 3:6–13, 25.

86. Ether 3:27.

shall seal them up also with the things which ye shall write."[87] By means not clearly specified, these stones came into the hands of the first King Mosiah, the grandfather of the second King Mosiah.[88] The later Mosiah used the Jaredite stones to translate the twenty-four gold plates as the Lord intended.[89] The two stones were the "interpreters" that Joseph Smith recovered along with the plates in 1827.[90] They came by a long passage from the post-Babel Jaredites through the two Kings Mosiah to Moroni, and then into the stone box where Smith found them.[91]

The seer stones and the twenty-four gold plates of Ether, however, came with strings attached. The knowledge on the plates was dangerous. As he passed along the sacred relics, Alma warned Helaman that the plates of Ether contained forbidden information that originated with the devil. Helaman was to hold back "all their oaths and their covenants, and their agreements in their secret abominations; yea, and all their signs and their wonders, ye shall keep from this people, that they know them not, lest peradventure they should fall into darkness also and be destroyed."[92] This part of Mosiah's translation had to be suppressed, since such knowledge could lead the Nephites to destruction if let loose in their society. Moroni's later summary of Jaredite history omitted the toxic portions.

---

87. Ether 3:23.

88. Mosiah 28:13.

89. Mosiah 28:13.

90. Exodus 28:30; Leviticus 8:8; Deuteronomy 33:8; Numbers 27:21. The spectacles were first referred to as "Urim and Thummim" in 1832—though in a somewhat speculative manner—by W. W. Phelps, the editor of the early Mormon newspaper. ("Hosea Chapter III," *The Evening and the Morning Star*, July 1832, 6; "Selected. The Excellence of Scripture," *Evening and Morning Star*, August 1832, 19; "The Book of Mormon," *The Evening and the Morning Star*, January 1833, 58.) Soon, the identification of the spectacles with the Urim and Thummim was solidified. For examples, see Oliver Cowdery to William W. Phelps, 7 September 1834, in *Latter Day Saints' Messenger and Advocate*, October 1834, 14; William W. Phelps to Oliver Cowdery, 25 December 1834, in *Latter Day Saints' Messenger and Advocate*, February 1835, 65; Revelation, June 1829—E, copied between 25 November 1834 and Summer 1835, in Robin Scott Jensen et al., eds., *Revelations and Translations, Volume 1: Manuscript Revelation Books*, vol. 1 of the Revelations and Translations series of *The Joseph Smith Papers*, ed. Dean C. Jessee et al. (Salt Lake City: Church Historians' Press, 2009), 655; see also p. 410. Joseph Smith later followed this usage. See, for example, Joseph Smith, "Church History," *Times and Seasons* 3 (March 1842): 707. See also Edward Stevenson, "One of the Three Witnesses," *Deseret News*, 30 November 1881; David Whitmer, *Kansas City Journal*, 5 June 1881.

91. For an example of the varied interpretations of the records of Ether, see Valentin Arts, "A Third Jaredite Record: The Sealed Portion of the Gold Plates," *Journal of Book of Mormon Studies* 11, no. 1 (2002): 50–59.

92. Alma 37:27.

On the other hand, the records descending from the Jaredites contained knowledge that was forbidden for another reason, not for its poisonous effect but because of its spiritual intensity. The brother of Jared had recorded his vision of all the earth's inhabitants from the beginning to the end of the world, written in a language no one could read.[93] Then he had been told to seal it up until the Lord would reveal it in his own due time.[94] This secluded knowledge had a precedent; the brother of Jared had previously had experience with holy knowledge. The veil was only taken from his eyes when the finger of the Lord touched sixteen stones that Jared needed to light the barges that would cross the ocean to the Americas.[95] The sight terrified him, as he feared he had looked upon forbidden holiness: "I saw the finger of the Lord, and I feared lest he should smite me."[96] Too much holiness was more than ordinary humans could bear. The brother of Jared's vision was sealed for similar reasons. It was not to come into view until the people would "repent of their iniquity, and become clean before the Lord."[97] Mosiah withheld this vision when he made his translation. It was opened to the public after Christ came to the Nephites and then closed again after the Nephites degenerated. Moroni was commanded "to hide them up again in the earth."[98] The gentiles would see the account only when they were "sanctified" in Christ.[99]

In keeping with the esoteric tradition of powerful knowledge, both evil and glorious information had to be hid from view. In Masonic lore, the ineffable name of God with its true pronunciation was written on a triangular gold plate by Enoch and reserved only for advanced initiates to know.[100] That aura of potent, forbidden knowledge lingered over the gold plates after they came to Joseph Smith. As much as two-thirds of the plates Joseph Smith received were sealed, either physically or by command, and kept from unworthy eyes. They were a mute testimony to the power of books. Words might redeem a people as the Book of Mormon

---

93. Ether 3:22.

94. Ether 3:25, 27.

95. Ether 3:19.

96. Ether 3:8.

97. Ether 4:6.

98. Ether 4:3.

99. Ether 4:6–7.

100. *Richardson's Monitor of Freemasonry* (New York: Fitzgerald, 1860), 155.

was expected to redeem the Lamanites; a book might also overwhelm a people with evil or holy knowledge.

After abridging the Jaredite history and writing a few words of his own, Mormon's son Moroni buried the plates. With no one left to receive the plates, they went into the ground to await their resurrection in another age. Moroni rested their future, and the meaning of the whole Nephite enterprise, with a subsequent discoverer and translator centuries down the line. The best he could do was to plead plaintively that these readers from the distant future would take his account seriously. When you receive these things, he wrote, "I would exhort you that ye would ask God, the Eternal Father, in the name of Christ, if these things are not true."[101] He warned these unknown future readers that they would see him "at the bar of God," and that God would say to them: "Did I not declare my words unto you, which were written by this man, like as one crying from the dead, yea, even as one speaking out of the dust?"[102] After inscribing these and a few more words of admonition, Moroni brought the book to a conclusion and bid his future readers farewell.[103]

Conclusion

The plates came to Joseph Smith with this heavy history weighing them down. One can look at the Book of Mormon as a work of religious fantasy or, as the Latter-day Saints do, as actually inscribed in reformed Egyptian on the golden surfaces of the plates. Either way, the Book of Mormon came with a long and complex account of its own textual history. The book tells of the plates' purpose, their manufacture, their inscription, their transmission. The writers faithfully noted the passage of the plates from one generation to the next. Through the entire course of Nephite history, not a single conveyance of the plates from one record keeper to another was omitted. The voices of the purported authors constantly interjected themselves into the history, explaining the sources of their writings, informing future readers of their purpose and importance, and expressing regret that so much was left out. The descriptions of the two sets of plates on the title

101. Moroni 10:4.

102. Moroni 10:27.

103. Moroni 10:28–34.

page—Nephi's and Mormon's—were typical of the whole book. Readers were constantly given a view of a book in the making.

The total effect was to make the book a transparently human production: people had put this book together. Writers introduced themselves, spoke of their personal situations when they wrote, and then frequently intruded to remind readers they were composing the narrative. The Book of Mormon authors seemed to conceive of all scripture this way. Nephi criticized future believers in the Bible for forgetting the human origins of scripture:

> O fools, they shall have a Bible; and it shall proceed forth from the Jews, mine ancient covenant people. And what thank they the Jews for the Bible which they receive from them? Yea, what do the Gentiles mean? Do they remember the travails, and the labors, and the pains of the Jews, and their diligence unto me, in bringing forth salvation unto the Gentiles?[104]

The Bible brought forth salvation to be sure; it was the word of God. But it was also the book of a people. No reader of the Book of Mormon could forget that fact about scripture, as human fingerprints were all over its pages. On the title page, Mormon stated frankly that "if there are faults they are the mistakes of men."

And yet these words of men were also the words of God. The combination of humanity and divinity in the Book of Mormon suggests a theological and epistemological principle: God does his work through human agents. Though the prophet-writers were mired in their humanity, they spoke for the heavens. Their words held the mysteries of godliness and offered hope of salvation. These very human words were the standard by which people would be judged. Despite any faults, the title page went on to say, the book had to be taken seriously. "Condemn not the things of God, that ye may be found spotless at the judgment-seat of Christ."

Ultimately that may be the meaning of the gold plates in the rise of early Mormonism. In the plates' backstory, the angel did not hand the plates to Joseph Smith. He had to dig them out of the ground, where presumably Moroni had buried them 1400 years earlier. They emerged from human history, not from the heavens. They were the product of an

104. 2 Nephi 29:4.

ancient Israelite people, just as the Bible was the product of the Jews. That is the way God works, the plates insist—through humans. Someone had to inscribe all those words into the surfaces of the metal plates, and once they were in Joseph Smith's hands, he had to figure out what the inscriptions said. Heaven hovered over it all in the form of the angel, but humans did the work. In the world of the plate-makers, that was how God conveyed his will to humankind. For early Mormons, the plates themselves, though unseen, were the foundational text of the religion that they were creating with their prophet and translator Joseph Smith.

3

Textual Criticism and the Book of Mormon

Grant Hardy

IT SEEMS SAFE to assume that without the Book of Mormon, there would be no Mormonism. In the America of the Second Great Awakening, many people claimed to have seen visions, heard voices, encountered spiritual beings, or received revelations. What made Joseph Smith stand out, however, was his account of a book written on thin gold plates that were delivered to him by an angel and, almost as improbably, the fact that he produced and published a nearly six-hundred-page "translation" of that record. The Book of Mormon received wide notice after its 1830 release, and missionaries carried it throughout the United States and abroad as tangible evidence of Smith's remarkable claims.[1] Believers were quickly labeled "Mormonites," a derisive nickname that was later shortened to "Mormons."[2] Smith founded a church within days of bound copies of the Book of Mormon becoming available, and converts accepted the new scripture as fully canonical, that is, of equal authority with the Bible—something virtually unheard of among Christian denominations.[3] Almost

1. For a general introduction to the Book of Mormon and its role as a witness of revelation from God through a prophet, see Terryl L. Givens, *By the Hand of Mormon: The American Scripture that Launched a New World Religion* (New York: Oxford University Press, 2002).

2. See Mark Lyman Staker, *Hearken, O Ye People: The Historical Setting of Joseph Smith's Ohio Revelations* (Salt Lake City: Greg Kofford Books, 2009), 73–74.

3. For comparisons and contrasts, see David F. Holland, *Sacred Borders: Continuing Revelation and Canonical Restraint in Early America* (New York: Oxford University Press, 2011).

two hundred years later, the Church of Jesus Christ of Latter-day Saints (hereafter LDS church) claims over fifteen million members, and tens of thousands of missionaries still take the Book of Mormon around the globe, in over a hundred languages, testifying that it is God's word for the modern world.[4]

In the Latter-day Saint movement, the Book of Mormon is *the* foundational text. Indeed, without the Book of Mormon, it is doubtful whether anyone today would care much about Joseph Smith, apart from the sorts of scholars who study Ann Lee, Jemima Wilkinson, Nimrod Hughes, Robert Matthews, or other religious visionaries in early American history. But people do care, and the last few decades have seen the emergence of Mormon Studies, a small but vibrant academic field that has grown to include detailed textual analysis of documents connected with Smith and his associates, as can be seen in the publications of the Joseph Smith Papers Project. These primary sources are essential to the study of the founding era of Mormonism, and a fuller awareness of their sometimes complex production histories can greatly enrich our understanding of the development of that American faith tradition.

Yet the Book of Mormon is different from most of the other writings discussed in this volume in at least four ways. First, its textual history is not particularly complicated. It was dictated, one time through, over a three-month period from April to June of 1829.[5] Twenty-eight percent of that dictation—commonly known as the Original Manuscript (hereafter O)—survives, as does nearly the whole of a second copy made for the printer: the Printer's Manuscript (hereafter P). The first edition of the Book of Mormon was typeset from P, and partially from O, with relatively few changes. A second edition of 1837 included numerous grammatical and stylistic corrections made by Smith, but only a handful of significant changes, and a third edition in 1840 offered a few corrections based on O. Subsequent editions have included a limited number of grammatical adjustments and corrections of inadvertent errors that have come to light through closer scrutiny of the two manuscripts. However, aside from

4. As of 31 December 2016, the LDS church had 15,882,417 members in 30,304 congregations around the world. "Facts and Statistics," *Mormon Newsroom*, http://www.mormonnewsroom.org/facts-and-statistics.

5. About 116 pages of translation that had been dictated in the spring of 1828 were stolen a few months later when they were in the care of Martin Harris, one of Smith's scribes. Virtually all of the Book of Mormon as we have it today was produced from April to June of 1829.

grammatical updating, the Book of Mormon currently published by the LDS church is essentially the same as that dictated in 1829. This stands in contrast to the extensive revisions and additions that have characterized Joseph Smith's revelations as published in the Doctrine and Covenants (the church's third book of scripture) and his journals as published in the official *History of the Church*, or the laconic notes from multiple sources that have to be pieced together to reconstruct his Nauvoo sermons.

The second distinctive quality of the Book of Mormon is its length, complexity, and originality. Other revelations of Joseph Smith—consisting of commandments, exhortations, doctrinal explications, and organizational instructions—may run to a few pages, but the Book of Mormon is a single, coherent narrative that relates the history of the Nephites over a thousand-year period, as told by three major narrators who integrate a variety of source materials and genres into their account, as can be seen in Richard Bushman's chapter in the present volume.[6] Apart from twenty-three chapters (out of a total of 239) that basically reproduce chapters from Isaiah, Matthew, and Malachi in the King James Version of the Bible, the content is original, which is quite different from Smith's "New Translation," or revision, of the Bible, and from his purported translation of a lost book of the Old Testament patriarch Abraham now found in the Pearl of Great Price (Mormonism's fourth and final book of scripture).[7] The scope and complexity of the narrative make the Book of Mormon easily the most impressive document that Smith ever produced. And that is all the more striking given that it was his first publication.[8]

A third difference is that Joseph Smith's role in the Book of Mormon narrative is rather peripheral. That is to say, he is not a character in the story. It is not told from his perspective as a nineteenth-century American

6. See Richard Lyman Bushman, "The Gold Plates as Foundational Text," chapter 2 herein. See also Grant Hardy, *Understanding the Book of Mormon: A Reader's Guide* (New York: Oxford University Press, 2010).

7. In addition to the 23 full chapters from the Bible, the Ten Commandments are quoted in Mosiah 12–13, and Micah 5:8–15 is reproduced in 3 Nephi 21.

8. According to Michael Hubbard MacKay et al., eds., *The Joseph Smith Papers, Documents, Volume 1: July 1828–June 1831* (Salt Lake City: Church Historian's Press, 2013), the only documents produced by Smith prior to his 1829 dictation of the Book of Mormon were three brief revelations that later became Doctrine and Covenants sections 3, 4, and 5. And the earliest extant copies of the first two were created after the Book of Mormon was published.

farmer, and he did not claim to be the author.[9] Most of the other documents in the Joseph Smith Papers are ones that he wrote, dictated, commissioned, or otherwise took responsibility for, or, in the case of later revelations, were formulated in his own mind rather than coming through a seer stone. Obviously, the question of how much of Smith is in the Book of Mormon is ultimately a matter of faith (or doubt). Some Latter-day Saints believe that Smith miraculously read a pre-existing translation word for word from a seer stone, while other Mormons believe that he received spiritual impressions that he put into his own words as he dictated. Outsiders generally view the Book of Mormon as Smith's creation from first to last, though one that incorporated bits of the Bible, popular culture, and experiences from his own life. Most historians will be reading the Book of Mormon as a window into Smith's mind, looking for clues as to his perceptions and responses to social, economic, political, and religious controversies of the day.[10] Yet the new scripture did not speak directly about such matters, and in any case, it provides only a snapshot of what one seemingly unremarkable twenty-three-year-old thought during a three-month period. The Book of Mormon, even when read as carefully as possible, does not offer much information about the development of the new religion, because there are not enough textual changes over time. It would be useful, of course, to undertake reception studies to see how others responded to this American scripture, but because the text itself is quite stable and comes at the very beginning of Mormonism, it functions as more of a starting point, or a theological baseline, from which to measure further innovations.

And finally, the Book of Mormon was regarded by Joseph Smith and his followers as canonized scripture—complete, sacred, and

9. Although the title page of the first edition of the Book of Mormon named Joseph Smith as its "AUTHOR AND PROPRIETOR," this was done to meet copyright requirements. It is clear that Smith was not meant to be understood as the book's author from the actual contents of the book, the way early church members understood the book, and the way church missionaries presented it to others. See An Act for the Encouragement of Learning, by Securing Copies of Maps, Charts, and Books, to the Authors and Proprietors of Such Copies during the Times Therein Mentioned [31 May 1790], *Public Statutes at Large of the United States of America . . .*, ed. Richard Peters, vol. 1 (Boston: Charles C. Little and James Brown, 1845), 1st Cong., 2nd Sess., chap. 15, pp. 124–26; see also Nathaniel Hinckley Wadsworth, "Copyright Laws and the 1830 Book of Mormon," *BYU Studies* 45, no. 3 (2006): 77–99.

10. See, for example, Dan Vogel, *Joseph Smith: The Making of a Prophet* (Salt Lake City: Signature Books, 2004).

authoritative—from the moment it was dictated.[11] Interestingly, this did not preclude extensive grammatical updating in later editions, but the Book of Mormon is the only document produced by Smith that had such status immediately. Later revelations were transcribed, revised, selected, and incorporated into the canonical collections of the Doctrine and Covenants and Pearl of Great Price over the course of years, if not decades. These other Mormon scriptures have been reduced and expanded in the past two centuries, and further changes or even additions are possible, at least in theory. But the Book of Mormon, as constituted in 1830, was described by Smith as the "keystone of our religion." As such, it has received extraordinary scrutiny for some time.

As early as 1898, a disillusioned Latter-day Saint named Lamoni Call counted some two thousand changes that had been made since the first edition, and he published a study enumerating the differences book by book. For instance, he noted that in 3 Nephi he had found 136 cases where *which* had been changed to *who*; twenty-three of *sayeth* to *said*; fifteen of *which* to *whom*; seven of *is* to *are*; six of *they* to *those*; six of *was* to *were*; and so forth. He consequently reasoned, "While the changes are only grammatical for the most part, when we consider how the book was translated [that is, by purportedly miraculous means], to my mind even grammatical changes are unpardonable." In contrasting what he saw in the Book of Mormon with the claims made for it, Call asked, "where, in the name of that Great God that created heaven and earth is 'the perfection of God's works'?"[12]

Wilford C. Wood's 1958 facsimile reprint of the 1830 edition made it easier to compare the first edition with current printings, and the first systematic textual comparison was published in 1965 by noted critics Jerald and Sandra Tanner with the descriptive title *3,913 Changes in the Book of Mormon: A Photo Reprint of the Original 1830 Edition of the Book of Mormon with All the Changes Marked.*[13] The book was presented as an exposé since the Tanners shared Lamoni Call's belief that grammatical errors would

11. They were keenly aware that the first 116 pages of the dictation had been stolen and lost, but the book's narrators had helpfully included substitute material, so the story that is told is complete. See Words of Mormon 1:6–8 and the preface to the 1830 edition.

12. Lamoni Call, *2000 Changes in the Book of Mormon* (Bountiful, Utah: 1898), 46, 83, 99.

13. Wilford C. Wood, ed., *Joseph Smith Begins His Work: Book of Mormon 1830 First Edition Reproduced from Uncut Sheets* (Salt Lake City: Wilford C. Wood, 1958); Jerald Tanner and Sandra Tanner, *3,913 Changes in the Book of Mormon* (Salt Lake City: Utah Lighthouse Ministry, 1965).

have been impossible in a book that had actually been revealed by God. The 1960s and 1970s saw the first academic studies of the text of the Book of Mormon, including several master's theses and scholarly articles.[14] Textual criticism of the scripture began in earnest in the 1980s with a preliminary three-volume critical text, published by the Foundation for Ancient Research and Mormon Studies (FARMS). This has since been superseded by the Book of Mormon Critical Text Project of Royal Skousen, a Professor of Linguistics and English Language at Brigham Young University, who remains the preeminent figure in the field.[15] Volumes from the Critical Text Project began to appear in 2001, and will be discussed below.[16] In fact, much of what follows is drawn from Skousen's work.

---

14. Jeffrey R. Holland, "An Analysis of Selected Changes in Major Editions of the Book of Mormon, 1830–1920" (master's thesis, Brigham Young University, 1966); Richard P. Howard, *Restoration Scriptures: A Study of Their Textual Development* (Independence, Missouri: Herald Publishing House, 1969), 23–69; Dean C. Jessee, "The Original Book of Mormon Manuscript," *BYU Studies* 10, no. 3 (1970): 259–78; Janet Jenson, "Variations between Copies of the First Edition of the Book of Mormon," *BYU Studies* 13, no. 2 (1973): 214–22; Stanley R. Larson, "A Study of Some Textual Variations in the Book of Mormon: Comparing the Original and the Printer's Manuscripts and the 1830, the 1837, and the 1840 Editions" (master's thesis, Brigham Young University, 1974); Stanley R. Larson, "Textual Variants in Book of Mormon Manuscripts," *Dialogue: A Journal of Mormon Thought* 10, no. 4 (1977): 8–30; Stanley R. Larson, "Conjectural Emendation and the Text of the Book of Mormon," *BYU Studies* 18, no. 4 (1978): 563–69; Hugh G. Stocks, "The Book of Mormon, 1830–1879: A Publishing History" (master's thesis, University of California at Los Angeles, 1979).

15. Foundation for Ancient Research and Mormon Studies, *The Book of Mormon Critical Text: A Tool for Scholarly Reference,* 3 vols. (Provo, Utah: FARMS, 1984–1987); Hugh G. Stocks, "The Book of Mormon in English, 1870–1920: A Publishing History and Analytical Bibliography," (PhD diss., University of California at Los Angeles, 1986); Royal Skousen, "Towards a Critical Edition of the Book of Mormon" *BYU Studies* 30, no. 1 (1990): 41–69; Royal Skousen, "The Original Language of the Book of Mormon: Upstate New York Dialect, King James English, or Hebrew?" *Journal of Book of Mormon Studies* 3, no. 1 (1994): 28–39; and Royal Skousen, "Changes in the Book of Mormon," *Interpreter: A Journal of Mormon Scripture* 11 (2014): 161–76. For overviews of the Critical Text Project, see M. Gerald Bradford and Alison V. P. Coutts, eds., *Uncovering the Original Text of the Book of Mormon: History and Findings of the Critical Text Project* (Provo, Utah: FARMS, 2002), and Royal Skousen, "Restoring the Original Text of the Book of Mormon," *Interpreter: A Journal of Mormon Scripture* 14 (2015): 107–17.

16. The Book of Mormon Critical Text Project consists of the following volumes. Each part is a separate book, and all the books are in quarto size:

Volume 1. *The Original Manuscript of the Book of Mormon: Typographical Facsimile of the Extant Text*
Volume 2. *The Printer's Manuscript of the Book of Mormon: Typographical Facsimile of the Entire Text in Two Parts*
Volume 3. *The History of the Text of the Book of Mormon,* in six parts
Volume 4. *Analysis of Textual Variants of the Book of Mormon,* in six parts
Volume 5. *A Complete Electronic Collation of the Book of Mormon*

Analytical Sources and Methods

In 2001, Skousen published typographical facsimiles of O and P (the latter in two books), based on close personal examination and multi-spectral imaging where needed.[17] Each of these large quarto volumes presents a typeset, line-by-line version of the text with interlinear corrections represented as such. The original and revising scribes are identified, as are the typesetter's notes in pencil and ink, and his take marks (indicating points at which he took a break from setting type, so that he could find his place when he returned). In addition, there are a multitude of transcription symbols indicating exactly what one might see in looking at the manuscripts with a magnifying glass. These symbols indicate intralinear insertions of words or even characters, supralinear insertions of words and characters, strike-throughs and cross-outs, erasures, overwrites, letters that are missing a stroke or a dot or a crossing, letters that have extra strokes or dots or crossings, spacing adjustments, places where the text is completely or partially illegible, and lacunae. And finally, there are extensive footnotes describing exactly what is on the pages, including information on changes in the ink flow or sharpness of the quill, along with paper tears, ink smears, splotches, seepage, and stray marks. There are even footnotes such as "dot for *i* of *plains* over the *n*," "crossing for 2nd *t* in JS's *that* too high," and "final *s* in 1st *Gentiles* ends in an extensive flourish under *iles*."[18] The result is that the work of the scribes can almost be followed in real time.

For example, at 1 Nephi 7:2 in O, one of the two unidentified scribes, presumably trying to keep straight new names and stories, starts to write *Lehi*, but catches his error after inscribing the *e*, crosses out the *L* and overwrites the name as *Nephi*. And here is the beginning of a line from the same manuscript in Skousen's transcript (erasures are indicated by angle brackets, overwrites by curly brackets): "sa{<y>|i}t{h}{<L>o|th(-)}e Lord in an exce|p|table time have I heard thee." Oliver

---

Volumes 1, 2, and 4 have been published thus far. The first two parts of Volume 3, which provide a detailed analysis of the grammar of the earliest text, were published in 2016.

17. Royal Skousen, ed., *The Original Manuscript of the Book of Mormon: Typographical Facsimile of the Extant Text* (Provo, Utah: FARMS, 2001); Royal Skousen, ed., *The Printer's Manuscript of the Book of Mormon: Typographical Facsimile of the Entire Text in Two Parts* (Provo, Utah: FARMS, 2001).

18. These examples are taken from three consecutive pages in Skousen, *Printer's Manuscript*, 1:87–89.

Cowdery, the scribe taking dictation, was having a difficult time with the familiar phrase "thus saith the Lord."[19] He first wrote *say* (perhaps intending *sayeth*), then he erased the *y* and wrote an *i* in its place. When he completed the word *saith*, he went back and partially overwrote the *h* to make it clearer (this type of correction is frequent in Cowdery's handwriting). He began to write "Lord" as the next word, but then caught his error, erased the *L* (but left the *o*), and overwrote with *th* (though the *h* is missing a stroke), and added the *e*. Finally, he wrote *Lord* and continued on. Three words later, the *p* within two parallel lines indicates that the letter was intralinearly inserted as a correction, probably almost immediately; the word itself is a misspelling of "acceptable." And so it continues line by line through the three lengthy books that make up volumes 1 and 2 of the Critical Text Project.

As Skousen himself explained, "Normally, transcripts of manuscripts do not provide the level of detail given here in volumes 1 and 2. However, the Book of Mormon is a religious, foundational text; and the reading of each sentence is of more importance to a religious community than it would be in the normal secular literary work or historical document."[20] This is also the reason the Joseph Smith Papers published a typographical facsimile edition (with full transcripts) of P in 2015.[21] The Joseph Smith Papers version is more streamlined than Skousen's. For example, it does not differentiate forms of cancellation. However, unlike Skousen's transcript, it differentiates between immediate revisions, made before anything else was inscribed, and inserted revisions. It also color codes the handwriting. Furthermore, the two quarto volumes include full-page color photographs for each page of the manuscript. A third volume of photographs and transcripts of the extant portions of O is planned.

19. Skousen, *Original Manuscript*, 157; the line is from 1 Nephi 21:8, which is itself borrowed from Isaiah 49:8.

20. Skousen, *Original Manuscript*, 26.

21. Royal Skousen and Robin Scott Jensen, eds., *Revelations and Translations, Volume 3, Part 1: Printer's Manuscript of the Book of Mormon, 1 Nephi 1–Alma 35*, facsimile edition, part 1 of vol. 3 of the Revelations and Translations series of *The Joseph Smith Papers*, ed. Ronald K. Esplin and Matthew J. Grow (Salt Lake City: Church Historian's Press, 2015); Royal Skousen and Robin Scott Jensen, eds., *Revelations and Translations, Volume 3, Part 2: Printer's Manuscript of the Book of Mormon, Alma 36–Moroni 10*, facsimile edition, part 2 of vol. 3 of the Revelations and Translations series of *The Joseph Smith Papers*, ed. Ronald K. Esplin and Matthew J. Grow (Salt Lake City: Church Historian's Press, 2015).

In 1841 Joseph Smith placed O into the cornerstone of the Nauvoo House for safekeeping. When it was recovered in 1882, most of it had been destroyed by water and mold. Today only 28% survives, with the greatest number of pages coming from the book of 1 Nephi and the middle of the book of Alma. Most of the handwriting is Oliver Cowdery's, though two unidentified scribes also contributed to 1 Nephi. There is no punctuation in the manuscript, apart from a few dashes in the preface to 2 Nephi. Cowdery occasionally corrected the work of the other two scribes and even added a few phrases himself to O as he was copying for P. The majority of these emendations were unnecessary but have nevertheless been preserved in the current official edition of 1981.[22]

Unlike O, P has survived intact, apart from three worn-away lines at the bottom of the first leaf. Oliver Cowdery wrote 85% of it, with another 15% by an unknown scribe, and a few lines here and there by Joseph Smith's brother Hyrum. Although Oliver Cowdery was fairly careful in his copywork, comparison with O reveals that he still made about three errors per page (typical examples, from 2 Nephi 7:1–9, can be seen in Figure 3.1). The manuscript shows evidence of immediate corrections by the original scribes, editing where scribes appear to have proofed each other's work against O, and numerous marks—mostly in pencil—made by John Gilbert, the 1830 typesetter. Gilbert added punctuation and paragraphing to the text and corrected a few obvious errors. Skousen has also demonstrated that one-sixth of the 1830 edition (Helaman 13:17 to Mormon 9:37) was actually set from O rather than P, which means that for these pages the 1830 edition and P are both first-hand copies of O—an observation that has significant implications for scholars trying to reconstruct the missing portions of O.[23]

P also contains nearly two thousand corrections made by Joseph Smith as he was revising the text for the second edition (1837). Almost all of these are grammatical in nature, beginning with 952 instances—nearly half the total—of *which* being changed to *who* or *whom*. Also very common are changes of *saith* to *said; hath* to *has* or *have; they* to *those; was* to *were*; and *is* to *are*. Smith also regularly excised extraneous instances of *that*, and

22. Royal Skousen, "Oliver Cowdery as Book of Mormon Scribe," in *Days Never to be Forgotten: Oliver Cowdery*, ed. Alexander L. Baugh (Provo, Utah: Religious Studies Center, Brigham Young University, 2009), 51–70; see also Skousen, *Original Manuscript*, 3–38.

23. Skousen, "Oliver Cowdery as Book of Mormon Scribe"; see also Skousen, *Printer's Manuscript*, 1:3–36; and Skousen and Jensen, *Revelations and Translations*, vol. 3, pt. 1, pp. 3–11.

FIGURE 3.1. 2 Nephi 7:1–9. Ultraviolet photograph of original manuscript of the Book of Mormon, p. 59 fragment.
Used by permission of Wilford Wood Foundation.

deleted forty-seven repetitions of *it came to pass*. In a few cases, he revised P to match the 1830 edition, but there is no evidence that he consulted O in 1837.[24] Figures 3.2 and 3.3, which correspond to Mosiah 25:4–19 in P, show a shift in handwriting between Oliver Cowdery and an unidentifed scribe, three supralinear corrections made by Cowdery and the unidentified scribe, pilcrows added by John Gilbert indicating paragraphs for the 1830 edition, and fourteen corrections made by Smith in his editing for the 1837 edition—most of which are changes from "which" to "who" but also including a deletion of "it came to pass that."

Four editions of the Book of Mormon were published during Joseph Smith's life—in 1830, 1837, 1840, and 1841—though the last was published

24. Full discussions of grammatical variants, as well as authoritative counts of changes, can be found in Royal Skousen, *History of the Text of the Book of Mormon, Parts One and Two: Grammatical Variation*, 2 vols. (Provo, Utah: FARMS; BYU Studies, 2016), particularly 1:35–43. These books constitute parts 1 and 2 of volume 3 of Skousen's Critical Text Project.

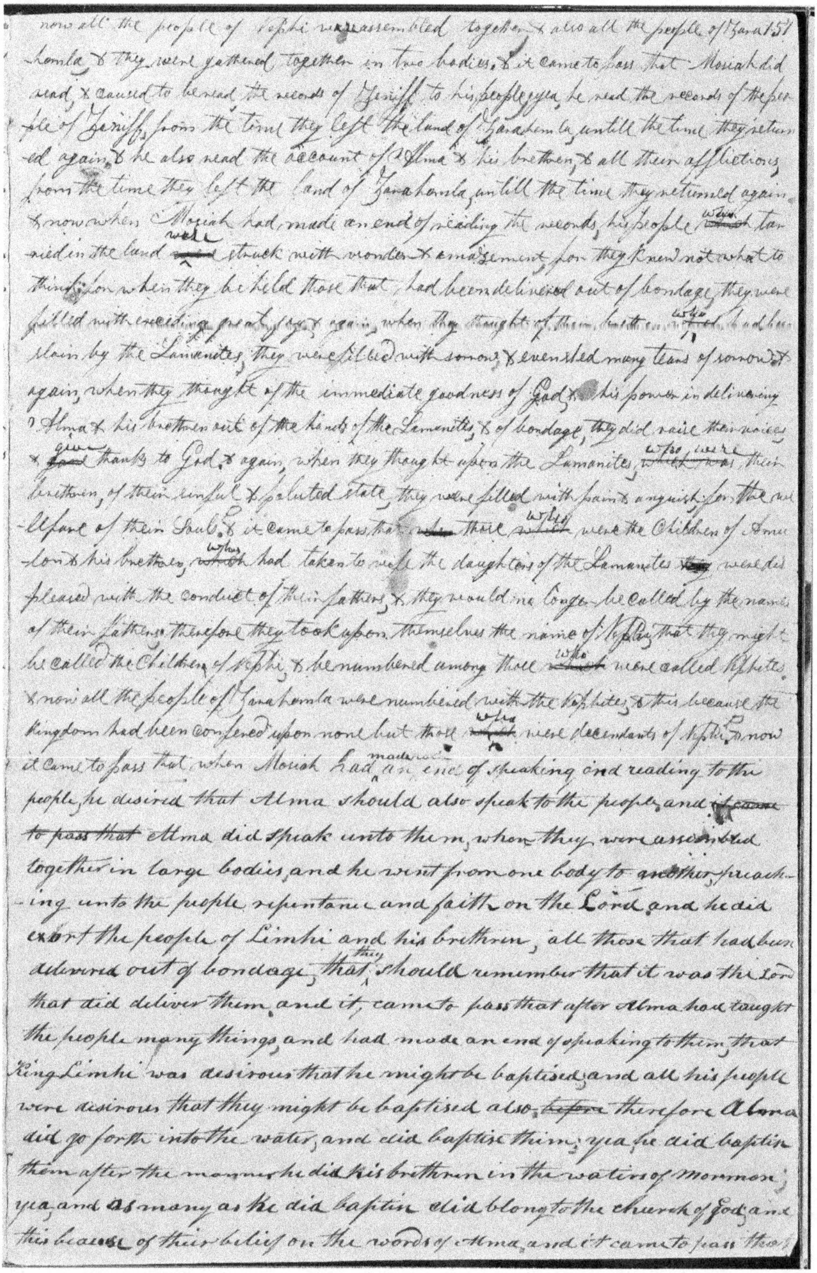

now all the people of Nephi were assembled together & also all the people of Zara 157
hemla & they were gathered together in two bodies & it came to pass that Mosiah did
read & caused to be read the records of Zeniff to his people yea he read the records of the peo
ple of Zeniff from the time they left the land of Zarahemla untill the time they return
ed again & he also read the account of Alma & his brethren & all their afflictions
from the time they left the land of Zarahemla untill the time they returned again
& now when Mosiah had made an end of reading the records his people ~~which~~ who tar
ried in the land ~~was~~ were struck with wonder & amazement for they knew not what to
think for when they beheld those that had been delivered out of bondage they were
filled with exceding great joy & again when they thought of their brethren ~~which~~ who had been
slain by the Lamanites they were filled with sorrow & even shed many tears of sorrow &
again when they thought of the immediate goodness of God & his power in delivering
Alma & his brethren out of the hands of the Lamanites & of bondage they did raise their voices
& ~~give~~ gave thanks to God & again when they thought upon the Lamanites ~~which was~~ who were their
brethren of their sinful & poluted state they were filled with pain & anguish for the we
lfare of their souls & it came to pass that those ~~which~~ who were the children of Amu
lon & his brethren ~~which~~ who had taken to wife the daughters of the Lamanites ~~they~~ were dis
pleased with the conduct of their fathers & they would no longer be called by the names
of their fathers therefore they took upon themselves the name of Nephi that they might
be called the children of Nephi & be numbered among those ~~which~~ who were called Nephites
& now all the people of Zarahemla were numbered with the Nephites & this because the
kingdom had been confered upon none but those ~~which~~ who were decendants of Nephi & now
it came to pass that when Mosiah had made an end of speaking and reading to the
people he desired that Alma should also speak to the people and ~~it came~~
~~to pass that~~ Alma did speak unto them when they were assembled
together in large bodies and he went from one body to another preach
ing unto the people repentance and faith on the Lord and he did
exort the people of Limhi and his brethren all those that had been
delivered out of bondage that they should remember that it was the Lord
that did deliver them and it came to pass that after Alma had taught
the people many things and had made an end of speaking to them that
King Limhi was desirous that he might be baptised and all his people
were desirous that they might be baptised also ~~before~~ therefore Alma
did go forth into the water and did baptise them yea he did baptise
them after the manner he did his brethren in the waters of Mormon
yea and as many as he did baptise did belong to the church of God and
this because of their belief on the words of Alma and it came to pass that

FIGURE 3.2 AND FIGURE 3.3. Mosiah 25:4–19. Printer's manuscript of the Book of Mormon, p. 157, and transcript.

Courtesy Community of Christ Archives, Independence, MO. Transcript from *The Joseph Smith Papers*, Revelations and Translations Series, vol. 3, p. 332.

PRINTER'S MANUSCRIPT
Mosiah, ch. 11
[Mosiah 25:4–19]

now all the people of Nephi w{as**er**}**e** assembled together, & also all the people of Zara 157 [recto]
-hemla, & they were gathered together in two bodies. & it came to pass that Mosiah did
read, & caused to be read, the records of Zeniff to his people; yea, he read the records of the peo-
-ple of Zeniff, from the time they left the land of Zarahemla, untill the time[465] they return
-ed again{;\.} & he also read the account of Alma & his brethren, & all their afflictions,
from the time they left the land of Zarahemla, untill the time they returned again.
who
& now when Mosiah had made an end of reading the records, his people ~~which~~ tar
w{as**er**}**e**
-ried in the land ~~were~~ struck with wonder & amazement, for they knew not what to
think{;\:} for when they beheld those that had been delivered out of bondage, they were
who
{h\f}illed with exceding great joy. & again, when they thought of their brethren ~~which~~ had been
slain by the Lamanites, they were filled with sorrow, & even shed many[466] tears of sorrow. &
again, when they thought of the immediate goodness of God, & his power in delivering
Alma & his brethren out of the hands of the Lamanites, & of bondage, they did raise their voices,
give **who were**
& ~~gave~~ thanks to God. & again, when they thought upon the Lamanites, ~~which was~~ their
brethren, of their sinful & poluted state, they were filled with pain & anguish, for the we
¶[467] **who**
-llfare of their Souls. & it came to pass that ~~when~~ those ~~which~~ were the children of Amu
who
-lon & his brethren, ~~which~~ had taken to wife the daughters of the Lamanites ~~they~~ were dis
-pleased with the conduct of their fathers, & they would no longer be called by the names
of their fathers; therefore they took upon themselves the name of Nephi, that they might
who
be called the children of Nephi, & be numbered among those ~~which~~ were called Nephites.
& now all the people of Zarahemla were numbered with the Nephites, & this because the
who ¶[468]
kingdom had been confered upon none but those ~~which~~ were decendants of Nephi. & now
made ~~⊘ade~~
it came to pass that when Mosiah /[469]had an end of speaking and reading to the
people, he desired that Alma should also speak to the people. and ~~it came~~
~~to pass that~~ Alma did speak unto them, when they were assembled
together in large bodies, and he went from one body to another, preach-[470]
-ing unto the people repentance and faith on the Lord. and he did
ex{⊘\o}rt the people of Limhi and his brethren, all those that had been
they
delivered out of bondage, that should remember that it was the Lord
that did deliver them. and it came to pass that after Alma had taught
the people many things, and had made an end of speaking to them, that
King Limhi was desirous that he might be baptised; and all his people
were desirous that they might be baptised also. ~~before~~ therefore Alma
did go forth into the water, and did baptise thim{,\:} yea, he did baptise
th{i\e}m after the manner he did {⊘\h}is brethren in the watirs of Mormon;
yea, and {is\a}s many as {t\h}e did baptise did blong to the church of {g\G}od; and
this bca{u⊘\us}e of their belief on the words of Alma. and it came to pass that

FIGURE 3.2 AND FIGURE 3.3. (Continued)

ORIGINAL INSCRIPTION
Oliver Cowdery
Scribe 2

REVISIONS
Oliver Cowdery
Joseph Smith
Compositor
Scribe 2
Hyrum Smith
Unidentified

465. 1837 omits "the time".

466. Uninked "|" etched into the paper between "ma" and "ny". This mark corresponds to the end of a line on page 207 of the 1830 edition.

467. Pilcrow corresponds to a new paragraph on page 208 of the 1830 edition.

468. Pilcrow corresponds to a new paragraph on page 208 of the 1830 edition.

469. Oliver Cowdery handwriting ends; scribe 2 begins.

470. Uninked "|" etched into the paper. This mark corresponds to the end of a line on page 208 of the 1830 edition.

in England without Smith's direct involvement. Full-color photographic renditions of all four have been posted at the Joseph Smith Papers website.[25] Online versions of two dozen more editions have been collected at KC Kern's *Book of Mormon Online: A Comprehensive Resource for the Study of the Book of Mormon.*[26] The 1879 edition was particularly important for the formatting of the book as scripture, since that was the first time the text was divided into numbered verses, and the original chapters were subdivided into smaller, more manageable chapters closer in length to the King James Bible.[27] The most important editions thereafter in the LDS tradition were those of 1920 (for which the editorial committee's marked-up copy is extant) and 1981, which is the current official edition.[28] Royal Skousen has created an electronic collation of the Book of Mormon documenting every difference between the two manuscripts and the twenty most significant editions, which he will release at the conclusion of his Critical Text Project. In the meantime, significant variants in all these editions are cited in the 4,060 pages of his *Analysis of Textual Variants of the Book of Mormon.*[29]

The loss of 72% of O is unfortunate and irreparable, but in general it can be determined when the text was changed and by whom, from the moment scribes first took down Smith's original dictation to the present day. Furthermore, careful scrutiny of the manuscripts and comparisons with early editions can reveal which changes were accidental and which were deliberate, and informed conjectures can be made as to the motivations behind the intentional revisions. Given these primary source materials, it is possible—to a large extent—to reconstruct the text in its original form, which is what Royal Skousen has done in his *Book of Mormon: The*

25. *The Joseph Smith Papers,* http://josephsmithpapers.org/the-papers/revelations-and-translations/jsppr4.

26. *The Book of Mormon Online,* http://bookofmormon.online/fax.

27. The 1852 edition had added numbers to the paragraphs, but the division of the text into Bible-length verses was new to the 1879 edition. These are the chapters and verses still used today.

28. A few minor revisions in spelling and punctuation were introduced in 2013.

29. Royal Skousen, *Analysis of Textual Variants on the Book of Mormon,* 6 vols. (Provo, Utah: FARMS, 2004–2009). All six volumes are also available in an electronic version at http://www.mormoninterpreter.com/books/volume-4-of-the-critical-text-of-the-book-of-mormon-analysis-of-textual-variants-of-the-book-of-mormon/ or at https://bookofmormoncentral.org/content/analysis-textual-variants-book-mormon.

Earliest Text.[30] Scholarly studies of the origin and development of the Book of Mormon should be based on this version.

In addition, Skousen has explained the reasoning behind each of the editorial decisions he made for the *Earliest Text* in his *Analysis of Textual Variants*, a series of six large volumes published from 2004 to 2009. There he presents detailed arguments based on his close examination of the manuscripts, his reconstruction of the actions and intentions of different scribes and editors, comparisons with other passages elsewhere in the text, statistics, biblical parallels, biblical languages, early English usage and dialects, the writing habits of particular scribes, pronunciation (some mistakes occurred in the initial transcription because dictated words sounded alike), and typical errors of the eye or hand made in copying.[31] It is a tour de force of scrupulous textual criticism. Of course, there is still more work to do. Skousen has not given much attention to the internal structure or intratextual allusions of the text—as revealed in close readings—or to the hundreds of examples of phrases from the King James Bible that have been incorporated into the Book of Mormon, and the way that they have been modified or recontextualized in the process.[32] And the relationship of the language of the Book of Mormon to terms and concepts prevalent in the nineteenth century has yet to be worked out.

Alma Chapter 30 as a Typical Example

It is not unreasonable to ask what might be gained from several decades of incredibly detailed textual criticism of the Book of Mormon. Is there any payoff to this astonishing amount of effort? For Latter-day Saints, who believe that the book is a work of scripture that was revealed by God in a rather direct fashion, every word is precious and potentially significant. This perspective, then, justifies the five full pages in *Analysis of Textual Variants*

30. Royal Skousen, ed., *The Book of Mormon: The Earliest Text* (New Haven: Yale University Press, 2009). The text is available in a read-only electronic version at http://bookofmormoncentral.org/content/book-mormon-earliest-text.

31. See Grant Hardy, "Scholarship for the Ages," *Journal of Book of Mormon Studies* 15, no. 1 (2006): 43–53.

32. For a version of the Book of Mormon that highlights its structure and interconnections, see Grant Hardy, ed., *The Book of Mormon: A Reader's Edition* (Urbana: University of Illinois Press, 2003), or Grant Hardy, ed., *The Book of Mormon: Maxwell Institute Study Edition* (Provo, Utah: Neal A. Maxwell Institute for Religious Scholarship, Brigham Young University, forthcoming in 2018).

that Skousen devoted to determining whether a single word in what is now Helaman 15:8 should be *thing* or *things*.[33] There are other possible benefits as well, for both believers and outsiders alike.[34] This chapter will organize these into broad categories, with examples from throughout the text. But to provide a better sense of the evidence, it may be useful to begin with a somewhat comprehensive examination of one significant but not atypical chapter, what is now Alma 30, which will also be used throughout the rest of this chapter.

Alma 30 tells the story of a confrontation between the high priest Alma and a popular dissenting preacher named Korihor, who is described as an "Anti-Christ," meaning he denies there is any validity to the Nephite prophets' message of a Savior who is yet to come. Korihor regards such teachings as the "foolish traditions of your fathers" and asserts that "no man can know of anything which is to come." Furthermore, he argues that there is no need for an atonement since there is no afterlife; in this life people can, and will, do whatever they like; and he insists that institutional religion is a scheme to oppress the common people and enrich the clergy. Eventually Korihor is arrested and brought before Alma, where he disavows any belief in God. Alma responds by claiming that prophets, scriptures, and all of nature testify of God, but Korihor refuses to believe unless he is shown a sign. Alma tells him that the sign he seeks will be his being struck dumb. When this happens, Korihor confesses through writing that he had been misled by the devil, and he meets his end when he is reduced to begging for food and is accidentally trampled to death in a crowd.

The manuscript evidence for Alma 30 is as follows. The chapter takes up a little more than four pages of O (two leaves, front and back), with the right-hand upper third of each leaf missing. There are thirty-five lines per page, and Oliver Cowdery was the scribe. In the portions of the pages that are extant, he made about eleven supralinear corrections, twelve intralinear corrections, thirty cancellations by strikethrough or cross-out, thirty-five cancellations by erasure, and 280 partial or full overwrites. (This is characteristic of Cowdery's scribal habits—in trying

33. Skousen, *Analysis of Textual Variants*, 5: 3140–45.

34. Royal Skousen has discussed thirty variants that he finds particularly valuable, which differ from the current official edition, in his article "Some Textual Changes for a Scholarly Study of the Book of Mormon," *BYU Studies* 51, no. 4 (2012): 99–117.

to make his writing as legible as possible, he went back and rewrote two or three letters per line.)[35]

In P the chapter is also written by Cowdery, and again there is evidence that he was taking pains to get the words exactly right, though the process of copying from a written page is much easier than taking live dictation. Cowdery made ten immediate supralinear corrections and seven somewhat later, along with ten intralinear corrections, fourteen strikes, seven erasures, and more than 360 overwrites. In addition, Joseph Smith's 1837 editing in P included ten changes of *saith* to *said*, eight of *which* to *who*, six of *hath* to *have* or *has*, and three deletions of *that*. Smith also added a set of parentheses and a question mark. He changed an *is* to *are*, an *if* to *will*, a *never* to *ever* (to remedy a double negative), and a *causeth* to *causes*; he also deleted both a *food* and an *it came to pass that he*.[36]

These may seem like a great number of changes, but none of them significantly revises or modifies the main line of narrative itself. Cowdery's insertions, cross-outs, and erasures were attempts to create a precise transcript of the original oral dictation and an accurate second copy. Smith's later corrections mostly concern diction. Royal Skousen has discussed the most significant changes in Alma 30 in his *Analysis of Textual Variants*. A summary of some of his specific findings is provided below, followed by analytic observations, supplemented with additional examples from elsewhere in the text, arranged under six general headings.[37]

v. 1 O – *Chapter XVI*

The ink flow for *XVI* is more even than for *Chapter*, suggesting that the chapter number was added later, which accords with evidence throughout the manuscript.

v. 2 O – *greatness of their* [*number* > *numbers*]

Oliver Cowdery [hereafter OC] corrected *number* to *numbers* almost immediately, intralinearly.

v. 5 O – *and it came to pass in the commencement of the seventeenth year*
P – *and it came to pass in the seventeenth year*

35. Skousen, *Original Manuscript*, 281–92.

36. Skousen, *Printer's Manuscript*, 2:539–48; Skousen and Jensen, *Revelations and Translations*, vol. 3, pt. 1, pp. 507–17.

37. Skousen, *Analysis of Textual Variants*, 4:2210–43.

OC accidentally omitted *the commencement of* in copying; the original reading was restored in 1981.

v. 7 O – *for it was strictly contrary to the commandments of God*
P – *for it was strictly contrary to the commands of God*
OC miscopied the word *commandments* as *commands*; all printed editions from 1830 to 1981 retain the mistake.

v. 10 O – *yea for all* [*these* > *this*] *wickedness they were punished*
OC corrected *these* to *this* almost immediately, supralinearly.

v. 11 O – *therefore a man was punished only for the* [*crime* > *crimes*] *which he had done*
OC corrected *crime* to *crimes*, intralinearly, perhaps immediately or perhaps later.

v. 12 O – *whose name was Korihor—and the law could have no hold upon him—& he began to preach*
P – *whose name was Korihor—and the law could have no hold upon him—*[*& he* > *Joseph Smith (hereafter JS) &*] *began to preach*
1837 – *whose name was Korihor—and the law could have no hold upon him—began to preach*
1830 edition followed O and P; JS crossed out *he* in P in 1837; 1837 edition deleted *& he*, which is probably what JS intended.

v. 16 O – *because of the* [*traditions* > *tradition*] *of your fathers which leads you away*
P, 1830, 1837 – *because of the tradition of your fathers which lead you away*
1840 – *because of the traditions of your fathers which lead you away*
OC erased the *s* at the end of *traditions* in an immediate correction to O, but then miscopied *leads* as *lead* in P. JS reconciled the resulting subject–verb disagreement in 1840 by changing *tradition* to *traditions*; this is the 1981 reading.

v. 17 P – *Ammon which was a high priest over that people*
O is not extant here and Skousen, based on spacing considerations, suggests that it might have read *the high priest*.

v. 24 O – *behold I say* [*there* > *these*] *are in bondage*
P – *behold I say* [*there* > *they*] *are in bondage*
OC immediately overwrote the *r* in *there* as an *s*, but then miscopied the word in P as *there*, after which he changed it to *they*, which is the reading of 1830–1981.

v. 28 O – *which never was nor never will be*

P – *which never was nor [never >*JS *ever] will be*

JS deleted a double negative by changing *nor never* to *nor ever* in his editing of P for the 1837 edition.

v. 30 P – *yea he went on to blasphemy*

1830 – *yea he went on to blaspheme*

O is not extant; John Gilbert, the 1830 typesetter, replaced *blasphemy* with *blaspheme,* which is the reading of all subsequent editions.

v. 31 O – *for the sake of glutting [by > in] the labors of the people*

1920 – *for the sake of glutting on the labors of the people*

OC first wrote *by,* then crossed it out and inserted *in* supralinearly, probably immediately. The *in* of the early editions was changed to *on* in 1920 as a deliberate change, since it is marked in the 1920 committee copy. This is the 1981 reading.

v. 35 O – *believest thou that we deceive this people & that causeth such joy in their hearts*

P – *believest thou that we deceive this people that causeth such joy in their hearts*

OC missed the & in copying P; it was inserted into O after the line had been written and is very faint and hard to see in the gutter of the tightly-stitched gathering. In fact, Skousen missed it as well in preparing his facsimile transcript of O. He hypothesized that an & was missing from the line, and when he was later examining the gutter in the ultraviolet photograph for the opposing page, he saw the inserted & there, thus confirming his conjectural emendation.

v. 35 O – *and that [causes > causeth] such joy in their hearts*

P – *and that [causeth >*JS *causes] such joy in their hearts*

OC immediately changed *causes* to *causeth* by overwriting the *s* with a *t* and adding an *h* inline; in his editing for the 1837 edition, JS changed the *causeth* in P to *causes,* the reading of all editions since 1837.

v. 39 P – *[if>*JS *will] ye deny again that there is a God and also deny the Christ* [NULL >JS?]

O is not extant here; in his 1837 editing JS changed *if* to *will* and added a question mark to complete the sentence. In its original form, the line could be punctuated with ellipses since the implied threat ends mid-sentence.

v. 41 O – *I have all things as a testimony that these things are true and ye* [NULL > *also*] *have all things as a testimony unto you that they are true*
OC omitted *also* in taking the initial dictation and then immediately inserted it supralinearly.

v. 49 O – *and I say that in the name of God that ye shall be struck dumb*
P – *and I say* [*that* >JS NULL] *in the name of God that ye shall be struck dumb*
1837–1981 – *and I say that in the name of God ye shall be struck dumb*
JS crossed out the first *that* when he was editing for the 1837 edition, but the typesetter accidently deleted the second *that*.

v. 51 O – *art thou convinced of the power of* [*gd* > NULL] *God*
P – *art thou convinced of the power of a God*
1840 – *art thou convinced of the power of God*
OC originally miswrote *God* as *gd*, then crossed it out and wrote the full word *God*; in copying for P, he misread the erased *gd* as *a*; the 1830 and 1837 editions read *power of a God*, then the extra *a* was deleted in 1840.

v. 52 O – *and I always knew that there was a God*
P – *and I also knew that there was a God*
When copying for P, OC misread *always* as *also*; the mistake appeared in all printed editions until the original reading was restored in 1981.

v. 53 O – *and he saith unto me there* [*was* > *is*] *no God*
OC originally wrote *was* and then corrected it to *is* supralinearly, probably fairly soon thereafter.

v. 58 O – *and Korihor did go about from house to house a begging food for his support*
P – *and Korihor did go about from house to house a begging* [*food* >JS NULL] *for his support*
1837–1981 – *and Korihor did go about from house to house begging food for his support*
The 1837 typsetter missed JS's deletion of *food* and kept the word in the text.

In Alma 30, there were immediate corrections done by the original scribe; accidental omissions and copying errors (only some of which were remedied in later editions); stylistic revisions for the 1837, 1840, and 1920 editions; mistakes made by typesetters; and additional errors that were introduced in attempting to correct previous mistakes. None of these changes appear nefarious or agenda-driven, but rather seem to indicate that the transcription, copying, typesetting, and editing were subject to ordinary human fallibilities. They are also all rather minor—suggesting that the people involved were trying hard to be as accurate as possible, even as Joseph Smith slightly regularized the diction.

Observations and Implications

The sorts of changes seen in Alma 30 occur throughout the Book of Mormon. Most readers will probably be less interested in a comprehensive categorizing of errors and changes than in what these variants might mean for our understanding of how the text came into being, how it has been transmitted over time, and what that says about the place of this scripture within the Latter-day Saint faith. The discussion that follows will use examples just seen in Alma 30, as well as textual variants from elsewhere in the Book of Mormon.

The Original Dictation

Both Mormons and non-Mormons have long been intrigued by the very unusual process that brought forth the Book of Mormon. According to eyewitnesses, Smith would place a seer stone into the crown of his hat and then, with his face in the hat to occlude outside light, he would dictate a few phrases at a time. A scribe would write the words as he or she heard them and then read them back to Smith, who would correct any errors before moving on to the next block of text.[38] About a decade into his Book of Mormon Critical Text Project, which began in 1988, Royal Skousen published an article describing what might be learned about the production of the Book of Mormon from a careful inspection of O. He offered five observations that largely confirm the reports of eyewitnesses. Skousen provided detailed evidence that (1) O was written from dictation, (2) Smith

38. Richard S. Van Wagoner and Steven C. Walker, "Joseph Smith: The Gift of Seeing," *Dialogue: A Journal of Mormon Thought* 15, no. 2 (1982): 48–68; Michael Hubbard Mackay and Gerrit J. Dirkmaat, *From Darkness Unto Light: Joseph Smith's Translation and Publication of the Book of Mormon* (Provo, Utah: Religious Studies Center, Brigham Young University; Salt Lake City: Deseret Book, 2015). Smith's wife Emma was his first scribe; unfortunately, none of her handwriting appears in the extant portions of the Original Manuscript. Images of the seer stone, long in possession of the LDS church, were first made public in Skousen and Jensen, *Revelations and Translations,* vol. 3, pt. 1, pp. xx–xxi.

was dictating at least twenty to thirty words at a time, (3) Smith spelled out unusual names at their first occurrence, (4) the scribe repeated the text back to Smith, and (5) the chapter numbers were not part of the original dictation—that is, Smith verbally indicated where narrative divisions occurred and had his scribe write the word *chapter*, and then the numbers were added later to the manuscript.[39]

Relevant evidence for several aspects of the dictation process can be readily discerned in Alma 30, especially in the immediate or nearly immediate insertions in O, which apparently were made when Cowdery read back to Smith words that had just been written, and then implemented corrections from Smith. Of particular interest are the changes that do not rectify obvious grammatical problems. For instance, the original word *number* in v. 2 works just as well as the revised *numbers*. The same holds for the changes from *crime* to *crimes* (v. 11), *traditions* to *tradition* (v. 16), *causes* to *causeth* (v. 35), and *was* to *is* (v. 53)—though the last example makes a difference in whether the phrase should be considered an indirect or a direct quotation. Furthermore, the inclusion of *also* in v. 41 is not absolutely necessary syntactically. It appears that Cowdery was listening intently to Smith's dictation and corrections, while Smith was equally attentive to Cowdery's reading the words back to him, enough so that both men were catching differences in plurals and verb endings. Evidence from O suggests that they were expending considerable effort to get the words exactly right.

Nevertheless, contrary to what some of the witnesses assumed, Smith occasionally did continue on with his dictation even when mistakes were still in O. This is clearly seen in O at 1 Nephi 7:5, where one of the unidentified scribes first wrote: "the Lord did soften the heart of Ishmael and his hole insomuch that they did take their journey with us," and then, apparently realizing that he had made a mistake, tried to correct the error by inserting another instance of the word *hole* above the first. But "hole hole" does not make much sense either, and Oliver Cowdery interpreted this as *household*

39. Royal Skousen, "Translating the Book of Mormon: Evidence from the Original Manuscript," in *Book of Mormon Authorship Revisited: The Evidence for Ancient Origins*, ed. Noel B. Reynolds (Provo, Utah: FARMS, 1997), 61–93. An interesting piece of evidence for oral dictation of even the biblical quotations occurs in P at 2 Nephi 23:14. Cowdery apparently copied P directly from O (which is no longer extant for this passage) where he had transcribed a phrase from Isaiah 13:14 as "it shall be as the chaste roe." At some later point Cowdery realized his error and after crossing out *chaste*, inserted *chased* above the line.

when he copied it into P. The originally dictated words were probably "whole household."[40] Similarly, at 1 Nephi 13:24, O has the problematic *gospel of the land*, which Cowdery miscopied into P as *gospel of the Lord*. The intended phrase was more likely *gospel of the Lamb*, which occurs four more times in the same chapter.[41]

Of particular interest in reconstructing the dictation process is Alma 45:22, which reads as follows:

> Therefore, Helaman and his brethren went forth to establish the church again in all the land, *yea, in every city throughout all the land which was possessed by the people of Nephi. And it came to pass that they did appoint priests and teachers* throughout all the land, over all the churches.

In O, Oliver Cowdery was the scribe for this page, aside from the twenty-eight words italicized in the above verse, which are in Joseph Smith's handwriting. Apparently Smith took over, mid-sentence, at a time when Cowdery was momentarily incapacitated—he had possibly started to doze off—and Smith needed to get the words down before they were lost. This is the only such occurrence in the surviving portion of the manuscript.[42]

Copying and Publication

Whether or not any divine intervention occurred in the original dictation, from the time the text was first committed to paper, it was clearly subject to very human influences as scribes, typesetters, and editors made inadvertent mistakes and then tried to correct them. Alma 30, seen in Figure 3.4 and Figure 3.5, contains examples of Oliver Cowdery missing or miscopying words in vv. 5, 7, 24, 35, 51, and 52. Joseph Smith made an incomplete correction in 1837 to v. 12, and in v. 16 there is an interesting example where Cowdery immediately caught an error as he was first writing O, but then made a mistake five words later in copying P, which led to Joseph Smith inserting a correction in 1840 that actually

40. Skousen, *Analysis of Textual Variants*, 1:142–43.

41. Skousen, *Analysis of Textual Variants*, 1:275–76.

42. Skousen, "Translating the Book of Mormon," 72–75; note that there was no punctuation in O itself.

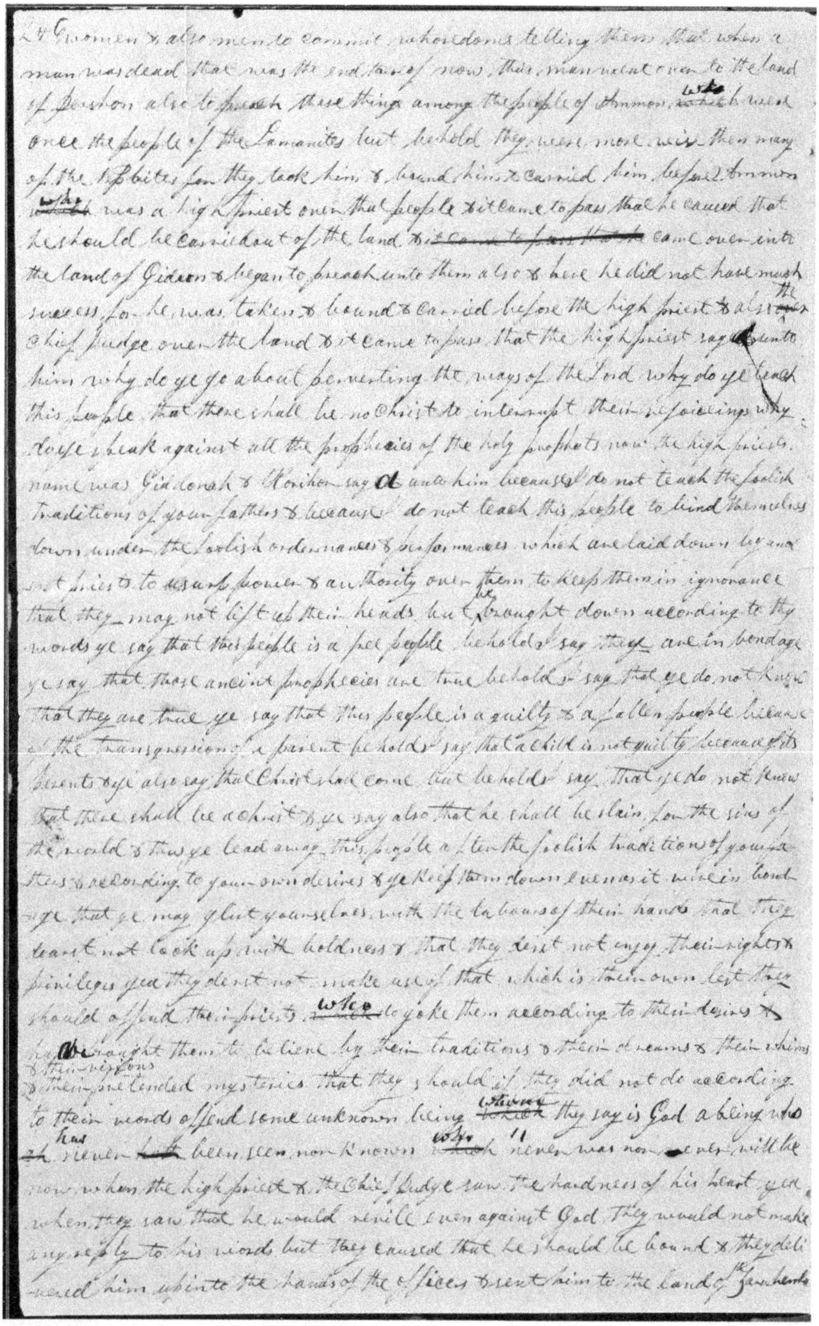

& women & also men to commit whoredoms telling them that when a
man was dead that was the end thereof now this man went over to the land
of Jershon also to preach these things among the people of Ammon who were
once the people of the Lamanites but behold they were more wise than many
of the Nephites for they took him & bound him & carried him before Ammon
who was a high priest over that people & it came to pass that he caused that
he should be carried out of the land & it came to pass that he came over into
the land of Gideon & began to preach unto them also & here he did not have much
success for he was taken & bound & carried before the high priest & also the
chief judge over the land & it came to pass that the high priest said unto
him why do ye go about perverting the ways of the Lord why do ye teach
this people that there shall be no Christ to interrupt their rejoicings why
do ye speak against all the prophecies of the holy prophets now the high priests
name was Giddonah & Korihor said unto him because I do not teach the foolish
traditions of your fathers & because I do not teach this people to bind themselves
down under the foolish ordinances & performances which are laid down by ancient
priests to usurp power & authority over them to keep them in ignorance
that they may not lift up their heads but be brought down according to thy
words ye say that this people is a free people behold I say they are in bondage
ye say that those ancient prophecies are true behold I say that ye do not know
that they are true ye say that this people is a guilty & a fallen people because
of the transgression of a parent behold I say that a child is not guilty because of its
parents & ye also say that Christ shall come but behold I say that ye do not know
that there shall be a Christ & ye say also that he shall be slain for the sins of
the world & thus ye lead away this people after the foolish traditions of your fa
thers & according to your own desires & ye keep them down even as it were in bond
age that ye may glut yourselves with the labours of their hands that they
durst not look up with boldness & that they durst not enjoy their rights &
privileges yea they durst not make use of that which is their own lest they
should offend their priests who do yoke them according to their desires &
have brought them to believe by their traditions & their dreams & their whims
& their visions & their pretended mysteries that they should if they did not do according
to their words offend some unknown being who they say is God a being who
has never been seen nor known who never was nor ever will be
now when the high priest & the chief judge saw the hardness of his heart yea
when they saw that he would revile even against God they would not make
any reply to his words but they caused that he should be bound & they deli
vered him up into the hands of the officers & sent him to the land of Zarahemla

FIGURE 3.4 AND FIGURE 3.5. Alma 30:18–29. Printer's manuscript of the Book of Mormon, p. 246, and transcript.

Courtesy Community of Christ Archives, Independence, MO. Transcript from *The Joseph Smith Papers*, Revelations and Translations Series, vol. 3, p. 511.

PRINTER'S MANUSCRIPT
Alma, ch. 16
[Alma 30:18–29]

246 [verso] women & also men to commit whoredoms telling them that when a
man was dead that was the end thereof now thiis man went over to the land
w{0\h}o
of Jershon also to preach these things among the people of Ammon ~~which~~ were
once the people of the Lamanites but behold they were more wise then many
of the Nephites for they took him & bound him & carried him before Ammon
who
~~which~~ was a high priest over that people & it came to pass that he caused that
he should be carried out of the land & ~~it came to pass that he~~ came over into
the land of Gideon & began to preach unto them also & here he did not have much
the
success for he was taken & bound & carried before the high priest & also ~~over~~
^
chief Judge over the land & it came to pass that the high priest say{eth**d**} unto
him why do ye go about perverting the ways of the Lord why do ye teach
this people that there shall be no christ to interrupt their rejoiceing⟨s⟩ why
do ye speak against all the prophe{s\c}ies of the holy prophets now the high priests
name was Giddonah & {0\K}orihor say{eth**d**} unto him because I do not teach the foolish
traditions of your fathers & because I do not teach this people to bind themselves
down under the foolish ordernances & performances which are laid down by anci
-ent priests to {~~u0~~\us}urp power & authority over them to keep them in ignorance
be
that they may not lift up their heads but brought down according to thy
^
words ye say that this people is a free people behold I say the{re\y}[799] are in bondage
ye say that those ancint prophecies are true behold I say that ye do not know
that they are true ye say that this people is a guilty & a fallen people because
of the transgression of a parent behold I say that a child is not guilty because of its
parents & ye also say that Christ shall come but behold I say that ye do not know
that there shall be a christ & ye say also that he shall be slain for the sins of
the world & thus ye lead away this people after the foolish traditions of your fa-
-thers & according to your own desires & ye keep them down even as it were in bond-
-age that ye may glut yourselves with the labours of their hands that they
dearst not look up with boldness & that they derst not enjoy their rights &
privileges yea they derst not make use of that which is their own lest they
who
should offend their priests ~~which~~ do yoke them according to their desires &
ha{th\{**d\v**}}**e** brought them to believe by their traditions & their dreams & their whims
& their visions
& their pretended mysteries that they should if they did not do according
^
whom
to their words offend some unknown being ~~which~~ they say is God a being wh{i**o**}
has **who** ^
~~-ch~~ never ~~hath~~ been seen nor known ~~which~~ never was nor ~~n~~ever will be
now when the high priest & the chief Judge saw the hardness of his heart yea
when they saw that he would revile even against God they would not make
any reply to his words but they caused that he should be bound & they deli
-vered him up into the hands of the officers & sent him to the land of Zarahemla

ORIGINAL INSCRIPTION
Oliver Cowdery

REVISIONS
Oliver Cowdery
Joseph Smith
Compositor
Scribe 2
Hyrum Smith
Unidentified

799. Original: "there" changed to "these".

FIGURE 3.4 AND FIGURE 3.5. (Continued)

restored the first error in O. John Gilbert, the 1830 typesetter, made an unnecessary correction in v. 30, while the 1837 typesetter scrambled Smith's 1837 revision to v. 49, and entirely missed Smith's correction at v. 58.[43] Some of these mistakes were recognized and rectified in later editions, but several were not.

Most of these are rather minor discrepancies, though a few might make a difference in the sort of close reading appropriate to sacred texts. If one were trying to gauge the social context for the Korihor story, or to track the activities of the high priest Alma, it might be important that there was continual peace in "*the commencement of* the seventeenth year," rather than just in "the seventeenth year." And there may be some distinction between Alma's pronouncing judgment "in the name of God," rather than the curse itself occurring "in the name of God" (v. 49).

Oliver Cowdery did not make many deliberate revisions as he was copying P, but he did make a few elsewhere, and those might matter for readers who are interested in the exact wording of the original dictation (whether regarded as originating with God or with Joseph Smith). The seven most significant examples are as follows, with Cowdery's revisions and additions in italics

1 Nephi 3:16 – because of the commandments *of the Lord*
1 Nephi 7:17 – according to my faith which is in [me > *thee*]
1 Nephi 11:6 – Son of the most high *God*
1 Nephi 11:36 – the pride of the world; *and it fell*, and the fall thereof was exceeding great
1 Nephi 12:4 – saw the earth [that it rent the rocks > *and the rocks that they rent*]
Alma 17:8 – preach the word *of God* unto the Lamanites
Alma 59:9 – into the hands of the Lamanites *than to retake it from them*

43. Or, at least this is what the manuscript evidence suggests. As is usually the case with textual criticism, the details can be much more complicated. For instance, at Alma 30:49, where Smith's deletion of the first *that* in P (*and I say* [*that* >JS NULL] *in the name of God that ye shall be struck dumb*) led to the deletion of the second *that* in the 1837 edition (*and I say that in the name of God ye shall be struck dumb*), presumably the 1837 typesetter made a mistake. But it is also possible that Smith changed his mind, or that Cowdery accidentally omitted the wrong *that* in the marked-up 1830 copy-text they were preparing for the 1837 typesetting.

John Gilbert also made a number of changes as he typeset the first edition. These include revising "hath visited me" to "hath visited men" in 2 Nephi 4:26 and expanding "my beloved" to "my beloved brethren" in Jacob 4:11.

When scribes and editors made deliberate changes, they were usually trying to regularize the grammar or correct obvious transcription errors, but they sometimes missed problematic readings, were thrown off by unclear handwriting, or introduced new problems by correcting words that were fine as is. Royal Skousen has tabulated the conjectural emendations that Oliver Cowdery, two unidentified scribes, John Gilbert, and Joseph Smith made in O, P, and the first three editions. In Skousen's judgment nearly three-quarters of them were either erroneous or unnecessary.[44]

The Nature of the Text

As Skousen worked to reconstruct the original text of the Book of Mormon, he made several observations based on his analysis of textual variants. He discovered that in the earliest form of the text, quotations of biblical chapters are sometimes closer to the King James Bible than they are in later editions. That is to say, later editors, either through accidental errors or deliberate attempts to update the language, rendered Book of Mormon quotations of the Bible less precise. For example, in 2 Nephi 24:25—quoting Isaiah 14:25 exactly—O included the phrase "I will *break* the Assyrian in my land," which Oliver Cowdery miscopied into P as "I will *bring* the Assyrian in my land." This has been the reading in every edition since 1830. Similarly, the quotation of the Lord's Prayer in the earliest version of 3 Nephi 13:9–13 included the King James wording "our father which art in heaven" and "thy will be done in earth," which Joseph Smith updated in 1837 to "our father *who* is in heaven" and "thy will be done *on* earth."[45]

---

44. Royal Skousen, "Conjectural Emendation in the Book of Mormon," *FARMS Review* 18, no. 1 (2006): 187–231; and personal communication with the author, 26 January 2016. His full results will be published in Part 6 of Volume 3 of the Book of Mormon Critical Text Project.

45. Royal Skousen, "Textual Variants in the Isaiah Passages of the Book of Mormon," in *Isaiah in the Book of Mormon*, ed. Donald W. Parry and John W. Welch (Provo, Utah: FARMS, 1998), 369–90; Skousen, "Some Textual Changes," 103–6; Skousen, *Analysis of Textual Variants*, 2:799–800 and 5:3381–82. For a careful analysis of the Book of Mormon's use of Isaiah, see David P. Wright, "Isaiah in the Book of Mormon: or Joseph Smith in Isaiah," in *American Apocrypha: Essays on the Book of Mormon*, ed., Dan Vogel and Brent Lee Metcalfe (Salt Lake City: Signature Books, 2002), 157–234. Wright believes that the book is a nineteenth-century text authored by Smith.

Skousen has also documented how the language of the original text of the Book of Mormon was more consistent than that of later versions. In its earliest form, there are only occurrences of *whatsoever*, never *whatever*; always *if it so be that* rather than *if it be so that; observe to keep the commandments* rather than *observe the commandments*; and *thus ended* [a period of time] rather than *thus endeth* [a period of time]—despite the fact that examples of the latter expressions all appear in the current edition.[46] He has identified examples in the earliest text of nonbiblical, archaic usages from the sixteenth and seventeenth centuries that were obsolete by the nineteenth century, which have been gradually edited out of the printed editions. These include *to counsel* meaning "to counsel with," *but if* meaning "unless," *depart* meaning "part," and *detect* meaning "to expose."[47] And he has pointed to possible Hebraisms that are clearer in the original text, including more than a dozen instances of *if–and* conditional clauses that were subsequently edited out. For instance, Moroni 10:4 originally read "if ye shall ask with a sincere heart with real intent having faith in Christ and he will manifest the truth of it unto you." In 1837 Joseph Smith deleted the extraneous *and*.[48]

Turning back to Alma 30, Cowdery's miscopying of *commands of God* for *commandments of God* is clearly seen when comparing O and P (v. 7), but it is also worth noting that the earliest text of the Book of Mormon almost always prefers *commandments of God* (70 times) to *commands of God* (just twice, both in the book of Jacob). There are a few nonbiblical phrases that were much more characteristic of Early Modern English than the English of Smith's time, including "save it were" (vv. 33, 34, 52) and "nor never" (v. 28). And the phrase *if ye deny again that there is a God and also deny the Christ* (v. 39) can be interpreted as a Hebrew-like conditional clause that is equivalent to a negative imperative. In any case, Smith changed it in 1837

---

46. Royal Skousen, "The Systematic Text of the Book of Mormon," in *Uncovering the Original Text of the Book of Mormon*, ed. M. Gerald Bradford and Alison V. P. Coutts (Provo, Utah: FARMS, 2002), 50–51. The entire article offers a useful overview of the sorts of observations Skousen has made about the earliest text.

47. Royal Skousen, "The Archaic Vocabulary of the Book of Mormon," *Insights: A Window on the Ancient World, The Newsletter of the Foundation for Ancient Research and Mormon Studies (FARMS) at Brigham Young University* 25, no. 5 (2005), 2–7 (available at http://publications.mi.byu.edu/fullscreen/?pub=1316&index=3); Skousen, "Conjectural Emendation," 193–97; Skousen, *Analysis of Textual Variants*, 3:1390–91.

48. Skousen, "Translating the Book of Mormon," 88–90.

to a simple question: *Will ye deny again that there is a God and also deny the Christ?*[49] Some Mormon interpreters have seen Skousen's findings of archaic usage and grammar as evidence that Joseph Smith could not have composed the Book of Mormon on his own.[50] Some further speculate that through the seer stone, God revealed to Smith a preexisting translation in a language that was based in the vocabulary and grammar of Early Modern English, but which nevertheless drew upon the phrasing of the King James Bible and other elements of nineteenth-century American culture.

The Nature of the Narrative

While Skousen systematically covers every variant in the text, his observations focus on recovering the original words and seldom involve the perspectives of literary criticism. However, there are several interesting possibilities here. The chapter numbers in O were written in later, as with Alma 30, and the same is true of P. Apparently when Smith was dictating, he would tell his scribe to write the word *chapter* and then continue on, perhaps assuming that numbers could be inserted afterward. At one point in O, the word *chapter* is followed by the title of a new book—suggesting that Smith had not planned out the macrostructure of the text beforehand—and in P the scribe adding the chapter numbers got confused and accidentally put an X where a IX should have gone. (The typesetter caught the error and penciled in the correct numbers for the subsequent chapters.)[51] The current LDS edition uses the shorter chapters introduced in the 1879 edition, but close readings of the narrative should take into account the original chapter divisions. Thus the Korihor story in Alma 30 was originally at the beginning of Alma XVI, which continued until the end of the current chapter 35. This means that in the mind of the original author—whoever that may have been—Korihor's confrontation with Alma was

49. Skousen, *Analysis of Textual Variants,* 4:2233–34; see also his discussion of 1 Nephi 19:20–21 at 1:416–20.

50. See Stanford Carmack, "Why the Oxford English Dictionary (and Not Webster's 1828)," *Interpreter: A Journal of Mormon Scripture* 15 (2015): 65–77, as well as his "Joseph Smith Read the Words," *Interpreter* 18 (2016): 41–64, and his essay "The Nature of the Nonstandard English in the Book of Mormon," in Skousen, *History of the Text,* 1:45–98. Skousen's own summary of the evidence will appear in the introduction to his *History of the Text of the Book of Mormon: Original Language,* forthcoming from FARMS and BYU Studies in 2018.

51. Skousen, "Translating the Book of Mormon," 85–87. The original chapter numbers were in Roman numerals, while modern chapters are designated by Arabic numerals.

intended to be read as an introduction to the account of Alma's mission to the Zoramites (chaps. 31–35).[52]

Sometimes the results of textual criticism may strengthen the case for deliberate internal allusions made by the narrators. It is striking that the phrase *press forward* (or *pressing forward*) occurs in only two passages: five times in 1 Nephi 8:21–30 describing Lehi's dream about people catching hold of an iron rod that would lead them to the tree of life, and twice at 2 Nephi 31:20, where Nephi appears to be alluding to that earlier imagery as he adds some clarifying information.[53] That distinctive usage pattern was made even clearer when it was discovered that the next verse (1 Nephi 8:31), which has always been printed as "multitudes *feeling* their way" was actually "multitudes *pressing* their way" in O. Similarly, Nephi's concluding testimony at 2 Nephi 33:4, that "the words which I have written in weakness will *be made* strong unto them," in P initially read "the words which I have written in weakness will *he make* strong unto them," giving God a more active role in fulfilling the prophecy. The P variant also strengthens the connection to 2 Nephi 3:21, where God himself says, in a revelation attributed to Joseph of Egypt, "and the weakness of their words will I make strong in their faith." And finally, a lengthy description of God at Helaman 14:12 in the current edition—"Jesus Christ, the Son of God, the Father of heaven and of earth, the Creator of all things from the beginning"—almost exactly repeats an earlier phrase from Mosiah 3:8 (20 of 21 words), but the restoration of a missing *of* from the earliest extant version of Mosiah (in P) makes the phrases completely identical.[54]

Skousen's conjecture that Alma 30:17 may have originally had "*the* high priest" rather than "*a* high priest" (the reading in P) is matched by other textual variants that conceivably might influence the way that one understands Book of Mormon characters and narratives. (In each case below, the textual evidence stands at odds with the current edition.) For example,

---

52. For an example of what such an integrated reading might look like, see Heather Hardy, "Alma's Experiment in Faith: A Broader Context," *Dialogue* 44, no. 3 (2011): 67–91. Brant Gardner also pays attention to the original chapter divisions in his six-volume *Second Witness* commentary series (Draper, Utah: Greg Kofford Books, 2007).

53. Actually, there is an eighth occurrence at Ether 14:12, which seems to be a stray usage having nothing to do with Lehi or Nephi.

54. John W. Welch first noted the connection between the two verses in "Textual Consistency," in *Reexploring the Book of Mormon*, ed. John W. Welch (Salt Lake City, Deseret Book; Provo, Utah: FARMS, 1992), 22; Skousen discussed the textual evidence in his *Analysis of Textual Variants*, 2:1167–68.

does King Benjamin at Mosiah 2:15 have a "*clear* conscience" (1981) or a "*clean* conscience" (P)? At Alma 8:23 was there a singular "*church* of God throughout the land" (1830, 1981) or numerous "*churches* of God throughout the land" (P)? Was Amalickiah at Alma 47:13 "*a* second leader" (P, 1981) or "*the* second leader" (O)? At Alma 51:7, was there rejoicing only among "*many of* the people of liberty (P, 1981) or more generally "among the people of liberty" (O)? Was Pahoran at Helaman 1:5 appointed to be "chief judge over the people" (1837, 1981) or "*a* chief judge over the people" (O, P)? Does Ether 1:41, which speaks of the Brother of Jared's *families* (1830, 1981), imply that he was a polygamist, or does the earlier reading of *family* (P) make him a monogamist?[55]

One of the most ambitious attempts to integrate textual criticism and theological interpretation was an essay by Brent Metcalfe in which he presented evidence for a hypothesis that had been developed over the previous two decades—namely, that after Martin Harris lost the initial pages (approximately 116) of the manuscript, Smith continued dictating where he had left off, in the book of Mosiah. Smith and Cowdery produced Mosiah through the end of the Book of Mormon, and then afterwards returned to an alternate version of the first generations of the Nephites in First Nephi through Words of Mormon. In other words, the Book of Mormon was dictated out of chronological order, and out of the order in which the text is currently printed. (Most scholars of the Book of Mormon, both in and out of the LDS church, agree with this reconstruction of events.) Metcalfe then argued that doctrines develop not from the beginning of the narrative to the end, but from the last pages to the first. So ideas that are somewhat obscure in the middle get clearer as the story moves toward its conclusion—including teachings concerning the coming of Christ to the Nephites, the meaning of baptism, the relationship between the Messiah and Jesus, and whether the word *churches* refers to congregations or denominations. That same clarity can be found in the first 150 pages of the Book of Mormon, which were dictated last. Metcalfe used this as evidence in an argument that the book originated in the mind of Joseph Smith. Whether one accepts that conclusion or not, his article is a fine

55. Skousen accepts the emendation "clear conscience" in his Yale edition, but for every other example cited here he follows the earliest reading of the text. In addition, the name *Pahoran* was originally *Parhoron*; see Skousen, *Analysis of Textual Variants*, 4:2635–37.

example of how close attention to the production of the text can influence theological analysis.[56]

The Mind of Joseph Smith

There will always be disagreement about how much of Joseph Smith is in the original text of the Book of Mormon, yet all readers can agree that it is possible to see Smith's mind at work in his 1837 and 1840 revisions. The first thing to notice is the pervasive grammatical and stylistic updating—not only the unique revisions presented above in verses 12, 16, 28, 35, 39, 49, and 58 of Alma chapter 30, but also the generic emendations to the chapter: the ten changes of *saith* to *said*, eight of *which* to *who*, six of *hath* to *have* or *has*, and three deletions of *that*. John Gilbert, the typesetter, later recounted that as he was preparing the 1830 edition, he asked about a grammatical error in the manuscript and was told by Martin Harris, "The Old Testament is ungrammatical, set it as written."[57] Seven years later, however, Smith was uncomfortable with the grammar of the first edition.

Smith's 1837 editing was attentive, but inconsistent. He changed verb forms in some places but left identical forms intact elsewhere; he sometimes misinterpreted handwriting (as when, at 2 Nephi 1:26, he sees "say th-" at the end of a line and instead of recognizing *th-* as the beginning of a hyphenated word, he reads it as *saith*); his attempts to smooth out diction could actually cause new problems (at 2 Nephi 4:17, he removed a *notwithstanding* that had to be added back in 1920); and he occasionally changed his mind (at 1 Nephi 3:3, he emended the 1830 *my forefathers* to *thy forefathers* in 1837, and then changed it back to *my forefathers* in 1840). His revisions of *which* to *who* were somewhat mechanistically done, so there are instances where he started to cross out *which* and then changed

56. Brent Lee Metcalfe, "The Priority of Mosiah: A Prelude to Book of Mormon Exegesis," in *New Approaches to the Book of Mormon: Explorations in Critical Methodology* (Salt Lake City: Signature Books, 1993), 395–444.

57. Dan Vogel, ed., *Early Mormon Documents*, 5 vols. (Salt Lake City: Signature Books, 1996–2003), 2:544, cf. 536, 550; see also Royal Skousen, "Worthy of Another Look: John Gilbert's 1892 Account of the 1830 Printing of the Book of Mormon," *Journal of Book of Mormon Studies* 21, no. 2 (2012): 63.

his mind, and in at least a few cases the original *which* makes better sense than the newly inserted *who*.[58]

More significant are Smith's deliberate, non-stylistic changes, the most famous of which are six verses where he changed a title of God, as seen in Figure 3.6 (Smith's 1837 additions or deletions are italicized):

1 Nephi 11:18 – the mother *of the Son* of God
1 Nephi 11:21 – the Lamb of God, yea, even *the Son of* the Eternal Father
1 Nephi 11:32 – *the Son of* the everlasting God
1 Nephi 13:40 – the Lamb of God is *the Son of* the Eternal Father
Alma 5:48 – the Son [of > ,] the Only Begotten of the Father
Alma 13:9 – the Son [of > ,] the Only Begotten of the Father

These revisions, however, probably represent simple clarifications rather than a development of Christology. Several other verses in the Book of Mormon refer to Jesus Christ as God or the Father, and Smith left these intact, further indicating that he did not revise the text consistently.[59]

In addition to the six changes above, there are only a handful of verses where Smith did more than correct grammar or smooth out diction (again, his 1837 additions or substitutions are italicized):

1 Nephi 8:4 – methought I saw *in my dream* a dark and dreary wilderness
1 Nephi 12:8 – and [Jesus Christ > *the Messiah*] which is the Lamb of God
1 Nephi 19:20 – had not the Lord been merciful to show unto me concerning them, even as he had prophets of old, *I should have perished also*
1 Nephi 21:20 – after thou hast lost the [other > *first*] [in a quotation of Isaiah 49:20]
2 Nephi 4:12 – after *my father* Lehi had spoken to all his household
Mosiah 21:28 – king [Benjamin > *Mosiah*] had a gift from God

58. For Smith's aborted replacements of *which*, see Skousen and Jensen, *Revelations and Translations*, vol. 3, pt. 1, p. 419; and pt. 2, pp. 45, 51, 85, 235. Verses where the original *which* is a better reading include 1 Nephi 13:12; Alma 12:29, 13:5; and Helaman 5:41.

59. 2 Nephi 25:12; Mosiah 3:8, 7:27, 15:1–2, 16:15; Alma 11:38–39; Helaman 14:12, 16:18; Mormon 9:12; Ether 3:14, 4:7, 4:12; see the discussion in Skousen, *Analysis of Textual Variants*, 1:230–33. The extraneous *of* in the last two examples appears to have been a transcription error; elsewhere in the Book of Mormon there is no mention of "the Only Begotten" having a son himself. For more on Smith's inconsistent revisions, see Skousen, *History of the Text*, 1:35–43.

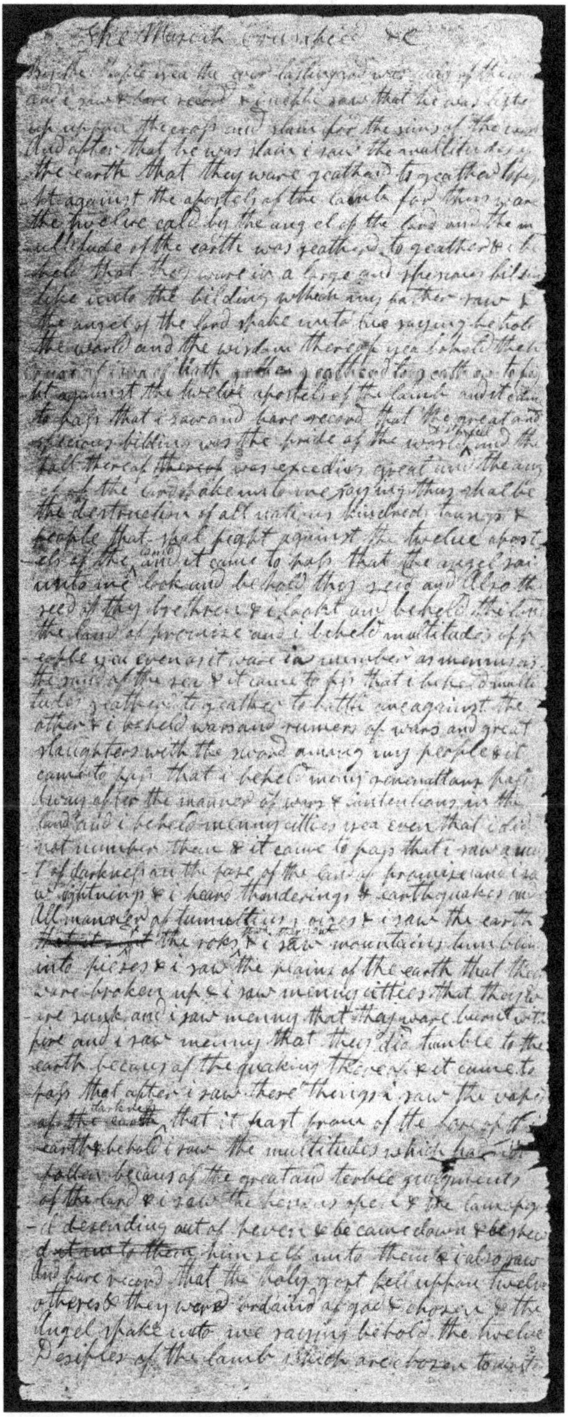

FIGURE 3.6. 1 Nephi 11:32–12:8. Original manuscript of the Book of Mormon. Church History Library, Salt Lake City.

None of these emendations make much of a difference to the narrative, with the possible exception of the last, but even that turns out to be unnecessary according to Book of Mormon chronology.[60]

Smith made even fewer substantive, deliberate changes for the 1840 edition. In fact, only two have real significance. At 1 Nephi 20:1 is the one instance in Smith's Book of Mormon editing of the sort of lengthy additions and innovative theologizing that characterized his 1830–1833 revision of the King James Bible (known as the Joseph Smith Translation) or of his own revelations. The verse is a quotation of Isaiah 48:1, which includes the phrase "are come forth out of the waters of Judah." In 1840, Smith added a parenthetical gloss immediately thereafter: *(or out of the waters of baptism)*. In 1920 the parentheses were deleted, so most Latter-day Saints today are unaware that this phrase was not part of the original Book of Mormon.

The second significant 1840 revision was Smith's change in 2 Nephi 30:6 of "many generations shall not pass away among them save they shall be a *white* and a delightsome people" to "many generations . . . save they shall be a *pure* and a delightsome people." This may indeed be indicative of Smith's racial views in 1840, though he left intact a half dozen other verses where skin color is seen as a pertinent issue in relations between Nephites and Lamanites. Because the LDS textual tradition took the 1837 edition as its base text rather than the 1840 edition (for complicated historical and geographical reasons), this particular revision was lost to the main denomination of Mormonism until it was restored in 1981, along with a few other 1840 readings.[61] It appears that the motivation was not so much to avoid embarrassing racial implications as to canonize one of Smith's deliberate emendations.

It is also worth noting some of the errors that Smith did not correct in either 1837 or 1840. Since 1830, the book of Alma has included references to two dissident groups of Nephites: the Amlicites found in chapters 2–3, and the Amalekites of chapters 21–27 and 43. Textual criticism, however, strongly suggests that these were the same people, who became disjoined through a spelling error.[62] This changes the narrative arc of the book of Alma, and if Joseph Smith was a master storyteller, it is odd that he never caught the

60. See Skousen, *Analysis of Textual Variants*, 3:1418–21.

61. Skousen, *Earliest Text*, 739–744; Skousen, *Analysis of Textual Variants*, 2:895–99.

62. Skousen, *Analysis of Textual Variants*, 3:1605–9.

mistake (though it is also strange that for the rest of his life, he almost never used Book of Mormon characters or stories in either his writings or his sermons).[63] Similarly, the 1837 edition added nine words to 3 Nephi 22:4 (which is quoting Isaiah 54:4): "for thou shalt forget the shame of thy youth, *and shalt not remember the reproach of thy youth*, and shalt not remember the reproach of thy widowhood any more." But rather than being a veiled reference to the censure Smith had experienced as a teenager, both for his religious claims and his short-lived career as a treasure seeker, it appears that this is a simple case of dittography—when the typesetter's eye skipped back from the second *of thy* to the first *of thy*, and he inadvertently copied the same line twice. Yet Smith did not correct this mistake in his editing for the 1840 edition.

In examining the changes made for the 1837 edition, it is possible to see Joseph Smith as a reader of the Book of Mormon, and it is striking how constrained he seemed to be in his revisions. He worked through the text making grammatical improvements, in a less than systematic fashion, but hardly any of this work resembled the theological innovations or narrative expansions that characterized his editing of the Bible or the Doctrine and Covenants. Very few of his 1837 revisions reinterpret or explain the text, and he never inserted additional information derived from new revelations. Nevertheless, it is remarkable that he was willing to update the language of a book that had been dictated in a fairly exact form, which he asserted had come from God. The 1837 Book of Mormon was the beginning of a translation of the text into modern English, which contrasts with the attitude of the LDS church today, where such efforts are strongly discouraged.[64] Even the punctuation, which was added by the non-Mormon typesetter and hence had little claim to canonical status, has been retained mostly unchanged.

---

63. See, for example, Grant Underwood, "Book of Mormon Usage in Early LDS Theology," *Dialogue: A Journal of Mormon Thought* 17, no. 3 (1984), 35–74. On p. 53, Underwood notes that "in the 173 Nauvoo discourses of the prophet Joseph Smith [spanning from 1839 to his death in 1844] for which contemporary records exist, only two Book of Mormon passages have been cited while dozens of biblical passages were."

64. The official handbook on church policy states in section 21.1.8, "The Church discourages rewriting the Book of Mormon into familiar or modern English. The First Presidency has said, 'When a sacred text is translated into another language or rewritten into more familiar language, there are substantial risks that this process may introduce doctrinal errors or obscure evidence of its ancient origin. To guard against these risks, the First Presidency and Council of the Twelve give close personal supervision to the translation of scriptures from English into other languages and have not authorized efforts to express the doctrinal content of the Book of Mormon in familiar or modern English.' " *Handbook 2: Administering the Church* (Salt Lake City: Church of Jesus Christ of Latter-day Saints, 2010), 181.

Conclusion

Since the death of Joseph Smith in 1844, the LDS church has not continued the type of widespread grammatical and stylistic updating that Smith practiced in 1837, even as the somewhat awkward, archaic language of the Book of Mormon has become increasingly removed from common English over the last two centuries. Instead, the LDS church has acted mostly as a conservator of the Book of Mormon as Smith left it, and they greatly value uniformity, so at any given time there is only one official, authorized English version of the Book of Mormon, which takes precedence over any previous editions. These editions have never included footnotes identifying textual variants or explaining changes over time. Thanks to the Book of Mormon Critical Text Project and the Joseph Smith Papers, Latter-day Saints now have much more access to information about the history of their signature scripture, and perhaps future official editions will incorporate the results of those scholarly endeavors.

Scholars working on the Book of Mormon should consult Skousen's *Earliest Text* first, which reconstructs Smith's original dictation as accurately as possible. The facsimile transcripts in Skousen's *Original Manuscript* and *Printer's Manuscript* volumes are invaluable for detailed studies of specific passages from those sources, though the color-coding of the transcript in the Skousen and Jensen edition of the Printer's Manuscript[65] makes it much easier to see the later additions and corrections made by John Gilbert, Oliver Cowdery, and especially Joseph Smith's revisions for the 1837 edition. Moreover, the photographs in the Skousen and Jensen volume can be used in conjunction with Skousen's facsimile transcripts. And finally, any significant changes in the text can be quickly and precisely tracked by means of Skousen's *Analysis of Textual Variants*.

Critics have long pointed to changes in the Book of Mormon as evidence against its claims of miraculous origins, but whatever the ultimate worth of such claims, it is clear from textual criticism that the Original

65. Royal Skousen and Robin Scott Jensen, eds., *Revelations and Translations, Volume 3, Part 1: Printer's Manuscript of the Book of Mormon, 1 Nephi 1–Alma 35*, facsimile edition, part 1 of vol. 3 of the Revelations and Translations series of *The Joseph Smith Papers*, ed. Ronald K. Esplin and Matthew J. Grow (Salt Lake City: Church Historian's Press, 2015); Royal Skousen and Robin Scott Jensen, eds., *Revelations and Translations, Volume 3, Part 2: Printer's Manuscript of the Book of Mormon, Alma 36–Moroni 10*, facsimile edition, part 2 of vol. 3 of the Revelations and Translations series of *The Joseph Smith Papers*, ed. Ronald K. Esplin and Matthew J. Grow (Salt Lake City: Church Historian's Press, 2015).

Manuscript was a painstaking transcript of Smith's dictation—essentially an oral performance—in 1829. From that time, the text was regarded as complete and mostly fixed, apart from inadvertent errors arising from copying and typesetting mistakes (many of which have been corrected) and the extensive grammatical and stylistic updating undertaken by Smith in 1837. There have been relatively few deliberate, substantive changes, and fewer still that have any significant effect on either the theology or the rather complicated narrative, which shows signs of having been carefully composed. The exact wording of the earliest text will matter a great deal to scholars who regard the book as an important work of American literature or world scripture, and to believers who see it as a gift from God pointing the way to salvation. For both sets of readers—and the two groups are not mutually exclusive—careful reading and detailed interpretation, as well as the textual criticism that makes them possible, are essential.

4

Intertextuality and the Purpose of Joseph Smith's New Translation of the Bible

Thomas A. Wayment

ALMOST ONE YEAR after completing the Book of Mormon translation, Joseph Smith initiated a new and ambitious translation project—a new "translation" of the entire Bible. Although this translation has been thoroughly discussed, the reasons he began the undertaking have never been fully understood. In broad terms, Smith and his scribes—Oliver Cowdery, Emma Smith, John Whitmer, and Jesse Gause—retranslated the entire Bible from Genesis to Revelation using a King James Version (KJV) and then rewording, expanding, and otherwise revising the English text in fairly significant ways. The term *translation*, as applied by Joseph Smith, is the word that has traditionally been used to describe this project, but it would be more appropriate to describe it as a Bible revision. No dictionaries were used, no primary source materials were consulted, and neither Smith nor any of his scribes had any appreciable skill in ancient languages, thus making it more of a revised English edition than a traditional translation.

Within a few months of the publication of the Book of Mormon, Smith and his associates began this major new project with the Bible.[1] In June

1. Title Page of Book of Mormon, circa early June 1829, in Michael Hubbard MacKay, Gerrit J. Dirkmaat, Grant Underwood, Robert J. Woodford, and William G. Hartley, eds., *Documents, Volume 1: July 1828–June 1831*, vol. 1 of the Documents series of *The Joseph Smith Papers*, ed. Dean C. Jessee, Ronald K. Esplin, Richard Lyman Bushman, and Matthew J. Grow (Salt Lake

of 1830, they produced the first document that would initiate and become part of what would come to be called the "Joseph Smith Translation," or JST.[2] The manuscripts that comprise the JST began to appear in June of 1830 and continued over the course of a three-year period, ultimately resulting in four distinct manuscripts and a marked-up Bible. All of the JST manuscripts, seen in Table 4.1, survive with very little damage, as does the Bible that was used in the translation process.

Scholars have divided the changes made to the Bible into several broad categories: (1) expansions of biblical narratives, (2) edits to make the text of the Bible more understandable, (3) harmonizations between the gospels, (4) additions of new discourses that appear to have the modern reader in mind, and (5) expansions of narratives to include new theological insights.[3] One problem with such a categorizing scheme for the JST is that it overlooks the original impetus for making such changes. A further complicating factor is that the purpose and scope of the JST appear to have evolved and grown over time. This essay will engage the question of why Smith and his scribes began a major revision of the Bible in the first place.

Based on the documents that have survived, this chapter argues that the very beginning of what would become the JST was not initially conceived of as the beginning of a complete revision of the Bible. Rather, the work was a natural consequence of Smith pursuing further information regarding Moses and the creation of the world that was implied in a revelation that he received in the late spring or early summer of 1830.[4] This revelation now constitutes the first chapter of the Book of Moses in the Pearl of Great

City: Church Historian's Press, 2013), 63–65, (hereafter *JSP*, D1). For a discussion of copyright procedure and practice in New York, see Nathaniel Hinckley Wadsworth, "Copyright Laws and the 1830 Book of Mormon," *BYU Studies* 45 (2006): 77–99. For information regarding the date of publication of the Book of Mormon, see History Drafts, 1838–circa 1841, vol. A-1, p. 34, in Karen Lynn Davidson, David J. Whittaker, Mark Ashurst-McGee, and Richard L. Jensen, eds., *Histories, Volume 1: Joseph Smith Histories, 1832–1844*, vol. 1 of the Histories series of *The Joseph Smith Papers*, ed. Dean C. Jessee, Ronald K. Esplin, and Richard Lyman Bushman (Salt Lake City: Church Historian's Press, 2012), 352–54.

2. Joseph Smith used the title "New Translation" to refer to his revision of the Bible on several occasions. See, for example, Letter to Church Leaders in Jackson County, Missouri, 25 June 1833, in Gerrit J. Dirkmaat, Brent M. Rodgers, Grant Underwood, Robert J. Woodford, and William G. Hartley, eds., *Joseph Smith Papers, Documents Series, Volume 3: February 1833–March 1834* (Salt Lake City: Church Historian's Press, 2014), 147–58.

3. Compare, for example, Scott H. Faulring, Kent P. Jackson, and Robert J. Matthews, eds., *Joseph Smith's New Translation of the Bible: Original Manuscripts* (Provo, Utah: Religious Studies Center, Brigham Young University, 2004), 8–11.

4. This is the position taken in *JSP*, D1:150–56.

Table 4.1. Extant pages of the Joseph Smith Translation manuscript

Date	Manuscript Description	Contents	Title
June 1830–March 1831	Hand-copied and dictated manuscript containing fifty-nine pages of text. Pages are numbered 1–61 (numbering skips 37–40).	Genesis 1–24:41	OT1
8 March 1831–June 1831(?)	Hand-copied and dictated manuscript where Smith began work on the New Testament. Sixty-five pages, numbered 1–63 (page numbers 56 and 57 are repeated).	Matthew 1–26:71	NT1
4 April 1831–July 1832	Four hand-copied folios or gatherings, comprising 203 pages of manuscript. Contains a copy of NT1, and then afterwards became the living dictated text for the remainder of the New Testament.	Matthew 1:1–Revelation	NT2
March 1831–2 July 1833	Three hand-copied folios comprising 119 pages. Contains a copy of OT1, and then afterwards became the living dictated text for Genesis 24:42 and after.	Genesis 1:1–Malachi	OT2
June 1830–2 July 1833	1828 King James Version of the Bible. This Bible was used throughout the translation process. Parts of the Old Testament (after Genesis 24:42) and the New Testament (after John 6:1) contain markings to show the reader the location of altered English text.	John 6:1–Revelation; Genesis 24:42–Malachi	Marked Bible

Price, the fourth of the four "standard works" that make up the canon of scripture for the Church of Jesus Christ of Latter-day Saints. Knowing this context will in turn have consequences for understanding the translation process as it applied to the JST. As Smith and his scribes began expanding the opening chapters of Genesis, another interest emerged, namely the re-envisioning of the Old Testament as a Christian text. This is evidenced primarily through Smith restructuring the early Genesis chapters to include

God and Jesus working side by side to develop a universal plan of salvation for humankind. In the revised narrative, God presents Moses with a panoramic vision of earth from its creation to a Christian millennium. God lays out a plan for the salvation of humankind in which Jesus Christ acts as the mediator of that plan. Additionally, there exist two cases in the New Testament in which Smith inadvertently revised the same passage twice, thus producing two different translations. The passages that were revised twice provide evidence that the purpose in revising the Bible shifted over time to include other concerns. As the project developed over a three-year period, new interests emerged, and the passages that were translated twice show a strong interest in making the text of the Bible more readable to an early nineteenth-century audience.

Moses 1

Moses 1 presents the reader with a sweeping vision in which Moses and God speak face to face and wherein Moses receives instruction about the purpose of human life on the earth. Satan also appears to Moses and demands to be worshiped, which Moses refuses. The encounter with Satan and a vision of hell serve as a contrast to beholding the glory of God. Then, "being filled with the Holy Ghost which beareth record of the Father & the Son," Moses sees God again and God reveals to Moses his divine plan of salvation. The text concludes with a tantalizing promise of further information.[5]

Moses 1 as a Discrete Text

The text now published as Moses 1 in the Pearl of Great Price—one of the "standard works" in the Mormon canon—appears to have been originally produced as a separate and distinct document.[6] And, this was prior to the revision of Genesis 1:1–6:13 (Moses 2–8 in the Pearl

5. For an edited version of the earliest extant manuscript, see *JSP*, D1:150–56.

6. In citing references to the JST, Latter-day Saint scholars employ two methods. First, because JST Genesis 1–6 was later canonized as the Book of Moses, it is common practice to refer to the Genesis 1–6 materials using their location in the Book of Moses. All other JST changes are cited using their biblical reference. The reason for citing Moses instead of Genesis is that the modern division of chapters in the Book of Moses makes the significant changes to Genesis easier to identify rather than referring, for example, to JST OT2, page 2.

of Great Price), the rest of Genesis, and the rest of the Bible.[7] In contrast to the Bible revision that followed, what is now designated Moses 1, seen in Figure 4.1 and Figure 4.2, purports to be a "revelation"—the name used for Smith's "Thus saith the Lord" communications. That revelation (Moses 1) is not directly associated with any biblical text: in fact, one of its key features is the lack of clear biblical parallels that are both continuous and consistent beyond echoes of and allusions to scriptural texts.[8] Moreover, the manuscript tradition for Moses 1:1–42 is unique in comparison to the remainder of the JST, where a consistent revision of text follows the biblical text sequentially. Given this unique feature of Moses 1, it appears that somewhere in the late spring or early summer of 1830, Smith produced a document that promised to reveal a first-person conversation that took place between God and Moses. That document ended with a warning not to share its contents with anyone, and an assurance that further information regarding the conversation would be forthcoming. The promise of more information about Moses led Smith and his scribes to turn to the most obvious source for more information: the Bible.

The document in question—the earliest known version or copy of Moses 1—is inscribed on two leaves measuring 12 3/4 inches high by 7 3/ 4 inches wide (32 × 20 cm) and bears a title at the top of the first page: "A Revelation given to Joseph the Revelator June 1830."[9] The handwriting of the title is well executed and is intentionally declarative of the document's purpose. This title may have been inserted later, after the document was initially begun with the words, "The words of God which he ~~gave~~ <spake> unto Moses."[10] Those words are written larger and are offset from the text below, suggesting they initially functioned as a title before the scribe added

7. The only full-scale study on Moses 1 and the origins of the text is E. Douglas Clark, "A Prologue to Genesis: Moses 1 in Light of Jewish Traditions," *BYU Studies* 45 (2006): 129–42. Clark argues that Moses 1 forms an independent unit of tradition that is akin to the second-century BCE book of Jubilees. He sees it as a larger introduction to the book of Genesis. He notes the work of Hugh Nibley, who also sees Moses 1:2–8 as an introduction. Hugh Nibley, *Teachings of the Pearl of Great Price: Transcripts of Lectures Presented to an Honors Book of Mormon Class at Brigham Young University, Winter Semester 1986* (Provo, Utah: Foundation for Ancient Research and Mormon Studies, 2004), 205.

8. The standard discussion on intertextuality of scripture is still Richard Hays, *Echoes of Scripture in the Letters of Paul* (New Haven: Yale University Press, 1993).

9. Visions of Moses, June 1830, in *JSP*, D1:150–56.

10. The angle brackets are used throughout this chapter to represent insertions, either inline or interlinear.

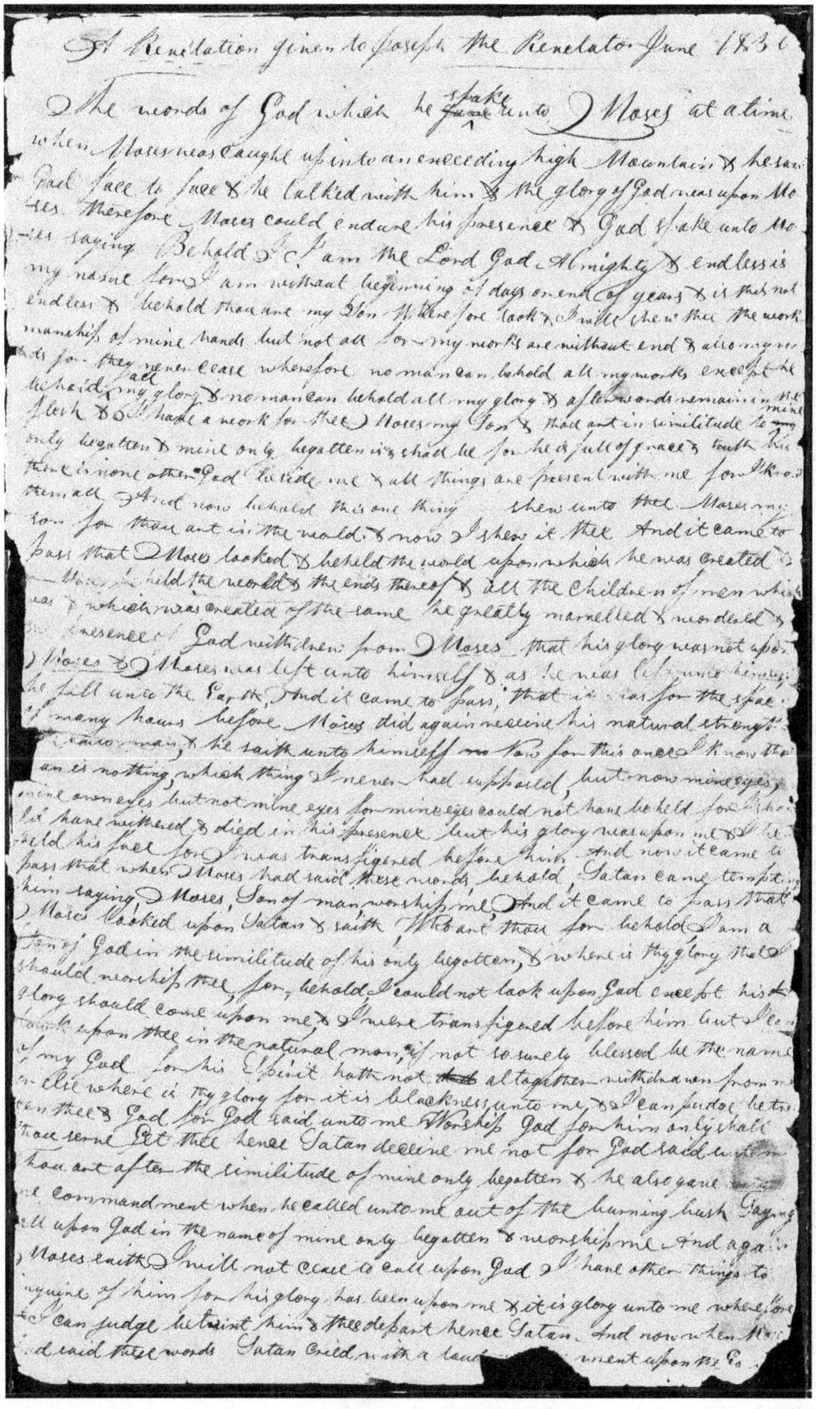

A Revelation given to Joseph the Revelator June 1830

The words of God which he spake unto Moses at a time
when Moses was caught up into an exceeding high Mountain & he saw
God face to face & he talked with him & the glory of God was upon Moses therefore Moses could endure his presence & God spake unto Moses saying Behold I am the Lord God Almighty & endless is
my name for I am without beginning of days or end of years & is this not
endless & behold thou art my Son wherefore look & I will shew thee the work-
manship of mine hands but not all for my works are without end & also my words for they never cease wherefore no man can behold all my works except he
behold all my glory & no man can behold all my glory & afterwards remain in the
flesh & I have a work for thee Moses my Son & thou art in similitude to mine
only begotten & mine only begotten is & shall be for he is full of grace & truth but
there is none other God beside me & all things are present with me for I know
them all And now behold this one thing I shew unto thee Moses my
son for thou art in the world & now I shew it thee And it came to
pass that Moses looked & beheld the world upon which he was created &
Moses beheld the world & the ends thereof & all the children of men which
was & which was created of the same he greatly marvelled & wondered &
the presence of God withdrew from Moses that his glory was not upon
Moses & Moses was left unto himself & as he was left unto himself
he fell unto the Earth And it came to pass that it was for the space
of many hours before Moses did again receive his natural strength
like unto man & he saith unto himself now for this once I know that
man is nothing which thing I never had supposed but now mine eyes
mine own eyes but not mine eyes for mine eyes could not have beheld for I should
have withered & died in his presence but his glory was upon me & I beheld his face for I was transfigured before him And now it came to
pass that when Moses had said these words behold Satan came tempting
him saying Moses Son of man worship me And it came to pass that
Moses looked upon Satan & saith who art thou for behold I am a
son of God in the similitude of his only begotten & where is thy glory that I
should worship thee for behold I could not look upon God except his
glory should come upon me & I were transfigured before him but I can
look upon thee in the natural man is it not so surely blessed be the name
of my God for his Spirit hath not altogether withdrawn from me
or else where is thy glory for it is blackness unto me & I can judge between thee & God for God said unto me Worship God for him only shalt
thou serve Get thee hence Satan deceive me not for God said unto me
thou art after the similitude of mine only begotten & he also gave me
commandment when he called unto me out of the burning bush saying
call upon God in the name of mine only begotten & worship me And again
Moses saith I will not cease to call upon God I have other things to
inquire of him for his glory has been upon me & it is glory unto me wherefore
I can judge betwixt him & thee depart hence Satan And now when Moses
had said these words Satan cried with a loud [illegible] went upon the Ea

FIGURE 4.1 AND FIGURE 4.2. Moses 1:1–36. OT1, pp. 1–2.
Courtesy Community of Christ Archives, Independence, MO.

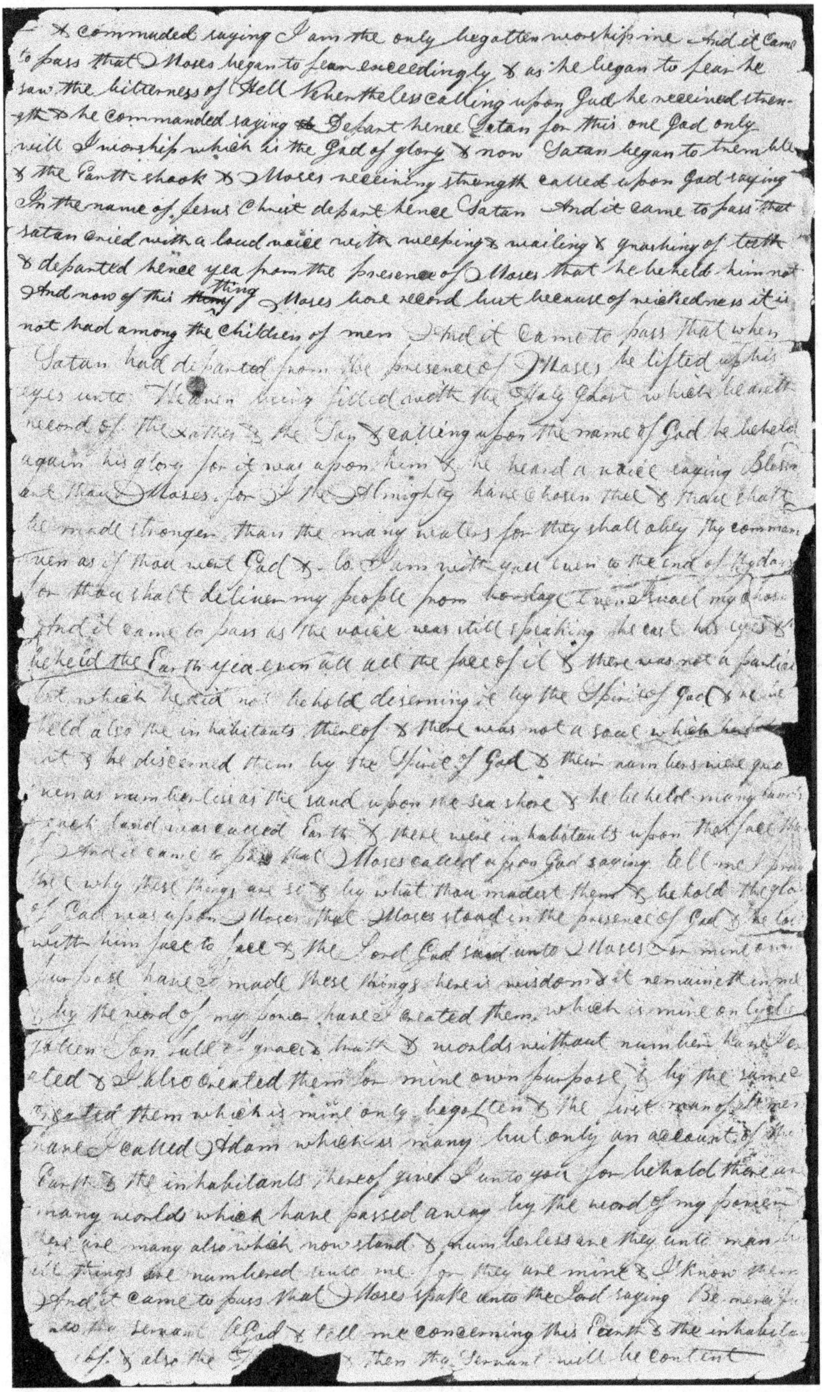

& commanded saying I am the only begotten worship me And it Came
to pass that Moses began to fear exceedingly & as he began to fear he
saw the bitterness of Hell Nevertheless calling upon God he received strength & he commanded saying Depart hence Satan for this one God only
will I worship which is the God of glory & now Satan began to tremble
& the Earth shook & Moses receiving strength called upon God saying
In the name of Jesus Christ depart hence Satan And it came to pass that
Satan cried with a loud voice with weeping & wailing & gnashing of teeth
& departed hence yea from the presence of Moses that he beheld him not
And now of this ~~story~~ thing Moses bore record but because of wickedness it is
not had among the children of men And it Came to pass that when
Satan had departed from the presence of Moses he lifted up his
eyes unto Heaven being filled with the Holy Ghost which beareth
record of the Father & the Son & calling upon the name of God he beheld
again his glory for it was upon him & he heard a voice saying Blessed
art thou Moses for I the Almighty have chosen thee & thou shalt
be made stronger than the many waters for they shall obey thy comman-
[d] even as if thou wert God & lo I am with you even to the end of thy days
for thou shalt deliver my people from bondage even Israel my chosen
And it came to pass as the voice was still speaking he cast his eyes &
beheld the Earth yea even all all the face of it & there was not a particle
[of i]t which he did not behold discerning it by the Spirit of God & he beheld also the inhabitants thereof & there was not a soul which he beheld
[no]t & he discerned them by the Spirit of God & their numbers were grea[t]
even as numberless as the sand upon the sea shore & he beheld many lands
[&] each land was called Earth & there were inhabitants upon the face the[re-]
of And it came to pass that Moses called upon God saying tell me I pray
thee why these things are so & by what thou madest them & behold the glo[ry]
of God was upon Moses that Moses stood in the presence of God & he tal[ked]
with him face to face & the Lord God said unto Moses for mine own
purpose have I made these things here is wisdom & it remaineth in me
& by the word of my power have I created them which is mine only begotten Son full of grace & truth & worlds without number have I created & I also created them for mine own purpose & by the same I
created them which is mine only begotten & the first man of all men
have I called Adam which is many but only an account of this
Earth & the inhabitants thereof give I unto you for behold there are
many worlds which have passed away by the word of my power &
there are many also which now stand & numberless are they unto man bu[t]
all things are numbered unto me for they are mine & I know them
And it came to pass that Moses spake unto the Lord saying Be merciful
unto thy servant O God & tell me concerning this Earth & the inhabita[nts]
thereof & also the [heavens] & then thy servant will be content

FIGURE 4.1 AND FIGURE 4.2. (Continued)

the more formal title to the document once the text was copied. The uppermost title appears somewhat cramped in the remaining head of the page, although one cannot be certain that it is a later insertion because both titles are in the handwriting of Oliver Cowdery. Beneath the uppermost title is a partial and apparently rapidly formed underline (for the title). The second line begins the first sentence of what would become Moses 1 and functions in concert with the body of the document.[11] It is simply the beginning of the document written in titular fashion.

The scribal features of the physical artifact containing the revelation of Moses 1 offer clues about whether the document preserves the original inscription of this text or a copy thereof. This is important because if it is an original document, then its physical connection to the manuscripts of the JST (OT1) would argue that Smith likely produced the text intending to revise the Bible, since every page with the exception of the first directly engages the book of Genesis. In this case, one might reasonably conclude that Moses 1 and the Bible revision were intentionally linear in their relationship and share a similar purpose. If the document is an original but was later joined to the JST documents as a type of introduction, then the idea of a linear, temporal connection would be unnecessary. Conversely, if the document is a copy, then it can be assumed that it was joined to OT1—the document that would become the starting point for the JST—sometime later in 1830. In this case, Joseph Smith and his scribal assistants sought to join the revelation of Moses 1 with their revision of the Bible. In either case, Moses 1 potentially forms the starting point for the three-year production known as the JST. A further benefit of this discussion would be the possible recovery of original intent, an intent that was later melded into a larger Bible revision project that engaged other interests and purposes.

Manuscript Moses 1 as a Copied Text

Because Smith's scribes and his document production practices varied over time, it is difficult to do a comparative analysis of the earliest extant version of Moses 1 to determine whether it is an original. Indeed, very few

11. For the title on page 3 following the document preserving Moses 1, it reads, "A Revelation given to the Elders of the Church of Christ | on the First Book of Moses ~~given to Joseph the Seer~~." Faulring, Jackson, and Matthews, *Joseph Smith's New Translation of the Bible,* note that the strikethrough bar must have been inscribed before December 1830 because the stricken words were not copied by John Whitmer in the manuscript commonly designated OT2.

original Smith documents have survived from the period between 1830 and 1833—the years in which he produced the JST—and for the most part scholars are left to work with copies.[12] Thus it will be important here to propose a methodology for analyzing Moses 1 as an original using standard document analysis practices. An initial analysis of the document preserving Moses 1 indicates that it is a copy of an earlier original—even though in this instance the copy may have been made within a few days of the original. Also, in some instances corrections may have been made to the copy because it became the live version of the document rather than the original. The evidence is not overwhelmingly conclusive, but overall it points to the document being a copy.

Among the features that point to the document in question being a copy is the spacing of words and the size of the handwriting as the scribe approached line ends. Typically, a scribe who is completely unfamiliar with a text, particularly one that is being orally dictated, will produce a fairly ragged right margin because the scribe is unable to anticipate what is coming; it is impossible to foresee whether those words will fit on a line or whether a word is too long and will have to be continued on to the next line.[13] If the dictation is slow enough, then a scribe can reasonably compensate in some instances. In contrast, when copying a document the scribe can visualize near the end of a line whether a number of words will fit on the given line if the size of handwriting is reduced. This is evident in several instances in Moses 1 where the scribe, Oliver Cowdery, decreased the size of the inscription of some words at the ends of lines because he realized that he could fit the word in. For example, in the third line from the top of page 1, the phrase "he saw" is clearly cramped so that it fits the end of the line. This is also apparent with the inscription of "talked" on page 2 and "thou shalt write" on page 3.

Inspecting the types of corrections made in a manuscript is another method for determining whether the text in question was an original or a copy, particularly when the purpose of the correction can be discerned or the handwriting of the correction identified. On line 24 of the first page, Cowdery wrote "~~no~~ Now" suggesting that he knew it began a quotation and that, following convention, he therefore needed to capitalize the

12. See *JSP*, D1:3–150.

13. In the Book of Mormon manuscripts, which were also dictated, Cowdery does frequently use the full length of lines.

quotation's first word.[14] That the error was corrected in the line, rather than above the line, suggests that the correction was made while making a copy, rather than during the original inscription. Other corrections in the manuscript were added after the line of text had been written, which is demonstrated by the fact that the correction was made above the line. Writing above the line may have occurred as soon as the scribe had finished a few more words of the line of text, or it may have occurred significantly later. For example, in one passage, "behold my glory" was revised to "behold <all> my glory" (with "all" inserted above the line). In another, "similitude to my only begotten" was revised to "similitude to ~~my~~ <mine> only begotten" (with "my" revised to "mine" above the line). In the second example, the phrase "mine only begotten" also appears at the bottom of the same page and makes this appear as a later correction made to maintain internal consistency. The interlinear corrections suggest that the text was reread after completion and either the original author (Smith) dictated corrections at that point, or the scribe (Cowdery) made corrections after comparing the copy to the original.

Some corrections in the document are more puzzling, such as an end-of-line error that reads "upon God except his {*illegible*} | glory"—with a now illegible word or character that has been cancelled by being stricken.[15] The position of the correction suggests that Cowdery began to write "glory" at the end of the line, though this is uncertain. It is possible that the scribe's eyes skipped to another line of the manuscript where "except his" or "his" occurred but where "his" was followed by a different word. Such errors—known as *homoioarchton*—are strong indicators of a copied manuscript because they show that the scribe skipped between similar words during the visual collation of copy work. A different error occurred when Cowdery wrote, "for his Spirit hath not ~~d.d~~ altogether withdrawn."[16] The cancellation may be the correction of a dictation error, although the manuscript otherwise seems to have been copied by looking at an exemplar, with Smith saying something like "for his spirit hath not de. . . ." and then correcting it to

14. Cowdery began to write "worship" but changed it to "Worship" toward the bottom of page 1. This word began a quotation.

15. Faulring, Jackson, and Matthews concur that this word is illegible (*Joseph Smith's New Translation of the Bible*, 84).

16. The Faulring, Jackson, and Matthews transcript reads, "for his Spirit hath not ~~did~~ altogether withdrawn" (*Joseph Smith's New Translation of the Bible*, 84).

"for his spirit hath not altogether withdrawn"—thus changing the verb in the sentence from what was originally proposed.[17]

A host of minor errors and corrections in the manuscript suggest a copied document. On the next to last line on the first page there is a correction at the very beginning of the line: a "d" or an "i" that has been cancelled with a strikethrough mark.[18] On the first line of the second page there is a dash or some other kind of horizontal stroke, the purpose of which is unclear. On the fourth line of the second page, a word at the beginning of a quotation from Moses was capitalized, suggesting that the scribe knew a quotation was being introduced. On line 10 of the second page, a spelling error was corrected above the line: "And now of this ~~thng~~ <thing>."[19] An error occurred when Cowdery wrote "even all all" on line 21 of the second page.[20] An error on line 10 of the third page seems to be a visual copying error, where "like unto them" is corrected intralinearly to "like unto ~~them~~ thee."[21] The division of words over line breaks almost always follows the conventional practice of dividing words between syllables.[22] With few exceptions, a word was only irregularly divided when the scribe had failed to anticipate the length of the word or apparently succumbed to mere carelessness. In the case of Moses 1, the majority of words were divided as one would expect—which further illustrates that the manuscript was a copy.[23]

There are a few unusual features of the manuscript, including a significant change of ink on line 11 of the second page. The ink becomes dramatically lighter, suggesting that something changed physically in the

---

17. Although I have not seen it suggested elsewhere, we must allow for the possibility that the manuscript in question was itself a copy made through the process of dictation.

18. Faulring, Jackson, and Matthews read it as "e" (*Joseph Smith's New Translation of the Bible*, 84).

19. The reading could also be "~~they.~~"

20. In *Joseph Smith's New Translation of the Bible*, Faulring, Jackson, and Matthews note several other potential scribal errors, such as "Holy G~~o~~host" (85), but it appears that what is noted as an "o" is hesitation before "h" and it is not sufficient to warrant the reading "o." They also give "& ~~b~~" in the middle of the second page (85), but this appears to be a stricken word that is illegible.

21. The Faulring, Jackson, and Matthews transcript reads "like unto ~~theee~~ thee" (*Joseph Smith's New Translation of the Bible*, 86).

22. Exceptions in this document are "betw-een", "concer-ning", and "wh-ich".

23. "Mo-ses," "work-manship," "wo-[r]ds," "shou-ld," "betw-een," "stren-gth," and "cre-ated," "there-of" (2 instances), "be-gotten," "concer-ning," "wh-ich."

copying process. The change in ink occurs at the end of a sentence, one that is not marked with terminal punctuation, and thus may provide evidence that this was a stopping place in the production of the text. The scribe before and after the change in ink is Cowdery. There is also a visual sense break on line 7 of the second page where the scribe left an enlarged blank space to convey the end of a sentence: "Satan [*space*] And it came to pass." Inscribed dots on the manuscript may also indicate stopping places in the production process. After "there is none other" on line 14 of the first page, an elevated point follows the word "other." It appears that the dot is an intentionally inscribed point representing a pause of some sort that is not otherwise at the end of a sentence.[24] Usually, this type of mark serves as a placeholder in the manuscript or to signal a pause in its production. Its purpose in this example is uncertain, but coming as it does in mid-sentence implies a pause in production.

While the foregoing elements indicate that the manuscript is a copy, several other aspects of the document argue against this view, which will be treated briefly here. One is the insertion of "Amen" at the end of Moses 1 to signal the end of the text. The word occurs at the end of the last line on the third page, and an insertion point is used to mark it. One might expect such an ending to have been part of the original and thus not an addition to the copy, although it easily may have been added later. There are also a few phrases that sound original. For example, the phrase "now I shew it thee" has the ring of oral dictation where one might instead expect something like "now I show it unto thee" in a copied manuscript—though Joseph Smith and his contemporaries occasionally wrote "shew."[25] Still, most textual and inscriptional clues in the manuscript indicate production as a result of copying. The document preserving the earliest extant text of Moses 1, which forms part of the larger OT1, is a copy of an earlier revelation.

---

24. The manuscript is punctuated randomly beginning after "he fell unto the earth," on the first page. The manuscript is punctuated for fourteen lines, thirteen of which follow the above first appearance. It appears to be in the handwriting of Whitmer and in the same ink, although it was clearly not inked at the same time the scribe was writing the main text. The ink is heavy, the pen having been recently dipped in the inkwell, whereas the main text of the page shows fading ink from when the scribe first dipped the pen and then the ink gradually fades.

25. See, for example, Joseph Smith, journal, 8 July 1838, Church History Library, The Church of Jesus Christ of Latter-day Saints, Salt Lake City.

The Significance of Moses 1 as a Copy

Moses 1 is not a directive to the fledgling church or to its members specifically. It is not a "thus saith the Lord" communication of the type Smith often used. Instead, it reports an extra-canonical experience in which Moses sees a vision of the creation of the world and experiences opposition from Satan. Specifically, Moses 1 poses an important metaphysical question through the character of Moses, who "called upon God, saying: Tell me, I pray thee, why these things are so, and by what thou madest them?"[26] This question ultimately laid the foundation for a revision of the Bible wherein Joseph Smith sought the answer to this question in the opening chapters of Genesis. A direct causal link can be seen in the opening verse of the JST, which connects with the revision of Genesis 1:1. The revision promises Moses greater knowledge regarding the heavens and the earth: "Behold, I reveal unto you this heaven, and this earth." The antecedent of "this" can only be to Moses 1:36, "tell me concerning this earth . . . and also the heavens." Thus, Moses 1 creates a need for further information, and Moses 2, which represents the revision of Genesis 1, provides a textual source that gives the reader an answer through Moses.

As to a direct genetic link between Moses 1 and Joseph Smith's Bible revision, the surviving evidence points to the fact that Smith's revelations in the months leading up to the production of Moses 1 manifest an interest in the themes of God as creator and an overarching plan for human salvation. Smith continued to address these topics on multiple occasions after the translation of the Book of Mormon was completed. Each surviving piece of evidence suggests that the above-mentioned topics were subjects of theological discussion in early 1830 and that Moses 1 was a part of that discussion—representing, perhaps, Smith's personal contemplations or prayers.

A revelation Smith dictated between June and August 1829 invokes similar themes as those found in Moses 1:

> Yea, even I, I am he, the beginning and the end: Yea, Alpha and Omega, Christ the Lord, the Redeemer of the world. I having accomplished and finished the will of him whose I am, even the Father: having done this that I might subdue all things unto myself: Retaining all power, even to the destroying of Satan and his

---

26. OT1, p. 2 (Moses 1:30).

> works at the end of the world, and the last great day of judgment, which I shall pass upon the inhabitants thereof, judging every man according to his works and the deeds which he hath done. And surely every man must repent or suffer, for I, God, am endless.[27]

In particular, this passage features Jesus Christ performing a central role in the salvation of the human family.

The themes of Moses 1 are even more prevalent in another revelation given during the first half of 1830:

> Behold I the Lord am God I Created the Heavens & the Earth & all things that in them is wherefore they are mine & I sway my scepter over all the Earth & ye are in my hands to will & to do that I can deliver out of evry difficulty & affliction according to your faith & diligence & uprightness Before me. . . . Behold my way is before you & the means I will prepare & the Blessing I hold in mine own hand & if ye are faithful I will pour out upon you even as much as ye are able to Bear & thus it shall be.[28]

This revelation also offered the first hint that Smith was considering other truths that might be restored.

In April 1830, about two months before the revelation of Moses 1, Smith directly declared to the fledgling church instructions that would become its articles of organization. The themes of Moses 1 are again touched upon, particularly in this text's emphasis on God as the creator:

> Wherefore, by these things, we know that there is a God in heaven, who is infinite and eternal, from everlasting to everlasting the same unchangeable God. The Maker of heaven and earth, and all things that in them is, and that he is all power, and all wisdom, and all understanding, and that he created man male and female after his own image and in his own likeness created he them.[29]

---

27. Revelation, circa Summer 1829, in *JSP*, D1:89.

28. Revelation, circa early 1830, in *JSP*, D1:108–12.

29. Articles and Covenants, circa April 1830, in *JSP*, D1:121–22.

These earlier, related revelations forged the context in which Joseph Smith produced Moses 1, which directly declared how creation indeed had a purpose and how Satan had attempted to hinder the work of God. This document may have further encouraged Smith and his scribal assistants to re-envision the biblical narrative in a way that brought these themes to the fore.[30] Moses 1 contains themes that are nearly identical to the revelations from the same time period: "Behold, I am the Lord God Almighty, and Endless is my name; for I am without beginning of days or end of years; and is not this endless?"[31] Additionally, when God calls Moses as a prophet, the JST adopts a similar theme: "And I have a work for thee, Moses, my son; and thou art in the similitude of mine only begotten; and mine only begotten is and shall be the Savior."[32] This same chapter further developed this theme, "And worlds without number have I created; and I also created them for mine own purpose; and by the Son I created them, which is mine only begotten."[33] The crowning statement is realized near the end of Moses 1 when the Lord explains to Moses, "for behold this is my work to my glory to the immortality & the eternal life of man."[34]

Ultimately, the evidence is lacking to fully explain what led Smith and his scribal assistants to revise the Bible, but the surviving evidence indicates that Moses 1 was tied definitively to the Bible revision. There is no direct evidence to support the claim that Smith felt commanded to revise or translate the Bible anew; rather, his work endeavored to revise the Bible in a way that would bring it into harmony with the 1829–1830 revelations on the themes that had occupied Smith's interests during that period. To state the matter more obviously, it is at least possible that the Bible revision was, in its infancy, a kind of editing project to bring existing canonical texts into harmony with newly given revelatory texts. That the surviving text of Moses 1 is apparently a copy means that Smith's theological interests in a plan of salvation for humankind eventually provided an impetus

30. Matthews and others would later argue that the JST restored the original text of the Bible. See Robert J. Matthews, *"A Plainer Translation": Joseph Smith's Translation of the Bible—A History and Commentary* (Provo, Utah: Brigham Young University Press, 1975), 21–54. The themes introduced by Matthews are further developed in Faulring, Jackson, and Matthews, *Joseph Smith's New Translation of the Bible*, 17–25.

31. OT1, p. 1 (Moses 1:3).

32. OT1, p. 1 (Moses 1:6).

33. OT1, p. 2 (Moses 1:33).

34. OT1, p. 3 (Moses 1:39).

for him and his assistants to revise the Bible according to their early theological interests and questions. Seeing Moses 1 as a document that was added to the Bible revision project provides an important piece of evidence in understanding the origins and initial interests of the JST.

A Christian Interest In Revising The Old Testament

A defining feature of the Genesis revision is the prevalence of Christian terms like the "only begotten," "Son," and "Savior" that begin to structure and shape the emerging narrative. Such terms might appear to be anachronistic from the purely biblical vantage point, and the revision of the early chapters of Genesis is so extensive that the reader engages the text as a Christian story rather than the beginning of the Pentateuch. Such a major revision took time and care to accomplish. By focusing on the Christian elements that process introduced into the text, readers can assess a possible second purpose of the JST: a revision of the Bible to introduce Jesus Christ as Creator and Savior who works alongside God for the salvation of humanity.

It is not entirely clear how aware Joseph Smith was of the overall intent of his revisions on the broader topic of reorienting the biblical narrative. It may be that he purposefully intended to re-envision the Old Testament as a Christian salvation epic. Or, in searching to expand the Moses narrative that appears to have been the genesis of the JST project in its initial stages, Smith, a nineteenth-century Christian himself, simply transformed the text using terminology that was familiar from his own worldview. Distinguishing between Smith's intent in revising and what may have been unintended results is difficult with respect to the inclusion of Christian phrases, terms, and stories into the Genesis account. Smith's intent in revising the Bible through a Christian lens probably stands somewhere between these two poles. Whether the reality is one or the other is probably not recoverable using the textual tools currently available, but the Bible revision's clear engagement of a salvation epic offered through a Savior—Jesus Christ—makes it a distinct possibility that this was one of the early interests of the JST project.

This study cannot engage the larger issue of how such a revision would be viewed in the period of the Early Republic and how that intellectual environment shaped the questions that Smith would have been inclined to ask. However, it can briefly consider whether a New Testament theology shaped the developing revision and whether the Christianizing of the Old Testament represents a continued focus in the JST.[35] To state the matter in different terms, it is possible to detect a Christian framework in the inspired revision of the book of Genesis and then assess what that developing framework might reveal about the purpose of the JST.

Jesus and Satan in Genesis

One means of assessing the infusion of Christian materials into the Genesis epic is to attempt to unravel the complicated story of the "only begotten" and his conflict with the adversary. As Bible scholars have long noted, Satan is nowhere mentioned in the book of Genesis and in fact makes only brief appearances in the entire Old Testament. Satan is a mostly post-Babylonian captivity (538 BCE) actor in the biblical story. The majority of all references to Satan are found in the book of Job, but he also appears by name in 1 Chronicles, Zechariah, and Psalms. Nowhere else is Satan or the devil mentioned by name in the Old Testament.[36] But Satan appears a staggering twenty-eight times in the Book of Moses, more than in any other single book of scripture. By introducing him into the Genesis material, Smith reshaped the narrative to read like a combat story between God and Satan like that envisioned in the book of Revelation.

Specifically, Smith's revised account builds upon the New Testament themes of the combat with Satan found in Revelation 12:9: "And the great dragon was cast out, that old serpent, called the Devil, and Satan, which deceiveth the whole world: he was cast out into the earth, and his angels were cast out with him." The expulsion of Satan, as depicted in Revelation, ultimately leads to an adversarial relationship between him and humanity. This conflict imagery is also found in 1 Peter 5:8, which urges Christians to "Be sober, be vigilant; because your adversary the devil, as a roaring lion, walketh about, seeking whom he may devour." Smith's Bible revision

35. The larger question of Smith's place in the development of canon has been discussed by David F. Holland, *Sacred Borders: Continuing Revelation and Canonical Restraint in Early America* (Oxford: Oxford University Press, 2011), 144–47. Philip L. Barlow, "Joseph Smith's Use of the Bible, 1820–1829," *Journal of the American Academy of Religion* 57 (1989): 741, has similarly noted the phenomenon of reading the Old Testament through a New Testament lens.

36. See Neil Forsyth, *The Old Enemy: Satan and the Combat Myth* (Princeton, New Jersey: Princeton University Press, 1987), 107–23.

saw similar themes of the devil's influence in the story of when the serpent "beguiled" Eve.[37] In Smith's more pragmatic theology, the serpent becomes an agent of Satan, "& Satan put it into the heart of the serpent for he had drew away many after him & he sought to beguile ~~Eve~~ Eve for he knew not the mind of God Wherefore he sought to destroy the world . . .. & he spake by the mouth of the Serpant)."[38]

By seeing the theme of spiritual warfare in the story of Eve and the serpent, Smith fundamentally redirected the flow of the creation account. Whereas God directs action in the Genesis account, in the JST he encounters an enemy who subverts his plan, leads Cain astray, and otherwise opposes the goodness of God. This shift in emphasis also opens a door to the addition of Christian concepts like a Savior, baptism, the "only begotten," the agency of humankind, and personal sin that requires repentance. Passages such as "& I have a work for thee Moses my Son & thou art in the similitude ~~to my~~ <mine> only begotten & mine only begotten is & shall be for he is full of grace & truth bu[t] there is no God beside me & all things are present with me for I know them all" embrace the centrality of Christ in salvation and provide a conceptual framework for the early Bible revision project.[39]

A Christian Plan of Salvation

The outline of Smith's early interest in recasting the biblical narrative as a Christian salvation epic includes the creation of humanity in the likeness of God and the only begotten, belief in the Son of God as a pathway to salvation, baptism in the name of Jesus Christ, a universal plan of salvation for humankind, and personal agency that leads individuals to choose good or evil. The JST builds upon the centrality of the Son of God as an object of faith: "& as many as believed in the Son & repented of their sins should be saved & as many as believed not & repented not should be damned & the words went forth out of the mouth of God in a firm decree Wherefore they must be fulfilled."[40] This in turn encourages the reader to see the influence of the Son as a force of goodness and Satan as a force of wickedness.

---

37. Genesis 3:13.

38. Genesis 3:1.

39. Moses 1:6.

40. Moses 5:15.

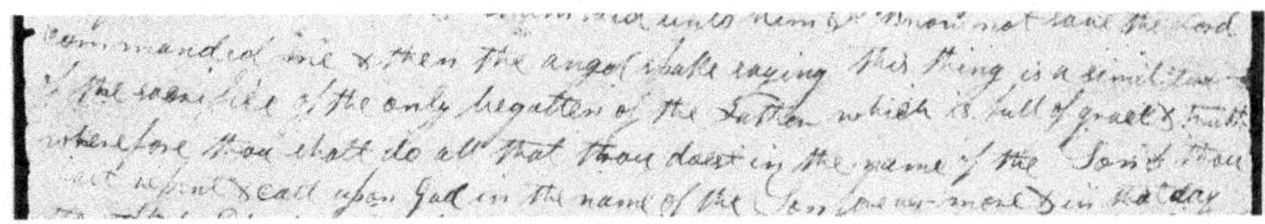
commanded me & then the angel spake saying this thing is a similitude
of the sacrifice of the only begotten of the Father which is full of grace & truth
wherefore thou shalt do all that thou doest in the name of the Son & thou
shalt repent & call upon God in the name of the Son forever more & in that day

FIGURE 4.3. Moses 5:1–17. OT1, p. 8.
Courtesy Community of Christ Archives, Independence, MO.

Within this salvation epic, a key feature is the reframing of the story of Moses and the burning bush from the book of Exodus, a story that then lays a clear foundation for the post-Sinai revelation to be Christian in its outlook. In the burning bush story, the JST reads, "& he also gave unto me commandment when he called unto me out of the burning bush Saying [c]all upon God in the name of mine only begotten & worship me." The presence of the "only begotten" in this text thereby reinterprets Sinai.[41] Subsequently, Smith's version, seen in Figure 4.3, reorients the entire law of animal sacrifice to prefigure the death of Jesus: "this thing is a similitude of the sacrifice of the only begotten of the Father."[42]

Perhaps the most powerful re-envisioning comes following an expansion regarding Cain, his descendant Lamech, and the beginning of evil traditions on the earth, which echo the Gospel of Mark: "& thus the Gospel began to be preached from the beginning being declared by Holy Angels sent forth from the presence of God."[43] Even though the JST does not define "gospel" specifically, it does appear to rely on the reader's knowledge of the term from the New Testament. In the JST revision of the Old Testament, the message becomes inextricably linked with the teachings of the New Testament.

The Significance of a Christianized Old Testament

Returning to the question of intent, it remains unclear whether Christianizing Genesis was a purposeful aim of the JST, a result of a Christian prophet re-envisioning the Old Testament narratives through a process of inspiration, or a result of Smith's own New Testament worldview. This process of Christianizing appears to taper off at the end of the

41. Moses 1:17.

42. Moses 5:7.

43. Moses 5:58.

revision of Genesis, but it is fairly consistent throughout. For example, Noah teaches the gospel of Jesus Christ, Melchizedek takes a sacrament of bread and wine, Abraham speaks of his anointing and baptism, and Joseph of Egypt learns a prophecy of Shilo that is intended to convey information about the coming Messiah.[44] This effort to reconceptualize the Genesis story may, upon closer scrutiny, demonstrate some of the early prophetic genius of Smith and his contemporaries in making the narratives of the Old Testament more accessible to a Christian audience. Just as the visions of Moses in Moses 1 eventually served to harmonize the Bible with Smith's earlier revelations, the JST revisions in Genesis reframed the Old Testament in ways that brought it more into harmony with the New Testament.

Two New Testament Passages Translated Twice

With Joseph Smith's revision of the New Testament, a new set of historical circumstances and textual issues further shape the way the process of biblical revision may be understood. Around 7 March 1831 Smith dictated a commandment wherein he was instructed to cease translating the Old Testament and to move directly to translating the New Testament. Working with Sidney Rigdon, Smith began translating the New Testament on the very next day, thus giving a clear revelatory "thus saith the Lord" purpose to the translation of the New Testament. Additionally, the process of translating the Old Testament—insofar as Smith and Rigdon had made progress on that front—had demonstrated that expansively editing and altering the biblical text required a tremendous amount of time. The actual practice of revising the text for nearly a year may have significantly expanded the original scope of the project over time.

In revising the New Testament, Smith and Rigdon accidentally translated two passages that had been translated previously. For both passages, this resulted in two editions of a single text that in many respects are quite different. This occurrence provides a window through which the

44. See JST revisions for Genesis 6:4, 14:8, 17:3, and 50:25. Many Latter-day Saint scholars consider these revisions to be restorations of redacted text. See, for example, Matthews, *Plainer Translation*, 233–54; Faulring, Jackson, and Matthews, *Joseph Smith's New Translation of the Bible*, 8–13; and Philip L. Barlow, "Joseph Smith's Revision of the Bible: Fraudulent, Pathologic, or Prophetic?" *Harvard Theological Review* 83 (1990): 45–64.

development of the scope and intent of Smith's revision of the Bible over time can be viewed.[45]

The process by which Smith produced two translations of the same passages is not extraordinary, but nonetheless noteworthy. When Smith and Rigdon began translating the New Testament in earnest on 8 March 1831, the manuscript they produced, hereafter designated NT1 (see Table 4.1), included Smith's reworking of Matthew 1:1–26:71. In June of 1831, Smith, Rigdon, and several other early Mormon leaders traveled to Missouri, where they spent part of that summer. While they were away, John Whitmer began producing a copy of NT1 that is now commonly referred to as NT2. When Joseph Smith returned from Missouri to Ohio and resumed his work on the Bible revision, NT2 became the live copy of the JST. Apparently unbeknownst to Smith, John Whitmer had only copied through to Matthew 26:1—either by mistake or neglect or a lack of time. Presumably Smith and Rigdon had forgotten exactly where they had left off their work, and they resumed translating at Matthew 26:1 rather than with Matthew 27:1. It is somewhat surprising that Smith did not remember that he had already translated Matthew 26 in its entirety, but his absence for several months may be enough to explain his forgetfulness.[46] The second passage that was translated twice, 2 Peter 3:4–6 seen in Figure 4.4 and Figure 4.5, is not so easily explained in terms of any known sequence of events like the interruption of work in Matthew. The duplicate translations occur on different pages and may have been the result of simple human error.[47]

Comparing the Parallel Revisions

When compared side by side, it becomes readily apparent that the two translations of Matthew 26 differ significantly.[48] Some verses were passed

45. This occurrence was first brought to the attention of Latter-day Saint readers by Kent P. Jackson and Peter M. Jasinski, "The Process of Inspired Translation: Two Passages Translated Twice in the Joseph Smith Translation of the Bible," *BYU Studies* 42 (2003): 35–64. Jackson and Jasinski focused on the theological impact of the two different translations of the same passage. Little else has been done on these two passages that were translated twice.

46. Jackson and Jasinski treat the process of duplication in much greater detail (Jackson and Jasinski, "Process of Inspired Translation," 36–41).

47. Jackson and Jasinski, "Process of Inspired Translation," 56–57.

48. Where the two translations are similar is in the alteration of the KJV italics where in one instance italicized words are changed in precisely the same way: "There came unto him a woman having an alabaster box of very precious ointment, and poured it on his head, as he

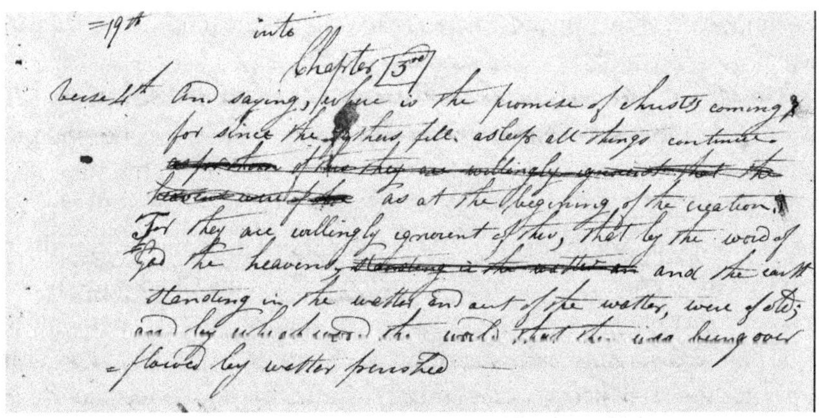
=19th into
Chapter [3rd]
verse 4th And saying, where is the promise of christs coming?
for since the fathers fell asleep all things continue
~~[illegible]~~
~~[illegible]~~ as at the beginning of the creation.
For they are willingly ignorant of this, that by the word of
God the heavens, ~~standing in the water an~~ and the earth
standing in the water, and out of the water, were of old;
and by which word the world that then was being over
-flowed by water perished —

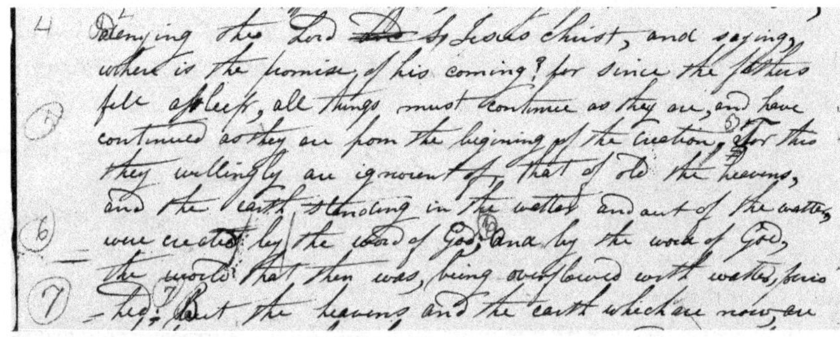
4 Denying the Lord ~~God~~ & Jesus Christ, and saying,
where is the promise of his coming? for since the fathers
(5) fell asleep, all things must continue as they are, and have
continued as they are from the begining of the creation. For this
they willingly are ignorant of, that of old the heavens,
and the earth, standing in the water and out of the water,
(6) were created by the word of God; and by the word of God,
the world that then was, being overflowed with water, peris-
(7) -hed; But the heavens and the earth which are now, are

FIGURE 4.4 AND FIGURE 4.5. 2 Peter 3:4–6. NT2, Folio 4, pp. 145–146. Courtesy Community of Christ Archives, Independence, MO.

over without revision in NT1 while other verses were omitted from NT2. Significant wording additions in NT1 were not reflected in NT2, and revisions with historical and theological significance in NT1 are sometimes not even hinted at in NT2. Ultimately, these different versions demonstrate that the process of translation in the New Testament was closely connected with Smith's efforts to edit the Bible for readability while at the same time attending to a variety of theological interests. Moreover, the changes confirm that Smith was not editing with a consistent plan or methodology in mind. This further suggests that the translation project had significantly expanded from its inception at Moses 1—when the plan seems to have been to bring the Bible into harmony with Smith's recent revelations. Instead, Smith seems to have edited according to what he felt

sat at meat." The final two words appear in italics in the printed KJV, which Smith changed in both NT1 and NT2 to "in the house."

was important at the time that he was carrying out the translation of a particular passage.

The editing of Matthew 26:2 illustrates this well: "Ye know that after two days is the feast of the passover, and the Son of man is betrayed to be crucified." Smith changed the archaic pronoun "Ye" in his June 1831 translation (NT1) but not in his September 1831 translation (NT2) of the same verse. Additionally, in the earlier translation the awkward "is betrayed to be crucified"—which accurately reflects the Greek word order and construction—is rendered into a clearer English causal statement "is to be betrayed and crucified." Grammatically speaking, Smith's rendition separates the act of betrayal from the act of crucifixion, whereas the Greek as rendered in the KJV connects the two events so that the act of betrayal leads to the crucifixion. The first revision, therefore, demonstrates an interest in grammatical issues whereas the later revision does not preserve any of these changes.

The passages that were translated twice relate in interesting ways to parallel gospel passages, and in several instances the changes introduced into the translated passages have clear biblical connections. These occur at Matthew 26:26 (NT1), which echoes the language of John 13:34 and 1 Corinthians 11:24; Matthew 26:27 (NT1), which reflects Mark 14:22; Matthew 26:28 (NT1), which is quite similar to Luke 22:19; Matthew 26:28 (NT2), which reflects John 13:34; Matthew 26:50 (NT2), which is reminiscent of Luke 22:48; Matthew 26:54 (NT1), which echoes Luke 22:51; Matthew 26:62, which in NT1 includes language from John 1:22 and in NT2 includes language from John 18:34; and Matthew 26:63 (NT1), which includes language from Mark 14:61.

From this list of instances in which the new translation was so largely influenced from parallel canonical sources, it becomes apparent that Joseph Smith had no obvious agenda in the translating process. In other words, he did not, for example, edit Matthew to include all of the unique material from the Gospel of John, nor did he include all of Mark's unique material. The process appears to be more haphazard; Smith was more inclined to draw upon parallel biblical passages when he was working on NT1 earlier in the year than he was when he was working on NT2 later in the year. This may be related to the amount of time he had at his disposal during the two different periods of translation, or it may simply reflect a change in thinking or even interest. In either case, there is clear evidence in the duplicate translation of Matthew 26 that at least one component of the translation process, particularly manifest in NT1, was to revise the books of the Bible to be in greater harmony with each other—especially with New Testament texts.

Examples of this editing process can be seen in several passages, shown below, where angle brackets mark insertions or other revisions. For example, Smith significantly revised Matthew 26:26: "And as they were eating, Jesus took bread, and blessed it, and brake it, and gave it to the disciples, and said, Take, eat <of it; and a commandment I give unto you, and this is the commandment which I give unto you, that as you see me do, you shall do likewise in remembrance of> my body." The addition to the verse relies openly upon two phrases, one from the Gospel of John ("A new commandment I give unto you") and one from the first epistle to the Corinthians ("this do in remembrance of me").[49] In at least one sense, the New Testament revision integrated an amalgamation of biblical texts. The Bible revision in these cases was an admixture of biblical passages and the language of Smith. Moreover, the apparent randomness of the process suggests that Smith drew upon his memory to aid him in the revision process. It is possible that he had his scribes searching for parallel passages in the Bible, although there is no surviving evidence to verify that he did so.

Two other occurrences in the revision demonstrate that it was not exclusively a harmonizing amalgamation of biblical texts. Some changes have historical implications. An important change to Matthew 26:47 in NT1 puts Judas in charge of the plot to kill Jesus: "And while he yet spake, <behold,> Judas, one of the twelve, came, and with him a great multitude with swords and staves, <having authority> from the chief priests and elders of the people." This overt shift in placing the authority to arrest Jesus in Judas's hands was not reflected in NT2, but it was related to another revision. Smith later added a significant portion to the end of his translation of Mark 14:28:

> But after that I am risen, I will go before you into Galilee. <And he said unto Judas Iscariot, what thou doest, do quickly; but beware of innocent blood. Nevertheless, Judas Iscariot, even one of the twelve, went unto the chief priests to betray Jesus unto them; for he turned away from him, and was offended because of his words. And when the chief priests heard of him, they were glad, and promised to

49. John 13:34; 1 Corinthians 11:24.

give him money; and he sought how he might conveniently betray Jesus.>

This addition similarly implicated Judas as the one responsible for Jesus's death, suggesting this culpability was a theme of continued interested for Smith.

A common type of JST revision occurs at Matthew 26:45, which fills a logical gap in the story: "Then cometh he to his disciples, and saith unto them, Sleep on now, and take rest: <and they did so. And when they awoke, Jesus saith unto them,> behold, the hour is at hand, and the Son of man is betrayed into the hands of sinners." This type of gap-filling emendation occurs frequently throughout the revision of both the Old and New Testament, but what is interesting in this case is that it is only evident in NT1. This would suggest that Smith was relying on his own impressions of what made sense in the Bible and what needed further clarification. The verse in question does contain a logical break or a textual seam. Christian scribes were similarly confronted with the abruptness of "sleep on now, and take rest; behold, the hour is at hand." But that Smith would only make the change in one manuscript and not the other raises the question of how the revision process worked. One possibility is that Smith simply had or took more time earlier in the year (with NT1) than he had later in the year (when completing NT2), and was likely to change the Bible more significantly when he had more time as he did in Genesis and the New Testament gospels. When his time was more limited, his changes to the text tended to be less imposing and significant.

The Significance of the Duplicate Translations

Over time, Joseph Smith's revision of the Bible developed into an expansive project that engaged new interests and approaches to the biblical text that were different from the project's original goals. When Joseph and his scribes inadvertently translated the same passages twice, they fortuitously provided a window through which their goals and interests in revising the text may be viewed. From the surviving evidence, it appears that by the time the project reached the New Testament, Joseph had increased his interests to include an improvement of the readability of the KJV text, as well as a focused attention on providing descriptions of motive and reasons for which biblical characters acted in certain ways.

Conclusions

From the evidence discussed above, two features regarding Joseph Smith's revision of the Bible emerge as indications of the purposes and processes behind the translation. First, the production of Moses 1 can, with some caution, be considered part of the justification for beginning a new translation project. It has been noted before that there is no known commandment, no "thus saith the Lord" instruction directing Smith to translate the Bible anew. Instead, he dictated several other revelatory texts that initiated an interest in the themes of God as creator and an eternal plan of salvation for all humankind. The text of Moses 1 seems to imply that Moses received an account of these and related topics while on a mountain—perhaps Sinai. Smith and others of his day commonly believed that Moses was the author of Genesis, so it is reasonable that Smith would associate the promise of new information found in Moses 1 with the creation narrative in the beginning of Genesis.

The revelation narrates conversations between Moses and God wherein Moses learns the eternal destiny of humanity—and that God has many important secrets he intends to reveal to Moses. The original document recording this revelation, which was eventually copied into OT1, the beginning of the JST, laid a foundation for Smith's subsequent editing of the Bible. There is no explicit documentation that Moses 1 exerted a causal influence on Smith in creating the JST, but the surviving evidence suggests a relationship. Thus, in one sense the purpose of the JST was to bring the English Bible into harmony with the revelations Smith had dictated prior to June 1830. Today this would be considered an editorial emendation, but Smith and his associates saw it as a "translation" process similar to the "translation" of the Book of Mormon—or at least similar enough to warrant using the same word to describe both productions.

In seeking to recover information about Moses through revising the Bible, Smith also reframed a significant portion of the book of Genesis as a Christian story. Reading the Old Testament through a New Testament lens was not unique to Smith and his associates, but the extent to which he revised the text of the Bible with explicitly Christian themes was unique. This substantial revision raises the possibility that soon after Smith began revising the Bible, a second purpose began to take shape: revising Genesis so that it explained the fall of Satan and his subsequent attempts to lead humanity astray. This redirection also allowed Smith to introduce Jesus Christ into the story and to resolve the conflict between God and Satan through the story of the "only begotten" Son who would redeem humanity.

In the two examples where Smith translated a biblical passage twice, there is evidence that the translation process relied heavily on incorporating passages from other canonical texts into the material that was being translated. This revision aspired to make the Bible more internally consistent and to smooth out the differences between canonical texts. This effort to reconcile the Bible certainly fits well within the era when the individuality of the gospel authors was not a subject of intense scholarly scrutiny. Instead, Joseph Smith seems to have viewed all revelation, prophetic writing, and scripture—both ancient and modern—as consistent manifestations of the eternal and divine gospel of Jesus Christ. Smith therefore edited the Bible to make it conform to his own revelations and to give it greater internal consistency.

Identifying the origins of Joseph Smith's revision of the Bible, particularly being able to understand the beginnings and initial purpose of the JST, is an important step to understanding how Smith and his associates intended their work to be received. Looking broadly at the JST, scholars have sought to find in the text an origin for later theological developments in Mormonism.[50] As the evidence presented here suggests, the Bible revision appears to have originally had an interest to harmonize the text to Smith's theological interests prior to and at the time he organized the Church of Christ. This would indicate that Smith was willing to revise canonical texts according to his revelatory interests from the beginning. In other words, canonical texts became subject to harmonizing in Smith's religious thinking prior to June 1830. The Bible revision project would go on to harmonize the Old and New Testaments, particularly the gospels, and over time adopted other interests as well, including clarifying passages that were difficult to understand and introducing new theological ideas.

50. For representative views, see Philip L. Barlow, *Mormons and the Bible: The Place of the Latter-day Saints in American Religion* (Oxford: Oxford University Press, 1991), 54–56; Robert J. Matthews, "The Role of the Joseph Smith Translation in the Restoration," in *Plain and Precious Truths Restored: The Doctrinal and Historical Significance of the Joseph Smith Translation,* ed. Robert L. Millet and Robert J. Matthews (Salt Lake City: Deseret Book, 1995), 42; Matthews, *Plainer Translation,* 12. Faulring, Jackson, and Matthews offer the most recent categorization of types of changes (*Joseph Smith's New Translation of the Bible,* 8–10).

5

The Dictation, Compilation, and Canonization of Joseph Smith's Revelations

Grant Underwood

MEMBERS OF THE Church of Jesus Christ of Latter-day Saints believe that church founder Joseph Smith, like the biblical Moses, was a "prophet." As such, they consider him to have been God's earthly representative and periodically to have communicated the word and will of God to the church and to the world. Latter-day Saints canonized many of Joseph Smith's "revelations" as scripture.

The first, and arguably the most influential, scriptural revelation published by Joseph Smith was the Book of Mormon. This sprawling saga is primarily the story of Israelites who migrated to the Americas six hundred years before Christ and lived there for the next thousand years. At just under six hundred printed pages, the book provides enough historical narrative to give readers a sense of societal ebb and flow, but its primary interest is theological, to restore the "plain and precious" truths of the pure Christian gospel that had been lost to the world.[1] Smith described

1. See Terryl L. Givens, *The Book of Mormon: A Very Short Introduction* (New York: Oxford University Press, 2009); and Grant Hardy, *Understanding the Book of Mormon: A Reader's Guide* (New York: Oxford University Press, 2010). Early nineteenth-century America was an era characterized by a cacophony of competing religious voices, all claiming to base their beliefs on the Bible. According to noted historian Gordon Wood, the Book of Mormon served to "cut through these controversies and brought the Bible up to date. It was written in plain biblical style for plain people. It answered perplexing questions of theology, clarified obscure passages of the Bible, and carried its story into the New World. And it did all this

the Book of Mormon as a "translation" of an ancient American record written on golden plates, yet at the time he knew nothing of ancient languages. He claimed that his translation of the Book of Mormon came by revelation or, as he phrased it in the book's preface, "by the gift and power of God."[2] Smith dictated two other major translation-revelations—his "New Translation" of the Bible and the Book of Abraham. The New Translation of the Bible, like the Book of Mormon, was not a translation in the usual sense of the word. Smith did not render the biblical languages into English. Instead, he selectively revised and amplified the King James Version wherever he felt inspired to do so. In similar fashion, he also "translated" or discerned by revelation an account by the Old Testament patriarch Abraham of his earliest years and what he learned from God of the cosmos and its creation.

The focus of this chapter, however, is on the shorter revelation texts that Joseph Smith did *not* present as translations of ancient documents but that he dictated in the earliest years of Mormon history. Smith dictated over one hundred of these "commandments" or "revelations" to establish the church and guide its members. The majority of these texts, ranging in length from a paragraph to a dozen or more manuscript pages, ultimately became distinct "sections" or chapters in the canonical compilation published in 1835 as the first edition of the Doctrine and Covenants, a volume about half the length of the Book of Mormon but considerably longer than the Book of Abraham.[3]

The General Nature of "Revelation"

To begin at the beginning is to interrogate the term *revelation*. According to the *Oxford English Dictionary*, the term has two meanings when used in a religious sense. It can refer either to "the disclosure or communication of

---

with the assurance of divine authority." Gordon S. Wood, "Evangelical America and Early Mormonism," *New York History* 61 (October 1980): 381.

2. "Preface," *Book of Mormon* (Palmyra, New York: 1830), [3].

3. Originally titled *Doctrine and Covenants of the Church of the Latter Day Saints: Carefully Selected from the Revelations of God and Compiled by Joseph Smith Junior, Oliver Cowdery, Sidney Rigdon, Frederick G. Williams, Presiding Elders of Said Church*, the volume is reproduced in its entirety in Robin Scott Jensen, Richard E. Turley Jr., and Riley M. Lorimer, eds., *Revelations and Translations, Volume 2: Published Revelations*, vol. 2 of the Revelations and Translations series of *The Joseph Smith Papers*, eds. Dean C. Jessee, Ronald K. Esplin, and Richard Lyman Bushman (Salt Lake City: Church Historian's Press, 2011), 311–593.

knowledge, instructions, etc., by divine or supernatural means," or it can identify the consequence of that action—"something disclosed or communicated by divine or supernatural means."[4] Noah Webster expressed it in more explicitly Christian terms in his 1828 dictionary. The act of revelation is "the disclosure or communication of truth to men by God himself, or by his authorized agents, the prophets and apostles." Latter-day Saints fit what Joseph Smith experienced into this first definition. Indeed, one of his titles was "revelator."[5] Mormons would also describe the revelations produced by the revelator in terms similar to Webster's second definition: "that which is revealed; appropriately, the sacred truths which God has communicated to man for his instruction and direction."[6] That is how Latter-day Saints view the contents of the Doctrine and Covenants.

Absent in these dictionary definitions and in early Mormonism, however, is the kind of formal theological definition that speaks of revelation more expansively as God's self-disclosure in the created universe or in the person of Jesus Christ. As theologian David Tracy has noted, "In modern Christian thought since the Romantics and Hegel, revelation has been construed primarily on some form of encounter model as an event of divine self-manifestation to humanity."[7] Although Joseph Smith affirmed that Deity revealed himself both in the design of the natural world and in shaping the course of human history, when Smith and his followers used the word "revelation(s)" they typically had in mind specific conceptual communications or *verbal* revelations.

4. *Oxford English Dictionary*, online ed., s.v. "revelation."

5. Although the *OED* acknowledges *revealer, revelationist*, and even *revelationer* to describe one who reveals something or "makes" a revelation, Latter-day Saints opted for the traditional term *revelator*, following the centuries-old custom of referring to the author of the final book in the New Testament as "John the Revelator." An early Latter-day Saint revelation declared that Joseph Smith was to be "a Seer, a revelator, a translator, & a prophet" to "the whole church." "A Revelation given at Hiram Portage Co Nov 11th 1831," in Robin Scott Jensen, Robert J. Woodford, and Steven C. Harper, eds., *Manuscript Revelation Books*, facsimile edition, vol. 1 of the Revelations and Translations series of *The Joseph Smith Papers*, eds. Dean C. Jessee, Ronald K. Esplin, and Richard Lyman Bushman (Salt Lake City: Church Historian's Press, 2009), 219. Wherever possible, quotations from Joseph Smith's revelation texts will be referenced to the current section-and-verse configuration in the modern Doctrine and Covenants (D&C). This quotation is found in D&C 107:91–92.

6. Noah Webster, ed., *An American Dictionary of the English Language* (New York: 1828), s.v. "revelation."

7. David Tracy, "Writing," in *Critical Terms for Religious Studies*, ed. Mark C. Taylor (Chicago: University of Chicago Press, 1998), 386.

Even when limiting revelation to such verbal or "propositional" communications, the question arises as to their nature as understood by Joseph Smith himself and by his followers, then and even now. Do Latter-day Saints understand revelations to be the actual words of God spoken in conversation with the prophet which he then communicated verbatim to the public, or do they have a sense in which the link between the *experience* of revelation and the *communication* of that experience in a written text is not so mechanical or linear?[8] The latter conceptualization suggests that the prophet has a role to play in the wording of the revelations; the former that he is merely the microphone through which God speaks his own words to the world. At a popular level, it is not uncommon for religious believers, including Latter-day Saints, to assume that revelations, especially when canonized as scripture, are the exact words God used in speaking to the prophet and that they are impervious to human influence and effect.

Some Latter-day Saints, though, along with theologically reflective believers elsewhere, have articulated more nuanced views of scriptural revelations. It was the view of Joseph Smith's contemporary and church apostle Orson Pratt that "Joseph the Prophet, in writing the [revelations of the Doctrine and Covenants], received the ideas from God, but clothed those ideas with such words as came to his mind."[9] Twentieth-century Mormon apostle John A. Widtsoe concurred: "Seldom are divine revelations dictated to man . . .. Instead, ideas are impressed upon the mind of the recipient, who then delivers the ideas in his own language."[10] Widtsoe's church-leader colleague B. H. Roberts added that while Smith's revelations were "expressed in such language as the Prophet could command, in such phraseology as he was master of and common to the time and locality where

8. Horace Bushnell, an American contemporary of Joseph Smith, argued that there exists "an immediate, personal knowledge of God, attainable through a dimension of experience deeper than language and discursive thought." Scripture, therefore, ends up being less a set of propositional truths than the "grand poem of salvation." Because words have their origin in the world of finite, sensory perception, they can never fully capture the infinite, divine reality to which they gesture as symbols and metaphors. E. Brooks Holifield, *Theology in America: Christian Thought from the Age of the Puritans to the Civil War* (New Haven: Yale University Press, 2003), 457–58.

9. Orson Pratt, "Minutes of the School of the Prophets," Salt Lake Stake, 9 December 1872, Church History Library, The Church of Jesus Christ of Latter-day Saints, Salt Lake City (hereafter cited as CHL).

10. John A. Widtsoe, "The Articles of Faith: X. Eternal Increase," *Improvement Era* 40, no. 10 (October 1937): 600–601.

he lived," that "phraseology" was sometimes "modified" and lifted "above the ordinary level of the Prophet's thoughts and language, because of the inspiration of God that was upon him."[11] Widtsoe, too, felt that Smith's ordinary language was enhanced by inspiration: "When therefore a passage of wondrous beauty or feeling occurs in a divine message, it is the natural result of the exalted feeling induced by inspiration which makes it easy to clothe the revealed truth in beautiful words and sentences."[12] From the perspective of these leaders, then, Latter-day Saints can affirm that the scriptural "word of God" produced by the prophet Joseph Smith was both divine *and* human, just as early Christians said of the incarnate Word of God himself.[13]

Such perspectives on revelation are not unique to Latter-day Saints. Catholic father Jean Levie captured the viewpoint succinctly in the title of one of his books: *The Bible: Word of God in Words of Men.*[14] Evangelical scholar Donald Hagner agrees; otherwise, "the genuinely human factor of the biblical documents is in effect denied in favor of a Bible that floated down from heaven by parachute untouched by human hands or the historical process."[15] Even if some Latter-day Saints reject this view, Joseph Smith as revelator seemed fully aware of the finitude of his revelation texts. On one occasion he expressed to a close associate his yearning for a time yet future when "we may stand together and gase upon Eternal wisdom engraven upon the hevens," when God will lift "the dark curtain until we may read the sound of Eternity to the fullness and satisfaction of our immortal souls." At present, however, the contrast between transcendentally perceiving "Eternal wisdom" and having to communicate it through finite, human language was frustrating: "Oh Lord God deliver us

---

11. B. H. Roberts, *A Comprehensive History of The Church of Jesus Christ of Latter-day Saints*, 6 vols. (Salt Lake City: Deseret News Press, 1930), 1:133.

12. Widtsoe, "Articles of Faith," 601.

13. The Church of Jesus Christ of Latter-day Saints has no official statement on the nature of Joseph Smith's revelations or on the genesis of scripture. Thus it is not surprising that all church leaders do not view the matter in the same fashion as those cited above. Influential twentieth-century church leader Bruce R. McConkie, for example, wrote that most of the sections of the Doctrine and Covenants "came to Joseph Smith by direct revelation, the recorded words being those of the Lord Jesus Christ himself." Bruce R. McConkie, *Mormon Doctrine* (Salt Lake City: Bookcraft, 1958), 191.

14. Jean Levie, S. J., *The Bible, Word of God in Words of Men* (London: Chapman, 1961).

15. Donald Hagner, "The Battle for Inerrancy: An Errant Trend among the Inerrancists," *The Reformed Journal* 34, no. 4 (April 1984): 21.

in thy due time from the little narrow prison almost as it were totel darkness of paper pen and ink and a crooked broken scattered and imperfect language."[16] Elsewhere Smith signaled the qualitative difference between revelatory experience and the textual report of that encounter by reportedly remarking, "Could you gaze in heaven 5 minute. you would know more—than you would can know by read[ing] all that ever was writtn on the subject."[17] Even the revealed "Preface" to the Doctrine and Covenants highlights the communicative gap between infinite God and finite prophet when it affirms that the volume's revelations "were given unto my Servents in their weakness after the manner of their Language that they might come to understanding."[18]

Whether or not those in the Judeo-Christian traditions recognize the "human factor" in revelation—whether believers view scripture as the inspired "word of God," though expressed in the time-bound words of human prophets, or instead as the very words of God himself—there is a widespread sense among believers in divine revelation that God guarantees the veridical reliability of scripture. This is a perspective shared by

---

16. Joseph Smith to W. W. Phelps, 27 November 1832, in Matthew C. Godfrey, Mark Ashurst-McGee, Grant Underwood, Robert J. Woodford, and William G. Hartley, eds., *Documents, Volume 2: July 1831–January 1833*, vol. 2 of the Documents series of *The Joseph Smith Papers*, eds. Dean C. Jessee, Ronald K. Esplin, Richard Lyman Bushman, and Matthew J. Grow (Salt Lake City: Church Historian's Press, 2013), 320.

17. Joseph Smith, Journal, 9 October 1843, in Andrew H. Hedges, Alex D. Smith, and Brent M. Rogers, eds., *Journals, Volume 3: May 1843–June 1844*, vol. 3 of the Journals series of *The Joseph Smith Papers*, eds. Ronald K. Esplin and Matthew J. Grow (Salt Lake City: Church Historian's Press, 2015), 109. This entry in Smith's journal includes a report of his speech given at a church conference that day. The quotation is introduced with the word *reportedly* because Smith almost always spoke extemporaneously and lived before the advent of accurate recording devices or even before Latter-day Saints were using shorthand to capture his sermons. Typically, one or more of his clerks took notes while he spoke, sometimes fleshing them out later. Willard Richards, his private secretary and clerk at the time, provided this report. For the remainder of this chapter, rather than repeatedly qualifying quotations with *reportedly*, unless otherwise specified, all reported remarks will be understood to be clerical notes and memories rather than verbatim transcripts of Smith's exact words.

18. "Revelation Given in Hiram Nov[m]·1st· 1831," in Jensen et al., *Manuscript Revelation Books*, 223, 225 (D&C 1:24). An alternative interpretation of this statement views it simply as expressing the longstanding Christian doctrine of "accommodation." This is the notion that God speaks to prophets in their own tongue and idiom. The words are still his, but he chooses them to accommodate finite, culturally conditioned human language. Calvin developed this doctrine of "accommodation" to its fullest. Ford Lewis Battles, "God Was Accommodating Himself to Human Capacity," in *Readings in Calvin's Theology*, ed. Donald K. McKim (Grand Rapids, Michigan: Baker Book, 1984), 21–42.

Latter-day Saints then and now.[19] Joseph Smith himself declared, "I never told you I was perfect—but there is no error in the revelations which I have taught."[20] Nonbelievers, of course, see all scriptural revelations as entirely human compositions whose authors simply invoke divine authorship for their own words. Ultimately, the subjective character of any attempt to affirm or deny a document's connection to Deity is self-evident. The question of the ultimate origin of a purported revelation is ultimately beyond the scope of academic analysis.

The Specific Character of Joseph Smith's Revelations

As with the Book of Mormon—Smith's founding work of revelation—and as was the case with many of his composed letters, journal entries, and other documents, Joseph Smith *dictated* to scribes or clerks virtually all his revelations (or the *texts* of those revelations, as will be used interchangeably here to keep in mind the distinction between the Mormon prophet's inner experience of divine revelation and the words he used to convey and express that revelation) rather than writing them out himself. One who assisted him briefly in this endeavor described the process in this way: "The scribe seats himself at a desk or table, with pen, ink, and paper. The subject of inquiry being understood, the Prophet and Revelator inquires of God. He spiritually sees, hears, and feels, and then speaks as he is moved upon by the Holy Ghost, the 'thus saith the Lord,' sentence after sentence."[21] This recollection suggests an immediacy that may not have been universal. Exactly how much time elapsed between Joseph Smith receiving or experiencing a revelation and his dictating a text for that revelation is rarely known. Circumstantially, it appears that often the time was short, or even immediate—sometimes given in social settings

---

19. During Joseph Smith's lifetime relatively little discussion of the revelatory process took place among his followers. The Latter-day Saints rarely noted in their diaries or letters the reception of a revelation, almost as if it were nothing extraordinary. They seem to have assumed the divinity of the revelation and either lacked information about how revelations were received or felt that the means of reception was not particularly important.

20. Andrew F. Ehat and Lyndon W. Cook, eds., *The Words of Joseph Smith: The Contemporary Accounts of the Nauvoo Discourses of the Prophet Joseph* (Provo, Utah: Religious Studies Center, Brigham Young University, 1980), 369, entry for 12 May 1844.

21. William E. McLellin, "Revelations," *Ensign of Liberty*, August 1849, 98.

in answer to a question.[22] But in some instances days or weeks seemed to have passed. In a few cases, such as the 12 July 1843 revelation regarding polygamy, the texts appear to combine a series of divine impressions and communications received over several weeks or maybe even years.[23] It is even possible that the earliest revelations that predate the formal organization of the church may not have been committed to writing until after the divine directive "there Shall a Record be kept" was issued in April 1830.[24]

Whatever the time lapse between revelatory experience and dictated revelation text, Joseph Smith often phrased his revelations in the first-person voice of Deity. Moreover, the wording of the revelation texts consistently echoes the literary cadences of the King James Version of the Bible, and using specific phrases from the Old and New Testaments is common. This may have enabled Latter-day Saints to more readily recognize what they considered to be God's voice in Joseph Smith's revelations and to embrace them as the scriptural word of God. On the other hand, historians have demonstrated how biblically saturated the discursive culture of antebellum America was. The eminent historian Perry Miller wrote that the Old Testament was "so omnipresent in the American culture of 1800 or 1820 that historians have as much difficulty taking cognizance of it as of the air the people breathed."[25] Of course the New Testament was as or even more ubiquitous. Given this cultural context, it is less surprising that Joseph Smith's revelation texts are suffused with the concepts, images, and language of the King James Version.

Consistent with the biblically inflected, divine-voice style of the revelation texts is the description of the revelations given by Richard Lyman Bushman, Smith's biographer: "the speaker stands above and outside Joseph, sharply separated emotionally and intellectually." The revelations even contain rebukes of the very prophet dictating them. "There is no effort to conceal or rationalize, no sign of Joseph justifying himself to prospective

22. See, for example, Revelation, 8 July 1838–A, in *Documents, Volume 6*, of *The Joseph Smith Papers*.

23. See Brian D. Hales and Laura H. Hales, *Joseph Smith's Polygamy: Toward a Better Understanding* (Salt Lake City: Greg Kofford Books, 2015), vol. 2, 64–73.

24. "17th· Commandment AD April 6 1830," in Jensen et al., *Manuscript Revelation Books*, 27 (D&C 21:1).

25. Perry Miller, "The Old Testament in Colonial America," in *Historical Viewpoints*, ed. John A. Garraty (New York: Harper and Row, 1970), 7. See also Phillip L. Barlow, *Mormons and the Bible: The Place of the Latter-day Saints in American Religion*, revised ed. (New York: Oxford University Press, 2013).

followers. The words flow directly from the messenger to Joseph and have the single purpose of setting Joseph straight."[26] Moreover, Smith's followers could distinguish his revelation texts from his general counsel as the president of the church. They "accepted the voice in the revelations as the voice of God, investing in the revelations the highest authority, even above Joseph Smith's counsel. In the revelations, they believed, God himself spoke, not a man."[27] A clear example of this may be seen in the behavior of John Whitmer, a close friend of Joseph Smith. Whitmer recounted how the governing church elders and Joseph Smith himself told him he was the man to serve as the church's historian. Whitmer, however, demurred, replying that if it were the will of the Lord, "I desire that he would manifest it through Joseph the Seer."[28] Smith soon dictated a revelation appointing Whitmer as church historian. When recorded by Whitmer himself, he introduced it as a revelation "given to John [Whitmer] in consequenc[e] of not feeling reconsiled to write at the request of Joseph with[o]ut a commandment &c"[29] This elevation of Smith's revelation texts above his ordinary declarations is expressly stated in one of the earliest revelations itself:

> I, Jesus Christ, your Lord and your God, have spoken it. These words are not of men, nor of man, but of me: Wherefore you shall testify they are of me, and not of man; for it is my voice which speaketh them unto you: For they are given by my Spirit unto you: And by my power you can read them one to another; and save it were by my power, you could not have them: Wherefore you can testify that you have heard my voice, and know my words.[30]

---

26. Richard Lyman Bushman, *Joseph Smith: Rough Stone Rolling*, with the assistance of Jed Woodworth (New York: Knopf, 2005), 69.

27. Richard Lyman Bushman, *Believing History: Latter-day Saint Essays*, eds. Reid L. Neilson and Jed Woodworth (New York: Columbia University Press, 2004), 258–59.

28. Whitmer, History, 24, in Karen Lynn Davidson, Richard L. Jensen, and David J. Whittaker, eds., *Histories, Volume 2: Assigned Historical Writings, 1831–1847*, vol. 2 of the Histories series of *The Joseph Smith Papers*, eds. Dean C. Jessee, Ronald K. Esplin, and Richard Lyman Bushman (Salt Lake City: Church Historian's Press, 2012), 36.

29. "50th Commandment March 8th. 1831," heading, in Jensen et al., *Manuscript Revelation Books*, 131. In the earliest years of Mormonism, Latter-day Saints used "commandment(s)" interchangeably with "revelation(s)."

30. Revelation, June 1829, in *Book of Commandments, for the Government of the Church of Christ, Organized according to Law, on the 6th of April, 1830* (Zion [Independence], Missouri: W. W. Phelps, 1833), 36–41.

The words of the revelation were seen as God's, not as Smith's.[31]

Preserving and Publishing the Revelations

A year and a half into the church's history, firm plans were made to compile and publish Joseph Smith's revelations in book form.[32] By then, the Mormon prophet had already dictated dozens of revelation texts. The printed compilation, *A Book of Commandments, for the Government of the Church of Christ* (hereafter Book of Commandments), was nearing completion in summer 1833, when the press was vandalized by local antagonists and printing was interrupted. Some Latter-day Saints, though, were able to salvage the printed sheets, each of which had sixteen pages printed on each side, preserving the first 160 pages. The evidence is clear that a sixth sheet was anticipated.[33] Those fortunate enough to gather the scattered sheets had them individually bound for personal use, but a publicly available, complete edition of Joseph Smith's revelations was still needed. The Mormon prophet and his associates were not to be deterred, and two years later, in 1835, they published the *Doctrine and Covenants of the Church of the Latter Day Saints: Carefully Selected from the Revelations of God, and compiled by* Joseph Smith Junior, Oliver Cowdery, Sidney Rigdon, Frederick G. Williams, *[*Presiding Elders of said Church.*] Proprietors* (hereafter "Doctrine and Covenants"). The new compilation contained all the revelations printed for the Book of Commandments as well as over thirty more revelations Joseph Smith dictated between summer 1831 (the date of the last typeset revelation in the Book of Commandments) and summer 1835

31. For more on how Smith's revelations presented themselves in God's voice or spirit, see Grant Underwood, "Revelation, Text, and Revision: Insights from the Book of Commandments and Revelations," *BYU Studies*, vol. 48, no. 3 (2009): 80.

32. The earlier notion that the revelations were only for Mormon consumption changed at this time, but apparently not without misgivings on the part of some. William McLellin, who attended the decision-making meetings, later claimed that it took "hours" to make the decision, in part because David Whitmer and "a few of the brethren" doubted that it was the will of the Lord to publish the revelations (see Godfrey et al., *Documents, Volume 2*, 95). Nonetheless, Joseph Smith dictated a revelation that specifically justified the change: "Commanded to be kept from the world in the day that they were given," they "now are to go forth unto all flesh." "A Revelation Recd. Nov 3, 1831," Jensen et al., *Manuscript Revelation Books*, 213 (D&C 133:60–61).

33. The extant five signatures of the incomplete Book of Commandments are reproduced in Jensen et al., *Revelations and Translation, Volume 2*, 13–170. Detailed discussion of the printing of the book and the envisioned sixth gathering is found in Jensen et al., *Revelation and Translations, Volume 2*, 4–12, 173–77.

(when the Doctrine and Covenants was completed).[34] Making these revelations available to the young and growing church was vital, since much of their content pertained to the church's developing polity and practice. The subtitle of the Book of Commandments indicated that the revelations were given for the "government of the church." In like manner, the editor's preface to the Doctrine and Covenants introduced the revelations as containing "items or principles for the regulation of the church."[35] Words like "government" and "regulation" make clear that the revelation compilations were designed to serve a purpose similar to that performed by the procedural "handbooks" and "disciplines" of other denominations. Latter-day Saints were expected to look to the Doctrine and Covenants more for guidance on church procedures and initiatives than as a source for church doctrine. But the content of the revelations themselves may invite some readers to read them in yet another way.

While the Book of Mormon, Bible revision, and Book of Abraham are primarily theological expositions embedded in historical narratives, many of the revelations in the Book of Commandments and Doctrine and Covenants are practical, even pedestrian in nature. The appearance of such considerations in revelation works to dissolve the distinction between sacred and profane. "All things unto me are Spiritual," announces a revelation, "& not at any time have I given unto you a law which was temporal."[36] Not surprisingly, therefore, church finances or emigration plans

34. A second edition of the Doctrine and Covenants was prepared between 1841 and 1844, and was published within two months of Joseph Smith's death on 27 June 1844. Essentially, the 1844 edition was a reprint of the first edition with the addition of five other revelation texts, two letters that Smith addressed to the church that were considered canonical, and a post-martyrdom tribute to the Mormon prophet. In the 1870s, a generation after Smith's death, Latter-day Saint leaders canonized another two dozen selections from historical records that contained additional revelation texts from Smith and other Smith-related documents deemed canonical, and added a revelation from Brigham Young, thus bringing the total number of Latter-day Saint Doctrine and Covenants sections from 111 to 136. A final Smith selection and an account of an early twentieth-century vision written by his prophet-nephew, Joseph F. Smith, were added to the 1981 Latter-day Saint edition of the Doctrine and Covenants, bringing the total to 138, the same number found in the church's latest, 2013, edition. Beginning in the 1860s, the Reorganized Church of Jesus Christ of Latter Day Saints (known today as Community of Christ) began publishing its own editions of the Doctrine and Covenants, adding revelation texts from its prophet-leaders who followed Joseph Smith. In 2010, Community of Christ canonized its latest revelation as section 165.

35. "Preface," *Doctrine and Covenants*, 1835 ed., [iii], in Jensen et al., *Revelations and Translations, Volume 2*, 313.

36. "29th Commandment AD 1830," Jensen et al., *Manuscript Revelation Books*, 49 (D&C 29:34).

intermingle with God's will on prayer or Sabbath observance. One revelation contains a profound, if brief, commentary on Christ's atoning sacrifice, followed later by an injunction to Smith's friend Martin Harris to "pay the printer's debt."[37] The wide range of matters discussed in the revelations, especially their practicality and immediacy, made them particularly meaningful to Smith's followers, but this earthy quality also made them the object of non-Mormon disparagement. "No association with the sacred phrases of scripture," wrote Josiah Quincy, "could keep the inspirations of this man from getting down upon the hard pan of practical affairs."[38] A few of the revelations in the Doctrine and Covenants soar to lofty philosophical or theological heights, but for the most part they focus on accomplishing the church's mission and formulating its polity.

The rather lengthy and sometimes complicated process by which the revelation texts traveled from the lips of the prophet to the pages of the Doctrine and Covenants is worth examining in detail. Once a revelation was dictated, it was often hand copied either by the individual to whom it was directed or by an interested Latter-day Saint if it was addressed to the church generally. Extant journals from some of the church's earliest missionaries, for instance, contain handwritten copies of key revelation texts such as "Articles and Covenants" and "Laws of the Church of Christ."[39] Such was the eagerness of the Latter-day Saints to make personal copies of the revelations that it seemed to a frustrated Joseph Smith as if they were "snatched from under my hand as soon as given."[40] Before the church was a year old, revelation directed John Whitmer to "assist [Joseph Smith] in Transcribing [copying] all things which shall be given him" and "to Keep the Church Record & History continually."[41] As a result, Whitmer faithfully

37. Revelation, March 1830, in *Book of Commandments*, in Jensen et al., *Revelations and Translations, Volume 2*, 54 (D&C 19).

38. Josiah Quincy, *Figures of the Past: From the Leaves of Old Journals* (Boston: Roberts Brothers, 1888), 387.

39. See Articles and Covenants, ca. Apr. 1830 (D&C 20), in Michael Hubbard MacKay, Gerrit J. Dirkmaat, Grant Underwood, Robert J. Woodford, and William G. Hartley, eds., *Documents, Volume 1: July 1828–June 1831*, vol. 1 of the Documents series of *The Joseph Smith Papers*, eds. Dean C. Jessee, Ronald K. Esplin, Richard Lyman Bushman, and Matthew J. Grow (Salt Lake City: Church Historian's Press, 2013), 116–26; Revelation, 9 February 1831, in MacKay et al., *Documents, Volume 1*, 245–56 (D&C 42:1–72); and Revelation, 23 February 1831, in MacKay et al., *Documents, Volume 1*, 264–67 (D&C 42:74–93).

40. Joseph Smith to William W. Phelps, 31 July 1832, in Godfrey et al., *Documents, Volume 2*, 266.

41. Revelation, ca. 8 March 1831 (D&C 48), in Jensen et al., *Manuscript Revelation Books*, 131–33.

began copying the revelation texts into a ledger-book repository titled "A Book of Commandments & Revelations of the Lord given to Joseph the Seer & others by the Inspiration of God & gift & power of the Holy Ghost" (hereafter BCR).[42] Not long thereafter Joseph Smith and his associates made plans to acquire a printing press and publish the revelations. By the time detailed plans were laid in November 1831, Whitmer had filled over a hundred manuscript pages in the BCR with transcripts of more than sixty revelation texts. It was the one place where a virtually complete collection of the revelations could be found. Not surprisingly, over the next two years the BCR provided the primary textual basis for printing the revelations, and it supplied in shortened form the name for that first compilation—the Book of Commandments.[43]

At the conclusion of the November meetings, Whitmer and Oliver Cowdery, another close associate of Joseph Smith, were charged with carrying the BCR to the recently designated Mormon "Zion" and gathering place in Independence, Missouri. There the printing operation was to be located. At the time, Zion was a frontier area on what was then the western edge of the United States. Before the transportation revolution in nineteenth-century America took full effect, travel between the church's interim headquarters in Kirtland, Ohio, and Zion was arduous and time consuming. For a variety of reasons, Whitmer and Cowdery spent six weeks making the journey; a fast trip still required two weeks.[44] Revelation texts dictated subsequent to the departure of Whitmer and Cowdery had to be delivered to church printers in Missouri either by church elders traveling there or by mail, which required basically the same amount of transportation time. The lengthy chain of transmission from prophet to printers is captured in a notation in the BCR. Whitmer concluded his transcription of a revelation he was registering in the BCR with this explanation: "Given by Joseph the seer. & written by Sidney [Rigdon] the Scribe & counsellor & transcribed by Frederick [G. Williams] assistant scribe & counsellor. & copied by Orson Hyde the clerk of the presidency: And Recorded by John

---

42. Reproduced in both photographical and typographical facsimile in Jensen et al., *Manuscript Revelation Books*, 8–405.

43. See Jensen et al., *Revelations and Translations, Volume 2*.

44. William G. Hartley, "Letters and Mail between Kirtland and Independence: A Mormon Postal History, 1831–33," *Journal of Mormon History* 35 (Summer 2009): 163–89.

Whitmer the Lords Clerk."[45] The passage identifies Rigdon as the scribe for the original dictation manuscript, which was dated 6 December 1832. Because the BCR was in Missouri by the time Smith dictated this revelation, it had to be copied into the successor volume to the BCR (historically known as the "Kirtland Revelation Book") by Whitmer's scribal successor Frederick Williams. At some point thereafter, Orson Hyde made the copy that was delivered to Missouri, where Whitmer finally copied it into the BCR. Because Whitmer inscribed the revelation in the BCR immediately following one dated August 1833, he could not have transcribed it before that time. Thus, the better part of a year passed before this revelation found its way into the BCR.[46]

Revising the Revelations

Time was not the only factor that influenced publication of the revelations. More significant still, and more revealing for what it suggests about the process of producing the Doctrine and Covenants and how the revelation texts were viewed, is the matter of emendation and revision. At the November 1831 conference where plans were finalized for publishing the revelations, "some conversation was had concerning Revelations and language."[47] Apparently some saw more humanity in the revelations' divine–human mix than seemed appropriate. "Your eyes have been upon my Servent Joseph," chastised a revelation dictated at the time, "& his language you have known, & his imperfections you have known, & you have sought in your hearts knowlege, that you might express beyond his language." The revelation then called for "the most wise" among them to attempt to compose a better-worded revelation.[48] When the experiment failed, the discontented elders apparently were satisfied. At some point in the conference they "arose in turn and bore witness to the truth of the Book of Commandments"[49] and agreed to sign "The Testimony of the

45. "Revelation given December 6, 1832 Kirtland Ohio," in Jensen et al., *Manuscript Revelation Books,* 331.

46. For more information on the chronology of the revisions, see Underwood, "Revelation, Text, and Revision," 72–75.

47. Joseph Smith et al., History, 1838–1856, vol. A-1, 161, CHL.

48. "Revelation given Nov 2nd 1831," in Jensen et al., *Manuscript Revelation Books,* 203 (D&C 67:5–8).

49. Minutes, 1–2 November 1831, in Godfrey et al., *Documents, Volume 2,* 98.

witnesses to the Book of the Lords commandments which he gave to his church through Joseph Smith Jr."[50]

Joseph Smith never pretended that he was simply God's stenographer or a human fax machine through which perfect, divine language descended to earth. The revelation to the disgruntled elders plainly acknowledged that the revelation texts contained "his language" and "imperfections." And the previously mentioned "preface" to the Book of Commandments dictated at the same conference freely acknowledged that the revelations were "given unto my Servents in their weakness after the manner of their Language."[51] That "manner" apparently included certain recognizable infelicities of expression, and human "weakness" was manifest both in the dictation and in the recording process, which entailed occasional errors of a scribal nature. Such matters, and the need to resolve them prior to publication, surfaced again at a meeting on 8 November 1831. After some discussion, the conference resolved that "Br Joseph Smith Jr. correct those errors or mistakes which he [may] discover by the holy Spirit."[52]

It has long been recognized that a number of "corrections" or revisions were made to the wording of revelation texts between the earliest printing of the texts in the church's Missouri periodical *The Evening and the Morning Star,* or in the Book of Commandments and their republication in the Kirtland reprint of the *Star,* or in Doctrine and Covenants. One revelation, for instance, tripled in size from the Book of Commandments version to the Doctrine and Covenants version.[53] Less well known is that the revelation texts were also edited prior to initial publication in the *Star* or Book of Commandments—and the extent of those earliest revisions was entirely unknown until the BCR was published in 2009. Hundreds of redactions, usually involving only a word or two but sometimes comprising an entire phrase or more, were inscribed in the BCR between 1831 and 1833. Thanks to the work of handwriting experts, it is also clear that the vast majority of revisions are in the handwriting of Sidney Rigdon, John Whitmer, Oliver Cowdery, and W. W. Phelps.[54] While it might be assumed that Smith

---

50. Revelation, in Jensen et al., *Manuscript Revelation Books,* 215.

51. "Revelation Given in Hiram Nov$^{\text{m.}}$ 1st·1831," in Jensen et al., *Manuscript Revelation Books,* 225 (D&C 1:24).

52. Minutes, 8 November 1831, in Godfrey et al., *Documents, Volume* 2, 123.

53. Now D&C 27.

54. For more information on the group of men who revised the revelations, see Underwood, "Revelation, Text, and Revision," 72.

dictated the changes, as he did the original revelation texts, the fact that for all but a few days in 1832 and 1833, Joseph Smith was in Ohio while the BCR—along with Whitmer, Cowdery, and Phelps—was nine hundred miles away in Missouri negates the likelihood of that being the common practice. Most of the revisions in the handwriting of Sidney Rigdon were made sometime during the twelve days of the November meetings, and some of them may have been made at Smith's behest. However, the far greater number of revisions—in the handwriting of Whitmer, Cowdery, and Phelps—were made in Missouri during 1832 and 1833, apparently without Joseph Smith's direct involvement.

Such data from the manuscripts themselves invite reconsideration of prior assumptions about Smith's role in revising the revelation texts and, therefore, about how he viewed the revelatory process itself. All of the men in whose handwriting the revisions appear had been charged by revelation at the conclusion of the November meetings with being "stewards over the revelations & commandments."[55] Five months later, Joseph Smith presided at a council meeting in Missouri at which "brs. William [Phelps], Oliver [Cowdery] & John [Whitmer] [were] appointed to review the Book of Commandments [BCR] & select for printing such as shall be deemed by them proper, as dictated by the spirit & make all necessary verbal corrections."[56] In July, he wrote to his Missouri associates about "correction" and "revisel" of the revealed New Translation texts.[57] Although "correction" typically implies changing wording to match a "correct" original, from what can be seen in the BCR, these stewards over the revelations understood "verbal corrections" and "revisel" more broadly to include a variety of textual improvements or revisions. Joseph Smith had a healthy awareness of the inadequacy of finite, human language, including his own, to perfectly communicate infinite, divine revelations, and he apparently welcomed assistance in the refinement of the language used to convey his revelations. Still, there were limits. Echoing Revelation 22, he warned his Missouri collaborators, "Be careful not to alter the sense of any of them for he that adds or diminishes to the prop[h]ecies must come under the

55. "Revelation, 12 November 1831," in Jensen, *Manuscript Revelation Books,* 221 (D&C 70:3).

56. Minutes, 30 April 1832, in Godfrey et al., *Documents, Volume 2,* 239.

57. Joseph Smith to William W. Phelps, 31 July 1832, in Godfrey et al., *Documents, Volume 2,* 267.

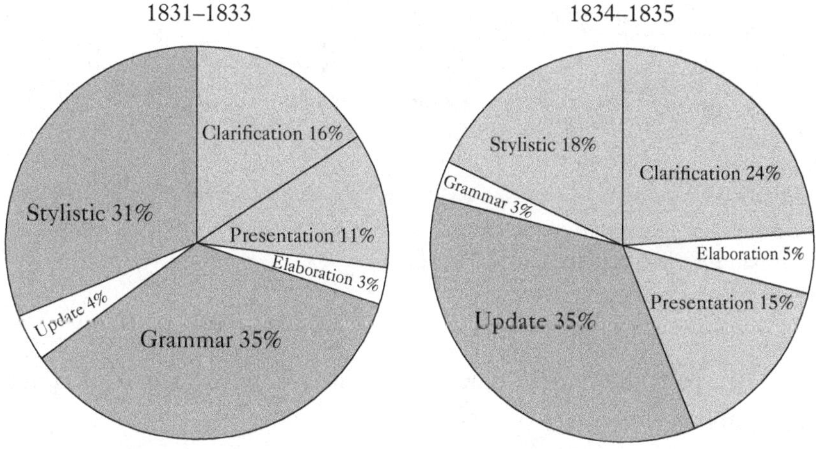

FIGURE 5.1. Types of Revisions.

condemnation writen therein."[58] Apparently, these men rarely crossed the boundary line, because the vast majority of their revisions were incorporated unchanged in the Doctrine and Covenants.

Analyzing the Revisions

Although an exhaustive analysis of all revisions made to Joseph Smith's revelation texts is beyond the scope of this chapter, a basic categorization of the various types of revisions is fairly straightforward. To provide a sense of the broad range of redactions, all revisions in the foundational and lengthy "Laws of the Church of Christ" were analyzed. This includes the 1831–1833 revisions made for the Book of Commandments, as well as changes made in 1834–1835 for the Doctrine and Covenants. Figure 5.1 illustrates the breakdown by category. Beyond revelations like "Laws of the Church of Christ" or "Articles and Covenants," few revelation texts include each kind of revision, but many include examples from one or more categories. A key observation from Figure 5.1 that seems to hold true when all revisions from each period are considered collectively is that grammatical changes were the dominant kind in 1831–1833, while revisions made to update church polity and practice were the most common type in

58. Joseph Smith to William W. Phelps, 31 July 1832, in Godfrey et al., *Documents, Volume 2*, 266–67.

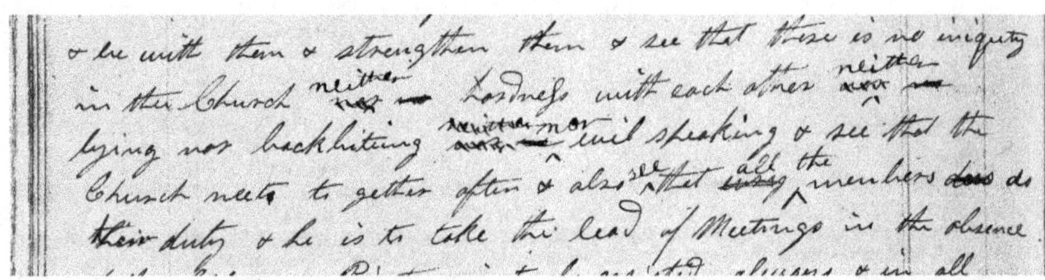

& be with them & strengthen them & see that there is no iniquity
in the Church neither hardness with each other neither
lying nor backbiting nor evil speaking & see that the
Church meets to gether often & also see that all the members do
their duty & he is to take the lead of Meetings in the absence

FIGURE 5.2. "Church Articles & Covenants" (D&C 20), in "Book of Commandments and Revelations," p. 56.
Church History Library, Salt Lake City.

1834–1835. In both periods, a concern to clarify wording or make wording more publicly presentable was also manifest.[59]

Figure 5.2 provides an example of grammatical and stylistic revisions. The unedited BCR transcript of Articles and Covenants identifies some of the duties of the Mormon ministerial office of "teacher" in these words: "see that there is no iniquty in the Church nor no hardness with each other nor no lying nor backbiting nor no evil speaking." Oliver Cowdery revised the grammatically incorrect "nor no" to "neither."[60] John Whitmer made refinements of a stylistic nature, just as Cowdery did later in the document regarding church-member relocation. Here Cowdery changed the last three words in the statement "Any member removeing from the Church where he belongs" to "where he resides."[61]

Revisions labeled "presentation" in Figure 5.1 target a particular kind of stylistic change common enough to merit its own category. Here the restatement seems to aim at communicating the same basic idea but in more refined language, to make it more "presentable." For example, the earlier wording of a February 1831 revelation text seen in Figure 5.3 grants the Latter-day Saints power to organize themselves according to civil laws "that your enemies may be under your feet in all things." At some point the potentially inflammatory nature of this language was recognized, and

59. For further examples, see Underwood, "Revelation, Text, and Revision," 67–71.

60. "Church Articles & Covenants," in Jensen et al., *Manuscript Revelation Books,* 83 (D&C 20:54).

61. "Church Articles & Covenants," in Jensen et al., *Manuscript Revelation Books,* 87 (D&C 20:84).

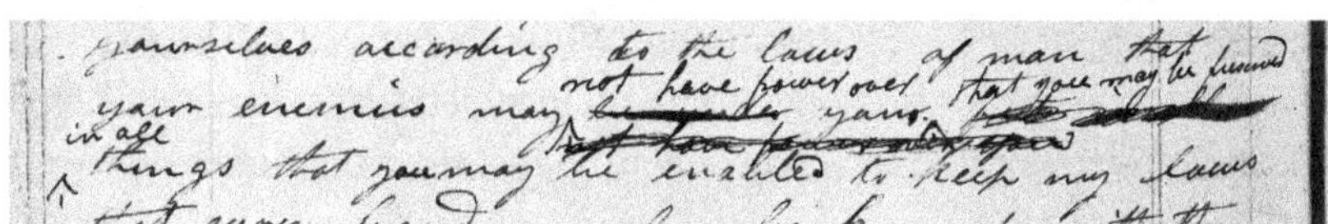

yourselves according to the laws of man that not have power over that you may be preserved
your enemies may you.
in all
things that you may be enabled to keep my laws

FIGURE 5.3. "46th Commandment Febu. 1831" (D&C 44), in "Book of Commandments and Revelations," p. 70.
Church History Library, Salt Lake City.

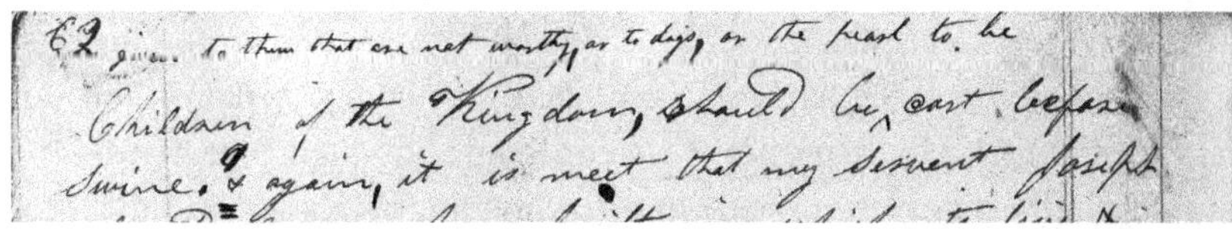

62 given to them that are not worthy, or to dogs, or the pearl to be
Children of the Kingdom, should be cast before
Swine. & again, it is meet that my servant Joseph

FIGURE 5.4. "Commandment given Feb. 4th 1831" (D&C 41), in "Book of Commandments and Revelations," p. 62.
Church History Library, Salt Lake City.

Sidney Rigdon revised the passage to read "that your enemies may not have power over you that you may be preserved in all things."[62]

Other revisions simply provide clarification by restating or expanding the wording. For example, the original BCR wording of an 1831 revelation was "Behold now it is called to day & verily it is a day of Sacrifice & a day for the tithing of my People for he that is tithed shall not be burned." In this case, Joseph Smith himself made the revisions. He inserted "until the coming of the son of man" to clarify what was meant by "to day." Also, he added "at his coming" to clarify *when* the tithe payer "shall not be burned."[63]

Some revisions can be classified as "elaborations." These seem to have no other purpose than merely to enrich and extend the text. Figure 5.4 shows a sentence that on its own is intelligible and grammatically correct and that echoes biblical language: "it is not meet that the things which belong to the Children of the Kingdom should be cast before Swine." However, between "should be" and "cast before Swine," John Whitmer inserted an additional line of text: "given to them that are not worthy, or to

62. "46th Commandment Febu. 1831," in Jensen et al., *Manuscript Revelation Books*, 113 (D&C 44:5).

63. "Revelation Kirtland Sept 11th 1831," in Jensen et al., *Manuscript Revelation Books*, 193 (D&C 64:23).

dogs, or the pearl to be."[64] Presumably, Whitmer felt that the text should more fully echo the Sermon on the Mount, in which Christ is remembered as saying, "Give not that which is holy unto the dogs, neither cast ye your pearls before swine."[65]

Although few redactions in BCR can be classified as "updating" the text, a much larger portion of the revisions in the 1834–1835 period fall into this category. Joseph Smith and his associates seemed anxious to ensure that the revelation texts published in the Doctrine and Covenants were current both ecclesiastically and doctrinally. In one revelation, "the first presidency of the chich [church]" and "this presidency" replaced the earlier "confrence of high priests."[66] A conference of high priests was the church's highest governing body in 1831 when this revelation was dictated, but by 1835 the "First Presidency" had been formed and was handling the matters discussed in this text. An even more dramatic example of bringing procedures and polity up to date occurred in the church's Articles and Covenants. Two brief paragraphs, constituting more than eighty words, were new to text in the Doctrine and Covenants.[67] The offices named in the added text—"bishops," "high counsellors," "high priests," and presidents "of the high priesthood"—did not exist when Articles and Covenants was first issued in 1830. Yet, by 1835, these officers had become crucial to the governance of the church.

Some revisions can be classified as doctrinal updates. For instance, Joseph Smith dictated a revelation text bearing the date of 1 March 1832 that included the perfectly acceptable phrase "saith your Redeemer even Jesus Christ." Sometime later that month an unusual document was

64. "Commandment given Feb·4th·1831," in Jensen et al., *Manuscript Revelation Books,* 93, 95 (D&C 41:6).

65. Matthew 7:6.

66. "A Revelation to Orson [Hyde] Luke [Johnson] & Lyman [Johnson] & William [E. McLellin]," in Jensen et al., *Manuscript Revelation Books,* 201 (D&C 68:22–23).

67. *Doctrine and Covenants,* 1835 ed., 16–17 (D&C 20:65–67). The additional verbiage first appeared in print in the January 1835 *Evening and Morning Star* reprint of the June 1832 issue where the church initially published Articles and Covenants. "The Articles and Covenants of the Church of Christ," *Evening and Morning Star,* June 1832 (January 1835), 4, in Jensen et al., *Revelations and Tranlsations, Volume 2,* 207. During the *Star*'s original print run from June 1832 through June 1833, one or more of the revelation texts appeared in each issue (except April). In September 1834, a decision was made to reprint those early issues and in doing so the editor promised to "make proper corrections" to the revelations ("Prospectus," *The Evening and the Morning Star,* September 1834, 192). As in the past, despite talk of correcting to "originals," "proper corrections" included updating the texts. Many of these corrections, as in the case above, were incorporated in the wording of the Doctrine and Covenants sections.

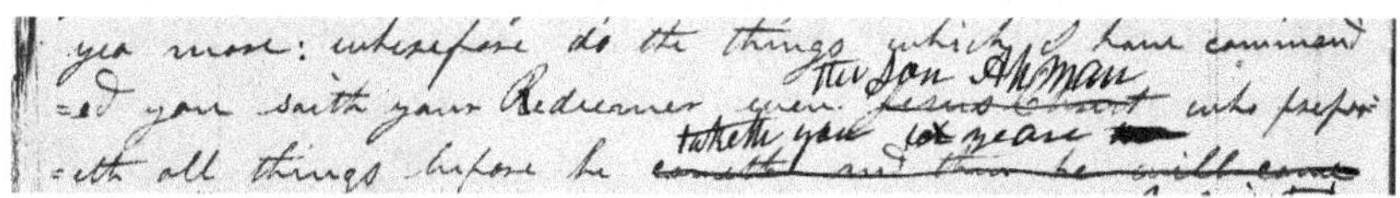

FIGURE 5.5. "Revelation given Kirtland March 1, 1832" (D&C 78), in "Book of Commandments and Revelations," p. 146.
Church History Library, Salt Lake City.

created titled "A Sample of Pure Language."[68] This brief item revealed that in the "pure language," the name of God was "Ahman" and the name of Jesus Christ was "Son Ahman." Shortly thereafter, a copy of the document, along with others Joseph had dictated after the BCR was taken to Missouri, were carried to Missouri. Later, when the revelation text was being revised for the Doctrine and Covenants, W. W. Phelps changed "your Redeemer even Jesus Christ" to "your Redeemer even the Son Ahman," seen in Figure 5.5.[69] Still more newly revealed doctrine was included from another, unknown source. To the title "Lord God, the Holy One of Israel" some fifty words of new descriptive text were added: "who hath established the foundations of Adam-ondi-Ahman; who hath appointed Michael, your prince, and established his feet, and set him upon high; and given him the keys of salvation under the counsel and direction of the Holy One who is without beginning of days or end of life."[70]

Finally, to gain some idea of how many revisions were made to the revelation texts, a detailed count was performed for "Laws of the Church of Christ." Two hundred and seventy-four words were deleted and 538 new words were added. The complete revelation text as printed in the Doctrine and Covenants numbered 2,659 words. Thus, approximately 25% of this revelation's wording was revised. Such a figure is on the high end, as some revelation texts passed virtually unrevised from the BCR to the Book of Commandments to the Doctrine and Covenants. The percentage of revised wording in many other revelations is in the single digits. Overall, though, revisions to the revelation texts of Joseph Smith constitute a

68. Jensen et al., *Manuscript Revelation Books,* 265.

69. "Revelation given Kirtland March 1, 1832," in Jensen et al., *Manuscript Revelation Books,* 269 (D&C 78:20).

70. See Jensen et al., *Revelations and Translations, Volume 2,* 515 (D&C 78:15–16). The earthly identity of Michael was first revealed at the end of 1833, and the earliest documented use of "Adam-ondi-Ahman" as the name of a geographical location in Missouri occurred in spring 1835. Thus, the textual amplification seems to have been made sometime in 1835.

significant feature of their transmission from the inscription of oral dictation to the published Doctrine and Covenants. This contrasts with the relatively few revisions visible on the extant pages of the original, dictation manuscript of the Book of Mormon.[71] However, in the case of the Doctrine and Covenants, virtually no additional revisions of any consequence were made to the hundred revelation texts in the first edition (1835) when republished in the second edition (1844). Apparently, Joseph Smith considered those texts suitably refined by 1835, and thereafter the wording was stable.[72]

Conclusion

Although Joseph Smith left no lengthy discussion of the matter, clues from his revelation texts suggest that the revelations were not experienced, or intended to be understood as, verbatim transmissions. Although Smith's revelations were viewed by early Latter-day Saints as offering "the foundation of the Church & the salvation of the world & the Keyes of the mysteries of the Kingdom, & the riches of Eternity," it was also recognized that they contained linguistic "imperfections" and stood in need of "corrections"[73] The texts of his revelations were not understood as infallible texts written in stone by the finger of God; they came instead through a finite and fallible prophet who, along with his associates, was not shorn of his humanity in exercising his prophetic office. Moreover, the revelation texts were not viewed as fixed and complete, beyond revision, but as articulations that could and should be updated to reflect the ongoing flow of revelation to the church. Focused as they were primarily on church polity and governance, the revelations were updated and refined as circumstance demanded. After 1835, the church continued to develop ecclesiastically and doctrinally. However, no attempts were made to keep revising

71. About 28 percent of the original manuscript is extant. Royal Skousen, editor of a multivolume, critical text edition of the Book of Mormon, argues that in the case of the Book of Mormon, from a believer's perspective divine "control" of the scripture's wording "was tight," though still "not iron-clad." Skousen, "Translating the Book of Mormon: Evidence from the Original Manuscript," in *Book of Mormon Authorship Revisited: The Evidence for Ancient Origins*, ed. Noel Reynolds (Provo, Utah: Foundation for Ancient Research and Mormon Studies, 1997), 90.

72. See note 34. Several of the eight new sections in the second edition of the Doctrine and Covenants, however, do incorporate revisions made to their underlying manuscript sources. See Jensen et al., *Revelations and Translations, Volume 2*, 645, 649, 674, 690.

73. The first quotation is from Minutes, 12 November 1831, in Godfrey et al., *Documents, Volume 2*, 138.

the revelations. The initial revisions laid the foundation. Thereafter, other forms and means were used to incorporate subsequent prophetic guidance. Thus, the first half decade of the church offers a unique and richly documented look at how Joseph Smith and some of the earliest Latter-day Saints understood revelation and the process of producing canonical articulations of those revelation texts, which in the end were considered fully divine if also noticeably human.

6

Joseph Smith's Missouri Prison Letters and the Mormon Textual Community

David W. Grua

ON 27 OCTOBER 1838, Governor Lilburn W. Boggs declared all Mormons enemies of the state of Missouri. To state militia commanders, Boggs wrote that the Latter-day Saints "must be exterminated or driven from the State if necessary for the public peace." Armed with Boggs's order, several thousand state militiamen occupied Latter-day Saint communities in northwestern Missouri, effectively ending the armed conflict between the Saints and anti-Mormons known as the 1838 Mormon War.[1] Church members learned that they would have until spring 1839 to leave the state, or face the consequences. Joseph Smith and other church leaders were taken into custody and charged with treason and other crimes allegedly committed during the recent conflict.[2] Smith spent the winter in the dungeon of a Missouri jail, while his followers—many of them living in makeshift refugee camps—endured cold, hunger, and frequent harassment from anti-Mormons. In spring, as many as ten thousand Latter-day Saints began

1. Lilburn W. Boggs, Jefferson City, MO, to John B. Clark, Fayette, MO, 27 October 1838, copy, Mormon War Papers, Missouri State Archives, Jefferson City, Missouri (hereafter MSA). On the Mormon War, see Stephen C. LeSueur, *The 1838 Mormon War in Missouri* (Columbia: University of Missouri Press, 1987); and Alexander L. Baugh, *Call to Arms: The 1838 Mormon Defense of Northern Missouri* (Provo, Utah: Joseph Fielding Smith Institute for Latter-day Saint History and BYU Studies, 2000).

2. Lilburn W. Boggs, Jefferson City, MO, to John B. Clark, 1 November 1838, copy; Samuel D. Lucas, "near Far West," MO, to Lilburn W. Boggs, 2 November 1838, copy, Mormon War Papers, MSA; Gordon A. Madsen, "Joseph Smith and the Missouri Court of Inquiry: Austin A. King's Quest for Hostages," *BYU Studies* 43, no. 4 (2004): 92–136.

the arduous journey out of Missouri, with a majority finding shelter in a western Illinois river town called Quincy.[3]

Boggs's order sent the Mormon community into a state of crisis. Smith's revelations had sacralized the state of Missouri as the "land of Zion," the future site of the biblical New Jerusalem.[4] Faced with expulsion from Zion, many Latter-day Saints questioned Smith's leadership, the reliability of his revelations, and the wisdom of continued adherence to the Mormon movement. It is unknown how many Mormons departed the faith during the winter of 1838–1839, yet disaffection was sufficiently widespread to merit comment in sources of the time.

Despite his confinement in the dungeon of a Missouri jail, Smith addressed these concerns in general epistles to the church, which he used as textual ligatures to bind the Mormon community together. These prison letters participated in the "long and variegated Christian literary tradition"—to use scholar of religion W. Clark Gilpin's words—of the letters written by prisoners of conscience.[5] Smith, like many of his Latter-day Saint readers, was familiar with this genre through Paul's epistles in the New Testament and the Reformation-era prison letters published in John Foxe's *Book of Martyrs*. Consistent with the prison epistolary tradition, Smith's letters framed the Saints' recent suffering in Missouri within the long story of God's persecuted people. Yet Smith went beyond the tradition by connecting suffering with a central theme in Mormon thought—revelation—concluding that suffering often preceded divine communication. Smith's prison letters unified and extended the community of Saints despite geographical separation, recontextualized tribulation as part of God's plan, and for many Latter-day Saints, provided the

---

3. William G. Hartley, "'Almost Too Intolerable a Burthen': The Winter Exodus from Missouri, 1838–1839," *Journal of Mormon History* 18, no. 2 (1992): 6–40; Richard E. Bennett, "'Quincy, the Home of our Adoption': A Study of Mormons in Quincy, Illinois, 1838–1840," in *A City of Refuge: Quincy, Illinois*, eds. Richard E. Bennett and Susan Easton Black (Salt Lake City: Millennial Press, 2000), 82–105.

4. See Holy Bible, Revelation 3:12; 21:2; Book of Mormon, 3 Nephi 21:23; Ether 13:2–13; Revelation, 20 July 1831, in Matthew C. Godfrey et al., eds., *Documents, Volume 2: July 1831–January 1833*, vol. 2 of the Documents series of *The Joseph Smith Papers*, ed. Dean C. Jessee et al. (Salt Lake City: Church Historian's Press, 2013), 5 (hereafter *JSP*, D2); and Mark Roscoe Ashurst-McGee, "Zion Rising: Joseph Smith's Early Social and Political Thought" (PhD diss., Arizona State University, 2008).

5. W. Clark Gilpin, "The Letter from Prison in Christian History and Theology," Religion and Culture Web Forum, January 2003, https://divinity.uchicago.edu/sites/default/files/imce/pdfs/webforum/012003/Gilpin_Commentary2.pdf, accessed 14 July 2016.

revelatory and textual sustenance necessary for the movement's ongoing vitality.

A Church in Crisis

The 1838 Mormon War that ended with Boggs's extermination order and Smith's imprisonment was rooted in what historian Steven C. Harper has called the "politics of revelation." For Mormons, Smith's claim to revelation was evidence of his divine calling as a prophet. For anti-Mormons, Smith's claim to revelation was evidence of his imposture and his followers' delusional fanaticism.[6] Anti-Mormon opposition had appeared whenever the Latter-day Saint population in a county approached a plurality. By October 1838, anti-Mormons had expelled Mormons from three Missouri counties[7] and were moving to repeat these measures in a fourth, Daviess County. Realizing that civil authorities would not protect the Daviess County Mormons, Smith and other church members opted for aggressive self-defense, burning buildings believed to be mob havens, confiscating goods, and expelling anti-Mormons from the county.[8] Subsequently, anti-Mormons took Mormon prisoners and attacked isolated Latter-day Saint homes and settlements, killing approximately forty Latter-day Saint men and boys while one non-Mormon died.[9] Based on exaggerated reports, Missouri Governor Lilburn W. Boggs issued the October 27 order authorizing the expulsion of the Mormons.

In November, Smith and sixty-three other Latter-day Saint men attended a preliminary hearing in Richmond, Missouri, before Judge

---

6. Steven C. Harper, "'Dictated by Christ': Joseph Smith and the Politics of Revelation," *Journal of the Early Republic* 26, no. 2 (Summer 2006): 275–304; J. Spencer Fluhman, *"A Peculiar People": Anti-Mormonism and the Making of Religion in Nineteenth-Century America* (Chapel Hill: University of North Carolina Press, 2013).

7. Anti-Mormons expelled the Saints from Jackson County in November 1833. In 1836, the Saints were asked to leave Clay County voluntarily rather than undergo forcible expulsion. In early October 1838, anti-Mormons successfully evicted Mormons living in De Witt, Carroll County. (Warren A. Jennings, "The Expulsion of the Mormons from Jackson County, Missouri," *Missouri Historical Review* 64 [October 1969]: 41–63; Stephen C. LeSueur, "Missouri's Failed Compromise: The Creation of Caldwell County for the Mormons," *Journal of Mormon History* 31, no. 2 [2005]: 113–44.)

8. LeSueur, *1838 Mormon War*, chap 7; Baugh, *Call to Arms*, chap. 7.

9. LeSueur, *1838 Mormon War*, chaps. 8–9; Baugh, *Call to Arms*, chaps. 8–10; John B. Clark, Jefferson City, MO, to Lilburn W. Boggs, Jefferson City, MO, 29 November 1838, copy, Mormon War Papers, MSA.

Austin A. King of the Fifth Judicial Circuit, for crimes allegedly committed during the conflict. King examined forty-two witnesses—including several disaffected Mormons—concerning an alleged insurrection against the state. Although seven defense witnesses testified, the Saints claimed that King would not permit testimony that substantially challenged the prosecution's case.[10]

At the conclusion of the hearing on 29 November 1838, King held that there was probable cause to believe that Smith and five other individuals—Sidney Rigdon, Hyrum Smith, Lyman Wight, Caleb Baldwin, and Alexander McRae—had committed treason. King ordered them confined to the Clay County jail to await a spring trial.[11] The jail in Liberty, Missouri, seen in Figure 6.1, was accessible only via a short flight of stairs that led to heavy, iron-studded double doors. Inside the doors was the upper room, at the center of which was a trap door that opened into the dungeon, a fourteen-by-fourteen space that spanned six-and-a-half feet from the stone floor to the wooden ceiling. Four-foot-thick walls, composed of stone and timber, separated the prisoners from the outside world. The dungeon's only sources of natural light were two narrow horizontal openings, each spanned by a solid iron bar. For the next four-and-half months, Smith and his fellow prisoners would subsist on insufficient rations, sleep on dirty straw mattresses, and endure what Smith later called "hell surrounded with demonds."[12]

Outside the jail, the Saints endured a cold winter crowded into houses and tents in Caldwell County, which the Missouri legislature had created just two years before in 1836 specifically for Mormons as a potential solution to the recurrent violence against the Saints.[13] In the winter of

10. Transcript of Proceedings, Richmond, MO, 12–29 November 1838, E. M. Violette Collection, Manuscript Collection, State Historical Society of Missouri, Columbia (hereafter SHSM), available at josephsmithpapers.org; Hyrum Smith, Testimony, Nauvoo, IL, 1 July 1843, pp. 18–19; see also Madsen, "Joseph Smith and the Missouri Court of Inquiry."

11. Transcript of Proceedings, Richmond, MO, 29 November 1838, pp. [123]–[124], E. M. Violette Collection, SHSM.

12. The best overview of Smith's experience in the Clay County jail remains Dean C. Jessee, "'Walls, Grates, and Screeking Iron Doors': The Prison Experience of Mormon Leaders in Missouri, 1838–1839," in *New Views of Mormon History* (Salt Lake City: University of Utah Press, 1987), 19–42; Letter to the Church and Edward Partridge, 20 March 1839, in Mark Ashurst-McGee et al., eds., *Documents, Volume 6: February 1838–August 1839*, vol. 6 of the Documents series of *The Joseph Smith Papers*, ed. Ronald K. Esplin et al. (Salt Lake City: Church Historian's Press, 2017), 361 (hereafter *JSP*, D6).

13. See LeSueur, "Missouri's Failed Compromise."

FIGURE 6.1. Clay County Jail, Liberty, MO, circa 1878.
Jacob Hicks photograph collection, Clay County Museum and Historical Society, Liberty, MO.

1838–1839, the state militia restricted travel outside of the county, effectively making a makeshift prison for church members. By early spring, the Saints began their migration out of the state toward Illinois. The sense of exile was palpable among the Mormon refugees. As nineteen-year-old Elizabeth Haven wrote to a cousin in Massachusetts soon after arriving in Illinois, the Saints had been "driven from the places of gathering out of the state from houses and lands, in poverty, to seek for habitations where they can find them." Comparing the Saints' expulsion and the exile of ancient Israelites in Babylon, Haven alluded to Psalm 137: "by the river of Babylon we can sit down [and] weep when we remember Zion." Haven conceded that "to look at our situation at this present time, it would seem that Zion is all destroyed," although she maintained faith that God would deliver the Saints.[14]

Other Mormons, however, were not as confident. Disaffection had been a growing problem since 1837, when dissidents led an unsuccessful

14. Elizabeth Haven, Quincy, IL, to Elizabeth Howe Bullard, Holliston, MA, 24 February 1839, Barlow Family Collection, CHL.

revolt against Smith's leadership in the midst of economic turmoil. Dissent continued to plague the church into 1838, even as the conflict with anti-Mormons in Missouri escalated.[15] In December 1838, Latter-day Saint Albert Perry Rockwood described "a sifting in the Church," with "many hav[ing] denied the faith," including some "that have long been in good standing."[16] Mormon apostle Parley P. Pratt agreed, claiming that "a vast many" had left the church during the 1838 crisis and its aftermath.[17] Missouri state officials evidently promised protection to any Latter-day Saint who disavowed the faith, exempting them from the governor's expulsion order and excluding them from criminal charges, thereby providing incentive not only to leave the church but also to cooperate with the government in the prosecution of Smith and others.[18]

The root of this disaffection was a loss of confidence in Smith and his prophetic calling. For example, former church leader John Corrill gave as the reason for his defection: "I can see nothing that convinces me that God has been our leader; calculation after calculation has failed, and plan after plan has been overthrown, and our prophet seemed not to know the event till too late."[19] Similarly, dissident Reed Peck assigned much of the blame for the conflict to Smith, concluding that "all his [Smith's] plan has been a total failure."[20] Apostle Parley P. Pratt denied rumors that the church as a whole had rejected the Prophet, but in so doing acknowledged the pervasiveness of such claims.[21]

---

15. Ronald K. Esplin, *The Emergence of Brigham Young and the Twelve to Mormon Leadership, 1830–1841*, Dissertations in Latter-day Saint History (Provo, Utah: Joseph Fielding Smith Institute for Latter-day Saint History and BYU Studies, 2006), chaps. 6–7.

16. Albert Perry Rockwood, Journal, 9 December 1838, CHL.

17. Parley P. Pratt, Richmond, MO, to "Dear Sister," 9 December 1838, copy, in Rockwood, Journal, CHL.

18. Rockwood, Journal, 2 December 1838; Charles C. Rich to Sarah Pea Rich, 21 December 1838, Charles C. Rich Collection, CHL; Sidney Rigdon et al., "To the Publick," 1839, p. 44[b], Joseph Smith Collection, CHL.

19. John Corrill, *Brief History*, 48, in Karen Lynn Davidson et al., eds., *Histories, Volume 2: Assigned Histories, 1831–1847*, vol. 2 of the Histories series of *The Joseph Smith Papers*, ed. Dean C. Jessee et al. (Salt Lake City: Church Historian's Press, 2012), 197 (hereafter *JSP*, H2).

20. Reed Peck, Quincy, IL, to "Dear Friends," 18 September 1838, p. 139, Mormon Material, Huntington Library, San Marino, CA.

21. Parley P. Pratt, Richmond, MO, to "Dear Sister," 9 December 1838, copy, in Rockwood, Journal, CHL.

Ultimately, a majority of Mormons remained committed to Smith and the church. For these individuals, Smith's arrest and imprisonment actually served as evidence of his prophetic call. For example, Albert Perry Rockwood reminded relatives in Massachusetts that "Christ told his deciple[s] they should be brought before rulers for his name sake, and if the Prophet should be condemned to die it would be no more than was done to Christ & his Apostles."[22] Mormon poet Eliza R. Snow anticipated the question of a friend in Ohio as to whether she "yet believe[d] Joseph Smith is a prophet?" To which Snow replied, "I have not seen or heard anything which caus'd me to doubt it even for a moment: If *possible*, I have *better* testimony that J. Smith is a prophet, than that Jeremiah was one, altho' he has not been kept in prison quite so long."[23] Smith and his imprisonment were therefore central to ways that Latter-day Saints navigated the aftermath of the crisis of 1838.

The Prison Letter Genre

"The prison," as literary scholar Rivkah Zim has noted, "figures as a crucible of suffering that induces self-knowledge and new wisdom."[24] From the apostle Paul's letter to the Philippians to Thomas Moore's letters written from the Tower of London to Martin Luther King's letter from the Birmingham jail, some of the most celebrated literature in the history of Western society has been written in prison, as inmates have committed to writing insights into the nature of suffering in poetry, treatises, and letters to friends, relatives, and supporters outside the prison walls. In Zim's view, "such carceral experience gives the writer authority, importance, and respect in the eyes of readers who may relate such experience to their understanding of the human condition."[25]

Joseph Smith's Missouri jail letters partook of this tradition and the authority his carceral setting imparted. Smith's prison letters sustained a community in the midst of crisis. "In the absence of a unified *physical* community," scholar Ruth Ahnert explains, prisoners use letters "to create

22. Rockwood, Journal, 19 December 1838. See Luke 21:12.

23. Eliza R. Snow, Caldwell Co., MO, to Isaac Streator, Streetsborough, OH, 22 February 1839, copy at CHL; see also Jeremiah chaps. 20, 26, 37–38.

24. Rivkah Zim, "Writing behind Bars: Literary Contexts and the Authority of Carceral Experience," *Huntington Library Quarterly* 72, no. 2 (June 2009): 296.

25. Zim, "Writing behind Bars," 291–92.

a coherent *textual* community."[26] Endowed with the authority of one writing from the "furnace of affliction,"[27] Smith drew upon the conventions of the prison letter genre to make sense of the crisis of 1838 for both himself and his followers.

Letters written from prison have long played an important role in Christian communities. For the apostle Paul, suffering for the sake of the gospel was a symbol of membership within a special community. As New Testament scholar N. T. Wright has argued, Paul's views on suffering stemmed from the history of the Jewish people, who believed they had been "called to be God's people in the midst of a wicked world." That call ensured that "God's people would indeed pass through slavery, torment, subjugation, humiliation and much besides, but that they would be vindicated at the end."[28] Imprisonment was part of what Paul expected to suffer. Several New Testament epistles attributed to Paul bore the markings of having been written from prison, and others addressed the significance of suffering.[29] Paul's prison letters were tangible dispatches written from within his own carceral crucibles, textually forging the early Christian movement's collective identity as the suffering people of the suffering Messiah.[30]

Imprisoned victims of oppressive Reformation-era regimes likewise utilized prison letters to maintain ties with family and friends and to articulate their willingness to suffer and even die for their beliefs. The authors of these letters regularly alluded to biblical passages and even adopted the basic format of Paul's New Testament epistles. Writers of prison letters placed themselves within what historian Brad Gregory has called the "historical community of men and women who were unjustly persecuted," a community that "was alive, reborn and thriving with the modern witness of fellow believers."[31] Just as Paul's letters textually formed a distinctive Christian identity, in contradistinction to broader Jewish and Roman

26. Ruth Ahnert, *The Rise of Prison Literature in the Sixteenth Century* (Cambridge: Cambridge University Press, 2013), 102.

27. See Isaiah 48:10.

28. N. T. Wright, *Paul and the Faithfulness of God* (Minneapolis: Fortress Press), 434.

29. See, for examples, Philippians 1:13–16; Colossians 4:3, 18; Romans 5:3; 8:18, 31–39; and 2 Corinthians 7:4; 11:26.

30. See David M. Carr, *Holy Resilience: The Bible's Traumatic Origins* (New Haven: Yale University Press, 2014), chaps. 9–10.

31. Brad S. Gregory, *Salvation at Stake: Christian Martyrdom in Early Modern Europe*. Harvard Historical Studies (Cambridge: Harvard University Press, 1999), 25, 119 (first quote), 123 (second quote), 127–29.

communities, Reformation-era writers from prison textually claimed the mantle of the persecuted early Christian church, often as part of an effort to delegitimize competing factions.[32]

Protestant Reformer John Foxe brought many prison missives together in his massive sixteenth-century martyrology, *The Actes and Monuments*, known popularly as the *Book of Martyrs*. The book narrates the history of Christian persecution from the Roman Empire through the Reformation, adopting a strong dualistic framework that divides humanity between God's suffering Saints and satanic persecuting forces and institutions. The *Book of Martyrs* was a publishing phenomenon, going through multiple editions and continuing to be updated and expanded by subsequent editors following Foxe's death in 1587.[33] The work was also influential among Protestants in America well into the nineteenth century.[34]

Joseph Smith and his Latter-day Saint readers would have been well aware of the literary genre of letters from prison and the cultural authority of such missives. As religious studies scholar Philip Barlow has noted, Smith was "immersed in biblical language, whether by personal study of scripture, by listening to sermons, by natural participation in the biblical idioms of family conversation, or by some combination of these."[35] Smith

---

32. Gregory, *Salvation at Stake*, 123; Adrian Chastain Weimer, *Martyrs' Mirror: Persecution and Holiness in Early New England* (Oxford: Oxford University Press, 2011), 9.

33. See John N. King, *Foxe's* Book of Martyrs *and Early Modern Print Culture* (Cambridge: Cambridge University Press, 2006); see also johnfoxe.org.

34. See Weimer, *Martyrs' Mirror*; *Abridgment of the Book of Martyrs: To Which are Prefixed, the Living Testimonies of the Church of God, and Faithful Martyrs, in Different Ages of the World; and the Corrupt Fruits of the False Church, in the Time of the Apostacy. To this Work is Annexed an Account of the Just Judgments of God on Persecutors, &c. Also A Christian Plea Against Persecution for the Cause of Conscience* (New York: Samuel Wood, 1810); *Book of Martyrs; or A History of the Lives, Sufferings, and Triumphant Deaths, of the Primitive as well as Protestant Martyrs; from the Commencement of Christianity to the Latest Periods of Pagan and Popish Persecution. To Which is Added an Account of the Inquisition, the Bartholomew Massacre in France, the General Persecution Under Louis XIV. The Massacre in the Irish Rebellion in the Year 1641, and the Recent Persecutions of the Protestants in the South of France, Originally Composed by the Rev. John Fox, M. A. and Now Improved by Important Alternations and Additions By Rev. Charles A. Goodrich* (Hartford: Philemon Canfield, 1830); see also Michael H. Harris, "Books on the Frontier: The Extent and Nature of Book Ownership in Southern Indiana, 1800–1850," *Library Quarterly* 42, no. 4 (October 1972): 425–27.

35. Philip L. Barlow, *Mormons and the Bible: The Place of the Latter-day Saints in American Religion*, updated ed. (Oxford: Oxford University Press, 2013), 24.

was sufficiently familiar with New Testament epistolary forms to reproduce some of their elements in his own letters.[36]

Latter-day Saint Edward Stevenson recalled that during an 1834 visit with church members in Pontiac, Michigan, Smith examined the Stevensons' "large Book of Martyrs," stating that "he [Smith] felt a degree of sympathy for those martyrs and expressed hopes for meny of those who had suffered death for their faith as far as they understood." According to Stevenson, Smith borrowed the book for a time, taking it with him to his home in Ohio so he could study it in greater detail.[37] By the time of his imprisonment four years later, Smith was therefore well acquainted with prison letters in both the Bible and the *Book of Martyrs*.

Smith's Prison Letters and Approaches to Text-Making

During his five and a half months in Missouri state custody from 31 October 1838 to 16 April 1839, Smith authored or coauthored twelve extant letters. These letters are an important subset of Smith's broader epistolary corpus,[38] and they provide an illuminating case study into Smith's various methods of text-making. Six were personal missives, five of which were addressed to his wife, Emma Smith, updating her on his situation and expressing his concerns for her and their children.[39] The other personal letter was written to Latter-day Saint Presendia Huntington Buell, who had sought Smith's counsel on whether to depart Missouri with the Saints or

36. For example, an 1831 missive addressed to his brother, Hyrum, Smith opened with "I <have> had much Concirn about you but I always remember you in your <my> prayers." This echoed Romans 1:9; Ephesians 1:16; and Philippians 1:4. Smith closed the letter with "may the grace of God be and abide with you all," echoing Romans 16:20, 24; 1 Corinthians 16:23; Ether 12:41; and Moroni 9:26. (Letter to Hyrum Smith, 3 March 1831, in Michael Hubbard MacKay et al., eds., *Documents, Volume 1: July 1828–June 1831*, vol. 1 of the Documents series of *The Joseph Smith Papers*, ed. Ronald K. Esplin et al. (Salt Lake City: Church Historian's Press, 2013), 273 (hereafter *JSP*, D1).

37. Edward Stevenson, Autobiography, transcript, CHL.

38. Smith authored or coauthored more than three hundred extant letters, all of them written during the last fifteen years of his life. ("Revelations, Letters, Reports of Discourses, Editorials, Minutes of Meetings, and Other Documents," in Mackay et al., eds., *JSP*, D1: xxii.)

39. Letter to Emma Smith, 4 November 1838, in *JSP*, D6:279; Letter to Emma Smith, 12 November 1838, in *JSP*, D6:290; Letter to Emma Smith, 1 December 1838, in *JSP*, D6:293; Letter to Emma Smith, 21 March 1839, in *JSP*, D6:372; Letter to Emma Smith, 4 April 1839, in *JSP*, D6:401.

remain in the state with her disaffected husband, Norman Buell.[40] Another four of the missives were directed to either the Saints at large or to church leaders, attempting to provide some semblance of stability in the midst of the expulsion crisis.[41] The remaining two letters were addressed to non-Mormons in hopes of cultivating sympathy.[42]

Private Letters

Smith's letters to his wife were typically written in response either to his or her movements. He wrote the first on 4 November 1838, informing her of his safe journey from Far West to Independence, Missouri.[43] He wrote the second on 12 November just prior to the commencement of the preliminary hearing in Richmond, Missouri, referring to himself and his companions as "prisoners in chains" and closing as her "husband . . . in bonds and tribulation"—a Pauline turn of phrase.[44] The third, seen in Figure 6.2, was a short note written on 1 December informing her of his commitment to the Clay County jail in Liberty.[45] No letters between the couple survive for the remaining weeks of 1838 or the first two months of 1839, likely because Emma visited Smith in the jail three times during that period.[46]

Following her move from Missouri to Illinois in February 1839, Emma Smith wrote her husband on 7 March, informing him of her safe arrival and describing her pain at having to leave him behind.[47] Smith responded on 21 March, reciprocating by comparing his loneliness with that of Joseph

---

40. Although only a copy of the letter to Buell survives, Smith concluded it by saying, "I wanted to communicate something and I wrote this." (Letter to Presendia Huntington Buell, 15 March 1839, in *JSP*, D6:352.)

41. Letter to the Church in Caldwell County, MO, 16 December 1838, in *JSP*, D6:294; Letter to Heber C. Kimball and Brigham Young, 16 January 1839, in *JSP*, D6:310; Letter to the Church and E. Partridge, 20 March 1839, in *JSP*, D6:356; Letter to Edward Partridge and the Church, ca. 22 March 1839, in *JSP*, D6:388.

42. Letter to the Citizens of Jackson County, MO, 5 November 1838, in *JSP*, D6:282; Letter to Isaac Galland, 22 March 1839, in *JSP*, D6:376.

43. Letter to E. Smith, 4 November 1838, in *JSP*, D6:279.

44. Letter to E. Smith, 12 November 1838, in *JSP*, D6:290.

45. Letter to E. Smith, 1 December 1838, in *JSP*, D6:293.

46. Emma Smith visited her husband on 8–9 and 20–22 December 1838 and on 21 January 1839. (*The History of the Reorganized Church of Jesus Christ of Latter Day Saints*, 4 vols. (Lamoni, IA: 1896–1902. Reprint, Independence, Missouri: Herald Publishing House, [after 1976]), 2:309, 315.)

47. Letter from Emma Smith, March 1839, in *JSP*, D6:338.

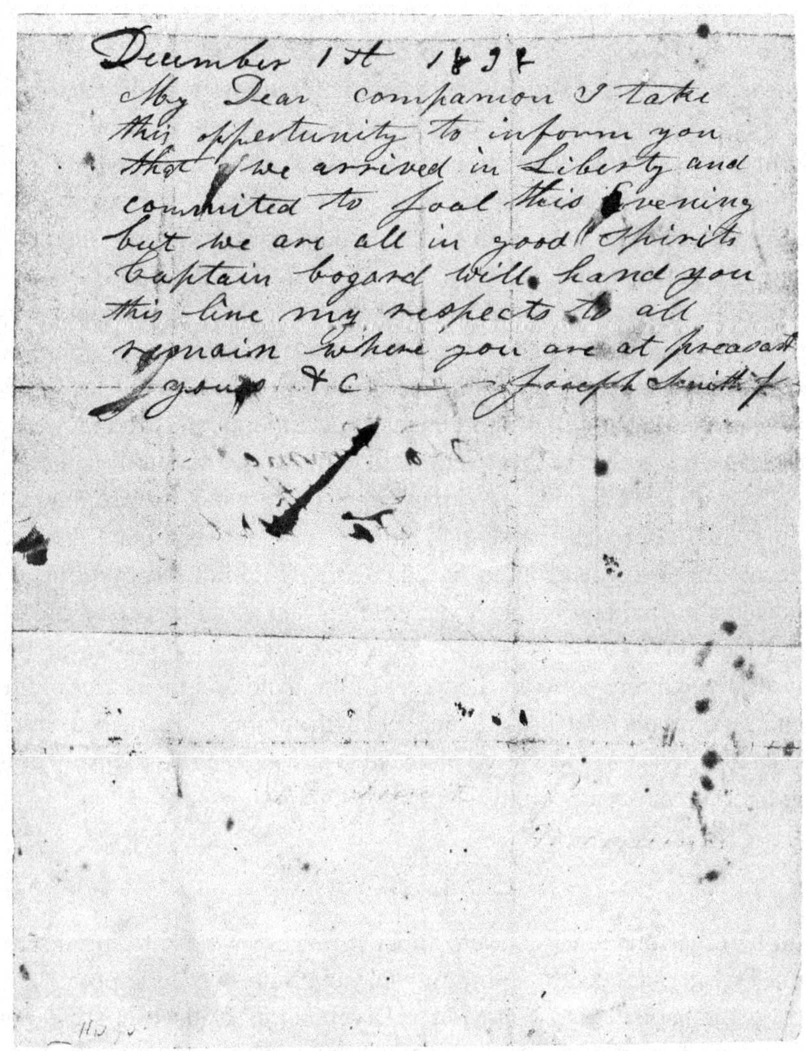

December 1st 1838
My Dear companion I take
this opportunity to inform you
that we arrived in Liberty and
committed to Joal this Evening
but we are all in good Spirits
captain bogard will hand you
this line my respects to all
remain where you are at present
yours &c — Joseph Smith Jr

FIGURE 6.2. Letter, Joseph Smith to Emma Smith, 1 December 1838.
Church History Library, Salt Lake City.

of Egypt, who queried whether his friends still remembered him.[48] Lastly, Smith wrote to his wife on 4 April, two days before he was removed from the jail and transported to a neighboring county for trial. He wrote that it had been "about five months and six days since I have been under the

48. Letter to E. Smith, 21 March 1839, in *JSP*, D6:372. See Genesis 43:7, 27; 45:3.

grimace, of a guard night and day, and within the walls grates and screeking ~~of~~ iron doors, of a lonesome dark durty prison." Smith doubted whether even angels, with all their supernatural power, could accurately describe his emotions or the "contemplations, of the mind under these circumstances," much less the earth-bound powers of the pen or tongue, to those "who never experiance what ~~I~~ we experience." He yearned for reunion so he could tell Emma his tale in person, sans the limiting mediation of paper, pen, and ink.[49]

Smith's prison letters to his wife are rare examples of documents written in his own hand. Only a small percentage of Smith's documentary corpus are holographs, and these are limited primarily to entries in his early journals, a handful of short business documents, and around twenty personal letters, most of these addressed to his wife.[50] As Smith explained in a May 1832 letter, he saw writing "in [his] own hand" as forming part of his "dut[i]es of a Husband and Father."[51] In historian Tamara Watkins Thornton's assessment, in an age increasingly dominated by print, an individual's own handwriting became closely tied with that person's identity. Nineteenth-century Americans came to see handwriting as "an almost mystical encounter between the writer of the hand and the reader of the hand, an intimate rendezvous of one soul with another."[52] As such, Smith's personal letters to his wife were intended to sustain their relationship during their forced separation.

Public Letters

Smith's other prison letters were public missives intended to sustain the broader Latter-day Saint community and cultivate outside support. The first general epistle was written on 16 December 1838, just over six weeks following his arrest and two weeks since his confinement in the Clay County jail. In the epistle, Smith condemned anti-Mormon religious and

49. Letter to E. Smith, 4 April 1839, in *JSP*, D6:401. Underlining in original.

50. See "Documents in Joseph Smith's Handwriting," http://www.josephsmithpapers.org/site/documents-in-joseph-smiths-handwriting, accessed 24 July 2016.

51. Conversely, he expected his wife to "communicate to [him] by [her] own hand," which would console him "to converse <with> [her] in this way in [his] lonely moments." (Letter to Emma Smith, 18 May 1834, in *JSP*, D4:50.)

52. Tamara Watkins Thornton, *Handwriting in America: A Cultural History* (New Haven: Yale University Press, 1996), 81.

civil elites as well as disaffected Mormon collaborators.[53] A month later, Smith's fellow prisoners Sidney Rigdon and Hyrum Smith—his counselors in the church's governing First Presidency—joined him in writing to church apostles Heber C. Kimball and Brigham Young, authorizing them to manage church affairs until the presidency's release.[54]

In late March 1839, after receiving letters from church leaders and family members who had recently relocated to Illinois, Smith and his fellow prisoners wrote two general epistles addressed to Bishop Edward Partridge and the Saints at large. The epistles explicitly framed the Saints' sufferings within the long history of God's persecuted people, promised church members that their ordeal would be temporary, and strongly affirmed that God continued to guide the church through Smith as a prophet.[55] Lastly, two letters were directed to outsiders. The first thanked the citizens of Jackson County for their kind reception of the Mormon prisoners in November 1838,[56] while the second informed Illinois land speculator Isaac Galland regarding the church's beliefs and the causes of the expulsion and discussed Galland's dual offer to sell land to displaced church members and influence public officials in the Saints' favor.[57]

Like most of Smith's writings, these prison epistles included extensive intertextual echoes, allusions, and quotations from the Bible.[58] As scholar of religion Philip Barlow has argued, Smith used "biblical building blocks" to produce "original religious creation[s]," drawing on the ancient scriptural texts to interpret the Saints' situation in the nineteenth century.[59] In religious historian Grant Underwood's words, Smith and other early

53. Letter to the Church in Caldwell County, MO, 16 December 1838, in *JSP*, D6:297–298.

54. Letter to Heber C. Kimball and Brigham Young, 16 January 1839, in *JSP*, D6:310.

55. Letter to the Church and E. Partridge, 20 March 1839, in *JSP*, D6:356; Letter to E. Partridge and the Church, ca. 22 March 1839, in *JSP*, D6:388.

56. Letter to the Citizens of Jackson County, MO, 5 November 1838, in *JSP*, D6:282. As no manuscript for this letter is extant, it is unknown who wrote it.

57. Letter to I. Galland, 22 March 1839, in *JSP*, D6:376.

58. On biblical intertextuality in the Book of Mormon and Smith's revelations, see Nicholas J. Frederick, *The Bible, Mormon Scripture, and the Rhetoric of Allusivity* (Teaneck, New Jersey: Farleigh Dickinson University Press, 2016); Seth Perry, "The Many Bibles of Joseph Smith: Textual, Prophetic, and Scholarly Authority in Early-National Bible Culture," *Journal of the American Academy of Religion* 84, no. 3 (September 2016): 750–75.

59. Barlow, *Mormons and the Bible*, 24–25. For example, in the general epistle written on 16 December 1838, Smith informally quoted Hebrews 10:26–29, a passage condemning those who "sin wilfully" after having "received the knowledge of the truth." Smith adapted the verses to apply to Mormon dissenters, who, in Smith's mind, were responsible for his

Mormons read the Bible typologically, meaning "the tendency to view the Old Testament as a book of anticipatory pictures of the person and work of Christ," or in Smith's case, the "restoration" of the primitive gospel and church in the latter days.[60] Just as God's people had suffered persecution anciently, his latter-day Saints would also endure suffering. For example, in the 16 December 1838 general epistle, shown in Figure 6.3, Smith quoted the Sermon on the Mount in Matthew 5:11–12, in which Jesus instructed his listeners to "rejoice" in persecution and to expect a great "reward in Heaven," since God's ancient prophets had also been persecuted. "Now brethren," Smith noted, "if any men ever had reason to claim this promise, we are the men."[61] In another instance, Smith wrote "Dearly and beloved Brethren we see that peralas times have come as was testified of," interpreting 2 Timothy 3:1 to refer to the persecution of the Saints.[62] Reading the Bible typologically allowed Smith to place his experience and that of his people within the long history of God's persecuted people.

Smith's prison epistles also alluded to Foxe's *Book of Martyrs*. In the 20 March 1839 general epistle, Smith declared that he was "held by the power of mobocracy under the exterminating reign of his excelancy the Governor Lilburn W. Boggs."[63] Referring to Boggs's "reign" echoed Foxe's use of that word to describe the regimes of persecuting monarchs such as the Roman Emperor Nero and the Catholic Queen Mary.[64] In another likely echo of the *Book of Martyrs*, Smith portrayed his religious opponents as "priests," a curious designation given that most if not all the leading anti-Mormons in Missouri were Protestants from denominations that had rejected the title and office of priest as a Catholic corruption,[65] while Smith's own

---

imprisonment. (Letter to the Church in Caldwell County, MO, 16 December 1838, in *JSP*, D6:309.)

60. Grant Underwood, *The Millenarian World of Early Mormonism* (Urbana: University of Illinois Press, 1993), 58–59.

61. Letter to the Church in Caldwell County, MO, 16 December 1838, in *JSP*, D6:302.

62. See Letter to the Church and E. Partridge, 20 March 1839, in *JSP*, D6:363; see also Letter to P. Buell, 15 March 1839, in *JSP*, D6:355.

63. Letter to the Church and E. Partridge, 20 March 1839, in *JSP*, D6:365.

64. *Book of Martyrs*, 69, 214.

65. Protestant Reformers rejected the office of priest because, in their view, the Catholic priesthood had created a hierarchy that falsely mediated between lay people and God. Martin Luther and others adopted instead the doctrine of the "Priesthood of All Believers" and cast ministers, pastors, and other leaders as part of, rather than distinct from, the laity. (See Cyril Eastwood, *The Priesthood of All Believers: An Examination of the Doctrine from the Reformation*

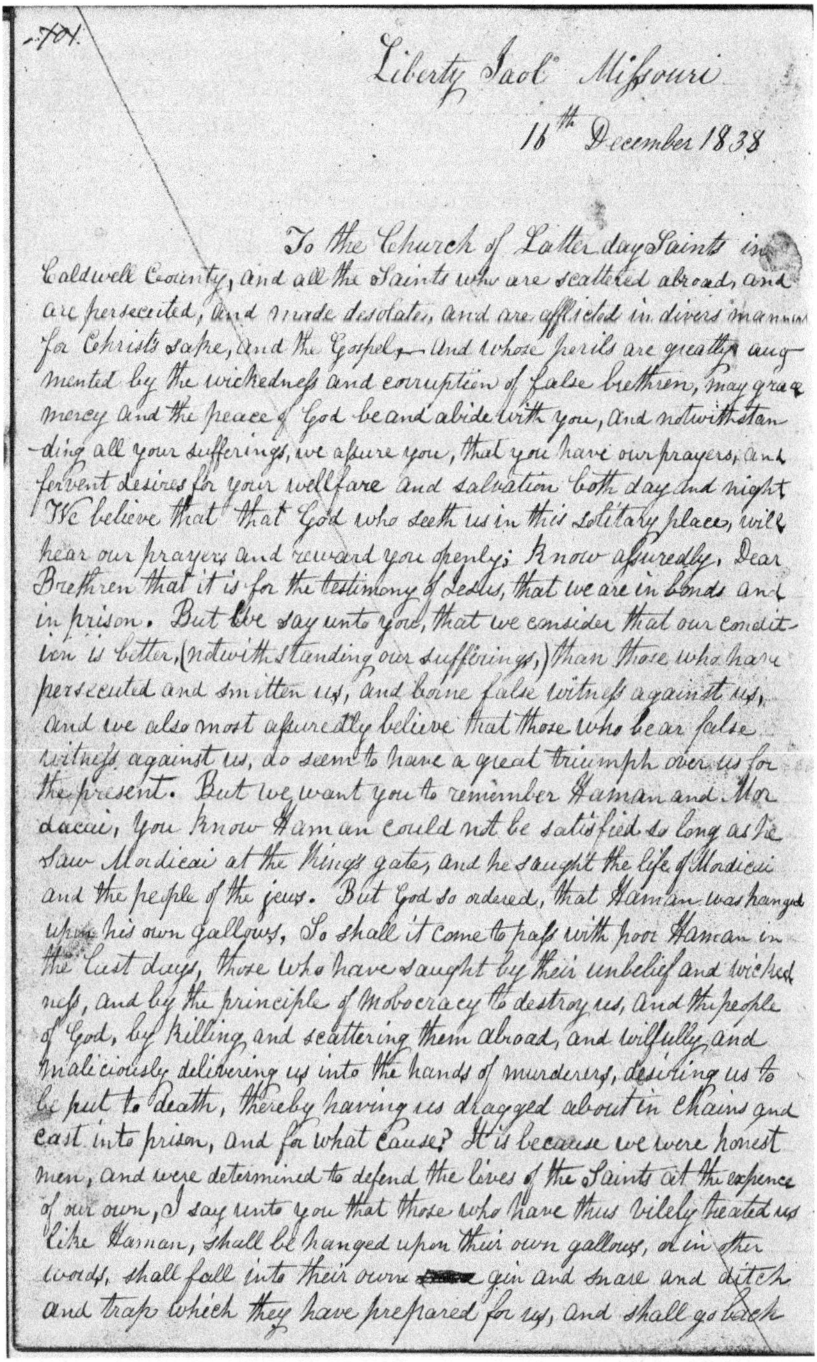

101.

Liberty Jail Missouri

16th December 1838

To the Church of Latter day Saints in Caldwell County, and all the Saints who are scattered abroad, and are persecuted, and made desolate, and are afflicted in divers manners for Christs sake, and the Gospel, And whose perils are greatly augmented by the wickedness and corruption of false brethren, may grace mercy and the peace of God be and abide with you, and notwithstanding all your sufferings, we assure you, that you have our prayers, and fervent desires for your wellfare and salvation both day and night We believe that that God who seeth us in this solitary place, will hear our prayers and reward you openly; know assuredly, Dear Brethren that it is for the testimony of Jesus, that we are in bonds and in prison. But we say unto you, that we consider that our condition is better, (notwithstanding our sufferings,) than those who have persecuted and smitten us, and borne false witness against us, and we also most assuredly believe that those who bear false witness against us, do seem to have a great triumph over us for the present. But we want you to remember Haman and Mordecai; You know Haman could not be satisfied so long as he saw Mordecai at the Kings gate, and he saught the life of Mordecai and the people of the jews. But God so ordered, that Haman was hanged upon his own gallows, So shall it come to pass with poor Haman in the last days, those who have saught by their unbelief and wickedness, and by the principle of Mobocracy to destroy us, and the people of God, by killing and scattering them abroad, and wilfully and maliciously delivering us into the hands of murderers, desiring us to be put to death, thereby having us dragged about in chains and cast into prison, and for what cause? It is because we were honest men, and were determined to defend the lives of the Saints at the expence of our own, I say unto you that those who have thus vilely treated us like Haman, shall be hanged upon their own gallows, or in other words, shall fall into their own gin and snare and ditch and trap which they have prepared for us, and shall go back

FIGURE 6.3. Joseph Smith's general epistle to the church, 16 December 1838, in "General" church record book, p. 101.

Church History Library, Salt Lake City.

ecclesiastical edifice included the office.[66] Casting the Saints' enemies as "priests" invoked Foxe's depiction of the state-sponsored persecutions of the Reformation era, when the Catholic priesthood prosecuted and executed violators of heresy laws.[67] Further extending this image, Smith wrote to his followers that "We have never dissembled, nor will we for the sake of our lives." Dissembling, or concealing personal convictions under pressure to avert suspicion, was a word commonly used in the *Book of Martyrs* to describe individuals who denied their faith under examination by religious authorities in order to avoid incarceration or execution.[68]

The majority of Smith's public prison letters have survived only as copies or in printed form, obscuring the details of their composition. However, manuscripts of the two March 1839 general epistles are extant, providing important insights into Smith's text-making process for letters intended for public consumption. Even before pen was set to paper, Smith and his companions doubtless discussed the themes that would be prominent in the epistles—the significance of persecution and suffering, the question of why God had allowed the catastrophe to occur, and how the Saints would survive the expulsion with their identity as a people intact. The March epistles—perhaps echoing the apostle Paul's epistolary practice of naming his companions in the greetings of his letters[69] —were rhetorically framed as joint compositions of all the prisoners, with frequent use of the first-person plural voice and with each man signing his name to the missives.

When it came to actually composing the documents, however, Smith was the dominant voice, dictating the words of the epistles to fellow prisoner and scribe Alexander McRae.[70] Likely reflecting Smith's own discomfort with the pen,[71] he had long preferred to dictate official documents to

---

to the Present Day [1960; repr., Eugene, Oregon: Wipf and Stock Publishers, 2009].) For names of prominent anti-Mormons, with their Protestant affiliations, see Sidney Rigdon et al., "To the Publick," pp. 16–17[a], 22[a], 26[a], [27b], [31b], Joseph Smith Collection, CHL.

66. See Revelation, ca. April 1830, in *JSP*, D1:124 [D&C 20:46–52].

67. For examples, see *Book of Martyrs*, 129, 206, 422, 518.

68. See *Book of Martyrs*, 324, 416, 464, 476, 477, 478.

69. See, for examples, 1 Corinthians 1:1; 2 Corinthians 1:1; and Galatians 1:1–2.

70. In Smith's 21 March 1839 letter to Emma Smith, he explicitly noted having "dectated" the 20 March 1839 general epistle. (Letter to E. Smith, 21 March 1839, in *JSP*, D6:373.)

71. Smith frequently commented on his discomfort with writing. In a June 1832 letter, for example, Smith apologized to Emma Smith for his "inability" to adequately convey his "ideas in writing." The following month, Smith recorded a prayer pleading for divine deliverance

scribes rather than write them himself.[72] "A prophet cannot be scribe," Joseph Smith remarked in 1843. "For a man to be a great man, he must not dwell upon small things; though he may enjoy them."[73] Based on eyewitness descriptions of Smith's dictation process it is possible to reconstruct how the March 1839 general epistles might have been produced. Accounts of Smith's writing process consistently describe a scenario in which a scribe would sit at a table with paper and writing instruments while Smith, seated nearby, would dictate each word and sentence deliberately. Parley P. Pratt, who witnessed this process on multiple occasions, recalled that "each sentence was uttered slowly and very distinctly, and with a pause between each, sufficiently long for it to be recorded, by an ordinary writer, in long hand."[74]

This slow and deliberate process may be evidenced in the two surviving manuscripts of the ca. 22 March 1839 general epistle: a rough draft and a fair copy, presented in Figures 6.4 and 6.5. Both documents were inscribed by Alexander McRae on the same size of paper (12 ½ × 7 ¾ inches), thereby allowing easy comparison.[75] The script of the rough draft is relatively loose, as if McRae were attempting to capture Smith's words

"from the little narrow prison," the "totel darkness of paper pen and ink," and the "crooked broken scattered and imperfect language." In Smith's view, only in the eternities would he be free from this linguistic imprisonment. (Letter to E. Smith, 6 June 1832, in *JSP*, D2:256; Letter to W. Phelps, 27 November 1834, in *JSP*, D2:320.)

72. Smith evidently dictated nearly all of the more than 500 pages—270,000 words—of the Book of Mormon manuscript in 1829. In addition, Smith appears to have dictated most if not all of the shorter texts known as "commandments" or "revelations." See Royal Skousen, "Translating the Book of Mormon: Evidence from the Original Manuscript," in *Book of Mormon Authorship Revisited: The Evidence of Ancient Origins* (Provo, Utah: FARMS, 1997), 71–93; Royal Skousen, *The Original Manuscript of the Book of Mormon: Typographical Facsimile of the Extant Text* (Provo, Utah: FARMS, 2001), 278; "Joseph Smith as Revelator and Translator," in Robin Scott Jensen et al., eds., *Revelations and Translations: Manuscript Revelation Books*, vol. 1 of the Revelations and Translation series of *The Joseph Smith Papers*, ed. Dean C. Jessee et al. (Salt Lake City: Church Historian's Press, 2011), xxii (hereafter *JSP*, R1); Robin Scott Jensen, "'Rely Upon the Things That Are Written': Text, Context, and the Creation of Mormon Revelatory Records" (master's thesis, University of Wisconsin-Milwaukee, 2009), 114–37.

73. Journal, 4 March 1843, in *JSP*, J2:296. Underlining in original.

74. Parley P. Pratt, *The Autobiography of Parley Parker Pratt, One of the Twelve Apostles of the Church of Jesus Christ of Latter-Day Saints*, ed. Parley P. Pratt Jr. (New York: Russell Brothers, 1874), 48; see also Jensen, "Text, Context," 129.

75. Joseph Smith et al., Liberty, MO, to Edward Partridge and the Church, Quincy, IL, ca. 22 March 1839, rough draft, Revelations Collection, CHL; Joseph Smith et al., Liberty, MO, to Edward Partridge and the Church, Quincy, IL, ca. 22 March 1839, fair copy, Revelations Collection, CHL.

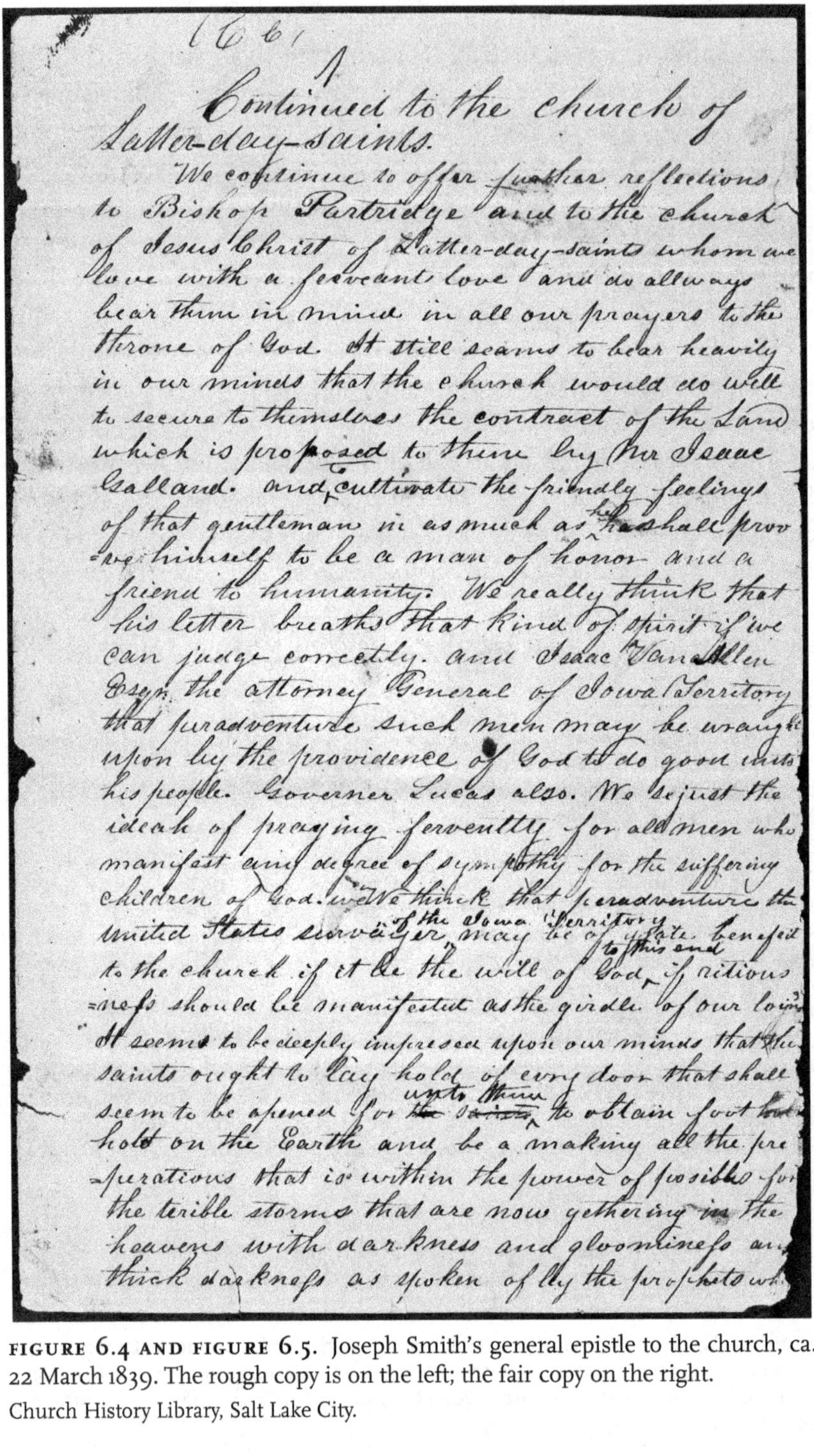

166

Continued to the church of Latter-day-saints.

We continue to offer further reflections to Bishop Partridge and to the church of Jesus Christ of Latter-day-saints whom we love with a fervent love and do allways bear them in mind in all our prayers to the throne of God. It still seams to bear heavily in our minds that the church would do well to secure to themselves the contract of the Land which is proposed to them by Mr Isaac Galland. and cultivate the friendly feelings of that gentleman in as much as he shall prove himself to be a man of honor and a friend to humanity. We really think that his letter breaths that kind of spirit if we can judge correctly. and Isaac Van Allen Esqr. the attorney General of Iowa Territory that peradventure such men may be wrought upon by the providence of God to do good unto his people. Governer Lucas also. We sugest the ideah of praying fervently for all men who manifest any degree of sympathy for the suffering children of God. We think that peradventure the united States survayer of the Iowa Territory may be of great benefit to the church if it be the will of God to this end if ritiousness should be manifested as the girdle of our loins. It seems to be deeply impressed upon our minds that the saints ought to lay hold of every door that shall seem to be opened unto them to obtain foot hold on the Earth and be a making all the preparations that is within the power of posibles for the terible storms that are now gethering in the heavens with darkness and gloominess and thick darkness as spoken of by the prophets wh

FIGURE 6.4 AND FIGURE 6.5. Joseph Smith's general epistle to the church, ca. 22 March 1839. The rough copy is on the left; the fair copy on the right.
Church History Library, Salt Lake City.

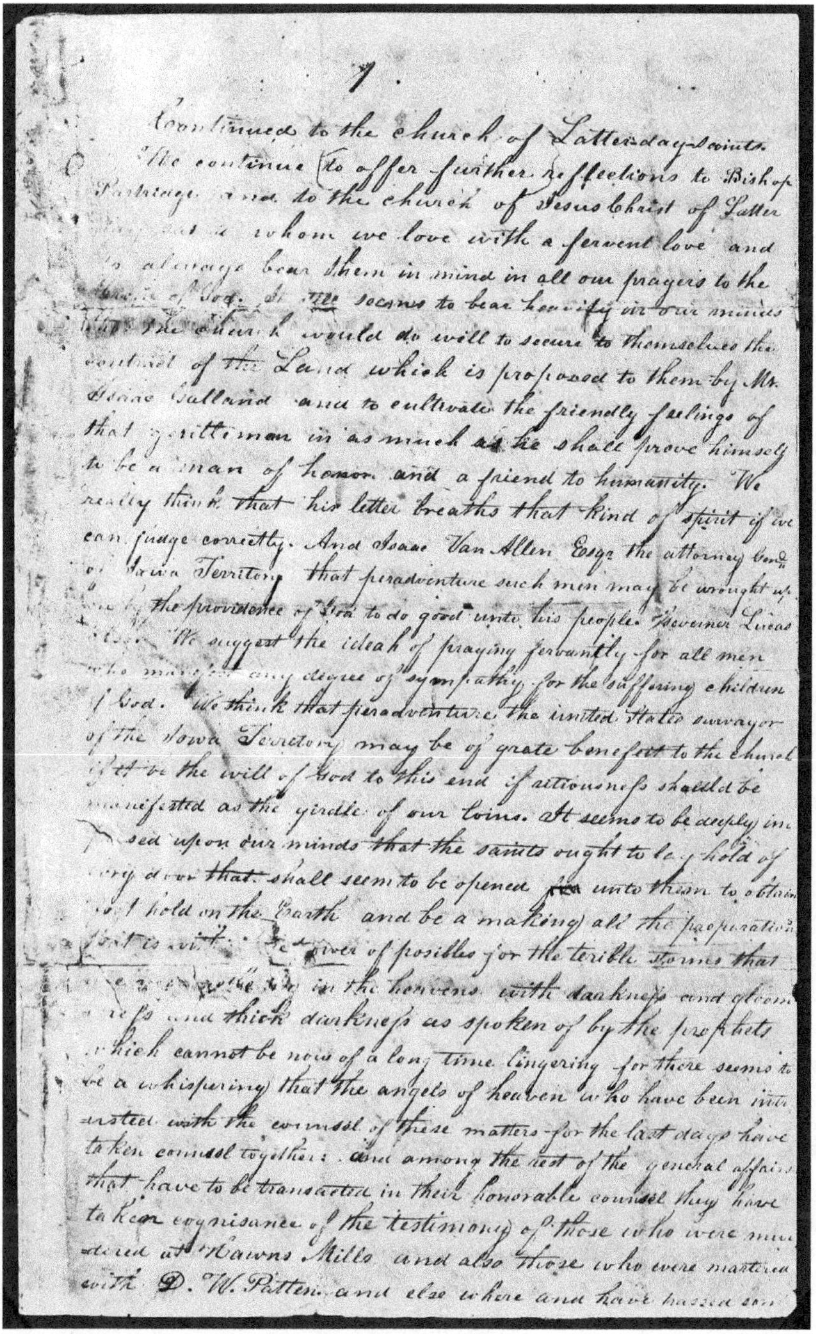

7.

Continued to the church of Latter-day-Saints.
We continue to offer further reflections to Bishop
Partridge and to the church of Jesus Christ of Latter
day saints whom we love with a fervent love and
do always bear them in mind in all our prayers to the
throne of God. It still seems to bear heavily on our minds
that the church would do well to secure to themselves the
contract of the Land which is proposed to them by Mr.
Isaac Galland and to cultivate the friendly feelings of
that gentleman in as much as he shall prove himself
to be a man of honor and a friend to humanity. We
really think that his letter breaths that kind of spirit if we
can judge correctly. And Isaac Van Allen Esqr the attorney Genl
of Iowa Territory that peradventure such men may be wrought upon
by the providence of God to do good unto his people. Governor Lucas
also. We suggest the ideah of praying fervently for all men
who manifest any degree of sympathy for the suffering children
of God. We think that peradventure the united states survayor
of the Iowa Territory may be of grate benefit to the church
if it be the will of God to this end if ritiousness should be
manifested as the girdle of our loins. It seems to be deeply impressed
upon our minds that the saints ought to lay hold of
every door that shall seem to be opened unto them to obtain
foot hold on the Earth and be a making all the preparation
that is within their power of posibles for the terible storms that
are now gathering in the heavens with darkness and gloominess
and thick darkness as spoken of by the prophets
which cannot be now of a long time lingering for there seems to
be a whispering that the angels of heaven who have been intrusted
with the counsel of these matters for the last days have
taken counsel together: and among the rest of the general affairs
that have to be transacted in their honorable counsel they have
taken cognisance of the testimony of those who were murdered
at Hawns Mills and also those who were martered
with D. W. Patten and else where and have passed som

FIGURE 6.4 AND FIGURE 6.5. (Continued)

as he spoke them. The script of the fair copy, in contrast, is significantly tighter, allowing McRae to fit on average two to three more words per line than the rough draft. Despite both drafts being written on paper of the same size, the rough draft is more than two pages longer than the fair copy.

Following the initial inscription of the dictation draft, Smith and McRae worked together to revise the rough manuscript, adding interlinear corrections and additions to correct misheard words,[76] insert words McRae had omitted presumably inadvertently as he sought to keep up with the dictation,[77] expand biblical allusions,[78] and add new words and phrases that augmented the meaning of the original inscription.[79] After completing these revisions, Smith and the other prisoners signed the epistle, and it was folded and addressed for mailing, signaling that Smith initially viewed this corrected draft as complete. For reasons that remain unclear, however, the epistle was then unfolded, and McRae made the fair copy, silently incorporating the corrections made on the revised dictation draft. Smith and McRae then read through the fair copy, making additional small corrections. Each of the prisoners then signed the fair copy, after which time it also was folded and addressed for mailing. Taking the ca. 22 March 1839 general epistle as a model therefore illuminates to some degree Smith's method of textual production for documents intended for broad circulation. The textual record for the other public prison letters is more fragmentary, but what has survived indicates that Smith used a similar method with the other compositions.[80]

Taken together, Smith's twelve extant prison letters offer an important window into Smith's various approaches to text-making. His private letters to his wife were personal and intimate, leading him to write them with

76. On page five, for example, McRae wrote "thine elder one." Smith afterward canceled "one" and inserted "son"—words that sound similar but are visually distinct—above the line.

77. For example, on page 8, McRae initially wrote "shackles and of hell" but later inserted "fetters" above the line between "and" and "of."

78. For example, on the second page McRae initially inscribed "the holy spirit which maketh intersession for us knight and day," an allusion to Romans 8:26. Above the line, McRae subsequently inserted "with groning's that cannot be uttered," augmenting the allusion to the Pauline text.

79. In another example, McRae initially wrote "all these things shall give thee experience" on page five. Smith afterward inserted "and shall be for thy good" above the line.

80. See Historical Introduction to Letter to the Church in Caldwell Co., MO. 16 December 1838, in *JSP*, D6:297–98; Historical Introduction to Letter to the Church and E. Partridge, 20 March 1839, in *JSP*, D6:358.

this own hand. For documents intended for broader circulation, Smith's process was more collaborative, encouraging contributions from his companions and utilizing their services as scribes. Nevertheless, it was also a process over which Smith maintained a substantial degree of control, from the dictation of the initial text to careful oversight of revisions and the preparation of subsequent drafts. This careful scrutiny was doubtless essential given Smith's need to directly address the displaced Latter-day Saints and the lingering questions regarding the root causes of the conflict, the viability of Smith's own prophetic leadership during the crisis, and the survival of the movement.

Suffering and Revelation

Smith responded to these questions in his prison letters, relying on the rhetorical authority inherent in the voice of the imprisoned sufferer. As noted, his letters paralleled other examples of the genre, revealing extensive biblical intertextuality and echoing language in Foxe's *Book of Martyrs*. Yet Smith's letters departed from the conventions of the genre in at least one important way by incorporating extended sections written not in Smith's voice, but rather the voice of Deity. Smith fused the genre of "thus saith the Lord" revelations he had established in earlier years with the genre of the prison letter.[81] The revelatory portions of Smith's letters offered comfort and counsel to Smith in his incarcerated condition and affirmed that his status as a prophet remained unchanged despite the catastrophic turn of events. Within the context of the crisis of confidence surrounding his leadership, these revelatory irruptions provided the faithful with evidence that he remained a prophet.

Smith had based much of his public persona as a Judeo-Christian prophet on his ability to produce new scripture, most notably in the Book of Mormon but also in the shorter texts known as commandments or revelations. As Smith's biographer Richard Lyman Bushman has observed, in the revelations "the voice is pure in that God alone is speaking; Joseph Smith, who spoke the words for God is totally absent from the rhetorical space. One relationship prevails in these revelations: God speaking to his

81. In a 27 November 1832 letter to church member William W. Phelps, Smith had similarly included a portion written in the voice of deity. (Letter to W. Phelps, 27 November 1832, in *JSP*, D2:315–21.)

people."[82] Once committed to writing, the texts were treated as scripture as his followers read them, made personal copies, and sought to apply the revelations' counsel to themselves. The texts were published in the church's newspapers and then in book form, dramatically increasing their circulation.[83]

In the revelations, as Bushman explains, Latter-day Saints "heard the pure voice of God speaking, not just the voice of Joseph their president and counselor. . . . The believers heard that voice and believed it; in times of stress, they wanted to hear it again."[84] Winter 1838–1839 was such a time of stress. As Elizabeth Haven wrote in February 1839, "When we shall enjoy the society of the Prophet, and know the will of the Lord concerning the church, we know not. We sigh and long for his deliverance. The word of the Lord is precious to us."[85] Albert Perry Rockwood similarly stated his frustration that "we have none to tell us what to do by direct Revelation." He spoke for many Mormons in stating, "We want our Prophet."[86]

Smith's letters answered Rockwood's plea by including multiple sections written in the voice of Deity. Near the end of the 16 December 1838 general epistle, Smith wrote an extended condemnation of the dissenters who had abandoned the faith in Missouri and had in many cases cooperated with the church's opponents. Smith then explained that he had received divine confirmation that "the keys of the kingdom"—a reference to Matthew 16:19, in which Jesus gave the apostle Peter authority to perform acts on earth that would be recognized in heaven—remained in Smith's possession. Smith followed with the text of the revelation: "'Fear not, but be of good cheer. For the keys ~~of~~ which I gave unto you are yet with

82. Richard Lyman Bushman, "The 'Little, Narrow Prison' of Language: The Rhetoric of Revelation," in *Believing History: Latter-day Saint Essays*, eds. Reid L. Neilson and Jed Woodworth (New York: Columbia University Press, 2004), 253.

83. See Jensen, "Text, Context"; *JSP*, R1; and Robin Scott Jensen et al., eds., *Revelations and Translations, Volume 2: Published Revelations*, vol. 2 of the Revelations and Translations series of *The Joseph Smith Papers*, ed. Dean C. Jessee et al. (Salt Lake City: Church Historian's Press, 2011).

84. Bushman, "Rhetoric of Revelation," 259.

85. Elizabeth Haven, Quincy, IL, to Elizabeth Howe Bullard, Holliston, MA, 24 February 1839, Barlow Family Collection, CHL; see also Melissa Dodge, Adams Co., IL, to William T. Morgan, Henderson, NY, 23 June 1839, William T. Morgan Correspondence, CHL.

86. Albert Perry Rockwood, Quincy, IL, to "Dearly Beloved Father," 1839, copy, Rockwood Journal, CHL.

you'!"[87] Smith recorded this revelation just over two weeks after the conclusion of the November preliminary hearing at which several disaffected former Mormons testified against him. The revelation doubtless buoyed Smith's confidence within the jail, and he likely knew that it would have a similar impact on church members who were wavering in their faith. God was still connected with his prophet, and his prophet was still connected with his people.

Following the opening greeting of the 20 March 1839 general epistle, Smith narrated the wrongs suffered by the Saints in Missouri. He called the conflict "a lamentable tail yea a sorriful tail" that had no parallel "among the nations where Kings and tyrants are enthroned" or "among the savages of the wilderness." Smith alluded to instances of the mob stealing food from starving church members, committing sexual violence against Latter-day Saint women, and mutilating the bodies of murdered Mormons. He then followed with a psalm reminiscent of biblical laments, asking God where he was and how long his hand would be stayed, how long his eye would behold, and how long his ear would hear the cries of the Saints "before thine hart shall be softened towards them and thy bowels be moved with compassion to-words them." Invoking God as the omnipotent creator, Smith pleaded with the Lord to vindicate the Saints.[88]

Smith then recounted the prisoners' unsuccessful efforts, both legal and extralegal, to obtain release, while maintaining that he was innocent of the charges against them. His continued incarceration was evidence of Missouri's perfidy rather than his guilt. He related that letters from the prisoners' family and friends had recently arrived at the jail. The receipt of correspondence caused overpowering emotions, that "the voice of inspiration steals along and whispers my son pease be unto thy soul." An extended section in the voice of Deity followed, promising Smith that his suffering would be temporary and that his friends would stand by him. The revelation proceeded to condemn those who had betrayed Smith and the church.[89]

The ca. 22 March 1839 epistle included two extended portions in the voice of Deity. The first was a meditation on Matthew 22:14, "For many are called, but few are chosen." The section warned against those who

87. Letter to the Church in Caldwell Co., MO, 16 December 1838, in *JSP*, D6:309.

88. Letter to the Church and E. Partridge, 20 March 1839, in *JSP*, D6:362.

89. Letter to the Church and E. Partridge, 20 March 1839, in *JSP*, D6:366–67.

"aspire to the honors of men," while counseling that those who are chosen exercise power "only by persuasion by long suffering by gentleness and meekness and love unfeigned [and] by kindness." The section also promised that the Holy Ghost would be the "constant companion" giving revelation to those who exercised power righteously. The second section narrated Smith's personal suffering in Missouri, including being torn from his family, falsely charged with crimes, and imprisoned. The voice of Deity promised him that "these things shall give thee experience and shall be for thy good," before reminding him that "the son of man hath descended below" all of Smith's afflictions. The voice then asked, "art thou greater than he?" This irruption of revelation concluded by admonishing that Smith should not fear men, as God was with him and would sustain him for the remainder of his life.[90]

Aside from these sections in the voice of Deity, portions of the letters written in Smith's own voice also reassured church members that despite the intense suffering experienced by the Saints in Missouri, God remained "the author" of Mormonism: "It is by him we received our birth, it was by his voice that we were called to ~~in~~ a dispensation of his gospel in the begining of the fullness of tim[e]s [and] it was by him we received the book of mormon." Smith conceded that "hell may poor forth its rage like the burning lavy [lava] of mount vesuvias or of Etna or of the most terible of the burning mountains." But, he concluded, "yet shall mormonism stand."[91] The conflict of 1838 was not evidence that God had abandoned the Saints or their prophet. Rather, Smith believed that suffering and persecution were actually part of the divine plan. God "hath said that he would have a tried people that he would purge them as gold now we think that this time he has chosen his own crusible wherein we have been tryed." The Saints' sufferings in Missouri had been "a tryal of [their] faith equal to that of Abraham," and other ancient people who suffered affliction for God's cause "will not have were off [whereof] to bost over [the Mormons] in the day of judgment." Yet just as God had provided Abraham a ram that served as proxy for Isaac in the commanded sacrifice, Smith held that the Lord would deliver the Saints from their troubles.[92]

90. Letter to E. Partridge and the Church, ca. 22 March 1839, in *JSP*, D6:395.

91. Letter to the Church and E. Partridge, 20 March 1839, in *JSP*, D6:370–71.

92. Letter to the Church and E. Partridge, 20 March 1839, in *JSP*, D6:367.

Expanding upon traditional understandings of suffering as a purifying act, Smith claimed that suffering persecution would lead to additional revelation. One of the principal attractions for early Mormon converts to Smith's message was the prospect that God had again opened the heavens and was pouring down new revelation and knowledge through his prophet. In his letter to Presendia Buell, Smith commented that his "heart bleeds continually" as he "contemplate[d] the distress of the Church." He yearned for reunion with his fellow Saints and stated that he "would not shrink at toil and hardship to render them comfort and consolation." He "want[ed] the blessing once more to lift [his] voice in the midst of the Saints" so he could "pour out [his] soul to God for their instruction" and more fully share with them the plan God had revealed for the church. He further explained that his suffering had given him new insights, even revelation. The Saints' troubles "will only give us that knowledge to understand the minds of the Ancients." New knowledge and wisdom had been brought forth out of the trial. "For my part," Smith concluded, "I think I never could have felt as I now do if I had not suffered the wrongs that I have suffered."[93]

Smith elucidated some of this new knowledge only a few days later. In the 20 March 1839 general epistle, Smith stated that opposition from Boggs and "his murderous crew" would not "hinder the Almighty from pooring down knoledge from ⟨heaven⟩ upon the heads of the Latter day saints." Smith further explained to church members that "after [their] tribulations" God would "give unto [them] knowledge . . . that has not been revealed since the world was untill now which our fathers have wated with anxious expectation to be revealed in the last times." Smith then introduced the earliest documented explicit reference to distinctive Mormon doctrines such as the plurality of gods and the divine council of heavenly beings, ideas that he claimed had been "held in reserve" for those "who have indured valiently for the Gospel of Jesus Christ."[94] In his prison letters, Smith therefore made sense of the Saints' suffering in Missouri by framing it as an essential part of God's unfolding plan to reveal new knowledge to his people in the last days.

93. Letter to P. Buell, 15 March 1839, in *JSP*, D6:355.

94. Letter to the Church and E. Partridge, 20 March 1839, in *JSP*, D6:369; see Samuel Brown, *In Heaven as It Is on Earth: Joseph Smith and the Early Mormon Conquest of Death* (New York: Oxford University Press, 2011).

Suffering and Textual Community

On 11 April 1839, Mary Fielding Smith wrote her husband, Hyrum Smith, that she and others in Quincy, Illinois, had "seen the Epistols to the Church and read them several times," referring to the 20 March and ca. 22 March letters. "They seem like food for the hungrey," she explained. "We have taken great pleasure on perusing them."[95] Her remarks provide a window into the textual community that existed among the Saints at a time when their physical community was shaken and scattered. As Elizabeth Haven wrote in February 1839, Mormons in Illinois yearned for "the society of the Prophet, and [to] know the will of the Lord concerning the church," as "the word of the Lord [was] precious to [them]."[96] Smith's followers treated his general prison epistles with deep reverence, as they pointed to his imprisonment and his prison letters as evidence of his character and of his prophetic authority in the midst of suffering and crisis. Church members viewed his prison letters as documents of special significance, copying and publishing them and eventually adding selections of the prison epistles to the Latter-day Saint scriptural canon.

That at least some Mormons saw the letters as evidence of Smith's prophetic authority is evident in a May 1839 letter written by Latter-day Saint David Foote. Writing to relatives in New York, Foote commented that they had doubtless "seen and heard many things" that had caused them "to doubt the truth of Mormonism," referring in part to newspaper accounts of the Missouri conflict that cast the Saints in an unfavorable light. He also referenced "many" fellow Saints who had "dissented from the church" and had "gone their own way" in the wake of the Missouri conflict. Foote then presented reasons to believe in Mormonism, including the religion's promise to "expand the mysteries of the kingdom." This would allow its adherents to "obtain to the ministering of angels and all the gifts of God mentioned in scripture," referring to revelation's key appeal to early Mormons.

Foote's most extensive proof of the truthfulness of Mormonism was Smith's willingness to suffer imprisonment for the cause. "Where is there a man," he asked, "that would suffer as much as Joseph Smith jr. has for

95. Mary Fielding Smith, Quincy, IL, to Hyrum Smith, 11 April 1839, Mary Fielding Smith Collection, CHL.

96. Elizabeth Haven, Quincy, IL, to Elizabeth Howe Bullard, Holliston, MA, 24 February 1839, Barlow Family Collection, CHL.

the sake of speculation"? Where in all of this was there any financial interest or gain to be had? Foote copied into his letter an eleven-line excerpt from the 16 December 1838 epistle, in which Smith assured the Saints that God was sustaining the prisoners in the jail. "We have never dissembled, nor will we for the sake of our lives." Foote took this assertion as evidence of Smith's sincerity: "Now if Joseph Smith jr. was not possessed with the spirit of God would he not long ago have given up his idea and called it a bad job[?]" Perhaps more significant for Foote, Smith's willingness to suffer in prison was evidence of his prophetic authority.[97]

Mormon apostle Parley P. Pratt interpreted the prison epistles as textual proof of Smith's prophetic calling. When Pratt published the ca. 22 March 1839 letter in the December 1840 issue of the *Millennial Star*, the church's newspaper in England, he stated that the epistle "exhibit[ed] the spirit of courage, boldness, faith, assurance, charity, wisdom, and virtue with which it pleased God to endow him." Pratt believed that Smith's prison letter served as an effective rejoinder to publications that "slandered and vilified" Smith's character. Pratt therefore saw the letter as a textual window into Smith's soul "under the most trying circumstances which it is possible for human nature to endure."[98]

These interpretations of Smith's general epistles by Foote and Pratt illuminate Mary Fielding Smith's remark that the letters were "food for the hungrey." They also help explain why several church members in the wake of the Missouri expulsion undertook the laborious task of copying by hand the prison epistles. As noted above, Smith himself worked with his fellow prisoners to make at least two copies of the letters within the prison, evidently with the intention of broadening their circulation, a practice historian David Hall refers to as scribal publication.[99] Furthermore, Smith directed Emma Smith to "have the [20 March 1839] Epistole coppyed immediately," so that Smith's parents could read it, and then forward it "to the Bretheren."[100] Extant copies indicate that Smith's directive was followed, with copies made by church leaders such as Edward Partridge as well as ordinary Saints like Albert Perry Rockwood, who appears to have sent his copies of the March general epistles to relatives in Massachusetts,

97. David Foote, Columbus, IL, to Thomas Clement, Dryden, NY, 14 May 1839, CHL.

98. See "Letter from Elder Jos. Smith," *Millennial Star*, December 1840, 1:193.

99. David D. Hall, *Ways of Writing: The Practice and Politics of Text-Making in Seventeenth-Century New England*. Material Texts (Philadelphia: University of Pennsylvania Press, 2008), 33.

100. Letter to E. Smith, 21 March 1839, in *JSP*, D6:375.

thereby extending the letters' circulation beyond the main body of Saints in Illinois.[101] Ultimately, as Hall explains, "texts had a currency that exceeded the specific number of copies." This occurred as texts were "copied and recopied, passed from hand to hand, mentioned in conversations and the stuff of rumor."[102] Reading, discussing, copying, and sharing copies or excerpts of Smith's epistles in Missouri, Illinois, and even as far as Massachusetts, sustained and extended the Saints' textual community beyond the main body of church members.

In 1840 the circulation of Smith's general epistles expanded substantially when they were printed in edited form in the church's Illinois newspaper, the *Times and Seasons*.[103] The founding editors, Ebenezer Robinson and Smith's younger brother Don Carlos Smith, announced in the first issue that they intended "to give a detailed history of the persecution of the church of Jesus Christ of Latter Day Saints, has had to endure in Missouri and elsewhere, for their religion." This the editors accomplished in a twelve-part series.[104] The printed prison letters appeared in multiple issues in 1840 alongside installments of the series, thereby supporting and augmenting the paper's overarching narrative that the Saints, most prominently Joseph Smith, had endured "unparalleled persecution" for the sake of the gospel.[105]

Conclusion

Once they entered the realm of print, Smith's prison letters were made available to the vast majority of Latter-day Saints and even among the non-Mormon population. The letters had played a key role in sustaining the

---

101. Partridge's copy, which is missing the first and last pages, is in MS 3595 at the CHL. Rockwood's copy is now housed at the Beineke Library at Yale University, along with other papers he had mailed to Massachusetts relatives in 1838–1839.

102. Hall, *Ways of Writing*, 35.

103. Terence A. Tanner, "The Mormon Press in Nauvoo, 1839–46," in *Kingdom on the Mississippi Revisited: Nauvoo in Mormon History*, ed. Roger D. Launius and John E. Hallwas (Urbana: University of Illinois Press, 1996), 94–96, 102. Letter to Isaac Galland, 22 March 1839, in *Times and Seasons*, February 1840, 1:51–56; Letter to the Church in Caldwell Co., MO, 16 December 1838, in *Times and Seasons*, April 1840, 1:82–86; Letter to the Church and Edward Partridge, 20 March 1839, in *Times and Seasons*, May 1840, 1:99–104; Letter to Edward Partridge and the Church, ca. 22 March 1839, *Times and Seasons*, July 1840, 1:131–34.

104. "Address," *Times and Seasons*, July/November 1839, 1:1; "A History, of the Persecution, of the Church of Jesus Christ, of Latter Day Saints in Missouri," December 1839–October 1840, in *JSP*, H2: 203–286.

105. "Prospectus," *Times and Seasons*, July/November 1839, 1:16.

Mormon textual community during a moment of crisis. Yet the letters would prove to be of enduring value to the Saints. Even before the March 1839 epistles had reached the Saints in Illinois, Smith directed that the originals be preserved in his papers.[106] Following Smith's death in 1844, his clerks copied the general prison epistles into the multi-volume manuscript of his personal history.[107] Outside of official church records, Latter-day Saints such as Eliza R. Snow continued to circulate manuscript copies of at least one of the general epistles through the early 1850s.[108] In 1854, after the church removed to Utah Territory, the history—including the letters—was published as part of serialized "The History of Joseph Smith" in the *Deseret News,* the church's Utah newspaper.[109]

Twenty years later, church historian Orson Pratt elevated the status of the March 1839 epistles even further by including those portions in the voice of Deity in a new edition of the Doctrine and Covenants, a compilation of Smith's written revelations. Although the letters had long been revered by the Saints, Pratt's inclusion of the revelatory irruptions—and the church's subsequent approval of his selections—meant that the letters had entered the Mormon canon of scripture alongside the Bible, the Book of Mormon, and more than one hundred of Smith's written revelations. The selections remain among the most-beloved sections of the Doctrine and Covenants, foundational scriptures that continue to sustain the Latter-day Saint textual community into the present.[110]

---

106. Letter to E. Smith, 21 March 1839, in *JSP,* D6:373.

107. Joseph Smith et al., History, vol. C-1, 868–73, 900–06, and 907–12.

108. Snow copied a partial version of the 20 March 1839 letter into her journal under the title, "A Voice from Prison." She further prefaced the document by stating the letter was "copied from the original, the first & last pages of which are lost, which accounts for the abruptness of beginning and end." Her starting point, however, does not match any known manuscript, suggesting that she had access to a version that has not survived. Snow copied the partial letter between two poems written in 1853. (See Eliza R. Snow, Journal, 1842–1882, [89]–[92], CHL.)

109. "History of Joseph Smith," *Deseret News,* 8 December 1853, p. 1; "History of Joseph Smith," *Deseret News,* 26 January 1854, p. 1; "History of Joseph Smith," *Deseret News,* 2 February 1854, p. 1.

110. See Dean C. Jessee and John W. Welch, "Revelations in Context: Joseph Smith's Letter from Liberty Jail, March 20, 1839," *BYU Studies* 39, no. 3 (2000): 130; Kathleen Flake, "Joseph Smith's Letter from Liberty Jail: A Study in Canonization," *Journal of Religion* 92, no. 4 (October 2012): 515–26.

7

The Textual Culture of the Nauvoo Female Relief Society Leadership and Minute Book

Jennifer Reeder

AT THE FIRST meeting of the Nauvoo Relief Society on 17 March 1842, female members elected their leadership—President Emma Smith, her two counselors, and other officers responsible for finances and minutes. Later, newly appointed secretary Eliza R. Snow recorded into the minute book the perceptive words of Joseph Smith: "Let this Presidency serve as a constitution—all their decisions be considered law; and acted upon as such. If any Officers are wanted to carry out the designs of the Institution, let them be appointed and set apart, . . . The minutes of your meetings will be precedents for you to act upon—your Constitutio[n] and law."[1] These words marked a standard by which the Relief Society established legitimacy and authenticity.

This living constitution[2]—the presidency as well as the minutes recorded in the Nauvoo Relief Society minute book—became the

1. Nauvoo Relief Society Minutes, 17 March 1842, 7, Church History Library, The Church of Jesus Christ of Latter-day Saints, Salt Lake City (hereafter CHL); Jill Mulvay Derr, Carol Cornwall Madsen, Kate Holbrook, and Matthew J. Grow, eds., *The First Fifty Years of Relief Society: Key Documents in Latter-day Saint Women's History* (Salt Lake City: Church Historian's Press, 2016), 31.

2. In 1844, Joseph Smith gave similar instructions to the Council of Fifty in a revelation which identified the council itself as the constitution of the Kingdom of God. A year later Brigham Young used the term "living constitution" to describe this arrangement, claiming that they were "the living body to enact laws for the government of this kingdom, we

establishment, the decree and judgment, the regulation of much more than the Latter-day Saint female association;[3] they determined an unparalleled course for Mormon women. The minute book established legitimacy with strict membership requirements, political and economic activity, theological discourse, and benevolent efforts. The ledger also provides a valuable—though incomplete—history of Mormon women in the Nauvoo era. Reading between the lines of the public record and the private relationships reveals additional insight into the transitions, disruptions, and politics of personality among Relief Society officers and members with male church hierarchy. This subtext indicates more than the inked words could ever tell.

The importance of the Nauvoo Relief Society minute book cannot be overstated; for more than a century it has been the object of much use, research, and thought by members of the Relief Society, Mormon church leadership, and scholars. The speeches of Joseph Smith to Relief Society members, recorded by Snow in the ledger, were published in the *Deseret News*, the church's Salt Lake City newspaper, in September 1855.[4] In 1882 Sarah Kimball compiled a history of the Nauvoo Relief Society at the fortieth anniversary of the organization, drawing on the minute book and her own memory.[5] Her use of the minute book set a precedent for recounting the history at 17 March anniversary celebrations in subsequent years.

The twentieth century produced various renditions of the Nauvoo minutes and scholarly studies on the Nauvoo Relief Society. The official 1931 Relief Society handbook included a detailed history and summary of the Nauvoo minutes.[6] For the organization's centennial, the Relief Society general board published *A Centenary of Relief Society: 1842–1942*

---

are a living constitution." Records of Council of Fifty or Kingdom of God, 1 March 1845, in Matthew J. Grow, Ronald K. Esplin, Mark Ashurst-McGee, Gerrit J. Dirkmaat, Jeffrey D. Mahas, eds., *The Joseph Smith Papers, Administrative Records: Council of Fifty, Minutes, March 1844–January 1846* (Salt Lake City: Church Historian's Press, 2016), 254.

3. See *Oxford English Dictionary Online*, s.v. "constitution," oed.com.

4. Joseph Smith, Discourse, 31 March 1842, in "History of Joseph Smith," *Deseret News* (Salt Lake City) (5 September 1855), 201; Joseph Smith, Discourse, 28 April 1842, in "History of Joseph Smith," *Deseret News* (19 September 1855), 217–18; both discourses in Derr et al., *First Fifty Years of Relief Society*, 198–208.

5. Sarah M. Kimball, "Early Relief Society Reminiscence," 17 March 1882, Relief Society Record, 1880–1892, 29–30, CHL, in Derr et al., *First Fifty Years of Relief Society*, 493–96.

6. The history was compiled by secretary Amy Brown Lyman who had access to the Nauvoo minute book. *Handbook of the Relief Society of the Church of Jesus Christ of Latter-day Saints* (Salt Lake City: General Board of the Relief Society, 1931), 15–31.

with excerpts from the Nauvoo minutes.[7] Fifty years later, in 1992, a more substantial history was published, *Women of Covenant: The Story of Relief Society*, illustrating the global expansion of the organization.[8] After the Nauvoo Relief Society minutes were included on the Joseph Smith Papers website in 2011, a compilation of Smith's sermons to the Nauvoo Relief Society was published in 2012 by Deseret Book, an LDS press.[9] In 2016, the Church Historian's Press published *The First Fifty Years of Relief Society: Key Documents in Latter-day Saint Women's History*, the first fully annotated version of the Nauvoo minutes, with biographical information for each member of the Nauvoo Relief Society, a foundational documentary collection for the study of nineteenth-century Mormon women's history.[10]

Both academic and devotional articles provide information about the Nauvoo Relief Society and its influence on generations of Mormon women.[11] Beyond the written words, both documentary and interpretive, the larger American context and the individual politics and personalities of the women comprising the original Society cannot be overlooked. This chapter will examine contemporaneous female societies and their records; the details of the founding of the Society and its formal, documented organization; the minute book itself—its creation and preservation; the forces that produced the minute book and the people who led the Society, including their complicated layers of relationships; and the transmission and reception of the minute book as a valuable Mormon document.

7. General Board of Relief Society, *A Centenary of Relief Society: 1842–1942* (Salt Lake City: Relief Society, 1942).

8. Jill Mulvay Derr, Janath Russell Cannon, and Maureen Ursenbach Beecher, *Women of Covenant: The Story of Relief Society* (Salt Lake City: Deseret Book, 1992).

9. See the Joseph Smith Papers website, josephsmithpapers.org; Jonathan Stapley, "Minute by Minute: Relief Society Documents and More," 25 March 2011, https://bycommonconsent.com/2011/03/25/minutes-by-minute-relief-society-documents-and-more/; and Sheri L. Dew and Virginia H. Pearce, eds., *Beginning of Better Days: Divine Instruction to Women from the Prophet Joseph Smith* (Salt Lake City: Deseret Book, 2012).

10. See Derr et al., *First Fifty Years of Relief Society*.

11. See, for example, Jill Mulvay Derr and Carol Cornwall Madsen, "Preserving the Record and Memory of the Female Relief Society of Nauvoo, 1842–1892," *Journal of Mormon History* 35, no. 3 (Summer 2009): 89–117.

Textual Culture and Documentary Context of the Nauvoo Relief Society

Emma Smith and members of the Nauvoo Relief Society were certainly not the first American women to speak and organize publicly. Early religious communities became locations where women could engage vocally. However, although females dominated the membership of most churches in the American colonies, many Christian traditions held that women should be "silent" in church.[12] The extent of female participation in formal religious settings was the subject of lively and bitter debates—and yet women did participate.[13] In the seventeenth century, for example, Anne Hutchinson encouraged women to engage in religious practice, to pray, teach their children, and speak in religious services.[14] The Great Awakening of the 1740s encouraged individual conversion, inciting women to act on personal religious impulses.[15] As early evangelical women gained experience speaking within religious communities, many extended their voices into political arenas. During the second half of the eighteenth century,

---

12. See 1 Timothy 2:11–12; 1 Corinthians 14:35; Ann Braude, "Women's History is American Religious History," in *Retelling U.S. Religious History*, ed. Thomas Tweed (Berkeley, California: Berkeley University Press, 1997), 87–107; Jon Butler, *Awash in a Sea of Faith: Christianizing the American People* (Cambridge, Massachusetts: Harvard University Press, 1990), 164–66, 170, 178; and Patricia U. Bonomi, *Under the Cope of Heaven: Religion, Society, and Politics in Colonial America* (New York: Oxford University Press, 2003), 105–15, 123–24.

13. See Ann Braude, *Sisters and Saints: Women and American Religion* (New York: Oxford University Press, 2007), 31–35; and Susan Juster, *Disorderly Women: Sexual Politics and Evangelicalism in Revolutionary New England* (Ithaca, New York: Cornell University Press, 1994).

14. As early as 1636, while attending neighbors' childbirths, Anne Hutchinson exhorted women in their travail, praying with them, reciting scripture and sharing spiritual insights, and discoursing about the covenant of grace. She began holding conventicles, meetings in her home with up to eighty attendees, where she spoke fervently on her individual interpretation of scripture. Hutchinson qualified her public speaking with biblical sources about daughters prophesying. See Joel 2:28; and Acts 2:17. See also John Winthrop, *A Short Story of the Rise, Reign, and Ruin of the Antinomians, Familists, and Libertines* (London: Ralph Smith, 1644), 35–36 [37–38]; Thomas Hutchinson, *The History of the Province of Massachusetts-Bay, from the Charter of King William and Queen Mary, in 1691, Until the Year 1750* (Boston: Thomas and John Fleet, 1767), 485; Michael P. Winship, *The Times and Trials of Anne Hutchinson: Puritans Divided* (Lawrence: University Press of Kansas, 2005), 85; Michael P. Winship, *Making Heretics: Militant Protestantism and Free Grace in Massachusetts, 1636–1641* (Princeton, New Jersey: Princeton University Press, 2002), 171; and Mary Beth Norton, *Founding Mothers and Fathers: Gendered Power and the Forming of American Society* (New York: Vintage, 1996), 374–97.

15. Juster, *Disorderly Women*, 3.

women joined public discourse at tea tables, salons, parlors, taverns, and coffee houses, contributing to the discourse of the Revolutionary era.[16]

The new republic and the Second Great Awakening produced a significant transition from the "Republican Mother" figure of the 1790s to the "True Woman" of the 1830s.[17] The Benevolent Empire, a popular movement rising from the confluence of new urban problems of poverty and evangelical efforts to contribute to the community, created opportunities for women to organize and promote religious and social causes.[18] Women began to manage benevolent societies with a missionary zeal aimed at "converting American Indians, carrying Christianity to the 'heathen,' and evangelizing the frontier."[19] Organizations such as the New York Female Moral Reform Society, the Female Association of Philadelphia for the Relief of Women and Children in Reduced Circumstances, and the Female Total Abstinence Society and Female Asylum in Boston afforded opportunities for women to contribute to moral reform and social concerns.[20] A close examination of women's associations during this time reveals an evangelical construction of womanhood and its influence on gender and class systems, combining religious practice with feminine benevolence, and democratic republicanism with market capitalism.[21]

These new women's organizations documented their activity. As early as 1797, the New York City Society for the Relief of the Poor Widows with Children began keeping records.[22] The Female Charitable Society was

16. Mary Kelley, *Learning to Stand and Speak: Women, Education, and Public Life in America's Republic* (Chapel Hill: University of North Carolina Press, 2006), 7–8; Anne Firor Scott, *Making the Invisible Woman Visible* (Urbana: University of Illinois Press, 1984); Nancy F. Cott, *The Bonds of Womanhood: "Woman's Sphere" in New England, 1780–1835* (New Haven: Yale University Press, 1997), 101–25.

17. Anne M. Boylan, *The Origins of Women's Activism: New York and Boston, 1797–1840* (Chapel Hill: University of North Carolina Press, 2002), 6.

18. Nancy A. Hardesty, *Women Called to Witness: Evangelical Feminism in the Nineteenth Century* (Nashville: Abingdon Press, 1984), 113.

19. Kelley, *Learning to Stand and Speak*, 7–8.

20. Linda K. Kerber, *Women of the Republic: Intellect and Ideology in Revolutionary America* (Chapel Hill: University of North Carolina Press), 111.

21. Boylan, *The Origins of Women's Activism*, 6–11, 124, 212.

22. "Society for the Relief of Women and Children," minute book, vol. 1, 1791–1813, New-York Historical Society, New York City, New York. By 1806, the women's group expanded to form the Orphan Asylum Society. Sparse holographic records for both groups are held at the New-York Historical Society. The Society for the Relief of Poor Widows with Children, ca. 1804–1881, minute book, vol. 1, 1791–1813, New-York Historical Society, New York City,

organized in Newark, New Jersey in 1803 with a constitution delineating their purpose and the responsibilities of members.[23] The Female Hebrew Benevolent Society in Philadelphia composed a constitution and bylaws in 1825.[24] Women published constitutions and reports in local newspapers to publicize efforts to elect officers and to fundraise.[25]

Most of these organizations compiled and preserved their minute books with detailed records of membership, donations, and meeting discussion. For example, the Association for the Relief of Respectable, Aged, Indigent Females in New York City, organized in 1814, preserved seven volumes of minutes and financial records.[26] Also in 1814, the Lynn, Massachusetts, Female Benevolent Society started keeping minutes of their meetings.[27] The Female Association of Philadelphia for the Relief of the Sick and Infirm Poor with Clothing preserved minutes, legal and financial reports, correspondence, and annual reports.[28] The Nauvoo Relief Society did the same.

The Founding of the Society

The Nauvoo Relief Society followed the stream of American nineteenth-century women. The idea began when seamstress Margaret Cook spoke with her employer, Sarah Kimball, about a recent public appeal for assistance for financial and material support for construction workers building

---

New York; Orphan Asylum Society/Graham Home for Children, 1806–1981, Records of Graham Windam, New-York Historical Society, New York City, New York.

23. Newark Female Charitable Society, Abby Eliza Condit Martin, and A. F. R. Martin, *The History of the Newark Female Charitable Society from the Date of Organization January 31, 1803, to January 31st, 1903* (Newark, New Jersey: Newark Female Charitable Society, 1903), New-York Historical Society, New York City, New York.

24. Female Hebrew Benevolent Society, *Constitution of the Female Hebrew Benevolent Society of Philadelphia* (Philadelphia: Lydia R. Bailey, 1838), Rosenbach Rare Books, American Jewish Historical Society, Center for Jewish History, New York City, New York.

25. Boylan, *The Origins of Women's Activism*, 18, 27.

26. Association for the Relief of Respectable Aged Indigent Females, Rare Book Collection, Butler Library, Columbia University, New York City, New York.

27. Lynn Female Benevolent Society, 1814–1914, Lynn Museum and Historical Society, on deposit at the Phillips Library, Peabody Essex Museum, Salem, Massachusetts. The collection includes a constitution, by-laws, treasurer's records, and meeting minutes.

28. Female Association of Philadelphia for the Relief of the Sick and Infirm Poor with Clothing Records, 1829–1978, Friends Historical Library, McCabe Library, Swathmore College, Philadelphia, Pennsylvania.

the Nauvoo temple and their families.[29] While Cook desired to contribute to the request for provisions, clothing, bedding, and general supplies, she had no financial means. Kimball offered to contribute material goods; Cook would provide her sewing services. They discussed organizing a sewing society. The following week, possibly 10 March 1842, Kimball invited several female acquaintances to her home.[30]

The Nauvoo women intended to produce a constitution and by-laws to gain credence. Kimball's neighbor, Phebe Rigdon, a well-educated woman, suggested that Eliza R. Snow, a friend not present at the meeting, be invited to compose a constitution.[31] The Snows and Rigdons had become acquainted in northern Ohio in the early 1830s when Sidney Rigdon, Phebe's husband, introduced the Snows to Joseph Smith and Mormonism.[32] Snow was a likely candidate for such an endeavor. She may have had the most experience as an actual secretary—she kept records for her father in his public office in Portage County, Ohio.[33] The Rigdons utilized Snow's intelligence and experience when she taught the Rigdon family school in 1839.[34] With Rigdon's recommendation, the women delegated Kimball to visit Snow and invite her to produce the incorporation material.

Snow produced a draft, then sought approval from Joseph Smith; contemporary female leaders of women's organizations often gained approval

---

29. See Willard Richards, "Tithings and Consecrations for the Temple of the Lord," *Times and Seasons* 3, no. 7 (1 February 1842): 677; Joseph Smith, "To the Brethren in Nauvoo City, Greeting," *Times and Seasons* 3, no. 9 (1 March 1842): 715.

30. Sarah M. Kimball, "Early Relief Society Reminiscence," 17 March 1882, Relief Society Record, 1880–1892, 29–30, CHL, in Derr et al., *First Fifty Years of Relief Society*, 493–96; Augusta Joyce Crocheron, *Representative Women of Deseret: A Book of Biographical Sketches* (Salt Lake City: J. C. Graham, 1884), 27.

31. Richard S. Van Wagoner, *Sidney Rigdon: A Portrait of Religious Excess* (Salt Lake City: Signature, 1994), 17; Kimball, "Early Relief Society Reminiscence," 29, in Derr et al., *First Fifty Years of Relief Society*, 495.

32. Eliza R. Snow, "Sketch of My Life," in Maureen Ursenbach Beecher, ed., *The Personal Writings of Eliza Roxcy Snow* (Logan: Utah State University Press, 2000), 9; Van Wagoner, *Sidney Rigdon*, 53.

33. Snow, "Sketch of My Life," 6. Oliver Snow was considered one of the most prominent citizens of Mantua, Ohio, where he and his family lived from 1805 until 1837. He served as county commissioner of Portage County for two terms, from 1809 to 1815. He also served several terms as justice of the peace. A town historian asserted, "It was rarely the case whilst he resided in Mantua that he was not holding some township office." Orrin Harmon, "Historical Facts Appertaining to the Township of Mantua," typescript, 1866, The Western Reserve Historical Society, Cleveland, Ohio, 28–29.

34. Snow, "Sketch of My Life," 15; Van Wagoner, *Sidney Rigdon*, 266.

from city fathers.[35] This document has not been found. According to Kimball, Smith "pronounced it the best constitution he had ever read," then proclaimed he had "something better" for the Mormon women. He wanted to organize them officially in the same way other early Mormon councils and quorums had been organized—after the pattern of the priesthood—with a president and two counselors, and with ecclesiastical sanction. Smith invited the women to the room over his red brick store the following Thursday afternoon.[36]

This meeting marks the beginning of the Nauvoo Relief Society minute book, seen in Figure 7.1. Men in attendance included Smith, the president of the church, and John Taylor and Willard Richards, members of the Quorum of Twelve Apostles. The women in attendance, listed in the minute book most likely according to the order in which they were seated, lived in two neighborhood clusters centered near the homes of Sarah Kimball, who initiated the meeting, and Emma Smith, wife of Joseph Smith.[37] Twenty women were voted in as members, and the men withdrew while the women deliberated over seven additional names. The men returned, and the group discussed the purpose of the organization: "That the Society of Sisters might provoke the brethren to good works in looking to the wants of the poor—searching after objects of charity, and in administering to their wants—to assist; by correcting the morals and strengthening the virtues of the female community."[38]

The officially sanctioned organization transformed into a broader purpose than the original intention of Kimball and Cook, which was to provide shirts for the men working on the temple. Perhaps "something better" reflected what Joseph Smith, John Taylor, and Wilford Woodruff had outlined two days previously in the *Times and Seasons*, a Nauvoo newspaper. In the newspaper, the men had identified the need to "feed the hungry, to clothe the naked, to provide for the widow, to dry up the tear of the orphan,

35. Boylan, *The Origins of Women's Activism*, 9.

36. Kimball, "Early Relief Society Reminiscence," 29, in Derr et al., *First Fifty Years of Relief Society*, 495; Crocheron, *Representative Women of Deseret*, 27.

37. Maureen Ursenbach Beecher created a chart of women who attended the founding Relief Society meeting in Nauvoo on 17 March 1842. Maureen Ursenbach Beecher, "The 'Leading Sisters': A Female Hierarchy in Nineteenth Century Mormon Society," *Journal of Mormon History* 9 (1982): 30–31.

38. Nauvoo Relief Society Minutes, 17 March 1842, 5–6, in Derr et al., *First Fifty Years of Relief Society*, 28–31.

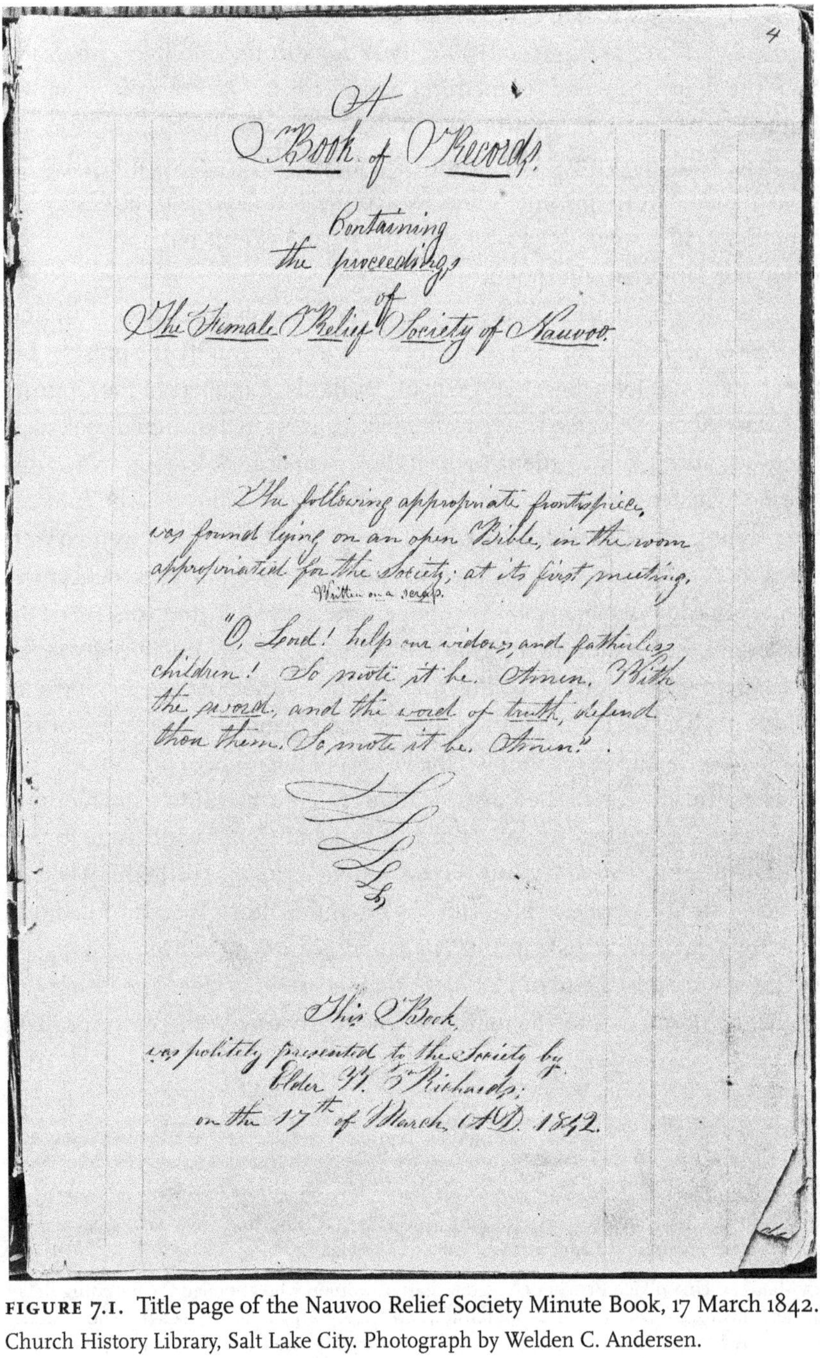

4

A
Book of Records.
Containing
the proceedings
of
The Female Relief Society of Nauvoo.

The following appropriate frontispiece,
was found lying on an open Bible, in the room
appropriated for the Society; at its first meeting.
Written on a scrap.

"O, Lord! help our widows, and fatherless
children! So mote it be. Amen. With
the sword, and the word of truth, defend
thou them. So mote it be. Amen."

This Book,
was politely presented to the Society by
Elder W. Richards;
on the 17th of March, A.D. 1842.

FIGURE 7.1. Title page of the Nauvoo Relief Society Minute Book, 17 March 1842. Church History Library, Salt Lake City. Photograph by Welden C. Andersen.

to comfort the afflicted," not just for temple builders.[39] After agreeing on their purpose, the women pursued a documented course as did so many other contemporary women's organizations: by keeping official minutes, they legitimized their associations at the same time they filled an evangelical sense of duty.[40] The minute book gave them an official record—a written mission statement and activity log. These minutes constituted what historian Anne M. Boylan has called a "rhetoric of female benevolence."[41]

The next order of business was to elect a president and officers, creating a leadership structure similar to that of the presidency of the church. The women voted with parliamentary procedure: Elizabeth Ann Whitney nominated Emma Hale Smith, portrayed in Figure 7.2, to be president; the nomination was seconded by Sophia Packard, and the motion passed unanimously.[42] Emma's high public profile and her proximity to Joseph Smith made her a prime candidate for the nomination according to common practice.[43] The "Presidentess Elect" then proposed Sarah M. Cleveland and Whitney to be her counselors. These three would stand as a living constitution according to Joseph Smith: "let this Presidency serve as a constitution—all their decisions be considered law; and acted upon as such." The women appointed additional officers, including a secretary, Eliza R. Snow, the author of the original constitution; an assistant secretary, Phebe M. Wheeler; and a treasurer, Elvira Cowles (later Holmes). The Society reiterated its purpose "to seek out and relieve the distressed," and donations were received from both men and women.[44]

The minutes recorded the solemn occasion of organization with attention to detail as well as ecclesiastical and democratic order and authority. By the second meeting, the minutes were already used. Presidentess Smith "rose and read from the Book of records, the proceedings of the first meeting of the Society."[45] At the third meeting, Joseph Smith reminded the

39. Editorial, *Times and Seasons* 3, no. 10 (15 March 1842): 732.

40. Boylan, *The Origins of Women's Activism*, 47.

41. Boylan, *The Origins of Women's Activism*, 18.

42. Nauvoo Relief Society Minutes, 17 March 1842, 7, in Derr et al., *First Fifty Years of Relief Society*, 31–32.

43. Boylan, *The Origins of Women's Activism*, 58.

44. Nauvoo Relief Society Minutes, 17 March 1842, 7–13, in Derr et al., *First Fifty Years of Relief Society*, 31–36.

45. Nauvoo Relief Society Minutes, 24 March 1842, 16, in Derr et al., *First Fifty Years of Relief Society*, 38.

FIGURE 7.2. Emma Hale Smith, circa 1842. Portrait by Sutcliffe Maudsley. Church History Library, Salt Lake City.

women to "observe the Constitution that the blessings of heaven may rest down upon us."[46] The precedent of the minute book as constitution and law had been set.

The Relief Society Record

When Kimball initially asked Snow to create a constitution for the women's sewing society in early March 1842, she presented Snow with a small notebook or "album" so she would have the means to write.[47] However, after drafting a version and before recording it in this particular book, Joseph Smith suggested to Snow that he had something better in mind, and a proper ledger was provided. The official Nauvoo Relief Society minute book veritably became an important document, better than the small album notebook, demonstrated by the weight and refinement of its physical description, analysis of the people and methods of those who wrote and maintained the record, and both what was included in the book and what was excluded.

Minute books contained the organizational records of the Mormon church as early as June 1830. From 1841 to 1845, the Book of the Law of the Lord included nine revelations and a portion of Joseph Smith's journal, as well as donations made to the Nauvoo temple and the Nauvoo House. The record contains the handwriting of different scribes.[48] By 1842, multiple scribes, secretaries, and recorders kept various types of records, including city council minutes, all within proximity of each other in the office of the Nauvoo red brick store, each providing additional context for the Relief Society minutes.[49]

A comparison could also be made between the Nauvoo Relief Society and the concurrent practice of Masonry in Nauvoo.[50] Again, proximity

---

46. Nauvoo Relief Society Minutes, 30 March 1842, 21, in Derr et al., *First Fifty Years of Relief Society*, 42–43.

47. The frontispiece states, "This Album was politely presented to Eliza R. Snow by Mrs. Sarah M. Kimball, City of Nauvoo, March, 1842." Eliza R. Snow, Nauvoo journal, frontispiece, March 1842, CHL.

48. Alex D. Smith, "The Book of the Law of the Lord," *Journal of Mormon History* 38, no. 4 (Fall 2012): 131–63.

49. This collection included council proceedings, elections, revenue, treasury, taxation, and judicial records, including meeting minutes, mayor's orders and proclamations, ordinances, memorials, motions, resolutions, petitions, committee reports, and claims. Nauvoo City Records, 1841–1845, CHL.

50. Nauvoo Masonic Lodge Minute Book, 1841–1846, CHL.

proved important as the women's organization met in the "lodge room" used for masonic inductions. References to order and office, relief of brotherhood (or sisterhood), examination of candidates, and growth by degree, in addition to the creation of a union of loyalty and commitment within Relief Society membership, echoed prevalent Masonic practices.[51] Just as each of these various institutions influenced the development and membership of the Relief Society, their records influenced the textual creation of the Nauvoo Relief Society minute book as suited to a legitimate organization with a significant public record.

Physical Description

Willard Richards, clerk to Joseph Smith and to the Quorum of the Twelve Apostles, scribed notes for the first Relief Society meeting prior to Snow's official appointment as secretary. He then presented the Society with a bound ledger book, seen in Figure 7.3, into which Snow copied the minutes of the first meeting. The brown suede leather cover and gold tooling around the edges, with a red leather label on the spine and the word "ledger" in gold lettering, signified official business, more refined than the simple album Kimball had earlier given to Snow. The book opened with a twelve-leaf gathering of tabbed index pages (unused), labeled alphabetically, followed by fifteen gatherings of eight leaves each.[52] Ultimately the pages would contain minutes from thirty-three meetings, recorded by the hands of four different scribes. The heavy cover and binding allowed the account book to lay open flat. The manuscript appears as a fair copy, likely produced from loose minutes hurriedly written during the meetings, as the handwriting and syntax in the ledger are fluid and complete.

---

51. See Michael W. Homer, *Joseph's Temples: The Dynamic Relationship Between Freemasonry and Mormonism* (Salt Lake City: University of Utah Press, 2014), 179–98; Don Bradley, "'The Grand Fundamental Principles of Mormonism': Joseph Smith's Unfinished Reformation," *Sunstone*, no. 141 (April 2006): 32–41; Cheryl L. Bruno, "Keeping a Secret: Freemasonry, Polygamy, and the Nauvoo Relief Society, 1842–1844," *Journal of Mormon History* 39, no. 4 (Fall 2013): 158–81.

52. The bound book measures 12⅜ × 8⅛ × 1 inches, with a tight-back case binding sewn on vellum tapes. For more detailed information on the physical characteristics of the book, see Derr et al., *First Fifty Years of Relief Society*, 23–24.

FIGURE 7.3. Nauvoo Relief Society Minute Book.
Church History Library, Salt Lake City.

Keepers of the Record

The titles given to those who created the Relief Society constitution and record demonstrate institutional as well as gendered expectations. There was one secretary, Eliza R. Snow, photographed in Figure 7.4; an assistant secretary, Phebe M. Wheeler; a temporary secretary, Hannah Ells; and one unknown scribe (a sister M. Peck), all four of whom took minutes for the Nauvoo Relief Society. There was also a treasurer, Elvira Cowles (later Holmes), who kept financial records. The minute keepers, their terms of service, and the pages they inscribed in the minute book are depicted in more detail in Table 7.1.

Although males held similar positions with various titles as clerks, scribes, or recorders in different organizations, often with overlapping roles, in Mormonism the women of the Relief Society were known only as secretaries and treasurers. In most women's organizations of the time, the secretary was often a single woman with significant visibility, whose

FIGURE 7.4. Eliza R. Snow, circa 1850s–1860s. Photographer unknown. Church History Library, Salt Lake City.

name often appeared on written and published documents.[53] The title *secretary* stems from the Latin word *secretus*, or secret—one entrusted with secrets.[54] The need for Relief Society confidentiality became apparent at the second meeting when Elizabeth Jones questioned "if the proceedings of this Society should be divulged out of the Society," to which President Emma Smith responded, "All proceedings that regard difficulties should be kept among the members," establishing a precedent of confidentiality.[55] As Relief Society treasurer, Holmes kept a record of donations, much like Richards or Clayton had done in their roles as temple recorders,

53. Boylan, *The Origins of Women's Activism*, 58.

54. "Secretary," *American Dictionary of the English Language*.

55. Nauvoo Relief Society Minutes, 24 March 1842, 17, in Derr et al., *First Fifty Years of Relief Society*, 39.

Table 7.1. Nauvoo Relief Society Secretaries

Minute Keeper	Dates	Pages	Number of Meetings
Eliza R. Snow, Secretary	17 March 1842–7 July 1843	4–96	19
Phebe M. Wheeler, Assistant Secretary	15 July–14 October 1843	97–122	11
Hannah M. Ells, Temporary Secretary	9 March–16 March 1844	123–27	4

then passed her calculations to Snow or Wheeler to record in the official minutes.

Production

It is not known precisely how Snow, Wheeler, and Ells recorded the minutes as they appear in the minute book. Snow never described the process, but the minutes she recorded are very neat with few corrections. She likely used the same method that other clerks and recorders used at the time, taking rough notes during the meeting. A loose copy would be prepared from those notes to be read for approval at the following meeting. Once those minutes were approved, a fair copy was written directly in the record book.[56] Each Relief Society meeting was carefully numbered, a practice not seen in other early Mormon minute books. Snow inadvertently left out minutes for the meeting numbered seventeenth, which would have fallen chronologically sometime between 31 August and 28 September 1842. The other secretaries followed Snow's example, although Wheeler was not as accurate as Snow; Wheeler recorded several meetings which inadvertently did not include the date.

It is important to recognize the subjective slant of each secretary's minutes, not only physically in the handwriting and misplacement of certain meetings and spelling of names, but also in the essence of the words recorded. Some meetings are recorded in the style of a business report, containing lists of names or donations with discussion of current needs.

56. See, for example, William Clayton's process to record the minutes of the Council of Fifty, in Grow et al., *Joseph Smith Papers: Administrative Records*, 1:12.

Others record the devotional sensation afforded by the practice of charismatic or spiritual gifts. Eliza R. Snow noted on 19 April 1842 that "nearly all present arose & spoke, and the spirit of the Lord like a purifying stream, refreshed every heart."[57] Secretary pro tem Hannah Ells recorded four meetings in 1844 in the form of a newspaper account, clearly stating the purpose of each meeting given to the reading of a document titled "The Voice of Innocence," with no additional social commentary. This document, written by church clerk William W. Phelps, was emended by Emma Smith, then published in the city newspaper, the *Nauvoo Neighbor,* as well as being read in four Relief Society meetings.[58] Ells did not copy the document into the Nauvoo minute book, as Snow had done with some important documents during her tenure as secretary. The only way to fully understand the subjectivity of each secretary is to examine their personal lives, experiences, backgrounds, and relationships with others as discussed later in this chapter.

Contents

The Nauvoo Relief Society minute book included minutes of sermons and discussions, lists of members' names, and records of benevolent needs and donations. Membership in the Relief Society was restrictive; women were recruited then required to apply, prove their worthiness, and be trained as members. On 31 March 1842, for example, the minutes include a transcript of a recommend for Elizabeth Jones as a Relief Society member in good standing, authorized to receive donations.[59]

The membership and donation lists in the minutes demonstrates the importance of keeping a detailed record of individual names. At the organization of the Church of Christ on 6 April 1830, Joseph Smith discussed the importance of recording names of members.[60] Similarly and more

57. Nauvoo Relief Society Minutes, 19 March 1842, 32, in Derr et al., *First Fifty Years of Relief Society*, 52.

58. William W. Phelps, "The Voice of Innocence from Nauvoo," February–March 1844, copy made by Thomas Bullock with revisions made by Emma Smith, CHL, in Derr et al., *First Fifty Years of Relief Society*, 151–56; "Virtue Will Triumph," *Nauvoo Neighbor*, 20 March 1844.

59. Nauvoo Relief Society Minutes, 31 March 1842, 25, in Derr et al., *First Fifty Years of Relief Society*, 45.

60. Articles and Covenants, ca. April 1830, in Michael Hubbard MacKay, Gerrit J. Dirkmaat, Grant Underwood, Robert J. Woodford, William G. Hartley, eds., *The Joseph Smith Papers: Documents, Volume 1: July 1828–June 1831* (Salt Lake City: Church Historian's Press, 2013), 126 [Doctrine and Covenants 20:82–83].

contemporary to the Nauvoo Relief Society, the Book of the Law of the Lord recorded names of faithful people who witnessed their loyalty and worthiness through their donations. The Relief Society records became a type of "book of life" or "book of record," recording names of those who would be saved and elevating the value of the Nauvoo minute book as a veritable record of salvation for the women of the church.[61]

Exchange of Services

Beyond a membership record, the Nauvoo Relief Society minutes record contributions and rendered service, common activities in contemporary benevolent associations. Through seeking donations, women who had previously been limited to a domestic sphere transitioned into public actors with a significant economic impact on the city. They shifted their work from household accounts to organizational budgets and local needs, learning valuable accounting strategies in the process.[62] The Relief Society minutes do not provide detailed disbursements, credits and debits; rather, as in the church's Book of the Law of the Lord, the focus is on *who* provided monetary or material assistance.

Supplemental Documents

In addition to minutes of discussion and lists of names and contributions, the Nauvoo Relief Society minutes contained important addenda outside of meeting notes. At the end of the first year, 1842, Snow copied into the ledger documents she felt were important for that year, including one epistle addressed to the Relief Society from several significant church leaders encouraging commitment to righteousness and loyalty to Joseph Smith as hallmarks of membership in the Relief Society.[63] Snow also transcribed into the minute book a certificate affirming the proper and virtuous conduct of Clarissa Marvel, whose character had been questioned earlier that year.[64]

---

61. Smith, "The Book of the Law of the Lord," 145–46.

62. Boylan, *The Origins of Women's Activism*, 29, 173.

63. See Kathleen Flake, "Ordering Antinomy: An Analysis of Early Mormonism's Priestly Offices, Councils, and Kinship," *Religion and American Culture: A Journal of Interpretation* 26, no. 2 (Summer 2016): 139–83.

64. Nauvoo Relief Society Minutes, 24 March 1842, 17; 31 March 1842, 23; 14 April 1842, 26, in Derr et al., *First Fifty Years of Relief Society*, 38–39, 43–44, 46.

Other ancillary documents illuminate the public activity of the Nauvoo Relief Society but were not attached to the actual minute book. Several of these are included in the documentary collection, *The First Fifty Years of Relief Society.*[65] These supplemental documents, though separate from the minute book, illustrate the political and civic activity of the Relief Society and demonstrate the public action of female officers, including Emma Smith, Sarah Cleveland, Elizabeth Ann Whitney, Eliza R. Snow, and Elvira Cowles Holmes, as the "living constitution."

Private Relationships Shaping the Relief Society

The value and meaning of the "constitution" proved to be much more than the written word. In her study of women's groups in New York and Boston at the turn of the nineteenth century, Boylan noted the confluence of public records and private relationships: "Organizational records, whether in the form of lovingly preserved complete sets of minutes or scattered references in . . . newspapers became richer and more revealing when paired with biographical information on the women who sat in the meetings, kept the minutes, reported on their labors, and initiated and carried out decisions." Such scrutiny redraws lines separating political and domestic affairs.[66] An examination of the biographical details of the female officers of the Relief Society reveals underlying complexities, including a very public social hierarchy meshed with private relationships, most highly influenced by the practice of plural marriage.

Social Hierarchy

The authority of the president, her counselors, and to a lesser degree the different women in the offices of secretary and treasurer, was made evident as each meeting was deliberately presided over by a member of the

---

65. See, for example, "Ladies' Relief Society," *Times and Seasons* 3, no. 11 (1 April 1842): 743; Eliza R. Snow, "The Female Relief Society of Nauvoo, What Is It?," *Times and Seasons* 3, no. 17 (1 July 1842): 846; Nauvoo Female Relief Society, petition, to Thomas Carlin, July 1842, CHL; Emma Smith et al., "Statement," *Times and Seasons* 3, no. 23 (1 October 1842): 940; Sarah M. Cleveland, "To the Presidency, and Ladies of the Female Relief Society of Nauvoo," *Times and Seasons* 4, no. 12 (1 May 1843): 187; "Female Relief Society," *Nauvoo Neighbor* 1, no. 2 (12 July 1843): 2; all in Derr et al., *First Fifty Years of Relief Society*, 132–48; and Eliza R. Snow, "Female Relief Society," *Times and Seasons* 4, no. 18 (1 August 1843): 287.

66. Boylan, *The Origins of Women's Activism*, 5, 136–37.

presidency. In 1842, Emma Smith was not present at three of the meetings, therefore first counselor Sarah Cleveland presided.[67] Cleveland submitted her resignation in May 1843 and moved away from Nauvoo.[68] Second counselor Elizabeth Ann Whitney then took charge, as Smith did not attend any of the fourteen meetings in 1843. In an undated meeting in September 1843, no member of the presidency was available to preside. Whitney asked Wheeler, assistant secretary, to lead the meeting.

The Relief Society social hierarchy demands attention to the public personas and personal experiences of each officer. President Emma Smith, wife of Joseph Smith, had been titled "Elect Lady" in an 1830 revelation.[69] Years later, Eliza R. Snow noted the reference of "Elect Lady" in the New Testament, stating that Joseph Smith taught them that "the same organization existed in the church anciently."[70] Emma acted as the First Lady of the church, accompanying her husband, the church's president, in official capacities. She worked as his scribe while translating the Book of Mormon. She provided essential service for the sick and poor. As a public figure, she made diplomatic appearances by welcoming esteemed visitors to Nauvoo, she rode in Nauvoo Legion parades, and she helped manage the red brick store.[71] Smith often missed meetings due to family responsibilities, exposing conflict between her public and domestic duties as dictated by contemporary culture.[72]

First counselor Sarah Cleveland had a personal relationship with the Smith family: she welcomed Emma and her children into her home in Quincy, Illinois, while Joseph was in Liberty Jail. Her daughter, Augusta

67. Nauvoo Relief Society Minutes, 19 April 1842, [30]; 7 July 1842, [73]; and 28 September 1842, [85], in Derr et al., *First Fifty Years of Relief Society*, 49, 87, 96.

68. Sarah M. Cleveland, "To the Presidency, and Ladies of the Female Relief Society of Nauvoo," *Times and Seasons* 4, no. 12 (1 May 1843): 187, in Derr et al., *First Fifty Years of Relief Society*, 145–46.

69. Revelation to Emma Smith, July 1830, "27th Commandment AD 1830," copied in Revelation Book 1, pp. 34–35, in MacKay et al., *Joseph Smith Papers: Documents*, 1:161–64; also in Derr et al., *First Fifty Years of Relief Society*, 17–21.

70. 2 John 1:1; Eliza R. Snow, "Female Relief Society, *Deseret Evening News*, 18 April 1868.

71. Derr et al., *First Fifty Years of Relief Society*, 17; Linda King Newell and Valeen Tippetts Avery, *Mormon Enigma: Emma Hale Smith* (Urbana: University of Illinois Press, 1994), 84–93, 102, 132.

72. Emma Smith was not present at seventeen meetings from 1842 to 1843, often due to sickness, travel, and other family issues. Derr et al., *First Fifty Years of Relief Society*, 8. See Boylan, *The Origins of Women's Activism*, 78.

Cleveland, married Joseph Lyman Smith, a cousin to Joseph Smith.[73] Sarah Cleveland was also a close acquaintance with Eliza R. Snow—both were born in Becket, Massachusetts, and both were well-educated.[74] Though Cleveland resigned her position when she relocated with her husband from Nauvoo in 1843, she remained a devout Latter-day Saint throughout her life.[75]

Similar to Cleveland, second counselor Elizabeth Ann Whitney had welcomed the Smith family into her home in Kirtland in 1831; then, when the destitute Whitney family arrived in Nauvoo nearly a decade later in 1840, they were reciprocally hosted by the Smith family.[76] Whitney and Smith held feasts for the poor in 1836, a particularly poignant preparation for their benevolent work in Nauvoo.[77] Whitney was widely known for her charismatic gifts of singing in tongues and healing.[78] At her death, she was remembered for her ability to provide relief "in such a rare degree" to Joseph Smith during periods of discouragement: "He would sit as it were spell bound and listen to the rich melody of her magnificent voice for the time so absorbed, as to forget his sorrows."[79] The manifestation of spiritual gifts in the Nauvoo Relief Society demonstrated Whitney's distinct contribution to a holy sisterhood, prompting Joseph Smith's invitation and instruction to women regarding spiritual manifestation on 28 April 1842. The minutes summarized that meeting: "The Spirit of the Lord was

---

73. Todd Compton, *In Sacred Loneliness: The Plural Wives of Joseph Smith* (Salt Lake City: Signature, 1997), 276, 281.

74. Andrew Jenson, *Latter-day Saint Biographical Encyclopedia* (Salt Lake City: Andrew Jenson Memorial Association; Deseret News, 1936), 4:183; "Sarah Marietta Kingsley Howe Cleveland," churchhistorianspress.org, accessed 7 October 2016.

75. Compton, *In Sacred Loneliness*, 280–87.

76. Emmeline B. Wells, "Elizabeth Ann Whitney," *Woman's Exponent* 10, no. 20 (15 March 1882): 153; Elizabeth Ann Whitney, "A Leaf from an Autobiography," *Woman's Exponent* 7, no. 7 (1 September 1878): 51.

77. Newell and Avery, *Mormon Enigma*, 54; Dean C. Jessee, Mark Ashurst-McGee, and Richard L. Jensen, eds., *The Joseph Smith Papers: Journals, Volume 1: 1832–1839* (Salt Lake City: Church Historian's Press, 2008), 146–47; Elizabeth Ann Whitney, "A Leaf from an Autobiography," *Woman's Exponent* 7, no. 9 (1 October 1878): 71; Elizabeth Ann Whitney, "A Leaf from an Autobiography," *Woman's Exponent* 7, no. 11 (1 November 1878): 83. See Jennifer Reeder and Kate Holbrook, eds., *At the Pulpit: 185 Years of Discourses of Latter-day Saint Women* (Salt Lake City: Church Historian's Press, 2017), 7–9.

78. Whitney, "A Leaf from an Autobiography," *Woman's Exponent* 7, no. 11 (1 November 1878): 83; Whitney, "A Leaf from an Autobiography," 7, no. 12 (15 November 1878): 91.

79. Emmeline B. Wells, "Elizabeth Ann Whitney," *Woman's Exponent* 10, no. 20 (15 March 1882): 154.

pour'd out in a very powerful manner, never to be forgotten by those present on that interesting occasion."[80]

Secretary Eliza R. Snow had a public reputation as a school teacher and poet. In the spring of 1836, she taught "a select school for young ladies" in Kirtland and lived with the Smith family. In 1837 she taught the Smith family school. After spending time with her family in Missouri, she returned to live with the Smith family in Nauvoo, where she again taught school.[81] Snow also lived with the Cleveland family and the Holmes family at different times in Nauvoo.

Phebe Mariette Wheeler, assistant secretary, lived with the Smith family in the Nauvoo fourth ward.[82] Though in August 1842 she temporarily left Nauvoo for Knoxville, Illinois, after a perceived problem with Emma Smith and Elizabeth Ann Whitney, she resumed her office as Relief Society assistant secretary in July 1843 when Snow left town, as seen in Figure 7.5.[83] Wheeler maintained the record until 14 October 1843. Little is known after this date; she appeared in Utah in 1868, where she participated actively in the Relief Society, serving as secretary in the Wanship, Utah, ward.[84]

Hannah Ells became a temporary secretary after Wheeler abdicated her office, recording minutes for the last four meetings of the Nauvoo Relief

---

80. Nauvoo Relief Society Minutes, 28 April 1842, 33–41, in Derr et al., *First Fifty Years of Relief Society*, 52–62. See Reeder and Holbrook, eds., *At the Pulpit*, 15–19.

81. Snow, "Sketch of My Life," 10–15, 18; see also Jill Mulvay Derr and Karen Lynn Davidson, eds., *Eliza R. Snow: The Complete Poetry* (Provo, Utah: Brigham Young University Press; Salt Lake City: University of Utah Press, 2009), 73–76.

82. Lyman De Platt, *Nauvoo: Early Mormon Records Series*, vol. 1 (Highland, Utah: [n.p.], 1980), 86.

83. Phebe M. Wheeler to Oliver Olney, 21 August 1842, Oliver H. Olney Papers, CHL; Nauvoo Relief Society Minutes, 15 July 1843, [98]; 28 July 1843, [102], in Derr et al., *First Fifty Years of Relief Society*, 108, 110.

84. "Sealings of couples, living and by proxy, 1851–1889," Endowment House, vol. E, no. 3413, Wilder Hatch and Phebe Mariette Wheeler, 22 August 1868, microfilm 1,149,515, Special Collections, Family History Library, The Church of Jesus Christ of Latter-day Saints, Salt Lake City. Phebe Hatch was living in Wanship, Utah in 1880. "Phebe Hatch," 1880 US census, Wanship, Summit County, Utah, ED 73, 2B. Her name is also recorded in the records of the Wanship Relief Society, beginning in 1872 through 1880, and she eventually served again as a Relief Society secretary of the Wanship Relief Society. See Wanship Ward, Summit Stake, Relief Society Minutes and Records, 1872–1972, vol. 1, 1872–1880, CHL; South Bountiful Ward, Woods Cross Stake, Relief Society Minutes and Records, 1878–1973, vol. 4, 1893–1899, CHL. Wheeler died in Bountiful at the home of her husband's cousin's son. Notice given in *Woman's Exponent* about her death mentioned she was the original assistant secretary of the Nauvoo Relief Society, but no laud is given her. "Bountiful Briefs," *Davis County Clipper*, 10 February 1899; "Memorable Anniversary," *Woman's Exponent* 27, no. 20 (15 March 1899): 116.

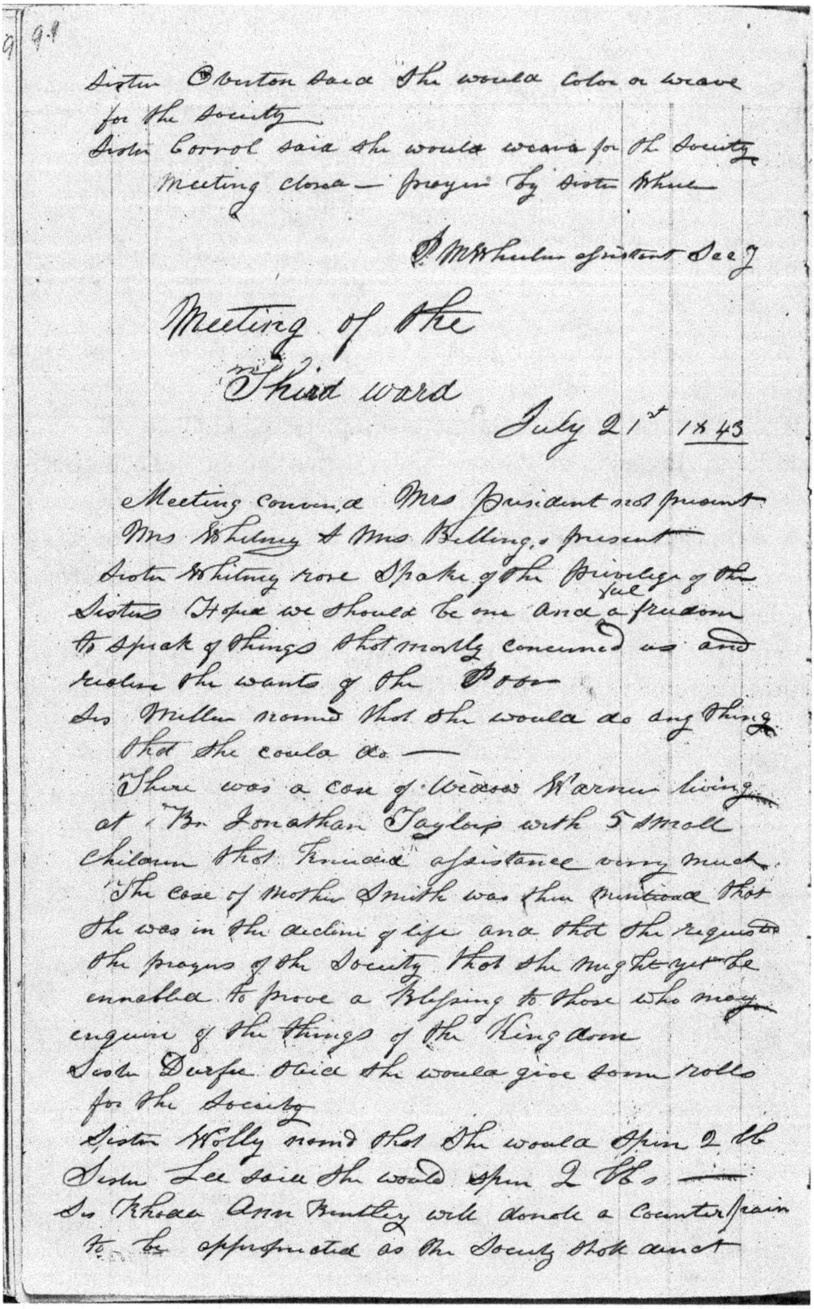

91

Sister Orton said She would color or weave
for the Society
Sister Corrol said she would weave for the Society
Meeting closed — prayer by Sister Wheeler

P M Wheeler assistant Secy

Meeting of the
Third ward

July 21st 1843

Meeting convened Mrs President not present
Mrs Whitney & Mrs Billings present
Sister Whitney rose Spake of the Privilege of the
Sisters Hoped we should be one and a feel freedom
to Speak of things that mostly concerned us and
relieve the wants of the Poor
Sis Miller named that She would do any thing
that She could do —
There was a case of Widow Warner living
at Br Jonathan Taylors with 5 small
children that needed assistance very much
The case of Mother Smith was then mentioned that
She was in the decline of life and that She requested
the prayers of the Society that she might yet be
enabled to prove a Blessing to those who may
enquire of the things of the Kingdom
Sister Durfee said She would give some rolls
for the Society
Sister Wolly named that She would Spin 2 lb
Sister Lee said She would Spin 2 lbs —
Sis Rhoda Ann Fuller will donate a Counterpain
to be appropriated as the Society shall direct

FIGURE 7.5. Nauvoo Relief Society Minutes, 21 July 1843, in handwriting of Phebe Wheeler.

Church History Library, Salt Lake City. Photograph by Welden C. Andersen.

Society. The English woman immigrated to Philadelphia in 1836 and then moved to Nauvoo in 1841.[85] Ells joined the Nauvoo Relief Society on 9 June 1842.[86] She boarded at Emma and Joseph Smith's home for two months in the summer of 1843 and for several months after Joseph Smith's death in 1844.[87] Ells remained close to fellow members of the Nauvoo Relief Society, including Jane Benbow and Phebe Woodruff.[88] She passed away in 1845 at Sarah Kimball's home in Nauvoo. Eliza R. Snow was present at her death.[89]

Finally, Elvira Cowles Holmes acted as treasurer of the Nauvoo Relief Society. The daughter of Nauvoo stake presidency counselor Austin Cowles, Holmes boarded in the Smith home and worked as a maid and a nanny. She became acquainted with Jonathon Holmes, a handyman and bodyguard to Joseph Smith, and they married on 1 December 1842.[90] Elvira Holmes and Eliza R. Snow were also close friends: Snow lived with the Holmes family in 1843.[91]

The public relationships among these Relief Society leaders is evident. It is also important to consider what is unsaid in recognizing the transitions between secretaries, illustrating the politics of personality in the Nauvoo Relief Society. Snow recorded in her personal journal that she left Nauvoo on 21 July 1843, after receiving a visit by a perturbed woman the day before, purportedly Emma Smith.[92] Wheeler, the assistant secretary,

---

85. See "Josiah Ells," 1840 US census, Hancock, Illinois, 183; "Millinery and Dress Making," *Times and Seasons* 2, no. 23 (1 October 1841): 566.

86. Nauvoo Relief Society Minutes, 9 June 1872, 68, in Derr et al., *First Fifty Years*, 83.

87. John Benbow, Affidavit, 8 August 1869, in "Plural Marriage," *The Historical Record* 6, nos. 3–5 (May 1887): 222–23.

88. Jane Holmes Benbow, also from England, became a member of the Relief Society on 19 April 1842. Nauvoo Relief Society Minutes, 19 April 1842, 30, in Derr et al., *First Fifty Years*, 50. See also Benbow, Affidavit, 8 August 1869, 222–23. Phebe Woodruff joined the Nauvoo Relief Society on 28 April 1844. Nauvoo Relief Society Minutes, 28 April 1842, 39, in Derr et al., *First Fifty Minutes*, 53. See also Hannah Ells to Phebe Woodruff, 4 May 1845 and Hannah Ells to Phebe Woodruff, 3 June 1845, Wilford Woodruff, Journals and Papers, CHL.

89. Eliza R. Snow to John Taylor, 12 December 1886, typescript, http://mormonpolygamydocuments.org/jsp-documents-book-47/, accessed 4 November 2016.

90. Nauvoo High Council Minutes, 30 March 1841; "Died," *Deseret Evening News* (Salt Lake City), 23 March 1871; Compton, *In Sacred Loneliness*, 543–48.

91. Eliza R. Snow, Nauvoo Journal and Notebook, CHL, in Beecher, *Personal Writings of Eliza R. Snow*, 64; Derr and Davidson, *Eliza R. Snow*, 218.

92. Snow, Nauvoo Journal and Notebook, in Beecher, *Personal Writings of Eliza R. Snow*, 80–81. See Newell and Avery, *Mormon Enigma*, 155.

was Snow's natural successor as secretary. Wheeler kept the minutes from July until October 1843, when she married Oliver H. Olney in Nauvoo on 19 October.[93] Wheeler's new husband had been excommunicated in 1842 and would eventually publish anti-Mormon literature in 1845.[94] Although the reason for her departure from the Relief Society was not recorded, perhaps her marriage to an unruly, vocal opponent of the church and Joseph Smith precluded the loyalty required of all Relief Society members. Minutes for the last meeting she recorded state that the meeting adjourned until the next week. She did not leave a trace of that meeting. The next recorded meeting was five months later, in March 1844, in the hand of Hannah Ells, and as seen in Figure 7.6.

Every member of the presidency and the officers lived near the Smith family at some point. Snow's relocations to different homes indicate significant relationships with home owners. She boarded with the Smith family in Kirtland and in Nauvoo, and at certain moments of tension she moved to live with Cleveland and Holmes, both officers in the presidency. Wheeler, Ells, and Holmes all lived at different times in the Smith household in Nauvoo. As previously mentioned, Emma Smith had lived with the Clevelands and with the Whitneys, and the Whitney family lived in a small house attached to the Smiths' red brick store. The Relief Society provided a geographical and emotional connection for these women to create and maintain relationships and care for each other.

While the Nauvoo Relief Society membership rolls provide a valuable resource about 1,336 women in 1840s Nauvoo, it is also important to examine the women not admitted to Relief Society.[95] Although Phebe Rigdon had been close to Emma Smith and had attended the initial planning meeting at Sarah Kimball's home, she never became a member of the Nauvoo Relief Society. Two of her daughters became members on the

93. Lyndon W. Cook, comp., *Nauvoo Deaths and Marriages: 1839–1845* (Orem, Utah: Grandin, 1994), 107; Phebe Wheeler Olney to "Uncle and Aunt Dunning," 24 January 1844, Oliver H. Olney Papers, CHL.

94. Joseph Smith History, vol. C-1, pp. 1295, 1312; "Try the Spirits," *Times and Seasons* 3, no. 11 (1 April 1842): 747–48; Oliver H. Olney, *The Absurdities of Mormonism Portrayed: A Brief Sketch* (Hancock, Illinois, 1843); Oliver H. Olney, *Spiritual Wifery at Nauvoo Exposed: Also a True Account of Transactions In and About Nauvoo* (St. Louis, 1845).

95. For membership numbers, see Derr et al., *First Fifty Years of Relief Society*, 25. According to Anne M. Boylan, such ineligibility of membership caused deep divisions between women in benevolent societies and those who were denied membership. Boylan, *The Origins of Women's Activism*, 17.

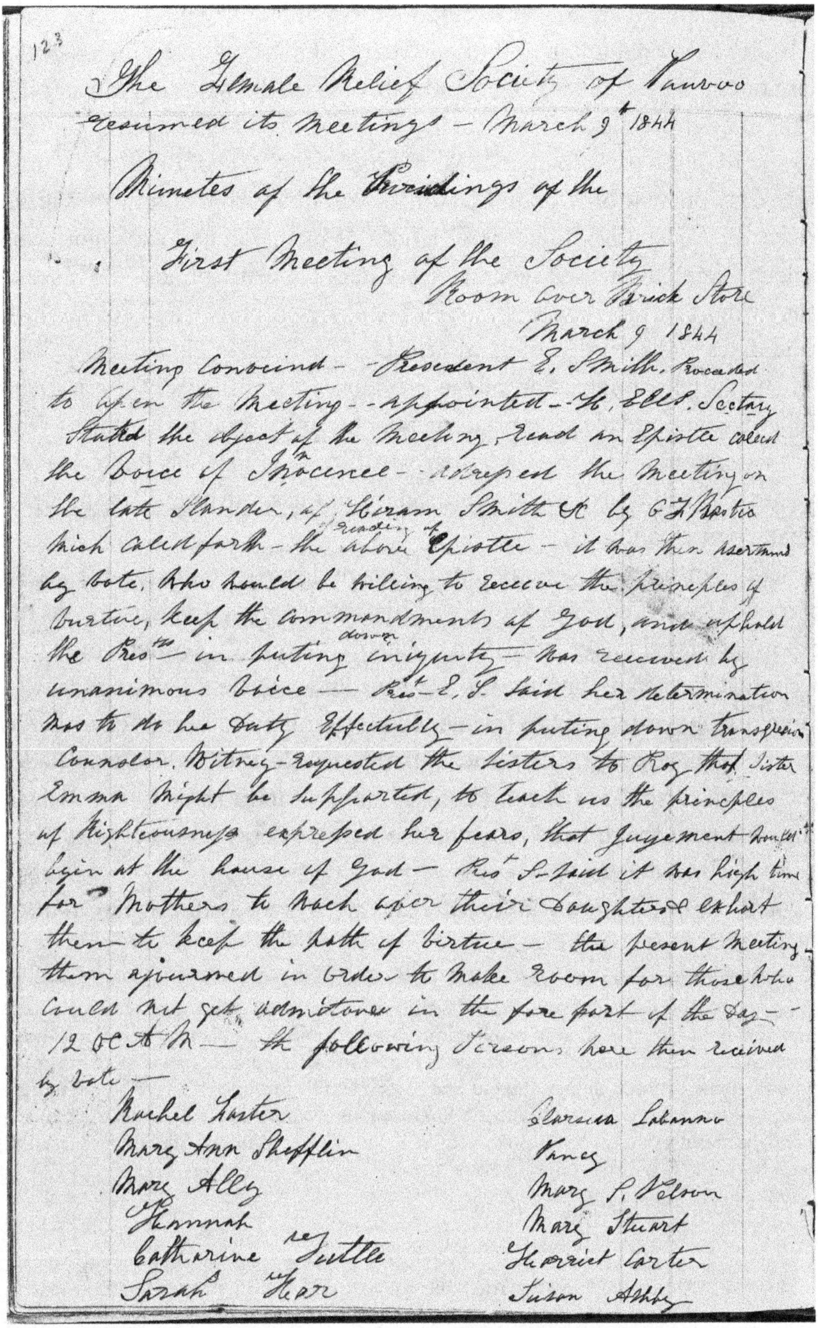

123

The Female Relief Society of Nauvoo resumed its meetings — March 9th 1844

Minutes of the Proceedings of the

First Meeting of the Society

Room over Brick Store
March 9 1844

Meeting convened — President E. Smith proceeded to open the meeting — appointed H. Ells. Sectary stated the object of the meeting, read an Epistle called the Voice of Innocence — addressed the meeting on the late slander, of Hiram Smith &c by O. F. Bostwic which called forth the reading of above Epistle — it was then ascertained by vote, who would be willing to receive the principles of virtue, keep the commandments of God, and uphold the Presdt— in puting down iniquity — was received by unanimous voice — Presdt E. S. said her determination was to do her duty effectually — in puting down transgression Counselor Witney — requested the sisters to pray that sister Emma might be supported, to teach us the principles of righteousness expressed her fears, that jugement would begin at the house of God — Presdt S — said it was high time for Mothers to watch over their daughters & exhort them to keep the path of virtue — the present meeting then ajourned in order to make room for those who could not get admittance in the fore part of the day — 12 OC A M — the following persons were then received by vote —

Rachel Foster
Mary Ann Shefflin
Mary Alley
Hannah
Catharine Settle
Sarah Hear

Clarissa Labanno
Nancy
Mary P. Nelson
Mary Stuart
Harriet Carter
Susan Ashby

FIGURE 7.6. Nauvoo Relief Society Minutes, 9 March 1844, in handwriting of Hannah Ells.

Church History Library, Salt Lake City. Photograph by Welden C. Andersen.

first day.[96] Jane Neyman was denied membership due to the inappropriate behavior of her daughters, yet fifteen years later she became the first president of the Beaver Relief Society in Utah.[97] While the wives of many significant male church leaders were active in the Nauvoo Relief Society, there is no record of the participation of Mary Ann Young, wife of Brigham Young; Ruth Clayton, wife of William Clayton; or Jennetta Richards, wife of Willard Richards. Boylan examined how "circles of inclusion and exclusion thus reflected and entrenched separate experiences of womanhood."[98] This also was evident in Mormonism's Relief Society. Acceptance and rejection of candidates was recorded in its minute book, as seen in Figure 7.7.

The social configuration of the presidency and officers of the Nauvoo Relief Society provides important details to understand its workings. The fact that women had to prove their worthiness to join the Relief Society suggests an attitude of social stratification, at the same time allowing democratic participation.[99]

Critics of Joseph Smith and Mormonism disparaged the Relief Society, perceiving a negative sense of social hierarchy among the women. In his exposé of Mormonism published in late 1842, John C. Bennett compared a cliquish proclivity among the Nauvoo Relief Society's members with three distinct orders of the female lodge, culminating in the "chambered sisters of charity."[100] In 1857, more than a decade after the Nauvoo Relief Society was disbanded, former church member John Hyde found fault in Eliza R. Snow, the link in Utah with the Nauvoo Relief Society: "Miss Eliza R. Snow, the Mormon poetess, a very talented woman, but outrageously bigoted, and one or two kindred souls, are the *nuclei* for all the female

---

96. In 1838, Phebe Rigdon and Emma Smith went to Liberty Jail together to visit their imprisoned husbands. Although two Rigdon daughters joined the Nauvoo Relief Society on 17 March 1842, there is no record of Phebe in the minutes. Perhaps this was due to the growing difficulties between Sidney Rigdon and Joseph Smith throughout 1842. Van Wagoner, *Sidney Rigdon*, 252–53, 290–302. Athalia Robinson and Nancy Rigdon's names were subsequently stricken out in different ink. Nauvoo Relief Society Minutes, March 17, 1842, 5, in Derr et al., *First Fifty Years of Relief Society*, 30.

97. See Reeder and Holbrook, *At the Pulpit*, 49–50.

98. Boylan, *The Origins of Women's Activism*, 38–39.

99. Joseph F. Darowski, "Seeking After the Ancient Order: Conferences and Councils in Early Church Governance, 1830–1834," in *A Firm Foundation: Church Organization and Administration*, ed. David J. Whittaker and Arnold K. Garr (Provo, Utah: Religious Studies Center, Brigham Young University; Salt Lake City: Deseret Book, 2011), 99.

100. John C. Bennett, *The History of the Saints; or, An Expose of Joe Smith and Mormonism* (Boston: Leland and Whiting, 1842), 217–25.

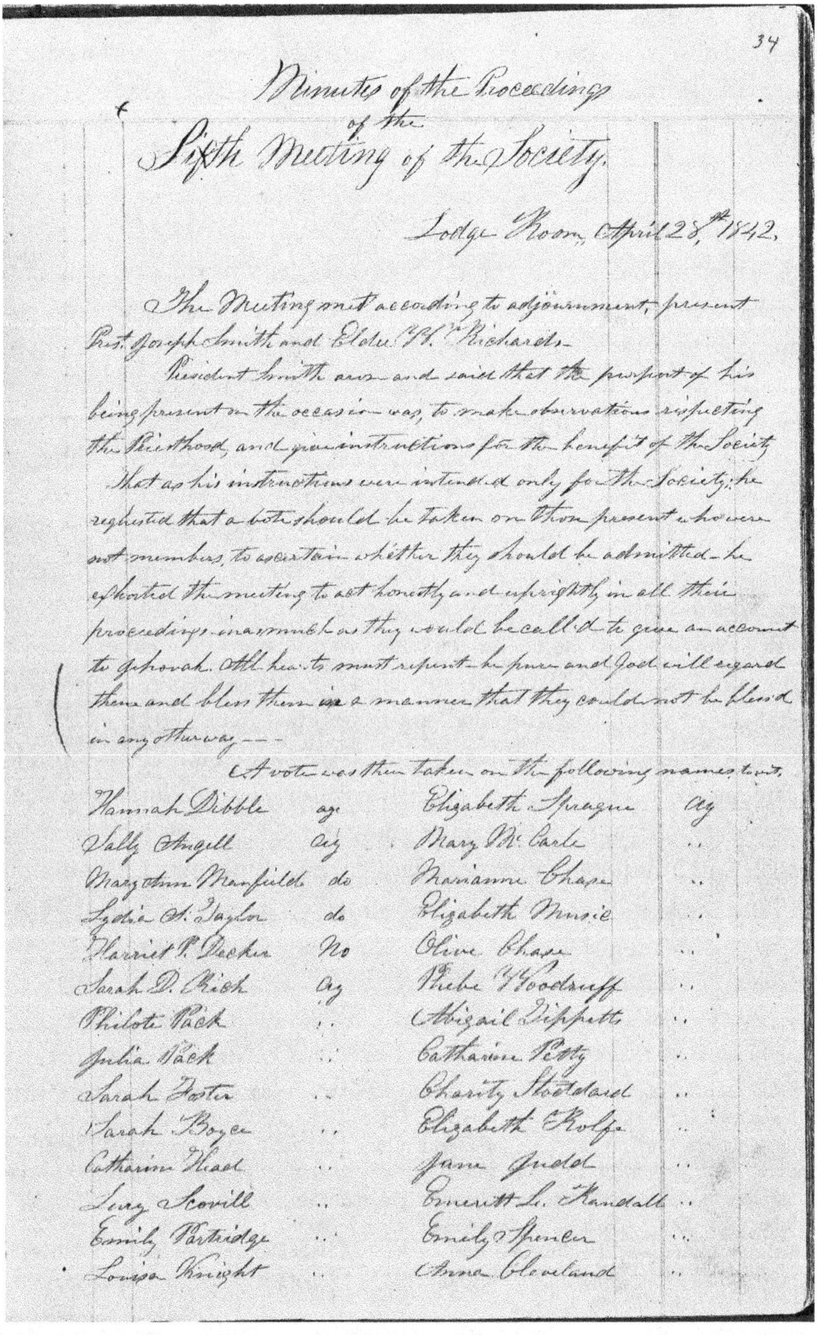

34

Minutes of the Proceedings of the Fifth Meeting of the Society.

Lodge Room, April 28th 1842.

The Meeting met according to adjournment, present Prest. Joseph Smith and Elder W. Richards.

President Smith arose and said that the purport of his being present on the occasion was, to make observations respecting the Priesthood, and give instructions for the benefit of the Society.

That as his instructions were intended only for the Society; he requested that a vote should be taken on those present who were not members, to ascertain whether they should be admitted—he exhorted the meeting to act honestly and uprightly in all their proceedings inasmuch as they would be call'd to give an account to Jehovah. All hearts must repent—be pure and God will regard them and bless them in a manner that they could not be bless'd in any other way—

A vote was then taken on the following names to wit,

Hannah Dibble	aye	Elizabeth Sprague	aye
Sally Angell	aye	Mary McCarle	..
Mary Ann Mansfield	do	Marianne Chase	..
Lydia A. Taylor	do	Elizabeth Music	..
Harriet P. Decker	No	Olive Chase	..
Sarah D. Rich	aye	Phebe Woodruff	..
Philote Pack	..	Abigail Tippetts	..
Julia Pack	..	Catharine Petty	..
Sarah Foster	..	Charity Stoddard	..
Sarah Boyce	..	Elizabeth Rolfe	..
Catharine Head	..	Jane Judd	..
Lucy Scovill	..	Emeritt L. Randall	..
Emily Partridge	..	Emily Spencer	..
Louisa Knight	..	Anna Cleveland	..

FIGURE 7.7. Nauvoo Relief Society Minutes, 28 April 1842, showing rejection of Harriet P. Decker.

Church History Library, Salt Lake City. Photograph by Welden C. Andersen.

intellect at Salt Lake. Let any recant from their creed, or oppose it, she and her band of second Amazons crush the intrepid one down."[101] Even critical observation of the Relief Society reveals impressions of hierarchical social underpinnings of the organization.

Polygamy

The Nauvoo Relief Society minute book exhibits a very deliberately constructed record regarding the contested issue of plural marriage in Nauvoo from 1842 to 1844. Beginning in 1841, Joseph Smith privately introduced what he considered a sacred religious ritual among trusted advisors and friends, some of whom were associated with Relief Society. Others took advantage of the complicated situation to cause internal division with spurious rumors. Publicly, the Relief Society addressed the Mormon stance on marriage between one man and one woman, and Emma Smith followed her charge to ensure the moral and genteel conduct of women in a civil society, as did other contemporary women's association of the time.[102]

Privately, Nauvoo Relief Society officers and members experienced a more complex history.[103] The presidency and other officers of the Nauvoo Relief Society each had a marital connection to Joseph Smith except for Phebe Wheeler, who herself had lived in the Smith home. Emma Smith, president, was his first and only publicly recognized wife. Plural marriages were not public information. First counselor Sarah Cleveland married Joseph Smith in June 1842.[104] Secretary Eliza R. Snow married Smith on 29 June 1842, and the wedding was witnessed by first counselor Sarah

---

101. John Hyde Jr., *Mormonism: Its Leaders and Designs* (New York: W. P. Fetridge, 1857), 128.

102. On 23 June 1842, "Mrs. President propos'd that a circular go forth from this society, expressive of our feelings in reference to Dr. [John C.] Bennett's character. . . said we had nothing to fear but God and keep the commandments, and in so doing we shall prosper." Nauvoo Relief Society Minutes, 23 June 1842, 68, in Derr et al., *First Fifty Years of Relief Society*, 84–85. The Relief Society published a statement against the Bennett scandal in the 1 October 1842 issue of the local newspaper, *Times and Seasons*. See Derr et al., *First Fifty Years of Relief Society*, 142–44. The four meetings of the 1844 Relief Society were dedicated to reading a document that spoke against immorality, "The Voice of Innocence." See Derr et al., *First Fifty Years of Relief Society*, 151–56.

103. According to Todd Compton, Joseph Smith was married plurally to at least twenty-three members of the Nauvoo Relief Society between 1841 and 1843. Compton, *In Sacred Loneliness*.

104. Andrew Jenson, "Joseph Smith's Plural Wives," ca. late 1880s, Andrew Jenson, Papers, CHL; Andrew Jenson, "Plural Marriage," *Historical Record* 6 (May 1887): 223, 234.

Cleveland.[105] Second counselor Elizabeth Ann Whitney's daughter, Sarah Whitney, married Smith on 27 July 1842.[106] Third secretary Hannah Ells was married to Joseph Smith in the summer of 1843.[107] It is unknown if Emma Smith knew of Ells's marriage to Joseph when she requested that Ells record the minutes of the final four meetings of the Relief Society. On 1 June 1843, the Relief Society treasurer, Elvira Cowles Holmes, also married Joseph Smith. Relief Society membership (not officers) also coincided with the plural marriage of many women to Joseph Smith. The society of women who were married to Smith proved strong. Augusta Joyce Crocheron, in writing the history of her friend Presendia Huntington Buell, a member of the Nauvoo Relief Society and a wife of Joseph Smith, connected the two communities: "The sisters who had entered into these covenants were in one sense separate and apart from all others. No tongue can describe, or pen portray the peculiar situation of these noble, self-sacrificing women, who through the providence of God helped to establish the principle of celestial marriage."[108]

Additionally, Sarah Kimball, who originated the concept of the Relief Society, had been approached by Smith in early 1842 when he requested her agreement to plural marriage. Kimball politely declined and asked him to invite someone else, to which Smith responded by asking her for referrals.[109] Kimball never held an office in the Nauvoo Relief Society, although she recorded her memory of the organization and became a significant Relief Society leader in Utah.

It is also interesting to note events occurring in Nauvoo connecting the Relief Society to polygamy that were obviously not recorded in the minute book. On 18 January 1843, during the winter hiatus of the Relief Society, the Smiths held a dinner party where both Hannah Ells and Eliza

105. Eliza Roxcy Snow Smith, Affidavit, 7 June 1869, Smith, Affidavits about Celestial Marriage, vol. 1, p. 25.

106. Sarah Ann Whitney Kimball, Affidavit, 19 June 1869, in Joseph F. Smith, Affidavits about Celestial Marriage, 1869–1915, vol. 1, p. 36, CHL; Elizabeth Ann Smith Whitney and Sarah Ann Smith Kimball, Affidavit, 13 August 1869, Smith, Affidavits about Celestial Marriage, vol. 2, pp. 25–28.

107. See John Benbow, Affidavit, 28 August 1869, Smith, Affidavits about Celestial Marriage, vol. 1, p. 74; vol. 4, p. 76.

108. Crocheron, *Representative Women of Deseret*, 30.

109. Crocheron, *Representative Women of Deseret*, 26.

R. Snow were in attendance.[110] Biographers of Emma Smith surmise that the topic of polygamy came up soon after the dinner.[111] Snow recorded in her personal journal that a month later, she relocated from the Smith home and moved in with Elvira Holmes.[112] Connected events occurred six months later when Hyrum Smith delivered the plural marriage revelation to Emma Smith on 12 July 1843.[113] Eliza R. Snow recorded her last minutes of the Relief Society on 7 July, and Phebe Wheeler took up the record at the following meeting on 15 July. During that time, Snow left Nauvoo to live with her sister in the Morley settlement, never appearing again in the Nauvoo minutes.[114] Such events are never clearly explicated in the minute book, but the timing strongly suggests complications.

Emma Smith grappled personally with polygamy and her husband's relationship with women she considered to be her friends and confidants. Her knowledge of some but not all plural marriages engaging her Relief Society constituents, while not expressly marked in the minute book for understandable reasons of propriety, certainly influenced the relationship among the women and the social climate of the organization. Many have deduced that plural marriage ended friendships as well as Relief Society participation, including the end of Snow's office as secretary.[115] While many of these women signed affidavits years later in Utah Territory witnessing their activity in plural marriage, in Nauvoo they did not speak of the complicated relationships they shared at the time they occurred. The matter became a contested battleground between public and private.[116] Thus these private relationships contributed to the tenuous complexity of personality played out in the minutes.

---

110. Joseph Smith, History, 1838–1856, vol. D-1, pp. 1453, 1455, CHL, on the Joseph Smith Papers website, josephsmithpapers.org, accessed 9 November 2016.

111. Newell and Avery, *Mormon Enigma*, 133–34.

112. Snow, Nauvoo Journal and Notebook, 11 February 1843, in Beecher, *Personal Writings of Eliza R. Snow*, 64.

113. Newell and Avery, *Mormon Enigma*, 151–52.

114. Snow, Nauvoo Journal and Notebook, 21 July 1843, in Beecher, *Personal Writings of Eliza R. Snow*, 80.

115. Newell and Avery, *Mormon Enigma*, 147–55.

116. Joseph F. Smith, Affidavits about Celestial Marriage, 1869–1915, CHL; Derr et al., *First Fifty Years of Relief Society*, 11.

Transmission and Reception of the Minute Book

The Nauvoo Relief Society minute book comes to an abrupt end on 16 March 1844. There is no explanation of the organization's termination nor a suspension of its meetings, but many circumstances must be considered. Zina Jacobs [Young] recorded in her journal that she met with the sisters later in 1844 at the Masonic Hall.[117] Perhaps there were additional meetings but no secretary to record minutes. Soon after the formation of the Nauvoo Relief Society, women also gathered in branches outside of Nauvoo, including in LaHarpe, about 20 miles east of Nauvoo, and Lima, about 30 miles south. These groups of women sent contributions that were recorded by the Nauvoo Relief Society.[118] Perhaps these branches of Relief Society continued, although there are no extant minutes. It was not until 29 March 1845 that Brigham Young ordered an effectual shut down of the Relief Society in response to "the revival of the Female Relief Society." He warned both a High Priests quorum meeting and a Seventies meeting about women meeting in the name of Relief Society and the potential danger they could cause, undermining men and priesthood authority: "I will curse ev[e]ry man that lets his wife or daughters meet again [in Relief Society]."[119]

On 16 November 1846, Willard Richards began to collect all letters and documents "which in any way relate to the History of the Church of Jesus Christ of Latter Day Saints, cataloged by Thomas Bullock."[120] The Bullock inventory did not include the Nauvoo Relief Society minute book. Whether this was an inadvertent oversight or a specific exclusion of a women's auxiliary record from the institutional church history is unknown.[121] Somehow

117. Zina D. H. Young, Diaries, 1844–1845, 18 June 1844, CHL.

118. See Nauvoo Relief Society Minutes, 14 July 1842, [77]; 2 September 1843, [116], in Derr et al., *First Fifty Years of Relief Society*, 90, 121; Glen M. Leonard, *Nauvoo: A Place of Peace, A People of Promise* (Salt Lake City: Deseret Book; Provo, Utah: BYU Press, 2002), 251.

119. Brigham Young, Discourses, 29 March 1845, in Nauvoo High Priests Quorum Record, 1841–1845, 4–5, CHL, and in Record of Seventies, Book B, 1844–1848, 77–78, First Council of the Seventy Records, CHL; both in Derr et al., *First Fifty Years of Relief Society*, 168–71.

120. Historian's Office, History of the Church, 1838–ca. 1882, vol. 14, p. 11, CHL. See Dean C. Jessee, "The Writing of Joseph Smith's History," *BYU Studies* 11, no. 4 (Summer 1971): 468–69. Thomas Bullock, Schedule of Church Records, February 1846, Historian's Office, Catalogs and Inventories, CHL. The box was unpacked in Salt Lake City on 7 June 1853. See Jessee, "The Writing of Joseph Smith's History," 469–70.

121. The Council of Fifty records were also not included in Bullock's inventory. Grow et al., *Joseph Smith Papers: Administrative Records*, 1:5.

Snow retrieved the book from Ells after the last meeting and carried it across the plains to the Salt Lake Valley.[122]

While the official Relief Society minute book seemingly disappeared from the institutional record, Mormon women continued to gather in the spirit of the charge given them by Joseph Smith to relieve the poor and save souls.[123] Zina Jacobs [Young] recorded in her diary personal visits to female friends in 1844–1845 Nauvoo, most of whom shared Relief Society affiliation.[124] After leaving Nauvoo in 1846, Eliza R. Snow and Relief Society member Patty Sessions wrote about intimate blessing meetings and spiritual gifts manifested in Winter Quarters and while crossing the plains, echoes of charismatic practices learned in the Relief Society.[125] The ongoing private practice of polygamy created small communities of sister wives who provided physical care and emotional support to each other in otherwise extremely challenging circumstances.[126] The Nauvoo Relief Society, while not meeting officially, permeated Mormon female culture.

Utah Territory in the 1850s saw a resurgence of the same benevolent spirit that sparked the Nauvoo Relief Society. Instead of sewing shirts for temple construction workers, women provided clothing and supplies for their American Indian neighbors as well as poverty-stricken handcart pioneers.[127] On 29 March 1855, Thomas Bullock and George A. Smith, appointed Church Historian the previous year, visited Brigham Young with the intent to discuss sermons Joseph Smith had given to the Nauvoo Relief Society. Young suggested that the men visit Snow, "who delivered them the original Sermon in the Female R S Record," or the Nauvoo Relief

122. Snow was present when Ells passed away at Sarah Kimball's home in Nauvoo in 1845. Typescript, Eliza R. Snow to John Taylor, 12 December 1886, http://mormonpolygamydocuments.org/jsp-documents-book-47/, accessed 4 November 2016.

123. Nauvoo Relief Society Minutes, 9 June 1842, 63, in Derr et al., *First Fifty Years of Relief Society*, 79.

124. Maureen Ursenbach Beecher, ed., "'All Things Move in Order in the City': The Nauvoo Diary of Zina Diantha Huntington Jacobs," *BYU Studies* 19, no. 3 (Spring 1979): 285–320.

125. Maureen Ursenbach Beecher, "Women in Winter Quarters," in *Eliza and Her Sisters* (Salt Lake City: Aspen Books, 1991): 75–97; Patty Bartlett Sessions, *Mormon Midwife: The 1846–1888 Diaries of Patty Bartlett Sessions*, ed. Donna Toland Smart (Logan: Utah State University Press, 1997), 32–124; Eliza R. Snow, Trail Diary, in Beecher, *Personal Writings of Eliza R. Snow*, 148–70.

126. See Beecher, "Leading Sisters," 34; Laurel Thatcher Ulrich, *A House Full of Females: Plural Marriage and Women's Rights in Early Mormonism, 1835–1870* (New York: Knopf, 2017), 162–82.

127. See Derr et al., *First Fifty Years of Relief Society*, 177–234.

Society minute book.[128] Church Historian Smith then printed the Relief Society sermons in the *Deseret News* in September 1855,[129] insinuating institutional acknowledgment of the Relief Society record as an invaluable part of LDS history. In 1868 Brigham Young encouraged official Relief Society reorganization.[130] Like Joseph Smith in 1842, Young recognized the collective power of women. He charged Snow to revive the Relief Society, expanding the Utah reiteration to every settlement.

Snow reclaimed the minute book she had so carefully written and preserved; she breathed life back into this "living constitution"—both the ledger and the embodiment of the presidency and officers. She, along with Elizabeth Ann Whitney, the two remaining women from the original "living constitution" of the presidency and officers who moved West, assisted bishops in establishing local Relief Societies.[131] They read from the original minute book and instructed new presidents and secretaries to organize and record their own constitutions, adapted to local circumstances.[132] Snow and the next four general Relief Society presidents retained the Nauvoo minute book and used it as a guide.[133]

128. Historical Department, Office Journal, 1844–2012, vol. 17, 29 March 1845, 361, CHL.

129. Joseph Smith, Discourse, 31 March 1842, in "History of Joseph Smith," *Deseret News* (Salt Lake City), 5 September 1855; Joseph Smith, Discourse, 28 April 1842, in "History of Joseph Smith," *Deseret News*, 28 September 1855, both in Derr et al., *First Fifty Years of Relief Society*, 198–208.

130. See Brigham Young, "Remarks," 8 April 1868, *Deseret News* (Salt Lake City), 13 May 1868, 106–7, in Derr et al., *First Fifty Years of Relief Society*, 262–65.

131. Maureen Ursenbach Beecher noted that the female elite of the social hierarchy in Utah, forty years after the Nauvoo Relief Society, included Eliza R. Snow, Sarah Kimball, Elizabeth Ann Whitney, Bathsheba W. Smith, Zina D. H. Young, Presendia Kimball, Mary Isabella Horne, and Phebe Woodruff, all members of the original Relief Society. Beecher, "Leading Sisters," 33.

132. For example, in Lehi, Utah, "the Bishop [David Evans] then Requested Sister [Eliza R.] Snow to read the Records of the organization of the first female Relief Society at Nauvoo." Lehi Ward, Utah Stake, Relief Society Minutes, 1868–1879, 27 October 1868, CHL.

133. Upon Snow's death, Zina D. H. Young obtained the ledger, and she in turn passed it to her successor, Bathsheba W. Smith. Smith kept a handwritten copy of the 28 April 1842 meetings of the Nauvoo Relief Society in her personal collection. When she died, her daughter, Bathsheba Merrill, donated the volume to the Church Historian's Office. Emmeline B. Wells served as general Relief Society secretary under Smith, and with her access to the Nauvoo minute book, Wells handwrote her own copy, including notes in the margins. Susa Young Gates also made her own typescript copy of the minutes. Additionally, upon the death of Bathsheba W. Smith, Amy Brown Lyman made a copy of the minutes. "Minute Book in Historian's Office Tells of First Relief Society Meeting," *Deseret News* (Salt Lake City), 12 March 1932; "Fifth meeting of the Relief Society in Nauvoo," 28 April 1842, holograph, Bathsheba W. Smith Collection, 1842–1948, CHL; Emmeline B. Wells, "Copy of the Minutes

Supplementary material elements of the volume in its current state provide additional insight to the book as a living constitution. A brown cotton chemise, possibly made from dress lining material, was created to protect the volume, either in Nauvoo or in Utah. The historic use of such book covers stemmed from early Christian tradition when missionaries carried covered religious texts; the fabric or leather covering not only protected the text from constant movement but also symbolically represented the covering and unwrapping of the literal body of Christ—the "word" of God made flesh.[134] It is possible that secretary Ells, a seamstress and milliner with access to dress lining fabric, could have made the chemise.[135] This ephemeral item transformed the business ledger to a sacred record. Additionally, a collection of pressed purple flowers, presumably violets, is found in between two blank pages near the back of the book. It is not known where the flowers came from, nor when they were picked and pressed. These additions to the minute book suggest ways in which the book was used.

The "living constitution" of the Nauvoo Relief Society was well utilized in nineteenth-century Utah. The minute book was transported and copied around the Territory, and the stories of the Nauvoo presidency permeated Utah Relief Societies. In its new iteration, the Relief Society in the West embraced and identified itself with polygamy. Defense of religious freedom became an impetus for Mormon women as they shifted into progressive efforts with suffrage, education, and economic opportunity, following the trends of their American counterparts.

Mormons encouraged engagement with the past, both through their records and through their reverence for and commemoration of significant historic leaders and founders. Although Emma Smith and Sarah Cleveland did not follow the Saints to Utah, they, along with other members of the Nauvoo Relief Society presidency, continued to expound scripture and exhort truth through other women retelling their sermons and stories. In instructions for children and teachers published in 1890, guidance was given to teach children "reverence for the Prophet Joseph

---

of the Relief Society," Emmeline B. Wells Papers, L. Tom Perry Special Collections, Harold B. Lee Library, Brigham Young University, Provo, Utah; Jill Mulvay Derr and Carol Cornwall Madsen, "Preserving the Record and Memory of the Female Relief Society of Nauvoo, 1842–92," *Journal of Mormon History* 35, no. 3 (Summer 2009): 105–7, 113–14.

134. Conversation with Katie Smith, conservator and book historian at CHL, 17 February 2016.

135. "Millinery and Dress Making," *Times and Seasons* 2, no. 23 (1 October 1841): 566.

Smith, Sister Eliza R. Snow and the Holy Priesthood."[136] In 1899, the *Woman's Exponent* recommended that Relief Society members "preserve and make the [Nauvoo minutes] a part of the record kept of the society in their respective wards, that hereafter they may have them for reference."[137] Snow described the Nauvoo minute book as a "Treasure beyond price."[138] She and Whitney became the living embodiment of the Relief Society, and the Nauvoo Relief Society minute book bore witness of this work as an important early Mormon relic.

136. "Review of Primary Associations and Instructions," *Juvenile Instructor* 25 (15 November 1890): 685.

137. "Memorable Anniversary," *Woman's Exponent* 27, no. 20 (15 March 1899): 116.

138. "Minutes of a meeting held at Ephraim, Sanpete Co., Friday, June 25th, 1875," *Woman's Exponent* 4, no. 5 (15 August 1878): 42–43.

8

Joseph Smith's Sermons and the Early Mormon Documentary Record

William V. Smith

THE EARLIEST MORMON oral preaching, including the sermons of Mormon founder Joseph Smith, was structurally much like the homiletic tradition of antebellum American Protestants. It is therefore helpful to evaluate Mormon preaching's interaction with—and to some extent, its critique of—that Protestant sermon culture.[1] This chapter focuses on Smith's oral efforts and their documentation, showing how the documentary record of Smith's preaching formed against religious imperatives and cultural expectations, and in particular how the literary value system of Mormonism moved from a textually conservative one to a system shaped in part by Mormon judicial bodies. That movement contributed to an important evolution in the way Mormon sermon documents were produced and preserved.[2]

1. The terms *Latter-day Saints, LDS, Saints,* and *Mormons* are all used to refer to members of The Church of Jesus Christ of Latter-day Saints (sometimes designated as the Utah branch of Mormonism). Prior to the death of Joseph Smith, the church was known variously as the Church of Christ, Mormonites, the Church of Latter Day Saints, the Church of Jesus Christ of Latter-Day Saints, and other variations. I use these terms without reference to era below.

2. Readers desiring a more formal acquaintance with documentary issues are invited to consult Mary-Jo Kline and Susan Holbrook Perdue, *A Guide to Documentary Editing,* 3rd ed. (Charlottesville: University of Virginia Press, 2008), Introduction. On documents surrounding Smith's preaching, see the seminal work by Dean C. Jessee, "Priceless Words and Fallible Memories: Joseph Smith as Seen in the Effort to Preserve His Discourses," *BYU Studies* 31, no. 2 (1991): 19–40. This chapter builds in part on Jessee's analysis.

Joseph Smith (1805–1844) founded Mormonism in 1830 in western New York, and became over the next two centuries the most historically revered preaching voice in the new religion.[3] Perhaps the most important observation on the state of the documentary record of Smith's preaching is that in contrast to most antebellum preachers, whose sermons are largely known through ego-documents, meaning texts produced by the preacher and not a scribe or secretary, Smith had only an indirect role in the creation of that record.[4] Indeed, early in his career he seemed to discourage the recording of sermons. Partly as a consequence of the resulting lacuna in a relatively robust record of early Mormonism, the collections of reports of Smith's sermons are small compared to his successors like Brigham Young, for whom corporate stenographic records and publications of speeches, if not complete in coverage, are routine and plentiful.

It took time and necessity to evolve a robust Mormon record-keeping ethos for sermons. In large part, the drift to a more liberal sermon culture resulted from the emphasis Smith put on new church councils and "courts" and the effort to keep accurate accounts of their activities. Counsel and instruction in such venues was reported as faithfully as any trial testimony. By the end of Joseph Smith's lifetime, the sermon had been elevated from oral expression—purposely unrecorded, uncirculated, and unprinted—to the permanent written word. Skilled clerks reported on and then published Smith's regular Sunday extempore excursions, while other observers unofficially took notes from the pews.

Moreover, the sermon began to acquire the status of revelation. Smith's dictation of "thus saith the Lord" revelation texts tapered off as his sermons became (in public and private), in broad terms, the new "revelation." During Joseph Smith's early religious career, he had pronounced numerous divine revelations that answered queries, expanded biblical passages, formed administrative bodies and policies, and directed various projects and liturgical practices. Smith's revelation texts were oral/aural entities,

---

3. The two most cited biographies of Smith are Richard L. Bushman, *Rough Stone Rolling: A Cultural Biography of Joseph Smith* (New York: Knopf, 2005), and Fawn M. Brodie, *No Man Knows my History: The Life of Joseph Smith the Mormon Prophet*, 2nd ed. (New York: Alfred A. Knopf, 1971).

4. Rudolf Dekker ed., *Egodocuments and History: Autobiographical Writing in its Social Context Since the Middle Ages* (Hilversum, Netherlands: Verloren, 2002). Critical work on the sermons of Charles Wesley demonstrates the relative uniqueness of Smith's preaching record. See Kenneth G. C. Newport, ed., *The Sermons of Charles Wesley: A Critical Edition with Introduction and Notes* (New York: Oxford University Press, 2001).

generally dictated to scribes who repeated his phrasing for approval as they wrote it on foolscap. Those texts were valued as sources of doctrine, interpretations of the Bible, and directives to individuals, groups, or the church at large. Smith's sermons, on the other hand, were rarely blessed as verbatim reports, and enjoyed virtually no redaction by him. The democratic creation of Smith's sermon corpus meant that long after his death, the content of his preaching was sometimes elevated to the Mormon canon.[5] The derivation of such scripture posthumously extended down to reports of Smith's "table talk," meaning that even the most informal preaching might evolve to written scripture, much as it did with traditions behind the New Testament Gospels.[6]

Finally, historic understanding and study of early Mormonism seems to require a thorough rethinking in light of oral/aural culture over against manuscript and print culture. Understanding the ways in which early Mormons thought about their religion and their prophet is deeply influenced by the gaps between oral archetypes, aural experience, note-taking, and the eventual print encoding of those events. To that end, perhaps the emerging discipline of Performance Criticism may make its way into the study of early Mormonism to help move beyond the bounds of an undifferentiated focus on manuscript and imprint.[7] New tools that work at the boundaries of orality, aurality, and scribality will have deeper impact as they are eventually extended to the earliest text-based traditions of Mormonism, a work that will augment the study of Mormonism as lived religion.[8]

5. There is some fascinating disjunction in the eventual creation of a largely fixed canon of Smith's revelations. In 1876, one of Smith's original apostles, Orson Pratt, created what is essentially the modern edition of Smith's revelations (the Doctrine and Covenants), and in doing so included several segments of such sermons from content audits together with sermon-letters composed by Smith and his assistants.

6. Smith was not the first to be subjected to posthumous reports of private remarks, which in his case might appear as reporting divine knowledge. See for example, Doctrine and Covenants, 129, 130, and literally, William Thompson, Statement, 23 August 1854, Joseph Smith History Documents, 1839–1860, CHL; see also Ann M. Blair, "Textbooks and Methods of Note-Taking in Early Modern Europe," in *Scholarly Knowledge: Textbooks in Early Modern Europe*, ed. Emidio Campi et al. (Geneva: Librairie Droz, 2008), 47.

7. For a lucid introduction see David Rhoads, "Performance Criticism: An Emerging Methodology in Second Testament Studies—Part I," *Biblical Theology Bulletin: Journal of Bible and Culture* 36, no. 3 (August 2006): 118–33; and David Rhoads, "Performance Criticism: An Emerging Methodology in Second Testament Studies—Part II," *Biblical Theology Bulletin: Journal of Bible and Culture* 36, no. 4 (November 2006): 164–84.

8. Many of these tools are presently being developed and employed in the study of the Pentateuch and the Gospels of the New Testament. Werner H. Kelber, *The Oral and the*

This chapter is divided into four sections. Section one (1830–1833) treats the background of Joseph Smith as a student of the religious culture of western New York, exploring how that background played out in his development as a preacher in his early Mormon career and how it interacted with the forces at work in a new religious tradition. Section two (1834–1838) considers the influence of church polity on Smith's preaching and how Smith's early experience and a growing structure for decision making and church discipline changed the early vision of preaching as ephemeral to one of more permanent value. Section three (1839–1844) briefly discusses the fruits of that change of vision and the implications of the nature of Smith's sermon documents for historiographical issues of reliability and methodology, as illustrated with examples from his preaching in these last years of his life.[9] The final section briefly discusses the posthumous transformation of Smith's manuscript sermons to print, further complicating the documentary state of those sermons.

Preaching in Early America and Early Mormonism

Preaching in antebellum America exhibited a variety of methodologies. Ministers sometimes made notes before or after preaching. Some wrote out their sermons and published them without any oral preaching event. Listeners in the pews might leave behind reports (audits) of the sermons they encountered. Many preachers spoke without any written preparation at all, and those sermons are largely lost to present human view except for the luck of a pew audit. Indeed, the extemporaneous sermon was a valued part of a number of Protestant traditions, and writing and publishing sermons had theological implications when set against Protestant views of scripture. Early Mormon preaching shared some of that worldview but, as it turned out, for somewhat different reasons.

Written Gospel: The Hermeneutics of Speaking and Writing in the Synoptic Tradition, Mark, Paul and Q (Philadelphia: Fortress Press, 1983); Werner H. Kelber and Samuel Byrskog, eds., *Jesus in Memory: Traditions in Oral and Scribal Perspectives* (Waco, Texas: Baylor University Press, 2009). On the interaction of aurality, manuscript, and print, see Meredith Marie Neuman, *Jeremiah's Scribes: Creating Sermon Literature in Puritan New England* (Philadelphia: University of Pennsylvania Press, 2013).

9. This last period is referred to as the Nauvoo era, after the Illinois town established by the Mormons following their forced exit from Missouri.

The Sermon in Antebellum America

From the Middle Ages and before, it was customary for Christian theologians to either leave behind written sermon notes or texts, or have assistants and students create notes of those events.[10] New England Puritans had similar habits, either by appointment or through spontaneous laity "audits"—which, as Meredith Neuman's work on Puritan preaching[11] has helpfully typologized, fell into three general categories. First are aural audits, where the auditor (that is, the person making a record of the sermon, perhaps an assigned clerk or secretary, or a spontaneous reporter in the pews) attempts to reproduce during the sermon an archetypal oral text. Next are content audits, where the auditor reports impressions during or after the sermon, possibly recalling some words or phrases from the event but alloying them with personal impressions or even critiques.[12] Finally, structural audits occur when the auditor lays out the logical progression and structure of the sermon.[13] Structural audits are often produced after the sermon event, based perhaps on notes taken regarding how a topic is dissected by the preacher or perhaps how a passage of scripture is divided and subdivided in the preacher's analysis (Ramist branching). These three manuscript categories not only help us understand Puritan sermons but also provide some theoretical contours for the methods used in creating Joseph Smith's public record of preaching.[14]

---

10. Blair, "Textbooks and Methods." An early example is illustrated in Peter W. Martens, *Origen and Scripture: The Contours of the Exegetical Life* (New York: Oxford University Press, 2011).

11. Neuman, *Jeremiah's Scribes.*

12. Obviously, first-order notes may count in any of Neuman's categories. Blair, "Textbooks and Methods," 39–40. First-order notes are notes taken during an event, rather than notes reconstructed later from either first-order notes and/or memory as a kind of fair, or clean copy, but these reconstructed manuscript notes also exist in what can only be described as rough form. I use the term *second-order notes* for any of these non-first-order manuscript productions. Both first- and second-order sermon notes exist for Smith's preaching, though largely the latter. Blair uses "higher-order" to describe a finer division of creation. See Ann M. Blair, *Too Much to Know: Managing Scholarly Information before the Modern Age* (New Haven: Yale University Press, 2010), 64–65, 68.

13. Neuman, *Jeremiah's Scribes,* 61–62, 88. Notes created after some settling in or notes created from first-order notes are content audits but also second-order notes.

14. Ann M. Blair defines useful terminology and methodology for understanding and documenting manuscript records of preaching. Blair, "Textbooks and Methods," 39–73; see also Olga Weijers, *Terminologie des Universitiès au XIIIe Siécle* (Rome: Edizioni dell'Ateneo, 1987), 361; and Blair, *Too Much to Know,* chap. 2.

The culture of sermon making in antebellum America was driven by a number of basic issues in tension, and some of these were centered in the notion of canon. Luther's *sola scriptura* placed the whole category of Christian literature (outside the Bible) at a lower, questionable, perhaps even dangerous level. Indeed, Luther placed those labels on certain parts of the traditional canon itself. The parallel view of *prima scriptura*, one that Smith may have seen through Methodism, allowed for a less strict boundary between preaching and canon. In any case, these ideas played out paradoxically to make the sermon both necessary and disposable. It also worked to make Evangelical Protestants mark preaching in print as less than canon and find careful justification for the inherent spiritual hubris of the published sermon.[15] As Neuman has put it, "... the knotty questions that lurk uncomfortably beneath [preaching] remain: What essentially is a sermon, and what kind of efficacy can its necessarily impaired, contingent language have in contrast to the coherent perfection of scripture?"[16]

The Protestant argument against the sermon having canonical status derived from the questionable prophetic status of the minister. That lesser status was thought to be proved by the lack of biblical prophetic gifts, which emerges from the "cessation" view that such gifts ceased after the deaths of the twelve apostles. Even the most riveting preachers were lauded with language that fell short of the biblical model; their finest sermons were described as "*almost* prophetic" or "*like* the voice of an angel." From this, Protestants registered reasons for a closed canon, guarding against ecclesial tyranny from above and untoward enthusiasm from below.[17] Smith's experiences were set over against this closed canon territory as he lamented the rejection of his early visions by a Methodist tutor. Smith's first vision experience found God declaring that ministers and creeds had corrupted the pure gospel, though later revelations

---

15. David F. Holland, *Sacred Borders: Continuing Revelation and Canonical Restraint in Early America* (New York: Oxford University Press, 2011), 115, 150; Neuman, *Jeremiah's Scribes*, 104.

16. Neuman, *Jeremiah's Scribes*, 9.

17. This is speaking generally. Preaching could go under the title of prophecy, and among Puritans that was an important category for lay auditors. Moreover, there were certainly charismatic preachers. But while a good minister might be understood as blessed by God in speaking, most preachers embraced plainness: take a text, derive doctrine, apply the doctrine. No one was making new revelation. Dawn Coleman, "The Antebellum American Sermon as Lived Religion," in Robert H. Ellison, ed., *A New History of the Sermon: The Nineteenth Century* (New York: Brill, 2010), 529–30; Holland, *Sacred Borders*, 28; Neuman, *Jeremiah's Scribes*, 2–5.

clarified that a set of sincere believers still occupied the various branches of Christianity, patrons whose good souls would resonate with the new restoration of an ancient uncorrupted faith. Smith's first visionary experience was treated with contempt not so much for its unusual nature but its seemingly authoritative declaration and consequent challenge to the Protestant safe-zone between "bishop" and "enthusiast."[18]

If Mormonism at its beginnings shattered the canonical boundary by offering an extensive new revelation (first seen as a confirmation of the Bible, and then in some sense as a corrective to its "translation"), that revelation mirrored the hope that Protestants held out for the Bible. Smith delivered a biblical doppelgänger in that sense: the Book of Mormon, purporting to consist of independent histories and extrabiblical teachings, given as a single block of revelation. The Mormons (along with many others) took pride in teasing out their inescapable truth that the Bible was inadequate to settle the challenging questions of a modern age. Drawing from biblical texts a logic for continuing revelation was a major theme in Smith's own preaching. At the same time, the Latter-day Saints appealed to other already circulating ideas—such as that the elites of Christianity had drifted from the primitive Christian patterns, falling by the wayside in their worldly accommodations and lukewarm commitment.[19]

Smith followed his five-hundred-page translation of golden plates with a stream of circumstantially (and sometimes cosmologically and often biblically) motivated divine communications that his followers saw as strengthening the call for new revelation. Early record books report over seventy of these diverse directives by the end of 1831. Many of these early revelations went well beyond the Book of Mormon, and together with later revelations were published in a rule of faith called the Doctrine and Covenants

18. See Karen Lynn Davidson et al., eds., *Histories, Volume 1: Joseph Smith Histories, 1832–1844*, vol. 1 of the Histories series of *The Joseph Smith Papers*, ed. Dean C. Jessee et al. (Salt Lake City: Church Historian's Press, 2012), 11–13, 53, 56n79 (hereafter *JSP*, H1); Richard L. Bushman, *Joseph Smith and the Beginnings of Mormonism* (Urbana: University of Illinois Press, 1985), 58–59.

19. Critics of Mormonism often used the term "gold bible" for the Book of Mormon. On critics of the establishment, see for example, John Walker and Alexander Campbell, *Infant Sprinkling* (Steubenville, Ohio: Wilson, 1820); James R. Wilburn, *The Hazard of the Die: Tolbert Fanning and the Restoration Movement* (Austin, Texas: Sweet Publishing, 1969). On the Bible in Mormonism see Philip L. Barlow, *Mormons and the Bible: The Place of the Latter-day Saints in American Religion*, 2nd ed. (New York: Oxford University Press, 2013).

(1835).[20] However, as the new religion began to develop its own practices and expectations, it moved inexorably into a position unmistakably parallel to, and yet separated from, Protestantism. In any case, after 1831 the rate of Joseph Smith's dictated communications from God decreased markedly. In their place were councils, exhortations, and sermons. Indeed, the effort defined in late 1831 to publish those revelations with a Mormon press at Independence, Missouri, seemed to anticipate this. Smith's shift from immediate revelation to group consensus was gradually formalized in permanent hierarchical structures.[21]

The Oral Sermon in Writing

Sermons among both antebellum Protestants and the earliest Mormons explicated and encouraged the heeding of scripture. If ministers took no pains to publish their own remarks, or at least leave behind sermon notes, that communication usually disappeared outside of the occasional auditor's notebook. Comparatively, sermon auditors were rarely moved to leave behind detailed reports. Frequently, ministers in American coastal population centers took to the printed word to circulate their preaching beyond the event itself. If reporting the Sunday sermon in the "provinces" was a relatively rare thing, it was still true that literally billions of pages

20. The 1835 text had 102 "sections," some of which combined various revelation texts together. In this work generally, references to the published compilation of Joseph Smith's revelations refer to the 2013 edition of the book: *The Doctrine and Covenants of the Church of Jesus Christ of Latter-day Saints* (Salt Lake City: The Church of Jesus Christ of Latter-day Saints, 2013). It is uncommon to use italics in naming Mormon books of scripture, and that convention is followed here. On Smith's earlier attempts to publish his revelations, see Robin Scott Jensen et al., eds., *Translations, Volume 2: Published Revelations,* vol. 2 of the Revelations and Translations series of *The Joseph Smith Papers,* ed. Dean C. Jessee et al. (Salt Lake City: Church Historian's Press, 2011), appendix 1 (hereafter *JSP,* R2).

21. Councils began as both decision-making bodies and church discipline functionaries, allowing for the restriction or expulsion of members who unrepentantly violated church law. Bushman, *Rough Stone Rolling,* chap. 13. William V. Smith, "Early Mormon Priesthood Revelations: Text, Impact, and Evolution," *Dialogue: A Journal of Mormon Thought* 46, no. 4 (Winter 2013): 1–84. As an example, see Lorenzo Barnes, Journal and Reminiscences, 1834–1839, vol. 2, CHL, p. 1. Instead of special revelation, which directed earlier members, people like Barnes were commissioned and dispatched to missions by councils of Mormon "high priests." Early on, councils could be vehicles for reception of Smith's revelations when the body was divided or requested Smith to ask God for direction. In one council, Cowdery suggested that the body could either grant or request a revelation text. See Matthew C. Godfrey et al., eds., *Documents, Volume 2: July 1831–January 1833,* vol. 2 of the Documents series of *The Joseph Smith Papers,* ed. Dean C. Jessee et al. (Salt Lake City: Church Historian's Press, 2013), 97 (hereafter *JSP,* D2).

of Christian homilies appeared in print every year during the boom of American religious pluralism in the early national period. The range of religious choice in antebellum America was unprecedented. Immigrants preserved the ethnic faiths of their ancestors, while others chose a particular faith for practical reasons, just as many chose to join the "ancient" lodges of Freemasonry for economic or social advantage. Some created new religions or synthesized existing faiths. Just as schools of thought developed in social theory, science, medicine, and philosophy, Americans created new brands of Christianity. Divergent religious thinking unfolded just as communal and marriage experiments found space in post-revolutionary America.[22]

In spite of this diversity, few religions of the period were founded both on new scripture texts as well as (eventually) the records of lay auditors of preaching. Smith was relatively exceptional on both counts.[23] The new scripture in the Book of Mormon functioned as prophetic credential and structural pattern, less so as quotidian wisdom.[24] Smith's preaching became the source of much of the most esoteric developments in Mormon cosmology, including baptism for the dead and the Mormon domestic heaven.

As a teenager, Smith attended a Methodist probationary class and heard revival exhorters—and may have been a volunteer himself—tasked with rousing the sensibilities of a congregation or revival camp following the ordained minister's sermon.[25] The exhorter was sometimes forbidden to read scripture, though that was not uniform. He (or she, since exhorters could be female) pressed the congregation to adhere to the minister's sermon, encouraging declarations of obedience, confession, and

22. See Daniel Walker Howe, "Charles Sellers, the Market Revolution, and the Shaping of Identity in Whig-Jacksonian America," in *God and Mammon: Protestants, Money and the Market*, ed. Mark A. Noll (New York: Oxford University Press, 2001), 54–74; Nathan O. Hatch, *The Democratization of American Christianity* (New Haven: Yale University Press, 1989), chap. 4; on ancient lodges, see Stephen C. Bullock, *Revolutionary Brotherhood: Freemasonry and the Transformation of the American Social Order, 1730–1840* (Chapel Hill: University of North Carolina Press, 1998), chap. 3.

23. Transcendentalists, Shakers, and Ellen G. White were important examples of preachers who founded contemporary religious traditions by employing, to one degree or another, the tool of the printing press. Holland, *Sacred Borders*.

24. On early preaching and the Book of Mormon, see Grant Underwood, "The Book of Mormon Usage in Early LDS Theology," *Dialogue: A Journal of Mormon Thought* 17 (Fall 1984): 35–74.

25. Bushman, *Rough Stone Rolling*, 36–38.

commitment. Exhorters were generally not ordained themselves, although their functions were sometimes performed by ministers.

Methodist practice and ideas had a profound influence on Mormonism throughout Joseph Smith's lifetime and later, perhaps especially with regard to sermon traditions. Smith's earliest documented Mormon preaching is clearly marked as exhortation, including his address at a church conference held on 9 June 1830. Reported by his Book of Mormon scribal assistant Oliver Cowdery, it read simply, "Ezekiel 14th read by br. Joseph Smith j^r and prayer by same Articles and Covenants read by Joseph Smith jr. and recieved by unanimous voice of the whole congregation . . .. Exhortation by Joseph Smith jr. and Oliver Cowdery." Mormons' reading of and assent to the Articles and Covenants was repeated in early church gatherings following a Protestant practice of creedal recitation. The report suggests that Smith had moved somewhat beyond the bounds of exhorter as it was often defined, since he appealed to the biblical theme-text directly. His speech was that of minister in part. Smith followed a pattern of preaching that, by Cowdery's words, must have seemed familiar to Protestant converts, and exhortation was a common practice in early Mormon preaching.[26]

By October 1831, Smith was teaching a small Ohio congregation the "ancient manner of conducting meetings as they were led by the Holy Ghost."[27] This event marked the beginning of more detailed reports of Smith's preaching within the context of council instruction. These "sermons" of council instruction created a style that filtered into much of Mormon preaching: Smith was setting rules and giving practical advice as well as offering theological declarations and exegetical explanations.[28]

---

26. The original 9 June 1830 audit is not extant. Before it was discarded or lost, it was copied into Minute Book 2. See Michael Hubbard Mackay et al., eds., *Documents, Volume 1: July 1828–June 1831,* vol. 1 of the Documents series of *The Joseph Smith Papers,* ed. Dean C. Jessee (Salt Lake City: Church Historian's Press, 2013), 141 (hereafter *JSP,* D1). On the Articles and Covenants, the earliest written charter of Mormonism, see *JSP,* D1:116–26. On exhortation, see, Jerry L. Tarver, "A Lost Form of Pulpit Address," *The Southern Speech Journal* 31, no. 3 (1966): 181–95. Mormon ecclesial officers were defined in terms of exhortation from the earliest period. See, for example, *JSP,* D1:124; Doctrine and Covenants 20:59.

27. Minutes, 11 October 1831, in *JSP,* D2:75.

28. Christopher C. Jones, "'We Latter-day Saints Are Methodists': The Influence of Methodism on Early Mormon Religiosity" (master's thesis, Brigham Young University, 2009); Also, Stephen J. Fleming, "'Congenial to Almost Every Shade of Radicalism': The Delaware Valley and the Success of Early Mormonism," *Religion and American Culture* 17, no. 2 (Winter 2007): 140; Raymond Bailey, "Building Men for Citizenship," in *Preaching in American History: Selected Issues in the American Pulpit (1630–1967),* ed. Dewitte Holland (New York: Abingdon Press, 1969), 143; James D. Bratt, *Antirevivalism in Antebellum*

Mormon preaching in missions seems to have centered on the existence of a new prophet in Smith and the return of the keys of the kingdom—together with the Book of Mormon as a confirming witness of ancient Christianity, the close approach of Christ's return and the necessity for a city of Zion, and the inadequacy of the Bible alone to authoritatively ensure the divine acceptance of sacraments like baptism and the Lord's Supper.[29] Preaching in the earliest Mormon congregations shared in those themes, and might be founded on a biblical passage followed by an exhortation to faithfulness.[30] But those early sermons went largely unrecorded.

Though its origin was in a new revelation, at a very early stage Mormonism experienced its own boundary issues between sermon and canon. Given its claims of new revelation, it was vital that regulation of that revelation should arise to prevent chaotic dissolution.[31] Indeed, a crisis of leadership arose just a few months after the April 1830 formal organization of the "Church of Christ," the earliest name associated with Mormonism, when Smith's revelations seemed to open the door to other believers to add their own canonical extensions.[32] In August 1830, one

---

America: A Collection of Religious Voices (Piscataway, New Jersey: Rutgers University Press, 2006), chap. 1.

29. The "keys" as seen in earliest Mormon preaching probably meant the power to see into heaven, to unlock its mysteries and reveal them to the church. See, for example, the narration of Mormon leader Edward Partridge's February 1833 sermon on Joseph Smith's powers as reported in a letter by Salmon Sherwood, *Sangamo Journal* (Springfield, Illinois), 6 April 1833, p. 2.

30. On early Mormon preaching, see, for example, William E. McLellin's journals in John W. Welch and Jan Shipps, eds., *Journals of William E. McLellin* (Provo, Utah: Brigham Young University Press, 1994); for Joseph Smith's brother Hyrum Smith's missionary journal, see Hyrum Smith, Diary and Accounts, 1831–1844, CHL; Wilford Woodruff's 1834 and 1835 journals in Scott G. Kenney, *Wilford Woodruff's Journal*, 9 vols. (Salt Lake City: Signature Books, 1983); Samuel H. Smith and Orson Hyde in Orson Hyde, Journal, February–December 1832, CHL; and Fleming, "Almost Every Shade of Radicalism." On the Missouri mob, see W. Paul Reeve, *Religion of a Different Color: Race and the Mormon Struggle for Whiteness* (New York: Oxford University Press, 2015), 114–26.

31. On Smith's developing exclusivity as revelator, see early dissident Ezra Booth's account in Ezra Booth, Nelson, OH, to Rev. Ira Eddy, 29 November 1831, in Ezra Booth, "Mormonism—Nos. VIII–IX," *Ohio Star* (Ravenna), 8 December1831, p. 1.

32. See Joseph Smith's early revelations to Oliver Cowdery in Robin Scott Jensen et al., eds., *Revelations and Translations: Manuscript Revelation Books*, facsimile ed., vol. 1 of the Revelations and Translation series of *The Joseph Smith Papers*, ed. Dean C. Jessee et al. (Salt Lake City: Church Historian's Press, 2009), 15, 19, 21 (page 21 missing) (hereafter *JSP*, MRB); Doctrine and Covenants 8, 9, 18:1–5; Robin Scott Jensen, "'Rely Upon the Things which are Written': Text, Context, and the Creation of Mormon Revelatory Records," (master's thesis, University of Wisconsin-Milwaukee, 2009), 158.

such believer, Hiram Page, began contributing revelations. At a September Mormon conference, Smith dictated a revelation that not only focused on Page but also on Oliver Cowdery, Smith's co-leader during the New York phase of the church (1830–1831).

This revelation formalized a hierarchy of value in religious expression. Though important in the new movement, Cowdery was not to "*write* by way of commandment,"[33] but he could render authoritative work from the pulpit. The meaning was clear: any written canon beyond the Bible was Joseph Smith's domain, while Cowdery's work was preaching.[34] Cowdery's preaching, since it was not to be written, could not really have the force of the canonical in any meaningful way, though he might "speak" by way of commandment, *as it would not, by revelatory regulation, be remembered in black and white.*[35] Canon is generally defined as written law, and though Cowdery's words might have the force of commandment, they lacked the force of portability. They were therefore limited by space and time and so suffered from a temporary physics. Other early Mormon preachers were under the same ban, which was only strengthened by the emphatic millenarian nature of the faith in its first nine years. That early sermons assured listeners of the limited time before Christ's second appearing seems obvious, and yet such preaching left few representing texts.[36] Perhaps the nearness of the end time made it seem that the topic needed no reinforcement.

---

33. Emphasis added. See *JSP*, MRB:51–53. Joseph Smith's revelations were redacted for publication and this was no exception. However, the important points of this text are found in the current printed edition in Doctrine and Covenants 28. On the act of creating revelation texts and their relation to the spoken revelations, see *JSP*, MRB:xxvii.

34. The Mormon definition of canon is more clouded yet, and there is no attempt to define it precisely here. For a working definition, we may use the LDS term "Standard Works," which came to mean the currently accepted four books: the Bible, Book of Mormon, Doctrine and Covenants, and Pearl of Great Price. The term *scripture* is even more nebulous and does not always coincide with the Standard Works. On Page, see Bushman, *Rough Stone Rolling*, 120–21. "Standard Works" was a term extracted from nineteenth-century discourse and originally referred to a broader set of references than Mormon scripture texts. George A. Smith, Discourse, Salt Lake City, 7 April 1867, in George D. Watt et al., eds., *Journal of Discourses*, 26 vols. (Liverpool: F. D. Richards, 1855–1886), 11:363.

35. Jensen, "Text, Context," 161–62; *JSP*, MRB:109–13; Doctrine and Covenants 43.

36. One brief report of a February 1835 sermon had Smith suggesting that only 56 years were left. Minutes, Discourse, and Blessings, 14–15 February 1835, in Matthew C. Godfrey et al., eds., *Documents, Volume 4: April 1834–September 1835*, vol. 4 of the Documents series of *The Joseph Smith Papers*, ed. Ronald K. Esplin et al. (Salt Lake City: Church Historian's Press, 2015), 225 (hereafter *JSP*, D4).

Thus, both cultural heritage and revelation within Mormonism placed the sermon in an even more restricted domain than it occupied in the parent faiths of early Latter-day Saints. It was important as exhortation, but clearly and specifically not regarded as canon and not to be written. The written word was pronounced superior to the spoken word, with some irony since Smith's revelations were first spoken, then written.[37] The partitioning of the authoritative sermon outside the category of authoritative printed material marked the sermon as lesser discourse among the earliest Mormons; the thin documentary record for Smith's own early extemporaneous preaching helps demonstrate the power of this communication hierarchy. The Page–Cowdery episode witnesses to the difficulty new religious traditions encounter in establishing this boundary between oral and scribal authority.

In a seeming reversal of position, a later (1 November 1831) revelation to Smith flirted with the homiletic expansion of canon. This revelation may seem to suggest a breaching of canonical walls by mere rank-and-file Mormon preachers: the ordained "high priest" preachers of Mormonism were to "proclaim the everlasting gospel by the Spirit of the living God, from people to people . . . in the congregations of the wicked, reasoning and expounding all scriptures unto them . . . and whatsoever they shall speak when moved upon by the Holy Ghost shall be scripture, shall be the will of Lord, shall be the mind of Lord, shall be the word of the Lord, shall be the voice of the Lord, and the power of God unto salvation."[38]

---

37. The process of recording Joseph Smith's revelations was apparently rather slow and painstaking, requiring the speaker to repeat phrases at times and speak with a slow cadence, referred to below as dictation speech. *JSP*, MRB:xxii; Jensen, "Text, Context," 1–3.

38. See *JSP*, MRB:199; Doctrine and Covenants 68:1–5. Few early Mormon women participated at the pulpit in this early period. It was not that the movement did not recruit erudite and thoughtful women. Eliza Snow, Elizabeth Whitney, Martha Coray and many others were capable, clear writers and thinkers. One outlet for some of that expressive power would come with the Female Relief Society of Nauvoo and its Utah daughter institutions and their eventual print outlets. In Protestantism as well, female preaching in nineteenth-century America carried high hurdles. Women were seen as too modest to allow men to stare at them in public. The elevated pulpit placed women in an indelicate position. Female preachers might therefore be seen in the category of actresses or prostitutes, who were seen as shameless fallen women. Catherine A. Brekus, *Strangers and Pilgrims: Female Preaching in America* (Raleigh: University of North Carolina Press, 1998), 14–16; Christine L. Krueger, *The Reader's Repentance: Women Preachers, Women Writers, and Nineteenth-Century Social Discourse* (Chicago: University of Chicago Press, 1992). On early Mormon women, see Jill Mulvay Derr et al., eds., *The First Fifty years of Relief Society: Key Documents in Latter-day Saint Women's History* (Salt Lake City: Church Historian's Press, 2016).

This language seems to suggest a breach of the sermon/canon boundary set in place in September 1830. However, the word "scripture" is used in two distinct ways in the 1831 revelation. Its first appearance in the revelation's text clearly had reference to the Bible. Its second appearance, while arguably somewhat shocking to most worldviews at the time, stops short of written canon. Indeed, when read in the context of the 1830 Page–Cowdery revelation, it may be (and was) regarded in the same light. Though they might be inspired, these sermons mentioned in the 1831 revelation were not in the same category as the Bible. They were not to be enshrined in writing. The ground broken here was in fact already plowed by Page–Cowdery. It merely broadened a portion of Cowdery's preaching rules to the church's newly introduced "high priests."[39] Sidney Rigdon, a Campbellite preacher who converted to Mormonism in 1830, while not mentioned by name in the 1831 revelation was by that time the Ohio preaching voice of Mormonism by experience and later by divine appointment.[40] Rigdon's preaching was rarely part of the Mormon written record at this stage.

The fence between orality and written canon, and Smith's careful regulation of the traffic between them, generally resisted change until the mid-1830s. But finally the boundary suggested by the September 1830 revelation was swept away. Having authoritative written words was vital to the effort to explain Mormonism to the population at large, based on Mormon claims of restoration and revelatory direction. The fact that change took so long was at least partly centered in Smith's reluctance to do his own writing.[41] Between 1831 and 1833, only about thirteen of Smith's sermons had been reported, and those reports were rarely more than a sentence or two.[42] With little formal education, Smith found written expression challenging

---

39. Smith, "Early Mormon Priesthood Revelations," 6–7.

40. See an 1833 revelation, *JSP*, MRB:559; Doctrine and Covenants 100. Cowdery, who returned to the Ohio headquarters from a Missouri assignment about the time of this 1833 revelation, gradually (but temporarily) resumed his position next to Joseph Smith in the hierarchy. *JSP*, H1:34.

41. The Book of Mormon frequently found fault with a paid ministry, and early Mormons extended this view in some degree to Joseph Smith's clerks and scribes. Cowdery, who penned most of the Book of Mormon, had no reimbursement for his labors beyond room and board. This issue was partly resolved in theory with the innovations of the Literary and United Firms in the first years of Mormonism. See *JSP*, R2:xxviii; Bushman, *Rough Stone Rolling*, 181, 185; Peter Crawley, *A Descriptive Bibliography of the Mormon Church*, 3 vols., (Provo, Utah: Religious Studies Center, Brigham Young University, 1997–2012), 1:18.

42. Minutes, 25–26 October 1831, in *JSP*, D2:83–85.

and so recruited others to pen his journals, histories, revelations, and finally his sermons as they came to form official communication.[43] As well, the movement to record sermons was delayed by the sensibilities of early Mormons, who saw sermons as necessary but lesser events in the fledgling church and who found little use for their detailed content in their recorded history.[44] Indeed, Mormon preaching was frequent, and its themes were common. Smith's revelations continually encouraged church elders and missionaries to unceasing preaching effort.[45] It was through the church's regulative minute books that sermons found a more robust presence in the written record.

Sermon Note-Taking in the Context of Developing Church Regulation

The *ex tempore* pattern of most Protestant preaching left little in the way of extended reports of those events, making them objects of mystery.[46] Within that mammoth genre, Joseph Smith represents an interesting

43. In Joseph Smith's lifetime and particularly his early years, the power of language manifested itself in many of his projects. His own frustration with it fueled some of the fascination with a "pure" language of heaven, Adam and Eve, and the angels. See Samuel M. Brown, "The Translator and the Ghostwriter: Joseph Smith and William W. Phelps," *Journal of Mormon History* 34, no. 1 (Winter 2008): 26–62. One exception to the general rule of extremely brief sermon records in the early 1830s was a four-paragraph Cowdery audit of an October 1831 instruction on ecclesial duty and salvation assurance.

44. Prophecy or testimony were mentioned by Whitmer (for example, see chapters 1 and 10 of Whitmer's history) but otherwise little or nothing beyond the preaching event (styled usually as calling to repentance). Davis Bitton, "Kirtland as a Center of Missionary Activity," *BYU Studies* 11, no. 4 (1971): 6. Richard Lloyd Anderson, "The Impact of the First Preaching in Ohio," *BYU Studies* 11, no. 4 (1971): 474–96. Barbara McFarlene Higdon, "The Role of Preaching in the Early Latter Day Saint Church, 1830–1846" (PhD diss., University of Missouri, 1961); S. George Ellsworth, "A History of Mormon Missions in the United States and Canada" (PhD diss., University of California, Berkeley, 1951).

45. Not only were biblical exemplars discussed, but nearly one hundred separate commands to preach appear in Smith's Doctrine and Covenants.

46. Charles Wesley seems typical. Newport, *Sermons of Charles Wesley*, 40. Alexander Campbell's most famous address, "Sermon on the Law" is found in what is most surely a very edited form by Campbell himself, thirty years after the fact. See *Millennial Harbinger* 3, no. 9 (September 1846): 493–521. On orality and print, Robert H. Ellison, *The Victorian Pulpit: Spoken and Written Sermons in Nineteenth-Century Britain* (Cranbury, New Jersey: Susquehanna University Press, 1998) and more generally, George P. Landow, *Elegant Jeremiahs: The Sage from Carlyle to Mailer* (Ithaca, New York: Cornell University Press, 1986). On orality and Joseph Smith, see Jensen, "Text, Context," 41–67. Colonial America's most influential theologian, Jonathan Edwards, found it impossible to preach without written text and never became proficient as an extemporaneous speaker.

trajectory.[47] Certainly, he compared and contrasted himself with the well-known Rigdon. Though Smith's earliest attempts went mostly unreported, almost surely he followed the pattern set by his early brush with Methodism, "taking a text"[48] in plain style, in keeping with his early experience. This evolved to a more free-form address within a few years, with Smith sometimes speaking to a topic and using a variety of biblical texts in support. He admitted that he found the theme-text practice confining, though he and other Mormons often paid homage to it.[49]

If Smith was becoming freer to experiment with the sermon traditions available to him, his followers were increasingly employed as record keepers of those sermons, especially if they were involved in church governance. As Smith developed deliberative bodies (the 1834 "high council" system was a landmark in government and discipline) to consider problems in church regulation, complaints of church members against each other, or other governing matters, he put in place strict rules regarding record keeping, a move founded on earlier revelations.[50] The Mormons were therefore recorders of their corporate doings by divine commandment and prophetic imperative. Meanwhile, in early 1835, Smith created a council of apostles modeled on the New Testament group. Instructing the group, he impressed his policy of reporting council proceedings:

> After the company were assembled, and the meeting opened by prayer of President J. Smith Junr., he (President Smith) arose and said, he had something to lay before the Council . . .. He had for himself, learned a fact, by experience, which on reflection, always gave him a deep sorrow. It is a fact . . . that if I now had in my possession every decision which has been had upon important items

47. The sermons of antebellum America remain an untapped area of study. Coleman, "Antebellum American Sermon," 521–22.

48. As a typical example of that method, one New York minister took for his text 1 Thessalonians 4:13. He gave his interpretation of the passage and then discussed the nature of sorrow and how this passage restricted what Christians should feel at the death of another person. E. J. Wheeler, *Pulpit and Grave: A Volume of Funeral Sermons and Addresses* (New York: Funk and Wagnalls, 1884), 103.

49. See reports of Joseph Smith's 11 June 1843 sermon. Also see Joseph Smith's almost unconscious wide-ranging use of biblical text in a sermon of 12 May 1844. Texts may be found at http://boap.org/LDS/Parallel.

50. *JSP*, MRB:639; Doctrine and Covenants 102; Jensen, "Text, Context," 69ff. See also, Smith, "Early Mormon Priesthood Revelations."

> of doctrine and duties which have been given since the commencement of this work, I would not part with it for any sum of money, but we have neglected to take minutes of such things, thinking, perhaps, that they would never benefit us afterwards, which, had we now, would decide almost any point of doctrine, which might be agitated.[51]

The minute book containing this report demonstrates the early interest in capturing the accumulating regulation of the little church. That capture began to include instructive remarks. This, combined with a more consistent effort at reporting Smith's own activities with a clerk-kept journal, made 1835 a more productive year for reporting (however briefly) Smith's preaching. Still, those audits were only robust when they formed part of regulatory councils.[52]

With Smith's decreasing output of revelation texts and the increase in breadth of his oral expression, some confusion of the two categories developed.[53] More observers saw revelation in Smith's remarks, and he used preaching as an important adjunct to his ministry—not just in the locally confined space initially allocated to Cowdery, but as a medium of instruction with more permanence and distribution. During an 1836 temple dedication, a pew audit of Smith's remarks shows that he reviewed his angelic call and ordination to the ministry, and also "testified of the Angel of the Lord's appearing unto him to call him to the work of the Lord, & also being ordained under the hands of the Angel of the covenant."[54] An April 1837 address declared the "order of heaven," according to a relatively long official content audit.[55]

Hence, over his career two closely linked forces acted to make Joseph Smith's sermons more than just Sunday exhortation: his own evolving vision of his communications and their value, and the nature of government in the maturing church. Records of decisions by church councils and associated explanations might stand as near canon, particularly when they

---

51. Minutes and Discourses, 27 February 1835, in *JSP*, D4:253.

52. A 2 May 1835 council reported some 500 words of Smith's instruction, while a Smith journal entry (now typically made by an assigned clerk) for a Tuesday evening sermon in November of the same year merely mentioned this preaching with no indication of content.

53. On Joseph Smith's revelation "schedule," see *JSP*, R2:ix.

54. Stephen Post, Journal, July 1835–March 1839, CHL, 27 March 1836.

55. *Latter Day Saints' Messenger and Advocate* 3 (Apr. 1837): 486–87.

launched new interpretation, doctrine, or practice (which, at least in theory, they could).[56] Smith's preaching outside the instructional scene still left behind only brief acknowledgments of those events, and it is to Smith's diary clerks that we owe much of the information about those sermons, if not their content. During the last period of Smith's life in Nauvoo, Illinois, his journal keepers began to make more extensive reports of sermons.

The Blooming of Sermon Records in the Nauvoo Period

Populist movements like Methodism followed old patterns of going "into the fields" to meet farmers, mechanics, and artisans on the ground. In like manner, Smith's early sermons were in small gatherings and typically delivered in homes or other shelters. Like other popular preachers, however, his draw soon outgrew the small schoolhouses and homes of fellow Mormons or interested listeners. At the end of his career, Smith, like many other divines of the early republic and their predecessors in the Atlantic world, spoke to large crowds in open-air venues. Trained or naturally gifted preachers like Anglican George Whitefield might preach for hours to extraordinary outdoor crowds without tiring significantly.[57] Unless the average speaker was trained for such efforts, the experience

56. See Joseph Smith's remarks of 27 February 1835 noted above. The Mormon "patriarchal blessing" stood in a kind of no man's land. More than the sermon-scripture of 1831, but less than canon (never published *en masse*), it was nevertheless written and kept as part of the official church record. See Samuel Brown, *In Heaven as It Is on Earth: Joseph Smith and the Early Mormon Conquest of Death* (New York: Oxford University Press, 2011), chap. 5; Irene M. Bates and E. Gary Smith, *Lost Legacy: The Mormon Office of Presiding Patriarch* (Urbana: University of Illinois Press, 1996); H. Michael Marquardt, *Early Patriarchal Blessings of The Church of Jesus Christ of Latter-day Saints* (Salt Lake City: Smith-Petit Foundation, 2007). Armand L. Mauss, *All Abraham's Children: Changing Mormon Conceptions of Race and Lineage* (Chicago: University of Illinois Press, 2003). Also, Gary Shepherd and Gordon Shepherd, *Binding Earth and Heaven: Patriarchal Blessings in the Prophetic Development of Early Mormonism* (University Park: Penn State University Press, 2012). Joseph Smith evolved in the way he saw the church landscape. The earliest cohort of Mormons from his New York career were less flexible. Peter Crawley, "The Passing of Mormon Primitivism," *Dialogue: A Journal of Mormon Thought* 13, no. 4 (Winter 1980): 26–37. Church discipline was modeled on civil judiciary in many respects. Smith, "Early Mormon Priesthood Revelations."

57. Whitefield gave upwards of 18,000 sermons, seventy-eight of which have appeared in print. A significant number remain unpublished, but the great majority have no remaining record. Benjamin Franklin notes in his autobiography (chapter 10) his impressive experience of hearing Whitefield preach with amazing clarity to tens of thousands in Philadelphia. Harry S. Stout, *The Divine Dramatist: George Whitefield and the Rise of Modern Evangelicalism* (New York: Eerdmans, 1991), 6–8. Also, Newport, *Sermons of Charles Wesley*, 40–41.

was exhausting. When Joseph Smith spoke to such large assemblies, he often complained of fatigue and "sore lungs,"[58] though he found some of the elocution techniques used to reach large audiences or impress congregations unbecoming of the Mormon preacher.[59] The transition to the outdoor church may have come by necessity for lack of chapel space, but it was never the preferred method ultimately. One reason the revival was feared by some American Protestants was its natural attraction for all kinds of people. The walls of the sanctuary contained the godly, but an outdoor church might mingle believers with the lowest members of society. Even atheists and scoffers were enabled to gain a voice if they were loud enough. Smith had his share of public scoffers at sermons, though he was quite capable of shouting them down in turn.[60]

Smith engaged classical preaching styles in his own way: if he didn't parse a single text in a sermon cycle,[61] he could and did mount extended examinations of topics, sometimes mixing eclectic collections of biblical passages with homespun advice or testimony of his angelic encounters. Two ambitious cycles expounded on "election," which ran from May 1843 through October 1843, and "resurrection," with various sermons beginning in March of 1844 and running through June of the same year, with both centered around Smith's explosive written revelation on polygamy in

58. For example, see his remarks in sermons of 13 August 1843 and 8 April 1844. Pew auditor Wilford Woodruff found it remarkable that Joseph Smith had enough strength to participate in strenuous activities following an open-air sermon.

59. Elocution instructors offered ministers training in addressing large outdoor venues. Such techniques and characteristic dramatic forms might make the speaker sound unnatural, using a higher register that may have been distasteful to Joseph Smith. He instructed: "the speaker should all ways speak in his Natureal tone of voice; & Not to keep in one loud strain; But to act without affectation." William P. McIntire, Notebook, 1840–1845, CHL, pp. [1]–[2]. On styles, see Coleman, "Antebellum American Sermon."

60. On aspects of the outdoor church in antebellum America see Robert Laurence Moore, *Selling God: American Religion in the Marketplace of Culture* (New York: Oxford University Press, 1994), 46–47. Smith related this experience from his 1840 preaching in Pennsylvania: "when I was preaching in Philadelphia a quaker wanted a sign-I told him to be still. after sermon he wanted a sign. I told the congregatin the man was an adulterer. 'a wicked & adulterous generation.' & the Lord to me in a revelation that any man who. wanted a sign was adulteros person. - It is true said one for I caught him in the very act. - which he afterward confessed when he was baptized." See Andrew H. Hedges et al., eds., *Journals, Volume 2: December 1841–April 1843*, vol. 2 of the Journals series of *The Joseph Smith Papers*, ed. Dean C. Jessee et al. (Salt Lake City: Church Historian's Press, 2011), 258.

61. Smith sometimes did develop something like *continua* around a passage. One source passage during this era came from Hebrews 6:2–6. For example, see Smith's sermons of 27 June 1839 and 12 May 1844. See http://boap.org/LDS/Parallel (accessed 4 August 2016).

July 1843.[62] These sermons had a far more robust group of auditors than those from any previous era.

Joseph Smith's later sermon form clearly registers his instructional regulation of church praxis, which transformed the habits acquired during his early experiences in Methodism. As council government matured and attitudes changed, Smith's preaching moved from early staples to the aforementioned sermon cycles ranging from foundational theology (including a radical cosmology/ontology) to an evolving exegesis of New Testament Letters. One of the more unusual examples of documenting Smith's preaching in Washington, DC, 5 February 1840, appears in a journalist's letter that rather mysteriously ended up in Mormon archives.[63] The letter, as seen in Figure 8.1 demonstrates Smith's brash piercing of the theological systems around him with an internal logic that tangles the ontological natures of God and humankind. Smith declared that God is eternal but that the human soul had no beginning or end, a serious breach of classical theism. For documentary purposes, it is an outlier from the usual homegrown audits. Its material value is high, but its content demonstrates an important consistency—it shows Smith's previous testimony habit, but also a more adventuresome theological journey—and an important transition in style and confidence.

In addition to a semi-conscious evolution of bureaucratic rules on recording and publishing the oral expressions of church leaders, a companion trend developed among Latter-day Saints in the early 1840s. Gradually, some recruits to the developing church saw Joseph Smith's sermons as having lasting value and even a kind of canonical rank.[64] Wilford Woodruff, Eliza R. Snow, and Martha Jane Knowlton were three of these. Woodruff began his rising career in Mormonism nearly four years after the New York organization of the church. He gradually became an unofficial auditor of some note, demonstrating a gradual increase in reporting

62. For more on the 1843 revelation and its link to preaching, see William V. Smith, *Textual Studies in the Doctrine and Covenants: The Plural Marriage Revelation* (Salt Lake City: Greg Kofford Books, forthcoming in 2017).

63. Suspected of being a Mormon "plant" to report Smith's preaching in a positive light, the letter was recently verified by historian Richard L. Jensen to be from well-known nineteenth-century journalist and Aaron Burr biographer, Matthew L. Davis. Another less detailed audit appeared in a New York Methodist paper, *Christian Advocate and Journal*, 6 March 1840, 1.

64. That status was generally informal, but for its development see Franklin D. Richards and James A. Little, *A Compendium of the Doctrines of the Gospel* (Salt Lake City: By the authors, 1882), iii.

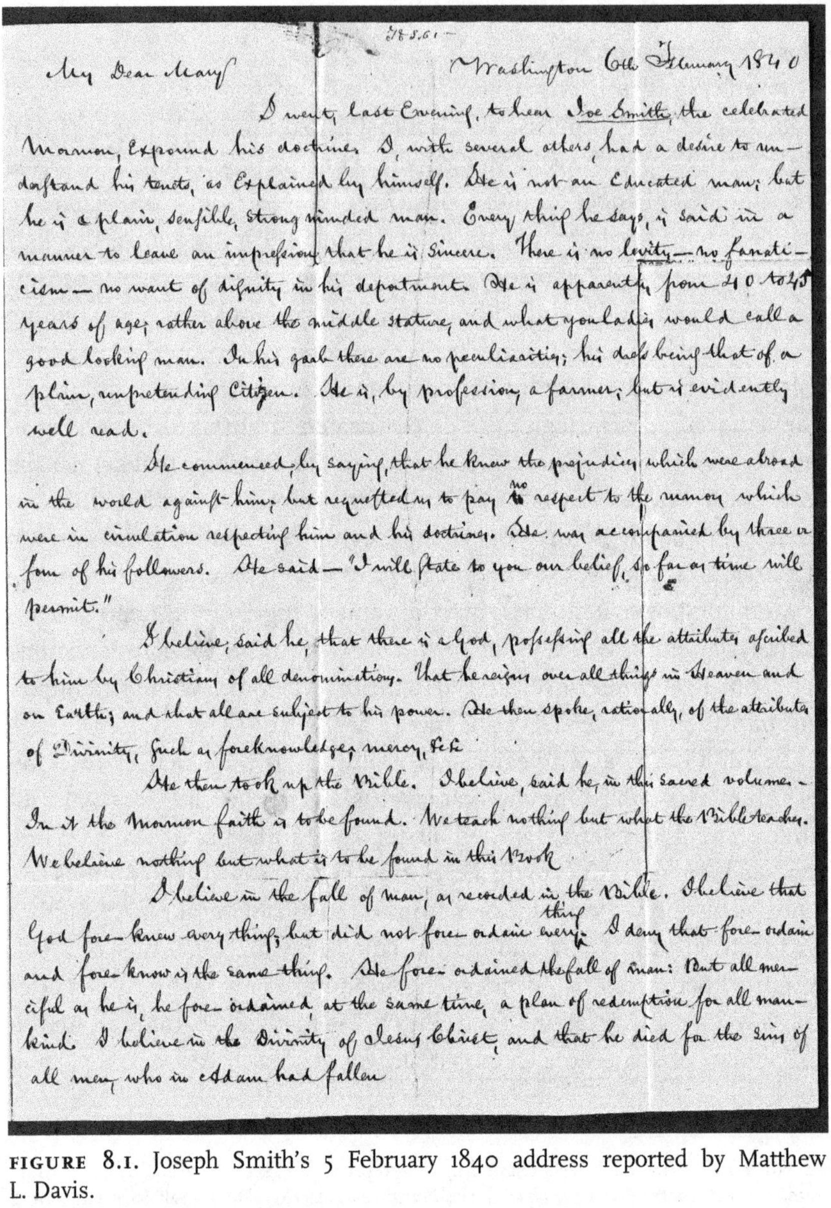

My Dear Mary

Washington 6th February 1840

I went, last Evening, to hear Joe Smith, the celebrated Mormon, Expound his doctrines. I, with several others, had a desire to understand his tenets, as Explained by himself. He is not an Educated man; but he is a plain, sensible, strong minded man. Every thing he says, is said in a manner to leave an impression that he is sincere. There is no levity — no fanaticism — no want of dignity in his deportment. He is apparently from 40 to 45 years of age; rather above the middle stature, and what you ladies would call a good looking man. In his garb there are no peculiarities; his dress being that of a plain, unpretending Citizen. He is, by profession, a farmer; but is evidently well read.

He commenced, by saying, that he knew the prejudices which were abroad in the world against him; but requested us to pay no respect to the rumors which were in circulation respecting him and his doctrines. He was accompanied by three or four of his followers. He said — "I will state to you our belief, so far as time will permit."

I believe, said he, that there is a God, possessing all the attributes ascribed to him by Christians of all denominations. That he reigns over all things in Heaven and on Earth; and that all are subject to his power. He then spoke, rationally, of the attributes of Divinity, such as foreknowledge, mercy, &c &c.

He then took up the Bible. I believe, said he, in this sacred volume. In it the Mormon faith is to be found. We teach nothing but what the Bible teaches. We believe nothing but what is to be found in this Book.

I believe in the fall of man, as recorded in the Bible. I believe that God fore-knew every thing, but did not fore-ordain every thing. I deny that fore-ordain and fore-know is the same thing. He fore-ordained the fall of man: But all merciful as he is, he fore-ordained, at the same time, a plan of redemption for all mankind. I believe in the Divinity of Jesus Christ, and that he died for the sins of all men, who in Adam had fallen

FIGURE 8.1. Joseph Smith's 5 February 1840 address reported by Matthew L. Davis.

Church History Library, Salt Lake City.

the details of his source material.[65] During the Nauvoo period from 1839 to 1844, Woodruff was occasionally the only person who left significant reports of Smith's sermons. Snow reported a much smaller set of examples, but they are mostly complementary to Woodruff's. Snow was the secretary for the Female Relief Society of Nauvoo and reported six of Smith's instructional sermons to the Society beginning at its organizational meeting in March 1842.[66] Knowlton left comparatively detailed reports of a few of Smith's sermons that were apparently later copied into a surviving notebook.[67]

Since early Mormon conferences acted as decision-making entities, as they did in the Protestant institutions they modeled, recording their proceedings was a natural extension of the emphasis to record denominational business.[68] The assigned reporting of church councils and their decisions led to reporting on certain kinds of sermons.[69] The outcomes of church conferences where such sermons, generally instructive episodes, were reported in print, again echoed Protestant tradition as well as church

65. While Woodruff recorded a number Joseph Smith's sermons, it is unclear whether he referenced his own reports after he penned them, though an occasional sermon by Woodruff himself refers to some of Joseph Smith's themes, such as the repeated stress on the opening text of Hebrews 6. Woodruff's early reporting was typical of many pew auditors: short on content, long on feeling. For example, he reported an April 1834 preaching event thus: "On the 27th of Apreil being the Lords day I attended meeting and herd several of the Brethren preach Brother Sidney Rigdon, Orson Hide. Orson Pratt and others spoke Joseph Smith closing during the meeting It appeared to me there was more light mad[e] manifest at that meeting respecting the gospel and Kingdom of God than I had ever received from the whole Sectarian world." Kenney, *Wilford Woodruff's Journal*, 1:9.

66. See Bushman, *Rough Stone Rolling*, 446–48; Brown, *In Heaven*, 190, 274–77. Jonathan A. Stapley and Kristine Wright, "Female Ritual Healing in Mormonism," *Journal of Mormon History* 37, no. 1 (Winter 2011): 6–7. Maureen Ursenbach Beecher et al., *Women of Covenant: The Story of Relief Society* (Salt Lake City: Deseret Book, 2010), chap. 1; Derr et al., eds., *The First Fifty Years of Relief Society*. On the Relief Society's Protestant pattern, see Daniel Walker Howe, *What Hath God Wrought: The Transformation of America, 1815–1848* (New York: Oxford University Press, 2007), 190–93.

67. Martha Jane Knowlton Coray, Notebook, undated, CHL.

68. One sees this trend in general church minute files. Reporting "conferences" was long a Protestant tradition, and likely in the Methodism that Joseph Smith saw working in upstate New York. For an interesting example, see "Minutes of a General Conference held by The Church of Latter Day Saints, at the Presbyterian Camp Ground Near Quincy, Adams County, Illinois, on Saturday the 4th of May 1839," Historian's Office, General Church Minutes, 1839–1877, CHL. Appointing capable clerks led to ever more detailed reports of these events.

69. Local church gatherings sometimes filled the same purpose, and records of those meetings were often published in early church periodicals.

regulation.[70] Conference proceedings evolved away from mostly business settings to preaching venues. With that evolution, preaching drifted in two ways: it became a higher-value enterprise, and it combined some of the inherited Protestant motifs with a pedagogical/instructional emphasis.

The Preacher's Intention and Textual Criticism

The most important textual contrast between Smith and many other antebellum American Protestant preachers lies at the document level: as noted already, Joseph Smith simply left few ego-documents. He exercised little review for the generated texts of his sermons and he kept no extensive personal notes of his own sermons. Largely, his intent can only be inferred by contextualizing witness reports with his contemporary statements or reported acts.[71] If a network of these statements exists as part of ongoing or repeated themes[72] engaged by him, then perhaps a more intentionally authentic text might be constructed. An interesting example of this is the topic of the Second Coming of Christ. An early (possibly 1832) revelation suggested that the reappearance of Christ might take place near Joseph Smith's eighty-fifth birthday. An 1835 reference to this suggests that Smith interpreted the experience as meaning the literal second coming would occur in 1890 or 1891. His later references to the experience suggest that his interpretation gradually changed in seeing this as a future personal experience rather than necessarily one of global impact. Indeed, a March 10, 1844 address is one such sermon. While Joseph Smith's view of this may have changed, many of his followers savored his earlier interpretation. This sort of rigidity, in a broader sense, probably explains much of what happened among believers following Smith's murder in terms of conflict over choosing a successor.

There are important difficulties for the textual critic when considering the archival status of Smith's sermons. Known texts of the same sermon

---

70. Conferences often made rulings of importance to the church at large. The U.S. mail service was a relatively cheap and easy way to codify rulings and get the word out. On Protestant imprints, consider the long-running *Journal of the General Conference of the Methodist Episcopal Church* (New York: Various publishers, 1796–).

71. James Thorpe, *Principles of Textual Criticism* (San Marino, California: Huntington Library, 1972), 202. Joseph Smith's acts and speech during the period from 1842 to 1844 are frequently centered in political matters and, *sub rosa*, his introduction and regulation of polygamy.

72. For example, see Howard Coray, Letter, Sanford, CO, to Martha Jane Lewis, 2 August 1889, CHL

rarely provide much word-for-word agreement, making their content auditors' perceptions fail at any verbatim image. This points one in a different direction, a direction that provides insights into problems of interpretation and reception. And it effectively doomed the enterprise of 1850s Mormon historians who hoped to approach a verbatim reconstruction of Smith and his preaching. Indeed, for preachers of the era generally, even when extensive speaker-prepared texts do exist, evidence shows that the actual sermon as it was delivered may have differed in both content and length.[73]

For preachers who published or reviewed/revised their own sermon texts, intention had important drawbacks and omissions: it not only failed to understand the sermon event, it did not speak to the preacher–audience experience, an aspect of preaching notorious for lack of study. Since the relevant documents for Joseph Smith were not produced by him and almost never edited by him, they stand at a certain degree of distance from him.[74] An illustration of the issue is found in reports of Smith's 3 October 1841 sermon, where a surviving manuscript and a published text differ in subject matter and detail. It is unclear that Smith redacted the manuscript for publication, but if the text was redacted by someone other than Smith (likely) it yet illustrates the point of distance. A version of the sermon appeared in the church bi-weekly magazine *Times and Seasons* for 15 October 1841. Markedly different sermon notes appear in the manuscript General Church Minutes.[75]

The following excerpts of the two reports show how different the two audits were. The published report of the sermon opens with,

> President Joseph Smith, by request of some of the Twelve, gave instructions on the doctrine of Baptism for the Dead; which was listened to with intense interest by the large assembly. The speaker presented "Baptism for the Dead" as the only way that men can appear as saviors on mount Zion. The proclamation of the first principles of

73. For example, Newport, *Sermons of Charles Wesley*, 41, 45–46.

74. Joseph Smith's sermon texts mirror some of the results if not the same issues met by female preachers in Britain and America. They tended toward strict orality in their work for reasons outside of any canonical angst. See Krueger, *Reader's Repentance*, 74–77; Brekus, *Strangers and Pilgrims*, 271–91, 339–41.

75. *Times and Seasons* 2 (15 October 1841): 577–78. Church minutes of the event are found in Historian's Office, General Church Minutes, 3 October 1841. The published text may be the work of Gustavus Hills while the manuscript is in the hand of Willard Richards.

> the gospel was a means of salvation to men individually, and it was the truth, not men that saved them; but men, by actively engaging in rites of salvation substitutionally, became instrumental in bringing multitudes of their kin into the kingdom of God.[76]

A manuscript for the same section reads,

> Saviors shall come up on. Mt Zion &c – . what is it & To preach only? No. In every dispensation something else to do besides preach to all– neglect the Baptism for the dead.– Could that man enter into the fullness of his rest? [illegible] cannot be saviors of man upon any other principle that be re[ce]ving revelation of all the things To trace our family by gene[a]olo[g]y & Rev[elation]– 1st principles of the Gospel no more to the B[aptism] for the Dead. then the dim[me]st Star is to the Glo[r]y of Yonder Son. All the kindred from the days of Adam dow[n] upon that princ[i]ple. Universalism is nothing.[77]

The published content audit is related to the aural audit of the second excerpt, but they show remarkable differences, some of which register as key themes in later Mormon practice and thought, such as the mention of genealogies.

Sermon Event and Perception

As Mormonism grew, literate followers were drawn into the fold. Joseph Smith was careful to cultivate some of this group as his record keepers. As he matured, Smith was no more likely to prepare written remarks, but he did engage in planning.[78] While again there are almost no real copy-texts

76. "Discourse, 3 October 1841, as Reported by Times and Seasons," p. 577, The Joseph Smith Papers, accessed 31 October 2016, http://www.josephsmithpapers.org/paper-summary/discourse-3-october-1841-as-reported-by-times-and-seasons/1?highlight=3%20October%201841

77. "Discourse, 3 October 1841, as Reported by Willard Richards," p. 1, The Joseph Smith Papers, accessed 31 October 2016, http://www.josephsmithpapers.org/paper-summary/discourse-3-october-1841-as-reported-by-willard-richards/1?highlight=3%20October%201841.

78. See his disclaimer as found in a sermon at the death of longtime friend Elias Higbee, delivered on 13 August 1843. However, sermons delivered on 7 and 8 April 1844 were planned in advance. A sermon on 20 March 1842, while not planned, partially replaced a planned address on baptism. For a transcript of the Higbee sermon, see http://boap.org/LDS/Parallel/1843/13Aug43.html. For the 7 and 8 April sermons, see http://boap.org/LDS/

(in terms of texts produced by Smith) to look to, there are in some cases several extensive audits of the same sermon and on occasion these are robust aural audits.

The best example of this is the collection of documents chronicling Smith's sermon of 7 April 1844 at a special conference of Mormons in Nauvoo. This sermon enjoys some of the best efforts at verbatim reporting of the entire cache of Joseph Smith's *extempore* efforts, and two of these independent reports exhibit close synchronization and considerable detail. The sermon was part of a cycle that summarized Mormon metaphysics with the intent to honor the Mormon dead and comfort the bereaved. (In fact, the sermon was so well known that it became known in early Mormon literature as "the King Follett Discourse" after Smith's friend King Follett was killed in a construction accident.) The sermon was reported by two official clerks, pictured in Figures 8.2 and 8.3, each attempting a verbatim transcription. These official reporters were joined by several pew auditors whose pew reports range through Neuman's categories of content audits and aural audits, at times blurring the distinction between the two categories.[79] These pew audits demonstrate the intrusion of the auditors own interpretive thoughts at times, while they tend to offer general confirmation of more robust reports. The striking content of the Follett sermon launched it on a career of suspicion, distrust, and even scorn, alternating with foundational respect and devotion both within Mormonism and among its dissenters and Protestant critics. The sermon was almost entirely a summary and expansion of a number of Smith's sermons over the previous four years, but those sermons were largely unpublished and therefore (like Cowdery's) unknown. Expanding uniquely on John 5, sermon audits captured Smith's distinctive cosmology, including a remarkable take on the potential deification of human beings.[80]

Parallel/1844/7Apr44.html and http://boap.org/LDS/Parallel/1844/8Apr44.html. For the March 20 sermon, see http://boap.org/LDS/Parallel/1842/20Mar42.html.

79. William Victor Smith, *Every Word Seasoned with Grace: A Textual Study of the Funeral Sermons of Joseph Smith*, chap. 7 (forthcoming). See also, William V. Smith, *The King Follett Sermon: A Social History* (Salt Lake City: BCC Press, forthcoming in 2018).

80. Some reports of the sermon can be found in digital form at http://www.josephsmithpapers.org/the-papers/documents/1844 (accessed 25 October 2016).

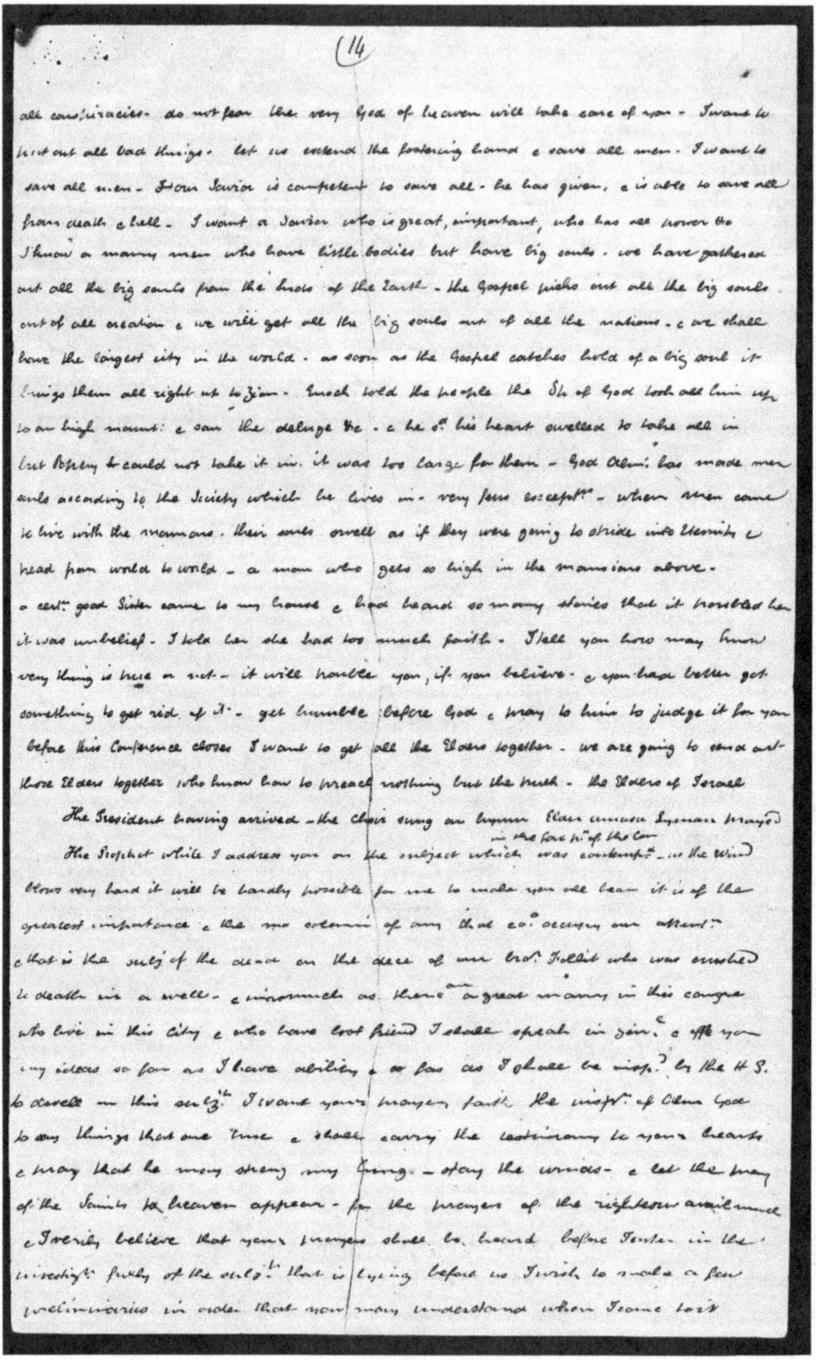

(14

all conspiracies- do not fear the very God of heaven will take care of you- I want to
kick out all bad things- let us extend the fostering hand & save all men- I want to
save all men- Your Savior is competent to save all- he has given, & is able to save all
from death & hell- I want a Savior who is great, important, who has all power &c
I know a many men who have little bodies but have big souls- we have gathered
out all the big souls from the ends of the Earth- the Gospel picks out all the big souls
out of all creation & we will get all the big souls out of all the nations- & we shall
have the largest city in the world- as soon as the Gospel catches hold of a big soul it
brings them all right up to Zion- Enoch told the people the Sp of God took all him up
to an high mount: & saw the deluge &c- & he sd his heart swelled to take all in
but Popery & could not take it in. it was too large for them- God Almi: has made men
souls according to the society which he lives in- very few exceptn- when men come
to live with the mormons. their souls swell as if they were going to stride into Eternity &
tread from world to world- a man who gets so high in the mansions above-
a certn good Sister came to my house & had heard so many stories that it troubled her
it was unbelief- I told her she had too much faith- I tell you how may know
every thing is true or not- it will trouble you, if you believe- & you had better get
something to get rid of it- get humble before God & pray to him to judge it for you
before this Conference closes I want to get all the Elders together- we are going to send out
those Elders together who know how to preach nothing but the truth- the Elders of Israel

The President having arrived- the Choir sung an hymn Elder Amasa Lyman prayed
in the fore pt of the Con

The Prophet while I address you on the subject which was contemplated- as the Wind
blows very hard it will be hardly possible for me to make you all hear it is of the
greatest importance & the mo solemn of any that cod occupy our attent.
that is the subj of the dead on the dece of our Brot. Follit who was crushed
to death in a well- & inasmuch as there are a great many in this congre
who live in this City & who have lost friends I shall speak in genl & offer you
my ideas so far as I have ability & so far as I shall be inspd by the H S.
to dwell on this subjt I want your prayers faith the inspn. of Alm God
to say things that are true & shall carry the testimony to your hearts
& pray that he may streng my lungs- stay the winds- & let the pray
of the Saints to heaven appear- for the prayers of the righteous avail much
& I verily believe that your prayers shall be heard before I enter in the
investign. fully of the subjt that is lying before us I wish to make a few
preliminaries in order that you may understand when I come to it

FIGURE 8.2 AND FIGURE 8.3. Thomas Bullock aural audit of Smith's 7 April 1844 sermon; William Clayton aural audit of Smith's 7 April 1844 sermon, in General Church minutes, 1839–1877.

Church History Library, Salt Lake City.

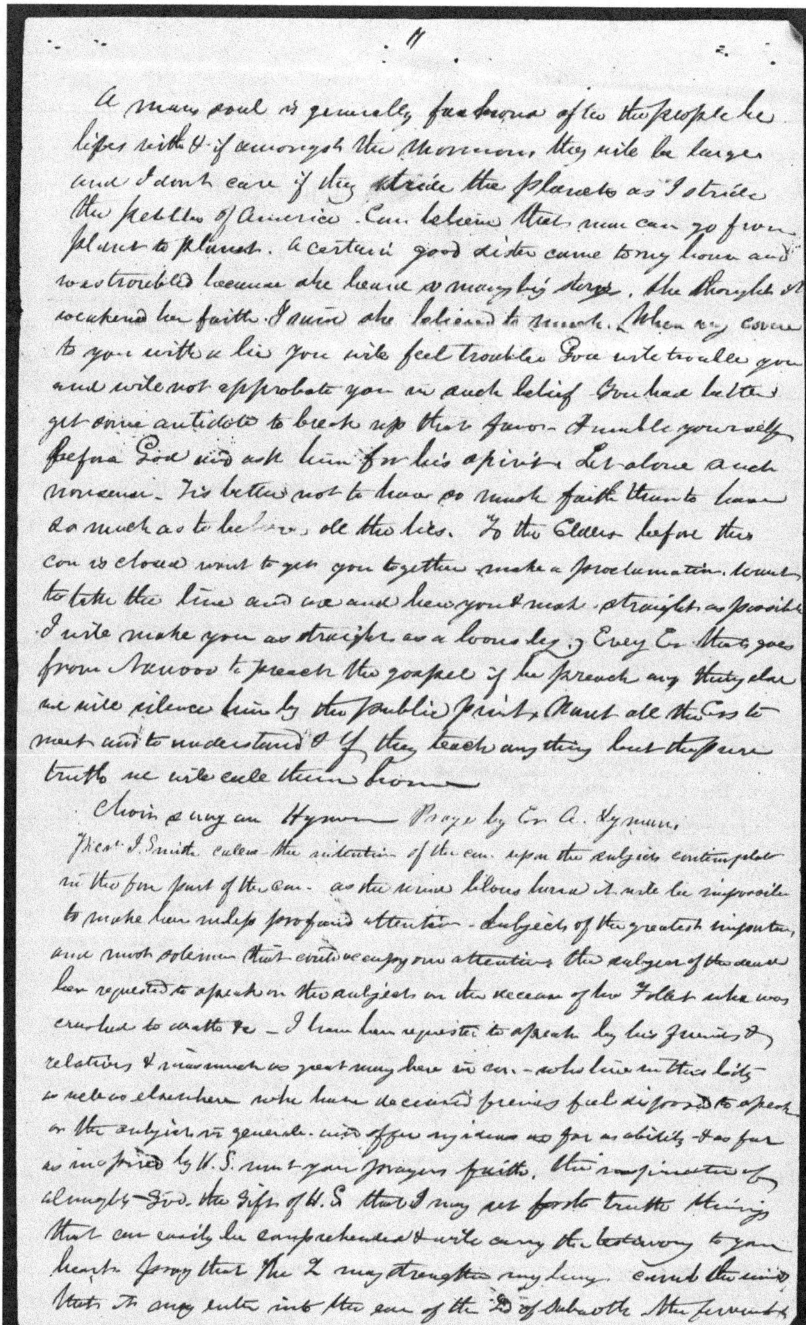

11   2.

A man soul is generally fashiond after the people he lives with & if amongst the Mormons they will be large and I dont care if they stride the planets as I stride the pebbles of America. Can believe that man can go from planet to planet. a certain good sister came to my house and was troubled because she heard so many big storys. She thought it weakend her faith. I said she believed to much. When any come to you with a lie you will feel troubled. God will trouble you and will not approbate you in such belief. You had better get some antidote to break up that fever. Humble yourself before God and ask him for his spirit. Let alone such nonsense. Tis better not to have so much faith than to have so much as to believe all the lies. To the Elders before this con is closed want to get you together make a proclamation. want to take the line and axe and hew you & make straight as possible. I will make you as straight as a loons leg. Every El. that goes from Nauvoo to preach the gospel if he preach any thing else we will silence him by the public print. want all the Els to meet and to understand & if they teach any thing but the pure truth we will call them home.

Choir sung an Hymn. Prayer by Er. A. Lyman.

Prest. J. Smith calls the attention of the con. upon the subject contemplated in the fore part of the con. as the wind blows very hard it will be impossible to make him unless profound attention. Subject of the greatest importance and most solemn that could occupy our attention. the subject of the dead been requested to speak on the subject on the decease of Br. Follett who was crushed to death &c. I have been requested to speak by his friends & relations & inasmuch as great many here in con. who live in this City as well as elsewhere who have deceased friends feel disposed to speak on the subject in general and offer my ideas as far as ability & as far as inspired by H. S. want your prayers faith, the inspiration of almighty God the gift of H. S. that I may set forth truth things that can easily be comprehended & will carry the testimony to your hearts. Pray that the L may strengthen my lungs. cause the winds that it may enter into the ear of the Ld of Sabaoth. The fervent

FIGURE 8.2 AND FIGURE 8.3. (Continued)

An Example from the Documentary Record

To illustrate how Smith's sermons were documented in the final period of his life, some examples form a useful template. James Adams (1783–1843), a friend and confidant of Smith's, died of an illness resembling cholera on 21 August 1843 at the Mormon headquarters in Nauvoo, Illinois. Public health in Nauvoo was at issue, partly for its endemic malaria that tended to weaken residents, making them more susceptible to other disease. Sickness in the city made Smith postpone his opportunity to eulogize Adams until 9 October 1843.

The Adams sermon then became part of a church conference proceeding, and evidently the conference clerk, Gustavus Hills, captured a selection of Smith's remarks in his notes. The proceedings of the conference later appeared in the church's religious serial, *Times and Seasons*, sometime in early November 1843.[81] The sermon report, as seen in Figure 8.4, opens with descriptive material almost certainly added for publication; however, the sermon report itself is primitive enough that it likely represents Hills's notes with some fidelity. Obvious expansions occur with word-for-word Bible passages. The provenance of this document is not in question, but its variance from the archetype in terms of length is significant. Hills's original notes are not extant.[82]

Smith's personal secretary, Willard Richards, who was keeping Smith's diary at the time, inserted notes of the sermon under the October 9 dateline, as seen in Figure 8.5. These notes probably originated with Richards, but the diary may not be a first-order version of the notes. The diary was normally written in "double space" format, in a small blank book purchased for use as a diary.[83] The notes are neatly formatted and the careful, compact script is unusual for Richards though the text is not polished.[84]

---

81. The issue was dated 15 September 1843, but the print shop crew was ill for a considerable time, shutting down the press. The 15 September issue was a catch-up printing and included minutes of the October conference.

82. From the time of Guttenberg, manuscripts that went through the printing process were often discarded when printing was completed. Blair, *Too Much to Know*, chap. 2.

83. The scribe may have left space between lines in case his master wished to make corrections, and occasionally Smith did review some of the diary entries. For Richards's notes, see Andrew H. Hedges et al., eds., *Journals, Volume 3: May 1843–June 1844*, vol. 3 of the Journals series of *The Joseph Smith Papers*, ed. Ronald K. Esplin and Matthew J. Grow (Salt Lake City: Church Historian's Press, 2015), 109–110.

84. Richards's work as a historian shows that he was capable of producing clear sentence construction and punctuation. The diary was rarely so careful, however, and this sermon text was no exception.

Elder Alpheus Cutler, on the part of the Temple Committee, represented the work of the Temple to be retarded for want of team work and provisions: also of iron, steel, powder and clothing—giving as his opinion that he walls could easily be completed next season, if these embarrassments were removed, and the brethren would come forward to sustain them in the work with the means that were in their hands.

Elder Reynolds Cahoon followed, seconding the remarks of elder Cutler, and setting forth the importance of the saints using their utmost exertions to fulfil the revelation concerning the Temple—earnestly exhorting the saints, here and abroad, to roll in the necessary means into the hands of the Committee, that the work may advance with rapidity.

President Hyrum Smith followed with pertinent remarks on the importance of the work—the ease with which it might be advanced to its completion—that it had already become a monument for the people abroad to gaze on with astonishment. He concluded with some advice to parents to restrain their children from vice and folly, and employ them in some business of profit to themselves, to the Temple, or elsewhere.

On motion by elder William Law, and seconded by President Hyrum Smith, Conference voted, That we, as conference, and individuals, will use all the means, exertions and influence in our power, to sustain the Temple Committee in advancing the work of the Temple.

President Joseph Smith presented and read to the Conference, a communication from Col. Frances M. Higbee, whose conduct had been called in question, in connection with elder Sidney Rigdon, and expressed himself satisfied that Col. Frances M. Higbee was free, even of reproach or suspicion, in that matter.

Conference adjourned for one hour.

Monday, 2 o'clock, P. M.

Conference reassembled, and listened with profound attention, to an impressive discourse from President Joseph Smith, commemorative of the decease of James Adams, Esq., late of this city, and an honorable, worthy, useful, and esteemed member of the Church of Jesus Christ of Latter Day Saints. He spoke of the importance of our understanding the reasons and causes of our exposure to the vicissitudes of life, and of death; and the designs and purposes of God, in our coming into the world, our sufferings here, and our departure hence—that it is but reasonable to suppose that God would reveal something in reference to the matter—the ignorance of the world in reference to their true condition, and relation. Reading the experience of others, or the revelations given to them, can never give us a comprehensive view of our condition and true relation to God. Knowledge of these things, can only be obtained by experience in these things, through the ordinance of God set forth for that purpose. He remarked that the disappointment of hopes and expectations at the resurrection, would be indescribably dreadful. That the organization of the spiritual and heavenly worlds, and of spiritual and heavenly beings was agreeably to the most perfect order and harmony—that their limits and bounds were fixed irrevocably, and voluntarily subscribed to by themselves—subscribed to upon the earth—hence the importance of embracing and subscribing to principles of eternal truth. He assured the saints that truth in reference to these matters, can, and may be known, through the revelations of God in the way of his ordinances, and in answer to prayer. The Hebrew church "came unto the spirits of just men made perfect, and unto an innumerable company of angels, unto God the Father of all, and to Jesus Christ the Mediator of the New Covenant;" but what they learned, has not been, and could not have been written. What object was gained by this communication with the spirits of the just, &c.? It was the established order of the kingdom of God—the keys of power and knowledge were with them to communicate to the saints—hence the importance of understanding the distinction between the spirits of the just, and angels. Spirits can only be revealed in flaming fire, or glory. Angels have advanced farther—their light and glory being tabernacled, and hence appear in bodily shape.

Concerning brother James Adams, he remarked, that it should appear strange that so good and so great a man was hated. The deceased ought never to have had an enemy. But so it was, wherever light shone, it stirred up darkness. Truth and error, good and evil, cannot be reconciled. Judge Adams had been a most intimate friend. He had anointed him to the Patriarchial power—to receive the keys of knowledge, and power, by revelation to himself. He had had revelations concerning his departure, and had gone to a more important work—of opening up a more effectual door for the dead. The spirits of the just are exalted to a greater and more glorious work—hence they are blessed in departing hence. Enveloped in flaming fire, they are not far from us, and know and understand our thoughts, feelings and motions, and are often pained therewith.

President Smith concluded with exhortations to the church to renew their exertions to

FIGURE 8.4. Gustavus Hills, "Minutes of a Special Conference," *Times and Seasons*, 15 September 1843, 331.

Church History Library, Salt Lake City.

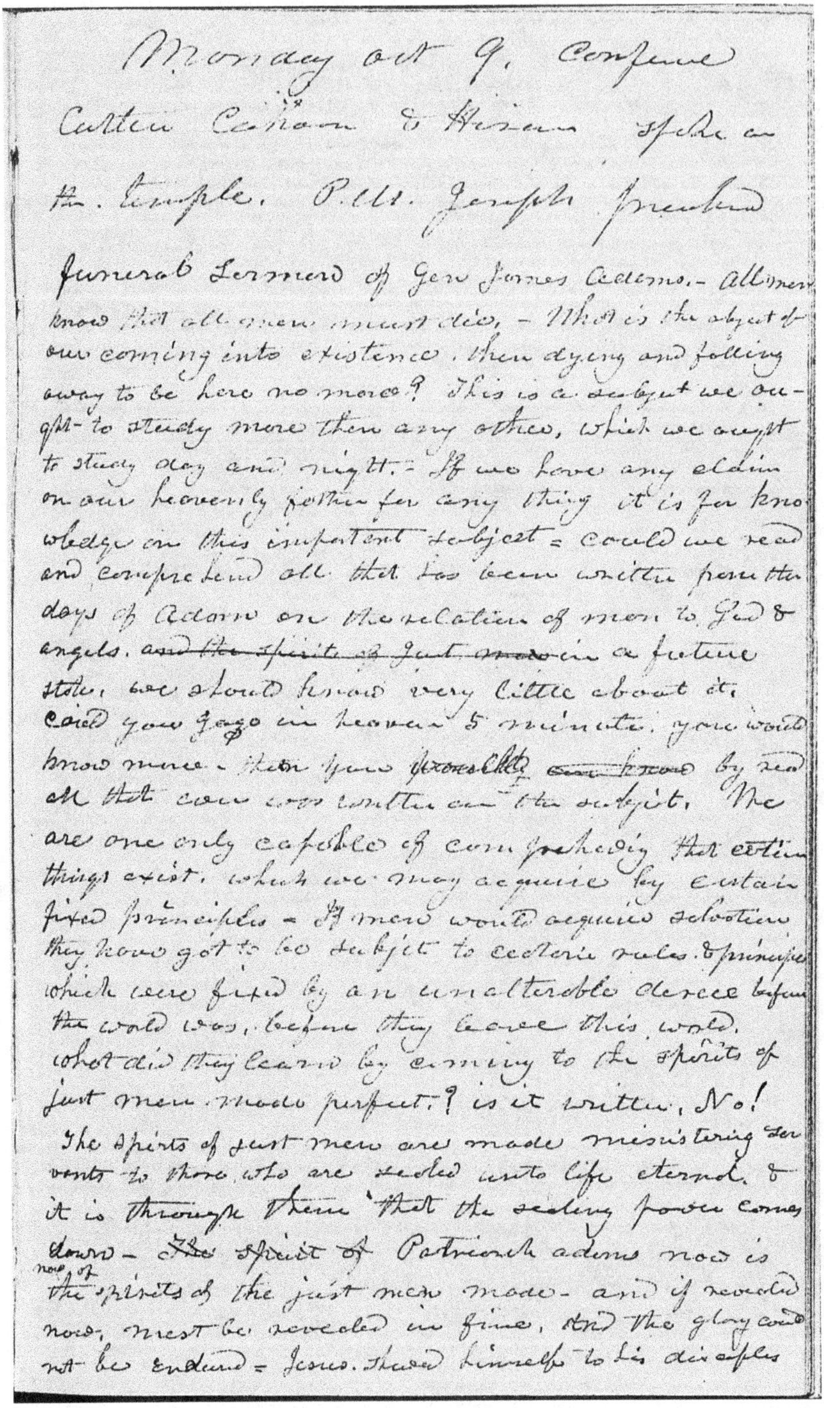

Monday Oct 9. Conference
Cutler Cahoon & Hiram Spoke on
the temple. P.M. Joseph preached
funeral sermon of Gen James Adams.— All men
know that all men must die, — What is the object of
our coming into existence. then dying and falling
away to be here no more? This is a subject we ought to study more than any other, which we ought
to study day and night.— If we have any claim
on our heavenly father for any thing it is for kno
wledge on this important subject = could we read
and comprehend all that has been written from the
days of Adam on the relation of man to God &
angels. ~~and the spirits of just men~~ in a future
state, we should know very little about it.
could you gaze in heaven 5 minutes. you would
know more — than you ~~possibly~~ ~~can know~~ by read
all that ever was written on the subject. We
are one only capable of comprehending that certain
things exist. which we may acquire by certain
fixed principles = If men would acquire salvation
they have got to be subject to certain rules & principles
which were fixed by an unalterable decree before
the world was, before they leave this world.
what did they learn by coming to the spirits of
just men made perfect.? is it written. No!
The spirits of just men are made ministering ser
vants to those who are sealed unto life eternal. &
it is through them that the sealing power comes
down — ~~The~~ Spirit of Patriarch Adams now is
one of the spirits of the just men made — and if revealed
now, must be revealed in fire. and the glory could
not be endured = Jesus. shewd himself to his disciples

FIGURE 8.5. Willard Richards's notes for Smith's sermon of 9 October 1843, in Joseph Smith journal, 9 October 1843, Joseph Smith Collection.
Church History Library, Salt Lake City.

The diary copy shows few redactions and at least some of these probably resulted from copying errors. The diary has been a part of the church's document collection since the time of the sermon.

Two other reports of the sermon exist. One is a reminiscence dictated by William C. Staines from memory to a church clerk on 24 April 1855, nearly twelve years after the sermon. Some of its text is wildly different from the other sources, but similar to some church discourse of the 1855 era. The other source is from British convert James Burgess. Burgess kept two short diaries during his time in Illinois, and he reported the Adams sermon in the second one. The content of the Burgess report is largely a subset of the Richards and Hills reports with a few important exceptions.[85] A canceled dittograph in the Burgess report suggests it was copied from a reconstruction of notes or from a document Burgess composed from memory. Burgess's unique dialogic insertions and exclamatory speech suggest that his own thoughtful considerations of Smith's sermons were deeply integrated into his reports.[86]

As is clear from these examples, each of the official and unofficial reports of the Adams funeral sermon is some editorial distance from any original notes and therefore any oral archetype. This is frequently the case in reports of Smith's sermons. Falling largely into Neuman's category of content audits, the Adams reports reflect the interplay of event and subjective impression, whether that interplay existed from first-order notes, or came to exist as notes that were fleshed out in manuscript. The Hills notes, at least, overlap Neuman's structural auditing category, marking the structural unfolding of the sermon.[87]

Exceptions to this pattern of content audits illustrated by the the Adams sermon include the King Follett Discourse mentioned above, and,

---

85. For example, as an illustration of Smith's point that angels need not appear as glorious apparitions, Burgess notes Hebrew 13:2: "an angel could come and appear as an other man for Paul says be careful to entertain ~~an~~ strangers for some have entertained Angels unawares."

86. James Burgess, Journal, October 1841–December 1848, vol. 2, CHL. The Burgess journal was not a professionally bound book. It was apparently constructed from lined paper, folded and sewn perhaps by Burgess himself. Keeping a record of Smith's sermons was an enterprise Burgess began in England, when he copied notes kept in 1840 by Mormon missionaries from Nauvoo. The provenance of the journal is somewhat obscure, though other entries suggest that it remained in Burgess's possession for decades. It has appeared in the LDS Church Library catalog for many years.

87. For transcriptions of the reports of the Adams sermon, see http://boap.org/LDS/1843/9Oct43.html (accessed 1 October 2016).

to varying degrees, Smith's sermons of 8 April 1844, 12 May 1844, 26 May 1844, and 16 June 1844. In these sermons one or more raw, extensive first-order aural audits exist that attempt verbatim capture of the preacher's words.[88] It is perhaps likely that Smith or his subordinates arranged for such reporting because of a new dissenting church staffed by former allies, which Smith mentioned at a number of these events. The dissenting group assigned words to Smith that he saw as inaccurate or wrongly contextualized.

These dissenters had once been intimates in church government, polygamy, temple ritual formation, and political strategy. As Smith acted to counter rumors and public complaints, it seems clear that the eventual publication of those remarks was part of an effort to tell his side of some issues without negative polemic.[89] There are a few other examples of sermons where textual evidence suggests that Smith made minor corrections to notes of a clerk and at least one example where he dictated an orally delivered sermon before the fact, a singular occurrence.[90] In general, beyond the appointment of men to keep track of his words and deeds, Smith took little direct interest in the methodologies employed in that task.

One other important force behind the increase in detailed audits of Smith's sermons has been hinted at above. Early Mormon convert and trusted follower Willard Richards was appointed as Smith's clerk and private secretary in December 1841, and commissioned to collate previous efforts to record Smith's life history as a religious figure. Richards systematized that work and led the effort to more carefully report Smith's acts

88. These audits are never exclusively aural. They contain scribal summaries at various points. Meanwhile, the character of longhand audits, even with a system of abbreviation, meant that much of what Smith said probably went unrecorded. Moreover, no longhand auditor was likely to include repetitions or rephrasings of thought. Extemporaneous speech can be a restless enterprise.

89. Clerks were always appointed for conferences and while subordinates arranged for the official reports, it is possible that Smith spoke more nearly at dictation speed on some of these occasions, a practice he was familiar with in his dictation of the Book of Mormon, and in later revelations. Medieval theologians/preachers used dictation speed when they desired auditors to recreate their words. Ann M. Blair, "Note-Taking as an Art of Transmission," *Critical Inquiry* 31 (Autumn 2004): 92.

90. On audits, see Neuman, *Jeremiah's Scribes*, 62. A manuscript of dictated text of the 5 October 1840 sermon is found in the Joseph Smith Collection, 1827–1844, CHL. It may be a copy of the original manuscript. Smith did not deliver the sermon; it was read over the pulpit by the clerk who penned it at Smith's dictation.

and words, including his sermons. Richards's work led to an expansion of a corps of clerks who reported and copied materials.[91]

No matter which period one considers, it is impossible to separate Joseph Smith from his engagement with the Bible. His sermons use biblical texts in straightforward as well as creative ways. At times Smith made explicit reference to one passage or another, but at other times he would paraphrase a passage in passing, borrow a phrase from one verse and combine it with another, and use the wording in a new sense without explicit citation. For example, Smith's 12 May 1844 sermon, a part of his last sermon cycle, is a dense mosaic of Old and New Testament passages. The pattern was frequent among Protestants. It was, as David Hall has written, a web of unattributed "patchwork quoting" meant to frame a central text. The difference with Smith was that he did not always use a particular text, but a central idea or two, around which he built an explication of a concept illustrated by biblical borrowing.[92] Smith's instructional sermon to church leaders, delivered on 2 July 1839, illustrates the point. The first half of the selection echoes patterns of early Christian hymning, while the second half offers a kind of hard-won autobiographical lesson. The whole demonstrates a certain poetic quality, which may have had as much to do with the pointed brevity of the auditor as with Smith. The selection is presented here with Smith's scriptural sources identified in brackets:

> Ye are not sent out to be taught but to teach [1 John 2:27]
> Let every word be seasoned with grace [Col. 4:6]
> Be vigilant, be sober [1 Pet. 5:8]
> It is a day of warning and
> not of many words [from his own 30 August 1831 revelation]
> Act honest before God and man. [2 Cor. 8:21]

---

91. Two years before Smith's death, a skilled "phonographer" (a purveyor of the Pitman shorthand system at the time) emigrated to Nauvoo. George D. Watt was the first Mormon convert in Britain (1837). Watt's skill seems to have been unappreciated by Richards, and he was never taken into the fold of Smith's clerks, though he was employed a year after Smith's death. Watt eventually broke through as a clerk to British Mission President George Q. Cannon in 1846. On Watt, see Ronald G. Watt, "Sailing 'the Old Ship Zion': The Life of George D. Watt," *BYU Studies* 18, no. 1 (1977): 48–65, esp. 51, 55. On Watt's attempt to teach Pittman shorthand in Nauvoo, see the Nauvoo newspaper, *The Wasp* 1, no. 52 (26 April 1842): 3. An example of Watt's early sermon reports can be seen online at https://dcms.lds.org/delivery/DeliveryManagerServlet?dps_pid=IE2343146 (accessed 4 August 2016). Though Watt did some reporting, he had no regular employment and occasionally asked Brigham Young for help. For example, see George D. Watt, Letter, Nauvoo, IL, to "the Twelve," 31 December 1844, Brigham Young Office Files, 1832–1878, CHL.

92. David D. Hall, *Worlds of Wonder, Days of Judgment* (New York: Knopf, 1989), 27–28.

> Beware of gentile sophestry
> such as bowing and scraping
> unto men in whom you have no confidence.
> Be honest open and frank
> in all your intercourse with mankind.[93]

The text was originally written by Wilford Woodruff, probably on 8 July 1839. Woodruff's report was later copied by Smith's future secretary Willard Richards in a small notebook. The selection above was taken from Richards' digest of Woodruff's notes.

A number of Smith's later instructional sermons circulated in this way, just as his early revelations did. The interesting development by Richards is illustrated by Woodruff's original audit. It read:

> Ye are not sent out to be taught but to teach.
> Let every man be Sober be vigilent &
> let all his words be seasoned with grace
> & keep in mind that it is a day of warning
> & not of many words.
> Act honest before God & man.
> Beware of gentile sophestry such as
> bowing & scaping unto men in
> wholm you have no Confidence.[94]

As seen in this example, Smith's preaching drew largely from biblical texts, though his sermons sometimes made silent or indirect reference to his Book of Abraham or used ideas from the Book of Mormon or his other revelations. Smith clearly favored some biblical passages but he used a variety of texts in the Old and New Testaments. He was consistently aware of the fact that nearly all his listeners came out of one Christian tradition or another and his sermons were styled in part to appeal to that heritage (which was, after all, his own).

---

93. Willard Richards, "Pocket Companion written in England," p. 13, Willard Richards, Journals and Papers, 1821–1854, CHL. Bowing and scraping was a cliché for subservient behavior.

94. Kenney, *Wilford Woodruff's Journal*, 1:343.

Smith occasionally drew attention to denominational views to contrast the Mormon position or note agreement with one tradition or another. His 10 March 1844 remarks on the theological question of election, reported with some detail by several auditors, doctrinally situated the Mormons as occupying a position between Methodists and Presbyterians on whether God had predistined some people to receive salvation. Woodruff's development as auditor is evident as a comparison with his report of Smith's sermon of 6 April 1837, seen in Figure 8.6.[95] The character of the 1844 report is something on the border between an aural audit and a content audit, though it is clearly a second-order manuscript. His report of the 1837 sermon appears to be one from memory, a second-order content audit. The July 1839 report seems to be a first-order example, probably again at the border of an aural and content audit. In other words, from 1837 to 1844 Woodruff had grown in his skill at, and commitment to, recording Joseph Smith's sermons. In this, Woodruff's sermon reports mirror the general evolution in the value of sermon literature among Mormons during Joseph Smith's lifetime. Finally, copying manuscript reports of sermons could significantly affect their form in eventual imprints.

Print Culture and Orality in Joseph Smith's Mormonism

While the sermon moved to a more valued position in the Nauvoo period of Mormonism (1839–1846), Joseph Smith's sermons were still oral events. Nuances such as dramatic pauses, repetition for emphasis, volume modulations, tonal inflections, sarcasm, sound effects, gestures, visual humor, audience cues, and audience response can be critical to understanding how contemporary listeners interpreted the sermons, but are virtually unrecorded in textual accounts of the events.[96] The text of Smith's

95. Woodruff's report should be compared to a published version already noted, probably an audit by clerk Warren Cowdery in *Latter Day Saints' Messenger and Advocate* 3 (April 1837): 486–87. For Woodruff's audit, see Kenney, *Wilford Woodruff's Journal*, 1:132.

96. Such visual and performative elements in sermon events were important to the experience. Coleman, "Antebellum American Sermon," 521–54; Teresa Toulouse, *The Art of Prophesying: New England Sermons and the Shaping of Belief* (Athens: University of Georgia Press, 1987); Stout, *Divine Dramatist*. Neuman, *Jeremiah's Scribes*, 30, 112. Crowd reaction might be noted in a Smith sermon audit, but also exaggerated or muted for print. Smith's sermon of 12 May 1844 is an important example, where late redaction made crowd reaction somewhat different from source reports. See, Smith, *Every Word Seasoned with Grace*, chap. 9.

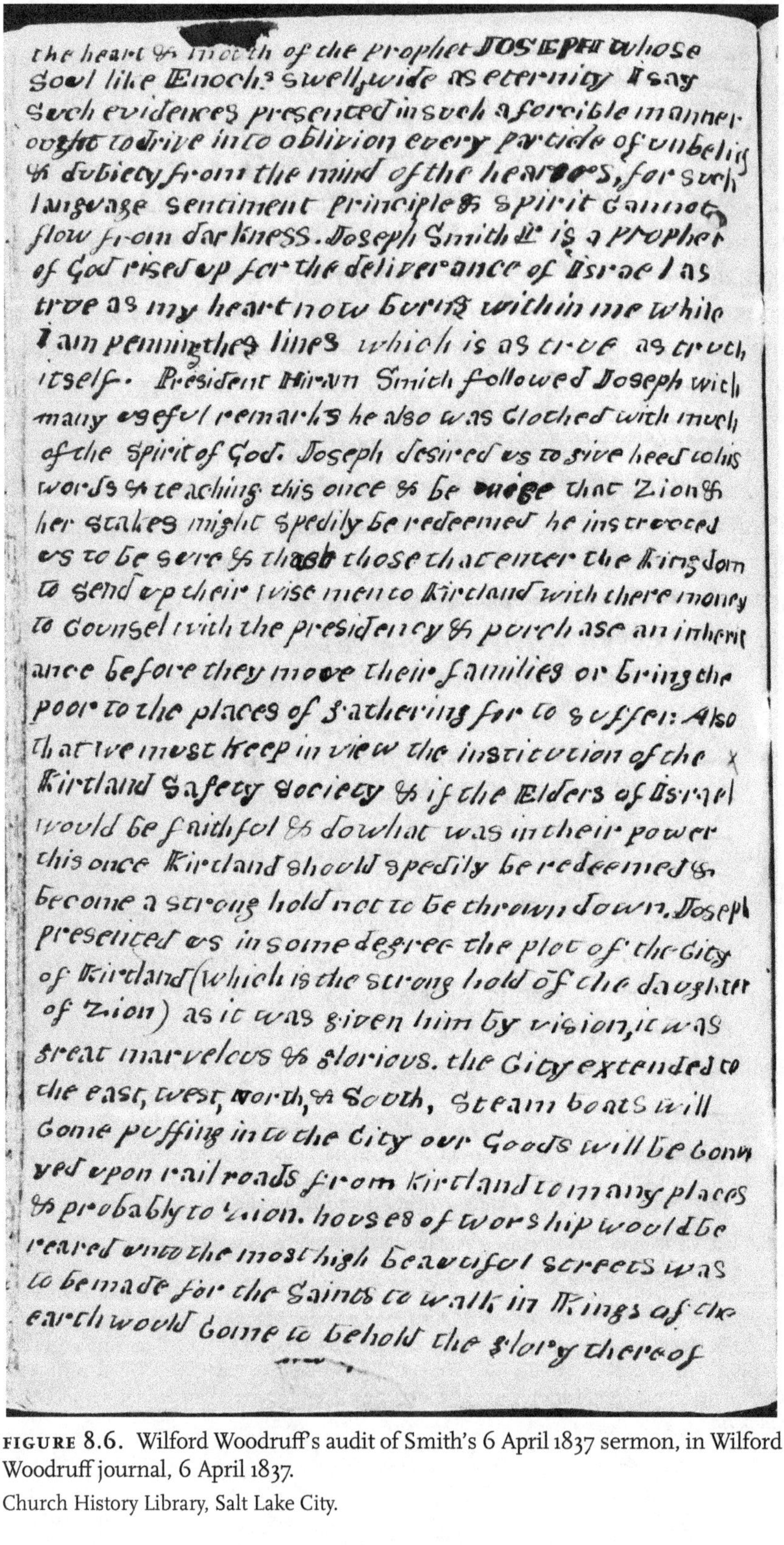

the heart & mouth of the prophet JOSEPH whose
soul like Enoch's swells wide as eternity I say
such evidences presented in such a forcible manner
ought to drive into oblivion every particle of unbelief
& dubiety from the mind of the hearers, for such
language sentiment principle & spirit cannot
flow from darkness. Joseph Smith Jr is a prophet
of God rised up for the deliverance of Israel as
true as my heart now burns within me while
I am penning these lines which is as true as truth
itself. President Hiram Smith followed Joseph with
many useful remarks he also was clothed with much
of the spirit of God. Joseph desired us to give heed to his
words & teaching this once & be wise that Zion &
her stakes might spedily be redeemed he instructed
us to be sure & those that enter the kingdom
to send up their wise men to Kirtland with there money
to counsel with the presidency & purchase an inherit
ance before they move their families or bring the
poor to the places of gathering for to suffer: Also
that we must keep in view the institution of the
Kirtland Safety society & if the Elders of Israel
would be faithful & do what was in their power
this once Kirtland should spedily be redeemed &
become a strong hold not to be thrown down. Joseph
presented us in some degree the plot of the city
of Kirtland (which is the strong hold of the daughter
of Zion) as it was given him by vision, it was
great marvelous & glorious. the city extended to
the east, west, north, & South, steam boats will
come puffing into the city our goods will be conve
yed upon rail roads from Kirtland to many places
& probably to Zion. houses of worship would be
reared unto the most high beautiful streets was
to be made for the Saints to walk in Kings of the
earth would come to behold the glory thereof

FIGURE 8.6. Wilford Woodruff's audit of Smith's 6 April 1837 sermon, in Wilford Woodruff journal, 6 April 1837.

Church History Library, Salt Lake City.

Mormon auditors was almost always intensely personal. The majority of the more extensive surviving sermon reports for Smith come from the 1839–1844 period and represent the experience, the interaction of orality and aurality, and the impress of the auditor's assessment of meaning for him or her. This made a posthumous drive to publish Smith's preaching problematic on several fronts.

Joseph Smith's sermon texts became largely fixed only in the 1850s as part of the construction of Smith's biography (as seen through the lens of Mormonism). Willard Richards, the church historian in Joseph Smith's last two years of life (1842–1844), and especially his successor George A. Smith, a cousin to Joseph Smith, who was appointed after Richards's death in 1854, assigned staff to gather accounts of Joseph Smith's addresses and create texts of these speeches by fusing and editing existing reports of a given sermon.

This process involved expanding such audits into readable, grammatically acceptable texts that conformed to Mormon policy and preaching as articulated in the 1850s. What the reader finds in these editorial constructions is affected to some degree by the choices and sensibilities of these editors and historians. These fusion texts, dating from a decade after Smith's death, formed the central historical texts of the sermons through which Joseph Smith's thought was circulated among readers of succeeding eras. While these fusion texts seemed to function according to design, they increased the distance to the respective sermon events, and readers may come away from them with a distorted idea of Smith's use of language and preaching praxis.[97]

Respectability was important to Smith's posthumous editors, who sometimes changed his usage to conform with standards of gentility in discourse. As a simple example, Joseph Smith used the colloquial form "Misoura" for Missouri. Audits suggest that he sometimes employed double negatives or used verb forms typical in rural and working-class America at the time. On a few occasions, redactors inserted or deleted material that reflected events or ideas that came after Smith's death. The editorial drive for respectability and the wish to supply Smith's imprimatur to ideas were other mechanisms that distanced readers from the original event.[98] Editors

97. See Jessee, "Priceless Words."

98. Jensen, "Text, Context," 81.

sometimes sought to lengthen the reports of Smith's sermons by filling in historical lacunae with material from reports of other sermons. Moreover, sermon redactors generally failed to distinguish between the types of manuscript audits they used or their own intrusions into the texts.[99]

A May 1844 preaching event, its aural audit, and subsequent redaction illustrate the point and enter a note of caution for the way Smith's sermon literature is deployed as a historiographical tool. A section of the first imprint of the sermon reads,

> For the last three years I have a record of all my acts and proceedings, for I have kept several good, faithful, and efficient clerks in constant employ; they have accompanied me everywhere, and carefully kept my history, and they have written down what I have done, where I have been, and what I have said; therefore my enemies cannot charge me with any day, time, or place, but what I have written testimony to prove my actions; and my enemies cannot prove anything against me.[100]

The original audit does not survive. However, a redacted manuscript dating from 1855 suggests something of the original audit, and how it was transformed to print.

> For the last three years I have a record of all my acts and proceedings <for I have kept several good <faithful> and efficient clerks in constant employ, they have accompanied me every where & carefully kept my history, and they have written down what I have done, where I have been & what I have said> there <fore my enemies> cannot charge me with any day ~~or~~ time <or place _ but what I have written testimony, to prove my actions, and my enemies> ~~for they~~ cannot prove anything against me.[101]

99. See Neuman, *Jeremiah's Scribes*, 30, 41, 45, 101; Stout, *New England Soul*, 4–5.

100. "History of Joseph Smith," *Deseret News* 7, no. 27 (9 September 1857): 210.

101. Joseph Smith, Sermon, 26 May 1844, Leo Hawkins manuscript, Joseph Smith Collection, CHL. This may be the first publication of Hawkins's manuscript showing Bullock's annotation.

The brackets < . . . > indicate interlinear insertions to the manuscript. This manuscript, a second-order text, is in the hand of Leo Hawkins, a clerk employed by the church's historian during the 1850s, the decade following Joseph Smith's death. Its first-order parent, a probable aural audit, is not extant but was created by clerk Thomas Bullock in Nauvoo. Bullock, a British convert who emigrated to Nauvoo in 1843, was almost immediately employed as one of Smith's clerks.[102] The insertions to the Hawkins manuscript were added by Bullock. Bullock's insertions are not historical, in several senses. Indeed, the complimentary adjectives like "faithful" were not atypical of Bullock's redactions of such items.[103] The redacted text implies that Smith purposely had his sermons, among other things, audited by "several good faithful clerks in constant employ."

There is no evidence that Smith made such a claim on this occasion. However, a search of the documentary record of the period shows that the skeleton of the claim is correct, though the timeline is exaggerated. Smith did employ clerks to do various acts of record keeping, but it was not until 1842 that a clerk consistently kept track of his daily movements in some detail, and it was not until April 1844 that Smith had several clerks auditing his preaching outside of the developed council audits. As the foregoing illustrates, using Smith's sermon corpus can be a fraught enterprise even with careful historiographical technique. The careful historian must always examine the documentary issues of these records, alert to the intrusion of auditor into archetype and the fundamental narrowness of flattened text that always fails to capture the preaching moment. When quoting such records, the auditor may be as significant to the source as the preacher and what is missing may be as significant as what is present.

Conclusion

Joseph Smith's sermon records, as a body, form an important aspect of early Mormonism's documentary record. The uneven nature of that record

102. For Bullock's assignment to record the sermon, see his journal entry for Sunday, 26 May 1844: "at the Stand [outdoor pulpit] recording J. Smith's sermon." Historian's Office, Journal, 1844–1879, CHL, p. 14.

103. While such redactions may sometimes appear self-serving, in this case at least, they had the religious purpose of supporting the reliability of the church historical record. A docket on the final page of the manuscript indicates that Brigham Young approved of the edited manuscript on 27 February 1856. Young was then the president of the church in Utah.

complicates the work of historians, textual scholars, and even devotional writers focusing on the period. The early protocol that set sermons as strictly oral literature makes it difficult to understand associated early Mormon liturgical habits and cultural themes. The gradually increasing overlap between revelation and instruction brought about ever more reliable reports of preaching and elevated preaching to the point that relatively detailed sermon audits were the norm, not the exception. Smith's sermons form a foundation for many common Mormon beliefs, like proxy Christian sacraments for the dead, the nature of grace, the protology of the human soul, and the nature of the afterlife. Subsequent redactions have sometimes become, like scripture, sources of proof-texts for behavior, teaching, and systematic belief within Mormonism. They likewise capture the attention of modern media voices and scholars who hope to understand modern Mormonism. Getting beyond the 1850s editions of those sermons that have long been the sources to which historians have turned and applying twenty-first century literary and historical tools to the documentary record is a fascinating work that is vital for any modern historian of early Mormonism.

9

Joseph Smith's Nauvoo Journals

Alex D. Smith and Andrew H. Hedges

THE MORMON PROPHET Joseph Smith's Nauvoo journals were anything but typical diaries. They did not record his innermost thoughts, feelings, and motivations; many entries captured only a fraction of his activities during a given day; and, most importantly, not a word in them was written by their subject. And yet, for the student of Mormon history, there are few records more valuable and informative. Despite ostensibly being one man's journals, these texts form a corporate history influenced more by the offices and personalities of their authors than by Smith himself. They chronicle the eventful final two and a half years of the prophet's life, shape the narrative of the Latter-day Saint story, and form the foundation for what is known of this important era in Mormon history.[1] However, in order to use Smith's journals critically, a historian should understand the particular reasons for which the various volumes were created, who produced them, and how.

Joseph Smith's Nauvoo journals are found in four documents: (1) the "Book of the Law of the Lord," (2) "President Joseph Smith's Journal," in four volumes, (3) Willard Richards's personal journal for 22–27 June 1844, and (4) William Clayton's "Daily Account of Joseph Smith's Activities (the first two documents are featured in Figure 9.1)." These records test the definition of *journal* and require contextualization as artifacts to be fully understood. This chapter will consider these documents

1. The authors express appreciation to Shannon Kelly for generously reviewing and improving this chapter, to Richard Lloyd Anderson and Brent M. Rogers for serving as co-editors of volumes 2 and 3 of *The Joseph Smith Papers*, Journals series, and to Dean C. Jessee, whose early work with Smith's journals provided the foundation for the *Papers*.

FIGURE 9.1. Nauvoo journals.
Church History Library, Salt Lake City. Photograph by Welden C. Andersen.

as discrete manuscripts, examining their creation and development over time. It will then conclude by analyzing the journals' content and evaluating their unique contributions to a better understanding of Smith's life and Nauvoo-era Mormon history.[2]

The Corpus of Joseph Smith's Journals

Joseph Smith began keeping his first known journal at the age of twenty-six in 1832, two years after he organized the Church of Christ. In a letter to church member William Phelps dated 27 November 1832, Smith wrote instructions that would come to shape his Nauvoo journals a decade later: "It is the duty of the lords clerk whom he has appointed to keep a

2. Complete transcripts of these journal texts are reproduced in Andrew H. Hedges et al., eds., *Journals, Volume 2: December 1841–April 1843*, vol. 2 of the Journal series of *The Joseph Smith Papers*, ed. Dean C. Jessee et al. (Salt Lake City: Church Historian's Press, 2011) (hereafter *JSP*, J2); and Andrew H. Hedges et al., eds., *Journals, Volume 3: May 1843–June 1844*, vol. 3 of the Journals series of *The Joseph Smith Papers*, ed. Ronald K. Esplin and Matthew J. Grow (Salt Lake City: Church Historian's Press, 2015) (hereafter *JSP*, J3). Portions of this chapter first appeared in *JSP*, J2; *JSP*, J3; and Alex D. Smith, "The Book of the Law of the Lord," *Journal of Mormon History* 38, no. 4 (Fall 2012): 131–63.

history and a general church record of all things that transpire in Zion."[3] Among other things, this history was to include an account of church members' "manner of life, their faith, and works." Smith evidently considered a personal journal to be a fulfillment of this injunction; on the same day he wrote this letter to Phelps, he began his first journal with the words "Joseph Smith Jrs Book for Record Baught on the 27th of November 1832 for the purpose to keep a minute account of all things that come under my obse[r]vation &c."[4]

Joseph Smith wrote in this first journal dutifully for nine days and then resumed after a break of ten months. Through the remainder of the 1830s, he had five journals in Ohio, Missouri, and Illinois, kept only sporadically between months and at times even years of silence. Even before the first of these journals was completed, Smith began employing scribes to record entries for him, often—but not always—dictating the content. Smith wrote in his journals with diminishing frequency, and his handwriting is found only in the first two.[5]

Though employing amanuenses for journal keeping was not unheard of in nineteenth-century America, Joseph Smith used scribes atypically. There is no evidence that he kept journals to later recollect his own activities or to pass down personal thoughts to posterity. From the outset he intended his journals as a history, and the texts can only be fully understood in that context. It is evident that Smith, and later his followers, believed that his story and that of the church he had organized were important and warranted documenting. By the time Smith's Nauvoo journals were being recorded, he was a nationally recognized figure. His use of clerks to keep his journal, however, apparently had never been for the traditional reasons such as illiteracy, convenience, or the demands of a busy schedule. Smith had not dictated daily diary entries but had increasingly distanced himself from his journal, eventually leaving his scribes and clerks virtually autonomous in deciding what to include. Nor had he retained a professional scribe or close family member for years on end, but rather transitioned frequently from one scribe to another. The clerks he employed were often

3. Joseph Smith, Kirtland, OH, to William W. Phelps, [Independence, MO], 27 November 1832, in Joseph Smith, "Letter Book A," 1832–1835, Joseph Smith Collection, 1827–1846, Church History Library, Salt Lake City, 1 (hereafter Joseph Smith Letterbook 1).

4. Joseph Smith, Book for Record, November 1832–December 1834, Joseph Smith Collection.

5. Mark Ashurst-McGee and Alex D. Smith, "The Joseph Smith Journals," *Ensign*, December 2007, 34–39.

selected based on their current ecclesiastical office, whether it was church clerk, historian, or institutional recorder. These practices, curious if Smith were keeping a personal diary but intuitive for a corporate history, demonstrate that he viewed his journal as the latter.

Joseph Smith's 1830s journals ended as the Latter-day Saints, having been driven from Missouri, began to gather at Commerce, Illinois (soon renamed Nauvoo). Joseph Smith left Commerce for Washington DC, in autumn 1839 to meet with United States president Martin Van Buren in an effort to seek redress for losses suffered by the Mormons in Missouri. Smith left James Mulholland, the scribe who had been keeping his journal prior to this time, home in Nauvoo—possibly due to the illness Mulholland suffered about this time. Within a week of Smith's departure, Mulholland had died.[6] Smith asked Robert D. Foster, who accompanied him on part of the trip east, to keep a journal, but the extent to which Foster complied is unclear; Smith wrote him in March 1840 that he wanted "to get hold of your journal very much," but no such record is known to exist.[7] Scribes were employed to compile and write the history of the church and to copy Smith's correspondence, but there is no evidence that anyone was keeping a record of his daily activities in Nauvoo until Smith appointed apostle Willard Richards to resume his journal in December 1841.

Richards had arrived in Nauvoo in August 1841 after a four-year mission to England. Joseph Smith found him to be "a man after his own heart, in all things, that he could trust with his business" and appointed him temple recorder and "Scribe for the private office of the President" on 13 December 1841. Richards began "the duties of his office" immediately, apparently writing the first entry of Smith's journal on the day of his appointment.[8] Richards, seen in Figure 9.2, kept Smith's journal for the remainder of the prophet's life, with the exception of the period from late June through late December 1842. Richards was absent at this time, and his assistant William Clayton, seen in Figure 9.3, kept the journal, with occasional assistance from colleagues Eliza R. Snow and Erastus Derby.

6. Emma Smith, Nauvoo, IL, to Joseph Smith, Washington DC, 6 December 1839, Charles Aldrich Autograph Collection, State Historical Society of Iowa, Des Moines.

7. Joseph Smith, Nauvoo, IL, to Robert D. Foster, Beverly, IL, 11 March 1840, Joseph Smith Collection.

8. Willard Richards, Nauvoo, IL, to Jennetta Richards, Richmond, MA, 26 February 1842, Church History Library, Salt Lake City; Joseph Smith, Journal, 13 December 1841, in *JSP*, J2:11.

FIGURE 9.2 AND FIGURE 9.3. Scribes of Joseph Smith's Nauvoo journals. Willard Richards (Top) and William Clayton (Bottom).

Church History Library, Salt Lake City.

Joseph Smith's Nauvoo journals cover the last twenty-six months of his life—a period marked by the continued growth of the church, significant doctrinal developments, the ongoing settlement of the Nauvoo community, and the maturing of Smith as a political and religious leader. Though not a comprehensive narrative of events, the journals are an essential source for reconstructing the events of Joseph Smith's life and the history of the church he founded.[9]

The Origin of the Nauvoo Journals

While incarcerated in the jail at Liberty, Missouri, Joseph Smith sent to the Latter-day Saints a now famous letter dated 20 March 1839, directing them to gather accounts and statements of losses incurred during their expulsion from Missouri during winter 1838–1839. The letter also suggested that a committee be formed to record these statements and to "gather up the libilous publications that are afloat and all that are in the magazines and in the Insiclopedias and all the libillious histories that are published and that are writing."[10] This effort was intended to promote national support for the Saints as they worked to petition the federal government for redress. After escaping from Missouri authorities, Smith arrived in Quincy, Illinois, on 22 April 1839, and the same day commissioned James Mulholland to begin keeping a new journal.[11]

Two weeks later, a general conference of the church near Quincy appointed Almon Babbitt, Erastus Snow, and Robert B. Thompson as the committee Joseph Smith had recommended in his letter from the jail in Liberty. The conference minutes confirmed the committee's purpose: "to gather up and obtain all the libelous reports and publications which have been circulated against our Church, as well as other historical

9. For additional biographical context, see "Joseph Smith and His Papers," in Dean C. Jessee et al., eds., *Journals, Volume 1: 1832–1839*, vol. 1 of the Journals series of *The Joseph Smith Papers*, ed. Dean C. Jessee et al. (Salt Lake City: Church Historian's Press, 2008), xv–xli (hereafter *JSP*, J1).

10. Joseph Smith et al., to the Church of Latter Day Saints at Quincy, IL, 20 March 1839, in Revelations Collection, 1831–ca. 1844, 1847, 1861, ca. 1876, Church History Library, Salt Lake City. Portions of this lengthy two-part letter were later canonized and are presently sections 121–123 of the LDS Doctrine and Covenants.

11. Joseph Smith, "Minute Book, 1839," Joseph Smith Collection. While the journal was begun on 22 April 1839, one retrospective entry precedes that entry. It reads: "Escaped Aprile 16th."

matter connected with said Church which they can possibly obtain."[12] The language of the direction suggests that the initial objective had already expanded beyond documenting the Missouri experience to encompass a larger history project. The following month, on 10–11 June, Mulholland recorded in both his own journal and Smith's that he had begun drafting—with Smith dictating—a history of the church.[13] Smith's and Mulholland's efforts between 11 June and 29 October resulted in draft notes and the first portion of the completed manuscript of Smith's 1838–1856 history, as well as the "Extract, from the Private Journal of Joseph Smith Jr.," published in the first issue of the *Times and Seasons* in November 1839.[14] Title notwithstanding, this latter publication was not truly a Joseph Smith journal or an extract of any known journal, but rather a brief summary of the events of the "Mormon War" in Missouri.

Joseph Smith's first Illinois journal, which was kept by James Mulholland until Smith departed for Washington in late October 1839,[15] follows Smith's move from Quincy to Commerce. The journal entries were recorded sporadically, and frequently summarized the events of three or four days in a few words. In one sense, excluding this first Illinois journal from the Nauvoo journals being considered in this chapter is merely a semantic distinction because Commerce, the location where the journal was kept, later became Nauvoo. However, because this journal is more appropriately linked contextually and temporally with Smith's other 1830s journals, it is not treated here. The extant historical sources show a gap in Smith's journal for two years after Mulholland's death—until 13 December 1841.

---

12. Minutes, 4 May 1839, General Church Minutes, 1839–1877, Church History Library, Salt Lake City.

13. James Mulholland, Journal, 10–13 June 1839, Joseph Smith Collection; Smith, Journal, 10–11 June 1839, in *JSP*, J1:340.

14. "History of Joseph Smith" (Mulholland draft), 1839, Church History Library, Salt Lake City; "Extract, from the Private Journal of Joseph Smith Jr.," *Times and Seasons*, November 1839, 1:2–9. For more discussion of these histories, see Jessee, "The Writing of Joseph Smith's History," 439–73; Dean C. Jessee, ed., *The Papers of Joseph Smith* (Salt Lake City: Deseret Book, 1989), 1:210–11, 230–31, 265–67; and *JSP*, J1:333, 340.

15. Sidney Rigdon, *Appeal to the American People: Being an Account of the Persecutions of the Church of Latter Day Saints and of the Barbarities Inflicted on Them by the Inhabitants of the State of Missouri* (Cincinnati: Glezen and Shephard, 1840), inside cover; Joseph Smith, Sidney Rigdon, and Hyrum Smith, Quincy, IL, to the Church of Jesus Christ of Latter-day Saints Scattered Abroad, 1 November 1839, photocopy of original in private possession.

While Joseph Smith's reasons for having his journal resumed at this particular time are not entirely clear, changes in the responsibilities of the church's Quorum of the Twelve Apostles may have played an important role. Members of the quorum began returning to Nauvoo in July 1841 after a two-year proselytizing mission in Great Britain. Before their British mission, the apostles' administrative responsibilities had been limited to overseeing scattered branches of the church that were outside of the organized "stakes of Zion" (the approved locations for the "gathering" of the Saints). Upon their return, however, Smith explained to a conference of the church on 16 August 1841 that the Twelve "should be authorized to assist in managing the affairs of the Kingdom in this place [Nauvoo]." A sustaining vote of the conference formalized the new arrangement, allowing Smith to delegate an increasing number of church administrative responsibilities to the Twelve in the coming months and years.[16]

Smith did not articulate, however, exactly what form these new duties would take and how the Twelve's expanded authority over the church generally would be manifest. An established Nauvoo stake presidency and high council were already functioning as an administrative head at the church's new central gathering place. Additionally, most of the Twelve had been separated from their families and new Illinois homes for two years or more, which made finding employment for these returning missionaries a priority. For some of the apostles with previous clerical and printing experience, a dual solution to expanding the quorum's authority and providing income came in the form of an apparently conscious decision by Smith to have the Twelve take control of the church's public image, its communications arm, and the creation and custody of its history.

Regulating the church's primary medium for communication (the Nauvoo newspaper, *Times and Seasons*) and resuming work on Joseph Smith's history soon became the occupations of Quorum of the Twelve members Wilford Woodruff, John Taylor, and Willard Richards. Ebenezer Robinson had recently resumed editorship of the *Times and Seasons* following the unexpected deaths of both of the paper's earlier editors, church clerk Robert B. Thompson and Joseph Smith's younger brother Don

16. General Church Minutes, 16 August 1841; Ronald K. Esplin, "The Emergence of Brigham Young and the Twelve to Mormon Leadership, 1830–1841" (PhD diss., Brigham Young University, 1981), 482, 500–6.

Carlos Smith.[17] In November 1841 the Twelve began to discuss taking over the printing establishment from Robinson, and a 28 January 1842 revelation directed the Twelve to "take in hand the Editorial department of the Times and Seasons."[18] With the church's purchase of the paper and printing office from Robinson, the Twelve selected Woodruff and Taylor to "edit the Times & Seasons & take charge of the whole establishment under the direction of Joseph the Seer."[19] Around this same time, Smith appointed Richards his scribe and the recorder for the temple, replacing the deceased Thompson as custodian of the Book of the Law of the Lord.[20] With these appointments, both the church's principal communications arm and the keeping of Smith's history fell under the direction of members of the Quorum of the Twelve.

"The Book of the Law of the Lord"

The large, enigmatic tome that is the Book of the Law of the Lord is a complex artifact. One of the most significant documents from the Nauvoo period in Mormon history, the book is at once a record of revelations, a register of donations for the construction of the temple, and the repository of Joseph Smith's journal entries between December 1841 and December 1842.[21] Despite the apparently disparate nature of these three texts—particularly the seemingly

---

17. "Death of General Don Carlos Smith," *Times and Seasons,* 16 August 1841, 2:503–4; "Death of Col. Robert B. Thompson," *Times and Seasons,* 1 September 1841, 2:519–20.

18. Quorum of the Twelve Apostles, Minutes, 1840–1844, Church History Library, Salt Lake City, 31 November 1841; Revelation, 28 January, 1842, in *JSP,* J2:38.

19. Wilford Woodruff, Journal, 1833–1898, Wilford Woodruff, Journals and Papers, 1828–1898, Church History Library, Salt Lake City, 3, 4, and 19 February 1842; see also *JSP,* J2:38.

20. Smith, Journal, 13 December 1841, in *JSP,* J2:11.

21. The "Law of the Lord" is listed in inventories of church records made in Salt Lake City in the 1850s. These entries show that the volume was housed for a time in Brigham Young's office. The book was eventually housed with the papers of Joseph Fielding Smith, apparently during his tenure as church historian and recorder (1921–1970), and became part of the First Presidency's papers when he became church president in 1970. In 2010, the First Presidency gave the Church History Library custody of the book. ("Inventory. Historian's Office. 4th April 1855," [1]; "Inventory. Historians Office. G. S. L. City April 1. 1857," [1]; "Historian's Office Inventory G. S. L. City March 19. 1858," [1]; "Historian's Office Catalogue Book March 1858," [11], Historian's Office, Catalogs and Inventories, 1846–1904, Church History Library, Salt Lake City; "Inventory of President Joseph Fielding Smith's Safe," 23 May 1970, First Presidency, General Administration Files, Church History Library, Salt Lake City; Letter of Transfer, Salt Lake City, UT, 8 January 2010, Church History Library, Salt Lake City.)

odd pairing of journal entries with financial accounts—there is an underlying relationship. The motivation for recording each of these texts in the Book of the Law of the Lord is, in one way or another, related to the Nauvoo temple. From the book's first entry to its last inscription, the temple and its construction are preeminent. Understanding the relationships between the revelations, journal entries, and donation records provides insights into Smith's developing vision of record keeping but requires a brief chronology of pivotal events relating to the church's financial records and to Smith's journal-keeping efforts.

Illinois law allowed every religious organization to elect up to ten trustees who would be legally responsible for the institution's property. Pursuant to this law, on 30 January 1841 a conference of the church elected Joseph Smith as the organization's "sole trustee," and notice of the election was filed with Hancock County, Illinois.[22] As trustee-in-trust, Smith was responsible for overseeing the church's financial matters; chief among them were donations for constructing the Nauvoo temple. William Clayton, one of Smith's clerks and the temple recorder, identified a correlation between Smith's role as trustee and the beginning of recording donations in the Book of the Law of the Lord. Clayton recalled, "President Joseph Smith was appointed, 'Sole Trustee in Trust for the Church of Jesus Christ of Latter Day Saints,' and consequently it became his prerogative to receive all the donations for the Church and the Temple."[23] Therefore, legal oversight for the church's finances in Illinois dovetailed with the instruction Smith had given almost a decade earlier to record donations of faithful members in a "book of the law of God."[24] Smith's need to record temple donations and his desire to have work on his history resumed combined when Willard Richards began recording both accounts in the Book of the Law of the Lord. On 13 December 1841, four months after Robert

22. "An Act Concerning Religious Societies," 6 February 1834, *Laws of the State of Illinois, Passed by the Ninth General Assembly, at Their First Session, Commencing December 1, 1834, and Ending February 13, 1835* (Vandalia, Illinois: William Walters, 1837), 147–48, sec. 1; Appointment, 2 February 1841, Hancock Co., IL, Bonds and Mortgages, vol. 1, p. 97, microfilm 954,776, U.S. and Canada Record Collection, Family History Library, Salt Lake City.

23. William Clayton, "History of the Nauvoo Temple," ca. 1845, Church History Library, Salt Lake City, 16–17.

24. Joseph Smith, Kirtland, OH, Letter to William W. Phelps, [Independence, MO], 27 November 1832, in Joseph Smith Letterbook 1, p. 1.

B. Thompson's death, Richards was appointed "Recorder for the Temple, and the Scribe for the private office of the President."[25]

The earliest entries in the book may be more appropriately termed "historical" entries rather than "journal" entries, as apparently the record was not immediately viewed as a journal for Joseph Smith but rather as a general history. A number of headings in the early part of the book indicate a developing conception of the book's purpose.[26] Page 26—the first in the book containing entries—bears no heading at the top of the page. On page 58—thirty-two pages after the entries begin—the contemporaneous heading appears: "Journal of President Joseph." Willard Richards moved in with the Smith family on 13 January 1842; the "Journal of President Joseph" heading preceding the 15 January entry therefore reflects Richards's increased proximity to Smith and a new function of the record.[27]

The journal entries and donations were kept concurrently, sometimes alternating every other page, until page 215. From that point on, Willard Richards kept Joseph Smith's journal in four small volumes with entries dated from 21 December 1842 to 22 June 1844. The record of donations in the Book of the Law of the Lord, meanwhile, continues from page 216 to the end of the volume.[28] Nearly 80% of the book is devoted to donation entries. The size of the Book of the Law of the Lord communicates its primary role as a financial ledger. It is a massive tome, measuring 17 by 11⅜ inches, with thick, leather-covered boards. The physical appearance immediately conveys the sense of a formal, official record. It was usually kept in the recorder's office, initially located in the "counting room" on the ground floor of Smith's brick store.[29]

On 29 June 1842, Willard Richards transferred the book to William Clayton. Richards went to join his wife Jennetta and their young son Heber in Massachusetts, leaving the book with Clayton, who was already

25. Smith, Journal, 13 December 1841, in *JSP*, J2:11.

26. These headings appear to have been written at the same time as the surrounding entries. Some appear in the middle of a manuscript page, and there is no indication that they were later insertions.

27. Willard Richards, Journal, 13 January 1843, Willard Richards Journals and Papers, 1821–1854, Church History Library, Salt Lake City.

28. Page numbers in the Book of the Law of the Lord were written by hand in the upper outside corners. While the last numbered page in the manuscript is 477, there are actually 478 pages because there are two pages numbered 453.

29. "Minutes of the General Conference of the Church," *Times and Seasons*, 15 April 1841, 2:386–87; Young et al., "Baptism for the Dead," *Times and Seasons*, 15 December 1841, 3:626.

assisting Richards in his clerical duties.[30] With the exception of correspondence copied briefly into the journal by Eliza R. Snow and Erastus H. Derby, the remainder of the manuscript is in Clayton's handwriting.[31]

The Book of the Law of the Lord also contains some internal evidence that its journal entries, revelations, and donation register are related and that there was a unifying motivation behind the book's creation. The imposing title "Book of the Law of the Lord" immediately raises the question of the book's purpose. The title appears to have been most directly an allusion to a biblical record bearing the various names of "Book of the Law of the Lord," "Book of the Law of God," or simply "Book of the Law." This record from ancient Israel contained the commandments and revelations by which the Israelites were to be judged—a natural naming precedent for Joseph Smith's book of revelations.[32] The Nauvoo volume was not, however, the first text referred to by this title in early Mormonism. A conference of the church in New Portage, Ohio, in September 1834, had made reference to an 1831 revelation containing "the rules and regulations of the Law," and the "Law of the Lord."[33] In this early context, the title appears to have been generically used to denote any modern revelatory text.

The title communicates that the book was designed with a sacred aspect in mind. It is uncertain precisely when the book's title page was inscribed or whether the title was selected prior to the writing of any text in the volume. The title was at least in part intended to relate to the revelations that Robert B. Thompson copied into the volume's first pages. The report of the church's Nauvoo conference in April 1841 referred to John C. Bennett's reading the first revelation from the Book of the Law of the Lord, identifying it by name a full eight months before Willard Richards began recording any financial donations or historical accounts.[34] It is unclear whether

---

30. Richards, Journal, 1 July 1842; Smith, Journal, 29 June 1842, in *JSP*, J2:71, 73.

31. "The Book of the Law of the Lord," Record Book, 1841–1845, Church History Library, Salt Lake City, 126–477 (hereafter Book of the Law of the Lord).

32. See, for example, 2 Chronicles 17:9, Nehemiah 9:3, Joshua 24:26, and Deuteronomy 30:10. A "book of the law of the Lord given by Moses" and presented to Josiah's scribe, Shaphan, was found during the temple's repair. (2 Chronicles 34:8–21; 2 Kings 22:3–130.)

33. Minutes, 8 September 1834, in Matthew C. Godfrey et al., eds., *Documents, Volume 4: April 1834–September 1835*, vol. 4 of the Documents series of *The Joseph Smith Papers*, ed. Ronald K. Esplin et al. (Salt Lake City: Church Historian's Press, 2016), 167.

34. "Minutes of the General Conference of the Church," *Times and Seasons*, 15 April 1841, 2:386–87.

the volume was originally intended to house more than just revelations, but evidence examined herein suggests that at some point Joseph Smith consciously linked all three texts within the book to its scriptural title.

Like the copied revelations and donations, Joseph Smith's journal was an integral part of the Book of the Law of the Lord. In the 1832 letter in which Smith instructed William Phelps to keep a history of the church, the title he repeatedly gave to the record, which was to include both an account of donations to the church as well as the church's history, was the "book of the law of God" or "the book of the law." Although no known volume bearing this title was created during the decade in which Smith gave that instruction, the combination of texts within the 1841 Book of the Law of the Lord suggests the connection was intentional and an attempt to fulfill the assignment in the 1832 letter. Excerpts from the letter to Phelps were not canonized until 1876, but whether Smith considered the instructions in the letter to be revealed commandments or not, the similarities between the description in the letter and the Book of the Law of the Lord, begun over eight years later, reflect the prophet's continuing belief that such a record was necessary.[35]

William Clayton's 1845 "History of the Nauvoo Temple" offers a possible explanation for the inclusion of the revelations recorded in the beginning of the Book of the Law of the Lord. When Willard Richards gave Clayton the Book of the Law of the Lord in June 1842, Clayton recorded Joseph Smith's instructions to him: "Brother Clayton I want you to take care of the records and papers, and from this time I appoint you Temple Recorder, and when I have any revelations to write, you shall write them."[36] Clayton's account demonstrates that Smith considered the recording of revelations to be a function of the office of temple recorder. Thompson's contribution in the beginning of the Book of the Law of the Lord was copying the revelations from draft versions—a different function than Clayton's, who inscribed revelations as Smith dictated them. Richards referred to himself throughout the Book of the Law of the Lord as "recorder" or "rec," implying that he viewed keeping the records in the Book of the Law of the Lord as part of his responsibilities as temple recorder.

35. Joseph Smith, Kirtland, OH, Letter to William W. Phelps, [Independence, MO], 27 November 1832, in Joseph Smith Letterbook 1, p. 1.

36. Clayton, "History of the Nauvoo Temple," 30.

That the Book of the Law of the Lord was intended for recording the names of the faithful is nowhere more explicit than in the journal entries of 16 and 23 August 1842—the only two entries in Joseph Smith's Illinois journals that were unquestionably dictated. Smith dictated these while in hiding from Missouri and Illinois law officers who were attempting to arrest him in connection with the attempted assassination of former Missouri governor Lilburn W. Boggs. When serving as governor, Boggs had ordered the removal of the Mormons from the state in 1838, and news of the attempt on his life met with little sympathy in Nauvoo. In his dictation, Smith recollected the names of those who had remained loyal to himself and the church. In the 16 August entry, while remarking on the good deeds of his wife Emma and close friends, Joseph Smith also reflected on his relationship with his brother Hyrum and stated, "Hyrum, thy name shall be written in the Book of the Law of the Lord, for those who come after thee to look upon, that they may pattern after thy works." Later in the same paragraph, Smith again alluded to the religious significance of the book: "The names of the faithful are what I wish to record in this place."[37] Smith's expression of his desire that the Saints follow Hyrum's example echoes language in the book of Galatians: "Cursed is every one that continueth not in all things which are written in the book of the law to do them."[38] Smith resumed the subject on 23 August: "While I contemplate the virtues and the good qualifications and characteristics of the faithful few, which I am now recording in the Book of the Law of the Lord."[39] The repeated reference to the title of the book, rather than to "my journal" or similar phrases, reflects a consciousness of the book's purpose.

In addition to the title and supporting journal entries, the concurrent donation entries evince a common function of the book's purpose. A note in Willard Richards's handwriting preceding the first donations recorded in the volume explains that they are "a Record of the consecrations and Tytheings of the church of Jesus christ of Latter Day Saints for the building of the Temple of God in the city of Nauvoo," seen in Figure 9.4.[40] The donation entries were listed by date of receipt and recorded the name

37. Smith, Journal, 16 August 1842, in *JSP*, J2:94.

38. Galatians 3:10.

39. Smith, Journal, 23 August 1842, in *JSP*, J2:115.

40. Book of the Law of the Lord, 27.

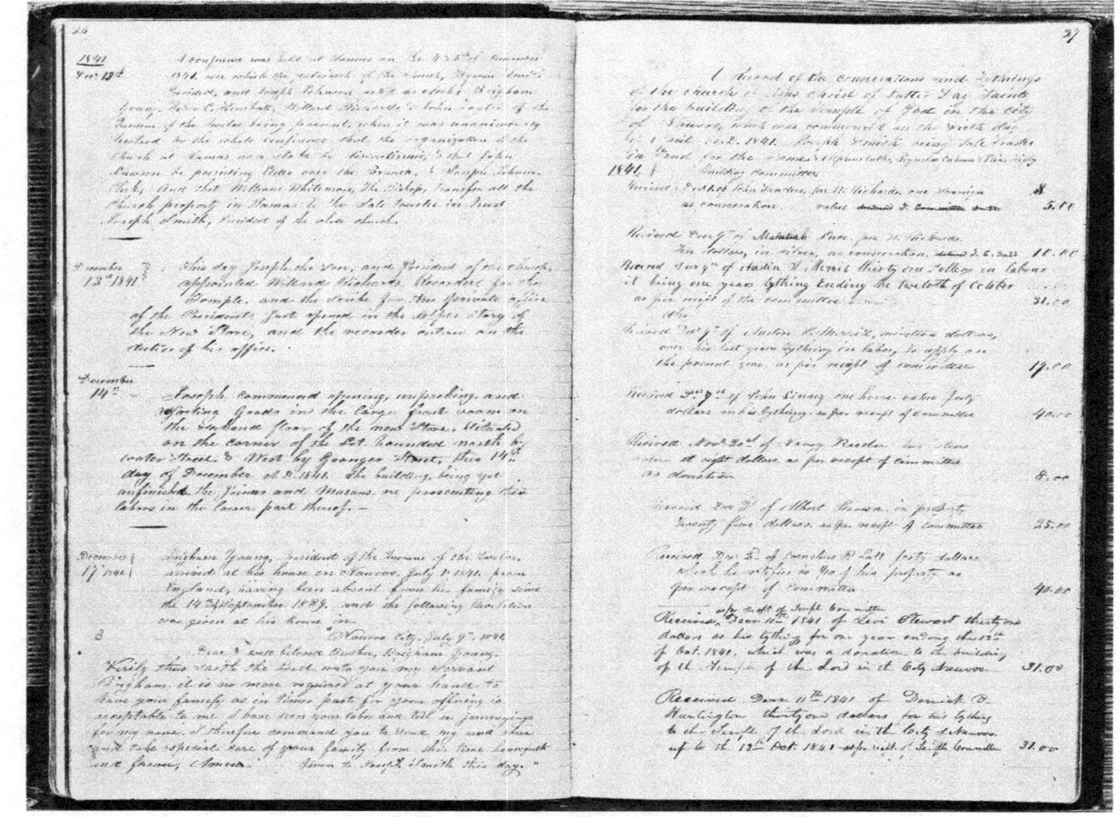

FIGURE 9.4. First pages of journal entries and donation records. Book of the Law of the Lord, pp. 26–27. Church History Library, Salt Lake City. Photograph by Welden C. Andersen.

of the donor, described the donation (which were most often in kind), and assigned its monetary value. It is noteworthy that while values were inscribed in a column running down the right side of each page, the totals were never tallied, implying that this was not an account book or ledger in the traditional sense.[41]

The book's emphasis on recording the names of faithful Saints was not limited to the journal entries but extended to some of the donation records. For instance, on 18 January 1842, Willard Richards recorded that one woman "offered a silver watch, purchased and saved by her own labor, as she stated to the Recorder. Beside supporting her children, her husband having neglected his family the past year; contrary to the principles of Righteousness, her offering was accepted. And returned to her again, for the purpose of assisting her to provide for her children. and the priviliges of the Font. Given her. & her children.— and may the blessings of Abrahams God rest upon her forever & ever Amen—".[42] Though extensive notes like this one were atypical in the tithing record, the phrase "priviliges of the Font"—referring to the temple's baptismal font, which was used for religious ritual, including individual healings—illustrates the relationship between temple access and documentation of worthiness in the Book of the Law of the Lord. The similarities between the records of donors and donations and the journal entries recounting the loyalty of faithful members suggest that the book was kept for the purposes Joseph Smith gave in his 1832 letter to Phelps.

The Book of the Law of the Lord was the church's first financial record to combine the element of spiritual worthiness with the concept of a "tithe."[43] Though the donations were initially to be entirely for the construction of the temple, it appears that Joseph Smith viewed the Book of the Law of

41. The exception to the rule that dollar amounts were never tallied occurred when itemized lists of donations were brought forward by a single person, spanning more than one page. The donations referred to above, brought by John Snider from his mission to Great Britain, are an example. These were then effectively treated as a single composite donation, with a total value inscribed.

42. Book of the Law of the Lord, 55.

43. Tithing donations recorded in the Book of the Law of the Lord frequently represent more than one-tenth of an individual's property or increase. A 13 December 1841 letter from the Quorum of the Twelve to the Saints defined tithing for the temple as "one tenth of all any one possessed at the commencement of the building, and one tenth part of all his increase from that time till the completion of the same, whether it be money or whatever he may be blessed with." (Brigham Young et al., "Baptism for the Dead," *Times and Seasons,* 15 December 1841, 3:626.)

the Lord as a literal fulfillment of his 1832 instruction to William Phelps to keep a "Book of the Law of God"—"a general church record . . . of all those who consecrate properties."[44] Expanding on the revelatory language in his 1832 letter to Phelps, which stated that church members "whose names are not found written in the book of the law . . . in that day shall not find an inheritance among the saints of the Most High," Smith introduced the principle that a physical record of worthiness—the tithing accounts in the Book of the Law of the Lord—was a requirement of eligibility for the blessings of the temple. In a meeting on 7 March 1844, addressing the topic of the future dedication of the Nauvoo temple, Smith stated: "Those whose names are found in the church book shall have the first claim . . . in that house.—I int[e]nd to keep the door at dedication myself— & not a man shall pass who had not paid his bonus."[45]

Despite ostensibly serving as Joseph Smith's personal journal, many of the entries focused on the temple. The operations of the temple committee were recorded regularly throughout the journal, including challenges committee members faced, complaints against their operation, and Smith's instructions to them.[46] Clayton's entry of 29 June 1842—the day Richards transferred the Law of the Lord to his custody—reads: "Heard the Recorder Read in the Law of the Lord."[47] This entry is one of very few in Smith's Nauvoo journals that gave explicit information about the degree of Smith's interaction with his own journal, and it suggests that he only rarely consulted the manuscript and may have been largely unfamiliar with its contents. Notably, in the entry of the following day, Clayton recorded two events that had occurred during the previous eight months but had gone

44. Joseph Smith, Kirtland, OH, Letter to William W. Phelps, [Independence, MO], 27 November 1832, in Joseph Smith Letterbook 1, pp. 1–2.

45. Smith, Journal, 7 March 1844, in *JSP*, J3:196. Smith's use of the term "church book" was a reference to the Book of the Law of the Lord. In December 1841, following his election as trustee for the church and repeated difficulties with donations not being properly recorded, Smith dictated that all tithing and temple donations be directed to him and recorded in the Book of the Law of the Lord by the temple recorder before any disbursements took place. (Brigham Young et al., "Baptism for the Dead," *Times and Seasons*, 15 December 1841, 3:626; Smith, Journal, 11 and 13 December 1841, 1 October and 28 November 1842, and 6 April 1843, in *JSP*, J2:14–15, 159–60, 169–70, 331–34.)

46. For examples of these issues, see the Joseph Smith journal entries of 11 and 13 December 1841; 1 October 1842; and 28 November 1842, in *JSP*, J2:14–15, 159–60, 169–70.

47. Smith, Journal, 29 June 1842, in *JSP*, J2:71.

unrecorded in the journal. Both related to the temple: the dedication of the baptismal font and a miraculous healing in it, and the deposit of items in the temple's cornerstone.[48]

Willard and Jennetta Richards reached Nauvoo on 30 October 1842, but Willard did not replace William Clayton as the keeper of Joseph Smith's journal until 21 December, almost two months later.[49] The reason for the delay is unclear, but in September, during Richards's absence, Clayton had been appointed to permanently replace Richards as temple recorder and, hence, as custodian of the Book of the Law of the Lord.[50] On 1 December 1842, a month after his return, Richards became involved in another project, when Smith instructed him to resume work on his history (the ramifications of Richards's new assignment on his keeping of Smith's journal will be discussed later in more detail herein).[51] Additionally, efforts to arrest Smith in connection with the Boggs assassination attempt had driven Smith into hiding for much of the last five months of 1842.[52] By October, Smith was no longer continually in hiding, but the persistent threat of arrest may have made keeping his journal a lower priority.

While Willard Richards was in the East, Joseph Smith and the temple building committee decided to move the temple recorder's office to the "committee house" near the construction site.[53] On 2 November, only a few days after Richards's return, William Clayton moved the temple committee books, including the Book of the Law of the Lord, to the new, small brick structure.[54] Clayton may have needed closer access to the temple

48. These additions may have been included at Joseph Smith's direction, following his review of the manuscript the previous day. Alternatively, William Clayton may have recorded these events in an effort to fulfill the responsibilities of his new office as temple recorder.

49. Woodruff, Journal, 1–5 November 1842.

50. Clayton, "History of the Nauvoo temple," 18.

51. Smith, Journal, 1 December 1842, in *JSP,* J2:171. In his "History of the Nauvoo Temple," Clayton explained his replacing Richards as the temple recorder: "This was done on account of E[lde]r Richards having more work than he could attend to, being engaged with the Church history and the president was anxious to have it progress as fast as possible." (Clayton, "History of the Nauvoo Temple," 30.)

52. *JSP,* J2, esp. 8 August 1842–6 January 1843.

53. Smith, Journal, 1 October 1842, in *JSP,* J2:160.

54. Clayton recorded in Joseph Smith's journal: "Spent this A.M in removing the books, desk &c from the store over to the house." A few years later, Clayton wrote in his "History of the Nauvoo Temple," "It was also agreed that the Recorders office should be moved to the committee house near the Temple for the better accommodation of the business. Accordingly

committee, and Richards may have needed more office space in Smith's counting room in the red brick store to work on the history. In any event, writing the history and keeping Smith's journal were now combined in Richards's work, while Clayton, as the temple recorder, became the keeper of the Book of the Law of the Lord.

The physical size of the Book of the Law of the Lord limited the record's usefulness as a repository for the initial inscriptions of Smith's sermons and discourses. Both its size and its role as a financial account book, which required that it be kept on hand for recording donations to the church, made it ill-suited for travel when Smith was away from Nauvoo. These limitations and the refinement in defining Richards's and Clayton's clerical responsibilities made obvious the advantages of transferring Smith's journal to smaller memorandum books.

Events in winter 1842–1843 surrounding the effort to extradite Joseph Smith to Missouri for alleged complicity in the shooting of Lilburn W. Boggs likely prompted the move of Smith's journal to a smaller set of books. In December 1842, a delegation of Smith's associates traveled to Springfield, Illinois, to seek counsel regarding Smith's bankruptcy. While there, the delegation members took the opportunity to discuss the extradition attempt and received the counsel that Smith should come to Springfield for a habeas corpus hearing. District attorney Justin Butterfield transmitted Governor Thomas Ford's assurance that Smith would be safe in Springfield and that the requisition from Missouri was "illegal and insufficient to cause your [Joseph Smith's] arrest."[55] Because both Willard Richards and William Clayton were members of the delegation, the Book of the Law of the Lord remained in Nauvoo, with no one keeping a contemporaneous account of Smith's activities. When they returned to Nauvoo, Clayton made an entry summarizing 9–20 December 1842—the last journal entry recorded in the Book of the Law of the Lord. This summary also included copied documents: Boggs's affidavit, Missouri Governor Thomas

---

the committee built a small brick office for the Recorder and on Wednesday November 2nd the Recorder moved his Records, books, papers &c to the new office and commenced business forthwith." (Smith, Journal, 2 November 1842, in *JSP*, J2:166; Clayton, "History of the Nauvoo Temple," 35.)

55. Smith, Journal, 9–20 December 1842, in *JSP*, J2:181, 183; Thomas Ford to Joseph Smith, 17 December 1842, in *JSP*, J2:179–81.

Reynolds's requisition of Smith and Orrin Porter Rockwell, and letters from Ford and Butterfield.[56]

The day after the Springfield party returned to Nauvoo, Joseph Smith appointed Willard Richards as his private secretary and historian, and Richards made the first journal entry in the first volume of a set of four small memorandum books. Having a portable journal would be advantageous when Smith traveled to Springfield for the recommended habeas corpus hearing. The experience of making the recent trip without Smith's journal and the subsequent need to record events and documents after the fact likely spurred the decision to keep the journal separate from the Book of the Law of the Lord.[57]

"President Joseph Smith's Journal"

Whereas the Book of the Law of the Lord is complicated, its successor journal, titled "President Joseph Smith's Journal," is relatively straightforward. Though this later journal also reveals the limitations inherent in a personal journal being kept by a second party, its style and content were closer to a journal's traditional function: describing the subject's actions and environment. The difference between the physical artifacts in which the earlier Smith journals and this new journal were kept is extreme and significant. Whereas the Book of the Law of the Lord is a large, cumbersome volume, the four books of "President Joseph Smith's Journal" are small leather-bound books measuring only 6½ by 4 inches, which communicates less formality and would have been significantly easier to transport.

Evidence indicates that these four memorandum books were considered multiple volumes of one journal rather than four separate journals. Smith's previous journals, kept during the 1830s, were recorded in bound books or notebooks labeled with different titles, such as "Sketch Book" or

---

56. Smith, Journal, 9–20 December 1842, in *JSP*, J2:176, 179, 181, 183.

57. Though the first entry of the new "President Joseph Smith's Journal" bears the date 21 December 1842—the day on which Smith appointed Richards his new secretary and historian—the first few entries may have been written retrospectively sometime between 21 and 27 December. Based on an analysis of ink and handwriting, the first entry that was obviously written contemporaneously is the entry for 27 December the day on which Smith and his companions departed for Springfield. The decision to have Smith submit to arrest by his associate Wilson Law and conveyed in Law's custody to Springfield, however, was made at least by 24 December because that day's entry discusses Smith's efforts to procure funds for the trip. (Smith, Journal, 21, 24, 26, and 27 January 1842, in *JSP*, J2:191, 193–95.)

"The Scriptory Book."[58] In contrast, the first and last of Willard Richards's memorandum books bear virtually identical titles, with the fourth explicitly identified as "vol 4". Similarly, the lack of titles for books 2 and 3 suggests that each was a continuation of the previous book. In fact, the first entry of book 2 commences at 4:00 p.m. on 10 March,[59] where the events of the earlier part of the same day were recorded in book 1.

Smith neither wrote nor dictated the text of the entries in the memorandum books; they were based on Willard Richards's observations. The entry for 22 September 1843, for example, noted only that Richards "saw Joseph pass in a waggon with Hiram."[60] Although the entries were secondhand, Richards, a frequent companion of Smith, was able to capture in detail the prophet's words and actions on many occasions.

Willard Richards had kept Joseph Smith's journal in the Book of the Law of the Lord in his earlier capacity as temple recorder. When he began keeping the journal on 21 December 1842, however, he did so as Smith's newly appointed secretary and historian. The change in titles may seem insignificant, but Richards was mindful of his new role: whereas he had identified himself as "recorder" and "scribe" in Smith's previous journal, he now referred to himself as "secretary." The shift of Richards's office from temple recorder and scribe to "private se[c]retary & historian,"[61] as well as the transfer of the journal out of the Book of the Law of the Lord, may have influenced what events Richards recorded in the memorandum books. Richards, as Joseph Smith's private secretary, may have placed less emphasis on at least some of the material he included in this journal—such as the protracted account of a medical malpractice suit over which Smith presided—were he still keeping Smith's journal in the book that also contained temple donation records.[62]

---

58. Source Note to Smith, Journal, 1835–1836; Source Note to Smith, Journal, March–September 1838; in *JSP*, J1:53, 225.

59. Smith, Journal, 10 March 1843, in *JSP*, J2:310.

60. Smith, Journal, 22 September 1843, in *JSP*, J3:102.

61. Smith, Journal, 21 December 1842, in *JSP*, J2:191.

62. Richards, who was also a doctor, filled more than forty manuscript pages of Smith's journal with graphic notes of the arguments and testimony in the *Dana v. Brink* case. This level of coverage probably reflects Richards's interest in the medical details more than Smith's, but the technical language about legal precedents and procedure is valuable in illustrating how Smith understood and applied the law.

Willard Richards's new title of historian was significant as well. On 1 December 1842 he acquired from William Phelps the documents being used to produce the "History of Joseph Smith" that was being serially published in the *Times and Seasons*, and by August 1843 Richards was drawing on Smith's earlier journals for that history.[63] Phelps had taken over responsibility for writing and compiling the multi-volume manuscript history some time following the death of church clerk Robert B. Thompson on 27 August 1841, and after Phelps's move to Nauvoo. Although Richards became custodian of the history materials on 1 December, Phelps continued to play a role on the project, and in late January 1843 Richards and Phelps began to resume work on the history in earnest.[64] The parallel timing of Richards's appointment to work on the history, the transfer of Smith's journal keeping from William Clayton to Richards, and the style and content of the material Richards wrote in the new volumes suggest that Richards likely expected that the contemporaneous journal entries he was keeping for Smith would eventually be used as the basis for the history.

Although Richards's new responsibility with the history project shaped the text that he recorded in "President Joseph Smith's Journal," the distinction between Smith's earlier Nauvoo journal and his commissioned history may not have been clearly defined. Indeed, the Book of the Law of the Lord shared a title with the history that Smith instructed Phelps to write in 1832, the heading of "journal" was only applied to it after numerous entries had been inscribed, and the journal's content was as corporate in nature as it was personal. In the days after Richards resumed keeping Smith's journal, William Clayton recorded in his own journal entries of 25 and 26 December 1842, that he spent the days "writing Josephs history with Dr Richards."[65] However, because no portion of Smith's manuscript history is in Clayton's hand, Clayton was probably referring to completing

63. Smith, Journal, 1 December 1842, and 20 January 1843, in *JSP*, J2:171, 246–47; see also "History of Joseph Smith," *Times and Seasons*, 15 March 1842, 3:726–28.

64. In his own journal, Phelps gave the date of 19 January 1843, for commencing work on the history. In Smith's journal entry of 20 January Richards wrote that Smith "gave some inst[r]uctions about Phelps & Richards uniting in writing the history of the chu[r]ch." (William W. Phelps, Diary and Notebook, ca. 1835–1836, 1843, 1864, Church History Library, Salt Lake City, 19 January 1843; Smith, Journal, 20 January 1843, in *JSP*, J2:246–47.)

65. William Clayton, Journal, 1842–1845, Church History Library, Salt Lake City, 25 and 26 December 1842.

the lengthy summary 9–20 December entry in Smith's journal kept in the Law of the Lord.

Further evidence that the Law of the Lord was viewed as part of Joseph Smith's history project is found in a Nauvoo-era manuscript version of Smith's 27 November 1832 letter to William Phelps.[66] This document, which reproduces only the excerpts from the letter that were later canonized as section 85 of the current Latter-day Saint edition of the Doctrine and Covenants, is titled "Extracts from the Law of the Lord page 240." The accompanying text, however, is found nowhere in the Book of the Law of the Lord. Rather, the reference is to the first volume of the manuscript for the serially published "History of Joseph Smith," implying a connection between Smith's history project and the Book of the Law of the Lord.[67]

It was proposed, at least for a time, to publish the Book of the Law of the Lord jointly with Joseph Smith's history of the church. An 1845 draft title page in Thomas Bullock's hand reads: "History of The Church of Jesus Christ of Latter Day Saints. also The Law of the Lord. and Biography of Joseph Smith, The Founder, First Apostle, and President of the Church. By Brigham Young President of the Church of Jesus Christ of Latter Day Saints."[68] While no history matching this description was ever published, efforts to pursue it went at least as far as legally filing for copyright.[69]

The Book of the Law of the Lord's ambitious and coherent purpose notwithstanding, the large volume proved an inefficient medium for journal keeping. The various texts it contained and the distinct offices held by the scribes maintaining those texts required a dissolution of the record into discrete artifacts. However, while the move of the journal portion to "President Joseph Smith's Journal" was advantageous for preparing the

66. "Extracts from the Law of the Lord," Revelations Collection.

67. Joseph Smith et al., History, 1838–1856, vols. A-1–F-1 (original), A-2–F-2 (fair copy), Church History Library, Salt Lake City, vol. A-1, 240.

68. Title Page, History of the Church, 15 August 1845, Historian's Office, Joseph Smith History Documents collection, Church History Library, Salt Lake City.

69. The copyright for the book was filed five days later on 20 August 1845 by William Pope, clerk of the federal court for the district of Illinois. It reads: "Brigham Young President of the Church of Jesus Christ of Latter Day Saints of this District hath deposited in this office the title of a Book, as follows to wit,: History of the Church of Jesus Christ of latter day saints: also the Law of the Lord and Biography of Joseph Smith, the Found[e]r First Apostle, and President of the church, By Brigham Young. President of the Church of Latter Day Saints–." (Copyright, 20 August 1845, Copyright Registry Records for Works Concerning the Mormons to 1870, Church History Library, Salt Lake City.)

prophet's history, it represented a retreat from Smith's vision for a physical history with salvific significance.

The solution to move the journal was also not without consequence with respect to the nature of Joseph Smith's journal. The smaller physical format of the volumes, for instance, was not as conducive to copying lengthy documents as were the larger pages in the Law of the Lord. Whereas copied correspondence and revelations were regular features in the previous journal, very few were recorded in "President Joseph Smith's Journal."[70] On the other hand, the convenient size of the new volumes and Willard Richards's predilection for capturing Smith's spoken words meant that this final journal contained numerous accounts of the prophet's public discourses and sermons, which were essentially absent from any of Smith's other journals.

The advantages of the smaller volumes extended beyond capturing Smith's discourses more efficiently. The ledger-size Book of the Law of the Lord likely remained in the recorder's office, and most journal entries were probably inscribed there. Textual clues—such as clean writing and relatively few edits or blank spaces—indicate that many, or even most, of the journal entries in the Book of the Law of the Lord were originally inscribed elsewhere and then copied into the volume. Four loose draft notes of source material that were later copied into the Law of the Lord are known to exist.[71] Conversely, only one draft note from which a later entry was copied into "President Joseph Smith's Journal" is known to exist, and most of the journal's entries contain textual evidence suggesting that they are not copies but

70. For example, when Clayton and Richards returned from Springfield in December 1842 bearing news regarding the efforts to extradite Smith to Missouri, Clayton copied into Smith's journal in the Book of the Law of the Lord documents obtained during the trip—Lilburn W. Boggs's affidavit, Missouri governor Thomas Reynolds's requisition, and letters by both Thomas Ford and Justin Butterfield. In a similar situation, when Smith's company was departing Springfield only a month later following his habeas corpus hearing, Clayton spent most of a day copying legal documents related to that trip. However, those documents were never recorded in "President Joseph Smith's Journal." (*JSP*, J2:176, 179–83, 235; Clayton, Journal, 6 January 1843.)

71. These draft notes, all in Richards's hand, were used with varying correlation to create journal entries in December 1841 and January, March, and December 1842. While only these four notes have been identified, there were likely many others that have not survived. (See Revelation, 22 December 1841, Revelations Collection; "Appendix 3: Willard Richards, Draft Notes of Joseph Smith's Activities," 1842, items 1–3, in *JSP*, J3:341–48.)

points of first inscription.[72] The memorandum volumes were small enough that Richards could have easily carried them with him, allowing him to record many of Smith's activities closer to the actual event—both temporally and spatially—than was possible earlier. From content to method of inscription, the final journal was markedly different from its predecessor.

Willard Richards employed various techniques in keeping the journal. For a few items, he made lightly penciled notes and returned later with a quill pen to expand the entry. In other places, the morning or afternoon portion of an entry was written in one ink and the evening portion in a different ink matching that of the following entry. These changes in writing media and in other aspects of the text indicate that many inscriptions were made on the very day of the events they described. Richards's notes of sermons and legal proceedings—an example of the latter is shown in Figure 9.5—bear evidence of both contemporaneous inscription and later revision. In some instances, Richards left blank spaces and even blank lines, apparently intending to add details later.

Willard Richards's handwriting in "President Joseph Smith's Journal" is frequently difficult to interpret and sometimes altogether illegible. Whether in settings like public meetings where Richards was frantically trying to keep up with a speaker or in the privacy of his office catching up on a day's events, Richards's penmanship in "President Joseph Smith's Journal" is uniformly less clean, precise, and formal than in his earlier inscriptions in the Book of the Law of the Lord. In this sense, it much more closely resembles that found in his own journal, suggesting that he did not intend Smith's final journal, at least in its manuscript form, for public scrutiny. His roughly scrawled writing and at times code-like notes further indicate that he viewed these small memorandum volumes as source material for Smith's history project.

Over time, Willard Richards settled somewhat into a pattern of generally recording the events of one day on one page—leaving some pages largely empty and others filled with cramped writing—with weather reported at the bottom of the page. He made an entry for almost every day during the last year and a half of Joseph Smith's life. The journal ended when Smith and his associates left Nauvoo on 22 June 1844, five days before he was killed at the jailhouse in Carthage, Illinois.

---

72. "Appendix 3: Willard Richards, Draft Notes of Joseph Smith's Activities," 1842, item 4, in *JSP*, J3:348–51.

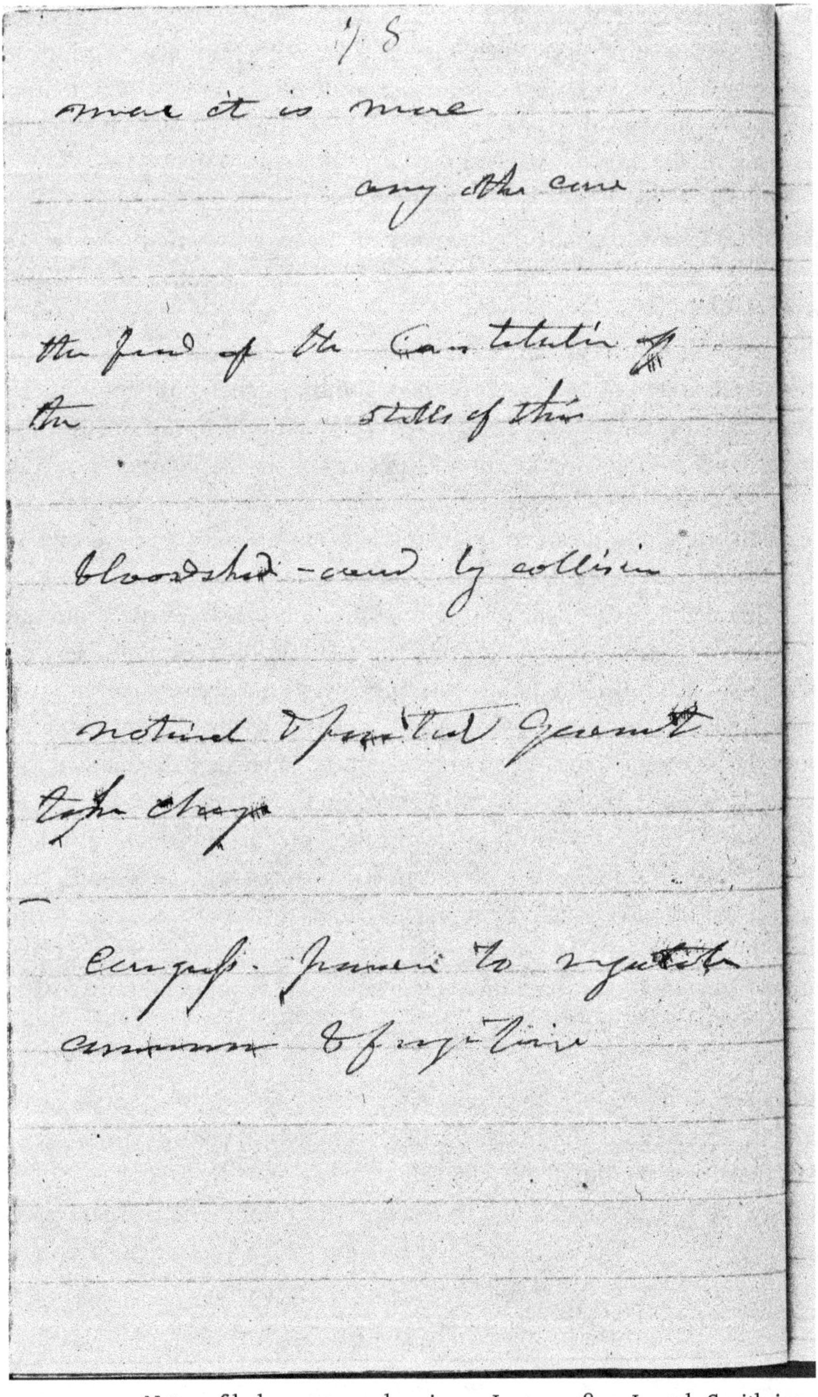

FIGURE 9.5. Notes of habeas corpus hearing, 5 January 1843. Joseph Smith journal, December 1842–June 1844, bk. 1, p. 78, Joseph Smith collection.
Church History Library, Salt Lake City. Photograph by Welden C. Andersen.

The Willard Richards Journal and the William Clayton Account of Smith's Activities

Though "President Joseph Smith's Journal" concluded on 22 June 1844, Willard Richards, evidently leaving Smith's journal in Nauvoo, accompanied Smith to Carthage and, during the final days of Smith's life, kept extensive notes of Smith's activities in Richards' own journal. Although Richards's personal journal would not intuitively be categorized as a Joseph Smith journal, the distinction between the two types of records became less tangible during these momentous days.

Richards probably considered it unnecessary to carry both his own and Smith's journal to Carthage, but the nature of the entries in his journal shifted dramatically during the days at the county seat. Prior to setting out for Carthage on 24 June, Richards's journal entries had been typically terse, never extending more than a few lines. The entries he was keeping in Smith's journal, on the other hand, had become much more detailed and lengthy beginning in late May, as tensions between the Mormons and their neighbors in the area were mounting. After leaving Smith's journal in Nauvoo, Richards extended his own journal entries for 25–27 June to many pages each—far more closely approximating the length of the entries he was keeping in Smith's journal prior to departing Nauvoo. This suggests that Richards intended to use his own journal to fill in Smith's at some later time.[73]

Although Willard Richards's lengthy journal entries during these days in June 1844 were not necessarily longer than some he had kept for Joseph Smith, the detail with which he captured events throughout each day was unparalleled in any Joseph Smith journal. Over the preceding years, it was not uncommon for Richards to designate part of an entry "A.M." or "P.M." or to sometimes note the specific time at which a meeting began or ended. During the days in Carthage, however, his notations became extremely precise and frequent. In the entry of 26 June, for instance, Richards indicated events taking place at a staggering twenty-five different times throughout the day.[74] Richards noted such things as the coming and going

73. Richards had done this same thing the previous year, when Smith took a trip to Ramus in the first week of April 1843. Richards did not accompany Smith, but later crafted entries about the trip in Smith's journal, using William Clayton's journal as source material, as Clayton had joined Smith on the trip. See "Appendix 2: William Clayton, Journal Excerpt, 1–4 April 1843," in *JSP*, J2:403–6.

74. Richards, Journal, 26 June 1844, in *JSP*, J3:314–15.

of visitors, correspondence received or sent, mealtimes, and conversations with guards.

It is unclear whether Smith instructed Richards to keep such an unusually detailed account, if Richards sensed the significance of the moment, or simply if the tedium of long days in the jail drove him to write. Whatever the cause, handwriting clues indicate that Richards made at least some of the inscriptions in pencil as events were unfolding and went back later to write over them in pen. Ink density suggests that the last thing he wrote while still in the jail was the time "4:15" in the entry of 27 June 1844. Richards may have written the remainder of that entry—which describes the mob rushing into the room and killing Hyrum Smith, with Joseph Smith, Richards, and John Taylor attempting to defend themselves—that same night at Artois Hamilton's hotel, where the wounded Taylor and the bodies of Joseph and Hyrum Smith had been conveyed. Though Richards never returned to complete that entry, the notes he kept of those days in the jail formed the basis of Smith's later history. In that sense, his journal during this period may be considered as filling the dual role of both his own and Smith's journal.

Also in June 1844, William Clayton, another close confidant of Joseph Smith and former scribe of his Nauvoo journals, began keeping a daily account of Smith's activities in a separate manuscript. Why Clayton created this account is unclear. The record does not include a title page or other written explanation identifying the purpose of its creation. Though the record contains daily entries from 14 to 22 June 1844, it is not part of Clayton's personal journal, which covers the same time period. Although Joseph Smith figures prominently in William Clayton's personal journal, he is demonstrably the principal subject of Clayton's "Daily Account." When Smith is not specifically identified, he is the implied subject, whereas references to Clayton are made by name. In contrast, in Clayton's personal journal the implied subject is Clayton, with Smith being referred to as "J." or "Prest. J."

The record ends with the entry of 22 June 1844, with blank pages left in the gathering, providing further evidence that the account was intended to capture Smith's activities. On the night of 22 June Clayton did not accompany Joseph and Hyrum Smith, Willard Richards, and Orrin Porter Rockwell when they crossed the Mississippi River into Iowa Territory, nor did he accompany the prophet and others when they departed for Carthage on 24 June. If this account was not meant to document the activities of Joseph Smith, Clayton likely would have continued recording entries in the former's absence. Clayton did not inscribe any entries after Smith's departure, further affirming that Smith is the main subject of this record.

The length of entries in the William Clayton account is roughly comparable to those recorded by Willard Richards in Joseph Smith's journal for this same period. As would be expected, many significant events—such as the arrival of visitors to Nauvoo, movements of militia units or mobs, and letters being sent to the governor—were treated in both manuscripts. The Clayton account, however, was more deliberate and comprehensive than Smith's journal in its coverage of the prophet's individual movements and personal involvement in events. Clayton frequently noted activities, such as early morning conversations, that are absent from Smith's journal. It is unknown whether this was because Clayton had more constant access to Smith or because Clayton's and Richards's journal-keeping styles differed.

The entries in William Clayton's account appear to have been made contemporaneously and depict no knowledge of events that occurred after the moment being described. For instance, Clayton employed the present tense when writing some sentences—such as "Prest. J is now in conversation," "Daniel Carns is gone on express," and "the balance will be sent in the morning"—indicating that he inscribed entries as events unfolded. If Clayton had been creating a historic reminiscence, as many Saints did in the days and weeks following the murders of Joseph and Hyrum Smith, he likely would not have concluded his narrative before recounting the broadly known and significant events in Carthage.

The account's focus on Joseph Smith may indicate that William Clayton was keeping the record at the former's instruction, though no known evidence suggests that Smith made such a request. It is unclear why Smith would have commissioned Clayton to produce this record when Smith's own journal was being regularly kept by Willard Richards with increasingly lengthy and detailed daily entries chronicling the eventful days of June 1844. One possibility is that Clayton's account was intended as a second witness of Smith's activities in case future legal documentation was needed. If Smith did not commission the record, it is unclear why Clayton would have taken it upon himself to keep such an account. Whatever its origin, the text provides an important detailed and contemporaneous account of Joseph Smith's life in the days leading up to his final trip to Carthage.

Nature and Significance of the Nauvoo Journals

The final years of Joseph Smith's life were marked by important developments in the growth of Nauvoo and in the doctrine and practices of The Church of Jesus Christ of Latter-day Saints. During this time, violence, both threatened and real, increased against Smith and other members of the church, culminating in the murders of Smith and his brother Hyrum in Carthage on 27 June 1844. This period was among the busiest and most complex of Joseph Smith's life as he functioned in the roles of president and trustee-in-trust of the church, mayor of Nauvoo, lieutenant general of the Nauvoo Legion, and candidate for the United States presidency.

Joseph Smith's Nauvoo journals differ materially from some of his earlier journals. Willard Richards's entries are often short and terse and provide only the barest outlines. William Clayton also wrote in an abbreviated style at times. However, the events, teachings, revelations, ordinances, and organizational changes documented in the journals constitute a significant contribution to foundational Mormon identity, beliefs, and practices. Perhaps most important, Joseph Smith's Nauvoo journals provide scholars and other interested readers with a much-needed window into his life, personality, and religious contributions.

Many journal entries deal with building the Nauvoo temple and the Nauvoo House. Despite support from many church members, both undertakings suffered from a lack of capital, complaints of mismanagement, and competition with private developers' projects. The economic jealousies between promoters of Nauvoo's commercial districts of the "Flats" and the "Hill," which plagued Joseph Smith's efforts to pay off land debts, also affected the building of the temple and the Nauvoo House. As a result, Smith publicly denounced other developers like Robert D. Foster, Amos Davis, and Hiram Kimball, whose business enterprises, he believed, impeded these church building projects.[75] Addressing workers' concerns, improving the methods for collecting funds, and keeping church members on task with these construction projects occupied much of the Mormon leader's time and energy.

At the same time, concerns for the temporal well-being of his family and members of the community vied for Smith's attention. By the end of 1842, Joseph and Emma Smith had four children to support, as well as others who lived in their home as household help or as wards. One means

75. See Smith, Journal, 21 February and 13 April 1843, in *JSP*, J2:268, 271, 273–76, 353, 355–56.

of providing for the family was Smith's store on Water Street.[76] Similarly, although he turned over the management of his farm to Cornelius Lott, Smith rode the three miles from Nauvoo to visit Lott and hoe potatoes during the summer. Both the store and the farm—as well as his other business concerns—affected the economic lives of numerous Nauvoo residents. "Let me assure you," wrote Emma Smith to Illinois governor Thomas Carlin in August 1842, "that there are many whole families that are entirely dependant upon the prosecution and success of Mr Smiths temporal business for their support."[77]

Administrative concerns also occupied a large part of Joseph Smith's time. As lieutenant general of the Nauvoo Legion, he oversaw the training, staffing, and supplying of more than two thousand troops of the Illinois militia. As a city councilman and later as mayor of Nauvoo, he helped draft ordinances and resolutions, attended city council meetings, and served as a judge for both the mayor's court and Nauvoo municipal court.[78] Cases involving slander, assault, petty thievery, and disorderly conduct occupied much of the court docket and are frequently referenced in the entries of Smith's journal.

When Willard Richards began inscribing Joseph Smith's journal in December 1841, Nauvoo and the surrounding area were experiencing a population boom. By January 1843, Smith estimated that twelve thousand church members lived in the area.[79] Many lived on land the church had purchased in summer 1839 on long terms from earlier settlers in the area and East Coast land speculators. Smith planned to make the required payments for some of these properties by selling lots to those moving into the city.[80] The numerous references throughout the journals to the buying and selling of these lands reflect Smith's prominent role in developing the community.

Joseph Smith directed and oversaw important innovations in the doctrine and organization of the church. These developments included publishing a new work of Mormon scripture: writings attributed to the biblical

76. See "Store (JS's brick store), Nauvoo, Hancock County, Illinois," in *JSP*, J3:372.

77. Emma Smith to Thomas Carlin, [17] August 1842, in *JSP*, J2:113.

78. See "Nauvoo City Officers," in *JSP*, J2:510–13.

79. Smith, Journal, 5 January 1843.

80. "An Epistle of the Twelve," and "Minutes," *Times and Seasons*, 15 October 1841, 2:567–70, 576–80.

patriarch Abraham that Smith said he translated from papyri he had obtained from an antiquities dealer several years earlier in Kirtland, Ohio.[81] The account included teachings about the priesthood, the Abrahamic covenant, premortal life, astronomy, and the creation of the earth. The narrative was considered significant enough for the church to accept the record into its official canon in 1880. The same status was eventually given to two lengthy letters Smith wrote during this time that further discuss the doctrine and practice of baptism for the dead—both of which were copied into the journal.[82]

During the years covered in these journals, Joseph Smith also delivered important discourses on a variety of topics ranging from gospel basics—such as obedience and gaining knowledge—to the second coming of Christ, the nature of God, and the ultimate destiny of the earth. Some of these discourses were copied into his journal, and a few were eventually canonized.[83] Smith also shared with a few trusted associates new rituals that would later be performed in the Nauvoo temple and that added to the ceremonies that had earlier been introduced in the Kirtland temple. Building on Sarah Granger Kimball's efforts to create a women's benevolent society, Smith also assisted in organizing the Female Relief Society of Nauvoo during this period.[84] The Relief Society, as it came to be known, quickly grew to a membership of over one thousand Mormon women in the Nauvoo area.[85]

By December 1842, the end of the first year covered in the Nauvoo journals, Joseph Smith had explained the doctrine of plural marriage to his closest associates and was practicing it himself.[86] Smith believed that

81. "The Book of Abraham," *Times and Seasons,* 1 March 1842, 3:704 [Abraham 1:1].

82. Joseph Smith to "all the saints in Nauvoo," 1 September 1842, in *JSP,* J2:131–33; Joseph Smith to "the Church," 6 September 1842, in *JSP,* J2:143–50.

83. Instruction, 2 April 1843, in Clayton, Journal, 2 April 1843; Smith, Journal, 2 April 1843, in *JSP,* J2:323–26.

84. "A Book of Records Containing the Proceedings of the Female Relief Society of Nauvoo," March 1842–March 1844, Church History Library, Salt Lake City, 17 March 1842.

85. Maurine Carr Ward, "'This Institution Is a Good One': The Female Relief Society of Nauvoo, 17 March 1842 to 16 March 1844," *Mormon Historical Studies* 3 (Fall 2002): 88.

86. Among the best-documented examples of plural marriage involving Joseph Smith during this period are his marriages to Sarah Ann Whitney and Eliza R. Snow. (Revelation, 27 July 1842, in Revelations Collection; Blessing, Joseph Smith to Sarah Ann Whitney, Nauvoo, IL, 23 March 1843, Whitney Family Documents, 1843–1844, 1912, Church History Library, Salt Lake City; Sarah Ann Whitney Kimball, Affidavit, Salt Lake Co., Utah Territory, 19 June 1869,

the ancient authority of Abraham and other biblical patriarchs and prophets had been conferred upon him as part of the latter-day restoration of the keys and power of the priesthood, and that his authorization of plural marriages was justified before God.[87] With certain checks in place,[88] a man might legitimately take plural wives "to multiply & replenish the earth, . . . & for thire exaltation in the eternal worlds," while Smith considered plural marriages that were undertaken without his direct approval unauthorized and adulterous.[89] Given the sensitivity of the topic, it is not surprising that clear references to plural marriage are virtually absent in Joseph Smith's Nauvoo journals. Some entries, however, may be best understood in light of the practice, although a significant amount of ambiguity remains even after a careful examination of the context and supporting sources.

More definitive references to plural marriage are apparent in several journal entries that discuss men attempting to seduce women by telling them that Joseph Smith sanctioned extramarital affairs. In these cases, though, the connection is an indirect one and demonstrates an abuse or misrepresentation of the practice as reflected in Smith's translations and revelations rather than the practice itself. Chief among those who invoked Smith's name "to carry on their iniquitous designs"[90]—and a prominent figure throughout Smith's Nauvoo journals—was John C. Bennett. Shortly after his conversion to Mormonism, Bennett had helped obtain the charter for the city and soon became a major general in the Nauvoo Legion, a prominent Mason, the mayor of Nauvoo, and a member of the church's

---

1:36, 4:36; Eliza R. Snow, Affidavit, Salt Lake Co., Utah Territory, 7 June 1869, 1:25, Joseph F. Smith, Affidavits about Celestial Marriage, 1869–1915, Church History Library, Salt Lake City; Eliza R. Snow, *Biography and Family Record of Lorenzo Snow, One of the Twelve Apostles of the Church of Jesus Christ of Latter-day Saints* [Salt Lake City: Deseret News Company, 1884], 68; Maureen Ursenbach Beecher, *The Personal Writings of Eliza Roxcy Snow,* Writings of Frontier Women 5 [Logan: Utah State University Press, 2000], 16–17.)

87. See Revelation, 12 July 1843, in Revelations Collection [D&C 132:44, 48].

88. Although reminiscent accounts must be used with caution, later affidavits attest to the highly regulated nature of plural marriage during Joseph Smith's lifetime. The most complete accounts generally refer to a specific ceremony, performed on a specific date, by an acknowledged holder of the priesthood, in the presence of witnesses, and according to specific regulations. (See, for example, Eliza R. Snow, Affidavit, Salt Lake Co., Utah Territory, 7 June 1869, 1:25, Joseph F. Smith, Affidavits about Celestial Marriage.)

89. See Revelation, 12 July 1843, in Revelations Collection [D&C 132:41–43, 63]; and *The Book of Mormon,* 3rd ed. (Nauvoo, Illinois: Robinson and Smith, 1840), 125 [Jacob 2:27–33].

90. Smith, Journal, 10 April 1842, in *JSP,* J2:50.

First Presidency. Bennett was eventually expelled from the Masonic lodge, dishonorably discharged from the Nauvoo Legion, and excommunicated from the church on charges of immorality.[91] Faced with censure from many directions, Bennett resigned as mayor, left Nauvoo, and wrote emotionally charged, hyperbolic letters to the *Sangamo Journal* and other newspapers accusing Smith and other church leaders with a variety of crimes and improprieties.[92] Bennett also lectured for pay against Joseph Smith and Mormonism in several eastern cities and eventually published a book attacking the church and its leader.[93]

The extent to which John C. Bennett's allegations influenced the final years of Joseph Smith's life is evident in the journals, and was not limited to the subject of plural marriage. With a dramatic accusation that would shape Smith's activities for almost half a year, Bennett charged Smith with masterminding the 6 May 1842 assassination attempt on Lilburn W. Boggs.[94] Although others had started this rumor, Bennett actively perpetuated it through his letters published in the *Sangamo Journal* and the St. Louis *Bulletin*.[95] Missouri authorities could do little on the basis of these allegations until Boggs himself signed an affidavit on 20 July 1842, accusing Smith of complicity in the attempted assassination and apparently based on Bennett's claims of insider knowledge about Smith's role. After Boggs wrote his affidavit, Missouri governor Thomas Reynolds requested that Illinois governor Thomas Carlin deliver Smith to Missouri authorities.[96] For the next five months Smith was in and out of hiding, evading authorities until federal district judge Nathaniel Pope ruled in early January 1843 that he be discharged from arrest. Arguably, more pages and

91. "Notice," *Times and Seasons*, 15 June 1842, 3:830.

92. See Bennett's letters printed in the 8, 15, and 22 July, 19 August, and 2 September 1842 issues of the *Sangamo Journal*.

93. See John C. Bennett, *History of the Saints; or, An Exposé of Joe Smith and Mormonism* (Boston: Leland and Whiting, 1842).

94. "Further Mormon Developments!! 2d Letter from Gen. Bennett," *Sangamo Journal (Springfield, IL)*, 15 July 1842, [2]; "Gen. Bennett's 4th Letter," and "Disclosures—the Attempted Murder of Boggs!" *Sangamo Journal (Springfield, IL)*, 22 July 1842, [2].

95. "Assassination of Ex-Governor Boggs of Missouri," *Quincy (IL) Whig*, 21 May 1842, [3]; John C. Bennett, 13 July 1842, Letter to the editor, *Bulletin* (St. Louis), 14 July 1842, [2]. See also *JSP*, J2:79n312.

96. Lilburn W. Boggs, Affidavit, 20 July 1842, and Thomas Reynolds, Requisition, 22 July1842, Joseph Smith Extradition Records, 1839–1843, Abraham Lincoln Presidential Library, Springfield, IL.

entries in Smith's Nauvoo journals are devoted to aspects of this extradition attempt than to any other single topic.[97]

The Nauvoo journals note both the momentous and the mundane. Several of Joseph Smith's dreams find their way into the journals, as do some of his reminiscences, opinions about current events, and accounts of various excursions. Mission calls, church disciplinary decisions, and references to local politics, economic developments, and newspaper articles find a place as well. Other topics covered in these journals include Smith's petition for bankruptcy, his emerging friendship with James Arlington Bennet, and discussions in the Illinois legislature about repealing or amending Nauvoo's charter. The journals also include copies of letters, reports of speeches and blessings, and other documents.

By September 1843, Willard Richards, the sole scribe of the final eighteen months of Smith's journals, was also serving as the church historian, church recorder, Nauvoo city recorder, and clerk of the municipal court. He appears to have either participated in or witnessed most of the events he documented, though at times he wrote retrospectively or used second-hand information.[98] Occasionally, such practices resulted in factual error.[99] Until late in the journal, many entries document relatively few events for each day rather than provide a comprehensive account of Joseph Smith's activities. Most entries in Richards's own journal for this period are even shorter, suggesting that the brevity of the entries in Smith's journal resulted more from Richards's laconic journal-keeping style than from a lack of familiarity with Smith's activities. Often Smith's undertakings are more thoroughly illuminated in other people's journals than they are in his own. Only on rare occasions was Richards not personally aware of

97. See "Appendix 1: Missouri Extradition Attempt, 1842–1843, Selected Documents," in *JSP*, J2:377–402.

98. In the 16 June 1843 entry, for example, Richards wrote that James Adams sent a letter from Springfield on that date, even though Richards was likely not aware of the letter until it arrived on 18 June. Similarly, Richards was probably trying to bring the journal up to date in April 1844 when he corrected the date of Emma Smith's return from St. Louis from 24 to 25 April. (Smith, Journal, 16 June 1843 and 24 and 25 April 1844, in *JSP*, J3:37, 234.)

99. In the 30 April 1844 entry, for instance, he wrote that a complaint was made against William and Wilson Law in the Masonic lodge. Lodge records indicate, however, that charges against Wilson Law and Robert D. Foster (rather than Wilson and William Law) were preferred on 2 May. (Smith, Journal, 30 April 1844, in *JSP*, J3:240; "Record of Na[u]voo Lodge under Dispensation," 1842–1846, Church History Library, Salt Lake City, 2 May 1844.)

Smith's actions, as when he remained in Nauvoo in June 1843 while Smith and his wife Emma visited relatives in Dixon, Illinois, and Joseph Smith was arrested on an 1838 charge of committing treason against the state of Missouri.[100] Longer, more detailed entries toward the end of the journal probably resulted from Richards's own interest in the growing number and seriousness of the threats against Smith beginning in January 1844.

For all their significance in Mormon history, Joseph Smith's candidacy for the presidency, the third attempt to extradite him to Missouri, the formation of the secretive new theocratic body "Council of Fifty," and the events in Carthage figure far less prominently in his journal than more mundane activities, such as business transactions, pleasure trips, visits with American Indians, conversations with friends, and observations on the weather. The journals also show Smith's engagement with many of the larger political and cultural issues of the time, such as abolitionism, the annexation of Texas, communitarianism, and a national bank. Willard Richards kept most entries quite brief, and his record is incomplete in many ways. Yet in their terse recital of any given day's events, his entries illustrate the variety of activities in which Smith was involved as well as his significance in the church, community, and region.

Despite the fact that Joseph Smith's final journals do not contain all the information readers might desire on many important topics and issues, the scope, focus, and complexity of their content depict relationships between events that simply would not be discernable without these journals. Though radically different in form and concept, the Book of the Law of the Lord and its successor "President Joseph Smith's Journal" are indispensable for understanding the final years of Smith's life in Nauvoo.

For today's researchers, the journal entries in the Book of the Law of the Lord are frequently the most primary sources for descriptions of Joseph Smith's daily activities during 1842. Certain details of events—such as the organization of the Female Relief Society of Nauvoo, John C. Bennett's expulsion from the church, the second attempt to extradite Smith to Missouri, the creation of the Nauvoo Masonic lodge, and the building of the temple and Nauvoo House—are found only in this book. Some of the earliest extant drafts of a few of Smith's revelations are found therein. It was the church's first tithing book, and its record of financial

100. See Smith, Journal, 14–29 June 1843, in *JSP*, J3:37–41, where references to Joseph Smith are few and apparently retrospective.

donations—providing valuations of common goods and services—is a rich cultural history resource. Internal evidence regarding the creation and development of the book gives clues about Smith's changing vision of record keeping. The Book of the Law of the Lord and later tithing volumes were a physical reflection of the Prophet's conception of a "book of life." Perhaps the book's greatest significance lies in its theological implication—a record decreed by revelation to record for heaven and earth the deeds and consecrations of the Saints.

"President Joseph Smith's Journal" is the product of Smith's final conception of a journal and, with the assistance of Willard Richards, is by far his most successful effort at capturing a consistent daily account of his activities—almost entirely free of the gaps and omissions present in his 1830s journals. Most importantly, this final journal functioned as the basis for this period of Smith's history. Copied in many cases verbatim or with slight alterations, the journal—even in its most abbreviated entries—provided the framework for the multi-volume history and was employed more than any other source for these years. Consequently, this journal is the foundation of our modern depiction of Smith's final years.

The Nauvoo journals provide glimpses into the richness and vibrancy of life in Nauvoo as well as the complexity of a community under tension, a society whose finer features are often blurred in broader historical narratives and thematic studies. They are an essential primary source for anyone interested in understanding one of the most significant periods, and certainly the most significant personality, in the history of Mormonism.

10

The Early Diaries of Wilford Woodruff, 1835–1839

Laurel Thatcher Ulrich

WILFORD WOODRUFF BEGAN keeping a daily diary shortly after his calling as a Mormon missionary in 1835.[1] He was an engaged witness to many formative events in Latter-day Saint history. He documented early temple rituals in Kirtland, summarized Joseph Smith's sermons in Nauvoo, and in 1844 participated in the raucous meeting in Boston, Massachusetts, that nominated Smith for the presidency of the United States. In 1847 he was at Brigham Young's elbow when he looked over the Salt Lake Valley and pronounced it the gathering place for the exiled Saints.

Woodruff's massive chronicle is not only an essential source for the study of nineteenth-century Mormonism, it is a great American diary. In his earliest volumes, he described travel in the United States, Canada, and Great Britain on foot and by rowboat, raft, canal boat, stage coach, ox cart, omnibus, aerial tramway, sailing ship, steamship, and railroad. He visited sites as different as the Big Bone Lick in Kentucky and the British Museum in London. On his missionary journeys, he drank wine with Rappites in Pennsylvania, harvested oysters with friends on Long Island Sound, and

1. The Church History Library, Salt Lake City (hereafter abbreviated as CHL), holds Woodruff's papers. A transcription of fifteen volumes of the journals in the oldest collection, Wilford Woodruff, Journals and Papers, 1828–1898, MS 1352, has been published as *Wilford Woodruff's Journal: 1833–1898*, ed. Scott G. Kenney, 9 vols. (Midvale, Utah: Signature Books, 1983–1985). Dean C. Jessee, "The Kirtland Diary of Wilford Woodruff," *Brigham Young University Studies* 12, no. 4 (1972): 365–99, provides a scholarly edition of a brief portion of the earliest volume in this collection.

ate sprats with Mormon converts in Lancashire. In a speech given in Salt Lake City in 1857, he bragged, "I have kept a Journal of almost evry day of my life for the last 24 years. I could tell each day what I had done, what Company I was in & what was transpiring around me." Although there are some things he chose not to document, he was a remarkably consistent chronicler of his own life and times. The geographic and social range of his experiences was impressive. In Connecticut, he conversed with Cinque, the Sierra Leonean leader of the *Amistad* mutiny. In Utah, he witnessed parleys with the Ute chief Walkara.[2]

Woodruff's diaries reflect religious commitment, democratic aspiration, enlightenment curiosity, sentimentality, and an ongoing personal struggle between faith and family.[3] Scholars have understandably focused on their rich content. This essay focuses on the material qualities of the earliest volumes, which reflect a host of writing practices common to his era. While maintaining consistent daily entries, he incorporated notes on speeches, minutes of meetings, acrostics, family registers, and memorials to the dead. His neat Roman print and the layout of some of his pages reflect the "pen-printing" of rural scribes. He marked important entries with ornamented frames and borders, employed Taylor and Pitman shorthand for sensitive material, and gradually developed a set of tiny symbols keyed to particular themes or actions. Understanding the cultural as well as the religious frameworks within which he worked helps us to understand both the man and the world around him.

While a full study of Woodruff's record-keeping processes is long overdue, this chapter focuses on their development between 1835 and 1839. On 1 July 1838, he described an event as "worthy to be recorded upon the ARCHIEVES OF HEAVEN. Or to be engraven with an iron pen & laid in a rock forever upon the EARTH."[4] That statement captures a well-known concept in early Mormonism, the notion that God spoke to his children through earthly artifacts. Mormons believed that Joseph Smith was called by an angel to translate metal plates almost too heavy to lift, a record

---

2. *Wilford Woodruff's Journals,* ed. Kenney, 1:105 (Bone Lick); 1:533–36 (British Museum); 2:264–65 (Rappites); 2:29 (sprats); 2:283 (oysters); 2:115 (Cinque); 4:20, 272–74 (Walkara); 5:36–37 (journal-keeping).

3. For an elaboration of these themes, see Laurel Thatcher Ulrich, *A House Full of Females: Plural Marriage and Women's Rights in Early Mormonism, 1835–1870* (New York: Knopf, 2017), especially chapters 1, 2, 6, and 11.

4. *Wilford Woodruff's Journals,* ed. Kenney, 1:263.

taken away by the angel when the translation was complete. The same thing was true in slightly different ways for the scriptures Joseph Smith translated from fragments of papyrus displayed in the upper story of the Kirtland Temple, or for the revelations printed in the Church's *Book of Commandments*. Whether given in the voice of God or the voices of ancient prophets, all these records came to believers' attention through the hands of scribes and printers, as well as from what believers would have called "the voice of the spirit."

Wilford Woodruff was both a preacher and, for a time, business manager of the Church's printing operation. His diary reflects more than a desire to capture the words of powerful preachers or data on travel, baptisms, and healings. With his pen, he documented the unfolding Latter-day movement with his own plebian heiroglyphics. The visual elements in Woodruff's diaries reveal his own hopes and struggles as well as cultural practices common to the era in which he lived.

"The First Book of Wilford"

Wilford Woodruff was born in 1807 in Northington (later Avon), Connecticut, then part of the larger township of Farmington, an area pioneered by his English ancestors. Educated in common schools and at the Farmington Academy, he worked for a time as a miller before moving in 1832 to Oswego County, New York, where he and his older brother Azmon acquired a farm and accepted baptism into the little "Church of Christ" (later the Church of Jesus Christ of Latter-day Saints). In the spring of 1834, Wilford left Azmon with the farm and traveled to Kirtland, Ohio, where he joined "Zion's Camp," an expedition led by Joseph Smith to relieve early Mormon settlers who had been expelled from their homes in Missouri. When the expedition dissolved, he accepted a calling as a missionary. He spent the next two years preaching in Arkansas, Tennessee, and Kentucky.[5]

Woodruff's earliest diaries survive in two separate collections in the Church History Library of the Church of Jesus Christ of Latter-day Saints. The presumably "canonical" version, catalogued as MS 1352, contains fifteen volumes extending from 1835 to 1898. Toward the end of his life

5. Thomas G. Alexander, *Things in Heaven and Earth: The Life and Times of Wilford Woodruff, a Mormon Prophet* (Salt Lake City: Signature Books, 1991), 2, 5, 11–14, 21, 27–18, 33–34.

Woodruff may have had a role in assembling these volumes.[6] Individual journals for 1835 and 1836, and very rough drafts of a few entries for 1837 and 1838, survive in a second collection now catalogued as MS 5506. Taken together, the two collections suggest that the presumed first volume in the 1352 collection was copied from earlier versions in the other.[7]

The survival of these materials reminds us that diary keeping can be a multi-layered process. That Woodruff was willing to invest time in recopying his already polished little diaries for 1835 and 1836 into a new and more substantial volume suggests that he was concerned about the continuity and preservation of his work. The existence of small packets containing rough drafts for 1837 and 1838 tells us that when traveling, he sometimes composed on-the-spot entries, as seen in Figure 10.1, that he later copied into more permanent form. In almost every instance the rough drafts begin when is leaving on a journey and end as he returns, with the succeeding entry in the finished volume often including some version of "spent the day writing," evidence that he not only tried to capture the essence of events as they occurred but recorded them in finished form as soon as possible.[8] Also in MS 5506 are separate records of appointments, expenditures, subscriptions to the church newspaper, and names of church members in the little branches he visited, suggesting that his habit of keeping tally of such things began early.[9]

Both the separate volumes for 1835 and 1836 and the fatter copy that includes 1837 measure 10 by 17 centimeters (roughly four by six inches), but the earlier journals are bound on the short side to create a horizontal format (as in the separate 1838 journal in the MS 1352 collection). Since

---

6. *Wilford Woodruff's Journals,* ed. Kenney, 9:547. The entry for 9 May 1898 says "Bro Nuttal assisted me in searching for two of my missing journals, which he found & made me a list of all my jurnals & put them in good shape."

7. Compare Wilford Woodruff, Journal, 18 August–11 October 1837; Journal, 9 May–9 July 1838; Journal, 30 July–21 August 1838 and 3 October 1839–4 March 1839, box 1, fd. 5, 6, 7, Wilford Woodruff, Collection, 1830–1898, MS 5506, CHL, with entries for those same dates in volumes 1 and 2 of Woodruff, Journals and Papers, CHL.

8. See *Wilford Woodruff's Journals,* ed. Kenney, 1:156, 182, entries for 1 August and 11 October 1837; 1:244, 271, entries for 9 May and 9 July 1838; 1:274, 281, entries for 30 July and 21 August 1838. The draft for 3 October 1838–4 March 1839 looks like a deviation from this pattern, but because he and his family were traveling together and in a very unsettled condition, he actually didn't make many entries during that period until after 4 March. See *Wilford Woodruff's Journals,* ed. Kenney, 1:298.

9. See Appointment Book, 1835–1836; Membership Record Book, 1835, box 2, fd. 6, items 1 and 2, Woodruff, Collection, 1830–1898, CHL.

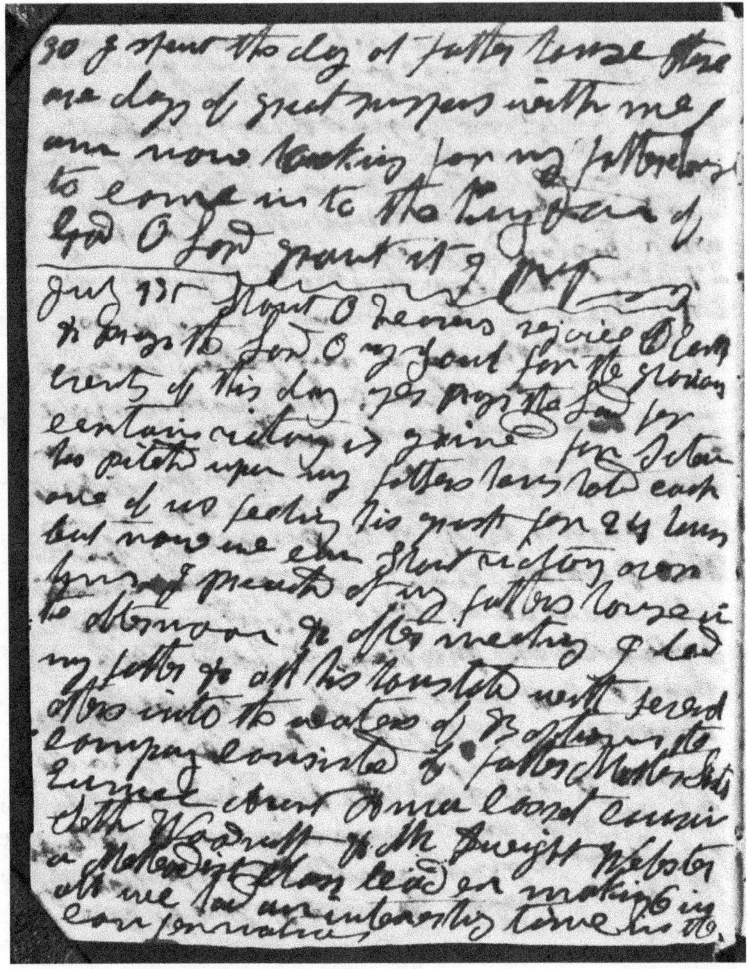

FIGURE 10.1. Rough draft journal entry, in Wilford Woodruff journal, 1 July 1838. Church History Library, Salt Lake City.

some of the material in the composite 1835–1837 journal postdates the entries it contains, it may have been rebound and perhaps even copied as late as 1842 in Nauvoo, when Woodruff was working as the business manager of the Church printing operation. Entries in his accounts for that year list several charges for book-binding.[10]

10. Wilford Woodruff, Journal, January 1841–Decemeber 1842, in Woodruff, Journals and Papers, CHL.

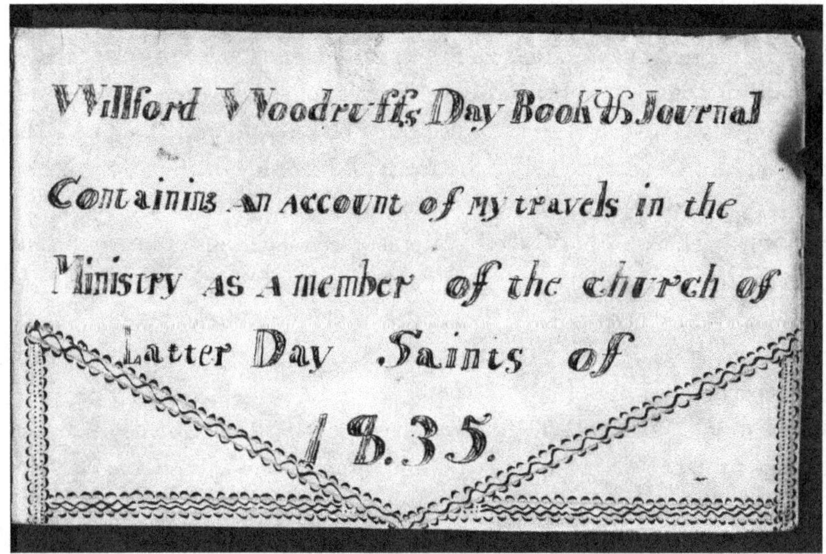

Willford Woodruffs Day Book & Journal
Containing an account of my travels in the
Ministry as a member of the church of
Latter Day Saints of
1835.

FIGURE 10.2. Title page of Wilford Woodruff journal, 1835.
Church History Library, Salt Lake City.

Both the original and recopied versions of the 1835 diary begin with a short autobiography, followed by Willford's announcement that, on 13 January 1835, he was about to "go forth into the world to preach the gospel of Jesus Christ." However, the titles differ. The 5506 version, written in ornamented but imperfect Roman letters, spread horizontally across the page as seen in Figure 10.2. It reads: "Willford Woodruffs Day Book & Journal Containing an Account of My travels in the Ministry as a member of the church of Latter Day Saints of 1835."[11] The composite volume, which of course contains three years entries, is simply labeled in cursive, "Wilford Woodruff's Journal Contain an Accouint of my life and travels from the time of my first connection with the Church of the Latter-day Saints." Perhaps over time, he came to see his record as an account of his life as well as his travels. His diary did expand in those years.

Above the recopied autobiography, he wrote, "The First Book of Willford," a perhaps half-serious, half-whimsical allusion to the Book of Mormon he carried, which opened with the "First Book of Nephi." Year after year, he repeated the label. His 1836 journal became "The second

11. See examples of Roman print with designs for ornamenting capital letters in Henry Dean, *Dean's Universal Penman, or, A Complete System of Examples for Writing* (New York: Geo. F. Hopkins, 1810).

Book of Willford for 1836," and the 1837 journal became the third.[12] Perhaps he was inspired by one of Joseph Smith's revelations, which assured newly called missionaries that "whatsoever they shall speak when moved upon by the Holy Ghost shall be scripture, shall be the will of the Lord, shall be the mind of the Lord, shall be the word of the Lord, shall be the voice of the Lord, and the power of God unto salvation."[13] Wilford believed he had not only been called to preach but to record the dealings of heaven in his own corner of earth. Like other men on a journey, he included accounts of distances between towns and the names of people who offered hospitality, but he knew that he was on a holy mission, and he struggled to find a form appropriate to his task.

Although Woodruff had an above-average education for a boy destined to be a miller like his father and grandfather before him, his mastery of "running hand" or cursive was incomplete. He filled the first pages in his 1835 diary with a hastily written and not very readable scrawl, then gradually shifted to a neat and minuscule Roman print, at first using printing only to highlight important words, often the active verb at the beginning of each sentence. Perhaps this helped him find things when he went back at the end of the year to create summaries. Gradually, hand printing took over, a great boon to future readers. It was not only easier to read than cursive, it took up less space in his small diaries. Although his handwriting had none of the polish and clarity evident in the work of English converts to Mormonism, like William Clayton, who was trained as clerk, he tried hard to create records that were both accurate and readable. Although he continued to use cursive in correspondence (and in rough drafts), printing became his standard diary mode.[14]

At some point he learned a form of shorthand developed in 1786 by an Englishman named Samuel Taylor and touted for its simplicity and its adapability to the the needs of "all classes." Woodruff may have been

---

12. *Wilford Woodruff's Journals,* ed. Kenney, 1:1, 3, 4, 55, 118, 276. His numbering was not always consistent. He labeled volume 2 in Woodruff, Journals and Papers, CHL, "The First Book of Wilford, Vol. 2."

13. Revelation, 1 November 1831—A, in Matthew C. Godfrey et al, *The Joseph Smith Papers,* Documents series, vol. 2: *July 1831–January 1833* (Salt Lake City, Utah: Church Historian's Press, 2013), p. 101 (D&C 68:4).

14. This conclusion is based on a close reading of early material in Woodruff, Collection, 1830–1898, CHL, alongside related materials in the "standard" collection of his diaries. For examples of his early experiments, see Wilford Woodruff, Daybook and Journal, 13 January–31 December 1835, box 1, fd. 4, item 1, Woodruff, Collection, 1830–1898, CHL.

attracted by the claim that it could be learned in a few lessons.[15] On 3 August 1835, he spent the day at the home of a fellow Mormon "writing & Studying Stenography from Wm. L. Sloss." On 19 August he filled a full page of his 1835 diary with an account, in Taylor shorthand, of a pair of dreams he had the evening before. The only words in recognizable English are "DREAM," which appears twice, and "After," which separates the accounts of the two dreams. In the first dream Woodruff found himself on horseback carrying a dead lion with its heels hanging over the horse's side. He had apparently gotten the lion from his mother. As he traveled, he passed other men carrying dead animals on their horses. They themelves were dressed in the skins of wild beasts and looked at him in an "eager" and perhaps threatening way. Taking a piece of the lion's raw flesh into his mouth, he found the taste offensive and spit it out, but some of it stuck to the roof of his mouth and he could not get rid of the bad taste. When he arrived at a house, a woman he did not know took the lion from him and told him it was not good to eat.

When he awoke, he lay meditating on the dream for "about an hour" until he again fell asleep. In the second dream, he was back in Connecticut, walking toward his father's grist mill, but when he tried to get in, the door shut before him. Although he called out, no one answered. Then he saw his brother Philo, who had been dead many years. Philo gave him a sword and pistol, while he took an axe, and together they walked toward the mill. At that point he awoke "and behld it was still a DREAM."[16] Although his account of these dreams filled a page in his 1835 diary seen in Figure 10.3, he barely mentioned them in the larger volume. The entry for 19 August in that copy reads: "Rode to Concord. Then returned to Br Taylors 14 mi." In shorthand he added "*I dream on the night of the 19 of Aug 1835. After meditating on the first dream, I dreamed another.*"[17]

Perhaps by the time he got around to copying the original version, the dream no longer seemed important to him. In the context of the 1835 diary, it is nevertheless fascinating because it echoes in interesting ways with his immediate situation and with his faith. For the past eight months, he had been traveling from small settlement to small settlement through

15. John Henry Cooke, *Taylor's System of Stenography, or Short-Hand Writing* (London: William Crofts, 1832), iii–v.

16. Woodruff, Daybook and Journal, 19 August 1835, shorthand transcription courtesy LaJean Carruth.

17. *Wilford Woodruff's Journals*, ed. Kenney, 1:41, entry for 19 August 1835.

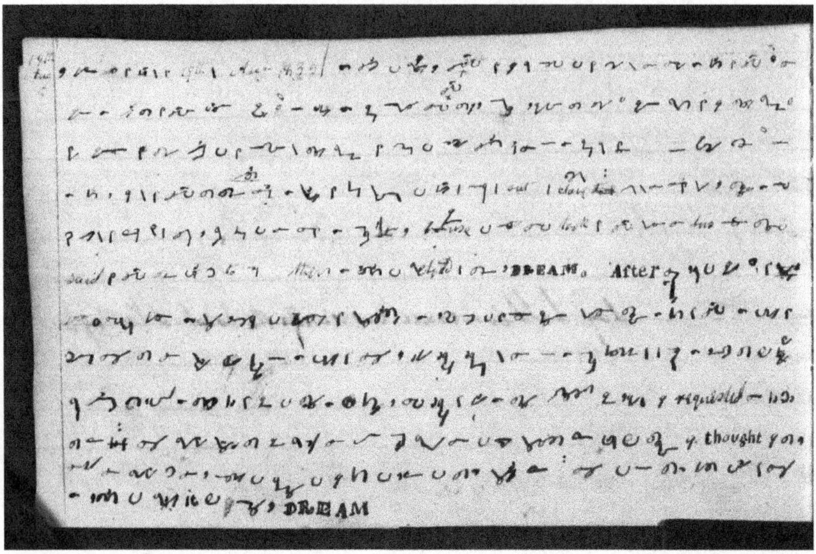

FIGURE 10.3. Dream in shorthand, in Wilford Woodruff journal, 19 August 1835. Church History Library, Salt Lake City.

what surely seemed to him a very wild country. On 17 January, he and his companion had stopped at Harmony, Missouri, a Protestant mission founded in 1821, where they were kindly received. But the next day, lost in the woods, they were only able to find their way to an Indian trading house by following "the hooting of some of the Osage tribe." Like other New Englanders venturing into the backcountry, Woodruff was both entranced and dismayed by the roughness of a country where in the dark of night there was no sound but "howling wolves." There is unintentional humor in his description of confronting "some dangerous reptiles which was two Sandapeads and three Terrantiallers. Their touch upon human flesh is considered immediate death. The Arkansaw abounds with them especially among the rocks."[18]

His dream also reverberates with early chapters in the Book of Mormon that describe an ancient prophet named Lehi wandering with his family in the wilderness, eating raw meat, and contemplating powerful dreams. Woodruff's dreams reflect his close association with his own brothers as

18. *Wilford Woodruff's Journals*, ed. Kenney, 1:18–19, 23; "Harmony Mission, Rich Hill, Missouri," *Journal of Presbyterian History* 60, no. 1 (1982): 80; Charles A. Anderson, "Journey to Indian Territory, 1833–1835: Letters of Cassandra Sawyer Lockwood," *Journal of the Presbyterian Historical Society* 23, no. 4 (1945): 214, 219.

well as his recent experience with the armed expedition to Missouri, which provided plenty of referents to his second dream. In his autobiography, he wrote about the men of "Zion's Camp" being "amed with dirks pistols sword & rifles for Self defence," and said that he gave his own sword to Joseph Smith.[19] More intriguing is the way the first dream begins and ends with a reference to a woman, first his own mother and then an apparent stranger.

As an unmarried man in his late twenties, Woodruff was careful not to express any untoward interest in female converts. So when writing about a young woman who fell ill after meeting one Sunday, he mixed his usual script with his newly acquired shorthand, simultaneously telling an innocuous story and another that in some settings might have raised eyebrows. (In the following transcription, the sentences in shorthand are in italics):

> Miss Elizabeth Wilson was attacked with violent sickness, *Elder Wells and myself assisted her throughout the night.* We thought she would soon depart but the Lord was merciful unto her. *Elizabeth was a lady possessing a generous heart a refined mind and adoring and expanded* thought *celebrated for her accomplishment and the knowledge and right she possesses and [uses] her qualification to the best advantage.* Elizabeth had much influence in the society of her acquaintance especially her sect.

The next day's report was mostly in shorthand:

> *I spent the night with Miss Elizabeth Wilson notwithstanding her low state of health I had an [interesting] discourse with her on spiritual subjects. She acknowledges us to be servants of God and that our precepts and doctrine are supported by the word of God and that we possessed the grater light in these last days.*[20]

Although he occasionally used shorthand just for the fun of it or to save space or time, in this case it helped him avoid any awkwardness he may have felt about giving so much attention to the accomplished Miss Wilson. That he "spent the night" with her does not suggest intimacy. In this era, sitting up or "watching" with someone who was ill was a common practice.

---

19. 1 Nephi 16–17; *Wilford Woodruff's Journals*, ed. Kenney, 1:9.

20. *Wilford Woodruff's Journals*, ed. Kenney, 1:63–64, entries for 28, 29, and 30 March 1836.

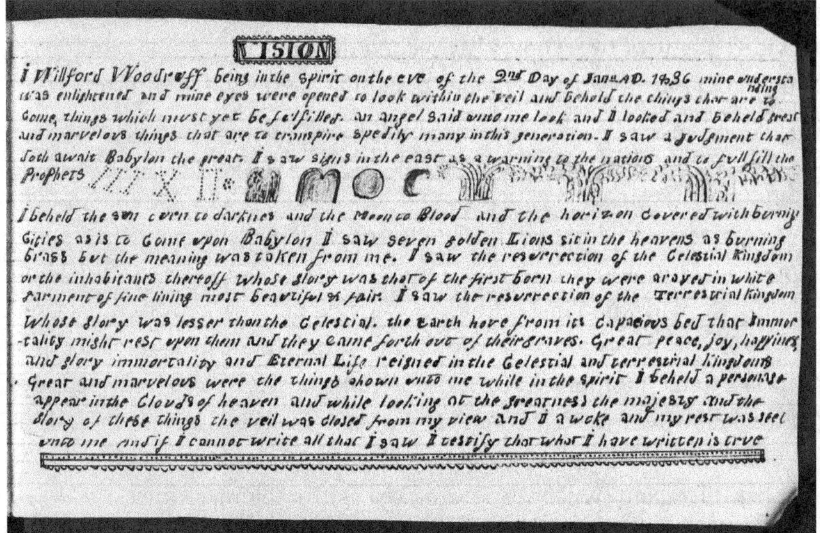

VISION

I Willford Woodruff being in the spirit on the eve of the 2nd Day of June AD. 1836 mine understa
was enlightened and mine eyes were opened to look within the veil and behold the things that are to
Come, things which must yet be fulfilled. an angel said unto me look and I looked and beheld great
and marvelous things that are to transpire spedily many in this generation. I saw a judgment that
doth await Babylon the great. I saw signs in the east as a warning to the nations and to fullfill the
Prophets III X II

I beheld the sun turn to darkness and the Moon to Blood and the horizon covered with burning
Cities as is to Come upon Babylon I saw seven golden Lions sit in the heavens as burning
brass but the meaning was taken from me. I saw the resurrection of the Celestial Kingdom
or the inhabitants thereoff whose glory was that of the first born they were arayed in white
garment of fine lining most beautiful & fair. I saw the resurrection of the Terrestrial Kingdom
Whose glory was lesser than the Celestial. the earth hove from its capacious bed that immor
-tality might rest upon them and they came forth out of their graves. Great peace, joy, happiness
and glory immortality and Eternal Life reigned in the Celestial and terrestrial kingdoms
. Great and marvelous were the things shown unto me while in the spirit I beheld a personage
appear in the Clouds of heaven and while looking at the greatness the majesty and the
glory of these things the veil was closed from my view and I awoke and my rest was swet
unto me and if I cannot write all that I saw I testify that what I have written is true

FIGURE 10.4. "Vision," at end of first Wilford Woodruff journal, undated entry. Church History Library, Salt Lake City.

Most of the 1836 journal appears pretty much verbatim in the later compilation. One exception seen in Figure 10.4 is his description of a moment of spiritual enlightment that he set off from the ordinary entries in his diary by adding an ornamented title and border to a narrative written in what must have been for him a scripture-like style. Under the word "Vision," written in capital letters, he began, "I Willford Woodruff being in the spirit on the even of the 2nd Day of June, AD. 1836, mine understanding was enlightened and mine eyes were open to look within the veil and behold the things that are to come." His description filled one full page and spilled backwards onto the empty page before it. He used two shades of ink to add a string of cryptic symbols: the Roman numerals III, X, and II drawn with small dots, followed by what look like stone tablets, then a sun, a crescent moon, and three striped rectangles with curving lines and squiggles emerging from them, probably his representation of fire and smoke rising from burning buildings. In recording such experiences, words were not enough. He reached for a symbolic language that conveyed the essence of the things he saw and felt but could not fully describe.[21]

21. Woodruff, Daybook and Journal, 1 January–31 December 1836, box 1, fd. 4, item 2, Woodruff, Collection, 1830–1898, CHL.

Wilford sought such experiences. In the spring of 1836, he received a letter "glorious in the first degree," from a friend who was in Ohio during the dedication of the Latter-day Saint temple in Kirtland. He reported that the heavens had been opened and "Angels & Jesus Christ was seen of them sitting at the right hand of the father."[22] In November of 1836, he and a companion named Abraham Smoot headed north, hoping to see such things for themselves. In Kirtland, he met and married Phebe Carter, a woman exactly his age, who had left her own parents and siblings in Maine in order to join the Saints in Ohio. In the spring of 1837, she and Wilford returned to New England and were soon serving a mission together in the Fox Islands off the coast of Maine. On 31 December 1837, he wrote "The spirit of God is like leaven in the midst of these Islands of the Sea."[23]

Woodruff's 1835–1837 diaries exemplify the combination of visionary faith and Yankee practicality familiar to students of early Mormonism. Thanks to his end-of-the-year tallies, we know that while serving in Tennessee and Kentucky in 1836, he traveled 6,557 miles, held 153 meetings, participated in four debates, baptized twenty-seven persons, blessed nineteen children, healed four persons, and escaped from the hands of three mobs; and that in 1837, he traveled in "uper Canada & in six of the United States," preached on "three Islands of the Sea," and baptized seventeen persons, including three sea captains and five of his own kin.[24]

He began the year 1838 with a new journal. In a first page filled with anticipation he prayed: "O may the God of Abram Isaac & Jacob stand by me and give me many souls as seals of my ministry during this year."[25] Before the year had passed that dream had been fulfilled more powerfully than he ever imagined.

---

22. *Wilford Woodruff's Journals*, ed. Kenney, 1:67, entries for 19 and 21 April 1836. Two days later, Wilford had an opportunity to hear the story for himself when he met with Apostle David Patten and his wife.

23. *Wilford Woodruff's Journals*, ed. Kenney, 1:193, entry for 31 December 1837.

24. *Wilford Woodruff's Journals*, ed. Kenney, 1:113, 114, entry for 31 December 1836; 1:214, entry for 31 December 1837; 1:314, entry for 31 December 1838.

25. *Wilford Woodruff's Journals*, ed. Kenney, 1:219, entry for 1 January 1838.

"Took the Parting Hand"

Woodruff's journal for 1838 survives intact in the MS 1352 collection of his papers. Rough drafts of a few important sections can also be found in the MS 5506 collection The contrast between the drafts, which were hastily written in cursive, and the neatly printed journal reinforces the importance of graphics in Woodruff's writing practice. The 1838 journal not only contains a virtuoso drawing representing the baptisms of his parents and the organization of the Farmington Branch of the church, but also introduces what became one of the most characteristic aspects of his work—the use of tiny drawings to accentuate or symbolize the content of individual entries. There are no such drawings in the 1835, 1836, and 1837 journals, although the individual emblems strung together in his account of his "vision" in 1836 illustrate a similar scale and quality.

The first of these symbols was a drawing of a tiny hand. Over the next five decades, he employed this emblem at least 3,800 times, mostly but not always in reference to having received or sent a letter.[26] Drawings of a fist with a pointing index finger are among the most common images in manuscript and book marginalia from the twelfth century onward, even appearing in handwritten books of recipes. At the most basic level, the "pointing hand" or *manicule,* simply says, "Look here."[27] Well before Wilford's time, it became a popular printer's device. Although sometimes used as paragraph marker, its most common function was indicated by one of its names—"pointer." In newspapers, it called attention to important notices, including lists of letters awaiting retrieval at local post offices. That the nineteenth-century postal service in the United States adopted as a symbol for "Return to the Sender" suggests its strong association with letters and with letter writing.[28]

---

26. Joshua M. Matson, "The Language of Symbols in the Wilford Woodruff Journals" (Honors Thesis, Brigham Young University, August 2013), 25, 28, 88.

27. James Wade, "Malory's Marginalia Reconsidered," *Arthuriana* 21, no. 3 (2011): 74, 75, 76; Linda Olson, "Reading Augustine's 'Confessiones' in Fourteenth-Century England: John De Grandisson's Fashioning of Text and Self," *Traditio* 52 (1997): 201–57; Wendy Wall, "Literacy and the Domestic Arts," *Huntington Library Quarterly* 73, no. 3 (2010): 407–08.

28. William Sherman, *Used Books: Marking Readers in Renaissance England* (Philadelphia: 2007), 29, 32–33, 39; Wade, "Malory's Marginalia Reconsidered," 74, 75, 76; Olson, "Reading Augustine's 'Confessiones,'" 201–57; Wall, "Literacy and the Domestic Arts," 407–8; Karen Ann Weyler, *Empowering Words: Outsiders and Authorship in Early America* (Athens: University of Georgia Press, 2013), 179–80; James W. Milgram, "Undeliverable

From antiquity on, some writers delineated the exact shape of the hand, portraying clasped fists with an index finger extended, and then adding details like fingernails, rings, and buttoned or ruffled cuffs. It is hard to imagine why someone would take so much trouble, when a cruder drawing would serve just as well as a pointer. In a strange way, these little hands functioned as markers of the writer's identity. In the early modern period, human hands were closely associated with mastery of information, showing the close relationship between reading, copying, and marking books, and associated mnemonic devices and gestural modes of communication, from mathematics to music. (Think of the hand signals still employed at some traffic stops.) It is not accidental that instructional works became known as *manuals* or *handbooks,* allusions lost in modern conceptions of reading. Historian of the book William Sherman writes,

> Unless we are wrestling with an unusually large volume or feeling our way through an unusually delicate book; unless we are reading a text in Braille or carefully transcribing passages into a notebook or laptop; and unless we are the kind of reader who follows along with our index fingers or gives them a good lick before turning the page, it is probably safe to say that we're not even conscious of our hands as we make our way through a text.

In early centuries, however, "readers picked up their books with an acute awareness of the symbolic and instrumental power of the hand."[29]

Even though Woodruff's hands were quickly drawn, with the fingers barely delineated, they clearly took more time to draw than an arrow or an asterisk, and they do point—usually to the right, sometimes to the left, and in one important case upward. It is not surprising that most of his hands had something to do with letters. Because he drew only one hand even on days when he received more than one letter, he actually had to go back and count in order to compose his year-end tallies of letters received, but at

---

Mail: Advertised Postmarks on U.S. Covers 1890–1931," *Postal History Journal* 153 (October 2012), 21–36.

29. Sherman, *Used Books,* 47–52; see also Claire Richter Sherman, *Writing on Hands: Memory and Knowledge in Early Modern Europe* (Carlisle, PA: The Trout Gallery, Dickinson College, with The Folger Shakespeare Library; Distributed by University of Washington Press, 2000); and the website of the related exhibition, http://www.handoc.com/writingonhands/about/generalinfo.html

least he knew where to look.[30] In the short run, the appearance of a hand on a page reminded him that he had accomplished an important task or reconnected with a person who mattered.

With or without a drawing, hands held a firm place in Woodruff's repertoire of symbols. His references to hands were expressive, reflecting deep connections with fellow church members, family, and friends. When leaving people he cared about, he wrote of taking "the parting hand."[31] When returning to Kirtland after his mission in the south, he wrote of his pleasure in being able "to again strike hands with president Joseph Smith Jr. & many other beloved saints of God." "Striking hands" probably described a particularly enthusiastic shake of the hand rather than a "high five," but the phrase conveyed something of the enthusiasm of the latter. Stopping for a night with his brothers in upstate New York on his way home to Connecticut, he described "taking my Brethren after the flesh by the hand." In Connecticut, he "had the happy privilege of again embracing" his only sister. They "saluted each other with a harty Shake of the hand," he wrote. Then added in shorthand, "and a kiss."[32]

Wilford Woodruff's reconnection with his sister Eunice awakened his nostalgia for a world long gone. When he had left Connecticut to become a farmer in New York, she was only twelve. Now she was a young lady of seventeen and a schoolteacher. Sitting in her schoolroom, he was struck with how much she looked like Philo, their brother who had died in his teens. Going with her to visit a house their parents had recently left, he grew morose. "All silent as death," he wrote. "I drop'd a tear. Eunice plucked a rose as we left."[33] Families had always lost loved ones to death, but in this period young people were also leaving ancestral homes in New England for cities, factories, or new farms in the West. The Mormon concept of gathering added spiritual meaning to westward migration, but it also complicated the struggle to maintain family unity. This tension was vividly portrayed in Woodruff's life. Aphek Woodruff, Wilford's father, had lost

30. Matson, "Language of Symbols," 25–28.

31. This phrase is especially common when he is traveling as an itinerant missionary or preacher, as during his first mission in Tennessee and Kentucky. *Wilford Woodruff's Journals*, ed. Kenney, 1:23, entry for 2 March 1836; 1:37, 39, entries for 16 and 23 July 1836; 1:40, entry for 4 August 1836; 1:63, 64, entries for 24 and 30 March 1837; 1: 65, entry for 4 April 1837; 1:93, 96, 98, entries for 5, 19, and 25 September 1837.

32. *Wilford Woodruff's Journals*, ed. Kenney, 1:107, entry for 25 November 1836; 1:149, entries for 4 and 22 June 1837; 1:155, entry for 30 July 1838; 1:274–75, entry for 2 August 1838.

33. *Wilford Woodruff's Journals*, ed. Kenney, 1:155–58.

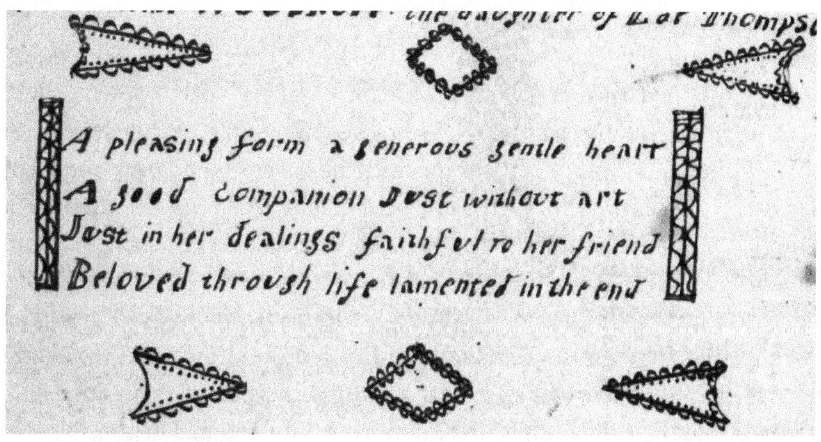

A pleasing form a generous gentle heart
A good companion Just without art
Just in her dealings faithful to her friend
Beloved through life lamented in the end

FIGURE 10.5. Border and epitaph on Beulah Thompson Woodruff's tombstone, in Wilford Woodruff journal, 6 July 1837.
Church History Library, Salt Lake City.

possession of the mill he had once owned, sliding downward from mill owner to hired operative. One consequence was the migration of all four of his living sons. Of his children, only Eunice remained in Connecticut, and she, like many other young women in this era, was living apart from her parents, teaching school.[34]

Continuing his journey, Wilford entered Avon, Connecticut, where there were droves of relatives—Woodruffs, Harts, and Thompsons—to greet him, and more scenes to remind him of time's passing. In the old burying ground, he copied the inscription on his mother's stone seen in Figure 10.5. He was only two years old when she died. She was twenty-six, four years younger than he and Phebe were now. He copied the epitaph into his diary, drawing tight borders on each side, then filling in the spaces above and below with ruffly triangles and diamonds:

> A pleasing form a generous gentle heart
> A good companion Just without art
> Just in her dealings faithful to her friend
> Beloved through life lamented in the end.[35]

---

34. Alexander, *Things in Heaven and Earth,* 11, 12.

35. *Wilford Woodruff's Journals,* ed. Kenney, 1:159–61, entry for 6 July 1837.

That Wilford had also used the phrase "generous heart" in his shorthand praise of Elizabeth Wilson meant only that he, like the author of his mother's epitaph, had mastered stock phrases.

At Farmington, he "was joyfully receieved and made heartily welcome" by his father and stepmother. He spent the next week going back and forth to nearby towns preaching in homes, schoolhouses, and occasionally a church. On 11 July, he preached at the Lovely Street School House in Avon. He and his Uncle Ozem and Aunt Hannah Woodruff and their son John stayed up late talking religion. At two a.m., the family told Wilford they were willing to embrace his faith, and he "led them fourth at the Same hour of the night and baptized them for the remission of their sins." The harvest of souls he had hoped to reap in New England had begun.[36]

Phebe, who had left Kirtland a few weeks later than her husband, arrived in Farmington in time to hear him preach at the schoolhouse on 16 July. Then the two of them "took the parting hand" with the Woodruff family and made their way to Maine, where they spent time with Phebe's family in Scarborough and then began their mission in the Fox Islands. By the spring of 1838, they and their companions had gathered a small body of converts willing to join them in migrating to Missouri, where many Latter-day Saints had now gathered. In June, while Phebe remained in Scarborough awaiting the birth of their first child, Wilford began a missionary journey through Massachusetts southward as far as New York City. On his return he stayed for a few days with his parents in Farmington. On 1 July he was at long last able to baptize his father, stepmother, and his sister Eunice into the new faith, and with Uncle Ozem and other converts organize a Farmington Branch of the church.[37]

When he returned to Scarborough on 6 July, he found Phebe still awaiting the birth of their child. He spent the next week editing and copying into his journal the rough draft he had made during his travels. When he recounted the baptisms he had performed on 1 July, he paused to create a memorial of the scene he had considered worthy to be recorded in the archives of heaven or engraved with an iron pen on a stone set in the earth. Using his pen, he gave material shape to what was for him both a profound manifestation of spiritual forces and a fulfillment of prophecy, as seen in Figures 10.6 and 10.7. On the left-hand page, inside an arched

36. *Wilford Woodruff's Journals,* ed. Kenney, 1:163, entry for 12 July 1837.

37. For more details on the Woodruff's activities in 1837–1838, see Ulrich, *House Full of Females,* Chapter 1.

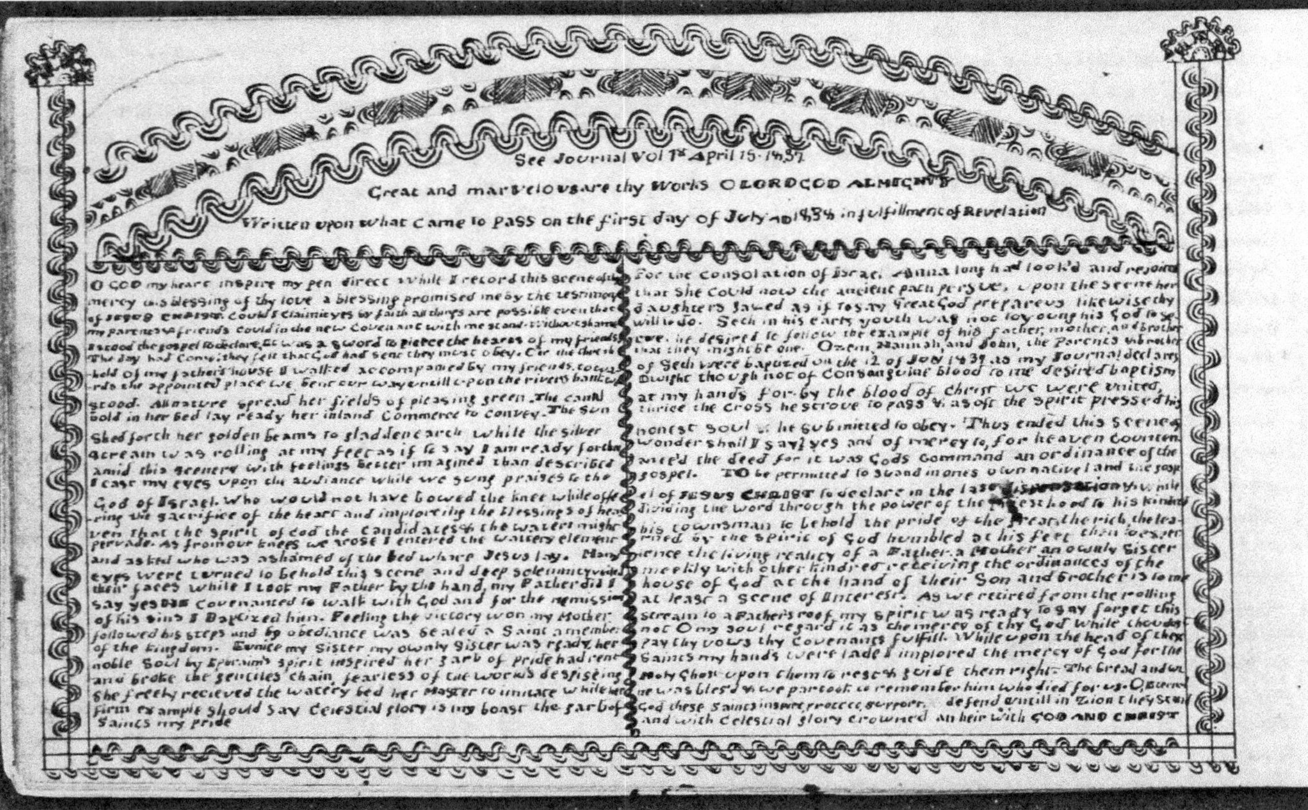

FIGURE 10.6 AND FIGURE 10.7. Inscriptions on the baptism of Azubah and Aphek Woodruff (left) and the formation of the Farmington, Connecticut Branch (right), in Wilford Woodruff journal, 1 July 1838.

Church History Library, Salt Lake City.

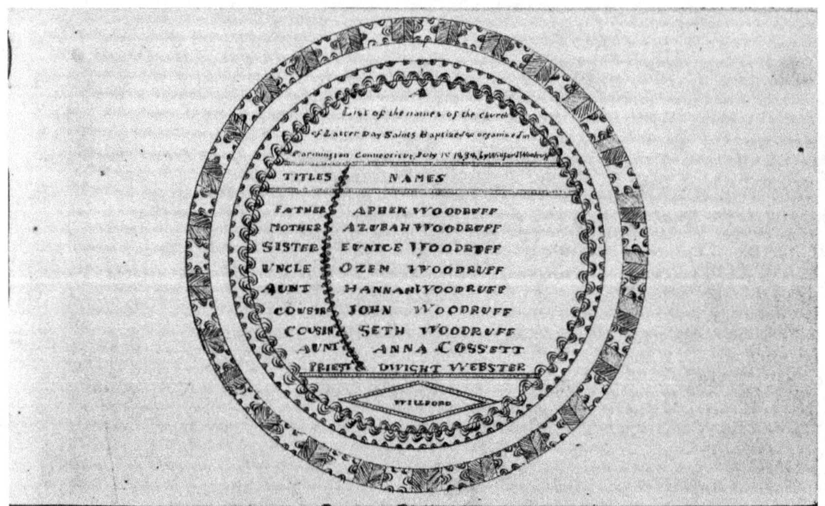

FIGURE 10.6 AND FIGURE 10.7. (Continued)

frame, he described the baptism of his parents, packing more than eight hundred words into a neatly framed space on a page less than four by six inches, in printing so small that it is almost impossible to read it without a magnifying glass. Perhaps he used one to create it. In the opening lines, he pleaded, "Oh GOD my heart inspire my pen direct While I record this scene of thy mercy." He not only relied on inspiration from God but on a straight edge and sharp pen. Looking closely, one can still see at the bottom corners the intersections of the lines that he drew. On the right-hand page he drew a circle, probably employing a compass. With the help of earthly instruments, he attempted to capture what had been for him a "scene of wonder."

Woodruff was obviously using techniques he had learned in school, perhaps during his time at an academy near his home in Farmington, Connecticut. From the eighteenth century onward, instruction in elite writing schools required "pieces" done in a combination of scripts, with geometrical patterns used as fillings for capital letters and as borders for important text.[38] Although Woodruff wouldn't have gotten very high

38. For examples of school exercises dating from 1773 to 1865, see Miscellaneous Specimens of American Penmanship, MS Typ 473.3, Houghton Library, Harvard University; for handwritten exercises added to published copybooks, see Charles W. Bazeley, *Elements of Analytical and Ornamental Penmanship* (Philadelphia: Desilver, 1830); and Eleazar Huntington, *The American Penman* (Hartford: By the author, 1825), both of which have

marks for his general penmanship, he had obviously acquired some sense of what was supposed to be done. In the two pages in which he memorialized the formation of the Farmington Branch, he outdid himself.

Woodruff built his elaborate drawing out of two simple elements—parallel lines and half circles, components introduced in basic writing and drawing lessons used in schools.[39] What look like continuous waves are actually concentric circles, broken in half and placed on opposite sides of a guiding line. Woodruff used basically the same technique for the foundation, the posts, the elliptical arch, the upper border, and the column marker, varying the concentric circles by size to create different effects. The center band in the arch alternated paired diagonals placed in opposition with still more tiny circles. Circles also crown the capstone of the posts. On the second page, he transformed the same elements into a circular frame. The miniaturization of the ornamentation, essential because of the size and shape of the page, disguises the routine nature of its elements, conveying an illusion of perfection belied under magnification.

Woodruff's allusion to a monument engraved with an iron pen is intriguing. On his way south from Scarborough, he had visited the site of the Battle of Bunker Hill in Charlestown, Massachusetts, just across the river from Boston. Perhaps the unfinished monument then in progress there triggered that idea.[40] Gravestones, like the ones in the burying

---

example of "running hand," Roman print, and repetitive filling patterns. The anonymous "Beauties of Penmanship," 1822, also at Houghton Library, has multiple filling patterns in its ornamented letters, including the various configurations of parallel lines and half circles evident in Woodruff's borders. None of these documents has compositions exactly like his. Additional examples of decorative pen-work taught in New England schools can be found in Jane Katcher, David Schorsh, and Ruth Wolfe, *Expressions of Innocence and Eloquence*, 2 vols., (Seattle: Marquand Books; New Haven: Yale University Press, 2007–2011), 1:136, 241, 249, 152, 355, 359; 2:19, 21. For "pen-printing" done by a Vermont contemporary, see Read Bain, "Educational Plans and Efforts by Methodists in Oregon to 1860," *The Quarterly of the Oregon Historical Society* 21, no. 2 (1920): 69; Robert W. G. Vail, "James Johns, Vermont Pen Printer," *The Papers of the Bibliographical Society of America* 27, no. 2 (1933): 89–132; and Paul Carnaham, "About the Cover Illustrations James Johns: Fastidious Vermont Chronicler," *Vermont History* 79, no. 2 (2011), cover and v–vii. Johns wrote and distributed a hand-lettered newspaper from 1833 to 1873 and many hand-printed poems. Some of his layouts look much like Woodruff's.

39. For example, see Rembrandt Peale, *Graphics: A Manual of Drawing and Writing for the Use of Schools and Families* (New York: J.P. Peaslee, 1835), 13–15, 22.

40. *Wilford Woodruff's Journals*, ed. Kenney, 1:247, entry for 11 May 1838. An association formed in 1823 to replace a deteriorating stone monument with a granite obelisk, had not yet succeeded in completing the monument, so Woodruff would have seen a work still in progress. The monument was dedicated in 1843. Woodruff visited it on subsequent visits to

ground where his mother was buried, were an even more familiar referent. They too were rocks engraved with iron tools, adhering to the rough shape that he gave to the first of his page—an elliptical arch supported by two posts or pillars. In Connecticut, ladder-back chairs and rural shop-signs had the same shape (and indeed the same men who turned the post for the chairs probably also made the signs). Posts and arches were also common elements in both printed and handmade family records in this period.[41]

Inside the ruffled circle he wrote the names of those he had gathered into a newly created branch of the church. The repetition of the name "Woodruff" reflects his joy in being able to administer the ordinance of baptism to "a Father, a Mother, an ownly Sister." By listing the relationship on the left and the name on the right he mimicked the pattern of family records created by village calligraphers through New England and by students in rural academies. Indeed his drawing *was* a kind of family record, recording spiritual as well as biological kinship. Wilford noted that although Dwight Webster, one of those he baptized in Farmington, was "not of consanguine blood to me," he and the others in the circles were "by the blood of Christ united." (He may or may not have suspected that his sister Eunice would eventually wed Webster.)[42]

In his ornamented pages, Woodruff used his own pen to meld Heaven and earth. At first glance, his fussy but almost mathematically regular design hardly conveys religious rapture. But the impulse was there. Under the curve of the elliptical arch, he wrote: "See Journal Vol 1st April 15, 1837 Great and marvelous are thy Works O LORD GOD ALMIGHTY Written upon what came to pass on the first day of July AD 1838 in fulfillment of Revelation." It wasn't just the fact that his relatives joined the church that gave this moment monumental significance. It was that their action fulfilled a promise that had been made at a "blessing meeting" held in the "House of the Lord" in Kirtland on 15 April 1837. On that day, Joseph Smith, Sr., the prophet's father and Patriarch of the church, promised Wilford

Boston. Bunker Hill Monument, National Park Service, Massachusetts, website at http://www.nps.gov/bost/learn/historyculture/bhm.htm

41. D. Brenton Simons and Peter Benes, eds., *The Art of Family: Genealogical Artifacts in New England* (Boston: New England Historic Genelogical Society, 2002), illustrations on pages 19, 20, 61, 63, 64, 65, 106, 107, 166, 167; Katcher et al., *Expressions of Innocence and Eloquence*, 1:69; 2:17, 112–13, 335.

42. Alexander, *Things in Heaven and Earth*, 70; *Wilford Woodruff's Journals*, ed. Kenney, 1:267.

Woordruff that if he lived by faith he might bring all of his relatives into the kingdom of God.[43]

The ornamented circle of names may also have reflected Wilford's experience at Kirtland. While there, he had visited an upper room of the temple where there was a display of mummies and fragments of papyrus that the church had purchased. One of the fragments, now known only by a drawing made at the time, was from a "Book of Breathings," an Egyptian text enclosed in a circle. From these fragments, Joseph Smith produced the Book of Abraham, an elaboration of the biblical story. The blessing Woodruff received in Kirtland had conferred upon him "the blessing of Abram Isaac and Jacob," a blessing that in Joseph Smith's words subtly altered the book of Genesis: "And I will make of thee a great nation . . .. and in thee (that is in thy Priesthood) and in thy seed (that is, thy Priesthood). . . shall all the families of the earth be blessed, even with the blessings of the Gospel, which are the blessings of salvation, even of life eternal."[44] Wilford's ornamented pages expressed a union of heavenly and earthly archives, of spiritual and biological kinship, and, beyond that, of priesthood and progeny.

"A Boon of Memory"

On 14 July 1838, at half past five in the morning, Phebe Woodruff passed through "that scene of Sickness which is common among women in every age of the world," and delivered a healthy baby girl. Her husband celebrated that occasion by filling two pages in an autograph album he had purchased for Phebe in Portland. The album had a bright red cover with an embossed gold lyre on the front and romantic engravings inside. It was a thoughtful, but perhaps also a painful, gift. In an era of high migration, people gave albums to friends who were about to move on. As she collected inscriptions, Phebe was reminded of how far she was going and how long it might be before she saw her siblings and friends in Maine.

On the title page, Wilford used a variant of the circle he had employed in his baptismal memorial to inscribe Phebe's name and the date of Sarah Emma's birth. On a separate page, he created a frame similar to the one in which he had described the baptism of his father and stepmother, adapting

---

43. *Wilford Woodruff's Journals,* ed. Kenney, 1:143.

44. Abraham 2:9, 11.

it to the size and shape of the page. Figure 10.8 shows the poem neatly printed inside described an album as a "boon of memory" and "cashier of friendship." In awkwardly poetic prose, he assured Phebe it would preserve the "speech of friends, of friends most dear," including her loving father, her fond mother, her noble brothers, and affectionate sisters. It at the same time reminded her that although "Natures laws are strong, spiritual laws are Stronger still, time breaks one, the other eternity perfects."[45]

Phebe certainly knew what that meant. She and Wilford were about to leave Scarborough to join their fellow Saints in Missouri. Anticipating that journey, Wilford wrote in his diary the day after his daughter's birth: "Our daughter Sarah Emma in half an hour after she was born performed a journey in the arms of Sister Sarah Foss through the garret, Chambers, & lower room, & principly through the whole house. Is not this an omen of her being an extensive traveler in her day?"[46] Wilford was determined to begin his journey to Missouri with Phebe, Sarah Emma, and as many of the Fox Island faithful as he could gather. But it wasn't going to be easy. Over the next few days, he helped Phebe's sister Sarah Foss with haying, then headed back to the Fox Islands to make sure that his little flock were prepared to join him in the migration. Back in Scarborough, all he could do was wait. He used his calligraphy talents to make "a family record for Brother Joseph Fabyan Carter," then an acrostic for sister Shuah; he read the journal of Lorenzo Dow, a famous New England itinerant; then he made another family record for Sarah Foss. For an example of a family record for Ezra Carter, see Figure 10.9. Later, when Sarah Emma came down with "a severe attack of the Hooping Cough," he continued to make preparations for the journey.[47]

The Woodruffs left Scarborough on 5 October 1838. During the long journey west, many of the Fox Island converts dropped out, resolving to winter over in a settled place before continuing. Wilford, Phebe, and their baby pressed on, determined to reach Terre Haute, Indiana, where Wilford's brother Asahel operated a bookstore. On 11 December 1838, they stopped at an inn in Menhaten, Indiana, not far from Terre Haute. Picking

45. Phoebe Whittemore Carter Woodruff, Autograph Book, 1838–1844, 1899, MS 90, CHL.

46. *Wilford Woodruff's Journals*, ed. Kenney, 1:271, entry for 14 July 1838.

47. *Wilford Woodruff's Journals*, ed. Kenney, 1:272, 273, 274, entries for 16–26 and 31 July; 1:274–81, 282, entries for 6–20, 27, 29 August 1838; 1:283, 284, entries for 8 and 9 September 1838).

Vera amicitia est sempiterna

ALBUM thou boon of memory
and of friendship, let thy name prove
dear henceforth, & thy garb be sacred.
As thy silent pages prove nemonical
to the reflecting mind let them teach
virtue and sincerity and oft console
the mind of <u>her</u> who is thy keeper.
Man hath promoted thee as the Casket
of friendship, yet oft hath man thy
name dishonord by crowding thy
storehouse with deceptive's ware and
should some fertile sophestry in its
variated course in thy repository
steal a place, yet let virtue wisdom
& truth prove the mainspring of thy
vaults. From thee we hear the
speach of friends, of friends most
dear, friends of our early youth
unto whom we are bound by consanguine laws. Thy pages speak of our buried
years unlock & before our minds portray
yr past scenes & teaches us to forget
not the undeviating course of a tender
father whose numerous hours were
spent to cheer our hearts & that our
minds with knowledge might be stored.
A fond mother cannot be denied a place
though distance space between us roll
she's near by ties & works, works which
none but a mother could perform. Noble
Brothers & affectionate Sister thy pen these pages have stained in memory of thy worth; the
recollection of thy deeds in our minds most occupy a conspicuous place while memory lives. We
speak of kindred warm, they are centripetal to
the heart by natures laws: Incidental friends
more numerous still, are appendages of our lives. Last of all though not least in interest a
bosom friend may speak, matrimonial law-
s should bind while others break. Natures laws are strong, spiritual laws are
stronger still, time breaks one the othe-
r eternity perfects. But what friendship's true, what love unsuled but that
which is eternal which from the love
of GOD doth FLOW. WILLFORD

FIGURE 10.8. "Vera amicitia est sempiteria," inscription 1 in Phebe Woodruff autograph book.
Church History Library, Salt Lake City.

up a local newspaper, Wilford discovered that his brother was dead. The writing in this entry for that day is as neat and precise as on any other page of his diary. Yet with a few graphic images he was able to convey the tumult of emotion that overcame him. There is no way of knowing precisely when he composed this page in his diary, but it must have been near enough

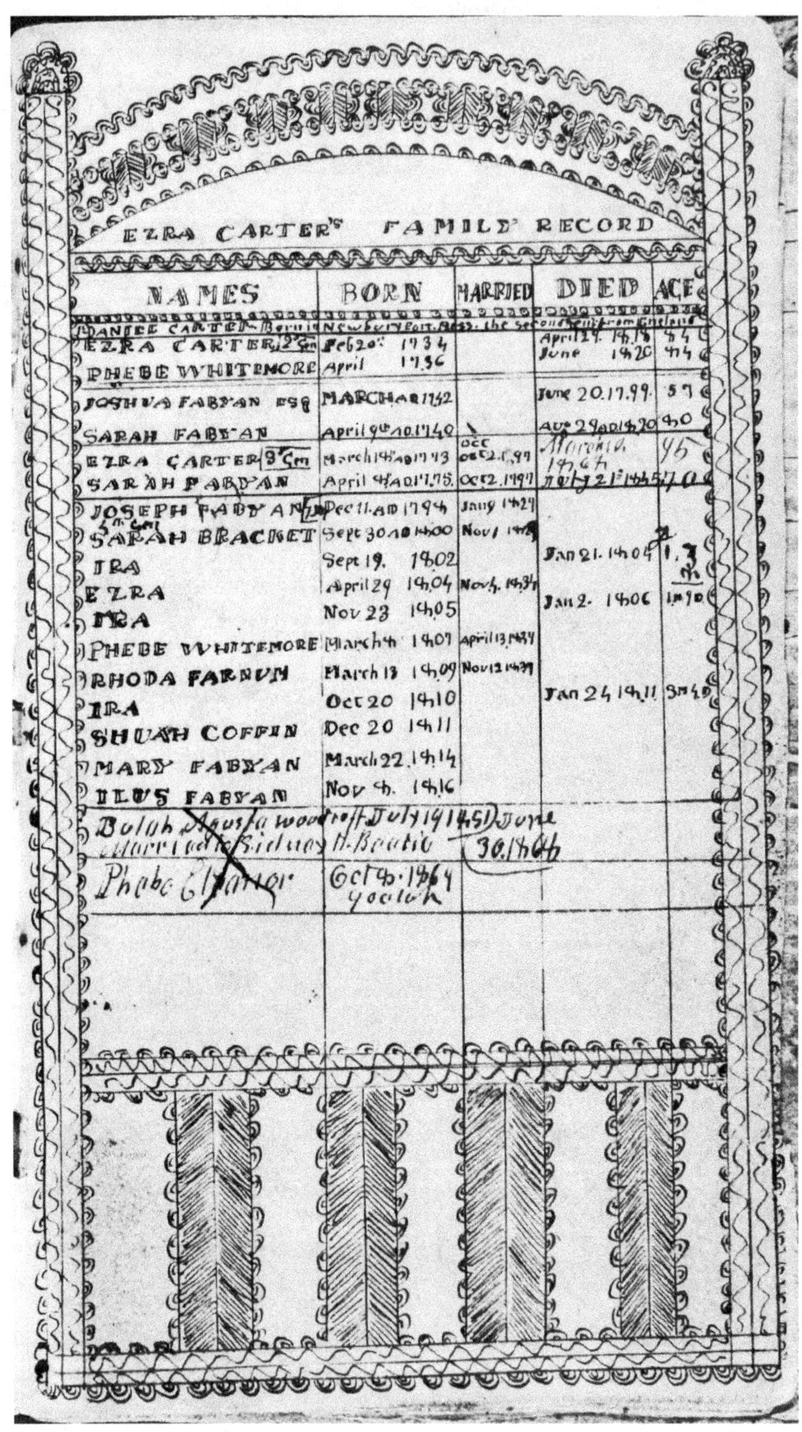

EZRA CARTER'S FAMILY RECORD

NAMES	BORN	MARRIED	DIED	AGE
Daniel Carter Born in Newburyport Mass. the second [illegible] from England				
EZRA CARTER 2d Gen	Feb 20th 1734		April 24. 1818	84
PHEBE WHITEMORE	April 1736		June 1820	84
JOSHUA FABYAN ESQ	MARCH AD 1742		June 20. 1799.	57
SARAH FABYAN	April 9th AD 1740		Aug 29 AD 1820	80
EZRA CARTER 3d Gen	March 14th AD 1773	Oct 2. 1797	March 1864	95
SARAH FABYAN	April 8th AD 1775.	Oct 2. 1797	July 21st 1845	70
JOSEPH FABYAN 4th Gen	Dec 11. AD 1798	Jan 9 1827		
SARAH BRACKET 5th Gen	Sept 30 AD 1800	Nov 1 18[illegible]		
IRA	Sept 19. 1802		Jan 21. 1804	1.3 m
EZRA	April 29 1804	Nov 4. 1834		
IRA	Nov 23 1805		Jan 2. 1806	1 m 9 d
PHEBE WHITEMORE	March 8 1807	April 13, 1834		
RHODA FARNUM	March 13 1809	Nov 12 1839		
IRA	Oct 20 1810		Jan 24 1811	3 m 4 d
SHUAH COFFIN	Dec 20 1811			
MARY FABYAN	March 22. 1814			
ILUS FABYAN	Nov 8. 1816			
Buloh Augusta Woodroff married Sidney H. Beatie	July 19 1851	June 30. 1866		
Phebe Eleanor	Oct 8. 1864 [illegible]			

FIGURE 10.9. Ezra Carter's Family Record, probably July 1838. Church History Library, Salt Lake City.

FIGURE 10.10. Description of Asahel Woodruff's death with row of upraised hands, in Wilford Woodruff journal, 11 December 1838.
Church History Library, Salt Lake City.

to the event for the feeling to be warm but long enough after the original shock for him to focus on the writing.[48]

It is a remarkably skillful composition, as seen in Figure 10.10. He began with his usual small printing, but when he came to the words, "Death of a Brother," he switched to capital letters, nearly doubling the size of the script as he continued with the words "Asahel H. Woodruff." Immediately below Asahel's name he sketched twelve upraised hands. These hands are indeed "pointers." They not only turn the reader's eyes to Asahel's name; they transform emotion into gesture. Raised hands convey both shock and surprise. They also signify prayer. Without the drawing, Wilford's words would have seemed flat. The ending might even have suggested that his primary concern was the value of Asahel's estate. It reads:

> The road was dry smooth & dusty & the weather warm. We travled to Manhaten & spent the night at an Inn whee I suddenly heard of the death of Brother Asahel H. Woodruff, who died at Terre Haute Indiana on the 18th of Oct 1838 at 3 oclock in the morning I also read in the Wabash Courier published at Terre Haute an account of the Administrators sale of the property of Brother Asahel. It was sold on the 4th of Dec for about $3,000 dollars. Mr. Robert A. Smith was his Administrator.

Although the text follows with a formulaic reflection on the transience of life, it moves on to another piece of news found in the *Wabash Courier*, "an account of the horrid butchery of eighteen latter Day Saints in Davis County Mo by the wicked mob," a story linked symbolically, though not textually, by the insertion of fourteen heavily inked exclamation points

48. *Wilford Woodruff's Journals*, ed. Kenney, 1:299, 301, 302, 304–5, entries for 3, 16, 20, 23 November 1838; 1:307–11, entries for 8–11 December 1838.

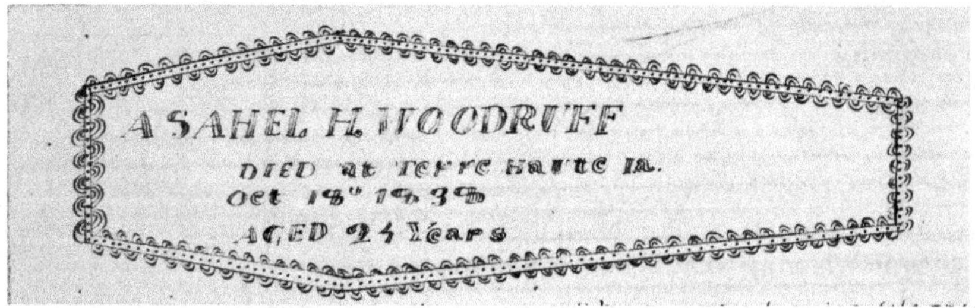

FIGURE 10.11. Ornamented outline of Asahel Woodruff's coffin, in Wilford Woodruff journal, 11 December 1838.
Church History Library, Salt Lake City.

followed by a sunburst. "O Lord hasten the day for the reign of righteousness," Wilford concluded.[49]

In Figure 10.11 on the next page, Wilford honored his brother by filling an artfully ornamented outline of a coffin with Asahel's name, age, and the date of his death. Then he penned a lamentation. "O Asahel among strangers thy lot was cast. Among them thou hast fallen & found a grave." He described the closeness he had developed with his younger brother through letters, even though they had not seen each other for seven years. Adding to his pain was his certainty that Asahel would have accepted baptism had they reached him in time. Wilford's only comfort was that he was able to meet with Asahel's business partner who gave him Asahel's journals and letters, objects Wilford considered of more value "than the gold of Opher or the rubies of Peru."[50]

Wilford and Phebe did not make it to Missouri, where the troubles reported in the *Wabash Courier* had led to the expulsion of their fellow saints. Instead the family spent the winter in Indiana, then in the spring joined the Missouri saints who had fled to Illinois. Wilford settled Phebe and Sarah Emma into a derelict fort across the Mississippi from the site of the future Mormon city of Nauvoo. Wilford now faced a new choice between faith and family. As a member of the Quorum of the Twelve apostles, he would soon be leaving to serve a mission in England. For the Woodruffs, the parting was difficult. Through physical tokens and small rituals, they resolved to remain together while apart.

---

49. *Wilford Woodruff's Journals*, ed. Kenney, 1:307, entry for 11 December 1838.

50. *Wilford Woodruff's Journals*, ed. Kenney, 1:309, entry for 12 December 1848.

As a surprise, Phebe tucked a lock of her own hair, perhaps fashioned into a wristband or ornament, into Wilford's luggage along with a poem. The poem, written in rhymed couplets, asked God to bless him with the wisdom of Solomon and the meekness of Moses. Then in a more practical vein the poem begged that he be supplied "with raiments, and with food."[51] Knowing that communication was going to be difficult, they had agreed to pray for each other every day at sunset, imagining that the sun in its revolutions would carry their messages. Leaving his unfilled diary for 1838–1839 where he knew Phebe would find it, Wilford added a greeting to the end of the last entry, "Phebe farewell Be of good cheer. . . . I leave these pages for your careful perusal while I am gone. I shall see thy face again in the flesh. I am gone to obey the command of JESUS CHRIST." Then he picked up the unfilled journal he had found in Asahel's papers and began a record of his travels. When he returned, he copied the entries he had written in Asahel's journal into the one he had left behind.[52]

What followed was a saga familiar in Latter-day Saint history. Wilford and the other apostles left their families to embark for an epic mission to England. However, it was a particularly difficult and disease-ridden time for the families left behind, who did the best they could to sustain themselves in a setting devastated by malaria. When Wilford left, Phebe was

---

51. "Phebe's Supplication," ca. August 1839, Wilford Woodruff, Collection, 1831–1905, MS 19509, CHL. In her note, Phebe referred to "the mysterious thing which was hid in the draw," likely a token made of hair. On the use of hair in the constructing of tokens exchanged between friends and lovers, see Lauren Hewes, "My Hairy Valentine," *Past Is Present: A Blog from the American Antiquarian Society*, 11 Febuary 2010, http://pastispresent.org/2010/curatorscorner/my-hairy-valentine/; and for a more general discussion of the practice, see Helen Sheumaker, *Love Entwined: The Curious History of Hairwork in America* (Philadelphia: University of Pennsylvania Press, 2007). Some people collected the hair itself into albums. At least one of these, made in Nauvoo, is in the collections of the Daughters of the Utah Pioneers, Pioneer Memorial Museum, Salt Lake City. For photographs of such albums, see Katcher et al., *Expressions of Innocence and Eloquence*, 1: endpapers, 89, 92–93, 96, 97, 99; and Jessica Helfand, *Scrapbooks: An American History* (New Haven and London: Yale University Press, 2008), x. Wilford collected locks of hair after Joseph and Hyrum's death, creating artifacts in which it was encased and sending some of it on to others.

52. Compare Wilford Woodruff, Journal, January 1838–1839, Wilford Woodruff, Collection, 1831–1905, CHL; with Wilford Woodruff, Journal, 8 August 1839–12 January 1840, Woodruff, Collection, 1830–1898. In both versions of the diary he misdated the first entry 8 October rather than 8 August. Later he or someone else corrected it. Since he surely he knew what day it was when he left, the misdating suggests that both versions may have been written somewhat later than the events they describe, perhaps in a rough draft. Except for the inscription leaving the old diary to Phebe, the content of the two versions is the same. In January 1840, he bought a new diary in England.

newly pregnant with their second child. Although Wilford, Jr. arrived in safety, his sister Sarah Emma died. During the two years Wilford was gone, they attempted to communicate through letters, but many crossed in the mail, if they arrived at all. So his diary and her letters tell related but contrasting stories.[53] When he returned in the summer of 1841, he attempted to memorialize her story inside another hand-drawn frame in her album.

When he inscribed the title page of Phebe's album in 1838, he was in buoyant spirits. He was now forced to confront the trials she had experienced in the years that had followed. In prose made awkward through his reach for eloquence, he noted the sacrifices she had made, not just for him, but "for truth and for thy God." He alluded to her willingness to leave her home and family while still single to join the saints in Kirtland, and then again, when she and Wilford packed a wagon for the ill-fated journey to Missouri. After his departure for England, her "noble soul hath been supported whilst thou hast with Zions children passed through tribulations deep." She had been alone in her "humble cot" with no one to wipe her tears or cheer her heart but her "offsprings" and God. Although they had been separated by "hills and daes, flood tides and seas," he hadn't gone to England for pleasure but to declare the word of God. He assured her that God had accepted her sacrifice and would reward her. He promised her that Sarah Emma would be restored to her embrace "clothed with immortality."[54]

Some albums in Mormon collections have inscriptions stretching over many decades. In contrast, more than half of the pages in Phebe's album are blank and almost all the inscriptions are dated 1838. Perhaps for her, the boon of memory it contained was too heavy to be overcome with later words.[55] With its empty pages, this album reminds us of both the power and the limitations of her husband's diary-keeping practice.

His end-of-the-year summaries tally miles traveled, ordinances performed, letters written, meetings conducted, and other ecclesaistical business. Although he inserted family records in the back pages of some volumes, he was not consistent in making entries about his own family relationships. In some ways, the penned monuments he created after

53. See Ulrich, *House Full of Females,* Chapter 2.

54. Phoebe Whittemore Carter Woodruff, Autograph Book, CHL.

55. For example, compare Phoebe Whittemore Carter Woodruff, Autograph Book, CHL; with Mary W. Woolley, Autograph Book, 1845–2013, MS 27006, CHL; Barbara N. Moses, Auotograph Book, ca. 1843–1919, MS 3465, CHL; and Sarah M. Kimball Autograph Book, 1850–1898, MS 131, CHL.

his parents' baptism also held paintful memories. His father remained with the church, but his stepmother and sister did not. Faith animated Woodruff's diary keeping. A passionate concern for his own family also shaped its pages, but counting baptisms was for him far easier than assessing his commitments as a son, brother, husband, and father. The triumphs and the trauma reflected in his early diaries highlight themes that have received too little attention in Mormon studies. In 1838, he created a two-page drawing that was both an ecclesiastical record and a family record, a monument to his highest hopes and his deepest disappointments.

11

A Textual and Archival Reexamination of Lucy Mack Smith's History

Sharalyn D. Howcroft

LUCY MACK SMITH (1775–1856), mother of Mormonism's founding prophet, Joseph Smith, witnessed several significant events in the unfolding of a nascent American religion. Next to her son Joseph, she was well acquainted with the people and events shaping early Mormonism. Her history depicts the religious fervor and conviction inherited by generations of Mack and Smith family ancestry. Contained within the history are events relayed nowhere else, including Joseph Smith's painful leg operation of his youth and the receptivity of the Smith family to the boy's accounts of America's early inhabitants depicted in the Book of Mormon. It begins with family genealogy and formative events in Lucy's life, then traverses the life of her prophet son. The history concludes with the assassination of her sons Joseph and Hyrum at the Hancock County jail in Carthage, Illinois.

Next to Joseph Smith's history, the Lucy Mack Smith history is one of the most widely utilized sources on the beginnings of Mormonism; thus, it is equally deserving of the type of scrutiny Joseph Smith's history has undergone. Like Joseph Smith's history, the Lucy Smith history incorporates documents with diverse authorship, requiring a deeper examination of the original manuscripts, the scribes writing the text, and the methods of production they employed.[1] This probing examination in turn will

1. Historian Dean Jessee's groundbreaking work on Joseph Smith's history identified scribal identification and compilation methodology as two essential components to supporting

enable scholars and historians to engage Lucy Mack Smith's history more critically. In the past, scholars uncritically used the official *History of the Church*, but now they draw upon its content more cautiously. Historians still quote from Lucy's history as if the words of the published history are just what Lucy said, yet the evidence concerning the production of Lucy's history is far more complicated. Historians Howard Searle and Lavina Fielding Anderson have written about the complex production of Lucy's history, but a closer look at the material and archival aspects of the manuscripts reveals an even more layered production history, one that should cause historians to begin using Lucy's history with caution much like that now applied to the "History of Joseph Smith."

This chapter reconsiders several aspects of the production of Lucy's history. It will examine the "original order"[2] of the history's rough manuscript as prescribed by its *amanuensis*, Martha Jane Knowlton Coray. New and revised identification of the handwriting in the rough manuscript and production methods utilized in the fair copy manuscript call for historians to reexamine the strategies used to compile the various versions. At times, historical sources conflict with textual evidence in the manuscripts. Even after Lucy's history was published, the provenance of the manuscript and other related documents reveal a good deal about the various stages in which the history was first created and subsequently preserved. Historian's Office methodologies for inventorying and preserving its records proffer new insights into the history's murky and seemingly contradictory custodial history.

Telling the Story

Lucy, as seen in Figure 11.1, was often asked to tell and retell the story of her family's involvement in the founding of the Latter-day Saint movement. These frequent requests for recitation of matters involving early Mormon history not recounted elsewhere "almost destroyed [Lucy's]

---

source integrity and authenticity. See Dean C. Jessee, "The Writing of Joseph Smith's History," *BYU Studies* 11, no. 4 (Summer 1971): 440.

2. Original order is "the organization and sequence of records established by the creator of the records." This shouldn't be confused with the order in which repositories receive acquired materials. Richard Pearce-Moses, "Original Order," in *A Glossary of Archival and Records Terminology* (Chicago: Society of American Archivists, 2005), 280.

FIGURE 11.1. Lucy Mack Smith, circa 1842. Portrait by Sutcliffe Maudsley. Church History Library, Salt Lake City.

lungs."[3] Presenting the story in print would allow her to refer enquirers to the published work.

Over time, Lucy would naturally develop a narrative; repeated rehearsal of events solidified their place in the narrative. New events were likely added to the narrative that she either experienced firsthand or likely borrowed from other Smith family records. Lucy's story did not represent her pure voice; rather, it was a biographical recapitulation constructed from events she and other family members experienced. Likewise, her history was shaped by memory and recitation, as well as several personal documents that were, as Lucy stated, "adapted to my purpose."[4]

Lucy Mack Smith inherited a sense of "social publication" from her New England forebears, whose practice of writing was bound closely to the practice of speaking.[5] Social publication was highly collaborative in nature and facilitated porous boundaries between the written and spoken word. Practicants of social publication could try out texts on audiences before they were widely disseminated.[6] Lucy took an active role in the common practice of social publication by publicly sharing an oral narrative of the Smith family that established a contextual framework for her written history. In February 1845, Lucy addressed a congregation at Bishop Jonathan Hale's residence in Nauvoo in which she "told her feelings and the trials and troubles she had passed through in establishing the Church of Christ and the persecutions & afflictions which her sons & husband had passed through and the cruel and unheard of martyrdom of Joseph & Hyrum which had took place so lately."[7] Committing the Smith family narrative to writing fit the construct of social authorship; that is, it drew upon pre-existing texts or oral sermons and manipulated them to create a new text.[8]

---

3. Lucy Mack Smith to William Smith, 23 January 1845, p. [4], Church History Library, The Church of Jesus Christ of Latter-day Saints, Salt Lake City (hereafter CHL).

4. Lucy Mack Smith, History, 1845, 8, CHL.

5. The eminent historian David D. Hall defined "social publication" as the early American practice of publishing a text through multiple scribal copies and reading texts aloud. See David D. Hall, *Ways of Writing: The Practice and Politics of Text-Making in Seventeenth-Century New England* (Philadelphia: University of Pennsylvania Press, 2008), 1, 23, 31.

6. Hall, *Ways of Writing*, 43.

7. Hosea Stout, Diary, February 23, 1845, in Juanita Brooks, ed., *On the Mormon Frontier: The Diary of Hosea Stout, 1844–1889*, 2 vols. (Salt Lake City: University of Utah Press, 1964), 1:22–23.

8. Ronald J. Zboray and Mary Saracino Zboray, *Everyday Ideas: Socioliterary Experience among Antebellum New Englanders* (Knoxville: University of Tennessee Press, 2006), 28, 47. Other

Other motivating factors contributed to the production of the Lucy Mack Smith history. Lucy stated she undertook the project based on instruction from the Quorum of the Twelve Apostles. Her personal incentive was to provide details about the beginning of the church that were not recorded in Joseph's history, and to obtain for her children a potential pecuniary gain if it were published.[9] Lucy contacted Martha Jane Knowlton Coray, a Nauvoo schoolteacher and well-known record keeper in her own right, to act as scribe for the history.[10] Martha's impetus was to secure information for herself and children about the Smith family, the intended result being a book of stories for children.[11]

Martha Coray, as seen in Figure 11.2, attributed her ability to transcribe Lucy's history to her early penchant for taking notes on anything she found interesting.[12] Martha's method for recording Lucy's history is described by her daughter Martha Lewis: "My dear mother went to her daily, and wrote until Mother Smith would grow weary. She then read over, several times, what she had written, making such changes and corrections as Mother Smith suggested."[13] This suggests that the history was not a simple narration from the lips of Lucy transcribed by Martha; rather, it was a complex process originating from Lucy's words. Martha read the inscribed text to Lucy several times to incorporate any recommended modifications.

---

contemporaneous Mormon records similarly incorporate other texts. Like Lucy's history, the autobiography of Newel Knight (ca. 1846–1847) contains interjections of Joseph Smith's history as published in *The Times and Seasons*. Production of the manuscript history of the church that began in 1839 relied upon a multitude of published and manuscript sources for its composition.

9. Lucy Mack Smith to William Smith, 23 January 1845, pp. [3]–[4], CHL.

10. Lavina Fielding Anderson, *Lucy's Book: A Critical Edition of Lucy Mack Smith's Family Memoir* (Salt Lake City: Signature Books, 2001), 86; Howard Coray, Autobiographical Sketch, 16, Howard Coray, Papers, ca. 1840–1941, CHL.

11. Martha Coray, Provo, Utah Territory, to Brigham Young, June 13, 1865, in Brigham Young Office Files, Brigham Young, Papers, 1832–1878, CHL. This motivation is corroborated by Corey's daughter Martha Lewis, who said her mother wanted to preserve the history of Joseph Smith to read to her children. It is plausible that Martha did not agree with Lucy's version of the origins of the history. Lucy's documentation on the history's origin is more contemporaneous to the writing of the history than Martha's, who was recounting its origins twenty years after its completion. For further information on the origins of Lucy's history, see Anderson, *Lucy's Book*, 85–88. (Anderson, *Lucy's Book*, 86, 88; Martha J. C. Lewis, "Martha Jane Knowlton Coray," *Improvement Era* 5, no. 6 [April 1902].)

12. Martha Coray, Provo, Utah Territory, to Brigham Young, 13 June 1865.

13. Lewis, "Martha Jane Knowlton Coray," 440.

The Beginnings of a Writing Enterprise

Martha had a writing compulsion from her youth. Born to Sidney and Harriet Knowlton, on 2 June 1821 in Covington, Kentucky, she evinced intellectual promise at an early age.[14] When around ten years old, Martha was put in charge of a Sunday School class whose members were considerably older than she was, and yet she was heartily praised for her ability. She was baptized a member in the Mormon church in early 1840, and met and married Howard Coray shortly thereafter.[15]

Categorized as a "rapid and lucid writer" with a broad knowledge base, Martha frequently attended meetings with pencil and paper in hand.[16] She took notes when clerks were absent, her prolific jottings encompassing discourses by notable members of church hierarchy. Apostle George A. Smith, Joseph Smith's cousin, said Martha had done more than any woman in the church to preserve the sayings of the founding prophet.[17] When items of historical importance were not available elsewhere, her notes were consulted by Church Historian Wilford Woodruff.[18] Martha thought her note-taking skill made the production of Lucy's history "an easy task."[19] Shortly after beginning Lucy's history, Martha received a blessing bestowing upon her traits essential to writing the history.[20]

---

14. "Very early in life she evinced a character in a degree somewhat rare for one of her sex—that is, of decidedly doing her own thinking, hence, before adopting any principle of religion, law or politics, whether proposed by father, husband, priest or king, she must clearly see and understand for herself the righteousness and consistency of the matter." ("Died," *Territorial Enquirer* [Provo, Utah Territory], 17 December 1881, [3].)

15. Inez S. Cooper, "Martha Jane Knowlton Coray," 2–3, in Coray Family Papers, L. Tom Perry Special Collections, Harold B. Lee Library, Brigham Young University, Provo, Utah.

16. Lewis, "Martha Jane Knowlton Coray."

17. *Territorial Enquirer* (Provo, Utah Territory), 17 December 1881, [3].

18. Lewis, "Martha Jane Knowlton Coray." Woodruff served as Assistant Church Historian from 1856 to 1881 and as Church Historian from 1881 to 1889. See Ben E. Park, "Developing a Historical Conscience: Wilford Woodruff and the Preservation of Church History," *Preserving the History of the Latter-day Saints*, ed. Richard E. Turley Jr. and Steven C. Harper (Provo, Utah: Religious Studies Center, Brigham Young University; Salt Lake City: Deseret Book, 2010), 117.

19. Martha Coray, Provo, Utah Territory, to Brigham Young, 13 June 1865.

20. The blessing ordained Martha to the power of assistant historian to Howard, noting she would be "enabled to wrt [write] in that manner which is best calculated to gain the atten[tion] of the reader that thy composition shall be filled with intelligence thy pen may be guided by inspiration that thy days may be spent in usefulness." See Lucy Mack Smith, Autobiography and Notes, 1850, p. 60, L. Tom Perry Special Collections, Harold B. Lee Library, Brigham Young University, Provo, Utah.

FIGURE 11.2 AND FIGURE 11.3. Martha Jane Coray, circa 1860s (Top); and Howard Coray with grandchildren, 1893 World's Fair in Chicago.

Martha Coray photograph by Savage & Ottinger, Coray Family Papers [MSS 1422], L. Tom Perry Special Collections, Brigham Young University, Provo, UT. Photograph cropped with black and white conversion. Howard Coray photograph by unknown photographer, Church History Library, Salt Lake City.

Howard Coray's initial introduction to record keeping and clerical work occurred shortly after his conversion to Mormonism. Born on 6 May 1817 to Silas and Mary Stephens Coray in Dansville, New York, he converted to the church in late March 1840. A month later, Howard, seen in Figure 11.3, went to Nauvoo, Illinois, to attend a church conference and meet Joseph Smith. This introduction secured him employment in Joseph Smith's office copying "a huge pile of letters into a book."[21]

Upon completion of this task, Smith requested that Howard work with Edwin D. Woolley to compile church history. Howard was reluctant to accept the offer due to his lack of experience writing books, but Smith persuaded him otherwise.[22] Howard's innate yet heretofore untapped capacity was vividly recognized in a patriarchal blessing he received in October 1840: "You shall become wise before you sleep in recording sacred histories, for you shall be called an historian. In these things you shall improve greatly insomuch that there shall be few greater."[23]

While Howard was put to work clerking for Joseph Smith, his wife's talents were soon engaged by the prophet's mother in a task that was no small undertaking. When Lucy's history commenced, Martha was a twenty-two-year-old mother of two young children—Howard, age two, and Martha, under one year. For Lucy, age sixty-nine, the vicissitudes of age were compounded by the grief of losing children. Her sons Joseph and Hyrum were recently murdered at the Hancock County jail in Carthage, Illinois, on 27 June 1844. Another son, Samuel Harrison Smith, died about a month later. Though indictments for the alleged murderers were secured in fall 1844, proceedings for the murder were postponed until May 1845.[24] Mormons received news of the delay with a jaded sense that justice would never occur. "We have not the least idea of any of the guilty will be punished by the law of Illinois," wrote George A. Smith. "God will execute

---

21. Howard Coray, Reminiscences, after 1883, 17, CHL. Howard's copyist efforts correlate with JS Letterbook 2.

22. Coray, Reminiscences, 4.

23. Hyrum Smith, Patriarchal Blessing to Howard Coray, Nauvoo, Illinois, 20 October 1840, 2–3, Coray Family Papers. The bottom panel of the leaf comprising the third and fourth pages of the original blessing is missing. The beginning of the above quoted passage, "You shall become wise before you sleep in recording sacred histories, for," is supplied from a late nineteenth-century copy of the blessing in the same folder as the original blessing.

24. Dallin H. Oaks and Marvin S. Hill, *Carthage Conspiracy: The Trial of the Accused Assassins of Joseph Smith* (Urbana: University of Illinois Press, 1975), 64.

his vengeance no doubt in due time."[25] Lucy may well have shared her nephew's sentiment.

In the midst of this sorrow and the uncertainty of justice, Martha Coray began working on Lucy's history in the winter of 1844 and 1845 as "Mother Smith's amanuensis." Martha stopped teaching school; later, Howard also stopped teaching to assist in writing the history.[26]

Approximately half of the manuscript was completed by late March 1845.[27] A month later, the Council of Fifty, a group tasked with laying the foundation of a theocratic government for Christ's millennial reign, discussed expanding the Nauvoo print shop to facilitate printing several religious works, including Lucy's history.[28] Apostle John Taylor, who was also a member of the Council of Fifty and one of the church's printers, read portions of Lucy's history at her request "to see it if was fit or ready for publication."[29] Smith filed for copyright in the State of Illinois by July, and in October announced to an assembled General Conference of Latter-day Saints that "she had written her history, and wished it printed."[30] Members of the Quorum of the Twelve expressed interest in purchasing the copyright of the history just a month after the General Conference.[31] On 14 January 1846, Howard Coray submitted a bill to the church for his services compiling and transcribing Lucy's history. Three days after submitting the bill, interim church trustees Newel K. Whitney and George Miller paid him in full.[32]

---

25. Quoted in Oaks and Hill, *Carthage Conspiracy*, 71.

26. Howard Coray, Autobiography, 26, Coray Family Papers.

27. Anderson, *Lucy's Book*, 89. Martha's notation, "here follows a long detail—see notes March 22 1845" is on page 2 of gathering 9 of the rough manuscript.

28. Council of Fifty Minutes, April 11, 1845, in Matthew J. Grow et al., *Council of Fifty, Minutes, March 1844–January 1846*, vol. 1 of the Administrative Records series of *The Joseph Smith Papers*, ed. Ronald K. Esplin et al. (Salt Lake City: Church Historian's Press, 2016), 412 (hereafter *JSP*, A1). For further information on the role of the Council of Fifty, see *JSP*, A1:xx–xxii.

29. Dean C. Jessee, "The John Taylor Nauvoo Journal," *BYU Studies* 23, no. 3 (Summer 1983): 52.

30. Copyright Records, Illinois, vol. 18 (1821–1848), July 18, 1845, cited in Searle, 372, note 29; *Times and Seasons* 6 (1 November 1845): 1014.

31. Historian's Office Journal, 10 November 1845, CHL.

32. Howard Coray, Statement of Costs, 14 January 1846, Newel K. Whitney, Papers, 1825–1906, L. Tom Perry Special Collections, Harold B. Lee Library, Brigham Young University, Provo, Utah; Daybook I, p. 194[b], Nauvoo Temple Building Committee Records, CHL.

Rough Draft Manuscripts and Their Compilation

Material evidence in the rough draft manuscript indicates Martha wrote and organized Lucy's history into eighteen books or gatherings of six to seven leaves (twelve to fourteen pages) each, except for the first gathering of nine leaves (eighteen pages).[33] The rough draft was compiled using two different sizes of paper. Pages from gatherings 1–7 measure 12 3/8 × 7 5/8 inches (31 × 19 cm) and were taken from a blank manuscript book. The paper is thicker, and each page has thirty-five blue horizontal lines. Pages from gatherings 8–18 measure 12 3/8 × 8 inches (31 × 20 cm), are comprised of thinner paper than previous gatherings, and have between thirty-three to thirty-five blue horizontal lines per page. Martha utilized the unlined space at the top of each page in gatherings 8–18 for two to three lines of text. Wear at gathering folds makes it difficult to determine if this paper originated in a bound volume.

The text is inscribed in brown, black, and blue ink, with interlineations in ink and graphite. Martha modified the history by inserting asterisks into the running text linking the reader to the fleshed-out text at the bottom of a page or at the back of a gathering. Slips of paper—loose, sewn, or attached to the pages of the gathering with adhesive wafers—were employed for larger additions of text throughout the manuscript.[34] Additionally, Martha used a manuscript version of the "digit" or "printer's fist" graphic, with text inscribed inside it to signal the addition of text on loose sheets with a corresponding fist.[35] The fists in gatherings four and six were inscribed in blue ink, suggesting they were applied to the manuscript after initial inscription.[36] The fists clearly show that the text was reworked, apparently with some editorial discretion on Martha's part.

---

33. This chapter narrative uses the terms *gathering* or *gatherings* to describe signatures in the rough manuscript; annotative references to these same gatherings are simplified to "bk."

34. Anderson incorrectly claims the loose half-sheets sewn along one side are evidence of notebooks Martha used to create the rough manuscript. The pin holes in these sheets and their spacing match pin hole spacing in the rough manuscript, indicating they are an integral part of the rough manuscript. (Anderson, *Lucy's Book*, 140.)

35. Examples of fists are in Lucy Mack Smith, History, 1844–1845, bk. 4, [9]; bk. 6, [10]; bk. 15, [2] and bk. 16, [8], CHL.

36. Smith, History, 1844–1845, bk. 4, [9]; bk. 6, [10].

Another noteworthy change is in the numbering of the manuscript. Gatherings 1–9 and 11 are numbered in the upper left corner of the first page and the upper right corner of the last page.[37] Gathering ten, though significantly damaged and incomplete, appears to be similarly numbered. Beginning with gathering 12, however, the pattern and location of numbering changes to the upper left and right corners of the first and last pages, possibly signaling that the rough manuscript is not one composition, but two different incomplete manuscripts. References to a reviser in gathering 10, which will be discussed later, may also signal the juncture between two rough manuscripts. A graphite notation in the handwriting of Martha Coray in the fourth page of gathering 13—"68 pages yet to write"—confirms that Martha copied the rough manuscript from an antecedent history draft.[38] The page count from this point to the end of the rough manuscript yields seventy pages, a discrepancy possibly attributed to pages of textual insertions interfiled in the precursor draft—another indication of extensive revisions to a draft version that predates the rough manuscript.

Handwriting identification confirms that Howard played a role in lightly editing approximately half of the rough manuscript.[39] Gatherings 1–9 were transcribed by Martha then later reviewed and corrected by Howard in blue ink. His insertions are most prolific in gathering one, pages 1–3, and appear thereafter in gathering three, pages 1–2 and gathering eight, page 9. Figure 11.4 shows some of Howard's insertions in gathering one. No textual insertions by Howard occur in gatherings 9–18, suggesting he was engaged in the history when Martha inscribed these gatherings.

Methods used for editing the rough manuscript transition in gathering ten, when Martha began writing instructions to a "reviser." This shift in composition links Howard's work on the history to no later than gathering

37. This should not be confused with pagination. Pages 2–8 in bk. 1 are numbered, after which pagination ceases in the rough manuscript.

38. Searle notes the possibility of "an earlier composition" begun by Lucy in late 1843 or early 1844 based on discrepancies in Lucy's age in the "unpolished preface" of the rough manuscript and when the Corays started working on the manuscript, not this graphite notation by Martha Coray. See Howard Searle, *Early Mormon Historiography: Writing the History of the Mormons, 1830–1858* (Los Angeles: University of California, 1979), 366–67.

39. The rough manuscript is not entirely in the handwriting of Martha Coray as previous treatment has suggested. (Searle, *Early Mormon Historiography*, 362.)

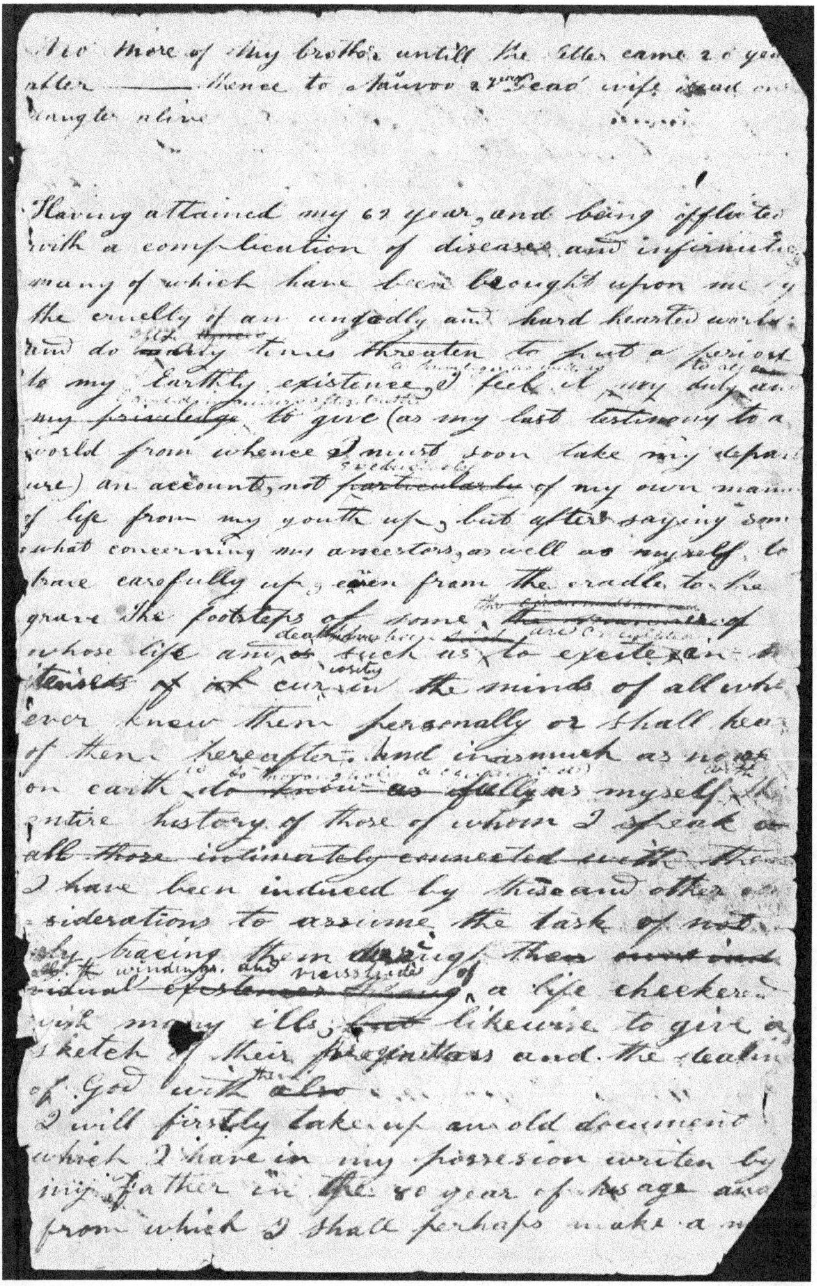

FIGURE 11.4. Lucy Mack Smith, History, 1844–1845, book 1, p. 1, with Howard Coray revisions. Church History Library, Salt Lake City.

ten.[40] The first instruction to the reviser is inscribed on page two of this gathering with an admonition to "look sharp."[41] These notes act as subtext between the scribe and the reviser—a one-way communication on how to build upon the narrative's existing textual architecture. In some instances, this subtext is reduced to simple instructions on adding text, such as a notation to "tell the whole story in full,"[42] or expansion using additional manuscript sources.[43] Other notes brief the reviser on the pacing of the narrative and infusing emotion into the text.[44] Notations continue through the rest of the rough manuscript,[45] indicating where the history should be augmented to form a usable narrative.

The rough manuscript also contains cross-referenced citations to numbered books. "Book 11th" was inscribed in the upper left corner of the first page of gathering 11 and placed where other gatherings were numbered, suggesting page eleven was likely folded back to make it an exterior page when initially inscribed. A notation on the eighth page in gathering 10 directed the reader to "see 11th book," but this cross-reference was later stricken with a line through the text.[46] A leaf titled "Histor[y] rough manuscript continued from book 18 page 8" correlates with these numbered books.[47]

---

40. A leaf that is non-contiguous with the rough manuscript contains text about "Lucy Smith's Dream" and instruction for "NB revisers." The final "s" is erased, likely indicating revision tasks were relegated to one individual.

41. This phrase originated from a story by Richard Steele published in *The Spectator* newspaper in 1711. It means "to keep watch vigilantly" or "to move or act quickly or energetically" See George A. Aitken, *Spectator* 2 (1898): 241; "To look sharp," *Oxford English Dictionary Online.*

42. Smith, History, 1844–1845, bk. 4, [9].

43. The top of bk. 15, [12] notes the inclusion of incidences from Don Carlos Smith's mission letters. The letters do not appear in the rough manuscript but were copied into the appendix of the fair copies with portions of Smith's mission journal. (Smith, History, 1845, 326–30.)

44. After describing the initial inclement living conditions at Commerce, IL, Martha wrote, "Here follows the story told by Aunt Mary if this be the correct time if not proceed as follows" (bk. 17, p. 7). A tender depiction of the death of Joseph Smith Sr. concludes with, "here the reviser will express sympathy at length." (Smith, History, 1844–1845, bk. 18, insert between [8] and [9].)

45. For notes to the reviser, see bk. 10, [2]; and bk. 18, [3] and [11]. Examples of interlineations containing similar revision language without invoking explicit instruction to the reviser are in bk. 14, [9]; bk. 15, [12]; bk. 16, [5]; and bk. 17, [7].

46. Another notebook reference on the same page is frustratingly obscured by an adhesive wafer: "see <slip> on book [wafer]."

47. Anderson takes this reference, in addition to the extant Coray notebook at Brigham Young University's L. Tom Perry Special Collections, to be evidence of precursor notebooks. (Anderson, *Lucy's Book*, 140.)

Though the rough manuscript suggests at least eighteen notebooks were used at various phases of composition, only one of the notebooks is extant.[48] Based on the content of this notebook, it appears the notebooks were exploited for multiple projects. Howard Coray initially used this notebook to write information on various historical figures of the Roman Empire, presumably as part of his teaching in Nauvoo, then transcribed excerpts from the missionary journals of John Smith, Lucy's brother-in-law, and George A. Smith, Lucy's nephew. Martha continued the journal transcription and then repurposed the notebook for writing information about the Smith family and documenting foundational content for Lucy's history. Texts copied for the history in the extant notebook were integrated into the history in successive drafting phases. Subject matter in the extant notebook correlates to text in the extremely fragmented gathering 10 of the rough manuscript. Text on pages 37–52 is inscribed in blue ink that possesses the same composition characteristics as the rough manuscript, such as references to the *Times and Seasons,* and the use of a printer's fist for inserted text.[49] This suggests that the excerpt from George A. Smith's mission journal, while not incorporated into Lucy's history, was inscribed before the extant rough manuscript, but pages 37–52 of the notebook were inscribed while the rough manuscript was in process. The text of George A. Smith's journal was apparently considered for the history but was ultimately replaced with passages from the journal of his missionary companion Don Carlos Smith, Lucy's son. Don Carlos's mission journal is not reflected in the extant rough manuscript, but was incorporated as an appendix item in the fair copies.

These notebooks did not have to be complete before the information they contained was integrated into drafts of the rough manuscript. Rather, the notebooks acted as a staging area for information copied into an undefined series of rough manuscripts, of which one complete or possibly two incomplete rough manuscripts are extant. Information from the notebooks was likely integrated at different times into versions of the rough manuscript, incrementally building the text with every subsequent draft. Although a substantial amount of text in the extant notebook correlates with the heavily damaged tenth gathering of the rough manuscript, the

48. Smith, Autobiography and Notes.

49. Smith, Autobiography and Notes, [7], [42]–[43], [46].

inscription of other disparate texts confirms the notebook's contents do not represent a contiguous phase of composition.

Several loose leaves in the Lucy Mack Smith history collection have a textual affiliation with the history and were incorporated after the extant rough manuscript but before Fair Copy 1. The clearest example of this is a series of visions of Joseph Smith Sr. Five of his seven visions were recorded in Lucy's history; four of them are represented in loose-leaf form.[50] No editorial revisions in the rough manuscript point to the integration of the visions into the history, but the vision texts are merged with the history by Fair Copy 1.[51] This indicates that Howard and Martha consolidated the visions with the rest of the history in a non-extant manuscript that followed the rough manuscript—either another rough manuscript or intermediate draft or drafts (not extant).

After its completion, most of the rough manuscript and some loose leaves were hand sewn into two groups. Nine needle holes near the gutter edge of gatherings 1–9 indicate they were hand sewn together; seven needle holes in gatherings 10–18 and the expansion notes for gatherings 1–18 indicate they were sewn together in a second group.[52] This division of gatherings coincides with the introduction of the "reviser" to the history. Additional leaves in the collection that were not part of the above-identified sewn gatherings possess a definite textual relationship with the history that is not contiguous with the narrative.[53] Pages covering events that are also recorded in gatherings 10 and 18 share a similar production method that deviates from the rest of the rough manuscript, and marked damage to these pages suggest they were at one time in physical proximity with each other. The manuscript is devoid of the type of redactions made by the

50. Visions one, three, six, and seven were recorded on loose leaves. The second vision was inscribed in Fair Copy 2 page 53 but is not extant in loose form. The visions were written one after the other, omitting visions four and five. The reason for their omission is unknown but likely intentional. Visions four and five are not represented in the rough manuscript or Fair Copy 2.

51. See the text for these visions in Fair Copy 2, pages 52, 53, 68, 70, and 72.

52. Searle suggests the possibility that rough manuscript pages were either removed from a journal before inscription or were later bound for preservation purposes (Searle, *Early Mormon Historiography*, 366). Evidence in bks. 1–9 of the rough manuscript indicates the pages were removed from a blank book, inscribed, and later rudimentarily sewn together, whereas bks. 10–18 were loose pages rudimentarily bound after inscription.

53. Leaves not sewn with the two groups of gatherings include corrections to bk. 2, p. 7; text continued from bk. 18, p. 8; and notes on Joseph Smith Sr.'s visions.

clerks in the Historian's Office who were appointed to revise Smith's history in the 1860s,[54] suggesting the rough manuscript either wasn't in the custody of the Historian's Office at the time or wasn't consulted because of its less polished state.

Previous historical analysis of the Lucy Mack Smith history has presented the rough draft as a contiguous manuscript with several miscellaneous pages of text that were affiliated with the history but not incorporated into it.[55] However, material evidence and clues about compilation methodology tentatively suggest that the extant rough manuscript was more complicated; it could be two incomplete drafts from different versions of the history later comingled and interfiled after being donated to the Historian's Office. If the transition of production methods in the rough manuscript represent Howard Coray's arrival in the writing initiative, then the rough manuscript is one seamless draft. On the other hand, if the divergent production methods signal different phases of writing the history, then the inscription of gatherings 10–18 of the rough manuscript may predate the inscription of gatherings 1–9.

In addition to the shift in production methodology between Howard and Martha Coray previously discussed, the Lucy Mack Smith collection evinces several dissimilar methods of securing information in writing before the history reached maturity. Initial gatherings have their textual origins in dictated text or non-extant records; other pieces, such as loose leaves in the collection, represent vignettes of history that Martha took from dictation or summarized from conversations with Lucy then cast aside for later use. Other loose leaves serve as memoranda of key events to be fleshed out in later drafts of text. Subtle variations in Martha's handwriting and the composition method of disparate parts of the history confirm that different segments of the Lucy Smith collection represent different phases of history production. Text from these loose leaves, like the notebooks, may have been implemented over a course of drafts that are not extant. The compilation process as explained here is shown in more detail in Figure 11.5. All of this confirms that Lucy's

54. The revision committee comprised Robert L. Campbell, George A. Smith, and Elias Smith.

55. Searle described the rough manuscript (what he refers to as "preliminary manuscript") as a contiguous manuscript of about 210 pages; Anderson, though she featured the rough draft as one manuscript, correctly concluded that the variety of damaged pages comprising rough notes, fragments, outlines, and intermediate manuscript "may actually be earlier or later material" than the rough draft. (Searle, *Early Mormon Historiography*, 363; Anderson, *Lucy's Book*, 141, 143.)

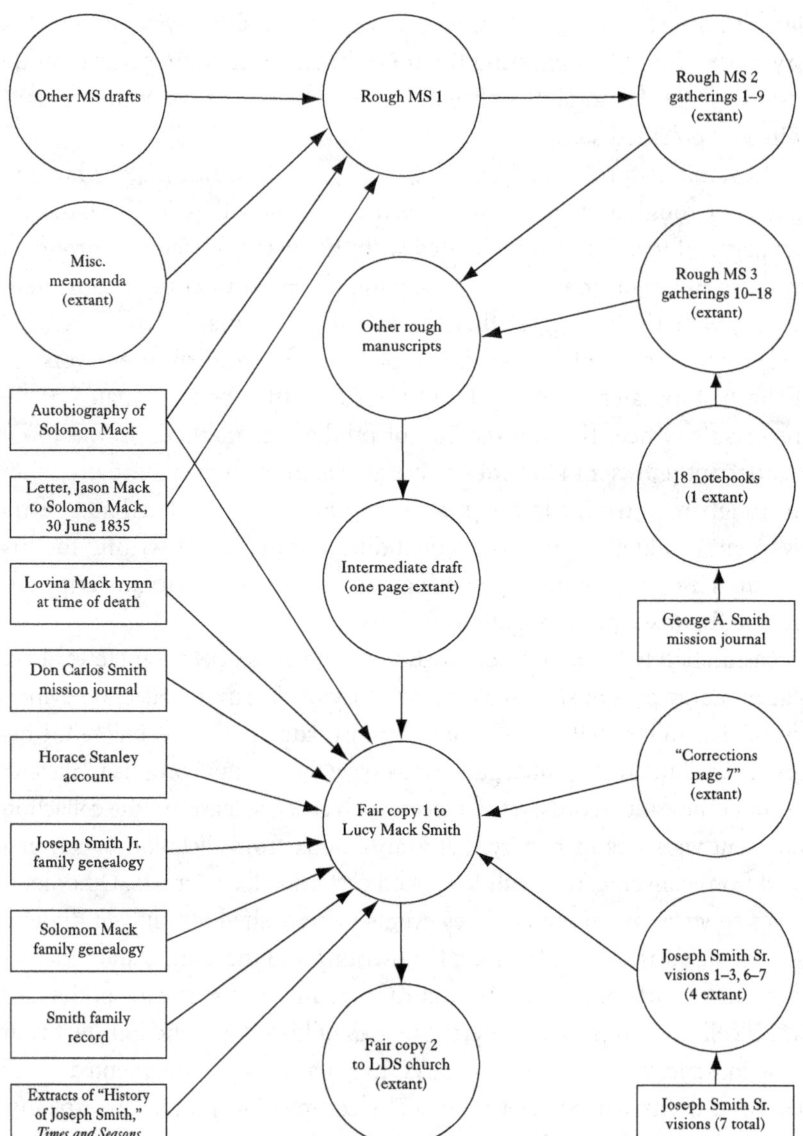

FIGURE 11.5. Sources used to compile the Lucy Mack Smith history. Texts not originating with the Corays are in rectangles; texts copied or otherwise recorded by the Corays are in circles. Arrows from non-Coray texts point to their first confirmed incorporation into the history, whereas arrows from Coray texts point to the next phase of history production. Most non-Coray texts likely merged with the history in early non-extant rough manuscripts and Fair Copy one. Texts from memoranda and notebooks were likely integrated into the history in successive drafting phases. Design by Matthew C. Howcroft.

history is the result of complex and somewhat unknown processes that historical sources do not explicate. The history was far from the result of a simple narration. As we shall see later in the chapter, previous treatment of Lucy's history and its text obscures this aspect of the manuscripts.[56]

Though statements by Martha Coray and Martha Lewis leave no ambiguity about the history being dictated, neither the extant notebook nor the rough manuscript represent first-generation aural dictation.[57] Although the extant rough manuscript uses first-person pronouns and colloquialisms and omits terminal punctuation,[58] these usual clues of dictation were likely inherited textual relics from previous rough drafts. Martha's notation in gathering 13—"68 pages yet to write"—confirms the rough draft is at least one version (or more) removed from the dictation transcript.

An Intermediate Manuscript

Lavina Fielding Anderson hypothesizes the existence of an intermediate draft based on two extant leaves: (1) a leaf in the handwriting of Martha Coray that depicts the death of Lucy's daughter-in-law, Jerusha Barden Smith (1805–1837);[59] and (2) a leaf, paginated 200 and 201, that contains two different inscriptions in the handwriting of Howard and Martha respectively.[60] Anderson's supposition is based on these leaves containing textual passages strongly resembling the fair copy text. Both leaves were excised from a volume and indeed show greater textual similarity

56. Lavina Fielding Anderson identified the relationship of the Lucy Mack Smith documents in a chart that begins with the Coray notebooks and ends with Anderson's own critical edition. The chart lists versions but omits texts incorporated into the history, whereas Figure 11.5 herein identifies versions and texts that end at Fair Copy 2. (Anderson, *Lucy's Book*, 218.)

57. Anderson asserts original dictation was committed to writing in "homemade notebooks" and on loose half-sheets that were then used to write the rough draft. Most of the content from the one extant notebook is a copied portion of the mission journal of George A. Smith and all loose half-sheets except for one are contiguous with the rough manuscript and not a separate entity. The one half-sheet describes in detail the death of Joseph Smith Sr., including pauses in speech that likely indicate it was dictated text. (Anderson, *Lucy's Book*, 140.)

58. Anderson, *Lucy's Book*, 142, 164.

59. Anderson, *Lucy's Book*, 145–47, 611 fn220. Richard Anderson claims the intermediate manuscript—what he refers to as the "Coray Rough Manuscript"—was taken to England, whereas Lavina Fielding Anderson claims the intermediate manuscript, most of it not extant, was used to produce two fair copies. (Anderson, *Lucy's Book*, 144.)

60. Page 200 correlates with chapter 39, pp. 177–78, in the 1853 edition. Anderson erroneously correlates the text with chapter 34. (Anderson, *Lucy's Book*, 145.)

to the fair copy than they do to the rough manuscript. However, textual correlation *and* material evidence are equally critical to establishing proof of an intermediate manuscript. The page containing text about the death of Jerusha is one in a series of unrelated disparate notes for the history recorded in piecemeal fashion. It is not, as Anderson asserts, evidence of an intermediate draft because it lacks the material evidence of a polished draft, but the text was integrated into a version of the history inscribed after the extant rough manuscript.

The second leaf contains inscription by Howard and Martha, the text on page 200 in Howard's handwriting correlating with pages 199–200 of the fair copy in Martha's handwriting.[61] The verso of the leaf in Martha's handwriting (page 201) does not continue with further draft text; rather, it is a continuation of text from gathering 18 of the rough manuscript. Close proximity of the pagination to the identical text in the fair copy and the abrupt termination of text at the end of page 200 both suggest the creation of an intermediate draft that was discontinued for unknown reasons in the extant manuscript. The leaf was salvaged and the blank page repurposed when the intermediate draft was discarded. If this is the case, it implies the Corays continued to add text to the rough manuscript(s) even after beginning the intermediate draft. In other words, Martha did not complete her inscription of a version of the rough manuscript before Howard commenced writing an intermediate draft; at some point, the two projects developed simultaneously.[62]

The Fair Copy Manuscripts

When the rough manuscript was completed by July or October 1845 at the latest, two fair copies were created. The first (hereafter "Fair Copy 1") was given to Lucy Mack Smith and is not extant; the second (hereafter

61. This nearly page-for-page copying method similarly occurred in Howard Coray's manuscripts of JS's history, wherein a four-page partial copy correlates with pp. 13–16 in the draft and fair copy histories. See Karen Lynn Davidson et al., eds., *Histories, Volume 1: Joseph Smith Histories, 1832–1844,* vol. 1 of the Histories series of *The Joseph Smith Papers,* ed. Dean C. Jessee et al. (Salt Lake City: Church Historian's Press, 2012), 191 (hereafter *JSP,* H1).

62. One could postulate that page 200 represents a leaf from Fair Copy 2 in its originally inscribed state were it not for its missing vertical margin line that is consistently inscribed on pages of Fair Copy 2. This evidence affirms that the inscription on page 200 is an intermediate draft as Anderson concluded.

"Fair Copy 2") was copied from the first and deposited with the church.[63] Previous attempts to reconstruct the chronology of composition have focused on the dating of the rough manuscript, with more speculative dating for the composition of the fair copies. However, new evidence provides more definitive dating for the fair copies. Lucy Mack Smith evidently solicited genealogical information from her relations as late as March 1845. The following month, her brother Solomon Mack Jr. responded with a lengthy letter that included Mack family genealogy.[64] This genealogy wasn't copied into the rough manuscript, but was recorded in chapter 9 of Fair Copy 2.[65] If Martha's claim that Fair Copy 2 is a copy of Fair Copy 1 is accurate, it means the inscription of chapter 9 in Fair Copy 1 occurred no earlier than April 1845. Furthermore, Martha docketed the Mack letter and added notations to its wrapper that are stylistically identical to the compilation methodology in the rough manuscript.[66] The combination of Martha's notations on the Solomon Mack Jr. letter and the letter's genealogical information later integrated in Fair Copy 1 indicates the rough manuscript remained in a state of flux in April 1845; the pieces used to produce the fair copies that were not integrated into the rough manuscript were still being gathered.

Although Lucy gave notice in the church's October 1845 General Conference that her history was written, it is more likely that her own involvement with the history had terminated by that time.[67] Scriveners

63. Martha Coray, Provo, Utah Territory, to Brigham Young, 13 June 1865. Additional evidence supporting this creation order of the manuscripts occurs in the differing text found in the fair copy and 1853 edition for Sophronia Smith's blessing and her genealogical information. (Anderson, *Lucy's Book*, 92–93.)

64. Solomon Mack, Gilsum, NH, to Lucy Mack Smith, Nauvoo, IL, 6 April 1845, CHL. At an unknown time, Emma Smith and Bathsheba Smith also provided genealogical information for the history. (Smith, History, 1844–1845, bk. 7, [11]; Emma Smith, List of Names, [ca. 1845], in Smith, History; Smith, Autobiography and Notes, [58].)

65. See page 37. A notation for Joseph Smith Jr.'s family genealogy is in the rough manuscript, bk. 7, [11] ("see Emmas paper names") that correlates with an undated paper slip in the Lucy Mack Smith history collection. The text is recorded on page 35 of Fair Copy 2.

66. The letter was docketed in its folded state: "Solomon Mack Jr's Children." After the letter was opened, Martha drew a digit with a notation to its side: "Joseph remained at home a short time and they began to harass him with writs again and." Inside the digit is written "book see." This notation was intended for the rough manuscript but ultimately not included there. See comparable editorial additions using a fist in Smith, History, 1844–1845, bk. 4, [9]; bk. 6, [10]; bk. 15, [2]; and bk. 16, [8].

67. Lavina Fielding Anderson notes the summer 1845 must have been dedicated to final revisions and possibly the beginnings of the fair copy, with a definite completion of the fair copy

Martha and Howard feverishly continued their work together on the history "till near the close of 1845,"[68] with Howard's bill signaling the completion of Lucy's history in its entirety no later than early January 1846.

Fair Copy 2, which is extant, consists of 377 inscribed pages measuring 12 5/8 × 7 7/8 inches; inscription comprises fifty-four chapters and an appendix. Howard Coray wrote pages 1–162, the last portion of page 307 that begins chapter 54, and pages 308–37. Martha inscribed pages 163–306, the first portion of page 307 concluding chapter 53, page 312, and the first three lines of text on page 313.[69] The versos of pages 162 and 317, both of which are not paginated, are blank. An excised leaf is visible between pages 89–90 and 162–63 containing text written by Howard and Martha, and between the termination of the narrative history and the appendix (pages 317–18).[70] Howard inscribed pagination in the upper exterior corners of each page. In addition to Howard's pagination sequence, Martha's segment contains an additional pagination sequence located at the top gutter edge of each page. Her pagination does not parallel Howard's sequence. Martha's pagination is alternately inscribed in graphite and ink on pages 163–302 respectively, then discontinued on pages 303–7 and 312–13. The nonparallel pagination is numbered 187–328. The excised leaves in Fair Copy 2 that precede Martha's segment and the alternate pagination sequence are physical and textual indicators of a different fair copy in its initial inscription that, for unknown reasons, replaced the same text in Fair Copy 2 prior to its presentation to the church.

In addition to these incommensurate pagination sequences, variations in the style used in chapter headings indicate Martha's fair copy segment was copied from a precursor manuscript. Segments of the fair copy penned by Howard generally have two to four blank horizontal lines before chapter headings and one to three blank lines after them. Chapter headings inscribed by Martha (chapters 33–35) follow this same general pattern, but the ones inscribed by Howard in Martha's segment (chapters 36–53, or

---

by 8 October 1845. If so, it does not explain why Howard took nearly three months after the conference to submit a bill for his work on the history. (Anderson, *Lucy's Book*, 90.)

68. Coray, Autobiography, [16]; Howard Coray, Statement of Costs, 14 January 1846.

69. Searle erroneously identified pages 312 and 313 as entirely inscribed by Howard Coray. (Searle, *Early Mormon Historiography*, 377.)

70. Two pages are numbered 273.

pages 179–302) show that he wrote them before Martha wrote the narrative text. Spacing above chapter headings ranges from three to twenty blank lines with one to three blank lines below.[71] Ample, variegated spacing before chapter headings in Martha's segment, as seen in Figures 11.6 and 11.7, suggest that Howard wrote the chapter headings and extrapolated what space was necessary to transfer the text from its precursor manuscript, after which Martha copied the text into the manuscript. This variation in spacing suggests the segment penned by Martha is an earlier copy of the history manuscript than the other pages Howard penned in Fair Copy 2.

The transition between text inscribed by Howard on page 162 and text inscribed by Martha on page 163 is critical to understanding the material and textual production of Fair Copy 2. Howard's inscription on page 162 terminates mid-sentence with eight blank lines remaining. The verso is not paginated, and the next leaf has been excised from the fair copy. Martha inscribed the following page, picking up the narrative precisely where Howard's incomplete sentence abruptly ended. Several factors signal that Martha's segment represents a separate and distinct fair copy that was repurposed to be incorporated into Fair Copy 2. First, the incomplete state of page 162, followed by the excised leaf, suggests Howard's inscription was cut off and filled in with text previously inscribed by Martha. The scribal transition is awkward. Second, there is a noticeable variation of blank lines before Howard's chapter headings in the segment penned by Martha (pages 163–302). Finally, the dual pagination beginning on page 163 shows that segment to be from a different manuscript. It is plausible this segment represents a portion of Fair Copy 1 in its initial scribal intention or perhaps yet another fair copy that was later integrated into Fair Copy 2. If so, it means that Fair Copy 2, in its original scribal intention, was predominantly produced by Howard Coray.

Although there is no way to conclusively prove that pages 163–302 were initially part of Fair Copy 1, an examination of the two extant drafts of Joseph Smith's history penned by Howard Coray in 1841 gives insight into strikingly similar production methods at work in both projects. Howard

71. Following the conclusion of chapter 46 on page 239, there are fourteen blank lines; the next page (240) has twenty-one blank lines prior to the chapter 47 heading. Nine blank lines precede the chapter 48 title and summary on page 245.

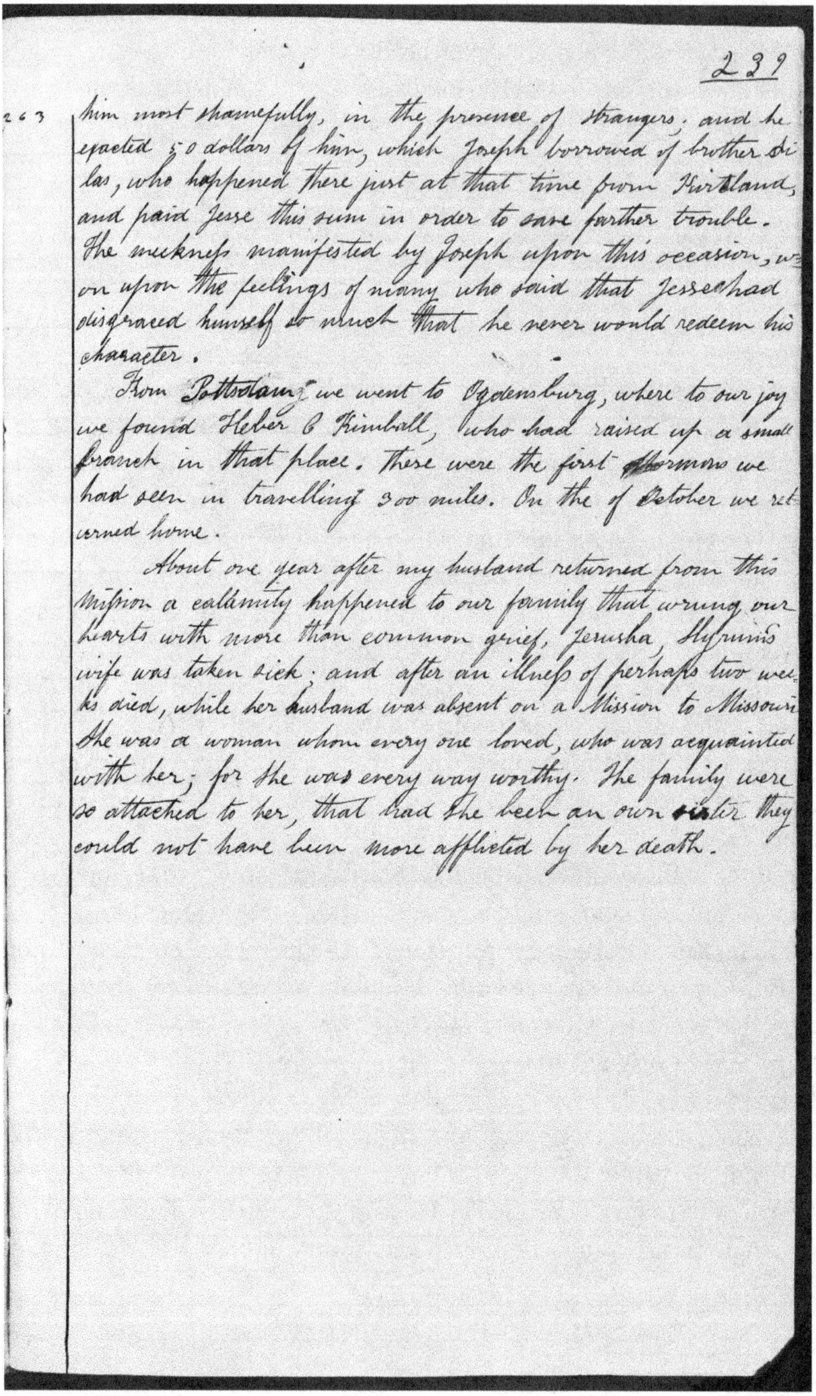

239

263 him most shamefully, in the presence of strangers. and he
exacted 50 dollars of him, which Joseph borrowed of brother Silas, who happened there just at that time from Kirtland,
and paid Jesse this sum in order to save farther trouble.
The meekness manifested by Joseph upon this occasion, w
on upon the feelings of many who said that Jessechad
disgraced himself so much that he never would redeem his
character.

From Pottsdam we went to Ogdensburg, where to our joy
we found Heber C Kimball, who had raised up a small
branch in that place. These were the first Mormons we
had seen in travelling 300 miles. On the of October we returned home.

About one year after my husband returned from this
Mission a calamity happened to our family that wrung our
hearts with more than common grief, Jerusha, Hyrum's
wife was taken sick; and after an illness of perhaps two weeks died, while her husband was absent on a Mission to Missouri
She was a woman whom every one loved, who was acquainted
with her; for she was every way worthy. The family were
so attached to her, that had she been an own sister they
could not have been more afflicted by her death.

FIGURE 11.6 AND FIGURE 11.7. Lucy Mack Smith, History, 1845, Fair Copy 2, pp. 239–240, showing copying methodology. Church History Library, Salt Lake City.

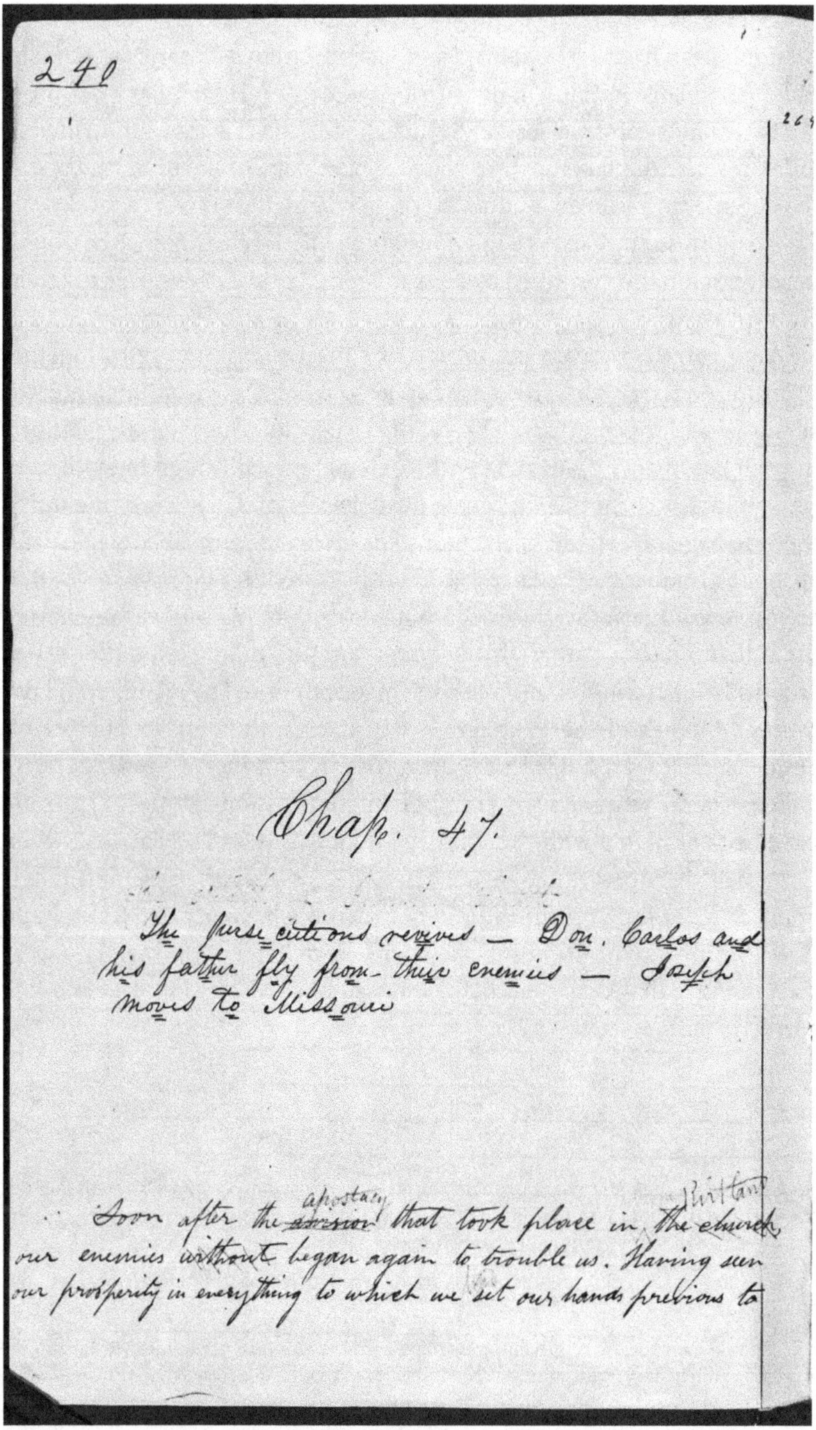

240

Chap. 47.

The persecutions revives — Don. Carlos and his father fly from their enemies — Joseph moves to Missouri

Soon after the ~~division~~ apostacy that took place in ~~the church~~ Kirtland our enemies without began again to trouble us. Having seen our prosperity in everything to which we set our hands previous to

FIGURE 11.6 AND FIGURE 11.7. (Continued)

Coray created two manuscripts for Joseph Smith's history—one being a version of the first sixty-one pages in Joseph Smith's history, vol. A-1, and the other incorporating changes from the earlier draft.[72] Comparison of the two manuscripts for Joseph Smith's history reveals that approximately ten percent of the fair copy is a page-for-page copy of the draft, the rest of the pages from each version trailing or preceding the other by a few lines.[73] This pattern is similar to the handwriting shifts occurring in Fair Copy 2 between segments inscribed by Howard and Martha, where page 163 trails Howard's text by a few lines.

After Fair Copy 2 was completed, the manuscript was sewn together in a rudimentary style. There are five needle holes at the gutter edge; the string is no longer extant. The manuscript was subsequently rebound in pasteboard covers adorned with paste paper, with calfskin leather on its spine and corners. The pastedown leaves and flyleaves, including the title page, are made of thinner paper than the inscribed pages. The absence of puncture marks on the leaf bearing the title page, as well as adhesive residue at the gutter edge, suggests that this leaf was not part of the initial binding but was likely adhered to the manuscript after it was rebound. Furthermore, the title page inscription—"The History of | Lucy Smith | Mother of the Prophet"—is in the handwriting of Historian's Office clerk Robert L. Campbell, who began working in the Historian's Office several years later.[74] Although the later minted title page could have been affiliated with the fair copy manuscript as early as 1854 when Campbell began working in the Historian's Office, it was more likely applied to the fair copy in 1866, when Campbell, George A. Smith, and Elias Smith—a committee tasked with revising Lucy's history—were comparing Fair Copy 2 with the 1853 published version and making corrections.[75]

72. Unlike the rough and fair copy manuscripts of Lucy's history, Howard's rough and fair copy manuscripts for Joseph Smith's history do not diverge as greatly textually. Most corrections were cosmetic or grammatical in nature.

73. For more information on Coray's efforts in writing Joseph Smith's history, see *JSP*, H1:198–202.

74. The title Campbell gave the fair copy manuscript is identical to the title Howard Coray ascribed to the history in his January 1846 bill, suggesting the fair copy at one time had a title page likely in Howard's handwriting (not extant).

75. Historian's Office, Journal, November 20, 1854, and April 30, 1866.

The Question of Authorship

When Orson Pratt published the history in 1853, first-person pronoun usage made it appear as though the history came directly from the lips of Lucy Smith. The title page identified Lucy as the author and professed the work was written under Joseph Smith's supervision. Subsequent publication of Lucy's history and supporting historical sources further cemented Lucy's role as the narrative's leading voice. To identify Lucy's history as a work of singular authorship, however, misrepresents its composite structure and Martha and Howard Coray's participation in its production. Whereas the Corays' presence in the rough draft was mostly in the subtext—functioning as scribe and reviser depicting events they didn't witness—their influence became more overt when Lucy's narrative touched on times their own lives had intersected with Joseph Smith's. Two occurrences illustrate this point. In a passage narrating Joseph Smith's return from Washington, D.C. after his failed attempt to petition Congress for Missouri redress in the spring of 1840, Martha inserted, "Here occurs the conference the arrival of H. Coray and his undertaking."[76] This addition referred to the April 1840 conference and Howard's initial scribal work for Joseph Smith. At another point in the narrative, in a passage describing Joseph Smith building a home in Nauvoo for his father, Joseph Smith Sr., Martha interrupted with unrelated text—"here H Coray's leg is broken and Emma's and Josep[h]s care and the revelation to build the Temple is given revise[r] take notice."[77] In the second instance, the broken

---

76. Smith, History, 1844–1845, bk. 18, [3].

77. Smith, History, 1844–1845, bk. 18, [3].This incident which occurred in June 1840, is described in Howard's autobiography:

"The Prophet and myself, after looking at his horses, and admiring them, that were just across the road from his house, we started thither, the Prophet at the same time put his arm over my shoulder. When we had reached about the middle of the road, he stopped and remarked, "brother Coray, I wish you was a little larger, I would like to have some fun with you." I replied, perhaps you can as it is,--not realizing what I was saying—Joseph a man of over 200lbs weight, while I scarcely 130lbs, made it not a little ridiculous, for me to think of engaging with him in any thing like a scuffle. However, as soon as I made this reply, he began to trip me; he took some kind of a lock on my right leg, from which I was unable to extricate it, and throwing me around, broke it some 3 inches above the ankle joint. He immediately carried me into the house, pulled off my boot, and found, at once, that my leg was decidedly broken; then got some splinters and bandaged it. A number of times that day did he come in to see me, endeavoring to console me as much as possible."

Drawing a parallel with Jacob who wrestled with an angel and received a blessing, Coray solicited a blessing from Joseph Smith, who deferred to his father, Joseph Smith Sr., the church patriarch.

leg incident and revelation were stripped from the fair copy. In the first instance, the reference to Howard was stripped from the fair copy, but the mention of the conference survives as a trace of editorial intrusions.

Clearly Martha and Howard differed in their level of comfort in weaving themselves into the historical narrative. Martha injected these brief personal accounts into Lucy's draft, only to have Howard cut them from the fair copy. It was one thing to inscribe subtext that functioned as scaffolding in a flurry of textual construction; it was another thing altogether to abandon the scaffolding and become a visible part of the textual construct. For Martha, who wrote these passages, it seemed appropriate. By 1845, the Corays were deeply embedded in the creation of records about the Smiths, both in the immediate past and the present. How could one become familiar with Smith family history without encountering the Corays as purveyors of that history? On the other hand, the history was intended to highlight events in the lives of the Smith family, not to showcase individuals whose lives intersected with the Smiths. So the paratextual insertions of the Corays were removed, and the evidence of their influence on the resulting narrative is now nearly invisible.

The influence of Martha and Howard Coray on the history is more conspicuous in the editorial manipulation of the Joseph Smith Sr. visions discussed above. Three of the visions (one, six, and seven) recorded on loose pages are written in the first person. The third vision flips from third-person to first-person point of view:

> he [Joseph Smith Sr.] dreamed that he was very sick and so lame he could scarcely walk he then asked his guide what he should do that he was sick and so lame <in my knee> that he knew not what to do his guide said get up and walk to a such garden that I shall shew you. . . limping along with great difficulty with much exertion I was enabled to reach the gate.[78]

It is unclear why the point of view repeatedly shifts in this vision. The dominant use of first-person point of view in the other visions suggests the visions (excluding vision three) were not dictated by Lucy but came from earlier manuscripts written by Joseph Smith Sr. prior to his death

78. This vision is housed in the Lucy Mack Smith history collection at the CHL.

in 1840.[79] Martha copied these manuscripts on loose pages placed with the history, but the visions were not inscribed in the rough manuscript. Howard Coray integrated them into the Fair Copy, making readers believe Lucy was retelling the visions as her spouse had explained them to her, but retained the first-person narrative voice.[80] In doing so, Howard made Lucy the interpretive lens through which readers confronted Joseph Smith Sr.'s visions.

This editorial license was well within the range of possibilities for scribal publication. As stated before, Lucy's history is an example of scribal publication that heavily draws upon pre-existing texts to flesh out the lives of the extended Smith family. Extracts from the writings of Lucy's father Solomon Mack were incorporated into gatherings one and two of the rough manuscript,[81] while information regarding her brother Stephen Mack was embellished with an undated account from Horace Stanley.[82] Family letters appear in both manuscripts.[83] Lucy compensated for her limited knowledge about her husband prior to their marriage by interjecting "a transcript from the record of the family of Smiths."[84] Citations to Joseph Smith Jr.'s published history occur throughout the manuscript.[85]

---

79. Joseph Smith Sr. died on 14 September 1840. (See Asael Smith Family Bible, 1795–1950, p. 12, CHL.)

80. Page 52 of Fair Copy 2 states Joseph Smith Sr. "had the following Vision; which I <shall> relate in his own words as he told it to me the next morning."

81. Lucy's introduction to her father's text in the rough manuscript describes it as "an old document which I have in my possesion writen by my Father in the 80 year of his age," while concluding statements refer to it as "my Fathers narrative." The fair copy text refers to it as "my father's journal." The text resembles portions of *A Narrative of the Life of Solomon Mack* (1811), but contains several unpublished incidences in first-person narrative, indicating that Lucy accessed writings that predate the published pamphlet. (Smith, History, rough manuscript, bk. 1, pp. 1, [7]; fair copy, p. 8; Richard Lloyd Anderson, *Joseph Smith's New England Heritage: Influences of Grandfathers Solomon Mack and Asael Smith,* rev. ed. [Salt Lake City: Deseret Book; Provo, Utah: Brigham Young University Press, 2003], 39.)

82. Smith, History, 1845, 20–21.

83. Smith, History, 1844–1845, bk. 1, [8]–[9]; Smith, History, 1845, 46–48.

84. This quoted text is recorded on a manuscript leaf describing the seventh vision of Joseph Smith Sr. in the Lucy Mack Smith history collection. Smith and Mack family genealogical data in the Smith family record was utilized to fill the deficiency of information. This data is not represented in the rough manuscript but appears in Fair Copy 2. (Smith, History, 1845, 29–37.)

85. *Times and Seasons* references begin in bk. 13, [7], and continue through bk. 18.

The liberal manipulation and repurposing of text had undeniable repercussions on the history—Lucy's pure, unadulterated voice is intermittent and sometimes simply non-existent.[86] This mashup of text was typical of the "heterogenous and provisional" text-making of New England, where "a writer's voice could fluctuate within the compass of a single text and, more certainly, from one act of writing to the next."[87] The deliberate comingling of multiple texts with disparate authorship in the history created a new textual narrative that congealed Smith family experience into a foundational text of Mormon collective memory spanning from Smith family progenitors to the death of its founding prophet. To Lucy, it become a "testimony" of the injustices the Mormons experienced to be presented "before angels, and the spirits of the just made perfect, before Archangels and Seraphims, Cherubims and Gods."[88]

A Tangled Web of Provenance

The provenance of the Lucy Mack Smith collection can only be understood by a close examination of historical sources and a consideration of changing archival methodologies. Statements about when the history was deposited in the Historian's Office—along with seemingly contradictory explanations by editors and publishers—have contributed to a misunderstood provenance.[89] Efforts to trace the custodial history of Lucy's history have been based on teasing meaning from these statements, with no reliable conclusions. For most users of the collection, the present assemblage of the rough manuscript, fair copy, and miscellaneous papers has oversimplified perceptions of the collection's integrity.[90] Material and textual

86. Anderson claims the addition of material not authored by Lucy, particularly Joseph Smith's history, "makes Lucy sound as if she is simply walking off-stage while someone else performs," resulting in a text with "greater impersonality." (Anderson, *Lucy's Book*, 139.)

87. Hall, *Ways of Writing*, 23.

88. Smith, History, 1845, 316.

89. According to Brigham Young, a copy of the history was in church possession since Nauvoo; see "Hearken, O Ye Latter-day Saints," *Millennial Star* 27, no. 42 (October 21, 1865): 658. Coray descendants claim Martha gave her original manuscript to Brigham Young after the Corays arrived in Salt Lake City. Likewise, Joseph F. Smith's preface to the 1901 publication in the *Improvement Era* notes Martha's transmission of the history to Brigham Young, but doesn't identify a specific date. (Cooper, "Martha Jane Knowlton Coray," 3; "History of the Prophet Joseph," *Improvement Era* 5, no. 1 [November 1901]: 1.)

90. Lavina Fielding Anderson acknowledges confusion over when the church acquired the manuscript, concluding that the most reasonable explanation is the rough draft and fair copy were kept together (Anderson 132). Searle, based on a Historian's Office journal entry

clues in the history manuscript, together with an understanding of the Historian's Office's record-keeping practices, indicate a disparate provenance. I argue that the Lucy Mack Smith History collection is an artificial compilation of manuscript records. In fact, the current collection is a confluence of at least three different streams of provenance.

This is most noticeable with Fair Copy 2. As we have seen, Howard Coray submitted a bill to the church for compiling and transcribing Lucy Mack Smith's history on 14 January 1846, and received payment a few days later.[91] Howard likely transferred possession of Fair Copy 2 to the church around the same time or shortly thereafter.[92] Historian's Office clerk Thomas Bullock packed Fair Copy 2 in the "large box" for the trek west within weeks of Coray receiving payment.[93] The first inventory of Historian's Office records lists a simple, descriptive title—"Mother Smith's history." Beginning in the 1850s, inventories listed either this descriptive title for the fair copy or a derivative title based on the half title of the 1853 Liverpool publication—"Joseph Smith the Prophet."[94] Miscellaneous graphite notations by George A. Smith and Robert L. Campbell throughout the manuscript volume indicate it was consulted heavily by the Historian's Office in the 1860s while revising Lucy's history for a new publication to replace the original one.[95] An identification number inscribed on the front pastedown leaf of Fair Copy 2 links it to a records-accessioning initiative for both

---

identifying "Mother Smith's history in M.S.," asserts the rough draft and fair copy were in the possession of the Historian's Office by 1855. (Searle, *Early Mormon Historiography*, 384; Historian's Office, Journal, October 17, 1855.)

91. See note 32 above.

92. Brigham Young recalled obtaining a copy of the history while in Nauvoo. Coray referred to "the written manuscript" in the possession of the Historian's Office as late as 1855. ("Hearken, O Ye Latter-day Saints," 658; Martha Coray, E.T. City, to George A. Smith, Salt Lake City, Utah Territory, June 5, 1855, in George A. Smith Papers, 1834–1877, CHL.)

93. Thomas Bullock, Journal, August 1845–July 1846, February 4, 1846, CHL; Schedule of Church Records, Nauvoo, IL, February 1846, CHL.

94. See in particular inventories dated April 1, 1857, April 4, 1855, March 19, 1858, and July 1858, Historian's Office, Catalogs and Inventories, 1846–1904, CHL.

95. Coray descendant Robert Cooper states, "The revised copy [Fair Copy 2] was kept by George A. Smith until his death in 1875 when it went into the keeping of Joseph F. Smith." Although Cooper offers no source citation for this information, it seems plausible that George A. Smith, one of the individuals assigned by Brigham Young to revise the manuscript, would retain custody of the record until his death, when the manuscript went into the possession of Church Historian Joseph F. Smith. (Robert P. Cooper, "Martha Jane Knowlton Coray and the History of Joseph Smith by his Mother," 3, 1965, photocopy at CHL.)

printed books and manuscript records occurring in the Historian's Office from ca. 1890 to 1930.[96] In contrast, the rough manuscript does not have any graphite notations from Historian's Office clerks, suggesting it was not in the possession of the Historian's Office in the 1860s when revisions to the history occurred, or wasn't consulted due to its less polished state.

The provenance of the rough draft manuscript is more complex, requiring contextual knowledge of record-keeping practices in the Historian's Office over several decades and the convergence of archives professionalization in the United States with practices in the Historian's Office. During the mid-1850s, manuscripts in the Historian's Office were organized chronologically for the writing of the History of Joseph Smith.[97] By the late nineteenth and early twentieth centuries, this methodology was replaced with filing documents by name and subject.[98] This filing methodology was heavily utilized in the manuscript collections of libraries and historical societies throughout the United States beginning in the mid to late nineteenth century and reflected the application of library classification techniques to manuscript records.[99] Organizing manuscripts by name or subject increased access to relevant manuscripts that a chronological filing would miss, particularly when using reminiscent accounts of events. The benefit of this classification system was that it decreased the amount of research required to identify relevant records in a pre–information system environment. On the other hand, this arrangement system destroyed provenance and custodial history.[100] A regrettable result was that organic

96. Entry 8602, "Library Record," in Historian's Office, Library Accession Records, ca. 1890–1930, CHL.

97. Historian's Office, Journal, May 16, 1849, April 20, 1854, May 15, 1854, and December 2, 1868; Historical Department, Office Journal, 1844–2012, CHL.

98. For references to the name and subject file methodology, see Historian's Office, Library Accession Records.

99. Susan E. Davis, "Descriptive Standards and the Archival Profession," *Historical Aspects of Cataloging and Classification,* ed. Martin D. Joachim, 2 vols. (Binghamton, New York: Haworth Press, 2003), 2:294. The earliest American institution to use library techniques for cataloging manuscripts was the Massachusetts Historical Society, created in 1791.

100. The principle of provenance dictates that manuscripts or records with differing provenance remain separate for contextual purposes. Items created or received by an individual or organization are kept in one collection. Name and subject file organization does the exact opposite; that is, records with differing provenance are put together and the papers of an individual or organization are spread through many collections. See Richard Pierce-Moses, *A Glossary of Archival and Records Terminology* (Chicago: Society of American Archivists, 2005), 317–18.

collections were splintered and scattered among many new and artificial collections.

The Lucy Mack Smith history collection represents a unique nexus of name and subject file methodology and the subsequent implementation of current archival standards in the Historian's Office. Merging the rough draft and fair copy manuscripts into one collection reflects name file organization; however, the presence of miscellaneous papers in the collection suggests the miscellany was donated to the Historian's Office with a segment of Lucy's history substantial enough to warrant the integration of the whole donation with the rest of the history. Had name and subject methodologies been fully enforced in the collection, various Coray miscellany would reside in Church History Library collections that are the last remaining relics of the name and subject file era.[101]

A second donation—that of the rough manuscript—may have been given by Martha herself. Coray descendant Robert P. Cooper claimed Martha kept the original history manuscript in her possession until after arriving in Salt Lake City in 1851, when she gave it to Brigham Young.[102] Although there is no documentation or clues within the collection to substantiate a Coray transfer to Young, Martha did alert Church Historian and Recorder George A. Smith in 1855 of "loose papers" in her possession that had not been published by Orson Pratt in Liverpool in 1853.[103] In 1866, Martha visited Brigham Young's office to consult with George A. Smith, Elias Smith, and others who were revising the history.[104] These encounters provided opportunities for Martha to transfer custody of whatever remnants of the history remained in her possession.

A third, perhaps more conclusive, donation of manuscripts was made by the Corays' children in the early 1900s. Helena "Nellie" Coray Alexander wrote to her father Howard in September 1904, questioning if the history

---

101. Based on the name and subject file methodology, manuscript versions of Doctrine and Covenants 77, 87, and 105 in the Lucy Mack Smith history collection would be transferred to the Revelations Collection and Howard Coray's priesthood license signed by Joseph Smith would be in the Joseph Smith Collection. The patriarchal blessing for Martha Coray and the leaf from a Joseph Smith discourse would be in subject files for patriarchal blessings and discourses (now dismantled and recataloged using current archival practices for arrangement and description).

102. Cooper, "Martha Jane Knowlton Coray and the History of Joseph Smith by his Mother," 3.

103. Martha Coray, E.T. City, to George A. Smith, Salt Lake City, Utah Territory, 5 June 1855. The 1853 edition of Lucy's history was typeset from Fair Copy 1.

104. Historian's Office, Journal, 12 April 1866.

manuscript in family possession should be sold to Joseph Smith III "if he could be ensured that Joseph F. had not had access to it."[105]

Nellie's letter confirms family possession of original manuscripts allegedly not consulted by the Historian's Office for the *Improvement Era* reprint of the history. The extant rough manuscript does not include revisions by Historian's Office clerks, suggesting it may have been the manuscript in question. Given the unknown number of potential drafts that were created for the history, however, it is equally plausible this could be yet another copy.[106]

Other historical sources substantiate familial retention of manuscripts later incorporated into the collection. Daughter Martha Lewis recorded attending a ward meeting with her father in 1906 where the bishop read her father's ordination certificate signed by Joseph Smith.[107] This certificate is part of the collection. Another odd piece of miscellany in the collection is a Joseph Smith III signature ripped from a letter of correspondence. It obviously has no relation to Lucy's history, but the pattern of tearing out signatures from correspondence correlates with Martha Lewis's efforts to copy her husband's 1868–1869 missionary journal in 1909. Pasted to the cover of the copied journal is a signature of Theodore Lewis torn from a letter.[108]

Historian's Office methodologies for organizing and preserving manuscripts suggests the priesthood license and Joseph Smith III signature were acquired with material easily identifiable as Lucy's history and merged with other records already in the possession of the Historian's Office. Had these pieces come to the Historian's Office separate from the history, the license would reside in the Joseph Smith collection and the signature may have been discarded. Instead, their presence in the Lucy Mack Smith history collection suggests the rough manuscript and miscellaneous manuscripts were donated in the early twentieth century,

105. Nellie [Helena K. Coray Alexander], Provo, UT, to Howard Coray, 21 September 1904, pp. [3]–[4], Coray Family Papers. Joseph F. Smith, president of the Church of Jesus Christ of Latter-day Saints, likely deemed the manuscript "worthless" because an authorized edition of the history was published serially from 1901–1903 in the *Improvement Era* that corrected many of the alleged errors perpetuated in the unauthorized 1853 edition.

106. See Figure 11.5 herein explaining the textual makeup of the history.

107. Martha Lewis, Journal, 29 April 1906, Theodore B. Lewis Collection, 1868–1825, CHL.

108. Theodore B. Lewis, Journal (copy), 1868–1869, Theodore B. Lewis Collection.

either around 1917—the year the multi-volume journal of Theodore and Martha Lewis terminated—or in 1929 when Lewis died.[109] Through this tangled provenance, we see that user's perceptions of the collection have been unknowingly shaped by institutional developments spanning 1845 to the 1920s.

Publication and Interpretation

If the history's production methods and custodial history both proved to be more complicated than was previously understood, perhaps it should not be surprising that the book's various editions published for lay and academic audiences alike have misrepresented the relationship of the extant manuscripts. A brief overview of these various editions of the book, with their editorial introductions, is important to establish context and help readers understand how this chapter builds on this previous scholarship but also diverges from them in several of its interpretations. Much of the publication and reception history of the book has been adequately covered in previous scholarship. But, as has been shown, there is more to the story as it relates to scribal intention, original manuscript order, production methodology, and provenance of the rough manuscript and Fair Copy 2.

Lucy lived until 1856, but her copy (Fair Copy 1) was likely in the possession of Orson Pratt by mid-March 1853.[110] Pratt took the manuscript with him to Liverpool, England, and had it published by the fall—without seeking authorization from church president Brigham Young.[111] After the 1853 edition, early efforts to publish the history focused on its public dissemination, with limited scrutiny of its text and origins.

In 1880, the Reorganized Church of Jesus Christ of Latter Day Saints (hereafter RLDS church) published an edition of Lucy's history with

109. Martha Lewis died of a paralytic stroke. ("Pioneer Utah Woman Dies at Daughter's Home," *Salt Lake Tribune*, October 27, 1929.)

110. Conflicting accounts document how the manuscript got from Lucy Smith to Orson Pratt. Martha Coray claimed Arthur Millikin, Lucy's son-in-law, obtained the copy from Lucy, the copy being further transmitted to Almon Babbit and then to Isaac Sheen. Pratt purchased the manuscript from Almon Babbitt for $200, not $1000 as Brigham Young professed. (Anderson, *Lucy's Book*, 95; Martha Coray, Provo, Utah Territory, to Brigham Young, June 13, 1865; Historian's Office, Letterpress Copybooks, 1854–1879, 1885–1886, vol. 2, p. 683, CHL.)

111. For more information on the fair copy manuscript taken to Liverpool, see Anderson, *Lucy's Book*, 97.

Pratt's preface and a new preface, but excluded the poems of Eliza R. Snow in the appendix. Lorenzo Snow, who became president of the Church of Jesus Christ of Latter-day Saints (hereafter LDS church) in 1898, authorized the publication of the history in serialized form in a church magazine with a preface by Joseph F. Smith, his counselor in the church's First Presidency.[112] In 1945, LDS author Preston Nibley compiled and reprinted the *Improvement Era* version in book form with slight revisions. Photomechanical reprints of the 1853 edition were produced by Modern Microfilm Company in 1965, Arno Press and the *New York Times* in 1969, and Grandin Book Company in 1995. Scot and Maurine Proctor produced a "revised and enhanced" critical edition of the history in 1996 that predominantly used the 1853 edition, seamlessly transferring back and forth between the rough manuscript and the published edition without informing the reader of the switch. Their purpose was to create a history "accessible and inviting to a wide audience" without the encumbrance of scholarly and textual apparatus and without a scholarly statement of editorial method.[113]

In 1996, amateur historian Dan Vogel made the first attempt to publish a text of Lucy's history applying rigorous documentary editing standards, resulting in *Early Mormon Documents*, volume one.[114] This volume featured a selection of the rough draft manuscript and the 1853 published edition in parallel columns, omitting revelation texts and portions of Joseph Smith's published history that were copied into Lucy's history. Vogel's compilation only covered the history of Mormon origins prior to 1831, so his selection eliminated chapters 1–7 and 9 of the published edition; his featured text concluded with text in chapter 39 from the published edition and gathering 11 page 3 of the rough manuscript.[115] Vogel claimed the rough manuscript (what he calls the "preliminary manuscript") was written by Martha and possibly revised with the help of Lucy and Howard, with Howard preparing the two final, or "fair copy" versions. Vogel's interpretation differs slightly from that of Lavina Fielding Anderson, who stresses that Martha Coray

112. *Improvement Era* (Salt Lake City, Utah), 1901–1903.

113. Scot Facer Proctor and Maurine Jensen Proctor, eds., *The Revised and Enhanced History of Joseph Smith by His Mother* (Salt Lake City: Bookcraft, 1996), xxxiii.

114. Dan Vogel, ed., *Early Mormon Documents*, 5 vols. (Salt Lake City: Signature Books, 1996–2003), 1:227–450.

115. Anderson, *Lucy's Book*, 162.

transcribed the rough manuscript in its entirety.[116] Vogel does not identify sources supporting his claim that Howard and Lucy possibly revised the rough manuscript; however, his claim is partially substantiated by textual evidence of Howard's editing. Fair Copy 2 was not presented to the LDS church in a leather bound volume as Vogel asserts, but was likely bound in the 1850s or 1860s in territorial Utah.

Like Vogel's work, Lavina Fielding Anderson's critical text of the history published in 2001, *Lucy's Book*, features the rough manuscript and published versions in parallel columns. However, Anderson's edition produces both in their entirety instead of just selections, along with a wealth of textual and contextual annotation. It is the most in-depth treatment of the history to date. Anderson painstakingly pieced together the narrative text of the rough manuscript using the 1853 edition as her guide.[117] She carefully navigated historical sources with contradictory statements about the custodial history of the manuscripts. If Anderson had an in-depth understanding of the institutional history of the Historian's Office,[118] it likely would have influenced her perception of provenance.[119]

The approach taken by Vogel and Anderson facilitates textual comparison but does not explicate production methods. It conflates and collapses all texts preceding the fair copies into one manuscript to arrive at a text resembling the published edition. This blending of texts steers reader perception of manuscript order and interpretation of the rough manuscript versions. Final production supersedes original intention by becoming the

---

116. Anderson, *Lucy's Book*, 88–89. Anderson's handwriting identification for the rough manuscript was based upon prior treatment of Lucy's history by Richard L. Anderson and Howard Searle. (Richard L. Anderson, "Circumstantial Confirmation of the First Vision through Reminiscences," *BYU Studies* 9, no. 3 [Spring 1969]: 387–88; fn 6 in Howard Searle, *Early Mormon Historiography*, 360.)

117. David J. Wittaker, former curator of Western and Mormon Manuscripts at Brigham Young University, loaned Anderson photocopies of the rough manuscript he had purchased from Deseret Book in the 1980s. Anderson was neither granted access to the fair copy manuscript nor given permission to publish it by the LDS Church Historical Department. Scholars who understand the inherent limitations of photocopies when attempting to discern production methods for manuscript texts will undoubtedly conclude Anderson's work is nothing short of miraculous. (Anderson, *Lucy's Book*, 1, 68.)

118. The Historian's Office was created in 1842 to gather, maintain, and preserve the records of the LDS church.

119. Anderson ultimately determined that the rough manuscript and fair copy were kept together. For an in-depth study of conflicting sources on the history's provenance, see Anderson, *Lucy's Book*, 132–34.

framework for understanding the history's text. This methodology, albeit helpful for textual comparison purposes, neglects the fundamental archival principle of original order and misrepresents the various versions of the extant (and non-extant) manuscripts and how they relate to each other in the history's production process. Recognizing and reconstructing the original order clarifies the history's production beyond what historical sources explicitly state. A careful analysis of handwriting and of material and textual clues in the extant manuscripts provides strong indications of original order and compilation methodologies, also illuminating historical sources and scholarly interpretations as well as calling into question or even unveiling inaccuracies in historical sources and scholarly interpretations.

Conclusions

Examining Lucy Mack Smith's history from an archival and textual perspective illuminates the original order of the rough manuscript and offers details about production methodology not described in historical sources. Reconstruction of original order and close scrutiny of handwriting substantiates a composition methodology wherein Martha inscribed approximately half of the rough manuscript before Howard began his work compiling the history. Howard made editorial corrections to Martha's inscription, then continued the history implementing different production methods. Because of this, the rough manuscript is possibly an amalgamation of two separate rough manuscripts with origins in earlier, non-extant drafts. Martha's notations in the rough manuscript support the use of a precursor manuscript that was copied to create the extant rough manuscript. Loose leaves in the collection with textual affiliation to the history were integrated into a non-extant version or versions of the history that succeed the rough manuscript. The lack of textual indicators for dictated text suggests the rough manuscript is not the dictated urtext described in historical sources.

Furthermore, Fair Copy 2 is an amalgamation of two different manuscripts. The contiguous segment in Martha Coray's handwriting possibly represents a part of Fair Copy 1 or (more likely) a fragment of another fair copy draft, wherein Howard created the chapter headings at one time and extrapolated how many pages Martha needed for inscription. Martha thereafter copied the text onto the fair copy pages. Scrutiny of texts implemented in the history indicates the narrative was a work of social publication. Even after the history was completed and published, its complicated provenance was repeatedly misinterpreted. Given what is known about the history and professionalization of the Historian's Office, we can determine that the Lucy Mack Smith history collection is the convergence of two or three disparate donations of material. The sum total of all this information discloses production and preservation methods heretofore unknown in the history manuscripts, enabling a closer, more critical reading and use of this foundational text of early Mormonism.

12

The Image as Text and Context in Early Mormon History

Jeffrey G. Cannon

PHOTOGRAPHY HAD NOT yet come into its own when Joseph and Hyrum Smith were murdered on 27 June 1844. Paint and canvas remained the preferred medium for portraying history and prominence of their subject. No photographs of either man are known to have survived, if any were taken at all. This chapter discusses the Latter-day Saints' use of photography and other visual media to record and remember the history of the movement under Joseph Smith by the generation of Mormons who knew him personally and had reason to remember him in specific ways.

Historians often illustrate their work with pictures of historical events, persons, and locales. More than just illustrations, however, images can serve effectively as primary source material to tell the story of the past. Richard Neitzel Holzapfel and T. Jeffery Cottle have rightly argued that careful use of photographs will enhance Mormon scholarship. They follow W. Randall Dixon and William W. Slaughter in arguing that images themselves can and should be used to bolster or even make scholarly arguments rather than simply illustrate a text.[1] As with textual sources, images that are used to document Mormonism's foundations must be properly read and critiqued. Not only is careful attention needed, but also

1. William W. Slaughter and W. Randall Dixon, "Utah Under Glass: An Introduction to Four Prominent Pioneer Photographers of 19th-Century Utah," *Pioneer* 2 (Summer 1977): 28–39; Richard Neitzel Holzapfel and T. Jeffery Cottle, "The City of Joseph in Focus: The Use and Abuse of Historic Photographs," *BYU Studies* 32, nos. 1 and 2 (1992): 249–68.

a correct understanding of the contexts and purposes of the images' creation and preservation. Nevertheless, Mormon historians, who are primarily Americanists, follow the trend of other Americanists in being slow to adopt photographs and other images as primary source material.[2]

The volume of visual primary source material for early Mormon history is significant but admittedly smaller than that of manuscript or print sources. A few portraits of early Mormons remain, including the series by English profile painter Sutcliffe Maudsley, which includes Joseph and Hyrum; as well as their respective wives Emma Hale Smith and Mary Fielding Smith; their mother, Lucy Mack Smith; and other prominent Mormons. David Rogers's oil portraits of Joseph and Emma Smith were executed in 1842 and are probably the finest artistic depictions of the couple made from life, though without photographic portraits it is difficult to judge their accuracy. Emma later said that a good depiction of her husband was never made.[3] Depictions of both the major and minor events of Joseph Smith's life and Mormon history were, with a few exceptions, left to later generations. None of the artists was actually present at the events they depicted.

Early Uses of Imagery after the Death of Joseph Smith

Joseph Smith's prophetic career began with a vision, and Brigham Young's did as well. On 8 August 1844, Young stood in the grove east of the temple to address the people of Nauvoo and the surrounding Mormon communities who were still mourning the loss of their prophet. Several in the crowd later recalled that as Young laid out his claims to leadership they witnessed Smith's visage fall upon him, apparently endowing him with the likeness of the dead prophet as a divine illustration of the transfer of

2. For Americanist historians' use of photography and the earlier adoption by other scholars, see Joshua Brown, "Historians and Photography," *American Art* 21, no. 3 (Fall 2007): 9–13. Americanist historians are not the only ones left open to such a critique. T. Jack Thompson has been critical of the general lack of critical examination of missionary photography in general but especially in Africa. See T. Jack Thompson, *Light on Darkness? Missionary Photography of Africa in the Nineteenth and Early Twentieth Centuries* (Grand Rapids, Michigan: Eerdmans, 2012), 3.

3. Junius F. Wells, "Portraits of Joseph Smith the Prophet," *Instructor*, February 1930, 79.

authority.[4] But others had no such memory, and many rejected Young's claims. Some claimed that Young and others invented the vision, initially through Young's showmanship and talent as a mimic and later through misremembered or intentionally fabricated "reminiscences" of the event.[5] For the rest of Young's life, he and his followers continued to assert the authority of the Apostles to lead the church in Smith's absence. Challenges to Young's authority came from every side: former colleagues in church leadership, members of the Smith family, and even from fellow apostles. In response to those challenges, Young and his followers turned, in part, to painting, sculpture, and photography in their efforts to illustrate and argue the transfer of Joseph Smith's authority to the Quorum of the Twelve Apostles and to Young, the quorum's president. As technologies and attitudes changed, they used different imagery to document and control the narrative of early Mormon history in ways that supported their claims. Images which survive from this time must be understood in this context.

Paint and Canvas

With photography still in its infancy and paint the preferred medium, Latter-day Saints naturally turned to painters to portray their history. Most painters made their living from portraiture, but history painting was the ideal to which they aspired.[6] The church under Brigham Young made use of both portraiture and history painting, producing several notable examples. Their production and display are indicative of the messaging Young and his followers created during that time.

One example, as seen in Figure 12.1, is a portrait of Brigham Young that hung in the temple at Nauvoo. Young and other apostles used some of the rooms of the unfinished temple to administer certain rites. Their ability to perform closely guarded rituals Joseph Smith initiated before his death was a central component of Young's argument for apostolic leadership.[7]

4. Lynne Watkins Jorgensen and *BYU Studies* staff, "The Mantle of the Prophet Joseph Passed to Brother Brigham: A Collective Spiritual Witness," *BYU Studies* 36, no. 4 (1996–1997): 125–204.

5. Richard S. Van Wagoner, "The Making of a Mormon Myth: The 1844 Transfiguration of Brigham Young," *Dialogue: A Journal of Mormon Thought* 28, no. 4 (Winter 1995): 159–82.

6. Alan Trachtenberg, *Reading American Photographs: Images As History—Matthew Brady to Walker Evans* (New York: Hill and Wang, 1989), 35–36.

7. Thomas Bullock, Minutes, 8 August 1844, General Church Minutes, 1839–1877, Church History Library, The Church of Jesus Christ of Latter-day Saints, Salt Lake City (hereafter

FIGURE 12.1. Brigham Young, July 1845. "Delivering the Law of the Lord," by Selah Van Sickle.

Pioneer Memorial Museum, International Society Daughters of Utah Pioneers, Salt Lake City.

CHL). For more on Joseph Smith's temple rites as an essential condition to apostolic succession, see Andrew F. Ehat, "Joseph Smith's Introduction of Temple Ordinances and the 1844 Mormon Succession Question" (master's thesis, Brigham Young University, 1982).

Temple initiates often received the sacrament intended to give them access into the "celestial" kingdom of heaven at the hands of Brigham Young, who spent night and day in the temple performing those rites for Latter-day Saints preparing to flee the city.[8] Upon entering the "celestial room" that represented their future salvation, initiates were confronted with a wall of portraits. In the center, the huge painting of Young stood before them. Painted by Selah Van Sickle, the image portrayed Young almost life-sized with his hand resting atop "The Book of the Law of the Lord." Begun under Joseph Smith, the book contained revelations, journal entries, and financial contributions to the church. Having one's name recorded inside was a significant recognition of faithfulness and a promise of eternal reward.[9] Also on the table were the Book of Mormon and the "History of Joseph Smith." The painting's message was clear: those who hoped to enter heaven must do so with the consent of Brigham Young. His authority was not only derived from the volumes on the table but was also manifest in his ability to interpret and even edit them.

Conspicuously absent from the room where the painting hung was a prominent image of the church's founding prophet. Paintings of other church leaders adorned the walls and cloth partitions, including Hyrum and two of Heber C. Kimball and George A. Smith, but there were none of Joseph Smith. Jill Major has argued that bad feelings between Young and Smith's widow Emma precluded the inclusion of an oil painting of Joseph in her possession.[10] While this may indeed be the case and it is consistent with what we know of the deteriorating relationship between Brigham Young and Emma Smith, the absence of a prominent Joseph Smith portrait may also be explained in other ways. If Emma Smith was asked for the painting, her refusal may simply have been the act of a grieving widow holding onto a cherished memento of her dead husband. Perhaps more tellingly, the absence of a prominent depiction of Joseph Smith communicated a carefully crafted message from Brigham Young and the Quorum of the Twelve Apostles. After all, a new portrait of Smith could have been commissioned just as the picture of Young had been.

---

8. John G. Turner, *Brigham Young: Pioneer Prophet* (Cambridge, Massachusetts: Harvard University Press, 2012), 130.

9. Alex D. Smith and Andrew H. Hedges, "Joseph Smith's Nauvoo Journals," pp. 239–250 herein.

10. Jill C. Major, "Artworks in the Celestial Room of the First Nauvoo Temple," *BYU Studies* 41, no. 2 (2002): 56–58.

The lack of a prominent Joseph Smith portrait in the temple is not because he was unimportant. His legacy could be seen in the building itself, the books Young had pictured on the table in his own portrait, and especially in the map of Nauvoo which hung on the western partition.[11] The map bore the only image of Joseph Smith in the room, a small engraving based on a profile portrait by Sutcliffe Maudsley. Smith's portrait was not as important, however, as the city itself, which Young renamed the City of Joseph in 1845. Smith mattered in Young's post-martyrdom Nauvoo iconography, but he was dead and the room's images pointed to the present and the future, not the past. With the foundation laid by Joseph Smith, it was now Young and the Quorum of the Twelve Apostles who would lead the Latter-day Saints to complete the project Smith had begun to build Zion. Like most foundations, what Smith laid down before his death supported the structure above it and remained unseen until some crack developed that necessitated repair. Just such a crack developed in later years, as will be seen below.

Young's emphasis on apostolic succession was not shared by everyone, but he found a way to keep those who disagreed with him in check. While Young's portrait in the temple overtly portrayed the book on Joseph Smith's life as being closed (i.e., the volume of the "History of Joseph Smith" resting on the table), Sutcliffe Maudsley was likely busy producing copies of his earlier images of Joseph Smith for individual Latter-day Saints.[12] Another Latter-day Saint from outside the Young-led hierarchy, Philo Dibble, took it upon himself to commission a painting of Joseph Smith. Dibble believed his 128-square foot painting of the events at Carthage had received a divine commission, being inspired by a dream of the Smiths' murder. He relayed the dream along with what he thought was its meaning to Brigham Young, who reportedly said, "go ahead and I will assist you." Young gave Dibble two dollars, with which Dibble bought the canvas for his painting.[13]

Church leaders and other prominent Nauvoo citizens took an interest in the history being portrayed in Dibble's work, which was executed by artists Robert Campbell, William Major, and others. Dibble identified

---

11. George D. Smith, ed., *An Intimate Chronicle: The Journals of William Clayton* (Salt Lake City: Signature Books, 1991), 206.

12. Steven Bule, *From Calico Printer to Portrait Painter: Sutcliffe Maudsley Nauvoo Profilist* (Orem, Utah: A Better Place, 2002), 26.

13. Noel A. Carmack, "'One of the Most Interesting Sceneries that can be Found in Zion': Philo Dibble's Museum and Panorama," *Nauvoo Journal* (Fall 1997): 26.

Campbell, an English-born convert, as the chief designer of two paintings: the one of the Smiths' martyrdom and the other portraying Joseph Smith's last address to the Nauvoo Legion. To give their work more authenticity, Campbell and the other artists invited potential subjects to sit for portraits to be used in the larger work.[14] Nevertheless, he took some artistic license, depicting some individuals in the Nauvoo scene who were not present during the events portrayed or giving them more prominent positions than some felt they deserved.[15] Concerns about Dibble's paintings were raised, but they were sufficiently allayed by March 1848 that church leaders gave the paintings official sanction.[16]

By then, Dibble had already presented the paintings for public display in Nauvoo. While Van Sickle's portrait of Brigham Young dominated the liturgical center of the Mormon *ecclesia* at Nauvoo, the Masonic lodge room where the theocratic Council of Fifty met featured a painting of Joseph Smith. It was not a portrait of the living Smith, however, but a portrayal of his death. The common message in both Dibble's painting of Carthage and Van Sickle's portrait of Young was that Smith was gone and Young was in charge.

Dibble's paintings, which no longer survive, were to be included in a larger project portraying the history of Mormonism. In the early nineteenth century, the panorama was a popular art form in America and Europe and its American center was St. Louis, a frequent stop for riverboats carrying Latter-day Saints up and down the Mississippi River. Panoramists painted landscapes and portrayed historical events on long canvas scrolls which would be unrolled before audiences, sometimes simulating the experience of a riverboat cruise or a ride through a geographic location while a lecturer described the images. Dibble's two paintings do not appear to have ever been incorporated into a longer piece, but he often displayed them

14. Carmack, "'One of the Most Interesting Sceneries that can be Found in Zion,'" 27.

15. Hosea Stout recorded in his journal that several officers of the Legion met at the home of Joseph W. Coolidge on 18 September 1845 to discuss the painting and their objections to it. "The officers were dissatisfied," he wrote, "with the plan for Br. Dibble was about to put in the likeness of officers who were not present & also some men who were to be put in conspicuous places on the scenery who were not officers and moreover betrayed the prophet & patriarch to death & also other men who had disgraced their calling as officers to all of these things I made objections and declared I would not be seen portrayed in a group of such men for it was a disgrace to my children." See Juanita Brooks, ed., *On the Mormon Frontier: The Diary of Hosea Stout, 1844–1889*, 2 vols., 2nd ed. (Salt Lake City: University of Utah Press and Utah State Historical Society, 1982), 1:61.

16. Carmack, "'One of the Most Interesting Sceneries that can be Found in Zion,' 27–28.

when he lectured on early church history. By the time he retired from lecturing in 1885, he had gained some competition from other Mormon panoramists, notably the Danish painter C. C. A. Christensen.[17]

Light and Metal Plates

While the painted panorama was a popular medium for display to large audiences, the photographic technology available kept images small and unsuitable for large public displays or decoration. Photographers, notably the celebrity-photographer Mathew Brady of New York, would display them in elaborate galleries set up in their studios, which became fashionable gathering places. But the small size of the images made viewing by more than one or two persons at a time awkward or impossible.[18] Consequently, they were not used in the same way as the large paintings that decorated public spaces like the temple in Nauvoo. The art on the walls inside the temple apparently did not include photographs. Neither are there any known photographs of the interior. However, a few examples exist of photographs taken of the temple's exterior and of some of the men depicted in the paintings inside.

Photography studios were popping up all over the United States following two announcements in 1839 of processes to chemically fix photographic images on solid surfaces.[19] Frenchman Louis-Jacques-Mandé Daguerre and Englishman Henry Fox Talbot had independently developed processes after years of experimentation. While technologies capable of temporarily projecting images onto a solid surface had existed for decades, Daguerre and Fox Talbot's innovations established a method for a lasting image to be fixed more permanently. Daguerre sold the rights to his process to the French government, which made knowledge of it free to all. Consequently, Daguerre's invention soon spread to pique and satisfy public interest the world over, while Fox Talbot remains relatively unknown.

The number of photographers using modifications of Daguerre's process was multiplying rapidly in 1844, when Joseph and Hyrum Smith died at Carthage, Illinois. The images made from this process, which were

17. Carmack, "'One of the Most Interesting Sceneries that can be Found in Zion,'" 33–34.

18. Trachtenberg, *Reading American Photographs,* 39–43.

19. The word "fix" rather than "affix" is used here following the example of photographic historians. The term describes an image to stay in place rather than adhering the image on a surface.

created by projecting light onto chemically treated metal plates, came to be known as *daguerreotypes*. Daguerrean photographers set up shop in cities and towns throughout the United States. Where resident photographers were not established, itinerants filled in. Nauvoo's first known resident photographer, Lucian Rose Foster, arrived in 1844 and soon began plying his trade on Main Street, taking images of church leaders and common citizens of the city.[20] The daguerreotype was so new that Foster found it necessary to explain it in his advertising.[21]

Across the country, some viewed the new technology with suspicion or even contempt, disparaging daguerreotypes as lacking the essential characteristics of true art. Photography was an adjunct to art rather than art itself, and photographers were often considered more tradesmen than artists. Indeed, many of them had come from the trades before launching into their photographic ventures. The photograph's economy, novelty, fidelity, and size, however, made it a popular alternative to the miniature painting often created as a memento of a loved one.[22]

Regardless of artistic merit, Foster's daguerrean photographs provide an interesting view of life in Nauvoo and early post-martyrdom Mormonism. Unfortunately, few examples of Foster's work remain, thus the glimpses they provide are offered with little context within the entirety of his body of work. Several of the examples that do remain are copies rather than original images. These copies were made decades later, when a new emphasis had been given to the Joseph Smith era as discussed below. Yet, even knowing that the examples we have are copies, the original images are still notable for what they capture and are worthy of examination.

Foster captured what is perhaps the most iconic view of 1840s Nauvoo as seen in Figure 12.2. The original has been lost, but the image has survived as a copy by Utah photographer Charles W. Carter. While the foreground of the image is dominated by a small outhouse, the intended subject was undoubtedly the temple. Taken from the flats on the Mississippi floodplain, the image shows the temple perched above the city on the bluffs while the homes of Nauvoo's residents lie below. Although no residents appear in Foster's photograph, the image reveals a good deal about the city's population. In comparison to the temple, the homes that can be

20. The exact timing of Foster's arrival to Nauvoo is unclear.

21. "Miniature Likenesses," *Nauvoo Neighbor*, 14 August 1844, 3.

22. Trachtenberg, *Reading American Photographs*, 13–22.

FIGURE 12.2. Nauvoo, Illinois, circa 1846. Carte-de-visite by Charles W. Carter copied from daguerreotype attributed to Lucian Foster.

Church History Library, Salt Lake City.

seen are not grand, reflecting the fact that the people had sacrificed for the sake of their religion personal resources that could have been used to beautify or expand their own homes. Many of Nauvoo's residents had left nicer homes to heed the call to gather, and some had settled Nauvoo after being forced from one or more homes in Mormon settlements in Ohio and Missouri. Their religion, like their temple and their city, was begun by Joseph Smith and was by then under the leadership of Brigham Young.

Young was himself photographed by Lucian Foster. Holzapfel and Shupe believe Young's journal positions the incident as occurring on 31 January 1846.[23] On that day Young recorded that "About noon—[he] Set while the artificial-est immitated the works of Nature from my Person."[24] Young's language here somewhat parallels Foster's in his advertisement in the *Nauvoo Neighbor*, describing the process as "a combination of nature and art."[25] Like the image of Nauvoo, Young's portrait (Figure 12.3), has survived only as a copy, this one being made about 1934, when it was published in the *Deseret News* after Young's daughter allowed it to be copied by the Church Historian's Office.[26] The location of the original is now unknown.

The photograph is an interesting study of both the man and the state of contemporaneous photographic practice. Photography manuals that circulated among the craft's practitioners advised them to collaborate with their subjects to determine pose, dress, and the use of props to communicate a subject's character and position in society. Foster's image of Young depicts a confident man dressed in a dark suit, wearing a tall hat, and holding a cane. The suit itself is unremarkable other than its selection as an obvious effort to present a respectable appearance; the hat and cane, on the other hand, lead the viewer to ponder their import. In particular, one wonders about the cane's provenance. After the death of the Smith brothers, canes were made from the rough pine used to make temporary coffins in which the bodies were transported from Carthage to Nauvoo. The canes were in

23. Richard Neitzel Holzapfel and R. Q. Shupe, *Brigham Young: Images of a Mormon Prophet* (Provo, Utah: Religious Studies Center, Brigham Young University, 2000), 91.

24. Brigham Young, Journal, Brigham Young Office Files, 1832–1878, CHL, 31 January 1846.

25. "Miniature Likenesses," *Nauvoo Neighbor*, 14 August 1844, 3.

26. The *Deseret News*'s writers, who presumably got the date from the Church Historian's Office staff, who got the information from Young's daughter, reported the date of the image between the fall of 1844 and the spring of 1845. ("Brigham: The Man and His Work," *Deseret News*, 28 July 1934, 2.)

FIGURE 12.3. Brigham Young, ca. 1845. Copy of daguerreotype by Lucian Foster. Church History Library, Salt Lake City.

a sense reliquaries, as they contained the hair of the fallen prophet in their handles, and were given to Young and others of the Smiths' close associates. Young's hat also calls to mind the old white hat which Joseph Smith was known to have worn in his early prophethood and in which he placed the seer stones he used to translate the Book of Mormon and receive other early revelations. Brigham Young is not known to have used a seer stone, but the hat itself was, perhaps, an indicator of Young's assumption of the role of seer for the church. Or, maybe, they were nothing more than a cane and a hat like any other.

FIGURE 12.4. Willard and Jennetta Richards family, 1845. Daguerreotype by Lucian Foster.
Church History Library, Salt Lake City.

The man perhaps best positioned to see Brigham Young's assumption of leadership was Willard Richards—Young's fellow apostle, the official church historian, and Joseph Smith's personal secretary. Richards's devotion had led him to accompany the doomed prophet to Carthage Jail, where he attempted to beat back the mobbers' guns with a heavy cane only to watch his friends die in a hailstorm of bullets. Following the deaths of the Smiths, Richards threw his support to Brigham Young and his fellow apostles, and was another church leader photographed by Lucian Foster in Nauvoo. Richards, his wife Jennetta, and their four-year-old son Heber John sat for a portrait by Foster on 26 March 1845 as seen in Figure 12.4.[27] The casual observer might see in the portrait a remarkably affectionate

27. Willard Richards, Journal, 26 March 1845, in Kent F. Richards, ed., *A Family of Faith: An Intimate View of Church History through the Journals of Three Generations of Apostles* (Salt Lake City: Deseret Book, 2013), 59.

family for the time period, with Jennetta sitting on Willard's lap and both parents holding the hands of the perhaps-fidgety young boy. But knowing the family's history, Clair Noall has observed that Jennetta's sitting on Willard's lap with her head on his shoulder seems to convey a sense of "he's mine." Their Mormon faith had caused not only months of separation as Willard had left Jennetta behind to hurry toward Nauvoo, where he stayed for months assisting Joseph Smith, but during that time Willard had also been initiated into Mormonism's secret plural marriage practices.

The collection of surviving Willard Richards portraits includes not only the image of him with Jennetta and Heber John but others demonstrating what he held most dear. While Jennetta is pictured with her head resting on Willard's shoulder in one portrait, Willard is in another portrait of the same period resting his head on a cane—the cane occupying the place of Jennetta (see Figure 9.2 on p. 235 herein). The same cane or a very similar one features prominently in several other pictures as well. By itself, the presence of a cane in Richards's photograph is unremarkable. Canes were common fashion accessories, and many photographs show men holding them. Yet Richards's retention of this one cane and his posture toward it seems almost affectionate. This particular cane appears to be special to him and may have been a gift from his beloved Joseph. A very similar-looking cane appears in a sketch of Joseph Smith in Springfield, Illinois, by Benjamin West in January 1843. That the cane was so prominently photographed with Richards suggests the object's treasured status, perhaps a relic of his dead friend and prophet. In addition, some believed the cane held special power either directly through its connection to Joseph Smith or indirectly through the priesthood power of the church he established. It became not only a symbol of Richards's and Smith's power but an instrument of it. In 1857, three years after Richards's death, Heber C. Kimball discussed Richards laying the cane on the sick and healing them by means of the relic.[28]

In some cases, the photographs themselves were relics. The technology of early photographs ensured that each one was unique. Each one-of-a-kind object could only be duplicated by photographing it over again. Doing so resulted in not only a loss in fidelity but also in reversing the images, as daguerrean photographs reversed their images horizontally across their vertical axis. Beyond their uniqueness which could endear them to their

28. Heber C. Kimball, 15 March 1857, in *Journal of Discourses,* 26 vols. (Liverpool: Various publishers, 1855–1886), 4:294.

owners, the small size of early photographs allowed them to be discreetly kept as personal keepsakes. Often cherished by a lover, family member, or dear friend, their size allowed them to be tucked away in a pocket or drawer to remember someone who was away or deceased. For example, the photograph of Brigham Young taken by Lucian Foster in Nauvoo was given to his wife, Clara Decker Young, and remained with the family after the deaths of both Brigham and Clara.[29]

Imagery in Early Utah

Young would be photographed again in December 1850, this time by Marsena Cannon, a native of Rochester, New Hampshire, who had joined with the Mormons in 1844 while operating a photography studio in Boston, Massachusetts.[30] Cannon left Boston and arrived in Salt Lake in 1850, just two months before photographing Young for the first of many times over the ensuing decade. Cannon would become a mainstay of Salt Lake photography during the 1850s and partnered with other photographers, including Louis Rice Chaffin and Charles Roscoe Savage. Many of the early photographs taken in Utah that are often attributed to Cannon may, in fact, be the work of these partners or their competitors. Cannon left Salt Lake for a colonizing mission to southern Utah in 1861 and returned in 1864. By then, several other photographers had established themselves in Salt Lake, and Cannon only briefly reopened his studio.[31]

The rise in local competition in Salt Lake City reflected a national trend: Photography was an increasingly popular novelty throughout the country. Many tried their hand as photographers, and even more had their "likenesses" taken by them. The public demand to see photographs was high. Without a means of publishing photographs in mass media, however, images were etched into wood, stone, or metal plates which were then used to print the images in books and newspapers. These

29. "Brigham Young—The Man and His Work," *Deseret News,* 28 July 1934, 2. The caption in this article states the image was given to Young by his wife Clara Decker Young, but as Holzapfel and Shupe propose, this is probably in error. More likely, Young gave the image to his wife (Holzapfel and Shupe, *Images of a Mormon Prophet,* 91).

30. No familial relationship is known to exist between Marsena Cannon and the author of this chapter.

31. Peter E. Palmquist and Thomas R. Kailbourn, eds., *Pioneer Photographers of the Far West: A Biographical Dictionary, 1840–1865* (Stanford, California: Stanford University Press, 2000), 148–50.

mass-produced images, which could be of varying quality and fidelity, could then be effectively used and exploited for different purposes, such as political propaganda.

Adapting Genres

As national tensions rose immediately prior to the American Civil War, some citizens employed the available technology to illustrate the nation's shared history. In 1850 the New York photographer Mathew Brady published his *Gallery of Illustrious Americans* featuring daguerreotypes of prominent, carefully selected American citizens rendered as lithographs by Francis D'Avignon.[32] Accompanying the images were short biographies penned by C. Edwards Lester, cataloging the men's public service and virtue. Amid the sectional crises which preceded the American Civil War, the photographer, the engraver, and the writer collaborated to emphasize Americans' common citizenship over their regional factionalisms. While *Gallery of Illustrious Americans* was an adaptation of the popular illustrated biographical encyclopedias of the time, it had a distinctively political reason for its publication, seeking to bolster national identity in a time of crisis.[33]

Brigham Young and other church leaders likewise adopted the genre of the illustrated biography for their own purposes. As seen in Figure 12.5, the apostles who were in Utah sat for a series of photographs by Marsena Cannon, which were then sent to England to be engraved by the English artist Frederick Piercy. Piercy's engravings were then printed on a broadside containing a picture of each member of the church's First Presidency and Quorum of the Twelve Apostles along with each man's signature and date of birth.[34] The publication, which did not mention Joseph Smith by name, clearly illustrated a continuity in the church he founded. It was well known among church members that Smith had helped organize the Quorum of the Twelve Apostles and that he had personally appointed several of its living members. As it had done in the Nauvoo temple, Brigham

32. Mathew Brady, Francis D'Avignon, and C. Edwards Lester, *Gallery of Illustrious Americans, Containing the Portraits and Biographical Sketches of Twenty-Four of the Most Eminent Citizens of the American Republic* (New York: Brady, D'Avignon and Company, 1850).

33. Trachtenberg, *Reading American Photographs,* 45–52.

34. Frederick Piercy and Marsena Cannon, broadside (Liverpool: Samuel W. Richards and Marsena Cannon, 1853).

FIGURE 12.5. Broadside of the First Presidency and Quorum of the Twelve Apostles. Published by Samuel W. Richards and Marsena Cannon in Liverpool England, 1853. The copy shown here includes the updated image of Brigham Young added in 1863.

Church History Library, Salt Lake City.

Young's image took the place of prominence, emphasizing his preeminent authority.

That the broadside was published and distributed in England is significant to understanding its purpose and milieu. Brigham Young and many of the other apostles had served as missionaries in Britain as early as 1837 under a charge from Joseph Smith.[35] But by 1853, a significant number of British converts from that era had quit the country to gather with the main body of the church in North America. Few of those left in Britain had ever met or seen the church's most senior leaders. For those in Britain as well as far-flung locales in the American Mountain West, where some copies found their way, the pictures provided a personal connection with the church's leaders and forged a common emotional bond for church members across the world, much like the images in *Illustrious Americans* were meant to do for antebellum Americans.

Further comparisons between the broadside of the apostles and *Illustrious Americans* are noteworthy. Lester's text identified his subjects in *Illustrious Americans* as "those American citizens, who . . . have rendered the most signal service to the Nation, since the death of the Father of the Republic."[36] Washington and the first generation of Americans were gone. Similarly, Joseph Smith was gone, and although Young and many of the other apostles pictured in the broadside knew Smith and had been appointed by him, Young's presence at the top of the page instead of Smith's clearly illustrates that a second generation had taken the reins. The apostleship of the men pictured had been conferred upon them after years of their own "signal service" to the church.[37]

Sales of the broadside must not have met expectations, however, and surplus copies still occupied the shelves at the British mission office more than ten years later. Brigham Young wrote to George Q. Cannon,[38] the mission president in England, instructing him to reissue the 1853 broadside with the pictures of the First Presidency and the Twelve Apostles. In

---

35. On the 1837–1841 mission see James B. Allen, Ronald K. Esplin, and David J. Whittaker, *Men with a Mission: The Quorum of the Twelve Apostles in the British Isles* (Salt Lake City: Deseret Book, 1992).

36. Quoted in Trachtenberg, *Reading American Photographs*, 49.

37. D. Michael Quinn, *The Mormon Hierarchy: Origins of Power* (Salt Lake City: Signature Books, 1994), 251.

38. George Q. Cannon was the older brother of the author's great-great grandfather Angus Munn Cannon and has no known familial relationship with the photographer Marsena Cannon.

their attempts to assert their apostolic authority as the leadership of the church, Young and his associates complicated the historical narrative the broadside portrayed. The men pictured had aged during the intervening decade; two had died and were replaced by new apostles.[39] Young, however, only instructed that one picture should be changed—his own. A new engraving was made of a now-bearded Young photographed by Charles W. Carter and pasted over the clean-shaven original on existing copies. Young instructed that individual copies of his new portrait should also be sent to Utah, where old copies could be similarly updated.[40]

By updating Young's image and not the others, the broadside may have communicated the importance of Young as first among his brethren. As he had done in Nauvoo, Young used imagery to assert his authority and that of the other apostles. And just as it had been in Nauvoo, Young's image was the most important one. Further demonstrating Young's preeminence, individual copies of his updated image were even printed as far afield as Dundee, Scotland. But the 1853 publication date remained unaltered on the broadside, as did the credits to Marsena Cannon and Frederick Piercy for their artistic contributions, although neither of them was responsible for the new image of Young. Thus, with the incorrect date attached to the new Young portrait, an inaccurate picture of the past was created, potentially affecting later scholarship and highlighting the importance of careful research regarding images.

Resurgence and Divergence in Historical Interests

The broadside's 1850s context was a period of renewed interest in the church's history and its connection to Joseph Smith, which continued after Young's death. Its publication coincided with a resurgence in historical interest which brought to the fore marked differences between Young's *de facto* official vision of the past and that of others. In 1853, work recommenced on the church history begun under Joseph Smith, while at the same time Apostle Orson Pratt was preparing to publish a history dictated by Joseph Smith's mother, Lucy Mack Smith. Pratt had not informed his apostolic associates of his plans, and Brigham Young's reaction to Pratt's

39. Willard Richards died in Salt Lake City on 11 March 1854 and was succeeded as second counselor in the First Presidency by Jedediah M. Grant on 7 April. Grant was never ordained to the apostleship. Parley P. Pratt was killed in Arkansas on 13 May 1857 but was not replaced until George Q. Cannon was ordained an apostle on 23 August 1860.

40. Holzapfel and Shupe, *Brigham Young: Images of a Mormon Prophet*, 164–65.

publication and Lucy Smith's version of events curtailed the history's reach and set in motion a series of events which lasted more than a decade.

As others have noted, the reaction to Mother Smith's history came from a place of insecurity on the part of Brigham Young and the apostles. The reasons for that insecurity seemed to be multiplying. Lucy's history focused on the Smith family and appeared to bolster the claims of familial succession that would reach their culmination in 1860, when Joseph Smith's son Joseph III took the reins of a newly reorganized church in the American Midwest. Lucy Smith's history also failed to mention the practice of polygamy by her son Joseph and others. When Joseph III took the leadership of the reorganized Church of Jesus Christ of Latter Day Saints (RLDS), it dashed the hopes of those who dreamed of Joseph Smith's sons taking up his mantle in Utah.[41] Joseph III further insulted the Utah church by committing himself and his new church to a longstanding denial that Joseph Smith Jr. ever had anything to do with polygamy.[42]

Efforts by the Church Historian's Office and Others

Responding to these challenges in the 1850s and 1860s, Brigham Young and his fellow apostles again turned to images to help legitimize the present, as they had done in 1840s Nauvoo. However, a renewed focus on the past can also be detected in the 1860s images. Whereas in Nauvoo the present trumped the past in a sort of natural progression from Smith to Young, and little emphasis was given to Joseph Smith, church leaders' later efforts self-consciously emphasized their ties to the founding prophet.

Under Joseph Smith's cousin, church historian George A. Smith, clerks working in the Church Historian's Office collected hundreds of photographs of Mormons who were connected to the early days of the movement. After George A.'s death in 1875, the photographs remained with his family and were added to and divided among family members. Two large collections that have found their way back into the holdings of the LDS Church History Library via George A. Smith's descendants can be traced to the efforts of the Historian's

41. The word "reorganized" was officially added to the name of the church in 1872. In 2001, the church again changed its name to become Community of Christ.

42. Jan Shipps, *Mormonism: The Story of a New Religious Tradition* (Urbana: University of Chicago Press, 1985), 91–106; Turner, *Brigham Young*, 335–37.

Office.[43] The emphasis on history in the photographs is clearly represented, emphasizing the connection between the church under Brigham Young and the church under Joseph Smith.

The images are mostly small albumen prints on paper known as *cartes de visite*. The albumen print was several technological generations removed from the Nauvoo-era daguerreotype, in a time when the field was advancing quickly. The ability to print photographs made from reusable negatives revolutionized photography. Photographs were no longer one-of-a-kind mementos exchanged between close family members and loved ones. Identical copies could be printed multiple times and distributed broadly. Images of friends, family, and prominent citizens were printed on paper and pasted onto cardstock. Although several standardized sizes were available, the carte de visite was the most popular at about 2 ½ by 4 inches. They were commonly collected in albums kept by individuals, families, and, like in the case of the Church Historian's Office, institutions.[44]

The studios most often credited for the images collected by the Historian's Office, as well as other collections in Utah from the time, are those of Edward Martin, Charles W. Carter, and partners Charles R. Savage and George M. Ottinger. The first of these to come to Utah was Edward Martin, who arrived as the captain of a tragedy-stricken handcart company in 1856. The George A. Smith-era Church Historian's Office photographs with the earliest dates (1856) are credited to Martin's studio. But because Martin did not begin advertising a photography department as part of his business until 1865, it appears he was engaged in the common practice of copying others' work for resale. He is not known to have ever actually operated a camera himself, but hired men like John Olsen instead.[45] Many of

---

43. These two collections are titled the "Bathsheba W. Bigler Smith Photograph Collection, circa 1865–1900" and the "George A. Smith Historical Photograph Collection, circa 1862–1873, 2003."

44. For a general history of photography, see Beaumont Newhall's classic *The History of Photography: From 1839 to the Present* (New York: Museum of Modern Art, 1984).

45. In 1866 Olsen was reportedly working as the "chief" of the photographic department, indicating at least some of the images bearing Martin's name may not have been taken by either Martin or Olsen. Other photography studios at the time, notably that of Mathew Brady, also employed mostly anonymous camera operators, whose work bore the names of their employers rather than their own. Martin's photographic department was only part of his larger business operations, which included sign and carriage painting as well as selling a large stock of merchanise. See Peter E. Palmquist and Thomas R. Kailbourn, *Pioneer Photographers of the Far West: A Biographical Dictionary, 1840–1865* (Stanford, California: Stanford University Press, 2000), 382–83.

Martin's photographs in the Smith collections are dated from 1867, when Martin advertised that he was "selling Card and other Pictures at Extremely Low Prices."[46] Among his inventory were "City and Mountain Views, also Portraits of Prominent Men For Sale."[47] The last of the dated photographs attributed to Martin's studio is dated in 1869, though he is thought to have included photography as a part of his business until about 1872.[48]

The next of the photographers to arrive in Utah was Charles Savage, who arrived in 1862 and two days later began a brief partnership with Marsena Cannon. His later partnership with the painter George Ottinger officially lasted about a decade, beginning in 1862, though Ottinger ceased playing an active role in the partnership around 1868 to focus on his painting. Savage continued as a photographer until around 1896.[49] In 1870 he formed the Pioneer Art Gallery, and upon moving in 1875 he renamed it the Art Bazaar, which burned in 1883, destroying all his negatives. A second fire destroyed the last two and a half decades of his negatives in 1911, two years after his death in 1909.[50]

Part of Savage's legacy was Charles Carter, who arrived in Utah in 1864 and almost immediately began working for Savage and Ottinger, with whom he remained for two years. After leaving Savage and Ottinger, Carter worked alone at times and sometimes with partners or assistants. Perhaps more than the others, he saw the historical utility of photography and copied photographs of important scenes taken by other photographers. It was he who reproduced the Lucian Foster image of Nauvoo and its temple on the hill. In March 1906 he sold his stock prints and nearly 2000 negatives to the LDS Bureau of Information.[51] Several of Carter's portraits were included in the Historian's Office collection made under George A. Smith's direction. Among them are several photographs of Joseph Smith's polygamous wives.

---

46. *Deseret News,* 6 August 1867, cited in Palmquist and Kailbourn, *Pioneer Photographers of the Far West,* 382.

47. *Deseret News,* 6 August 1867, cited in Palmquist and Kailbourn, *Pioneer Photographers of the Far West,* 382.

48. Palmquist and Kailbourn, *Pioneer Photographers of the Far West,* 382–83.

49. Palmquist and Kailbourn, *Pioneer Photographers of the Far West,* 476–79.

50. Palmquist and Kailbourn, *Pioneer Photographers of the Far West,* 476–79.

51. Palmquist and Kailbourn, *Pioneer Photographers of the Far West,* 156–57. More than 900 of Carter's images of nineteenth-century Mormonism are currently housed at the LDS CHL.

Documenting Early Mormon Polygamy

There can be no doubt that the most prominent feature of 1860s Mormonism in the minds of the general public was polygamy. Rumors of secret polygamous marriages had circulated under Joseph Smith, but under Brigham Young's leadership the church in Utah publicly announced it as a doctrine and practice in 1852. It was anathema to the majority of Americans and particularly to Joseph Smith's eldest son, Joseph Smith III, who had grown to adulthood in Nauvoo after Young and his followers had left for the Rocky Mountains. Nevertheless, Young, who claimed to have been repulsed by polygamy himself upon first learning of it, was fully converted by the time he took the reins of church leadership and emphasized its connection to his beloved Joseph.

As RLDS missionaries crisscrossed Mormon settlements in the West preaching against polygamy and denying Joseph Smith's connection to it, LDS leaders under the direction of Brigham Young collected evidence of the elder Smith's introduction of polygamy in opposition to the claims of the Reorganized church. Joseph Smith's polygamous wives swore out affidavits describing their involvement and their relationships with him.[52] Those affidavits remain a useful and oft-cited resource for piecing together the puzzle of Mormon polygamy in Nauvoo. Less well known is the series of photographs collected by the Church Historian's Office staff, which predate the affidavits and include notations by clerks identifying the women pictured and often giving the dates and briefly sketching the circumstances of their marriages to Smith.

Desdemona Fullmer, as photographed in Figure 12.6 and 12.7, is one such woman whose photographs not only tie her to Joseph Smith as a polygamous wife but also connect Brigham Young as a trusted and authorized participant in Nauvoo's secret, inner circle of polygamists. Fullmer's name is written on the back of one photograph of her, including the last name Smith and a note: "wife of Joseph Prophet."[53] The verso of the photograph in Figure 12.6 bears a note that she was "sealed to Jos. Smith 1841. December by Brigham Young" (see Figure 12.7).[54] This inscription not only

52. Joseph F. Smith, Affidavits about Celestial Marriage, 1869–1915, CHL.

53. Edward Martin, Photograph of Desdemona Fullmer Smith, 1867, Bathsheba W. Bigler Smith Photograph Collection, ca. 1865–1900, CHL.

54. Edward Martin, Photograph of Desdemona Fullmer, 1867, George A. Smith Historical Photograph Collection, ca. 1862–1873, 2003, CHL.

FIGURE 12.6 AND FIGURE 12.7. Desdemona Fullmer Smith, 1867. Photograph by Edward Martin.

Church History Library, Salt Lake City.

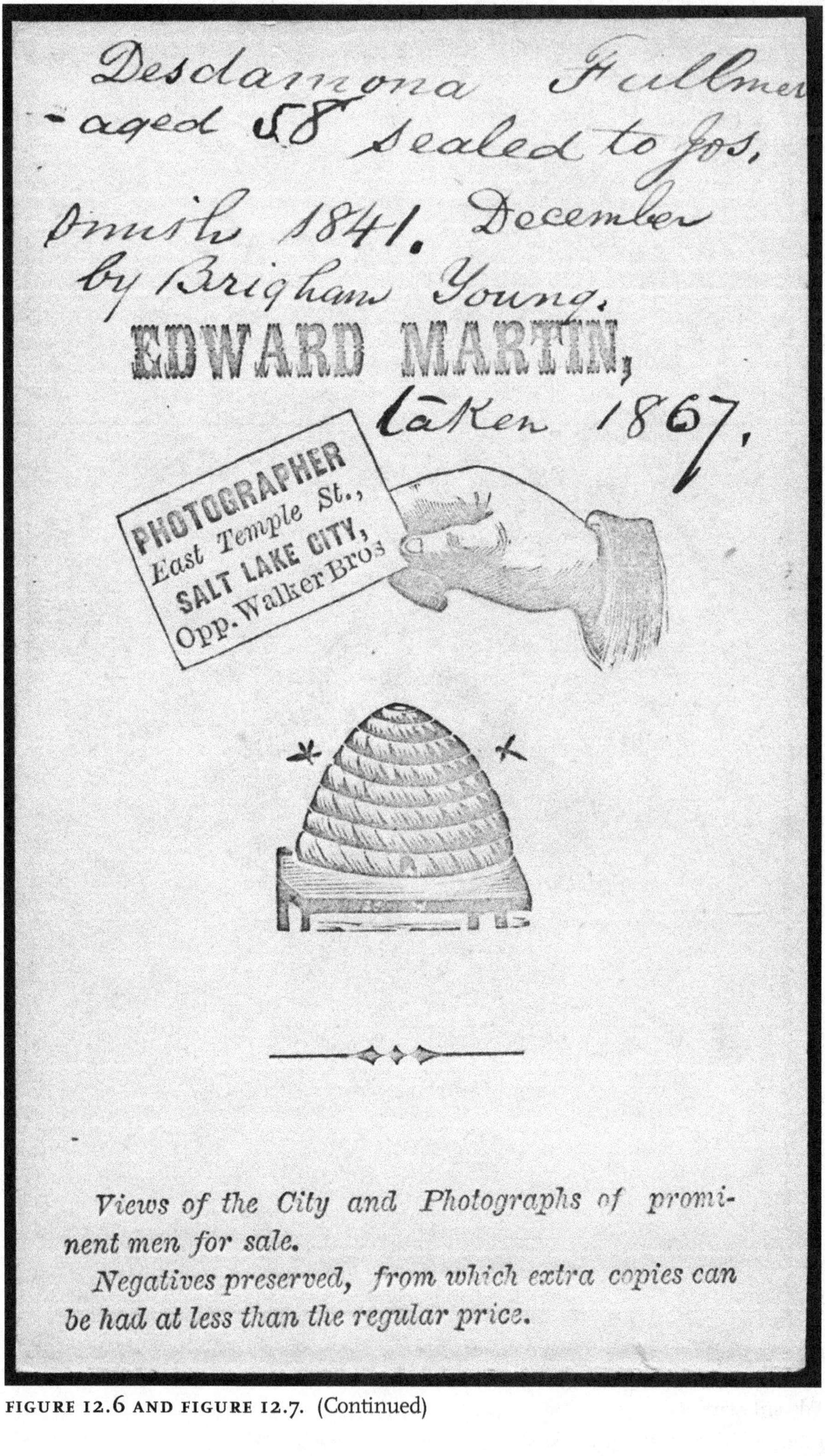

Desdamona Fullmer aged 58 sealed to Jos. Smith 1841. December by Brigham Young.

EDWARD MARTIN, taken 1867.

PHOTOGRAPHER
East Temple St.,
SALT LAKE CITY,
Opp. Walker Bros

Views of the City and Photographs of prominent men for sale.

Negatives preserved, from which extra copies can be had at less than the regular price.

FIGURE 12.6 AND FIGURE 12.7. (Continued)

notes the important fact of her sealing to Joseph Smith but also Brigham Young's intimate connection to both the practice and Joseph Smith at that early date. It is significant that Joseph Smith would turn to Young to perform the sealing, as the power to do so was held by very few, very close associates. Young's involvement also establishes a precedent for his future claims to authorize new plural marriages and take the leadership of the church.

Precise information about any of these women's relationships with their common husband is unknown. As secret polygamous wives, any intimate interactions would likely have been brief and irregular. Perhaps they hoped for a time when they could live out their relationship openly. However, Joseph's life was cut short and the women could not mourn their husband publicly. For wives Sarah Whitney Kimball and Lucy Walker, their personal grief in losing their prophet husband may have found some expression in the annotations "widow of Joseph Smith" included on the reverse side of a few of the photographs taken years later.[55]

Just as he assumed Smith's ecclesiastical roles, Young assumed the role of husband to many of his predecessor's polygamous wives, a fact which is indicated on some of the pictures. For example, Emily Partridge is given the married names of both Smith and Young on her portrait and identified as a "wife of Joseph Smith the prophet."[56] Though her surname as a wife of Brigham Young is included, her marriage to Young is not explicitly noted, perhaps because her relationship with the second church president was, by then, in the open. In any case, the larger point was her polygamous marriage to Smith. For those in Nauvoo's inner circle of church leaders and polygamists, Young's marriage to several of his predecessor's widows may have been perceived as one sign of his successorship. This was poignantly illustrated in ceremonies performed in the Nauvoo temple in which Young acted as proxy for Joseph Smith ratifying Smith's pre-temple sealings to several of his plural wives. The ceremonies were then followed by the women's sealing to Young for time.[57]

---

55. Edward Martin, Photograph of Sarah Whitney Kimball, Bathsheba Smith Photograph Collection; Edward Martin, Photograph of Lucy Walker Smith, Bathsheba Smith Photograph Collection.

56. Savage and Ottinger, Photograph of Emily Partridge, George A. Smith Historical Photograph Collection.

57. Turner, *Brigham Young,* 134, 137.

It should be noted that more than twenty years after Smith's death, the photographs of his wives and other associates show a more mature Mormonism than existed during Smith's lifetime. By then middle-aged or older, the men and women we see in the photographs are in very different stages of their lives. Many of the wives were quite young at the time of their marriages, and the photographs do not reflect the image of child brides conjured up in the minds of those who learn how young some of them in fact were. Similarly, Smith's other once-young associates, who preached his radical new reinterpretation of Christianity, had grown older too. Perhaps more than anything else, this fact demonstrates a central argument of this chapter, which is that the images created after Joseph Smith's death do more to illustrate the circumstances surrounding their sometimes much-later creation than the events they were intended to illustrate. Both Mormons and Mormonism had changed considerably in the intervening decades.

Claiming the First Generation of Mormonism

Other examples of the maturation that occurred are the photographs of two of Joseph Smith's earliest supporters, David Whitmer and Martin Harris. Whitmer was born in 1805, the same year as Joseph Smith. However, the enduring image is of a much older man—the man we see in photographs like the one George A. Smith received from Lydia Ann Cole on 2 July 1869. The photograph gives no indication of the photographer or where it was taken, but the verso notation states the picture was taken in 1868—thirty years after Whitmer's excommunication, while he was living in Richmond, Missouri. The photograph seen in Figure 12.8 was certainly included in the Church Historian's Office collection because of his connection to early Mormonism: "He is one of the <3> witnesses to the Book of Mormon" a clerk noted on the back as seen in Figure 12.9, though he was never a member of Brigham Young's brand of Mormonism.[58]

Whitmer's fellow Book of Mormon witness Martin Harris, who also left Mormonism under Smith but eventually returned under Young's administration, was also included in the collection. Although the notation on the back of an 1870 photograph of Harris gives no detail of his involvement with the Book of Mormon translation and other events from early church

58. George A. Smith Historical Photograph Collection.

FIGURE 12.8 AND FIGURE 12.9. David Whitmer, 1868. Photographer unknown. Church History Library, Salt Lake City.

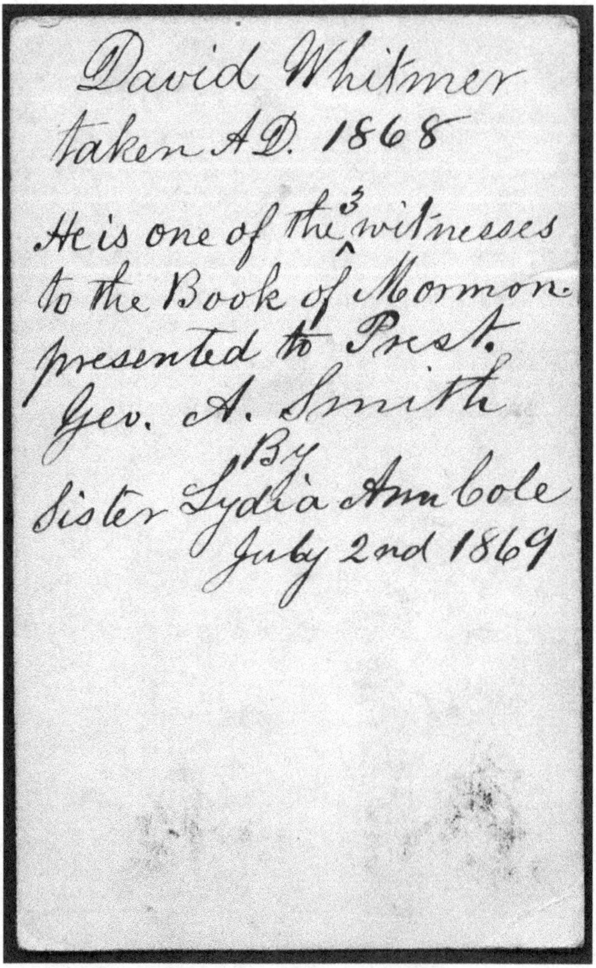

David Whitmer
taken A.D. 1868

He is one of the 3 witnesses
to the Book of Mormon
presented to Prest.
Geo. A. Smith
By
Sister Lydia Ann Cole
July 2nd 1869

FIGURE 12.8 AND FIGURE 12.9. (Continued)

history, the reason for his inclusion in the collection would have been obvious to many contemporaries. Not only was Harris connected to the Book of Mormon translation and early Mormonism, he married Brigham Young's niece Caroline after the death of his first wife, Lucy.[59]

Other early church members who never rose to high office or broadly recognized historical prominence were also included in the collection

59. The author is indebted to Jana Riess for this insight. Caroline Young Harris was the daughter of Brigham Young's brother John and John's wife Theodocia Kimball.

of photographs of George A. Smith's Historian's Office. This collection was never intended to be a representative sample of Mormons loyal to Brigham Young, though. Even the most average of Mormons included were not unremarkable in their sacrifice or connections to early events and prominent early members. Photographs of Freeborn DeMill and his wife Anna, the daughter of Joseph Sr. and Polly Peck Knight, each bear their names and a simple notation—"baptized 1830"—the continuity of these long-suffering rank-and-file members' church membership being the notable criterion for their inclusion.[60] The inclusion of these photographs in the collection emphasizes a broader connection between the Mormonism of Young's followers and the early days and trials of the movement under Joseph Smith. The DeMills had been members of the branch of the church from Colesville, New York—a wellspring of early converts. The DeMills briefly settled in Jackson County, Missouri, along with other Colesville Saints, in 1831; removed to Clay County in December 1833; relocated to Far West in 1837; and were finally driven out of the state with other church members in 1839, when they settled in Quincy, Illinois. In September 1850 they arrived in Salt Lake City, and less than two months later they left for Manti, where Anne died in 1878 and Freeborn died in 1881.[61]

Others who sacrificed were also included, along with explicit notes of their trials. Amanda Smith was noted to be both a "widow of Warren Smith who was killed at Haun's Mill" and to have been "sealed to Joseph the Seer." She was also noted to have one son killed and another wounded at Hawn's Mill.[62] Dimick Huntington was noted to have fought in the battle of Crooked River during the Missouri troubles.[63] Alexander McRae was for "six months a fellow prisoner with Jos. Smith in Mo."[64] The honor of being driven from Jackson County was also noted on the back of a photograph of Levi Jackman, who, in addition, was identified as being a member of the

60. Edward Martin, Photograph of Freeborn DeMill and Edward Martin, Photograph of Anne Knight DeMill, both in George A. Smith Historical Photograph Collection.

61. "Died," *Deseret News*, 7 August 1878, 432; "Obituary," *Deseret News*, 16 February 1881, 48.

62. Edward Martin, Photograph of Amanda Smith, George A. Smith Historical Photograph Collection.

63. Savage and Ottinger, Photograph of Dimick B. Huntington, 2 April 1867, George A. Smith Historical Photograph Collection.

64. Photograph of Alexander McRae, George A. Smith Historical Photograph Collection.

high council in Missouri and having fought at the Battle of the Blue, when the Mormon settlement at Blue River was attacked by a group of Missouri vigilantes in November 1833.[65]

Certainly, not every picture in the Church Historian's Office was meant to bolster Brigham Young's claims to leadership. Nor was every picture taken in early Utah meant to be included in the church historian's collection. However, understanding the milieu helps in understanding the pictures that were taken and preserved.

Claiming the Image and the Memory of Joseph Smith

Others in Utah also collected the popular carte de visite photographs. The Pack family acquired an album in the 1860s and continued filling it with photographs until around 1900. It is uncertain whether the current arrangement reflects the original positions of the images. However, if the arrangement has not been significantly changed, the prominence given to certain images by their order within the album may be significant. The album begins with photographs of LDS general authorities almost exclusively from Edward Martin's studio. The album itself may have been purchased from Martin with the church leaders' portraits already inserted. Interestingly, the first two "photographs" are two rare images of Joseph and Hyrum Smith, also baring the imprimatur of Edward Martin's photography studio. The Smiths were long dead before Martin set up his studio, so these photographs were not based upon the living men but their death masks.[66] Masks of both the living and the dead were often made at the time in preparation for the creation of a sculpture or other portrait. Masks of the Smith brothers were made by Nauvoo residents George Cannon and Ariah Coates Brower before the men were buried.[67] In Martin's pictures, clothing, hair, and even eyes have been painted on the faces immortalized by Cannon and Brower's castings. Martin advertised that his store on East Temple Street in Salt Lake City (today's Main Street) sold "everything that can't be found anywhere else." Indeed, only this one example of these particular images, seen in Figures 12.10, has been found.

65. Sutterley Brothers, Photograph of Levi Jackman, Bathsheba Smith Photograph Collection.

66. Someone in Martin's studio may have also copied the image from another artist's work.

67. George Cannon was the father of George Q. Cannon, already mentioned, and the great-great-great grandfather of the author.

FIGURE 12.10. Joseph Smith and Hyrum Smith portraits made from death masks. Pack family photograph album, circa 1860s–1900.
Church History Library, Salt Lake City.

Despite these images' apparent unpopularity, their creation is notable. The two men were unquestionably deceased when these likenesses were produced in Martin's studio, but they had in a way been brought to life through the medium of photography. Unlike painters or sculptors who could reach back into an imagined or real past to produce their art, photographers (at least in theory) could only reproduce what actually appeared before their cameras. Therefore, for a moment, Joseph and Hyrum Smith were made to appear as though they had been reanimated and transported from their graves in Nauvoo to the photographer's studio in Salt Lake City, exclusively among the followers of Brigham Young. Nevertheless, George A. Smith and the staff of the Church Historian's Office do not seem to have been interested in the eerie depiction.

As a cousin of Joseph Smith, George A. Smith may have known the founding prophet longer and more intimately than almost anyone else in the Utah church. His choices of which pictures of Joseph to include, as well as which to omit, are interesting. We are left to wonder which images were considered for inclusion but were rejected. George A.'s wife Bathsheba once commented that several images of Joseph displayed at a commemorative service were "libels and ought to be burned" and that they were "little better than caricatures."[68] Therefore we know that several inferior images of Joseph circulated in early Utah which George A. Smith and the Historian's Office staff may have chosen not to acquire. We also wonder which likenesses were originally included but were later removed or lost before the collection was reacquired by the CHO's successor, the Church History Department. Contrary to what one might expect, the fragments of George A.'s collection known to be extant include only one image of his cousin Joseph. It is a photographic copy made by the Provo, Utah studio of George Taylor & Co. of a profile image, possibly made by Dan Weggeland, based on an image by Sutcliffe Maudsley. Maudsley's profile was made from life and served as a basis for other posthumous depictions, including some that were probably among those panned by Bathsheba Smith. Another image in George A.'s collection is one of Hyrum—a photographic copy of a painting made while Hyrum was living in Kirtland.[69]

As a sort of epilogue to the CHO's collection, another image of Joseph Smith which may have been included by his cousin George A. arrived in Utah too late to be considered. It came as a direct challenge to the collection's message but quickly lost its adversarial might when it was coopted by Mormons in Utah. Ten years after George A.'s death, Joseph Smith III arrived in Utah in June 1885 with a very special image. He claimed the image in Figure 12.11 was a copy of an original daguerreotype of his father, taken in life. Such a thing was unknown in the territory, but Joseph III claimed he could provide it. He brought it along to attempt once again to stake his claim to his father's memory and to leadership in his father's church.

Utah was reeling from the federal government's anti-polygamy campaign, and John Taylor had gone into hiding in February. Joseph III, who had supported the political anti-polygamy efforts, now appeared in Utah to present an alternative, less legally fraught brand of Mormonism with him at the head.[70] The image of his father, he told his cousins as far back as 1860, was pivotal in his decision to take on the prophetic mantle. Less than three months after assuming leadership of the reorganized church, Joseph III's cousins, Joseph F. and Samuel H. B. Smith, visited him in Nauvoo. Samuel relayed part of their conversations in a letter to George A.

68. "Joseph Smith," *Salt Lake Herald*, 24 December 1894.

69. Photograph of painting of Hyrum Smith, Bathsheba Smith Photograph Collection, CHL.

70. For Joseph III's support of the anti-polygamy campaign, see Roger D. Launius, *Joseph Smith III: Pragmatic Prophet* (Urbana: University of Illinois Press, 1988), 247–72.

FIGURE 12.11. Joseph Smith. Ambrotype by Charles W. Carter copied from daguerreotype.
Church History Library, Salt Lake City.

> [H]e sais that the spirit has been working on his mind diring the last two years and he has felt all the time as though he had a work to do, . . . he further states that one day as he was pondering over in <in> his own mind why he didnot go to Salt Lake that he felt his Father's hands upon his heads<,> and then he [p. [3]] thought the reason why he dident go, and he told us a circumstance of his seeing his Father, he said that one day he went up stars to show some person's his Father's likness and after they had all turned, and ~~steppd~~ stepped out the door, he turned around ~~towad~~ towards the likness and he saw his Father, in ~~the likness~~ he then told us of ~~two~~ <two> or th[r]ee other visions he had had.[71]

71. Samuel H.B. Smith, Letter to George A. Smith, 10 July 1860, George A. Smith Papers, 1834–1877, CHL.

Joseph III clearly connected the image of his father to his own prophetic claims, and he brought that image with him to Utah.

For years, his mother, Emma, had maintained tight control over several Joseph Smith images, but after her death in April 1879 Joseph III made steps to publish them. He had copies made of them and submitted two albumen prints to the Library of Congress with an application for copyright on August 6. He may have seen an opportunity and moved to take it.

In 1879 things in Utah were still unsettled after Brigham Young's death two years earlier. The Utah church had not yet sustained a new president, and elsewhere other claimants to succeed Joseph Smith had either died or their movements had mostly petered out. Joseph III remained the last to claim direct succession from his father. Even the claims in Utah were to succeed Brigham Young rather than Joseph Smith Jr. directly. With the encouragement of others, Joseph III considered the possibility of presenting himself in Utah to take leadership, but eventually saw his chance slip away when John Taylor clinched his position as successor in 1880.[72]

Five years later, and with John Taylor in hiding, Joseph III made another trip west, photograph in hand. Although the consensus is that the image he brought is likely an edited photograph of the David Rogers painting executed in 1842, it saw broad circulation in Utah after he arrived in June 1885. In August the *Deseret News* announced that photographer Charles Carter had a daguerreotype of Joseph Smith in his possession and "has taken photographic copies of the daguerreotype, which he proposes to touch up with India ink and have copied again, until pictures as true to nature as possible and in various sizes can be produced."[73]

Interest in Joseph Smith images was obviously high. When the copies were ready for sale, the announcement appeared on the same page of the *Deseret News* with an advertisement for the October issue of the *Contributor* magazine advertising its own engraved portrait of Joseph Smith.[74] The magazine's editor, Junius F. Wells, noted that although their image was made from the same daguerreotype, Carter's version was superior. The quality of the artist's execution aside, Wells doubted that the daguerreotype had been made from life. According to Wells, "so far as we have been able

72. Launius, *Pragmatic Prophet*, 236–37.

73. "Portrait of the Prophet," *Deseret News*, 26 August 1885, 497. The header for this section notes that the news was copied from the daily paper of 18 August.

74. "The Only Correct Photograph of the Prophet Joseph Smith," *Deseret News*, 23 September 1885, 576.

to discover by diligent inquiry, no such portrait was ever taken." Instead, he wrote the daguerreotype was likely taken from the Rogers painting.[75]

If Joseph III hoped owning the legal rights to the image would secure him any increased prominence or ecclesiastical rights, he was mistaken. Wells's editorial failed to identify him as the daguerreotype's owner. He rejected both Joseph III's claims to succeed his father and that he had a daguerreotype of him. Although Carter identified Joseph III in his September advertisement, the photographs he produced and the subsequent drawings he commissioned based on the daguerreotype omitted his name.[76] Joseph III returned home with little to show for his efforts.[77]

Conclusion

Competing claims to church leadership following the death of Joseph Smith led Brigham Young and those who supported his claim to use various means to justify and bolster their position over the ensuing decades. Some of their rivals did the same. Visual media, and particularly the developing medium of photography, were important means they employed in their efforts. While paint remained the medium of choice for both portraiture and depicting history, Brigham Young and his followers rallied its powers for their ends. As photography became more popular and increasingly available in the mid-nineteenth century, it eclipsed paint as the preferred medium.

As the visual technology changed, so too did the visual argument for the succession claims of Brigham Young and the apostles. Initially, Young's early iconographic argument presented his ascension to church leadership as a logical progression from Joseph Smith. However, as others, particularly members of the Smith family and the Reorganized church, presented alternate historical narratives, the Utah church under Young's leadership changed its tack. By the 1860s, when RLDS claims directly contradicted the historical claims in Utah, photographs began appearing that

75. Junius F. Wells, "Our Engraving," *Contributor,* October 1885, 34–35.

76. Carter photographed several versions of the image. (Charles W. Carter Glass Negative Collection, ca. 1860–1900, CHL.)

77. When Carter's glass plate negatives were acquired by the LDS church, they included several images of Joseph Smith. One of them was likely the image Joseph III brought to Utah.

explicitly tied the Utah church and its practices to Joseph Smith and the earliest years of the movement.

More than just illustrations, these images serve as important sources in understanding early Mormonism. Knowing how and why these images were created is necessary for historians to use them appropriately as sources for researching the Mormon past. With very few images surviving from the Joseph Smith era, historians wanting to illustrate their writing naturally seize upon anything they can find, especially images of early Saints taken much later in life. Historians should be aware and make their readers aware that the archive of available images is strongly shaped by the decades-long battle over the memory of Joseph Smith and the right to succeed him.

13

Joseph Smith and the Conspicuous Scarcity of Early Mormon Documentation

Ronald O. Barney

A CULTURE-CHANGING INITIATIVE in the study of the life of Joseph Smith first appeared on bookstore shelves in 1984. Dean C. Jessee's compilation, *The Personal Writings of Joseph Smith,* was born of the careful scholarly work he had begun in the 1960s and was edited and annotated by the professional standards of the Association for Documentary Editing. With this work, Jessee helped create a consciousness among Mormon scholars and others regarding the importance of exacting textual and contextual preparation of historical documents for use in writing about the past. Followed in 1989 and 1992 by the first two of several volumes planned for *The Papers of Joseph Smith,* Jessee's excellent work demanded that all who entered the realm of Joseph Smith scholarship thereafter consider Smith's own "papers" as central to their probe.

Much more than just transcripts of Joseph Smith's documentary record, Jessee's production featured contextual apparatus, including a chronology, extensive biographical notes, and detailed maps. Jessee's work helped moderns see Joseph Smith "in much the same light as did those who received his letters or read the original documents."[1] He prepared his readers for a view of Joseph Smith by straightforwardly instructing them

1. Dean C. Jessee, ed., *Personal Writings of Joseph Smith,* rev. ed. (Salt Lake City and Provo, Utah: Deseret Book and Brigham Young University Press, 2002), xix.

that Smith must be considered in light of the full scope of his documentary record. For many, Jessee's challenging methodology stood in stark contrast with an unqualified reliance upon the *History of the Church*, which had been used for a century as devotional literature by his co-religionists.[2]

Smith's Autobiographical Effort

An authorized autobiography of Joseph Smith had originally been compiled between 1838 and 1856 as the manuscript for the "History of Joseph Smith," which was serialized in early church newspapers and later compiled by B. H. Roberts as the first six volumes of the *History of the Church* (1902–1912, with multiple reprints). For its time, it proved to be a remarkable record. But by presenting the Mormon prophet as seen by his closest associates who compiled the record, often in superlatives, the *History of the Church* portrayed a larger-than-life Joseph Smith found wanting by those who increasingly scrutinized the particulars of his life.[3] Jessee's labor of professionally presenting Smith's documentary record gave that record new life by couching the product in terms acceptable to the scholarly community.

Compiled as if it had been written by Joseph Smith in first-person narrative style, the several-thousand-page *History of the Church* also suggested that he was literarily prolific in telling his own story. However, Jessee cautioned that this was not quite the case:

> [W]hile the Mormon prophet produced a sizeable collection of papers, the question remains as to how clearly they reflect his own thoughts and personality. The answer lies in the documents themselves and becomes particularly clear when we note that the sources are not the past but only the raw materials whence we form our conception of the past, and in using them we inherit the limitations that produced them—the lack of personal writing, the wide use of

2. Joseph Smith et al., *History of the Church of Jesus Christ of Latter-day Saints*, ed. B. H. Roberts, 7 vols. (Salt Lake City: Deseret Book Company, 1946). The seventh volume of the set was a compilation of information about the period between Smith's death and Brigham Young's assumption of Smith's prophetic role.

3. The primary compilers for Smith's "History of Joseph Smith"—Willard Richards, Wilford Woodruff, and George A. Smith—as well as a number other clerks that influenced the text are described in Dean C. Jessee, "The Writing of Joseph Smith's History" *BYU Studies* 11, no. 4 (Summer 1971): 439–73.

> clerks taking dictation or even being assigned to write for him, and the editorial reworking of reports of what he did and said.[4]

Jessee's work disclosed the limited and filtered influence of Joseph Smith on his own papers. It turns out, Jessee wrote, that the young prophet had difficulty in transferring his thoughts to paper. In this light, Smith's use of clerks and scribes acquires new meaning as we attempt to pry open the past to understand his motives and behavior. "A complicated life and feelings of literary inadequacy explain this dependence," Jessee explained. Quoting from Smith's own letters, Jessee wrote that Smith "lamented his 'lack of fluency in address,' his 'imperfections of . . . writings' and his 'inability' to convey his ideas in writing. Communication seemed to him to present an insurmountable barrier. He wrote of the almost 'totel darkness of paper pen and ink and a crooked broken scattered and imperfect language.'"[5] Not understanding this important feature of Joseph Smith's personality, of course, could significantly distort one's expectations of the documentary record he left behind.

Jessee was the first to systematically bore into that record, culling subtleties that forced all thereafter to rethink how the most oft-used sources had influenced previous interpretations of Joseph Smith and his work. As noted above, Smith wrote little of his own autobiography.[6] Regarding his journals covering the years of 1832 to 1844—not to be confused with the *History of the Church* noted above—Jessee wrote: "Of the 1,587 manuscript pages comprising the Smith journal, 31 contain holograph writing, where he is known to have put his own thoughts on the paper. Another 250 were evidently dictated to scribes."[7] Clearly, Smith's journals did not uniformly qualify as the intimate expressions traditionally affixed to them.

Joseph Smith's sermons also posed a problem. The extant notes of the sermons are vital documents for understanding his mature doctrine, and for the last few years of his life were his primary means of delivering his

---

4. Jessee, *Personal Writings of Joseph Smith*, 2.

5. Jessee, *Personal Writings of Joseph Smith*, 2–3. Jessee quoted from Joseph Smith to Moses Nickerson, 19 November 1835; Joseph Smith to Emma Smith, 21 March 1839; Joseph Smith to Emma Smith, 6 June 1832; and Joseph Smith to W. W. Phelps, 27 November 1832 (all found in *Personal Writings of Joseph Smith*).

6. Dean C. Jessee, "The Writing of Joseph Smith's History," *BYU Studies* 11, no. 4 (Summer 1971): 440.

7. Dean C. Jessee, ed., *The Papers of Joseph Smith: Volume 2, Journal, 1832–1842* (Salt Lake City: Deseret Book Company, 1992), xxii–xxiii.

revelations to the church. But they were nothing near a complete record, as Jessee explained that it is likely that "not more than one in ten of Joseph Smith's discourses were recorded, and most of these come from the last three years of his life."[8]

Smith's Leadership Style

The scarcity of written copies of Joseph Smith's sermons and the significant activity of scribes and clerks in writing his first-person *History* point to a larger issue, one that Dean Jessee's meticulous work helped subsequent scholars to uncover: There are lacunae in this record. Some documentation that would be central to Joseph Smith's ministry is conspicuously absent. This essay considers three aspects of Joseph Smith's distinctive leadership style in forming and fostering what became The Church of Jesus Christ of Latter-day Saints.[9] The three aspects of Smith's peculiar personal character illustrated below are rooted in an acknowledgment of a conspicuous dearth of significant documentation—the kind of historical record that, had such material been created, would likely have rendered a rather different perspective on Mormon beginnings than presently exists. These three characteristics are:

(1) Contrary to what one might expect, Smith largely kept to himself the sacred experiences that bore on his validity as a religious leader.
(2) Rather than imposing himself upon his followers, as some have argued that he did, Smith often chose not to insert himself into church dialogue when one might think he would be most inclined to do so.
(3) Smith appears to have had an aversion, or at least little to no interest, in having his numerous sermons captured and distributed, which besides giving inspiration and encouragement to church members, also had become his principal medium for delivering his revelations to the church.

8. Dean C. Jessee, "Priceless Words and Fallible Memories: Joseph Smith as Seen in the Effort to Preserve His Discourses" *BYU Studies* 31, no. 2 (1991): 23. On the scarcity of sermon transcripts, see also William V. Smith, "Joseph Smith's Sermons and the Early Mormon Documentary Record," chap. 8 herein.

9. This essay relates to a larger work by this author about Joseph Smith and the historical record produced by and about him.

When considered together, these matters suggest clues to Smith's personality that must temper demands for him being a person preoccupied with chronicling his experiences in order to give him credibility as an authentic religious personality. In other words, one might expect someone in the early American republic with a story of great significance to have jumped into the public square via the stump or the printed word to advance his singular experience. Joseph Smith did not.

At the outset, we may ask why Joseph Smith refrained from inserting himself into the public forum in the manner of so many of his religious contemporaries to popularize his agenda. Smith himself later reflected upon the response he received when he first relayed his initial vision of Deity. The Methodist minister he told within a few days of his experience "treated my communication not only lightly but with great contempt." As word spread, he recounted, it "excited a great deal of prejudice against me."[10] Richard Lyman Bushman, Smith's biographer, speculated that, indeed, "he may have held back for fear of ridicule." But Bushman also posited that in Smith's early years it "may have been the natural reticence of a teenage boy keeping his own counsel."[11] Bushman's observation identifies a significant feature of Joseph Smith's personality that helps explain why he did not disseminate information about himself—especially his experiences of the sacred.

The evidence or lack thereof regarding the foundational events of Joseph Smith's church have been used by polemicists in attempts to prove or disprove his claims. These milestone events include his first vision of Deity, probably in 1820; his encounters with the angelic messenger of the golden plates, later identified as the Book of Mormon prophet Moroni, 1823–1827; and the bestowal of divine authority upon Joseph Smith and his associate Oliver Cowdery by John the Baptist and by the apostles Peter, James, and John. The adversarial contentions center on whether Smith had the experiences he later described or he had manufactured them. Setting aside the issue of whether he really experienced the things he claimed to, one can still ask *when* he started telling the stories that were only later

10. History Drafts, 1838–ca. 1841 [Draft 2], 4, in Karen Lynn Davidson, David J. Whittaker, Richard L. Jensen, and Mark R. Ashurst-McGee, eds., *Histories, Volume 1: Joseph Smith Histories, 1832–1844*, vol. 1 of the Histories series of *The Joseph Smith Papers*, eds. Dean C. Jessee, Ronald K. Esplin, and Richard Lyman Bushman (Salt Lake City: Church Historian's Press, 2012), 216.

11. Richard Lyman Bushman, *Joseph Smith: Rough Stone Rolling*, with the assistance of Jed Woodworth (New York: Knopf, 2005), 40.

committed to paper. While what is presented below may appear to be an affirmation of Joseph Smith and his experiences, its intent is to illustrate for the reader how Smith's personality influenced the records upon which we judge his life and his work.

I: Sacred Experience and Sense of Privacy

The primeval event of Mormonism, even though it was not heralded as such during most of Joseph Smith's lifetime, is what is known today as his "First Vision." Smith later claimed that he had seen the resurrected and glorified Jesus Christ and God, the Father, in 1820 or around that time. The fact that a paper trail describing this vision did not begin until circa Summer 1832—post-dating the event by twelve years—has stoked the polarized contests about the validity of his story for decades. Twelve years is a long time to conceal such an important moment, even if it were psychologically concocted. It is to Dean Jessee that we owe the debt of equipping scholars with historiographical perspective to better approach this and other features of early Mormonism rather than the positivist approach that some consider historical analysis.

Writing of Joseph Smith's vision, Fawn M. Brodie, whose significant biography of Smith in 1945 raised his profile among America's educated elite, credited him little when she postulated that "the awesome vision he described in later years was probably the elaboration of some half-remembered dream stimulated by the early revival excitement and reinforced by the rich folklore of visions circulating in his neighborhood." Her summary scrutiny, however, more starkly concluded that "it may have been sheer invention, created some time after 1830 when the need arose for a magnificent tradition."[12] Though Brodie was excommunicated by the Mormon church for her characterization of Smith—beginning with her dismissal of the "First Vision"—her artful analysis has affected all thereafter who have seriously written about him.

Brodie's conclusions are not unique. The debate about Smith's numinous claims were hatched in the decades that followed his death, especially among those who reconsidered their previous affiliation with Mormonism. Despite the lack of uniformity by those who challenged early Mormon claims, fragmented cells of his church individually regrouped,

12. Fawn M. Brodie, *No Man Knows My History: The Life of Joseph Smith*, 2nd ed. (New York: Knopf, 1975), 25.

fashioning identities based upon particulars of what they claimed were Smith's declarations. One who made an impact on sectors of Smith's disparate followers was David Whitmer. He had been one of Smith's most important allies during the church's infancy and, reasonably, someone who might be expected to intimately know the founder's secrets. Whitmer submitted to an interview about the early days of Mormonism in 1885 with Zenos Gurley, an advocate at the time of the Reorganized Church of Jesus Christ of Latter Day Saints (now the Community of Christ). At the time of the interview Whitmer had been estranged from Smith and what became the Utah division of Mormonism for almost half a century. Regarding the question of Smith's early acquisition of divine authority from heavenly messengers in 1829, the year traditionally accepted by the Mormon faithful, Gurley wrote that Whitmer told him: "I never heard that an angel had ordained Joseph and Oliver to the Aaronic priesthood until the year 1834[,] 5[,] or 6."[13] In other words, Whitmer believed that Joseph Smith made up the story in the mid-1830s; otherwise, Whitmer would undoubtedly have heard of it, given his early proximity to Smith.[14]

So how have Smith's sympathizers—or empathizers—explained the absence of contemporary verification of his prophetic record? For some the quandary regarding the lacuna of Smith's numinous experiences relies upon his own justification of his silence. In this specific case of the angel who empowered Smith and his scribe, Oliver Cowdery, with authority to baptize, the hostile social environment prohibited the telling of such a marvelous story: "we were forced to keep secret the circumstances of our having been baptized, and having received this priesthood; owing to a spirit of persecution which had already manifested itself in the neighborhood."[15] The contextual evidence suggests that this explanation is valid. As word spread regarding Smith's claims of accessing the divine, he received

13. Zenos Gurley, "Questions Asked of David Whitmer at His Home in Richmond Ray County Mo," 14–21 January 1885, MS 4633, Church History Library, Salt Lake City (hereafter the Church History Library will be abbreviated as CHL); see also David Whitmer, *An Address to All Believers in Christ* (Richmond, Missouri: By the author, 1887), 64.

14. Confusing this later declaration is one posed earlier by David Whitmer's collaborator at the time, William E. McLellin, who acknowledged Joseph Smith's acquisition of "Melchizedek" authority. This suggests that in 1848 they considered Smith's priesthood claims were valid. See [W. E. McLellin], "James J. Strang, of Voree, Wis.," *The Ensign of Liberty of the Church of Christ* (Kirtland, OH), April 1847, 31; [W. E. McLellin], "Our Principles in Kirtland," *The Ensign of the Liberty of the Church of Christ*, March 1848, 67.

15. History Drafts, 1838–ca. 1841 [Draft 2], 18, in Davidson et al., *Histories, Volume 1*, 296.

not only cold rejoinders but, over time, physical abuse. That same documentation also demands that fear of persecution was only one reason for Smith's reticence to reveal his experiences with the sacred.[16]

It is implausible in the minds of some that Smith, if he actually experienced the numinous occurrences he professed, did not run home to chisel his experiences in stone, or at least put them to paper, so that all would know of God's recent activity on earth. The evidence for the first years of his prophetic career suggests, however, that Smith instinctively kept quiet regarding many features of his ministry, befuddling many modern observers. The record suggests that he looked upon the events as demanding restraint on his part in divulging the sacral nature of what he had experienced.

Then there is the factor of memory. Not only did Joseph Smith wait twelve years to pen the account of his first vision of Deity—apparently written in 1832—he produced other written versions of the event before his death in 1844: in 1835, 1838, about 1841, and 1842.[17] In his 1838 account, his third rehearsal of the event that found its way onto paper, he stated that the vision occurred in the spring of 1820,[18] when he was fourteen by the calendar, suggesting that perhaps his scribe for this account participated in composing the language rather than the text being a precise transcription of Smith's oral dictation. His few other references to the moment use the phrase "about fourteen" to describe its timing.[19] Smith would be

16. Others have argued as much, but have addressed only Joseph Smith's reluctance to discuss his "First Vision." See, for example, Hugh Nibley, "Censoring Joseph Smith's Story" Part 1, *Improvement Era*, November 1961, 522; James B. Allen, "The Significance of Joseph Smith's 'First Vision' in Mormon Thought," *Dialogue: A Journal of Mormon Thought* 1, no. 3 (Autumn 1966): 34; Donna Hill, *Joseph Smith: The First Mormon* (New York: Doubleday & Company, 1977), 52–53; Richard L. Bushman, *Joseph Smith and the Beginnings of Mormonism* (Urbana and Chicago: University of Illinois Press, 1984), 58.

17. Jessee tackled contextualizing the accounts in 1969 in "The Early Accounts of Joseph Smith's First Vision," *BYU Studies* 9, no. 3 (Spring 1969): 275–94. See also a newly discovered circa 1841 version of the 1838 account in History Drafts, 1838–circa 1841, in Davidson et al., *Histories, Volume 1*, 208–19. Only since 2012 has the Coray history, ca. 1841, been available for scrutiny, in *JSP*, H1:187–463.

18. History Drafts, 1838–ca. 1841 [Draft 2], 3, in Davidson et al., *Histories, Volume 1*, 212.

19. Joseph Smith, Journal, 9 and 14 November 1835, in Dean C. Jessee, Mark Ashurst-McGee, and Richard L. Jensen, eds., *Journals, Volume 1: 1832–1838*, vol. 1 of the Journals series of *The Joseph Smith Papers*, eds. Dean C. Jessee, Ronald K. Esplin, and Richard Lyman Bushman (Salt Lake City: Church Historian's Press, 2008), 88, 100; "Church History," *Times and Seasons*, 1 March 1842, 706. A later interpolation by Frederick G. Williams into Joseph Smith's History stated without commentary that the event occurred "in the 16th year of my age." History, ca. Summer 1832, 3, in Davidson et al., *Histories, Volume 1*, 12.

something superhuman if his memory remained constant and undeviating year after year. Those who demand that each rehearsal of his first vision exactly overlay anything previously produced by him to consider his claims valid would have just another point with which to combat him. The believers would undoubtedly be more content with such a scenario. But in neither case do we get closer to understanding Smith's experiences or behavior.

That same 1838 account states that soon after experiencing his first vision, Smith explained what had happened to him to someone he thought would be sympathetic and understanding, a man of the cloth. Instead, according to Smith, the minister delivered a condescending rebuke to the boy that scorched his sensibilities.[20] This penetrating censure by a clergyman may have been one of the reasons that he did not initially share the experience with his parents. It is not known when he first revealed his encounter with the divine to his family, but—as far as we can tell—it was not until about 1832 that he first attempted to describe it on paper, apparently with the intent to distribute it.[21] Three years later, in November 1835, his scribe at the time recorded Smith's explanation of the phenomenon to a visitor. Then three years later when he was finally forced to prepare a report for public consumption, Smith produced what has become the formal, institutionally codified account of his "First Vision."[22] About 1841, he apparently considered, again, the language and structure of how he would present his story, as manifest in the effort of Howard Coray, one of his clerks, to refine the language of Smith's history.[23] And, again, in 1842, he portrayed the event for publication by a Boston lawyer who requested the story of Mormonism, as seen in Figure 13.1 [24] As Smith's rehearsals of the

---

20. History Drafts, 1838–ca. 1841 [Draft 2], 3–4, in Davidson et al., *Histories, Volume 1*, 214, 216, 218.

21. History, ca. Summer 1832, 1–3, in Davidson et al., *Histories, Volume 1*, 11–13. This account has become controversial when compared to the other three rehearsals of the event attributed to Joseph Smith. In the circa summer 1832 version he identified only the appearance of Jesus, whereas in the other stories he states that both Jesus Christ and God, the Father, were his visitors, a matter I address in my biography of Joseph Smith (work in progress). See also Mark Ashurst-McGee, "The Mosaic of Early Mormon Histories," chapter 7 herein.

22. While Smith explicitly stated in 1838 that bad press and hearsay had "induced" him to initiate his 1838–1856 history, the circa 1832 history may well have been produced for comparable reasons. See the author's forthcoming biography of Joseph Smith.

23. *JSP*, H1:191–92 (Draft 3).

24. "Church History," *Times and Seasons*, 1 March 1842, 706–7. See also Ronald O. Barney, "'There is the Greatest Excitement in This Country That I Ever Beheld': Mormonism's New

CHURCH HISTORY.

At the request of Mr. John Wentworth, Editor, and Proprietor of the "Chicago Democrat," I have written the following sketch of the rise, progress, persecution, and faith of the Latter-Day Saints, of which I have the honor, under God, of being the founder. Mr. Wentworth says, that he wishes to furnish Mr. Bastow, a friend of his, who is writing the history of New Hampshire, with this document. As Mr. Bastow has taken the proper steps to obtain correct information all that I shall ask at his hands, is, that he publish the account entire, ungarnished, and without misrepresentation.

I was born in the town of Sharon Windsor co., Vermont, on the 23d of December, A. D. 1805. When ten years old my parents removed to Palmyra New York, where we resided about four years, and from thence we removed to the town of Manchester.

My father was a farmer and taught me the art of husbandry. When about fourteen years of age I began to reflect upon the importance of being prepared for a future state, and upon enquiring the plan of salvation I found that there was a great clash in religious sentiment; if I went to one society they referred me to one plan, and another to another; each one pointing to his own particular creed as the summum bonum of perfection: considering that all could not be right, and that God could not be the author of so much confusion I determined to investigate the subject more fully, believing that if God had a church it would not be split up into factions, and that if he taught one society to worship one way, and administer in one set of ordinances, he would not teach another principles which were diametrically opposed. Believing the word of God I had confidence in the declaration of James; "If any man lack wisdom let him ask of God who giveth to all men liberally and upbraideth not and it shall be given him," I retired to a secret place in a grove and began to call upon the Lord, while fervently engaged in supplication my mind was taken away from the objects with which I was surrounded, and I was enwrapped in a

FIGURE 13.1. "Church History," *Times and Seasons*, 1 March 1842, p. 706. Church History Library, Salt Lake City.

accounts post-dated the event by twelve to twenty-two years, no one should be surprised that questions have been raised about the stories and the timing of their creation.

One of Joseph Smith's famous apologists in the mid-twentieth century, BYU's Hugh Nibley, was likely the first to describe the most probable explanation for the late narratives. Undoubtedly reflecting on Brodie's earlier insinuations regarding the absence of Smith's contemporaneous disclosure of his experiences, Nibley wrote: "One may ask, why should Joseph Smith have waited so long to tell his story officially. From his own explanation"—in the 1838 account of the First Vision that was published in 1842 in the *Times and Seasons*[25]—"it is apparent that he would not have told it publicly at all had he not been 'induced' to do so by all the scandal stories that were circulating." He continued, "What the present state of the evidence most strongly suggests is that Joseph Smith did tell his story to some of his followers at an early date." He "did this reluctantly, confining his report to bare essentials." Then, summarizing Smith's taciturn approach, he declared, "Throughout his life Joseph Smith was never eager to tell the story of his first vision."[26]

This posture is difficult for contemporary observers to understand, as for much of the twentieth century Mormon missionaries used the LDS Church's codified "First Vision" story among their initial testimonials regarding Joseph Smith and the restoration of Jesus' gospel.[27] Smith's 1838 rehearsal of

---

England Ministry of the Forgotten Eli P. Maginn" *Mormon Historical Studies* 15, no. 2 (Fall 2014): 222–34.

25. "History of Joseph Smith," *Times and Seasons*, 15 March 1842.

26. Hugh Nibley, "Censoring Joseph Smith's Story," *Improvement Era* 64, no. 11 (November 1961): 813. Peter Bauder, who visited Joseph Smith in 1830 at the Peter Whitmer Sr. home in Fayette Township, New York, interviewed Joseph Smith alone for "several hours . . . investigating his writings, church records, &c." but complained that "he could give me no christian experience"—a phenomenon that the "First Vision" would have completely satisfied had it been related. While Joseph Smith withheld his "First Vision" account from Bauder, he did tell him about the coming forth of the Book of Mormon, including Moroni's connection to the story. Peter Bauder, *The Kingdom and Gospel of Jesus Christ: Contrasted with That of an Anti-Christ. A Brief Review of Some of the Most Interesting Circumstances, Which Have Transpired Since the Institution of the Gospel of Christ, from the Days of the Apostles* (Canajoharie, New York: A. H. Calhoun, 1834), 36–38.

27. Others, such as Allen, have previously argued these points. James B. Allen, "Emergence of a Fundamental: The Expanding Role of Joseph Smith's First Vision of Mormon Religious Thought," in *Exploring the First Vision*, eds. Samuel Alonzo Dodge and Steven C. Harper (Provo, Utah: Religious Studies Center, 2012), 43–44. The "codified" account was produced in the mid-twentieth century as a missionary tract that remains in print.

his experiences—absent the context of his own sensibilities about the sacred nature of what had happened to him—became the burden of the Mormon proselytizing message. This is in contrast to the first cadre of Mormon missionaries who, by design, simply proclaimed "the first principles and ordinances of the gospel" and the Book of Mormon. Because Smith had protected distribution of the "First Vision" story until the early 1840s, it may have been known to but a limited number of early Mormons in the church's first decade. Indeed, the first description of the vision was not printed until 1840, when Orson Pratt published the story in Scotland as a missionary tract.[28] Thus, Hugh Nibley's 1961 statement that Smith resisted dissemination of his holiest personal experiences was likely received with surprise.

A Pattern of Reticence

The "present state of the evidence" that Nibley drew upon indeed suggests that Joseph Smith was sensitive to incurring the displeasure of Deity by divulging his heavenly or spiritual encounters. Smith generally followed this pattern regarding the protection of sacred matters for the remainder of his tenure as prophet. For instance, minutes of a 25 October 1831 gathering of church elders in Orange, Ohio, thirteen miles southwest of Kirtland, indicate Smith's refusal to discuss manifestations of God even among his closest associates. Present at the meeting were some of Smith's most trusted advisors, including Oliver Cowdery, his intimate collaborator in Mormonism's founding. So were Cowdery's fellow Book of Mormon witnesses, Martin Harris and David Whitmer, who had previously claimed to have seen an angel and handled the gold plates from which the Book of Mormon was derived. Others who claimed to have seen the angel and the plates were also there, including Smith's father and his older brother Hyrum. Sidney Rigdon and Frederick G. Williams, both of whom would soon become Smith's counselors in the church's governing body, the First

---

28. Orson Pratt, *A[n] Account of Several Remarkable Visions and of the Late Discovery of Ancient American Records* (Edinburgh: Ballantyne and Hughes, 1840), also published in Davidson et al., *Histories, Volume 1*, 517–46. From the late 1960s to the 1980s several scholarly defenders of Joseph Smith, including Dean Jessee, published treatments of the scope of Joseph Smith's rehearsals of the "First Vision" in order to disarm claims of critics, such as Wesley P. Walters and Jerald and Sandra Tanner, who contended that Joseph Smith fabricated accounts of his divine authorization. Others who published important affirmative clarifications of Joseph Smith's theophanies, besides Jessee, include James B. Allen, Milton V. Backman, and Richard L. Anderson, all BYU professors. The literature since the 1960s regarding the "First Vision" is so enormous and unwieldy that it precludes a bibliography here.

Presidency, were in attendance, as were several others who would later become charter members of the church's Quorum of the Twelve Apostles.

Yet when Hyrum proposed to Joseph that he relate to the small gathering "the information of the coming forth of the Book of Mormon" that all present "might know for themselves," Joseph replied that "it was not intended to tell the world all the particulars of the coming forth of the book of Mormon." The minutes, seen in Figure 13.2, further report Smith's statement "that it was not expedient for him to relate these things."[29] If there was ever a moment for him to share such an important matter with his closest associates, this was such a time. Yet he refused. Enough of the larger story had circulated that several of those in attendance could have substantiated Joseph Smith's account, thereby confirming his assertions among themselves. Oliver Cowdery, who had shared with Joseph Smith a number of the most supernatural experiences of Mormonism's founding and who took the minutes of the October 25 meeting, could have offered firsthand corroboration, as, indeed, could have the others who reported having seen the golden plates. Still, Smith resisted.[30]

Not only did he personally maintain this perplexing posture, Joseph Smith instructed his companions in their private experiences to do so as well. To a November 1835 gathering of some members of the newly appointed Quorum of the Twelve Apostles, Smith warned: "let us be faithful and silent brethren, <and> if God gives you a manifestation, Keep it to yourself."[31] Smith placed the apostles at the head of the church's

---

29. "The Conference Minutes, and Record Book, of Christ's Church of Latter Day Saints," 1838–ca. 1839, 1842, 1844, entry for 25 October 1831, LR 7874 21, CHL. A transcription of the minutes is found in *Far West Record: Minutes of the Church of Jesus Christ of Latter-day Saints, 1830–1844*, eds. Donald Q. Cannon and Lyndon W. Cook (Salt Lake City: Deseret Book Company, 1983), 23.

30. Except that it was by "the power of God," Joseph Smith never did explain exactly "how" he translated the Book of Mormon, though he was known to describe the circumstantial context of the "coming forth of the Book of Mormon" in numerous settings. See John W. Welch, "The Miraculous Translation of the Book of Mormon" in John W. Welch, ed., *Opening the Heavens: Account of Divine Manifestations, 1820–1844* (Provo, Utah: Brigham Young University Press and Deseret Book, 2005), 77–213. Cowdery, while in 1834 describing features of the coming forth of the Book of Mormon to W. W. Phelps, remained silent regarding the divine manifestations that he experienced incident to his initial association with Joseph Smith. Oliver Cowdery to W. W. Phelps, 7 September 1834, *Messenger and Advocate*, October 1834, 15–16; see also History Drafts, 1838–ca. 1841 [Draft 2], 14, in Davidson et al., *Histories, Volume 1*, 284. This is likely the event described in Joseph Smith's early history: History, ca. Summer 1832, [6], in Davidson et al., *Histories, Volume 1*, 16.

31. Joseph Smith, Journal, 12 November 1835, in Jessee et al., *Journals, Volume 1*, 98.

13

Br. Edmund Durfee said that he had professed religion for a number of years yet now felt to bear testimony of the goodness of God, & also to consecrate all to the Lord.

Br. Joseph Smith said that he had nothing to consecrate to the Lord of the things of the Earth, yet he felt to consecrate himself and family. Was thankful that God had given him a place among his saints, felt willing to labor for their good.

Br. Luke Johnson said that he was determined to be for God and none else come life or death also remembered his covenant that he would consecrate all that he had to the Lord.

Br. Hyrum Smith said that he thought best that the information of the coming forth of the book of Mormon be related by Joseph himself to the Elders present that all might know for themselves. |

Br. Joseph Smith jr. said that it was not intended to tell the world all the particulars of the coming forth of the book of Mormon, & also said that it was not expedient for him to relate these things &c. |

Br. Frederick G. Williams laid before the Conference the case of Sister Marsh & family who were somewhat destitute.

Br. Titus Billings said that he was surprised that the case of Sister Marsh should be brought to this Conference, as she and her family were provided for as well as her brethren around her.

Br. Joseph Smith Jr. said that he intended to do his duty before the Lord and hoped that the brethren would be patient as they lived a considerable distance. also said that the promise of God was that the greatest blessings which God had to bestow should be given to those who contributed to the support of his family while translating the fulness of the scriptures, also said until we have perfect love we are liable to fall and when we have a testimony that our names are sealed in the Lamb's Book of life we have perfect love & then it is impossible for false Christs to deceive us. also said that the Lord held the Church bound to provide for the families of the absent Elders while proclaiming the Gospel. further said that God had often sealed up the heavens because of covetousness in the Church. said that the Lord would cut his work short in righteousness and except the church receive the fulness of the scriptures that they would yet fall. |

FIGURE 13.2. The Conference Minutes and Record Book of Christ's Church of Latter Day Saints, 25 October 1831, p. 13.
Church History Library, Salt Lake City.

missionary force, and sent them into the field to lead the effort, but they were instructed not to witness to all they knew. Thus, rather than publicly bellowing his private communications with heaven, as would seem a reasonable course of action for a person trying to convince others of God's new revelation, Smith kept his own counsel and expected those in his inner circle to do the same.[32]

Just five months later, on 3 April 1836, when spiritual fervor erupted in the small but growing village of Kirtland during the dedicatory rites of the Mormon temple, Joseph Smith and Oliver Cowdery claimed to witness yet another phenomenal vision. In this case, at the time of the event, Smith dictated to his clerk, Cowdery's brother Warren, wording to suggest that something otherworldly had happened to them. The descriptive text, well known to modern Mormon observers, consists of the announcement that not only had Jesus of Nazareth appeared to Joseph Smith and Oliver Cowdery, but also the Old Testament–era figures of Moses, Elias, and Elijah. Smith claimed that these three bestowed divine authority upon him and Cowdery—empowering them with religious abilities previously unavailable.[33] Following the logic of Smith's critics, one would think that he would have quickly announced, at least to his followers, the Kirtland Temple visions of April 3. If he needed to bolster his waning influence—the motive ascribed to him—surely this could have supplied him with a weight and gravity previously undeclared.[34] However, he did not. While the

---

32. Joseph Smith, while he later was constrained to give particulars of the founding events of Mormonism, remained sensitive to the principle of keeping sacred things sacred. In an 1841 sermon, as recorded by Wilford Woodruff, he said, "The reason we do not have the secrets of the Lord revealed unto us is because we do not keep them but reveal them, we do not keep our own secrets but reveal our difficulties to the world even to our enemies[.] then how would we keep the secrets of the Lord[.] Joseph says[, '] I can keep a secret till dooms day[.']" Joseph Smith, in Wilford Woodruff, Journal, 19 November 1841, in Andrew F. Ehat and Lyndon W. Cook, eds., *The Words of Joseph Smith: The Contemporary Accounts of the Nauvoo Discourses of the Prophet Joseph* (Provo, Utah: Religious Studies Center, Brigham Young University, 1980), 81. Clearly, this principle of restraint had circulated among church members. Joseph Smith's brother Hyrum later publicly instructed, "Therefore beware what you teach! for the mysteries of God are not given to all men; and unto those to whom they are given they are placed under restrictions to impart only such as God will command them; and the residue is to be kept in a faithful breast, otherwise he will be brought under condemnation. By this God will prove his faithful servants, who will be called and numbered with the chosen." Hyrum Smith to "the brethren of the Church of Jesus Christ of Latterday Saints," in *Times and Seasons* 15 March 1844: 474.

33. Joseph Smith, Journal, 3 April 1836, in Jessee et al., *Journals, Volume 1*, 219–22.

34. ADD: Grant H. Palmer, *An Insider's View of Mormon Origins* (Salt Lake City: Signature Books, 2002), 230–31.

experience is recorded in his private journal, seen in Figure 13.3, there is no evidence that he publicized the fantastic and marvelous encounter except perhaps to a handful of the faithful.[35] There is no extant record indicating that he, or Oliver Cowdery for that matter, ever thereafter referred to the event, privately or publicly—although Smith's clerks later used his journals to draft his history and included the journal account in the history. It is likely that the church and the world first became aware of the story when a portion of the serialization of Smith's history appeared in November 1852 in Salt Lake City's *Deseret News*.[36] Unless one recognizes Smith's idiosyncratic disposition to conceal his personal experience with heaven, the absence of the event from his litany of truth claims, despite a contemporary private record of the incident, is contradictory and enigmatic.

A Private Personality

Was Joseph Smith's careful clutch of religious experiences learned or instinctual? Donald L. Enders, one of the leading scholars of this generation on Joseph Smith and his family, has argued that there was an instinctual component to the behavior. Contrary to modern sentimental portrayals of young Joseph running home from the grove where the "First Vision" was to have taken place, to tell his mother of the phenomenon, Enders argues in a forthcoming book on Joseph and his family that Joseph did not immediately share his remarkable experiences with his family. He cites a later redaction to what became the codified "First Vision" story, penned by Joseph Smith's scribe Willard Richards in December 1842, that includes language of the exchange between Joseph and his mother after the experience. Upon Joseph's return to the Smith family's nearby home, his mother observed an unusual countenance upon her son and asked "what the matter was?" Instead of pouring out his heart, Joseph replied "never mind[,] all is well—I am well enough—off. I then told my mother

35. At least some aspects of the visions were also known to William W. Phelps. William W. Phelps, Kirtland, Ohio, to Sally Phelps, Liberty, MO, April 1836, William W. Phelps, Papers, Brigham Young University, Provo, Utah. Phelps was an early scribe of Smith and played a significant role in Kirtland and the Mormons' early venture into Missouri. Bruce A. Van Orden, "'We'll Sing and We'll Shout!' Who is the Real W. W. Phelps?" *Mormon Historical Studies* 16, no. 1 (Spring 2015).

36. "Life of Joseph Smith," *Deseret News*, 6 November 1852. The account was later canonized as "Joseph Smith—History" in *The Pearl of Great Price*, one of the "standard works" of the Church of Jesus Christ of Latter-day Saints.

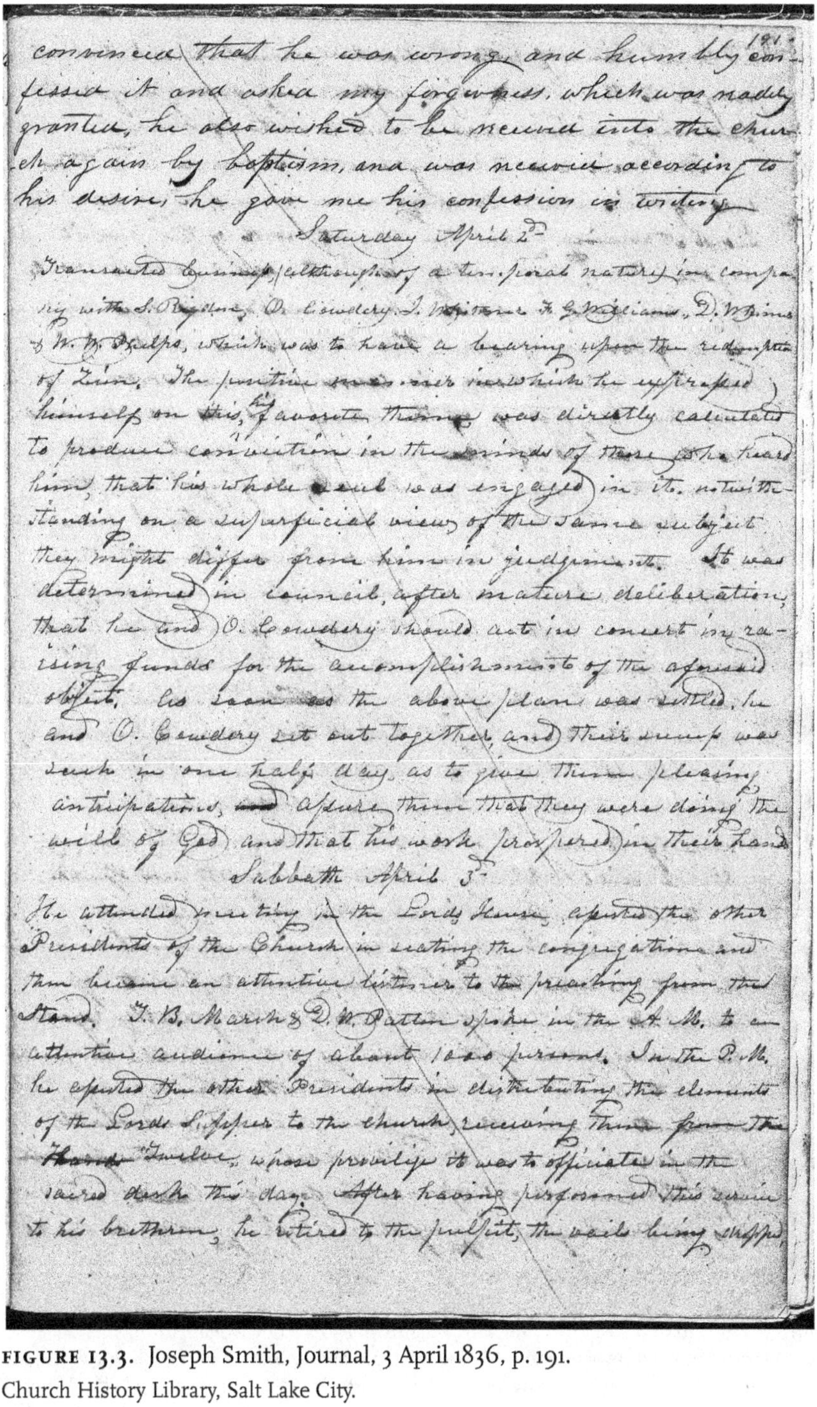

191

convinced that he was wrong and humbly confessed it and asked my forgiveness, which was readily granted, he also wished to be received into the church again by baptism, and was received according to his desire, he gave me his confession in writing.

Saturday April 2d

Transacted business, (although of a temporal nature) in company with S. Rigdon, O. Cowdery, J. Whitmer F. G. Williams, D. Whitmer & W. W. Phelps, which was to have a bearing upon the redemption of Zion. The positive manner in which he expressed himself on this, his favorite theme, was directly calculated to produce conviction in the minds of those who heard him, that his whole soul was engaged in it, notwithstanding on a superficial view of the same subject they might differ from him in judgement. It was determined in council, after mature deliberation, that he and O. Cowdery should act in concert in raising funds for the accomplishment of the aforesaid object. As soon as the above plan was settled, he and O. Cowdery set out together, and their success was such in one half day as to give them pleasing anticipations, and assure them that they were doing the will of God and that his work prospered in their hands.

Sabbath April 3d

He attended meeting in the Lords House, assisted the other Presidents of the Church in seating the congregation and then became an attentive listener to the preaching from the stand. T. B. Marsh & D. W. Patten spoke in the A. M. to an attentive audience of about 1000 persons. In the P. M. he assisted the other Presidents in distributing the elements of the Lords Supper to the church, receiving them from the ~~Holy~~ Twelve, whose privilege it was to officiate in the sacred desk this day. After having performed this service to his brethren, he retired to the pulpit, the veils being dropped,

FIGURE 13.3. Joseph Smith, Journal, 3 April 1836, p. 191. Church History Library, Salt Lake City.

I have learned for myself that Presbyterianism is not True." Nothing more was said or explained about the life-altering event.[37] There is no evidence, Enders explains, that Joseph told his mother that he had talked face-to-face with God. Certainly his mother never claimed to have heard such a declaration.[38]

This exchange after the "First Vision" is only the first instance demonstrating Joseph Smith's taciturn inclinations. One of the most well-known of all Mormon foundational stories is Joseph Smith's claim that an angel named Moroni appeared to him in September 1823 to reveal the location of the gold plates from which Smith later translated the Book of Mormon. A feature of Smith's account of the story again reveals his instinctual behavior. Enders points out that, as Joseph Smith recounted it, he would not have told his father about his initial encounter with the angel Moroni had not the angel directed him to do so. Using Joseph Smith's 9 November 1835 journal entry, wherein Smith related some of his remarkable experiences to an unusual visitor to his home, Enders notes that Smith was clear that he initially kept the events of a most remarkable night from his father. After recounting to the visitor the now-famous story of Moroni's appearance to him three times in one night in September 1823, Smith dictated to his scribe, "after the vision had all passed, I found that it was nearly day-light." Later that day, as the male family members labored in a nearby field, Joseph Smith exposed his physical weakness from little or no sleep the previous night. His father, noticing that he was not his usual self, asked whether Joseph were sick. He simply replied that he "had but little strength." So, as he explained, his father told him to "go to the house." One might think that this would have been a good time to tell his father of the phenomenal visions that had kept him up all night. Instead, as he recounted it, "I started [home] and went part way and was finally deprived ~~deprived~~ of my strength and fell, but how long I remained I do not know." It was during this incapacitation that "the Angel came to me again and

37. Dean C. Jessee, ed., *The Papers of Joseph Smith: Volume 1, Autobiographical and Historical Writings* (Salt Lake City: Deseret Book Company, 1989), 273; Davidson et al., *Histories, Volume 1*, 215.

38. See Donald L. Enders and Mark Lyman Staker, work in progress on the Smith family in New England and New York. Richard Bushman also acknowledges Smith's tendency to take care about what he said about his sacred experiences. Bushman, *Joseph Smith and the Beginnings of Mormonism*, 58. When Lucy Mack Smith wrote about her son's "First Vision," rather than including her personal observation of learning about the vision, she quoted the "History of Joseph Smith" entry from the *Times and Seasons*, 1 April 1842, p. 748.

commanded me to go and tell my Father, what I had seen and heard." It is reasonable to ask why the youth of seventeen initially refrained from telling his father of the previous night's visitations. Enders notes that according to Lucy Mack Smith, "he was afraid his father would not believe him."[39] Yet after he reported the occurrences to his father, the elder Joseph Smith "wept and told me that it was a vision from God to attend to it."[40] This event, near the beginning of his prophetic journey, indicates that his instinct for silence on spiritual matters found expression early, prompted perhaps by fear of ridicule.

While concern about how his experiences would be viewed influenced him significantly, another weighty attribute influenced Smith that precluded dissemination of much of what he experienced. This one was not innate, but learned from the Bible. Without question, Smith was "exceeding well versed in the scripture," as one early immigrant to Nauvoo, Illinois, declared while describing him to friends back home in England.[41] Smith would have been well familiar with instances where Jesus refrained from revealing sacred occurrences and his works to strangers and often cautioned those upon whom he worked his mysterious powers to "tell no one."[42] And as Smith translated the Book of Mormon, while still a young man, he may have taken note when the text declared: "It is given unto many to know the mysteries of God; nevertheless they are laid under a strict command, that they shall not impart only according to the portion of his word, which he doth grant unto the children of men."[43] The early revelations he received also confirmed the care that should be taken of

39. Lavina Fielding Anderson, ed., *Lucy's Book: A Critical Edition of Lucy Mack Smith's Family Memoir* (Salt Lake City: Signature Books, 2001), 340.

40. Joseph Smith, Journal, 9 November 1835, in Jessee et al., *Journals, Volume 1*, 89. Smith, in the history he initiated in 1838, included the anecdote of neglecting to tell his father of the angel's visit in what came to be popularized as Joseph Smith's public story. He stated that regaining his senses after falling over the fence, "The first thing that I can recollect was a voice speaking unto me calling me by name. I looked up and beheld the same messenger—standing over my head surrounded by light as before. He then again related unto me all that he had related to me the previous night, and commanded me to go to my father and tell him of the vision and commandments which I had received." History Drafts, 1838–ca. 1841 [Draft 2], 7, in Davidson et al., *Histories, Volume 1*, 230, 232. See also Lucy Mack Smith's account of the event in Anderson, *Lucy's Book*, 339–40.

41. William Clayton to "Beloved brethren and sisters," 10 December 1840, MS 5215, CHL.

42. See, for example, Matthew 8:4; 9:30; and especially 17:9.

43. Book of Mormon, 1830 ed., 255 (Alma 12:9, 1981 ed.).

divulging sacred matters. This religious protocol to keep sacred things close to the vest likely appealed to Smith's instinctual feelings about what had happened to him.[44]

A Dearth of Documentation

Because of a dearth of contemporary information describing Joseph Smith's early life, it is difficult to define the full scope of his religious experiences, and how or whether he related them. One telling indicator is found in an epistle to his followers that he had published in the church's periodical, the *Times and Seasons,* on 1 October 1842. Writing on 6 September 1842, Smith stated to his followers that in order for a complete restoration of the ancient religious world to the earth, including God's authority to perform efficacious religious ordinances such as baptism, "a whole, and complete, and perfect union, and welding together of dispensations, and keys, and powers, and glories should take place, and be revealed from the days of Adam even to the present time."[45] Thus, to restore both ancient Israel and primitive Christianity in a modern "dispensation of the fulness of times," the very players who staged God's work in biblical times were required to return to earth to bestow upon Smith all of the power and authority they themselves possessed during their mortal sojourns. The New Testament recounted that on the Mount of Transfiguration, Jesus—together with his apostles Peter, James, and John—had been visited by Moses and Elijah. Joseph Smith, in fact, claimed that all these and several others had appeared to him in visions.

Smith's September 1842 epistle not only fleetingly mentioned revelations from Jesus "at sundry times, and in divers places," but also announced that "divers angels" from "Adam, down to the present time" had manifested themselves to him. He identified several of them by name,

44. Others, such as James B. Allen, have also surmised that the sacred nature of Joseph Smith's experiences may have precluded his public disclosure of them (Allen, "Emergence of a Fundamental," 46). Subsequent revelatory instruction given to Joseph Smith, later codified into Mormon scripture, emphasized the importance of discreet care with divine manifestations: Revelation, summer 1828 (D&C 10:35); Revelation, April 1829 (D&C 6:12); Revelation, March 1830 (19:21); Moses 1:42; 4:32; Revelation, 22 June 1834 (D&C 105:23).

45. "Letter from Joseph Smith," 6 September 1842, in *Times and Seasons,* 1 October 1842, 935. This epistle was later canonized as Mormon scripture in 1876 in the Doctrine and Covenants as Section 128.

including Adam; Peter, James, and John; Gabriel; and even Raphael, a figure from the biblical Apocrypha.[46] Few claims by Judeo-Christian religious characters rival the spectacular pronouncements Joseph Smith advanced. And yet, though this brief expression about the biblical figures' appearances to Joseph Smith was made public, the details of these extraordinary spiritual experiences are nowhere to be found in Smith's writings or sermons. This may seem surprising, but is entirely consistent with the way that Smith treated other spiritual manifestations.

Another glaring issue relating to Joseph Smith's credibility in this light concerns the controversial absence of the higher (or Melchizedek) priesthood restoration narrative. Today's Mormons consider the appearance of the biblical apostles Peter, James, and John to Joseph Smith and Oliver Cowdery, probably in 1829, to be among the most important bestowals of heavenly empowerment handed to Joseph Smith. With this authority, modern Mormons believe, Joseph Smith could establish, organize, and perpetuate a church, while endowing the laity with power to be full partners in the process. Details of Joseph Smith's and Oliver Cowdery's reception of the lesser (or Aaronic) priesthood were written by Cowdery in 1834 and later by Smith in 1838.[47] While it appears that they may have once thought of relating the account of the appearance of the apostles, the fact is that the event was never prepared for distribution by Smith or Cowdery, whether they ever verbalized it to others or not.[48] The pattern for the absence of a narrative describing this important circumstance fits other refusals to discuss sacred matters.

---

46. "Letter from Joseph Smith," 6 September 1842, in *Times and Seasons,* 1 October 1842, 936. Joseph Smith confirmed this generalization of numerous visits from divine beings in his so-called Wentworth Letter. As a prelude to describing his encounter with the angel called Moroni, he revealed that he had "received many visits from the angels of God unfolding the majesty, and glory of the events that should transpire in the last days." "Church History," *Times and Seasons,* 1 March 1842, 707.

47. Oliver Cowdery to W. W. Phelps, 7 September 1834, in History, 1834–1836, 48–49, in Davidson et al., *Histories, Volume 1,* 42–43; History Drafts, 1838–ca. 1841 [Draft 2], in Davidson et al., *Histories, Volume 1,* 292–94.

48. John W. Welch, comp., *Opening the Heavens: Accounts of Divine Manifestations, 1820–1844* (Provo, Utah: Brigham Young University Press, 2005), summarizes, as a mechanism to defend Mormon claims to divine connections, numerous heavenly encounters in the early church period. See also Ronald O. Barney, "Priesthood Restoration Narratives in the Early Church" (MS in author's possession, 1991).

II. Publicity

Another unusual factor of Joseph Smith's personal behavior had to do with the manner in which he popularized his own role as leader of the fledgling church. In the most recent generation Smith has been "diagnosed" with numerous psychological disorders by those attempting to explain his unusual charisma, behavior, and influence over his followers.[49] These diagnoses include megalomania, symptoms of which are an insatiable quest for notoriety, power, and influence. To be sure, Smith understood and carried out his role as a prophet and leader. A contemporary non-Mormon observer, Peter Burnett—who had been one of Joseph Smith's lawyers in Missouri and who later became the first elected governor of the state of California—begrudgingly acknowledged Smith's talents and gifts, and wrote that Smith "deemed himself born to command, and he did command."[50] No one ever accused Smith of being a shrinking violet, and he assumed the prophetic role with confidence. But arguments made by some modern psychobiographers, including claims of dissociation, are based upon a surprisingly narrow and limited selection of documentary sources used to assign Smith patholological status. Such a person would likely manipulate and maneuver circumstances to elevate his visibility and status over his disciples. One of the primary arguments against Smith being a psychological misfit is that he refrained from inserting himself into the public square by literary means, even among his own people, when it was his prerogative to do so.

Many of Joseph Smith's contemporaries took full advantage of the opportunity to instruct, educate, and otherwise influence their followers through the printed word. Ellen G. White, the central figure of Seventh-day Adventism's founding in the middle of the nineteenth century, published 5,000 periodical articles and forty books—along with tens of thousands of manuscript pages she penned—much of which was divinely inspired revelatory material. Another famous divine of the time,

---

49. See, for example, Gary James Bergera, "Joseph Smith and the Hazards of Charismatic Leadership," in *The Prophet Puzzle: Interpretive Essays on Joseph Smith,* ed. Bryan Waterman (Salt Lake City: Signature Books, 1999); William D. Morain, *The Sword of Laban: Joseph Smith, Jr., and the Dissociated Mind* (Washington DC: American Psychiatric Press, 1998); and Robert D. Anderson, *Inside the Mind of Joseph Smith: Psychobiography and the Book of Mormon* (Salt Lake City: Signature Books, 1999).

50. Peter H. Burnett, *Recollections and Opinions of an Old Pioneer* (New York: D. Appleton and Co., 1880), 40.

Alexander Campbell, began a literary career that coincided with his ministry. He edited *The Christian Baptist* from 1823 to 1830, then published the *Millennial Harbinger* throughout the rest of his life to 1866. During the 1830s, as his rival Joseph Smith envisioned the expansion of his own church, each monthly issue of Campbell's magazine contained forty-eight pages, with Campbell himself contributing between ten and fourteen articles per number: a remarkable literary output.

The Mormons also had denominational publications, but in contrast to the examples of Ellen White and Alexander Campbell, Smith was only tangentially involved. Their first periodical was *The Evening and the Morning Star,* first published in June of 1832. By this time there were over a thousand followers of Joseph Smith, primarily located in two regions of the country, the old Western Reserve of Ohio and the western border of Missouri. Published by W. W. Phelps in Independence, Missouri, the *Star,* offering eight pages per issue, rallied the Mormons with new revelations received by Joseph Smith, as well as other information of religious and secular interest. Once the Mormons were forced from Missouri in July 1833, and the press destroyed, the periodical continued publication until September 1834 in Kirtland, Ohio, then the home of Smith. During this nearly two-and-one-half-year period one might expect regular installments from Smith providing instructive guidance to his followers that would further his designs and ultimately endear him to them personally. However, there was never such a strategic move. Indeed, besides the implicit understanding that the revelations printed therein came from Joseph Smith, his name appeared in the periodical during its entire run only about two dozen times, usually identified as one attending a conference meeting but never as a signatory providing instruction or personal information.[51] This is not the behavior one might expect to see from a man whose ambition was to conquer the minds and hearts of even a small sector of the frontier population of America. And while his literary presence increased somewhat in subsequent church periodicals such as the *Messenger and Advocate,* the *Elders' Journal,* and the *Times and Seasons,* it was infrequent. This was even the case when he was the official editor of the organ (the *Elders' Journal* and the *Times and Seasons*).[52] In the latter case, it is demonstrable it was

51. The last issue of the *Star* contained one of Smith's letters. However, it was Oliver Cowdery, the recipient of the letter and the editor of the *Star,* who published the letter.

52. Smith edited the *Elders' Journal* from October 1837 to August 1838 and edited the *Times and Seasons* from February 1842 to October 1842.

not Joseph Smith who wrote editorial pieces but rather one of his editorial assistants, particularly John Taylor.[53]

III. Sermon Record

By the time Joseph Smith appeared as part of America's religious demographic, the skill and method of delivering a sermon had become something of an art form.[54] The Mormons, including Joseph Smith, did not ignore this means of communications that had become standard in the young country's religious meetinghouses. Again, it was Dean Jessee who first identified for readers the scope of Joseph Smith's sermonizing. Jessee pointed out that private and institutional reports of 250 of Smith's sermons survive. Jessee postulated that if Smith delivered a statistically comparable number of sermons prior to his ministry in Nauvoo, he may have delivered as many as 450 over the course of his career, but accounts of what he said exist for barely half of the sermons he likely delivered. It is surprising that a man who calculated to create a religious environment of uniform polity and belief never commissioned his clerks to capture his language so that his instructions and teachings could be communicated in the print media for his followers and others. In contrast to many of his religious contemporaries, he delivered, but never disseminated, what he preached to his followers.

Like his discomfort in expressing himself on paper, noted above, Joseph Smith also discounted his verbal abilities in conveying his thoughts and emotions. Clearly his insecurity with verbal and written English affected his style as a prophet. "I cannot find words to express myself," he confessed

---

53. Joseph Smith scholar Richard L. Anderson clarified this posture by comparing two pamphlets published by Joseph Hyrum Parry in the mid-1880s. Parry revised his 1884 pamphlet, *Items of Church History, The Government of God, and The Gift of the Holy Ghost, Articles Written by the Prophet Joseph Smith* (Salt Lake City: Jos. Hyrum Parry & Co., 1884) in 1886 by crediting John Taylor with authorship of the essays previously attributed in the 1884 version to Joseph Smith. A printed note of errata tipped into the reprint stated: "The articles in this Pamphlet titled, 'The Gift of the Holy Ghost' and 'The Government of God,' though appearing in 'The History of Joseph Smith' were not written by the Prophet himself, but by President John Taylor, who at that time had charge of the 'Times and Seasons,' though the Prophet Joseph was the editor." Taylor was LDS Church president at the time of the correction.

54. See, for example, Phyllis M. Jones and Nicholas R. Jones, eds., *Salvation in New England: Selections from the Sermons of the First Preachers* (Austin: University of Texas Press, 1977), 3–24; Ellis Sandoz, ed., *Political Sermons of the American Founding Era, 1730–1805* 2nd ed., 2 vols. (Indianapolis: Liberty Fund, 1998).

to a congregation in April 1843. "I am not learned." He then lamented, "O that I had the the [*sic*] language of the archangel to express my feeling once to my frends. but I never expect to."[55] Despite this almost consuming plague of insecurity in articulation, the sermon became one of the most important means of his communication to the Latter-day Saints.

In April 1843, at the same time Smith explained to his followers that he had trouble expressing himself, Nauvoo acquired another immigrant from England, part of an incessant immigration cycle of British Saints arriving in America during the early 1840s. This one, however, happened to be the first convert to Mormonism in England, baptized at the beginning of the initial apostolic mission to Great Britain in 1837. Thirty-year-old George D. Watt was a man of letters who also knew the specialized skill of shorthand (phonography).[56] When Watt immigrated to Nauvoo he apparently arranged with Smith to lecture about shorthand to Nauvoo residents on the second level of Smith's store. A promotional ad in Nauvoo's newspaper, *The Wasp,* promised to introduce the new and superior system of Pitman shorthand:

> This system, which, from its simplicity, is remarkably easy of attainment and pleasing in practice, is so true and perfect a method of writing, that any word in *any* language, names, of persons and places, the precise pronunciation of a person, &c. can be expressed by it with perfect case and precision; be read at any distance of time without the possibility of mistake, and with a greater ease than longhand—it is, therefore, admirably adapted for every species of composition.[57]

To underscore its utility over existing practice, the notice in Nauvoo's newspaper stated that an apt comparison between the phonographic

55. Joseph Smith, Journal, 16 April 1843, in Andrew H. Hedges, Alex D. Smith, and Richard Lloyd Anderson, eds., *Journals, Volume 2: December 1841–April 1843,* vol. 2 of the Journal series of *The Joseph Smith Papers,* eds. Dean C. Jessee, Ronald K. Esplin, and Richard Lyman Bushman (Salt Lake City: Church Historian's Press, 2011), 361.

56. The same year that Watt became a Mormon, his countryman Sir Isaac Pitman introduced a modified shorthand method that would eventually replace the prevailing technique known as Taylor shorthand.

57. Advertisement, *The Wasp,* 26 April 1843.

Pitman and stenography was the advance of "railway locomotives" over "stage coaches."[58]

Prior to Watt's arrival in Nauvoo, Smith had delivered over a hundred sermons in and around Nauvoo. Observers today know about most of those Nauvoo sermons because persons in the audience penned some longhand notes of what he said, almost always notes of an abbreviated nature. Often a small paragraph would be used to describe the content of a lengthy speech. Occasionally, especially when the delivery was covered by one of Smith's clerks—like William Clayton, Willard Richards, or Thomas Bullock—a more detailed and comprehensive report was produced. Still, even these more comprehensive reports might represent a small percentage of what Smith actually related in a given sermon. One would think that Watt's arrival in Nauvoo might be looked upon by Smith as a godsend—finally, someone could capture his words for publication, distribution, or even archival purposes. It did not happen. Smith apparently never engaged the services of the man who taught those skills above his Red Brick store, though he delivered over fifty sermons in and around Nauvoo after Watt's arrival.

The absence of George D. Watt in Joseph Smith's stable of clerks is a glaring example of Smith's lack of interest in having his sermons captured, recorded, published, or read. Certainly the inspired direction he gave to the Saints after the spring of 1843 was no less important for the growing church than it had been at the outset. Yet he never employed Watt to make his words live on. When Brigham Young assumed leadership of the church after Joseph Smith's death, he recognized the value of Watt's abilities and put him to work. Watt became the trial clerk for the proceedings against those accused of murdering Smith, and then spent years in clerical service to Young.

In contrast to the lack of attention he showed to preserving his sermons, Joseph Smith went to some trouble to have his early revelations recorded, compiled, and published. The *Doctrine and Covenants*, the volume where Smith's revelations were published, contained the doctrines, polity, and protocols that thereafter governed the church. There was both a practical and an archival purpose in these revelations' publication. But after the initial printing of the revelations in 1835, the output of "thus saith the Lord"–type revelations that characterized many of his codified texts

58. Advertisement, *The Wasp*, 26 April 1843.

precipitously declined. While he added eight "revelations" to the Doctrine and Covenants in 1844 before his death, during the Nauvoo period Smith's revelations to the church were dispersed primarily by way of his sermons (though a few were distributed by way of epistle).[59] Yet even after the sermons had taken on this crucial revelatory role he made no effort to have their language or content captured for present or future use.[60]

This is not to suggest that Joseph Smith was not sanguine about what he said and how his words were received by the listener. Numerous followers declared that he spoke with compelling power. Although others, usually skeptical visitors, picked at his lack of polish and erudition, this did not keep him from the podium. He regarded his speaking opportunities with much gravity. He cared about how his words were received. Indeed, while there is not a demonstrable pattern of Joseph's examination of notes taken from his sermons, there is evidence that he reviewed the notes taken from at least one sermon that he delivered. Willard Richards, who kept Joseph Smith's journal at the time, wrote on 17 April 1843 that in the afternoon Smith "retu[rne]d home & listind to the reading of a synopsis of his sermon of last sabbath."[61] He may have reviewed others as well. Still, not only did Smith refrain from having his words secured by phonographic transcription, he also never spoke from a prepared text.[62] Many of the established clergy in early America wrote their sermons before verbalizing them, which explains why so many are available at present. Thereafter, what they delivered could be disseminated through publication and then preserved for posterity. Here, again, Smith bucked the norm by extemporaneously speaking to his listeners.

---

59. See, for example, Joseph Smith, Journal, 16 April 1843, in Hedges et al., *Journals, Volume 2*, 360; "Letter from Joseph Smith," 6 September 1842, in *Times and Seasons*, 1 October 1842, 934.

60. The texts of most of Joseph Smith's sermons included in *The History of the Church* were inserted after his death by the initial compilers of his history, in many cases from reports recorded in their own journals.

61. Joseph Smith, Journal, 17 April 1843, in Hedges et al., *Journals, Volume 2*, 363. The review probably concerned Joseph Smith's sermon delivered on 16 April 1843.

62. A note from one of Joseph Smith's clerks, Howard Coray, described one circumstance where Joseph Smith dictated a text included for delivery in preparation for the October 1840 general conference. Peculiarly, Joseph Smith did not deliver the sermon, leaving that duty to the clerk who took the dictation, Robert B. Thompson. But other than this unusual instance, no known preliminary sermon text is known to exist. Howard Coray, Autobiographical Sketches, undated, Howard Coray, Papers, ca. 1840–1941, MS 2043, CHL; Minutes, *Times and Seasons*, October 1840, 187.

Joseph Smith was apparently content to have the extent of his inspired words be the internalization of his message by the hearer. A sermon of 6 August 1843, captured in brief form by scribe Willard Richards, contains these words attributed to Smith: "every word that proceedeth from the mouth of Jehovah has such an influence over the human mind[,] the logical mind[,] that it is convincing without other testimony. faith cometh by hearing."[63] The expression, referencing Romans 10:17, suggests that Smith's primary ambition was to reveal the word of God resulting in the increase of faith for the hearer.

And there were often many hearers. Some, though not all, of his speaking ventures in Nauvoo may have attracted as many as a few thousand people. As there was never a meetinghouse in Nauvoo for regular worship, Joseph Smith's primary Nauvoo sermons were given outdoors, often from the "temple stand" just west of the edifice then under construction. Occasionally a few paragraphs of what he said would appear in the church periodical, the *Times and Seasons*. The local newspaper, *The Wasp*, later renamed *The Nauvoo Neighbor*, was another potential outlet for themes of his preaching. But he was satisfied with being a verbal rather than a literary prophet. Indeed, when Brigham Young returned to Nauvoo from the second apostolic mission to Great Britain, he wrote to the Saints who remained in England to say that if they wanted to access Joseph Smith's teachings, they would have to relocate to Nauvoo.

> We . . . have been instructed, by the Prophet of the Most High, even Joseph, the Seer and Revelator for the church, whose instructions to us, are as the voice of the Lord, and whose admonitions we ever regard as true and faithful, and worthy the confidence of all who profess the Gospel of Jesus Christ. . . . That the saints may enjoy the teachings of the Prophet; those teachings which can be had only at this place so that they may go on from knowledge to knowledge even to perfection.[64]

With convenient outlets such as the *Times and Seasons* and *The Wasp* in Nauvoo, and even the church's British periodical, the *Latter Day Saints'*

---

63. Ehat and Cook, *Words of Joseph Smith*, 237.

64. Brigham Young et al., *An Epistle of the Twelve, to the Church of Jesus Christ of Latter Day Saints, in Its Various Branches and Conferences in Europe* (Nauvoo, Illinois: 20 March 1842).

Millennial Star, it is curious that Smith chose for his sermons to benefit only those who heard them in person.

Conclusion

There are no modern explications of the reasons for Joseph Smith's behavior in his neglect to write, chronicle, produce, record, or disseminate much of the material we would expect from a religious leader. As has been noted above, Smith reacted with restraint, perhaps because he was reticent by nature or perhaps because he had become insecure from the criticism that he experienced. He was uncomfortable putting his thoughts on paper, was disinclined to reveal his experiences with the divine, was disinterested in inserting himself into the popular literary dialogue of the day, and, aching for greater facility with his verbal expression, chose not to have his sermons recorded for distribution or preservation. Brigham Young undoubtedly puzzled an audience when he told them in September 1859 that despite their familiarity with Joseph Smith during his mortal sojourn, there were "but few [who] were really acquainted with brother Joseph."[65] Young may very well have been speaking of these features of Smith's personality. Joseph Smith conceded as much when he told his followers, and everyone else thereafter, in his own oft-quoted valedictory delivered on 7 April 1844: "You don't know me—you never will. . . . when I am called at the trump & weighed in the balance you will know me then."[66]

65. Brigham Young, 1 September 1859, in *Journal of Discourses Delivered by President Brigham Young, His Two Counsellors, The Twelve Apostles, and Others*, vol. 7 (Liverpool: Amasa Lyman; London: Latter-day Saints' Book Depot, 1860), 243.

66. Joseph Smith Diary, kept by Willard Richards, 7 April 1844; Thomas Bullock, Report, 7 April 1844, in Ehat and Cook, *Words of Joseph Smith*, 343, 355.

Index

Page numbers in *italics* indicate illustrations.
The initials "JS" refer to Joseph Smith (1805–1844).